Fodor's see it™

italy

FODOR'S TRAVEL PUBLICATIONS
NEW YORK • TORONTO • LONDON • SYDNEY • AUCKLAND

WWW.FODORS.COM

Contents

KEY TO SYMBOLS

- Map reference
- Address
- Telephone number
- Opening times
- Admission prices
- Bus number
- Train station
- Ferry/boat
- Driving directions
- Tourist office
- Tours
- Guidebook
- Restaurant
- Café
- Shop
- Bar
- Toilets
- Number of rooms
- Parking
- No smoking
- Air-conditioning
- Swimming pool
- Gym
- Other useful information
- Shopping
- Entertainment
- Nightlife
- Sports
- Activities
- Health and beauty
- For children
- Cross reference
- Walk/tour start point

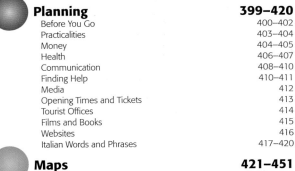
HOW TO USE THIS BOOK

Understanding Italy is an introduction to the country, its geography, economy and people. **Living Italy** gives an insight into Italy today, while **The Story of Italy** takes you through the country's past.

For detailed advice on getting to Italy—and getting around once you are there—turn to **On the Move**. For useful practical information, from weather forecasts to emergency services, turn to **Planning**.

Out and About gives you the chance to explore Italy through walks and drives.

The **Sights, What to Do, Eating and Staying** sections are divided geographically into nine regions and cities, which are shown on the map on the inside front cover. These regions always appear in the same order. Towns and places of interest are listed alphabetically within each region.

Map references for the **Sights** refer to the atlas section at the end of this book or to the individual town plans. For example, Milan has the reference ✚ 431 D4, indicating the page on which the map is found (431) and the grid square in which Milan sits (D4).

UNDERSTANDING ITALY

From well-kept beaches and dramatic mountain scenery to historic cities with a wealth of art and architecture, and small, picturesque villages, Italy offers something for all visitors. Since Turin hosted the Winter Olympics in 2006, this northern city has been the focal point of winter sports in Italy, and the growth of European budget airline routes has opened up other regions of the country not previously thought of as main holiday destinations. Just as Rome wasn't built in a day, so Italy cannot be explored in a single visit. The country is truly a year-round holiday destination, with a vibrant arts and music scene, world-class sporting events, colourful festivals, unforgettable food and some of the best shopping in Europe.

The 14th-century Castello degli Challand, on a lofty outcrop in the Alpine foothills near the Valle d'Aosta town of Verres (left); a view over the resort of Limone Sul Garda on Lake Garda (right)

LANDSCAPE

Italy is a mountainous Mediterranean country extending south from the Alps, with two major off-shore islands, Sicily and Sardinia, and several groups of smaller islands. It covers an area of about 300,000sq km (116,000sq miles) and has a coastline running for 7,600km (4,723 miles). It is over 1,500km (930 miles) long, a contrast to the width, which you can drive across in 3–4 hours.

The chain of the Apennine Mountains runs down the country from Genoa in the north to Reggio di Calabria in the south, covered in huge tracts of forest. North of Genoa lie the flat plains of the Po Valley, immensely fertile and intensively farmed. These mist-laden plains are backed by the Alps, stretching eastward from the border at Ventimiglia through to Slovenia, with the most scenic ranges, the Ortles and Dolomites, in the east. The stereotypical classic rolling hill landscape dotted with vines and lined with cypress trees is confined to central Italy, seen at its best in Tuscany and Umbria.

ECONOMY

Italy is a modern industrialized nation. Business and commerce revolve around Milan in the north, but the deep south remains one of Europe's most economically depressed areas.

Apart from natural gas, the country has few natural resources, with no substantial deposits of oil, iron or coal. Much of the land is unsuited to agriculture and Italy is a net food importer. Its economic strength lies in the processing and manufacturing of goods, primarily in family-owned firms. The major industries are car and precision machinery manufacture, textiles, clothing and footwear, ceramic and chemical production and food processing. Sixty-two per cent of the population is employed in tourism and the service industries. Major trading partners include the US and countries within the European Union, with car and fashion industries exporting worldwide.

POLITICS

The Republic of Italy was created in 1948; since then there have been well over 50 governments. The head of state is the president, chosen by an electoral college drawn from the houses of parliament and regional representatives. Decision-making lies with the lower house, the Chamber of Deputies, which is directly elected. The upper house, the Senate, is made up of six representatives from each region, plus a number of senators-for-life. The complicated proportional representation electoral system has been responsible for a series of coalition governments, many of which have been suspected of corruption at the highest level. The *Mani Pulite* (Clean Hands) investigation in the 1990s extinguished the *tangentopoli* (bribetown) climate, leading to the downfall of some of the old-established parties. Scandals continue, but there is a genuine feeling that Italy is moving forward.

THE NORTHWEST

Lombardy is heavily industrialized, but it also has beautiful valleys and Alpine foothills and some splendid historic towns. Among these are medieval Padua, Cremona, famous as the birthplace of Stradivari and Amati violins, the great Gonzaga stronghold of Mantova, and Bergamo. To the north lie the lakes—Orta, Iseo, Garda and Como, popular destinations for Italians and visitors alike.

Piedmont, at the foot of the Alps, borders France and is renowned for its winter skiing and summer walking, found at their best in the Parco Nazionale del Gran Paradiso, Italy's oldest national park. For culture there's Alba, a lovely mix of narrow streets and medieval, Renaissance and baroque buildings. This region is known for its stuffed pastas, and connoisseurs will enjoy the renowned red wine, Barolo, and the world-famous white truffles.

Liguria is Italy's Riviera, a tiny region between the Alps and the sea, tucked around the Gulf of Genoa and curving northwest towards France. The rugged coast, scattered with chic, glitzy resorts famous for their seafood, contrasts with the unspoiled and largely unknown interior. To sample the best of both, head for the Cinque Terre and Lerici, south of Genoa, or switch off for a few days in Portofino or Rapallo, both on the Riviera di Levante, east of the city.

The village of Baschi in Umbria (left); the morning haze over the lush vineyards of the Chianti district, famed for its production of fine red wine (right)

VENICE, THE NORTHEAST AND EMILIA-ROMAGNA

The Veneto is a rich and developed region spreading from the flatlands and lagoon northward into the Dolomites. Its cities include thriving Padua, with its medieval core, centuries-old university and tempting shopping; the Palladian delights of Vicenza, Europe's textile capital, and rich, historic Verona, but **Venice** is the main draw. Smaller towns worth exploring are Asolo, a medieval walled town in the foothills of the Dolomites, and Conegliano, a pleasing old town in the middle of the wine-growing area.

Friuli-Venezia-Giulia has mountain ranges in the north, spiritual retreats in the east and Adriatic lagoon land to the south. The ancient past is preserved in towns like Aquileia, with its 11th-century basilica and Roman remains, and Cividale del Friuli, home to some exceptional Lombard treasures. Trieste is the regional capital, its grandiose architecture balanced by the airiness of Udine.

Trentino-Alto-Adige is a German-Italian region in the far northeast, created in 1919. The Alto-Adige is German, while Trentino is distinctly Italian, a contrast of cultures evident in the region's main towns. Bolzano (Bozen), the trim capital of the Alto Adige, Bressanone (Brixen) and Merano (Meran) are markedly German in character, while Trento, with its castle, is undoubtedly Italian.

Emilia-Romagna is famous for its artistic towns and for its cuisine. Prosperous Bologna is the capital, and culture-lovers will find plenty to admire—the Byzantine mosaics of Ravenna, Parma's Lombard-Romanesque duomo and baptistery, and Ferrara's huge castle, fine palaces and museums. Lower-key delights lie in Piacenza and Pavarotti's home town of Modena.

FLORENCE, TUSCANY AND UMBRIA

Tuscany has an abundance of picturesque towns, attracting huge numbers of visitors each year, but leave time for the rural pleasures in the wooded hills of Chianti, famous for its wine, and the rolling honey-hued landscape, dotted with cypress trees. **Florence**, renowned as the cradle of the Renaissance, has long been on the tourist map. Topping the list of bigger towns is Siena, with its shell-shaped Campo and medieval architecture, closely followed by Pisa with its tower.

Umbria, whose capital is Perugia, is Italy's only landlocked region. Orvieto, with its famous cathedral, far in the west, is the other main town, while to the east lies Spoleto, a quiet, historic town that comes alive during its summer arts festival. Between these is a clutch of smaller towns: medieval Gubbio, Assisi, St. Francis's birthplace, laid-back Spello and Montefalco. Umbria also has blue waters at Lago di Trasimeno, dramatic gorges in the Valnerina and the towering mountains of the Sibillini.

ROME, LAZIO AND THE MARCHE

Lazio is a quiet and low-key region with a gentle landscape. Rome is close to many of the key sights—the stunning baroque gardens at Tivoli, the towns of the Alban Hills known as the Castelli Romani, and the ancient Roman port of Ostia. The Etruscan settlements of Cerveteri and Tarquinia are older still, and medieval Viterbo is culturally fascinating.

Rome, Italy's compelling capital, has a staggering wealth of monuments, museums, galleries and architecture spanning almost 3,000 years. There are outstanding examples of baroque sculpture and countless Renaissance masterpieces on display in its galleries and museums. Above all Rome is a vibrant modern capital, where life continues to buzz through the patchwork of its ancient, medieval and modern streets.

The Marche is tucked away inconspicuously in the east on the calf of Italy, across the Apennines. This is an unspoiled region with historic towns, long stretches of coastline and a green, hilly interior. The main attraction is Urbino, a classic Renaissance ducal town, but don't miss compact Ascoli Piceno in the eastern valley and the tiny fortress town of San Leo. There are plenty of family resorts to choose from—Pesaro is the most notable, with its old town and well-groomed, sandy beaches.

Naples from Castel San Elmo (left); Taormina, with the snowcapped peak of Mount Etna in the background (middle); and clear turquoise water near Capriccioni on the Costa Smeralda (right)

THE SOUTH

Campania has a vibrant capital—Naples—a coastline dotted with picturesque villages between Sorrento and Amalfi, the jewel-like islands of Ischia and Capri, and a wealth of archaeological sites: Pompei, Herculaneum and Paestum.

Molise is remote and undiscovered; nearby, the **Abruzzo** is better known, chiefly for its superb Parco Nazionale d'Abruzzo, Italy's third-largest park. The Gran Sasso massif is a magnet for outdoor enthusiasts and wilderness-lovers. L'Aquila is the region's bustling and prosperous capital.

Basilicata has superb mountain scenery, seen at its best in the Parco Nazionale del Pollino. Enjoy the coastline on both the Mar Tirenno and Golfo di Taranto, delve back in time in Matera to the east, an ancient settlement peppered with cave houses, or travel south for archaeology at Metaponto.

Calabria, Italy's toe, is an undeveloped region with a long coastline and mountains inland. The Sila range, with its rolling plateaux and dense woodlands, shouldn't be overlooked. Reggio di Calabria is the main ferry port for Sicily and its chief attraction is its outstanding archaeological museum.

Puglia, the heel of Italy, is more prosperous than other regions in the south. Highlights include the port of Bari, with its labyrinthine old town and Norman cathedral, exuberant Lecce, one of Italy's finest baroque towns, and Castel del Monte, an isolated, 13th-century Swabian castle. More relaxing is the Gargano peninsula, the spur of the boot, a limestone promontory dotted with fishing villages.

SICILY AND SARDINIA

Sicily, to the southwest of the toe of Italy, has enough to keep you busy for weeks. Palermo is the capital, its vitality rivalled only by grimy Catania and the ancient Greek settlement of Siracusa. There's more of archaeological interest at Greek Agrigento, Selinunte and Segesta. Taormina's main attraction is Mount Etna, one of the world's largest active volcanoes. Quieter, but equally attractive, are Noto, a superb baroque town built after the 1693 earthquake, the inland town of Enna and the north-coast fishing port of Cefalù, with its beaches and Norman cathedral.

Sardinia, 200km (124 miles) to the west of the mainland, is renowned for its idyllic coastline, clear waters, classy resorts and wild interior. Walled Cagliari is the capital, and Nora is the island's premier archaeological site with Phoenician, Carthaginian and Roman remains. There is an abundance of coastal resorts too—the Costa Smeralda in the northeast, the Riviera di Corallo in the northwest, and Cala Gonone, with mountainous cliffs and sea caves, in the east.

ITALY'S REGIONS

CH · FL · A · TRENTINO-ALTO-ADIGE · FRIULI-VENEZIA-GIULIA · SLO · VALLE D'AOSTA · LOMBARDIA · VENETO · HR · F · PIEMONTE · LIGURIA · EMILIA-ROMAGNA · MC · TOSCANA · MARCHE · Isola d'Elba · UMBRIA · F · ABRUZZO · LAZIO · MOLISE · CAMPANIA · PUGLIA · BASILICATA · SARDEGNA · CALABRIA · SICILIA

THE BEST ART CITIES

Florence (▷ 115–134) Buildings and art collections that provide an insight into the revolutionary Renaissance.

Naples (▷ 198–201) A variety of architecture, from Gothic to Baroque, and the city's classical art collections are among the finest in the country.

Ravenna (▷ 110) Some of the world's finest Byzantine mosaics.

Rome (▷ 157–180) Artistic delights spanning 2,000 years, encompassing architecture, sculpture, painting and mosaics.

Siena (▷ 152–153) A perfectly preserved medieval city with an artistic heritage and cityscape focused on the Italian Gothic.

Venice (▷ 81–102) A city built on water, crammed with treasures covering over 1,000 years of art history.

THE BEST COASTAL AREAS

The Amalfi Coast (▷ 318–319) A stretch of coast south of Naples, with towering cliffs, steep, green mountains and fabulous views over the azure sea.

Cinque Terre (▷ 279, 280–281) 'The Five Lands'—a string of higgledy-piggledy fishing and holiday villages, where cliffs, covered in terraced vineyards, lead down to hidden beaches.

Costa Smeralda (▷ 220) Sardinia's Emerald Coast, where natural beauty and clear waters combine with chic resorts.

Gargano Peninsula (▷ 322–323) The spur of the 'boot'—a limestone peninsula fringed with turquoise water, relaxed fishing villages and small resorts.

Riviera di Levante (▷ 80) A beautiful area south of Genoa, renowned for its up-market resorts and dramatic cliffs.

THE NORTHWEST

The Parco Nazionale del Gran Paradiso (▷ 76) Some excellent walking in majestic mountain scenery.
Milan (▷ 72–75) Explore the art and architecture and indulge in some of the world's best retail therapy.
Finestre Sul Po, Turin (▷ 345) Sit back and relax in this long-established riverside restaurant that serves unforgettable food in beautiful surroundings.
Bellagio (▷ 69) Tour around Lake Como by car or ferry from here.
Grand Hotel Villa Serbelloni, Bellagio (▷ 337) Stay at one of Italy's most beautiful lakeside hotels on Lake Como.
The Via dell'Amore, Cinque Terre (▷ 279) Walk along this cliff-side path in the Cinque Terre, particularly dramatic between Manarola and Riomaggiore.
Isole Barromee (▷ 70) Take a boat trip to these idyllic islands in Lago Maggiore.
Mantova (▷ 77) Survey some of the 500 rooms of the vast complex of the Palazzo Ducale, once the home of the Gonzagas.

When it comes to shopping for the latest styles, there's plenty of choice in Milan (left)

The marina in Bellagio (above)

VENICE

The Canal Grande (▷ 86–87) Take the *vaporetto* No. 1 down this famous waterway for a panoramic presentation of elegant architecture.
The Basilica di San Marco (▷ 84–85) Appreciate this mind-blowing overview of Venetian art and history.
The Accademia Bridge (▷ 87) Admire the view down the Canal Grande towards the great church of the Salute.
Antiche Carampane (▷ 341) Track down the Antiche Carampane, an off-the-beaten-track restaurant, for the best fish in the city.
Burano, Murano and Torcello (▷ 83, 89, 102) Spend a day exploring the lagoon islands.
The Scuola Grande di San Rocco (▷ 102) Take in Tintoretto's great cycle of paintings.
Rialto (▷ 97) Make a morning visit to the Rialto food markets and admire the fruit and vegetables piled high and the sparklingly fresh fish and seafood.
Pensione Accademia (▷ 373) Stay in the Pensione Accademia in Dorsoduro, the perfect Venetian base—but be sure to book ahead.
Shopping (▷ 240–242) Browse among the shops for handmade carnival masks and Murano glass.
Ca' Rezzonico (▷ 83) Visit this palace for a glimpse of the ostentation and grandiose style that characterized 18th-century Venetian life.

A vaporetto on the Canal Grande in Venice (above); Murano glassware by Stefano Toso (left)

THE NORTHEAST AND EMILIA-ROMAGNA

Bologna (▷ 105) Spend time strolling through the arcaded streets—don't miss the Strada Maggiore.
Verona (▷ 112–113) Admire the Roman Arena before exploring the area around the Piazza delle Erbe.
The Grande Strada delle Dolomiti (▷ 290–291) Drive along this route past mountain views, high passes and picturesque villages.
Villa Madruzzo, Trento (▷ 376) Drink in the mountain air while staying in country house comfort at the Villa Madruzzo.
Parma (▷ 109) Shop for *prosciutto di Parma* (Parma ham) and Parmigiano Reggiano (Parmesan cheese) before taking in the city's artistic treasures.
Ferrara (▷ 106) Take a tour of this historical town, once the Este powerbase—don't miss the Castello Estense.

Parmigiano Reggiano (right)

FLORENCE

The Duomo, Campanile and Battistero (▷ 118–121)
Appreciate this harmonious trio of Renaissance church buildings.
The Galleria degli Uffizi (▷ 122–123) Trace the development of
Italian painting and admire the treasures.
The Piazza della Signoria (▷ 131) Sit and enjoy a coffee while
overlooking the Palazzo Vecchio and the statues, the heart of
historic Florence and a great place for people-watching.
Il Latini (▷ 347) Enjoy a meal at this restaurant, famous for its
traditional Florentine cooking.
The Galleria Palatina, Palazzo Pitti (▷ 128–129) Admire the
superb Renaissance pictures and then relax with a picnic in the
Giardino di Boboli.
Shopping (▷ 247–248) Try the Via Tornabuoni and the Via della
Vigna Nuova for high fashion, or track down Florentine products
such as ceramics, leather and marbled paper.
San Lorenzo (▷ 134) Visit the Medici family church, and the
Biblioteca Laurenziana next door, before moving on to the Cappelle
Medicee with their superlative sculpture by Michelangelo.
Fiesole (▷ 141) Take an evening trip here for a quiet dinner and
great views of Florence lit up at night.
Soggiorno Antica Torre (▷ 379) Stay in the heart of the city in this
quintessentially Florentine hotel.

*The Duomo
(above) and
a statue in
Piazza
della
Signoria
(left) in
Florence*

TUSCANY AND UMBRIA

Siena (▷ 152–153) Wander around one of Italy's most perfect
medieval cities.
Southern Tuscany (▷ 302–303) Drive through this landscape of
rolling hills, olive groves and historic towns.
Granaro del Monte (▷ 351) Enjoy the very best of Umbrian
cooking in the heart of the Sibillini Mountains at the Granaro del
Monte in Norcia.
Montalcino and Montepulciano (▷ 143, 144) Sample the great
red wines of Montalcino and Montepulciano in their place of origin.
Assisi (▷ 137) Follow the pilgrim trail to this lovely Umbrian town that
is famously the birthplace of St. Francis.
Norcia (▷ 144–145) Drive up the Valnerina to Norcia to eat some of
Italy's finest pork products and pasta dishes rich in truffles.
Orvieto (▷ 146) Admire the fine façade of Orvieto's Duomo before
shopping for ceramics.
Grand Hotel Continental (▷ 384) Stay the night a couple of
minutes' walk from Siena's glorious Campo.

Orvieto's Duomo

ROME

The Basilica di San Pietro (▷ 160–161) Marvel at the
overwhelming opulence of this famous Roman Catholic landmark.
The Musei Vaticani (▷ 168–170) Don't miss one of the
world's greatest museums, home to Michelangelo's Sistine Chapel.
The Colosseo (▷ 162–163) See this ancient arena lit up at night.
The Piazza di Spagna (▷ 171) Stroll through the piazza before
climbing the Spanish Steps for great views across the city.
The Galleria Borghese (▷ 166) Spend a morning or afternoon
viewing this wonderful art collection, in verdant surroundings.
Antonio al Pantheon (▷ 354) Mix with the local clientele and
sample authentic Roman cuisine at Antonio al Pantheon.
Piazza Campo dei Fiori (▷ 171) Enjoy a taste of everyday Roman
life at this morning market.
San Giovanni in Laterano (▷ 176) Admire the baroque splendour
of Rome's cathedral.
The Pantheon (▷ 172) Step inside this impressive example of the
grandeur of ancient Rome.
Lancelot (▷ 387) Retreat to the cool space and warm welcome of
the Lancelot hotel at the end of a day's sightseeing.

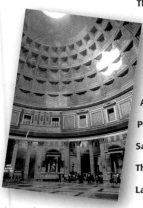

The Pantheon in Rome

LAZIO AND THE MARCHE

Tivoli (▷ 189) Take time out surrounded by the shade and rushing water of the Villa d'Este gardens.
Ascoli Piceno (▷ 182) Drive down the Tronto Valley to this relatively undiscovered jewel with its beguiling piazza.
La Vecchia Urbino (▷ 357) Eat the very best of the Marche's regional dishes in Urbino's top restaurant.
Sirene (▷ 390) Spend a night in magical Tivoli at the Hotel Sirene and be first at the Villa d'Este in the morning.

Piazza del Popolo in Ascoli Piceno (above)

THE SOUTH

Naples (▷ 198–201) Explore the treasures and streets of this vibrant city, where life is theatrical and emotions run high.
Pompei (▷ 204–207) Step back in time into a Roman town preserved by the eruption of Vesuvius in AD79.
The Amalfi Coast (▷ 209) Drive along the corniche road south of Naples, punctuated by pretty villages.
Caravella (▷ 359) Discover the secrets of modern southern Italian cooking at the renowned Caravella in Amalfi.
Constantinopoli 104 (▷ 394) Use this stylish hotel, with garden and swimming pool, as a base for exploring the Amalfi coast.

There are plenty of seafood restaurants to choose from along the Amalfi Coast (left)

SICILY AND SARDINIA

Palermo (▷ 215) Experience a brash fusion of architecture, art and culture in this fascinating city with a chequered history.
Monreale (▷ 214) Visit the Norman cathedral famed for its Greek, Byzantine and Sicilian mosaics.
Ristorante da Lorenzo, Taormina (▷ 363) Have a romantic summer meal on the terrace.
Stromboli (▷ 213) Climb the slopes on the Aeolian island and get close to an active volcano.
Agrigento (▷ 212) Watch the night draw in around the magnificent Greek temples.
Hotel Moderno, Erice (▷ 397) Stay in one of Sicily's most picturesque villages.

Palermo's narrow streets buzz with activity (below)

TOP 10 EXPERIENCES

Visit Rome for artistic delights spanning 2,000 years, encompassing architecture, sculpture, painting and mosaics (▷ 157–180).
Stroll out in the early evening anywhere in Italy and join the locals for the *passeggiata*.
Head for Venice, crammed with palaces, churches, museums and galleries built on the water; a unique visual experience (▷ 81–102).
Sample some of the local dishes—Italian cooking is regional, seasonal and fresh, and there is always something local on the menu (▷ 332–363).
Visit Florence, a city whose buildings and art collections are a product of the Renaissance at its most revolutionary (▷ 115–134).
Head for a bar and enjoy an excellent cup of coffee.
Shop for the best of Italian style or seek out sumptuous textiles, sophisticated stationery and a wide range of handmade gifts (▷ 222–224).
Take a walk in the country—from north to south there are beautiful areas waiting to be explored (▷ 278–329).
Browse in a food market, a feast of colour and aromas, and an inspiration for all cooks and food-lovers (▷ 222–223).
Swim in clear warm sea off sandy beaches or rocky coasts.

A marble copy of David—4m (13ft) high—by Michelangelo in Piazzale Michelangelo in Florence (left). The original (1501–1504) stands in the Galleria dell'Accademia in Florence

Living Italy

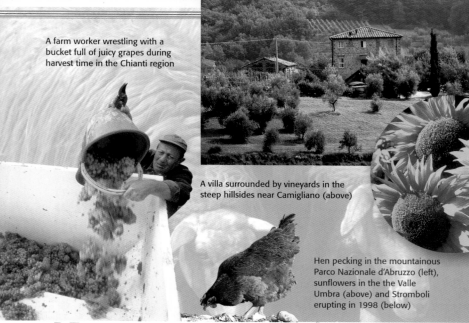

A farm worker wrestling with a bucket full of juicy grapes during harvest time in the Chianti region

A villa surrounded by vineyards in the steep hillsides near Camigliano (above)

Hen pecking in the mountainous Parco Nazionale d'Abruzzo (left), sunflowers in the the Valle Umbra (above) and Stromboli erupting in 1998 (below)

Nature and Landscape

Black runs

Italians love their volcanoes, so much so that they live and farm on their fertile slopes (asparagus is particularly popular) and even holiday on them. Plucky skiers can whiz down Etna, Europe's tallest and most active volcano and the focus for some well-managed ski resorts. The most popular among locals is Piano Provenzana, as the slopes on the northern side of Etna receive more snow. The other main ski town is Linguaglossa, which means 'big tongue of lava'. Of course the resorts face unique problems—the last eruption destroyed ski lifts and cable cars—but passes are cheap and you get the added bonus of some great views of the sea, with a literal whiff of danger thrown in.

Italy covers an area of about 300,000sq km (116,000sq miles) and is surprisingly mountainous, with the Alps forming a natural northern barrier and the Apennines running from the French border down the middle of the country to Sicily. South of the Alps is the Po Valley, the country's largest flat, fertile area, intensively farmed and irrigated. The central regions of Tuscany, Umbria and Lazio are hilly rather than mountainous, ideal for grape and olive cultivation. Farther south and on the islands of Sicily and Sardinia the climate is drier and harsher and the soil generally poorer, making agricultural production difficult. Although 1.4 million people are employed in farming, only 28 per cent of Italy is arable and most farms are small, with the average being only 7ha (17 acres).

Visitors to the major cities quickly become familiar with the problems of air pollution and over-aggressive housebuilding—seen at its worst in the villas constructed within the Agrigento archaeological park—and yet, there are signs that Italy is becoming eco-friendlier. The country has had a decent sprinkling of green MPs and senators—and even a couple of ministers—over the last 25 years, and the national parks are working hard to educate people about the importance of the countryside and endangered habitats.

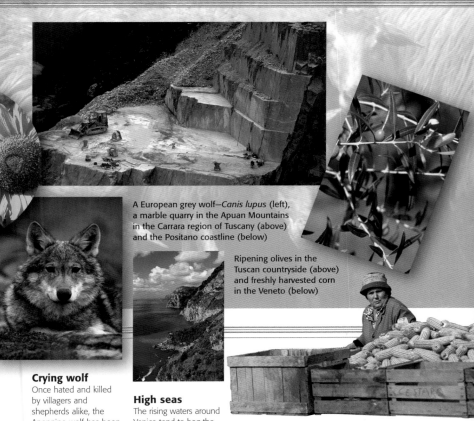

A European grey wolf—*Canis lupus* (left),
a marble quarry in the Apuan Mountains
in the Carrara region of Tuscany (above)
and the Positano coastline (below)

Ripening olives in the
Tuscan countryside (above)
and freshly harvested corn
in the Veneto (below)

Crying wolf

Once hated and killed
by villagers and
shepherds alike, the
Apennine wolf has been
nursed back from near
extinction in the 1970s.
There are now around
400 European wolves
living in Italy and
numbers are growing by
about 7 per cent a year.
If they continue to thrive,
environmentalists
believe that they could
spread throughout the
Alps and cross over into
nearby countries.
Success is most evident
in the Abruzzo National
Park, where Operation
St. Francis has educated
locals about the wolf
population, encouraging
them away from hunting
and leading to the
establishment of a wolf
museum in the park
village of Civitella
Alfedena (▷ 202). This
has also increased visitor
numbers to the area
and transformed the
economy of a once
decaying village—a
striking example of the
powers of ecotourism.

High seas

The rising waters around
Venice tend to hog the
headlines, but Italy, a
country surrounded by
water, could lose
4,500sq km (1,740sq
miles) of land to flooding
and rising seas by the
end of the century. Rapid
development and erratic
weather conditions in
vulnerable areas have
accelerated coastal
erosion. The sunny
southern beaches are
most at risk, with the
largest losses predicted
between the toe and the
heel of Italy around the
Gulf of Taranto.
Government officials will
soon be forced to act if
they want to preserve
the beaches and
profitable tourist industry.
Large-scale investment is
needed and there are
plans to build dikes to
protect areas at risk, but
in the long term they
may have to accept that
some beautiful parts of
Italy will return to the
sea.

Alpine assistance

To get close to the great
Italian outdoors, head for
a *via ferrata*. *Vie ferate*
are metal ladders, pegs,
bridges and ropes,
cemented onto the
mountainsides to help
walkers reach otherwise
inaccessible areas of the
Dolomites without
specialist climbing
equipment. They are not
for the faint-hearted
though—some sections
are vertical and you will
need a good head for
heights. Climbing aids
were first introduced
around 100 years ago,
used by soldiers during
the two World Wars, but
only became popular
with climbers from the
1930s onwards when
the Bochette Way was
opened. Today there are
dozens of routes,
maintained mostly by
the Club Alpino Italiano—
the Italian Alpine Club
(www.cai.it).

Olive branch

You can see olive groves
along the length of Italy,
from the shores of Lake
Garda through Tuscany to
Sicily, and the production
of olive oil is as varied
and complex as wine.
Half of Italy's output is
from Puglia and Calabria
in the south. Italian
olive trees have become
a victim of their own
beauty—they are
frequently stolen and
sold on to private
'collectors' to decorate
their gardens, both
abroad and in the north
of Italy, despite
legislation to protect
them. Unfortunately
many of the replanted
trees die within 12
months. The practice of
uprooting ancient olive
trees is particularly
prevalent in the south,
where thieves and
farmers use mechanical
diggers to prize up the
precious specimens.

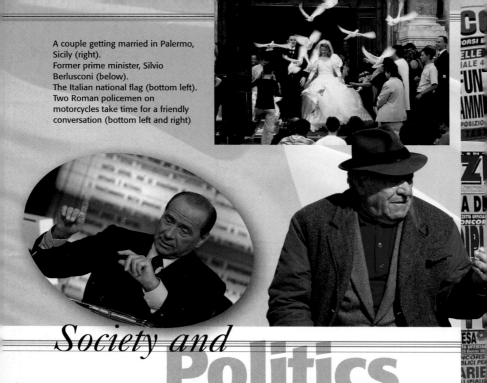

A couple getting married in Palermo, Sicily (right).
Former prime minister, Silvio Berlusconi (below).
The Italian national flag (bottom left).
Two Roman policemen on motorcycles take time for a friendly conversation (bottom left and right)

Society and Politics

Italy has some of the most densely populated areas in Europe, as Italians gravitate towards the cities for economic reasons, leaving their native regions behind. Women's roles are evolving, particularly in the north, with many continuing with their careers after marriage. Over the last 20 years the birth rate has fallen alarmingly, while the divorce rate has rocketed, affecting traditional patterns. Despite this, family and community ties remain strong. The impression of the family gathering to eat together regularly is still a very real one (51 per cent of Italians live within 15 minutes of their mother's home). The concept of family underpins all Italian relationships, whether it's between actual blood relations or simply in the construction of a familiar world of personal ties. Despite past political turmoil, the Italian way of life remains enviable—southern Italians in particular work fewer hours, have more holidays and enjoy a lower cost of living than their frenetic northern European counterparts.

Mamma's children

These days, the image of a prosperous, pasta-serving *mamma* surrounded by a house full of kids is way off the mark. Italy has one of the lowest birth rates in the world, at 9.1 per 1,000 inhabitants, and one of the lowest fertility rates, with 1.2 children born per adult woman (compared with 1.7 in the UK and 2.0 in the US). But parents continue to play a key role in their children's lives. At the last count 56 per cent of 25- to 29-year-olds still lived at home and the number is increasing. According to the Italian statistical institute, Eurispes, the figures are connected: 'Young people are getting married less, and until they do marry they prefer to live at home'.

Two men chatting animatedly in Piazza Navona, Rome (below left)

Emanuele Filiberto, his father Prince Vittorio Emanuele and his mother Princess Marina Doria attending Mass in May 2003 in the Pantheon in Rome (left)

A protester publicizing his cause by attaching himself to the Italian flag (below right)

A bicyclist navigating the busy streets of Milan, Italy's business capital (below)

The Berlusconi factor

Silvio Berlusconi has been surrounded by controversy throughout his business and political career, yet he became the most effective prime minister that Italy has had for decades. He is Italy's richest man and owns a media empire including three television stations, newspapers, an advertising agency and one of Italy's top soccer teams, AC Milan. He was born in Milan and made his first serious money in the city's property boom of the 1960s, before turning his attention to media with the deregulation of State-controlled television. He has supreme self-confidence and flair, which Italian voters admire, although this did not prevent him from losing the closest election in the history of the Italian Republic to Romano Prodi in April 2006.

New men

The role of husbands is beginning to change with the establishment of the Italian Association of Househusbands in the town of Pietrasanta in Tuscany. While working opportunities for women in Italy have improved, females still tend to do the majority of the household tasks. This is where the Association comes in, teaching men how to do housework, cook, clean, and even enjoy it. At the moment it has 2,000 members—mainly those who have chosen to leave the workplace or whose wives are the main breadwinners—and there is growing interest from around the country. Best of all, like Italian housewives, they can also claim pension benefits relating to their work at home.

New women

Most Italian businesses are family affairs and increasingly it is women who are taking their place in management and in boardrooms, not to mention political parties and the civil service. Perhaps a by-product of women raising their career expectations is that Italy now has one of the lowest birth rates in the industrial world. In the cities of the industrial north, though not so much in country areas or the south of Italy, the traditional role of women running the home while the men go out to work is being replaced by either the need for two incomes or a drive by university-educated young women to assert their independence and develop a career. Ten per cent of Italian MPs are women.

Royalty

If you thought the British Royal Family was having a rough time, pity the former Italian sovereigns. Exiled 50 years ago to Genoa after rather too fulsome support for Mussolini, the royals have long argued for their right to return home. Following a change of heart by the Italian parliament, they have made something of a comeback. Vittorio Emanuele, the son of Italy's last king, Umberto II, and just nine years old when he left, returned to Italy (albeit briefly) in December 2002 to talk with Pope John Paul II and swear allegiance to the Republic. Though the family has denied any possibility of wearing a crown again, this hasn't stopped Vittorio's son Emanuele Filiberto appearing in a television commercial for olives that make you 'feel like a king'.

POLIZIA

A banner advertizing the fashion designer Versace in Piazza di Spagna, Rome (right)

Shop for the latest fashions in Salvatore Ferragamo (below left)

A woman laden down with designer shopping bags in Milan (right), a sign for one of Buccellati's luxurious jewellery shops on Via dei Condotti in Rome (below right) and the Fiat 500, a compact style icon designed to cope with narrow streets and tight city parking (bottom)

High **Style**

Is it art?

Could Prada be the new Palladio? Or Gucci the new Giotto? Perhaps it's not too fanciful to say that Italian fashion is the new art. After all, the iconic Giorgio Armani had an entire exhibition at the Guggenheim Museum in New York devoted to the development of his work, which was treated in exactly the same way as the work of a classical Renaissance artist. Gianni Versace's creations have been on show in the same city's Metropolitan Museum of Art. Italy itself has also recognized the skills of its native sons, with the Palazzo Pitti in Florence exhibiting more than 60 Gianfranco Ferre outfits for its grand reopening. To see the art of high fashion for yourself, spend a little time window shopping in Milan.

There's a long-established Italian tradition of craftsmanship and luxurious living, dating right back to the glittering Renaissance courts. With this background, the native sense of style and the cult of the *bella figura*, it's not surprising that fashion and design are booming. Italians seem to infuse everything with elegance, whether it's gorgeous clothes or cars, interior or exterior building design, washing machines or typewriters (Olivetti's Lettera 22 and Lexikon 80 models are even part of the permanent collection of New York's Museum of Modern Art). The sense of style spills over into the media and the creative arts, too, evident in the cutting-edge sharpness of Italian magazines and the distinctive and unmistakable films of Italian-born Federico Fellini and Michelangelo Antonioni. Enterprising and creative Milan is one of the world's genuine style capitals, a hotbed for must-have fashion items and accessories—Gucci, Armani, Prada, Missoni, Versace—as well as affordable, zappy wardrobes from Max Mara and the super-giant Benetton. Refreshingly, there is no pigeonholing of designers according to industry: Donatella Versace has overseen every lifestyle element of the Italian-themed Palazzo Versace hotel in Australia, for example. Italian style is famous worldwide: The rich and stylish cruise the roads in Italian cars by Ferrari, Lamborghini and Maserati, and deck their houses with functional and sleek furniture, fabrics and gadgets.

An impressive line-up of shining vintage Lancias parked on the waterfront in Portofino (above). Giorgio Armani showing off his 2004 autumn Emporio Armani collection on the catwalks of Milan in March 2003 (left)

A woman zipping around the streets of Milan on a scooter (right) and a window display of gloves in Florence (below)

Pininfarina

The Pininfarina company was founded in 1930 by Battista Pininfarina, who was inspired by a meeting with Henry Ford and the entrepreneurial culture of America. His cars came to embody the idea of democracy in car design—an international approach, extremely unusual in Italy at that time, which marked him out as a unique designer. The company's down-to-earth approach means that it has been happy to work on 'normal' cars such as the Peugeot 205 and the Austin-Morris 1100 (its 1952 Ambassador also revolutionized the design of small cars in the US) as well as the more exciting and sporty names such as Ferrari, Alfa Romeo and the two-seater sports car, Enjoy, winner at the Geneva Motor Show 2003.

Benetton—a success story

Luciano Benetton is said to have sold his accordion to buy his sister a knitting machine, setting the ball rolling for the development of one of the retailing world's great success stories. Today, there are over 7,000 Benetton stores in more than 120 countries, selling affordable and stylish knitwear and much more besides. The company owns huge tracts of Argentina, where some of their 280,000 sheep are raised, and the wool from these animals only provides about 10 per cent of the company's annual requirements. On a global scale, Benetton has had far more impact than big Italian fashion names such as Armani, Missoni, Pucci, Gucci et al. Lines differ from country to country—and the Italian stores definitely have the cutting edge.

La bella figura

The concept of *bella figura* means many things—keeping up a good front, not making a fool of yourself, and above all, looking good. It's a little bit presence, and a little bit self-respect, and a little bit being careful not to let the side down. The opposite is *brutta figura*, as in the expression *fare una brutta figura*, to show oneself up. Around 60 per cent of Italian women buy a new wardrobe twice a year, their choice dictated by the latest shades and styles. When the seasons change, it is common for women to take a day off work just to rearrange their wardrobe. Italians spend up to 50 per cent of their disposable income on clothes and fashion, and designer wear is considered an option for all. It's not what you've got, but what you project that's important.

Little stinger

The Vespa was built and named by Enrico Piaggio—'*Sembra una vespa*' ('It looks like a wasp')—to meet post-war needs for an affordable means of getting around for the general public, both men and women, that kept their clothes clean (Piaggio now produces a range of clothes and accessories, too). The scooter owes its revolutionary construction to the aeronautic background of its designer, Corradino d'Ascanio. From humble beginnings it became a cult icon, its elegantly simple look coming to symbolize a sense of freedom and independence for each new generation, thanks to careful image adjustments. Consequently it has been a scene stealer in films from Fellini's *La Dolce Vita* right through to Austin Powers' *Goldmember*.

Restoration of Giotto's frescoes, in the Scrovegni Chapel, Padua (top).
A fresco in the Villa Imperiale, Sicily (left).
The Roman ruins in Herculaneum (right).
The Leaning Tower of Pisa (below)

Living with History

The role Italy's history plays in the 21st century is particularly apparent in the continued lively celebration of ancient annual festivals around the country. Physically, it's simply impossible to avoid the artistic remains and treasures of the country's many previous cultures, with the incorporation of ancient temples into modern churches and marvellous frescoes in tiny villages as well as the more monumental grandeur of the capital. With 31 UNESCO World Heritage Sites, Italy stands at the top of the international list for cultural importance. The artistic heritage spans over 4,000 years, comprising archaeological sites, monuments, churches and works of art. In the last 50 years Italy has made outstanding achievements in the field of restoration, preserving important treasures nationwide and rising superbly to challenges such as the aftermath of the 1997 earthquake in Umbria. However, the ongoing process of decay is still frightening. Many regions contain nearly abandoned towns and villages, churches have been looted and stand empty, and often the scaffolding around historic buildings remains in place for years. Until recently over 15,000 objects vanished from churches, palaces and museums annually, while archaeological sites have been ruthlessly pillaged. There's no easy answer in a country with so many top-flight treasures, but it's generally agreed there could be a better balance between the money poured into the major attractions and the neglect of a broad conservation infrastructure.

Fragile frescoes

In terms of restoration, there's probably more to do with regard to preserving frescoes than anything else. Buildings and stonework also require urgent restoration, but, with frescoes, time is of the essence. Fresco technique involves applying pigment to wet plaster, the drying process causing a chemical reaction that fixes the image permanently into the plaster. The condition of centuries-old frescoes deteriorates for a number of reasons; some problems go as far back as the artist's original application of the pigments, while others arise through damp and pollution. New techniques are being developed all the time, ensuring that, with proper attention, frescoes will survive indefinitely.

The ruins at Selinunte in Sicily (above).
Canal Grande in Venice (far right).
Neptune having a wash in Rome (below)

Fresco fragments from
the octagonal Baptistery
in Parma (left); the
Cattedrale di San Francesco
in Assisi (below)

Going underground

Underneath modern Rome is a buried, hidden city encountered by building developers who constantly unearth new remains whenever they start to dig. St. Peter's Basilica sits on top of a massive Roman necropolis, but to get a closer look at Rome's history head for the 12th-century Basilica of San Clemente near the Colosseum, below which you can see the original 4th-century and even earlier 1st-century buildings including a temple dedicated to the ancient god Mithras. So extensive are the remains that guided visits are now offered by several tour operators. These include Roma Sotteranea (www.underome.com), an association devoted to the underbelly of the capital.

Can you spot a fake?

If you fancy a masterwork but have no millions to spare, you could commission a genuine fake from artist-to-the-stars Daniele Donde, whose client list included the late Diana, Princess of Wales. Donde is the latest in a long line of fine Italian copyists, including Alceo Dossena (1878–1937). A sculptor and stonemason, Dossena was so good that unscrupulous dealers started to sell his work as the real thing, and experts and museums simply couldn't tell the difference. When the artist found out what was going on, he blew the whistle on the charade and took his dealer to court, claiming that he had been cheated out of thousands of lire. It is believed that many of his pieces are still collected and exhibited unwittingly as genuine originals today.

Sensitive statues

Michelangelo's *David*, in the Galleria dell'Accademia in Florence, has had a facelift—financed partly by big names such as Sting and Mel Gibson. As always, restoration of the 500-year-old masterpiece of sculpture is controversial. Early efforts included inserting metal pins in his broken left arm in the 16th century, cleaning by hydrochloric acid in the 19th century and the addition of a new toe in the 20th century when it was accidentally chiselled off. Modern restorers are more cautious: one walked out after an argument about the use of water-soaked poultices rather than careful dry brushing.

Acqua alta

Venice has been battling against water for 1,500 years—it has sunk more than 23cm (9in) over the last 100 years—and scientists now estimate that, unless dramatic action is taken, the city will be destroyed by the end of this century. Dedicated groups such as Venice in Peril (www.veniceinperil.org) and Save Venice (www.savevenice.org) raise awareness and international support, and the latest move by the Italian government is to install huge flood-control barriers, a series of 78 mobile gates that can be used during high tides. The Moses Project, as it is known, is not without its critics: Environmentalists claim it will cause irreparable damage to the area's ecosystem.

The Vilo Per Grango Easter Parade in Gargano (far left). Detail of Annibale Carracci's *Assumption of the Virgin* in the church of Santa Maria del Popolo, Rome (left). Crowds gathered outside the Basilica di San Pietro in Rome, waiting to catch a glimpse of Pope Benedict XVI (below). Detail of a fresco by Ghirlandaio in the church of Santa Trinità in Florence (bottom)

Catholic Italy

A new Pope

April 2005 was an extraordinary month in the life of the Roman Catholic Church. On 2 April, Pope John Paul II died after serving 26 years as head of the world's 1.1 billion Roman Catholics. Millions of pilgrims subsequently flocked to the Vatican to say their final farewell to the Pope, and to attend the emotional open-air service, which accompanied his funeral in the Basilica di San Pietro. The election of his successor then gripped the media for several weeks until, on 24 April, Cardinal Joseph Ratzinger emerged, taking the name Pope Benedict XVI. He was installed as the new pontiff in a Mass in Piazza San Pietro.

Although Church and State are theoretically separate in Italy, the Catholic Church is so well established that its position of strength seems unassailable. Around 85 per cent of native-born Italians are still nominally Roman Catholic, and celebrations such as First Communion remain a major event. Still important, too, is the tradition of *onomastico*, celebrating your saint's day as you would your own birthday (the saint who shares your first name). And yet many young Italians take divorce, birth control and abortion for granted and cracks are appearing—over 95 per cent of Italians are baptized, but fewer than 10 per cent attend Mass regularly. Many churches, not only in Rome but also in remote villages, are treasure houses of art from past ages of religious devotion. Some are funded by local government to conserve this heritage. Some churches are thus becoming monuments, museums and art galleries more than places of active worship. The 21st century will bring further challenges. Not least of these is growing immigration from Africa, Asia and the Middle East, resulting in increased numbers of practising Buddhists and Muslims in the country. This is bringing about political and social conflict, as seen in the divisive comments of the former prime minister, Silvio Berlusconi, about Islam following the terrorist attacks against the US on 11 September 2001. But the Church thinks in centuries, not decades, and continues to view modern apathy with equanimity.

A statue of the Madonna and Child outside a building in Burano, Venice (left). The Turin Shroud (right). A ceramic panel depicting St. Francis on Asissi's external walls (lower left). A mosaic crucifix in the church of San Clemente, Rome (lower right). A Swiss Guard (far right). The new pope meets his cardinals (below)

Superstitions

Some Italians can be very superstitious, and some bizarre practices have been incorporated into religious ceremonies, such as the annual display of the blood of St. Gennaro in Naples. If it liquefies during the service, the city is said to be blessed with prosperity for the coming year. And in Siracusa, a church has been built around a tiny image of the Virgin Mary that is supposed to weep miraculously. Italians have an inordinate veneration for objects linked to saints and associate them with miracles. Bones from the right hand of Santa Lucia are displayed on a special altar in the Duomo of Siracusa and are considered to be endowed with healing powers.

Papal audience

General audiences with the Pope are usually held on Wednesdays at 11am in St. Peter's Basilica, or in the *Aula Paolo VI*, the hall of Papal audiences, and are open to the public. In the summer they are held in St. Peter's Square or at the Pope's summer residence south of Rome, Castel Gandolfo. To participate in a general audience, you must apply for a ticket to the office of the Prefetto della Casa Pontificia, 00120 Città del Vaticano (tel 06 6988 3114) at least two weeks in advance. A few tickets are usually available the day before at the Bronze Door of St. Peter's Basilica. If you are a Catholic, you will be asked to bring a letter of introduction from your parish priest and you will need to show a passport or ID card to the Swiss Guard at the entrance.

Nazareth House

Italy has many pilgrimage sites, most holding saints' relics. But pilgrims to the town of Loreto come to see the Virgin Mary's house (▷ 184–185). According to pious legend, this humble cottage—scene of the Annunciation and Jesus' family home—was miraculously transported by angels from Nazareth to Loreto in the late 13th century. Recent investigations indicate that, after the Crusades, a noble Byzantine family called Angeli shipped the stones of the Holy House to Italy, where it was rebuilt. It has only three walls; the fourth side formed by a grotto dug out of the rock in Nazareth, a common arrangement for houses of that time. Technical comparisons show the Loreto house and the Nazareth grotto to be contiguous.

Vatican City state

Technically, the Vatican is not part of Italy, though it lies within the heart of Rome. It is a sovereign independent state which negotiates with governments around the world and is represented at the United Nations and in other political bodies. Vatican City is the smallest city-state in the world, one-third the size of Monaco, and has fewer than 1,000 permanent residents, mainly church officials and a security force, the Swiss Guard. It issues passports and produces its own euro coins and bank notes and its own stamps. The independence of Vatican City is guaranteed by the Lateran Treaty of 1929, amended in 1984, when the main change was that the Catholic Church would no longer be the official state religion of Italy. Nonetheless, its values and traditions are deeply ingrained in Italian culture and everyday living.

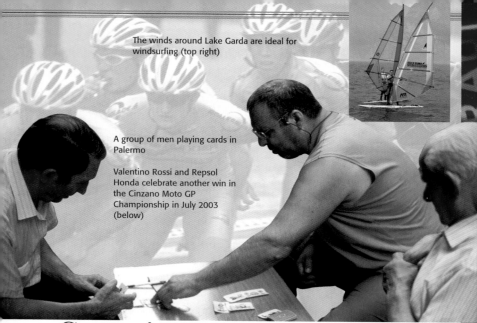

The winds around Lake Garda are ideal for windsurfing (top right)

A group of men playing cards in Palermo

Valentino Rossi and Repsol Honda celebrate another win in the Cinzano Moto GP Championship in July 2003 (below)

Sporting Life

Olympic spirit

The 2006 Winter Olympic Games have turned Turin into a world-class venue for winter sports. The preparations included a massive investment to upgrade skiing and skating facilities, and building the state-of-the-art Olympic Stadium. Torino Palaghiaccio is an impressive new skating complex, and the Olympic Palasport built for the ice hockey competitions has transformed the urban landscape. The village of Barbonecchia now has the best snowboard runs in Europe, and Cesana a bobsleigh and luge run that includes the Toro, or bull, a section of three successive curves. The hills of Pragelato offer cross-country skiing and ski jumping against a spectacular backdrop of Piedmont countryside.

Sport is part of daily life in Italy, a country that has its own daily newspapers devoted entirely to the subject—*La Gazzetta dello Sport* (the pink paper) and the *Corriere dello Sport*. The Italian Olympic Committee's president, Gianni Petrucci, has stressed the importance of promoting all sports within the country, but football (soccer) is the undisputed king by some distance (though when it comes to actually taking part, bicycling probably has the edge). Italy also has a passion for skiing, skating and other winter sports, which fully justified the selection of Turin as the venue for the 2006 Winter Olympics, and northern Italy now has some of the finest and most up-to-date winter sports facilities anywhere in Europe. But football continues to dominate the headlines, whether it's pay-TV negotiations delaying the start of the season, or the progress in European competitions of Italy's leading sides, AC Milan, Juventus and Inter Milan. There is interest in other sports, notably bicycling and motor racing. The Italians' obvious ability in ball games extends to basketball, handball, volleyball and tennis, not to mention rugby (the national side is now firmly established in the prestigious Six Nations tournament) and, perhaps more surprisingly, cricket.

Paragliding in Spello in Umbria (left)

Cyclists exploring the Italian Lakes near Lake Iseo (right)

Medieval football in front of Florence's Santa Croce during the Calcio Storico (left)

The fast-paced bareback horseracing of the Palio in Siena (left)

Sardinian stampede

There is plenty of horsemanship, historic costumes and partying at the dangerous downhill race the L'Ardia di San Costantino in Sedilo, Sardinia (5–7 July). Though the origins of the race are probably pagan, the race is said to commemorate Constantine's—and consequently Christianity's—victory in AD312 at the battle of Ponte Milvio (Milvio Bridge), the race recreating his historic battle charge. The riders and their horses meet up on a hill just outside the town's sanctuary and after various speeches and prayers for safety, they gallop at top speed down the slope, past the sanctuary and towards the finishing post in town (a dry fountain), with the man representing Constantine at the front—it's a safe bet who's going to win each year!

Driving skills

Italy has a passion for motor racing. It has bred some top Formula 1 drivers, including current stars Giancarlo Fisichella and Jarno Trulli, and the Ferrari team is the pride of Italy. If you are a fan, Italy offers several classic race weekends. The Grand Prix circuit at Monza, near Milan, is on the Formula 1 calendar usually in early September. You can also see the stars of Formula 1 in action on the San Marino Grand Prix circuit at Imola, usually in April, the start of the European motor-racing season. Lonigo, near Vicenza, hosts motorcycle races from the Speedway World Championship.

Packs of cards

Bridge players will know that the Italians are keen on their cards, but if you observe a card game in Italy, the deck and game may look strange. In place of clubs, hearts, spades and diamonds many areas also have coins, cups, swords and clubs. Packs—which have a marvellous medieval design and no queen— also vary regionally in their shape (Trento's are long, Naples' are small) and number (most games use 40, some use 52), and while some games like Scopa—a complicated capture game—are nationally popular, there are regional playoffs such as *madrasso* (similar to bridge) in Venice and *coteccio*, a trick-taking game, in Trieste.

Gladiator school

For the last 10 years the fun-loving Gruppo Storico Romano, based at the appropriately historical address of Via Appia Antica in Rome, has been running regular gladiator training classes with frighteningly authentic swordplay and in full gladiatorial regalia. The range of courses corresponds to your level of interest, from introductory training, two months of twice-weekly sessions (after which you can specialize in various weapons and styles), to total-immersion courses that last three days. At the end of a course, 'survivors' are given a medal and declared *tiro* (beginner gladiator). Rather like the craze for replacing a trip to the gym with toned-down fighting techniques, the idea of keeping fit and relieving stress is as strong among Gruppo members as their proud interest in Roman history.

Orvieto wine (below left); a masked figure during Carnevale in Venice (below right); Caffé del Greco in Milan (below)

The opening of Calcio Storico in Piazza della Signoria, Florence (above); a child dressed up for the Carnevale in Venice (left); the poster from Fellini's film *La Dolce Vita* (below)

La Dolce Vita

VINO BUONO
VERNACCIA DI S. GIMIGNANO

The perfect espresso

Whether it's made in a one-cup pot at home or comes from a gleaming machine in a bar, all Italian coffee is made by the espresso method. In bars, freshly ground coffee is put into a filter, compressed, and attached to the machine. Hot, not boiling, water is forced through, producing an intense, aromatic brew with a distinctive *crema* (cream) on top. Milk is frothed with steam from a separate nozzle and added for the perfect cappuccino. The roast varies from region to region, becoming increasingly potent the further south you go, but Romans claim to make the best coffee because their water is so good.

For centuries, visitors to Italy have found something invigorating about the country, whether it be the cultural aspects beloved of the Grand Tourists, or the personal growth outlined in E. M. Forster's *A Room with a View*. Family life, sociability, food and drink, civic pride and cultural interests all play their part in shaping the concept of *la dolce vita*—the sweet life—as does the obsession with style and design.

La dolce vita is a double-edged attitude, though, as outlined in Fellini's famous film, which did much to internationalize the philosophy: Fellini shows a post-war Italy enjoying a period of relative peace and stability and wallowing in a haze of decadence. But elements of the sweet lifestyle are on the wane, with increasing European homogenization threatening the survival of the traditional siesta and the *passeggiata*, the early evening stroll. Yet there is no doubt that Italians are pleasure people; a recent poll by Censis shows that more than a quarter of Italians are not happy with their sweet life.

Slow Food

The essence of Italian cooking is good ingredients, but no less important is the way meals are prepared, eaten and appreciated. To this end, the Slow Food movement was born in 1986 and has now grown into an international lobby, promoting the enjoyment of eating. It also campaigns to preserve ingredients threatened by environmental degradation, industrial standardization, and strict hygiene legislation. Members regard themselves as 'eco-gastronomes' whose main priority is to counter what they see as shabby eating habits, particularly junk food. Slow Food promotes its ideals through events and festivals, and publishes *The Ark of Taste*, a catalogue of products and dishes close to extinction (www.slowfood.com).

The Story of Italy

Greeks, Carthaginians, Etruscans

Surrounded by water and cut off from the European landmass by a mountain barrier, the boot-shaped peninsula of modern Italy was destined to develop into an exceptionally individual country. Despite being isolated from the north by the Alps, its shores were easily reached by eastern and southern invaders, the great early civilizations of the Phoenicians, who settled Carthage, and the Greeks. From their colonies in present-day Sicily and Sardinia, the Phoenicians established trade routes with Carthage, while the Greeks set up a new and magnificent empire in the south, totally assimilating the native people.

Farther north, the enigmatic Etruscans, whose history and language have barely been penetrated, were the dominant civilization. They lived in an area between the Tiber and Arno rivers and established a confederation of 12 sophisticated city-states, which traded with the Greek colonies in the south. As their power grew, they edged out the other northern indigenous peoples, the Ladini, the Ligurians and the Sabines. With the emergence of Rome, their civilization waned and their culture and influence were eclipsed by the growing Empire.

A wall painting in the Etruscan tombs at Monterozzi (right)

Magna Graecia

In the eighth century BC, the Greeks colonized southern Italy and Sicily, establishing hugely prosperous colonies (Magna Graecia). The cities of Siracusa, Sybaris, Metapontum and Tarentum became richer than many cities in Greece. By 400BC the Romans had moved in and sacked the most important, but some superb examples remain: Paestum, south of Salerno, Metapontum, with its archaeological museum, the theatres in Taormina (▷ 217) and Siracusa (▷ 216), and the temples at Segesta, Selinunte (▷ 214) and Agrigento (▷ 212) in Sicily.

1200 BC

An Etruscan plate in the Museum of Ancient Tuscany in Chiusi (above); a Carthaginian coin (above right); the amphitheatre at Segesta in Sicily (right)

The Etruscans

Much of what we know about the Etruscans comes from discoveries made in their necropolises, huge stone cities of the dead found at the sites of their main settlements in central Italy. Their cities of wood have long since gone, but the stone cemeteries remain. The tombs were lavish; some, as at Cerveteri and Orvieto, take the form of miniature houses lining paved streets, others, like Tarquinia, are beautifully decorated underground chambers. Elsewhere there are apartments full of funerary niches, known as *colombari*. These tombs for the afterlife were often filled with statues, jewellery and vases, and decorated with religious scenes of people hunting, fishing, playing games and dancing.

The Phoenicians

The Phoenicians came from modern-day Lebanon, emerging in the 12th century BC as what was to become the greatest trading nation of the ancient world. The Greeks called them Phoenicians after the valuable purple dye derived from molluscs that they exported all over the ancient world. They were middlemen as much as anything, buying in and selling on goods from all over the Mediterranean. The early Italian civilizations were good customers, and the Phoenicians, from their western power base of Carthage, established trading settlements in Sicily and southern Italy. To the north, the Etruscans were eager for luxury goods, particularly purple-dyed fabrics and Greek pottery, which were traded for Etruscan items such as jewellery and mirrors.

The Ladini

The far northern valleys of the Dolomites, where the regions of Trentino, Alto-Adige and the Veneto meet, is still home to one of Italy's oldest peoples. The Ladini, a distinct ethnic group with their own language and culture, have lived here since 4000BC. Their epics portray a history of battles, triumphs, disasters and treachery. Threatened by Germanic tribes from the north and marauders from the south, the Ladini were constantly at war, invoking their primitive divinities for help. When Christianity arrived, they blended the new religion with the old, investing Christian saints with their gods' powers. Ladino is still spoken in the area around the Sella Mountains, and the people preserve much of their culture and customs today.

Prehistoric buildings and bronzes

Little is known about the first Sardinians or where they came from. These prehistoric tribes that dominated the island between 1500 and 500BC are known as the Nuraghi, the same name given to their temples and necropolises, which are scattered all over the island. For years Sardinian peasants believed that they were the tombs of a race of giants from whom they were descended. Enigmatic structures, they are mainly round, with a vaulted interior, connected to an upper terrace by stairs and corridors. Equally mysterious are the hundreds of eighth-century BC statuettes that have also been found on the island—bizarre bronzes of gods, people and animals.

An Etruscan vase (left)

A detail of a Phoenician sarcophagus (left). The farewell of Admetos and Alketis, a scene on an Etruscan vase found at Vulci (right)

600BC

The Etruscan barrow tombs within the necropolis that surrounds the medieval town of Cerveteri (above)

The Hellenistic Greek theatre near Taormina, rebuilt by the Romans (above).
The sixth-century Etruscan bronze of Romulus and Remus in the Musei Capitolini in Rome (left)

Roman Empire

The Roman Empire prospered at the expense of the Etruscans, who were absorbed into Roman culture and finally displaced. The Romans went on to defeat the Carthaginians in the Mediterranean, winning large parts of North Africa and Spain along the way. After conquering Italy they spread out over the rest of the Mediterranean. As the generals, troops and administrators fanned out over Europe, their ideas and inventions formed the bedrock for much that is familiar in today's society. Fundamental concepts of law and order, justice, democracy, literature and philosophy, which had been pioneered by the Greeks, were adopted and developed by the Romans. They also gave those they conquered a taste for good plumbing, warm houses, paved roads and luxurious living. The Roman era lasted almost 1,000 years, evolving from a high-minded republic to a hedonistic empire. Periods of expansion and prosperity were tempered by civil unrest, and from AD300 the Empire was divided into separate eastern and western territories. By AD400, the emperors were reliant on the support of disenchanted mercenaries in their conquered territories, and the frontiers collapsed. The barbarians moved in and a dark veil descended over Italy.

Julius Caesar

Soldier, orator, first consul of Rome and financier, Julius Caesar looked fate in the eye in 49BC, when he left the battlefields of Gaul to challenge his rival Pompey for control of the Empire. He took his troops with him, and as he approached the River Rubicon, the boundary between Gaul and Italy, he was faced with a major decision. It was a heinous crime to enter Roman territory with an army without informing the Senate. He vacillated, unable to decide whether or not to risk all. Then came his famous words, 'Let the die be cast' and he crossed the river to march on Rome. By 44BC, he had been appointed ruler for life; a few months later he was dead, assassinated on the Ides of March.

Items from a Roman toilet set (left); Julius Caesar (102–44BC)

6OO BC

Mosaic of Neptune and Aphrodite in Herculaneum (Ercolano) (above). The amphitheatre in Pompei (right)

What the Romans did for us

Superbly practical, the Romans' inventions made life easier and more comfortable. Good road networks were essential to travel their huge empire. Some still exist, others are the foundation for today's highways. Aqueducts efficiently brought fresh water over long distances to prosperous cities. Bathing was now a feasible option and people benefited from hot and cold running water, steam baths and clean toilets. The latter were often communal—a great place to catch up on the gossip. Cold winters were made bearable by central heating, with hot air being circulated under the floors by a flue system. The Romans also invented dozens of small gadgets—reliable water clocks, cooking utensils, brushes, combs, mirrors, and comfortable chairs and beds.

Hannibal and the elephants

Even before the great Carthaginian general Hannibal arrived at the foothills of the Alps to invade Rome, his battle elephants had had an adventurous trip from their starting point in Spain. They had to cross the River Rhône, deep and fast, and evade the Roman sentries. The river was too deep for the elephants to wade through, so Hannibal had water wings made for them from inflated bladders, and floated them across. Thirty-seven elephants made it to the Alps and the crossing took 19 days, trudging through late snow and struggling on the slopes. The descent into Italy was too steep for many of the elephants, and most perished, while only a few of the remainder made it through the following winter.

Vestal Virgins

The Vestal Virgins were the custodians of the sacred fire, a perpetual flame of great religious significance. This cult involved the safety of the state, and the smoke emerging from the circular marble Temple of Vesta, goddess of the hearth, was a sign that all was well. There were six Vestals, girls of unblemished character recruited from irreproachable families. They served the goddess for 30 years: 10 learning their duties, 10 performing them, and 10 passing on their knowledge. Sacred to Vesta, they enjoyed incredible privileges, but led circumscribed lives, constantly watched by the chief priest and his spies. If a Vestal slipped, the punishments were severe. Breaking the vow of chastity was seen as betraying the faith of Rome and the offender was buried alive.

Hannibal, the famous Carthaginian general (247–182BC, left)

Rome in flames

According to legend, Emperor Nero played the fiddle and watched while Rome burned around him in AD64, having set fire to the city to see how Troy had looked in flames. It's a notorious tale, but fails to stand up to scrutiny, as violins were not invented for another 1,500 years. Two-thirds of the city did burn that year, though: Nero considered much of the city ugly and wanted to rebuild on a grand scale and rumours were rife that the fires had been started on his orders. To see the results, head for the ruins of Nero's Golden House, near the Colosseum in Rome, one of the largest and most ostentatious palaces in the world in its heyday.

Nero reigned for 13 years, 7 months and 28 days before he killed himself in AD68 (below)

AD 400

Detail of a fresco in a Pompei garden (above left)

Hubert Robert's (1733–1808) painting *The Fire of Rome, 18 July AD64* (above)

The Atrium Vestae in the Foro Romano, where the six Vestal Virgins lived for 30 years and kept the sacred flame burning at the Temple of Vesta, the symbol of Rome's continuity (above)

Dark Times

For the next 500 years chaos whirled through Italy. Ostrogoths, Visigoths and the ferocious Huns moved south, as the remnants of the Roman Empire were bitterly contested. The Ostrogoths under Theodoric emerged triumphant in the west, while the Byzantines held the east. The Ostrogoths continued moving west and in AD552 established a presence in southern Italy and Sardinia that was to last 500 years. To the north, the Lombards moved south into Italy, gradually extending their power. Franks eased east from Gaul, advantageously allying themselves with the emergent papacy, a crafty move that led to the Frankish ruler Charlemagne being crowned Emperor of the Holy Roman Empire by Pope Leo III in AD800. This empire covered central and northern Italy; to the south, the Byzantines had been joined by Arabs and Greeks. No dynasty or ruler was stable, nothing endured. Charlemagne's empire collapsed, and by 1000 Italy had no official ruler. Into the void swept the Normans, synthesizing their culture with the half-Arab, half-Byzantine south. The power of the papacy grew, the Holy Roman Empire rose again, and time was ripe for the start of two centuries of conflict on the issue of papal versus imperial supremacy. The Guelphs supported the pope, the Ghibellines the emperor, and Italy was torn between the two.

The sack of Rome

By AD410 the writing was on the wall for the tottering Western Empire. The Visigothic chief, Alaric, had blockaded Rome for two years, hoping for loot and prestige. The Western Roman Emperor, Honorius, now based in Ravenna, refused his demands, and Alaric, his patience finally snapping, let his troops loose on the already dying city. For three days, the Visigoths plundered, killed, raped and looted, finally moving south and devastating Rome. Alaric died soon after, and myth has him buried, together with a hoard of treasure, in a diverted riverbed in Calabria. The great Roman cities and civic buildings gradually decayed, but they were still used, and Latin continued to be widely spoken. The might of Rome collapsed, not with a bang but a whimper.

Atilla, King of the Huns (right inset), and a Byzantine mosaic of Emperor Justinian I (AD483–565) in the Basilica of San Vitale in Ravenna (right)

400

The Fall of Rome (AD410), illustrating the death of Alaric after the sack of Rome (below)

Cultural U-turn

The Lombards, a Germanic barbarian tribe, moved south into Italy in the sixth century AD. They arrived with barbaric customs, such as drinking out of their enemies' skulls, and set up their capital in Cividale del Friuli in the far northeast. Within a century they had moved farther south under the ruthless King Aistulf, taking Ravenna, and embraced Christianity and its culture. They left some of the most beautiful and serene artworks of the Dark Ages, gently smiling saints and charming reliefs, while their excavated tombs have yielded fabulous gold jewellery, crosses, swords and shield-holds. The designs are sinuous and intricate, the workmanship sophisticated. The Lombards were defeated by the Franks in 774, leaving a fascinating artistic legacy behind.

Larger-than-life ladies

Roman and Byzantine Ravenna produced two remarkable women, both captured in the city's stunning mosaics. Galla Placidia was half-sister to the fifth-century Roman Emperor Honorius, and was kidnapped by the Goths, creating a major scandal when she married one of her abductors and fought beside him in battle. The other leading lady was Theodora, wife of Emperor Justinian, who lived in the sixth century. Her previous professions as circus entertainer, sex-show performer and prostitute made tongues wag. Aristocratic Romans were horrified when the sagacious Justinian married her and she embarked on a consortship of bad conduct, marked by acquisitiveness, corruption and venality.

Red hair and food for the gods

Sweeping into southern Italy and Sicily in the 11th century, the Normans created one of the Mediterranean's most vibrant cultures. They intermarried with the dark-skinned southerners, leaving a genetic legacy that's still alive and well in Sicily. Carrot-coloured hair, straight Norman noses and startlingly blue eyes are found in even remote villages, and some Sicilian dialects still contain substantial numbers of French words and phrases. The Arab inheritance appeals to the tastebuds. Rice and oranges, extra-sweet desserts and pastries stuffed with nuts and candied fruit, and fish served with couscous are all Arab imports. Street food vendors sell dishes that wouldn't seem out of place in a souk, while combinations of sweet and savoury in meat and fish dishes reflect North African cuisine.

The coronation of Charlemagne

Charlemagne (747–814), king of the Franks and de facto ruler of Western Europe, came south in the winter of 800 to help Pope Leo III deal with the Lombards. On Christmas Day he attended Mass in Rome, and while he was kneeling in prayer the Pope picked up a crown and set it on Charlemagne's head, declaring him Emperor of Western Europe, apparently to Charlemagne's surprise. The story's probably apocryphal, and it's more likely that Pope and would-be Emperor cooked up the plan between them beforehand. The coronation was a boost to them both; it enhanced Charlemagne's reputation, while stressing the power of the papacy to make kings, increasing their temporal and spiritual clout.

Charlemagne (right)

Empress Placidia and her son depicted on an ivory diptych in Monza (left) and an icon of the canonized Byzantine Empress Theodora (above)

1280

A market stand in Pompei (left); the Basilica of San Vitale in Ravenna (below)

A Byzantine mosaic (cAD547) of Empress Theodora with her court of two ministers and seven women in the Basilica of San Vitale, Ravenna (left)

Northern Prosperity

Confusion continued into the 13th century, with the south and Sicily hotly contested by the French and the Aragonese, the papacy fleeing to Avignon, and the political power of the major rulers under pressure all over the country. But times were changing, and no more so than in central and northern Italy. By 1300, some 300 virtually independent city-states had emerged, with a concept of citizenship radically different from that of the traditional lord-and-vassal relationship. Growing wealth from commerce and trade provided a good breeding ground for the birth of a ruling class in many of these cities, but one where the ruling class constantly feuded among itself for supremacy. Fed up with the bloodshed and perpetual vendettas, by the 15th century many cities had opted for rule by a single overlord strong enough to maintain order. The day of the *signore* had arrived. These despotic rulers oiled up to the papacy, obtaining official titles to bolster their power, so that by the second half of the 15th century most city-states were under princely, rather than republican, rule. Italy was well on the way to taking the political shape it was to maintain up until unification in the 19th century.

The Marketplace in Naples during the Plague of 1656 (1672) by Carlo Coppola (left)

The Black Death of 1348

The Black Death, which wiped out between 25 and 50 per cent of Europe's population over four years, arrived in Italy from China via a Genoese ship returning from the Black Sea in spring 1348. Most people contracted the bubonic strain, transmitted by infected fleas carried by rats. The first symptom was the appearance of the dreaded buboes, pus-filled swellings around the neck, armpits or groin. Death followed within a week. With no defence and no understanding of the cause of the plague, people panicked and law and order broke down. It was at this time that the Florentine writer Giovanni Boccaccio wrote his great work *The Decameron*, documenting individual accounts of suffering.

1280

The Cappella Colleoni in Bergamo (above). A marble statue of Dante with an eagle at his feet in Florence's vast Piazza Santa Croce (right). Cypress trees adorn an otherwise bare hillside near Mount Amata (middle)

Condottiere—medieval mercenaries

The city-states were constantly battling it out for territorial, commercial and political advantage. Their populations were small, their citizens too busy for campaigns and sieges. The solution was the *condottiere*, a mercenary leader who offered himself, and his men, to the highest bidder. Attracted to the richer contracts, they amassed huge wealth and prestige, their deeds and deaths celebrated. Bartolomeo Colleoni, better known as 'The Invincible', was born in 1400. He fought for the Venetians and became their captain general, leaving behind the beautiful Colleoni Chapel in Bergamo and donating his wealth to the city of Venice, where he is commemorated by Verocchio's great equestrian statue.

The language of literature

After the fall of Rome, Latin was still widely spoken throughout Italy, but a Latin that was constantly evolving as the waves of invaders introduced new words from their own languages. During the more prosperous times of the 13th and 14th centuries, scholarship and literature once more found a place, and the earliest of the new writers all spoke the Tuscan dialect, rich in Latin roots. Dante, Boccaccio and Petrarch wrote in Tuscan, which became established as Italy's literary language and later became the country's official language. The other dialects clung on; many are still spoken today, though mass communication is eroding them fast, and there are few modern Italians who cannot speak 'pure' Italian as well as their local dialect.

Marco Polo

In 1295 Marco Polo returned to Venice after 25 years in China. He had learned many Eastern languages on his travels, but returned to find himself a stranger and a little rusty in his native tongue. He came to fame when he was captured in 1298 during the Battle of Curzola and imprisoned in Genoa, where he shared a cell with the writer Rustichello di Pisa. Enthralled by Marco's tales, Rustichello turned them into a book, *Divisament dou Monde* (Description of the World). A bestseller, it was translated from French into dozens of languages, and revealed the wonderful wealth of the Orient. The book soon became known as *Il Milioni*, while Marco earned the nickname of Messer Marco Milioni, for the millions of tall tales he told.

St. Francis of Assisi

St. Francis was born to wealthy parents in 1182, spending his youth drinking and womanizing. He continued in this way until a spell in prison turned him to God. In 1209 he decided to dedicate his life to preaching. His message was simple—do away with material goods, love God in poverty, chastity and obedience, and see the Lord's hand in the beauty of the world. He loved nature, and is famous for blessing birds and animals—beautifully depicted by Giotto in a fresco in Assisi (▷ 137). He attracted 12 followers and obtained papal permission to found a religious order, the Franciscans. In 1224, he received the wounds of Christ on his hands and feet and in his side, and died two years later. He was canonized in 1228.

The Italian writer Giovanni Boccaccio (1313–75), from a print by Cornelius Van Dalen (right)

Petrarch (1304–74), one of the earliest modern lyric poets (left middle). Marco Polo (left)

1450

The equestrian statue of Bartolomeo Colleoni (1400–75) in Venice

Frescoes by Ghirlandaio depicting the life of St. Francis of Assisi in Florence's Santa Trinità church (above)

Renaissance *Italy*

Booming economies and relatively stable governments were fertile ground for the flowering of the Renaissance—the 're-birth' of scholarship, architecture and the visual arts. The dynastic families and autocratic rulers of the most important states—Florence, the Papal States, Milan, Venice and Naples—were in competition to establish glittering courts, finance building schemes and patronize the finest minds and artists of the day. Smaller centres, such as Siena, Modena, Mantova, Ferrara and Urbino, were hot on their tails, resulting in an explosion of creativity all over the country.

The Renaissance started as an intellectual movement with the rediscovery of classical manuscripts and texts, which gave rise to the philosophical movement known as Neoplatonism. This influenced new architecture, new styles of painting and a new approach to sculpture inspired by the classical delight in human beauty. The restrictions that earlier thinking had imposed disappeared, leaving the way open for huge strides in every field, science and medicine in particular. No longer constrained by Aristotle's model of the universe, astronomers and cartographers re-examined existing theories of the universe and made more accurate maps. This provided the impetus for a wave of exploration and discovery.

David by Michelangelo in the Galleria dell'Accademia in Florence (right)

Patrons and artists

The Renaissance artist certainly didn't see himself as an inspired genius, seeking to express himself. His patrons paid him to do a job. Summoned to the great man's presence, artists would be confronted with a complete brief for the proposed commission, down to the last angel in the top right-hand corner. If the painting was secular, every figure in the complicated composition had an iconographical meaning, carefully configured by the philosophers—a mere artist was not deemed capable of working out the deeper significance of a piece. Pigments were expensive, so exact amounts of different tones were specified. Blue, derived from lapis lazuli, was the most expensive of them all; lots of blue means lots of money.

Leonardo da Vinci (1452–1519)

1450

Botticelli's *Birth of Venus* (c1485) in the Galleria degli Uffizi in Florence

Detail of a fresco in the elegant Renaissance Villa Farnesina (1511) in Rome (right middle)

Galileo Galilei

Galileo, astronomer and mathematician, made huge contributions to our understanding of the solar system. Born in Pisa in 1564, he pioneered 'experimental scientific method' and was the first to use a refracting telescope to make important discoveries. He supported Copernicus's theory that the Earth and planets moved around the sun, rejecting Aristotle's Earthcentric model. Galileo's Inquisition opponents prevailed over his supporters, and he was told to suppress his opinions—which he did not. At the age of 69, he again faced the authorities, who made him kneel and deny the Copernician theory. He spent his last years in Florence under house arrest, and wrote his greatest work. His dying words supposedly were: 'But it does move'.

Italian explorers and foreign financiers

Christopher Columbus was born in 1451, and lived in Genoa until his sea-faring career took him to Portugal and Spain, whose monarchs financed his discoveries. During his four voyages to the Caribbean (1492–1504) he unintentionally discovered the New World while searching for a sea route to Cathay (China). He died in 1506, convinced he had found the 'Indies'. The Florentine Amerigo Vespucci (1454–1512) was less naïve. He studied navigation, which allowed him to calculate the geographical location of Columbus's Indies more accurately, and on a Spanish expedition west in 1499 he observed that the land masses of North and South America were actually separate from Asia.

Niccolò Machiavelli

Machiavelli was born in Florence in 1469. A true patriot, he dreamed of a career in politics and began work as a diplomatic secretary for the Florentine republic, meeting important contemporary political figures. Once the Medici returned to power in 1512, he was out of a job, and turned to writing in the hope of attracting patronage. In 1513 he wrote *Principe* (*The Prince*), an intensely practical guide to the exercise of raw political power over a Renaissance principality. It cut no ice with the Medici, and the book's reputation continued to haunt him after they fell from power; he never again held public office. He died in 1527, his theories so twisted by public opinion that his name has become synonomous with political corruption.

Michelangelo and the Sistine ceiling

In 1508 Pope Julius II commissioned Michelangelo to decorate the ceiling of the Sistine Chapel in the Vatican. It was a huge task; the incentive was the sum of 3,000 ducats. The surface area is over 500sq m (5,500sq ft), all of which is painted with stories from the Book of Genesis, prophets and sibylls, and enclosed within a *trompe l'oeil* architectural framework. Executed in all temperatures as the artist lay or crouched on a scaffold some 20m (65ft) above the floor, it was physically gruelling work that took him four years to complete. He hated the task, which took him away from his sculpture, writing, 'I am attending to work as much as I can...I don't have a penny...I am unhappy and not in too good health…'.

Galileo Galilei
(1564–1642)

Christopher Columbus
(1451–1506)

Niccolò Machiavelli
(1469–1527)

1600

The Creation of Adam in the Sistine Chapel in Vatican City (above right); a delicate Madonna by Filippo Lippi, in the Galleria degli Uffizi in Florence (right); an altarpiece by Giovanni Bellini (c1430–1516) in San Zaccaria in Venice (below)

The legend of the Cross, by Piero della Francesca (above)

Foreign Domination

The Italian states didn't stay rich and independent for long. As early as 1494 the Duke of Milan made the fatal mistake of asking for French help, and the other European super-powers soon had considerably more than a foot in the door. Spain controlled Naples, Sardinia, Sicily, Milan and parts of Tuscany, the French were on the move in the north, and only the Papal States and Venice remained independent. Great chunks of Italy were bartered between the French and Spanish as alliances changed. Spain hung on for nearly 200 years, only to be replaced by Austrian domination as a result of the War of the Spanish Succession. The Austrians were perhaps the most progressive occupiers, preparing the way in the north for early industrialization.

With Napoleon's arrival on the scene it was all change once more, and by 1810 he was in command of the whole peninsula, setting up family members and trusted supporters as his puppet rulers. Napoleon introduced political reforms, such as representative assemblies, which were to have far-reaching consequences for the emerging middle class. After Waterloo, the Congress of Vienna attempted to re-establish the old order, but protest against oppression and occupation grew increasingly in the first half of the 19th century.

Earthquake in Sicily

In January 1639, the southeast corner of Sicily was devastated by a series of earthquakes. The shocks continued for three days, accompanied by a blood-red moon, fissures in the land and catastrophic tidal waves. Over 60,000 people perished and churches, civic buildings and houses were destroyed. The quake's epicentre was the Val di Noto to the southeast of Catania and Siracusa, which were extensively damaged. In the years that followed, many towns in the area were rebuilt, almost entirely in the baroque style. Today, they are considered to be the final flowering of the baroque in Europe—an innovative approach to town planning and urban building, Noto being the finest example.

1600

Raphael's *Marriage of the Virgin* and *The Virgin in Prayer* by Sassoferrato (1609–85, right); a baroque façade in Noto, rebuilt after the 1683 earthquake (below)

The Austrian legacy

The Austrians were big players in northern Italy throughout the 18th century and into the 19th century, their grip only loosening in 1859 following the war engineered by Count Camillo Cavour and Napoleon III. They hung on longer in the far northern South Tirol region, which only became part of Italy in 1919, when Mussolini renamed it the Alto-Adige. It's still almost completely Austrian in character. German is the first language, the towns and villages are sprinkled with onion-domed churches and traversed by arcaded streets, and all the street signs are in German. The food, in particular, is heavily Teutonic, with sauerkraut, knödel (dumplings) and strudel on the menu, and scarcely a whiff of pasta to be found.

Napoleon and the Popes

The conqueror of Europe kept the papacy well under control during his years of power. In 1798, French troops invaded Rome, demanding the abdication of the 82-year-old Pius VI; he refused, and was promptly deported to die in France. Five years later, Napoleon summoned Pius VII to Paris to officiate at his coronation. In 1809, Napoleon proclaimed the Papal States part of the French Empire and the Pope merely the Bishop of Rome. Pius excommunicated Napoleon, who retaliated by sending his troops to seize the pontiff and hustle him away to exile. He and his Cardinal of State left in such a hurry the Pope forgot his spectacles and the two venerable churchmen had less than 5 scudos (€2) between them.

Paolina Borghese

Napoleon's sister, Pauline, was married to Prince Borghese when she was 23, and became Princess Paolina. Beautiful, selfish and spoiled, she was famed in Roman society for her looks, lovers and style. Her wedding present to her husband was a near-nude statue of herself posing as Venus, sculpted by Canova. Rome buzzed with Paolina stories—her clothes and jewels, the huge servant who carried her to her bath, and the use of ladies-in-waiting as footstools. Her lovers were numerous: artists, actors, musicians and handsome young army officers. Generally disliked, she had one redeeming feature: her love for her brother. She shared his exile on Elba and gave him her jewels to help fund the Waterloo campaign.

The Grand Tour

Backpackers of the 21st century exploring the sights and delights of Italy are not the first visitors to fall for Italian pleasures. In the 18th century it was fashionable for young English gentlemen to go on the Grand Tour of Europe, including an Italian jaunt to enrich the mind. In practice it was a glorious excuse for profligate living. The days were spent sightseeing with the tutors, while the nights were given over to drinking, gambling and whoring. Shopping was a serious pursuit, and many of the statues, prints and paintings found in Britain's large country houses were brought home from the Tour. Artists were kept busy churning out portraits of the young gentry. With Joshua Reynolds charging over £150 in London, Roman portraits were a snip at £25.

Left to right: Count Camillo Cavour (1810–61); Napoleon Bonaparte (1769–1821); Pope Pius VII (in office 1800–23) and Lord Byron (1788–1824)

1860

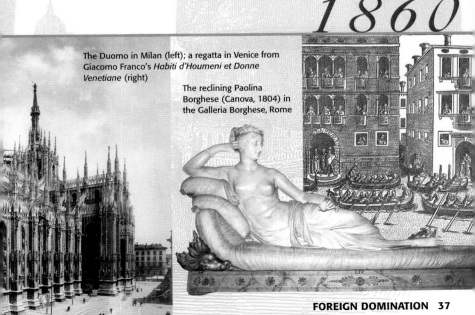

The Duomo in Milan (left); a regatta in Venice from Giacomo Franco's *Habiti d'Houmeni et Donne Venetiane* (right)

The reclining Paolina Borghese (Canova, 1804) in the Galleria Borghese, Rome

From Unification to World War II

Between 1848 and 1860 the movement to oust the occupiers and reform and unite the country grew. It was known as the Risorgimento, the new arising, and its key players were Giuseppe Mazzini, Giuseppe Garibaldi and Count Emilio Cavour. As ever in Italy, the story is complicated, but by 1860 Piemonte, Tuscany and Emilia were united. Garibaldi took Sicily and Naples, while a referendum secured Umbria and the Papal States. In 1861, the Kingdom of Italy was proclaimed, albeit without Rome and Venice. It was not until 1871 that the Unification of Italy was complete.

The 1880s saw the start of the new nation's colonial expansion into North Africa, which brought Abyssinia (present-day Ethiopia), Eritrea and Libya under Italian control. World War I was seen as a chance to get even with Austria for past wrongs, gaining Trieste and Trentino Alto-Adige at vast cost. Disillusioned with this, the middle classes turned to the Fascists and their leader, Benito Mussolini. He became dictator in 1925, ruling by the adage 'Everything within the State, nothing outside the State, nothing against the State'. Allied with Nazi Germany, Italy entered World War II in 1940. As the Nazis' dominance began to falter in Europe, Italy signed an armistice with the Allies in 1943 and Mussolini was finally captured from the Germans and executed in 1945.

Garibaldi and the one thousand

A guerrilla fighter and a man of the people, with a gift for motivating and enthusing the masses, Giuseppe Garibaldi (1807–82) was a key instigator in the Unification of Italy. He arrived in Sicily in 1860 with 1,000 soldiers, brightly clad in red shirts, and proclaimed himself dictator in the name of Vittorio Emanuele II. He defeated the Neapolitans and, helped by a popular uprising, captured Palermo. Crossing to the mainland, he then took Naples, handing both Sicily and Naples over to Vittorio Emanuele.

Giuseppe Garibaldi (above)

1860

Posters showing the Allies' flight towards the heel of Italy (above) and Hitler and Mussolini working together to erect a monument dedicated to peace, civilization and work (above right)

Austrian Italy

Before Unification, a big chunk of northeastern Italy, much of it German-speaking, belonged to the Austrian Empire. Some areas, such as the Veneto and Friuli, were soon acquired by Italy, but the South Tirol in particular, proud of its Austrian links and traditions, continued to look firmly towards Vienna, and was loath to change. Politicians in Rome, determined on a fully united Italy, felt differently, and put the reacquisition of the Austrian areas of the country at the top of its list of World War I objectives. At the cost of a huge war debt, 650,000 dead, and a million casualties, the politicians got their way in 1919 when the frontier was moved north to the Brenner Pass, and the South Tirol and Trentino became part of Italy.

The prisoner of the Vatican

Right up to the Unification of Italy, the Papal States sprawled across central Italy, successive popes hanging on to their temporal power. As elsewhere, the natives were restless and the Pope needed outside help to retain control. Garibaldi invaded twice during the Risorgimento, but the Pope, Pius IX, somehow hung on to Rome itself. Finally, in 1870, King Vittorio Emanuele seized the city and Rome became the capital of a united Italy. Furious, Pius refused to accept the loss of his holdings and retreated into the Vatican, declaring himself a prisoner. Later popes followed his example, never setting foot outside from election until death. The question was only settled by Mussolini's Lateran Treaty of 1929, which established Vatican City as the world's smallest independent state.

Vittorio Emanuele III, King of Italy in 1901 (left). Summer holidays at the Hotel Excelsior in Venice in 1931 (below)

Resistance

Southern Tuscany was one of Italy's strongest partisan regions during World War II, with anti-Fascist and anti-Nazi feeling running high. In 1943, as the Allies moved north from Monte Cassino, Resistance groups in the Val d'Orcia harried the Nazis incessantly, destroying whatever they could. The penalty was death, as it was for sheltering or feeding Allied soldiers on the run. In Florence, the Resistance was protected by the anti-Nazi German consul, but many farmers and peasants risked their lives and were imprisoned, transported or executed. Memorials can be found in many of the region's hilltop towns.

Monte Cassino monastery

Mussolini's end

By April 1945, the Allies were uncomfortably close to Mussolini's puppet Republic of Salò on Lake Garda, and the ex-Duce, together with his mistress, Claretta Petacci, tried to flee to Switzerland. They were caught at Lake Como by partisans and shot on 28 April. The next day the bodies were taken to the Piazzale Loreto in Milan and strung by their feet from the girders of a gas station, to be kicked, shot at and spat upon by a furious crowd. After a year's interment in Milan's municipal cemetery, Mussolini's body was stolen by surviving Fascists. It was finally returned to his widow in 1957 and buried at his birthplace, Predappio in Emilia, which became a magnet for Fascists.

1945

A giant figure towering above the Fiat Factory in Turin, lending a hand with construction (1917, below)

Hitler and Mussolini with Goering (left) and Count Ciano (right); the Italian Foreign Minister, at the Four Power Conference in Munich on 30 September 1938 (left)

Post-World War II

The years since 1945 have seen successive governments come and go, political scandal on a large scale, corruption in high places and terrorism. Despite this, Italy has boomed economically, establishing itself as a front-rank industrialized nation and a key player in influencing style across Europe, but the gulf between north and south remains.

Modern industry

Since World War II, Italy has become a major industrialized nation with a diversified economy. Heavy industry—particularly motor car production—drives the wealth of the north. The south is not so prosperous and survives on small-scale agriculture, wine production, fruit-growing and olive oil exports. The tourism boom has also become a significant part of regional economies and has helped to attract funding to improve roads and investment in hotels. But Italy's adoption of the euro is blamed by many traders for raising costs everywhere, just as cheaper eastern European countries are opening up their resorts and attracting holidaymakers in competition with Italy.

The former prime minister, Silvio Berlusconi (left), has been one of the major figures of post-war Italian politics

The Sicily Bridge

There have been years of discussion about building a suspension bridge that will cross the Straits of Messina between Sicily and mainland Italy. The project should be completed in 2011, at a cost of €4.4 billion. It will carry two railway lines and a 12-lane expressway and is designed to resist earthquakes of up to 7.1 on the Richter scale and wind speeds of 200kph (125mph). A key factor delaying the bridge-building is the loss of business and jobs for the people who operate the ferries that transport vehicles, passengers and trains.

Terrorist threats

In addition to the threat of violence from the Mafia, Italy, like many countries, faces the threat of terrorism from Islamic extremists. Italians were shocked when a suspect in the investigation into the 2005 London bombings turned up in Rome and was sent back to Britain to face trial. Coming after the attacks in Madrid and London, this alerted Italians to the possibility that Rome could also be a target for terrorism by Muslim extremists. The abduction of an Italian aid worker in Iraq and the death of a security official escorting her to freedom also added fuel to campaigns calling on Silvio Berlusconi to disengage Italy from the military operation in Iraq.

1945 to the present

Sophisticated women in Rome (above)

A swarm of scooters (right)

On the Move

ARRIVING

Arriving by Air

Many visitors to Italy arrive by air, their numbers increasing with the growth of low-cost airline routes from other European destinations and the increasing popularity of short breaks throughout the year. If you're flying direct from another continent you will arrive at Rome Fiumicino, the capital's main airport, or Milan Malpensa, serving Italy's economic capital and the Lakes. Rome and Milan each have a second airport: Rome Ciampino and Milan Linate.

Turin Caselle has doubled in size as a result of the world's attention on Turin as the venue for the 2006 Winter Olympic Games and now rivals Milan as the gateway to the north of Italy.

Venice Marco Polo is the main arrival point for northeastern Italy, and most visitors heading for Florence arrive at Pisa, an hour's journey by road or train from the city. Naples is the South's busiest international airport.

Rome Fiumicino (FCO) is 32km (20 miles) west of central Rome and has three terminals: A for domestic flights, B for domestic and some international, and C, with boarding gates connected to the terminal by monorail, for international flights only. All three terminals are big, so allow plenty of time for onward connections. There are interactive information points in arrival and departure areas.

Rome Ciampino (CIA) is 15km (9 miles) southeast of Rome, a short distance from the city ring-road which feeds into the motorway (expressway) network. This is the airport used by budget airlines as their gateway to Rome, though some also use Fiumicino. The departure area is rather small for the volume of traffic generated by budget airlines and can get very crowded at peak times in July and August.

Torino/Turin Caselle (TRN) is 16km (10 miles) north of the city centre. The airport has been expanded and modernized as a result of investment in connection with the 2006 Winter Olympic Games. The arrivals and departure areas have doubled in size with additional boarding

GETTING INTO CITIES FROM THE AIRPORT		
AIRPORT (CODE)	**ROME FIUMICINO (FCO)**	**ROME CIAMPINO (CIA)**
DISTANCE TO CITY	32km (20 miles)	15km (9 miles)
TAXI	Price: €45 Time: 30–45 min	Price: €45 Time: 30–45 min
TRAINS/ BOATS	Fiumicino to Termini Frequency: First train 7.37am, then hourly from 8am–10pm Price: €8.80 Journey time: 30 min Fiumicino to Trastevere, Tiburtina, Ostiense, then metro to Termini Frequency: Every 20 min from 6.27am–11.27am Price: €5 Journey time: 30–45 min	Bus to Ciampino town station, from where trains run to Termini Frequency: Every 15 min 6.30am–11pm Price: €2.40 Journey time: 20 min Anagnina Metro (Line A) to Termini Frequency: Buses run from the airport to Anagnina every 60 min Price: €1.10 Journey time: 20 min
BUS	Cotral buses from Fiumicino to Tiburtina Frequency: Every 90 min during the night Price: €3.60 Journey time: 45 min	There is a free shuttle bus available for disabled and elderly people. Reserve in advance, tel 06 6991 0000 There is no direct route into central Rome from Ciampino. The choice is either a combination of bus and metro or bus and train
CAR	Take Fiumicino–Rome motorway and travel eastwards	Take the Via Appia Nuova northwest into the heart of the city

gates, and the baggage handling facilities are the most modern in Europe. A new airport bus station is linked to the train station in an interchange facility that includes a remote check-in area to ease congestion in the main terminal at peak times. There is a 24-hour medical centre in the arrivals hall, and the new airport has been designed with the needs of people with disabilities in mind, with mobility-adapted toilets and special vehicles that can raise a wheelchair from the ground to the door of a plane. The main international car rental companies and several local ones are represented in the arrivals hall, and the airport has direct access to the motorway network linking the most important places in Piedmont, in northern Italy; southern France; and well-known holiday and ski resorts.

Pisa Galileo Galilei (PSA) is Florence's main entry point for most overseas visitors, 91km

ON THE MOVE

GETTING INTO CITIES FROM THE AIRPORT			
PISA (FLORENCE) (PSA)	**MILAN MALPENSA (MXP)**	**TURIN (TRN)**	**VENICE MARCO POLO (VCE)**
91km (57 miles) to Florence; 2km (1 mile) to Pisa	50km (31 miles)	16km (10 miles)	By water 7km (4 miles); overland 12km (7.5 miles)
Price: €120–150 to Florence; €6–8 to Pisa Time: 60–80 min to Florence; 10–20 min to Pisa	Price: €60–75 Time: 35–60 min	Price: €26–42 Time: 20–30 min	**Land taxi price:** €15–18 Time: 15–25 min **Water taxi price:** €70–90 Time: 20–35 min
Pisa Aeroporto–Firenze Santa Maria Novella Frequency: Every 60 min to Florence, stopping at Pisa Centrale Price: €4.85 Journey time: 75 min For Siena change at Empoli	Malpensa to Milano Nord Frequency: Every 30 min between 6.30am and 1.30am Price: €8 (discounted tickets for Alitalia passengers) Journey time: 40 min	Casalle airport station to Turin Dora Frequency: every 30 min between 6.50am and 9.20pm Price: N/A Journey time: 19 min	**Boat Alilaguna service** From the airport to the city via Murano and the Lido Frequency: Every 60 min Price: €10 Journey time: 30 min to Murano, 55 min to the Lido, 1 hour 10 min to the city
CPT No. 3 from Pisa airport to Pisa Frequency: Every 15 min Price: 50c Journey time: 10–15 min	Malpensa to Stazione Centrale Frequency: Every 20 min 5.20am–10.30pm Price: €7 Journey time: 45–60 min	Airport bus station to central Turin Porta Nuova train station. Frequency: Every 30 min 6.30–9am and 5.30–10.45pm, every 45 min 9–5.30pm and 10.45–11.30pm Price: N/A Journey time: 40 min with intermediate stops Bus tickets can be bought at newsstands, tourist information offices and ticket machines in the arrivals area. 50c extra charge when paying on the bus.	Airport bus (ATVO) to Piazzale Roma, ACTV bus No. 5 to Piazzale Roma Frequency: Airport bus (ATVO) every 20 min, ACTV bus No. 5 every 30 min Price: ATVO €2.70, ACTV 77c Journey time: ATVO 20 min, ACTV 20 min
From the airport follow the motorway Pisa–Firenze east to Florence	Take the link motorway southeast to the A8 (E62) and follow signs to the city centre	Driving into the city centre takes about 20 minutes (30 minutes in peak time). Turin airport has direct access to the highway linking the most important places in Piedmont, north Italy; the south of France; and Alpine ski resorts.	N/A

(57 miles) west of Florence. It has good road and train connections and handles internal and European flights. The spacious terminal has information desks, a train ticket office and adjoining railway station.

Milan Malpensa (MXP), Italy's main international gateway in the north, is 50km (31 miles) northwest of the city. It has two terminals: Terminal 1 handles domestic and international flights; Terminal 2 is mainly for

Inside the terminal building at Venice Marco Polo Airport

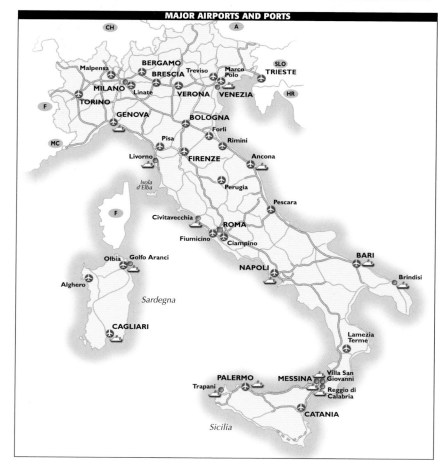

MAJOR AIRPORTS AND PORTS

CH
A
SLO

Malpensa
BERGAMO
Treviso
Marco Polo
TRIESTE

BRESCIA
Verona
HR

MILANO
Linate
VERONA
VENEZIA

TORINO

GENOVA
BOLOGNA

Forlì

Pisa
Rimini

Livorno
FIRENZE
Ancona

Isola d'Elba

Perugia

Pescara

Civitavecchia
ROMA

Fiumicino
Ciampino

BARI

Olbia
Golfo Aranci
NAPOLI
Brindisi

Alghero

Sardegna

CAGLIARI

Lamezia Terme

PALERMO
MESSINA
Villa San Giovanni

Trapani
Reggio di Calabria

CATANIA

Sicilia

F
F
MC

short to medium-haul flights and charters. Both terminals have information, hotel reservation and car rental desks.

Milan Linate (LIN), 7km (4 miles) from the city centre, handles domestic and European flights. It has a full range of airport services.

Naples Capodichino (NAP) lies 8km (5 miles) northeast of the city centre. This airport handles domestic and European scheduled and charter flights. An airport bus (every 30 min) runs to Piazza Garibaldi and Piazza Municipio; bus Nos 14 and 15 (every 15 min) run to Piazza Garibaldi.

Venice Marco Polo (VCE) is on the northern edge of the lagoon, 7km (4 miles) from the city by water and 12km (7.5 miles) by road. Serving the northeast of Italy, it handles mainly domestic and European flights. Its terminal is on three levels (ground floor for arrivals, first floor for check-in and departures, second floor for VIP lounges). Frequent and efficient water taxi and ferry services run to Venice.

Some charter and budget airlines use **Treviso San Angelo (TSF)**, a small airport 30km (18.5 miles) north of the city.

CAR RENTAL
The major car rental companies have offices at airports, train stations and major cities. You will usually get a better deal if you shop around and reserve from your own country. Local companies will often have airport pickup points, but you may be unable to reserve them from home. If you reserve with a tour operator, it will be able to arrange car rental in advance.

Before you leave, check your insurance and see if you will need additional cover. You will need to show your credit card when you pick up the car and to pay for additional charges.

Drivers of rental cars must be over 21 or 25 (depending on the company) and have a valid driver's licence. Any additional drivers may also have to sign the rental agreement. If you intend to go off public roads, check that the insurance covers this. You will be offered the choice of returning the car filled with fuel; it is cheaper to fill it up yourself just before you return it. Be sure to check thoroughly both inside and outside the vehicle for any damage. If you find any, report it at once and get a company representative to make a note.

USEFUL TELEPHONE NUMBERS AND WEBSITES

AIRPORTS
General www.worldairportguide.com
Florence tel 055 306 1300
www.aeroporto.firenze.it
Naples tel 081 789 6259
www.gesac.it
Milan Malpensa & Linate
tel 02 748 52200
www.sea-aeroportimilano.it
Pisa tel 050 849300
www.pisa-airport.com
Rome Ciampino tel 06 794941
www.adr.it
Rome Fiumicino tel 06 65951
www.adr.it
Treviso tel 0422 315111
www.trevisoairport.it
Turin tel 011 5676 361
www.aeroportoditorino.it
Venice Marco Polo tel 041 260 6111
www.veniceairport.it

AIRLINES
UK
Alitalia tel 0870 544 8259
www.alitalia.co.uk
BMI Baby tel 0870 264 2229
www.bmibaby.com
British Airways tel 0870 850 9850,
(UK); 199 712266 (IT) www.ba.com
easyJet tel 0905 821 0905 (UK);
848 887766 (IT) www.easyjet.com
Flybe tel 0870 701 0123
www.flybe.com
Meridiana tel 0845 355 5588 (UK);
0789 52 682 (IT) www.meridiana.it
MyTravelLite tel 0870 1564564
www.mytravellite.com
Ryanair tel 0906 270 5656 (UK);
899 678910 (IT) www.ryanair.com
Volare Airlines tel 0039 070 4603397
(UK); 0199 414 500 (IT)
www.volare-airlines.com

US
Alitalia tel 800 223 5730
www.alitaliausa.com
American Airlines tel 800 433 7300
www.aa.com
Continental tel 800 231 0856
www.continental.com
Delta tel 800 221 1212
www.delta-air.com
Northwest Airlines tel 800 447 4747
www.nwa.com
United tel 800 538 2929
www.ual.com
US Airways tel 800 428 4322
www.usairways.com

ON THE MOVE

Arriving by Ferry

If you are planning a trip to Sicily or Sardinia, or onwards to Greece, you may want to travel by ferry. With the exception of the short hop across the Straits of Messina to Sicily, it's best to reserve a crossing in advance. You need to arrive at the departure port anything between 2 and 6 hours before sailing; individual companies will provide details when you reserve. The major ferry ports are clearly marked by road signs with a ship symbol, the name of the destination port and the word *traghetti* (ferries). Overnight ferries have cabins available; these, too, should be reserved in advance.

For faster links to the main islands there's also the hydrofoil, though these services tend to be greatly reduced outside the peak summer season. Prices vary considerably, but reserving in advance may get you a good deal. The best way to research Italian ferries is through www.traghettionline.net/eng, a portal site linking virtually all the major operators, with an online

A ferry at Civitavecchia

reservations facility. For ferries to Greece, use www.ferries.gr.

Arriving by Rail

From Britain you can travel by train to Italy, routing, via the Channel Tunnel, through either Brussels or Paris. The journey time via Brussels is longer, but if you choose the Paris option, you have to change from the Gare du Nord to the Gare de Lyon. Direct trains run to **Rome**, **Florence**, **Milan**, **Turin** and **Venice**.

The choice of routes and fares is highly complex, but it's best to use the **Eurostar** as far as **Paris** or **Brussels** from where trains south are fast and frequent.

Eurostar trains link London with Paris and Brussels in under 3 hours. You must check in 30 minutes before departure and you are allowed two suitcases and one item of hand baggage. You need your passport to clear immigration and customs.

● The total journey time from London to Italian destinations varies from 11 to 15 hours.

FERRY INFORMATION AND TICKETS

Frequencies and timings of ferry services vary according to season and demand. A more detailed summary of Italian ferry services is available in the Thomas Cook European Rail Timetable, tables 2515 to 2755.

SICILY

Operator NGI, tel 090 9284091, 090 679141, www.ngi-spa.it, www.cormorano.net/ngi/orari.htm
Departure port Reggio di Calabria
Arrival port Messina
Frequency Every 20–40 min
Duration of crossing 40 min

Operator Tourist Ferry Boat, tel 090 371851, fax 090 51422, www.cormorano.net/tourist-ferry-boat/info_i.htm
Departure port Villa San Giovanni
Arrival port Messina
Frequency Every 20–40 min
Duration of crossing 25 min

Operator Tirrenia, tel 081 317 2999, www.tirrenia.it; Snav, tel 081 428 5555, www.snav.it
Departure port Naples
Arrival port Palermo
Frequency 1 daily
Duration of crossing 11 hours

Operator Grandi Navi Veloci, tel 899 199 069, www1.gnv.it
Departure port Genoa
Arrival port Palermo
Frequency 1 daily
Duration of crossing 20 hours

SARDINIA

Operator Tirrenia, tel 081 317 2999, www.tirrenia.it
Departure ports Civitavecchia, Genoa, Livorno
Arrival ports Cagliari, Olbia, Golfo Aranci
Frequency From Civitavecchia 1 daily to Cagliari (Fri, Sun via Arbatax), 3 daily to Olbia; from Genoa Jul–Sep 2 weekly

to Arbatax, daily to Olbia (Sun 2 sailings); from Naples 2 weekly; from Palermo to Cagliari 1 weekly
Duration of crossing Civitavecchia to Cagliari 15–17 hours, Civitavecchia to Olbia 9 hours; Genoa to Cagliari 21 hours, Genoa to Olbia 14 hours; Naples to Cagliari 17 hours; Palermo to Cagliari 14 hours

GREECE

Operators Superfast, Minoan Lines, Blue Star, Hellenic (www.superfast.com, www.bluestarferries.com, www.minoan.gr, www.hellenicferries.com)
Departure ports Ancona, Bari, Venice (Minoan Lines)
Arrival ports Patras, Igoumenitsa, Corfu (Blue Star, Minoan Lines)
Frequency Ancona 3 daily; Bari 1 daily; Venice 2 daily
Duration of crossing Ancona 19 hours; Bari 16 hours 30 min; Venice 22 hours

TRAIN INFORMATION AND TICKETS

RAIL

Eurostar EPS House, Waterloo Station, London SE1 8SE, tel 08705 186 186
www.eurostar.com
Rail Europe 179 Piccadilly, London W1V 0BA, tel 08705 848 848, www.raileurope.co.uk

Trenitalia (Italian State Railways) tel call centre 892021 (IT), tel 0870 751000 (Simply Rail) (UK), www.simplyrail.com
Venice-Simplon-Orient-Express Ltd Sea Containers House, 20, Upper Ground, London SE1 9PF, tel 020 7805 5100, www.orient-express.com

• Return ticket prices range from around €250 to around €300.

Both Eurostar and other fast European trains have facilities which include:

• 1st- and 2nd-class seating.
• Bar/restaurant cars.
• Trolley service on day trains.
• Baby-changing facilities.
• Air-conditioning.
• Telephone kiosks.
• Toilets in each carriage including some that are accessible to wheelchairs.

Smoking is banned inside station buildings and on all trains—even if old window stickers still indicate smoking is permitted.

Sleepers are available from Paris on direct routes to Rome, Milan, Florence and Venice. Accommodation varies from 3-, 4- and 6-berth couchettes to single and double sleepers with integral shower and toilet.

The **Orient Express,** the celebrated luxury train ride to Italy, runs from London to Venice. The journey time is 31 hours, and costs around €1,770 one way.

RAIL PASSES

Prices indicated below are subject to annual revision.
• **InterRail Passes** give you complete flexibility. A single-zone pass for standard or second-class travel is valid in Italy but also includes Greece, Turkey and Slovenia and some ferry services across the Adriatic between Italy and Greece. It costs £145 for travellers under 26 and £215 if you're over 26 (child under 12 £108). A two-zone pass is valid for 22 days and also allows you to use trains in France, Belgium,

Luxembourg and the Netherlands. It costs £205 for those under 26 and £295 if you're over 26 (child under 12 £148). For the complete freedom of Europe's rail network, an all-zone pass, valid for 1 month, costs £285 for those under 26 and £405 for those over 26 (child under 12 £203).

The InterRail pass gives discounts on cross-Channel services including Eurostar, and is available to European residents.
• **EurRail Passes** have similar validity to the InterRail pass for a period of consecutive days' travel and are available for residents of countries outside Europe.
• **Trenitalia Passes** are available to non-residents of Italy and are valid for unlimited rail travel on any four–ten days within a two-month period. They are good value for long distances, but bear in mind that train fares in Italy are relatively cheap compared to the rest of Europe, so it may be cheaper to buy single tickets for short journeys. A four-day second-class Trenitalia pass costs €174 adult, €145 youth aged 12–26, a ten-day pass €282 adult, €220 youth. Discounts are available for small groups of two to five people travelling together. Supplements must be paid for Italian Eurostar trains (€12 upgrade per journey) and for couchettes or beds on overnight trains.
• **RailPlus cards** give you a reduction of 25 per cent on international train fares and on journeys within Italy linked to an international ticket (€45 adult 26–60, €20 young people up to 26 and seniors over 60, valid for one year).

Arriving by Bus

Italy has few domestic long-distance bus routes, but there are international routes from major cities across Europe.
International buses to Italy from the UK are coordinated by Eurolines (tel 0870 514 3219 www.nationalexpress.com), a consortium of 30 independent long-distance bus companies. Regular services run from London Victoria Coach Station to 27 cities in Italy, though most journeys involve a change in Paris. The typical adult return fare London to Turin is £112, and London to Rome £142.
Destinations: Ancona, Bologna, Florence, Genoa, Milan, Naples, Padua, Parma, Pisa, Rimini, Rome, San Remo, Siena, Turin, Venice, Verona, with connections to other Italian destinations.
Journey time: London to Milan 22 hours, Florence 28 hours, Rome 30–32 hours, Naples 33–35 hours, all with a stop in Paris of 1½ hours.
Tickets can be reserved online or at National Express travel offices. A Eurolines Pass allows you unlimited coach travel between a choice of 35 cities across Europe, including internal Italian routes between Milan and Siena and Siena and Rome (15 days £149, 30 days £189, 40 days £219).

Arriving by Car

Driving to Italy, you will need a valid driver's licence, a vehicle registration document, a motor insurance certificate and a passport.

From the UK, you can take the ferry or use the Channel Tunnel. The main routes to Italy run through France, Switzerland and Germany. All cross the Alps; the St. Gotthard tunnel is free, but other passes range from €15–€25. To reach these take the E15 and E17 to Reims, then pick up the motorways. There are toll roads (turnpikes) all along the route (▷ 52–53). You should allow 11 to 14 hours' driving time to reach the north Italian border.

GETTING AROUND

Getting Around in Rome

ATAC runs Rome's public transport system, which includes the bus, tram and metro network, all frequent, cheap and reliable. You can navigate the city easily by using just a few lines.

INFORMATION

• The ATAC office is at Piazza dei Cinquecento (tel 800 431784, daily 7.30–7). Transport details, ticket information and free transport maps are available.
• Online at www.atac.roma.it

TICKETS

Buy tickets before boarding at *tabacchi* (tobacconists), shops and bars displaying the ATAC logo. Main stops and some metro stations have automatic ticket machines. You can save money by buying an 'integrated' ticket for use on buses, trams and trains.
• *Biglietto integrato a tempo* (BIT) €1—valid for 75 minutes for unlimited bus and tram travel plus one metro trip.
• *Biglietto integrato giornaliero* (BIG) €4—valid up to midnight on the day of use for unlimited travel on buses, trams, metro, Cotral and FS trains.
• *Carta integrata settimanale* (CIS) €16—valid for a week.
• **Validate** your ticket the first time it's used. The machines are inside buses and trams and just before escalators on the metro. BIT tickets must be validated again if you are using the BIT on the metro. The fine for not validating your ticket is €51 and is strictly enforced—no excuses.

BUSES

Single-decker buses cover most routes, with the historic centre served by small electric minibuses (routes 116, 117, 119). There are few seats and buses can be very crowded. Be wary of pickpockets.
• **Bus stops** *(fermata)* show the route number, the *capitolinea* (headstop where the service originates) and list the intermediate stops for buses using the stop. The stop where you are is circled.
• Bus drivers do not sell tickets, so buy a ticket before you board.

Night Buses

Services start at midnight and drop off at stops marked with a blue owl logo. Tickets are available on board.

Taxis

There are taxi stands throughout the city centre, and it is not usual to hail a taxi as it is cruising along the street. Official metered taxis are white or yellow. The meter starts running at €2.33 7am– 10pm Mon–Sat and €3.36 Sun and public holidays; €4.91 10pm– 7am daily. The meter clicks around in increments of 11c approximately every 20 seconds of the journey. You can phone for a taxi on 06 3570, 06 4944, 06 551, 06 6645 or 06 8822.

METRO (LA METROPOLITANA)

There are **two lines** which intersect at Termini, the main railway station.
• **Trains** run between 5.30am and 11.30pm.
• **Entrances** are marked with a large white M on a red background.
• **Ticket machines** are below street level; be sure to validate your ticket.
• **Information boards** indicate platforms.
• The metro is always very crowded. Use the **route maps** displayed in the carriages to find out which side the doors will open at your stop, and start working your way towards the door well before the train stops.

TRAMS

Trams are good for getting to the outskirts. The following routes are great for sightseeing:
3—Villa Borghese, Villa Giulia, modern art museum, zoo and Trastevere.
8—Trastevere.
19—Piazza del Risorgimento for San Pietro. Also serves Villa Borghese, Villa Giulia, the zoo and modern art museum.

DISCOUNTS

• Children under 10 travel free.
• Reductions for students holding ISIC cards.

TIPS

• Be aware of pickpockets, who tend to be children or teenagers.
• Keep shoulder bags and backpacks in front of you on buses and metro trains. Groups of women acting together frequently cause obstruction of doors as a distraction while rifling through bags to steal money or valuables.

SIGHTSEEING TOURS OF ROME

ATAC 110 City Tour Every 30 min. Hop on and off (stop 'n' go) ticket €13
ATAC Archeobus From Piazza Venezia hourly. Circuit of archaeological sights including the Via Appia Antica and the catacombs, 2 hours, €7.75.
Appian Line Piazza Esquilino 6/7, tel 06 4878 6604, fax 06 481 9712.

Green Line Tours Via del Viminale, tel 06 462 0651/06 482 8647/ 06 4877 2253, fax: 06 4782 3335, www.greenlinetours.com.
Stop 'n' Go CSR, Via Barberini 86, 00187 Roma, tel 06 4782 6379, fax 06 488 3167, www.romecitytours.com €12.

Getting Around in Other Major Cities

The metro, buses and trams are easy to use, but knowing some key words makes things easier (▷ 417–420). Information is provided on all services, and safety standards are high.

MILAN

www.atm-mi.it

Milan has an efficient integrated transport system comprising trams, buses and a metro. The metro is the easiest and fastest option, though you may have to combine it with a bus or tram.

Metro: 4 lines: red MM1, green MM2, yellow MM3 and blue *passante ferroviario*.

These intersect at the hub stations of Stazione Centrale, Duomo, Cadorna and Loreto.

Buses and trams: Routes cover the whole city and the follow the metro routes overground.

Tickets: A single (€1) is valid for 75 min from validation and can be used on the entire system for as many bus and tram trips as you want and one metro journey. A book of 10 tickets costs €9.20, and 1- and 2-day travel cards (€3 and €5.50) are also available. Tickets are sold at *tabacchi*, bars, newsstands and metro stations. The network runs 6am–12.30am, with night buses continuing until 1.30am.

FLORENCE

www.ATAF.net

Florence is largely pedestrianized and the historic heart can be crossed on foot in 30 min, so you're unlikely to have to use the bus system. It is useful if you're

A Eurotram on line 14 in Milan

staying on the outskirts.

Buses: Most lines either originate at or pass the railway station, a 15–20 min walk from Piazza della Signoria. They run 6am–midnight.

Tickets: €1 for 1 hour, €1.80 for 3 hours, €4.50 for 24 hours. Tickets are sold at *tabacchi*, bars and newsstands displaying ATAF signs.

VENICE

www.actv.it

Walking and taking the *vaporetti* (water buses) are the quickest ways to get around.

Water buses: There are two types, *vaporetti* (bigger and slower) and *motoscafi* (smaller and faster). All are numbered on the side and follow set routes. They leave from *pontile*, floating piers, marked with the stop name, service numbers and a route map. The same numbers sometimes go in two directions, so check you are heading the right way before you board; busy routes have separate boarding points for each direction.

Tickets: Sold at many *pontile* or at shops showing the ACTV sticker. A single ticket costs €3.50, but you can save money by buying a 24-hour (€10.50) or 72-hour (€22) ticket. Validate your ticket at the yellow machine on the *pontile* before boarding. There is a limited night service on most routes. ACTV produces a booklet, available at ticket booths *(orario)* containing routes, services and timetables.

AL VAPORETTO

Traghetti: These are gondola ferries that cross and recross the Canal Grande at seven points. The Canal only has three bridges, so taking a *traghetto* can save time and your feet. Follow the yellow street signs to the boarding points and watch your balance, as it is customary to stand up.

Tickets: Pay the gondolier (70c) on boarding.

NAPLES

www.campaniatrasporti.it

Naples is a big, congested city where the best option is to walk. You'll have to use the public transport system to reach outlying areas and the Bay of Naples, though. There are several integrated options run by ANM— buses, the Metropolitana, funiculars within the city and three suburban rail systems.

Buses: The best option for short journeys, though they can be very slow in heavy traffic.

The Metropolitana: Expanding to cover more of the city.

Funiculars: These run up the hill of the Vomero.

Out-of-town trains: The Circumvesuviana runs around the bay to Pompei and Sorrento; the Ferrovia Cumana runs west to Pozzuoli and Baia; the Circumflegrea goes to Cuma.

Tickets: Single tickets (€1) are valid for 90 min and allow any combination of bus and tram rides plus unlimited travel on two additional forms of transport. Tickets are sold at *tabacchi*, stations and the ANM booth on Piazza Garibaldi, which has timetables and route maps. A 24-hour pass is available (€2.32).

Driving

Italy's road system is comprehensive, with motorways (expressways) covering the entire peninsula from north to south and with trans-Apennine links at regular intervals. In addition, all regions have dual-carriageway (divided highway) and main-road alternatives and rural villages are connected by minor roads. Civil engineering is excellent, with bridges soaring over ravines and well-lit tunnels going through mountains. Given the country's north/south economic divide, the road network is at its best in the north, but even in the south driving is easy and a pleasure. However, driving in the cities, particularly in Rome, should be avoided.

Driving is ideal if you are concentrating on smaller towns and cities and rural areas. Although it's not for the faint-hearted, you can enjoy panoramic views from the road, famously along the Amalfi coast (▷ 318–319) and through the Dolomites (▷ 290–292).

Italian driving belies its fearsome reputation; once you grasp their rationale, you'll find Italian drivers less erratic and on the whole safer than drivers of many other nationalities.

The best bet is to steer clear of cities. One-way systems, narrow streets, lack of parking, traffic congestion and occasional aggression make city driving stressful. Be prepared for traffic jams in August when all of Italy is on holiday and everyone heads for the roads and motorways, particularly on weekends.

BRINGING YOUR OWN CAR
Before you leave:
● British drivers should adjust headlights for driving on the right.
● Contact your motor insurer or broker at least 1 month before you leave.
● Have your car serviced.
● Check the tyres.
● If you don't have a rear-view mirror on the left side, fit one before you go.
● Ensure you have adequate breakdown assistance cover (AA Five Star 0800 444500, www.theAA.com).

You will need:
● A valid driver's licence.
● The original vehicle registration document.

A vigile urbano (traffic policeman) in Piazza Venezia, Rome

● A motor insurance certificate; at least third-party insurance is compulsory.
● A first aid kit, fire extinguisher and spare bulbs.
● It is compulsory to carry a warning triangle (in case of breakdown) and display a nationality sticker (unless you have Euro-plates).
● If you're driving in winter you may need winter tyres or snow chains.

DOCUMENTS
Carry documents with you whenever you are driving; if you are stopped by the *polizia stradale, polizia municipale* or *carabinieri* they will want to see them. Both UK and US driver's licences are valid in Italy, but you should also carry a translation. In the UK, the new licences with photographs and the pink, EU-style ones include a translation, but if you hold an older, green licence, you can either update the licence or apply for an International Driving Permit. Holders of US driver's licences should also apply for an International Driving Permit. These permits are not compulsory, but can smooth out problems and act as another form of identification. Permits can be obtained from the Italian State Tourist Offices or through national motoring organizations such as the AA and AAA.

HOW TO NAVIGATE A ROUNDABOUT

This sign indicates that there is a roundabout (traffic circle) ahead. You must give way to traffic approaching from the left. If road markings allow you to approach without giving way, proceed, but look left before joining. Always look forward before moving on to the roundabout to check traffic is moving.

1. To take the first exit, signal right, approach in the right-hand lane, keep right and continue signalling right.
2. To take the intermediate exit, select the appropriate lane, signalling as necessary. Stay in this lane and signal right after you pass the exit before the one you want.
3. To take the last exit or go full circle, signal a left, approach in the left-hand lane, keep left until you need to exit and signal right after you pass the exit before the one you want.

RULES OF THE ROAD

● Drivers must be at least 18 and hold a full driver's licence.
● Drive on the right and give way to traffic from the right. However, at crossroads (intersections) displaying a precedence sign (inverted triangle bearing the words *dare precedenza*) give way to traffic coming from left and right.
● Seat belts must be worn in the front of a vehicle and (where fitted) in the back.
● Children under 4 must have a suitable restraint system. Those aged between 4 and 12 cannot travel in the front of the car without a fitted restraint system.
● Speed limits: built-up areas—50kph (31mph); outside built-up areas—110kph (68mph); motorways *(autostrade)*—130kph (81mph) (if your car is over 1100cc).

● Use dipped headlights in non-urban areas during the day and in towns or cities at night. These are compulsory when driving in tunnels, even if they are well lit.
● There are severe penalties for drinking and driving.
● Italy uses international road signs.

MOTORWAYS AND TOLL ROADS (EXPRESSWAYS AND TURNPIKES)

As you approach the *autostrada* take the ticket from the automatic box on the left-hand side of the car or press the red button to get one. The barrier will lift. Keep your ticket safe, as you will need it to pay when you leave the *autostrada*. Cash payment is normally made to the official in the booth; the amount is displayed on a screen

Autostrada *toll booths*

outside the pay window. If you are using a pass or paying by credit card, follow the signs into the Viacard booth.

Slip roads onto and off Italian *autostrade* are short. You may have to stop and wait for traffic to pass before you can join the motorway.

Italians are fast, disciplined drivers on the motorway. Only use the outer lanes for overtaking and be prepared to move continuously between lanes to allow faster drivers behind you to overtake; they often drive up close behind you. Use the indicator before you pull out and while you are overtaking.

Autostrade have regularly spaced service areas *(area di servizio)* with filling stations, bar/restaurant, shops and toilets.

ROAD SIGNS

stazione
Areas of public interest—this directs you to the station

zona industriale
Industrial area or zone

Long tunnel

Only vehicles with snow tyres or chains may proceed

SS 1 ROMA 84
Urban directions to state roads (SS)

A1 MILANO
(A) *Autostrada* (motorway/expressway)

BORGOSOLE 48 SS 16

SS 16 BORGOSOLE 48
(SS) State open road direction signs indicating destination, distance and road number

SS 8b PAVIA
MILANO Ticinese
A1 BOLOGNA
✈ Linate
90

MILANO
◎ centro
60

A7 GENOVA

Autostrada signs: Lane signs are positioned above the carriageway and may combine a variety of signs indicating direction and lane change, danger, orders, warnings, speed limits, information and directions to the city centre (such as Milano above). This allows you to select the appropriate lane for your itinerary and move into it safely and in plenty of time.

There are also occasional pull-off areas with shady trees and picnic tables, some with toilets.

The Italian *autostrada* network is run by several different companies, which means that both price and frequency of tolls vary greatly. On the whole, northern motorways tend to be more expensive, and you may find a *pedaggio* (toll station) coming up every few kilometres. South of Naples, the A1 *(Autostrada del Sole)* is State-subsidized and free. Motorcycles under 150cc are not allowed on the motorway.

PROBLEMS

If your car breaks down, turn on your hazard warning lights and place the warning triangle 50m (55 yards) behind the vehicle.

If you're driving your own car, obtain assistance from the Automobile Club d'Italia (ACI) by calling 116 and telling the operator where you are, the make of car and the licence plate number. This is not a free service, so it might be better to arrange breakdown cover with a motoring organization before you leave home.

If your rental car breaks down, call the rental company on the emergency number included with the car's paperwork.

If you have an accident call the police (113), but do not admit liability. Witnesses should remain to make statements and exchange details (name, address, car details, insurance company's name and address).

If you are stopped by the police (the *carabinieri*, the *polizia stradale* or the *polizia municipale*) they will want to see your papers. They may give no reason for stopping you, in which case it is likely to be a random spot check and once they realize you are a non-national they will probably wave you on. The commonest offence is speeding, for which there is a hefty on-the-spot fine. The police must issue fined drivers with a receipt.

ON THE MOVE

The chart below gives the distances in kilometres (green) and duration in hours and minutes (blue) of a car journey between key towns. The times are based on average driving speeds using the fastest roads. They do not allow for delays or rest breaks.

Distance/duration chart between key towns (cities given along the diagonal): Ancona, Aosta, Bologna, Bolzano (Bozen), Firenze, Genova, Lecce, Milano, Napoli, Padova, Perugia, Pisa, Ravenna, Reggio di Calabria, Roma, Siena, Torino, Trento, Trieste, Venezia, Verona.

Upper-right triangle (duration in hours and minutes, blue):

608	222	501	333	512	611	424	459	323	209	400	150	909	314	327	534	428	520	345	344
404	445	455	236	1158	200	919	411	608	401	450	1345	731	525	120	412	604	430	328	
257	129	309	812	220	553	125	242	156	104	1019	405	159	331	224	322	148	140		
357	427	1051	313	821	227	511	425	343	1248	633	427	430	042	420	246	142			
242	831	320	455	231	144	109	215	921	307	106	420	324	428	254	240				
1043	146	706	353	356	148	354	1133	518	312	201	354	547	413	310					
1014	441	913	735	909	740	523	609	819	1124	1018	1110	935	934						
744	239	434	255	306	1211	556	350	145	240	432	258	156							
655	346	533	527	503	233	430	844	748	852	718	704								
345	259	157	1122	507	301	356	154	213	039	103									
222	203	809	200	129	533	438	542	407	354										
242	959	345	128	326	352	456	321	308											
1038	344	245	416	310	341	207	226												
659	851	1310	1214	1318	1144	1130													
246	656	600	704	530	516														
450	354	458	324	310															
357	549	415	313																
348	214	109																	
159	257																		
123																			

Lower-left triangle (distances in kilometres, green):

612																		
215	395																	
498	465	281																
323	472	103	369															
510	245	293	425	227														
613	1214	817	1100	849	1079													
428	183	211	294	298	147	1030												
482	947	578	844	472	702	442	774											
326	407	116	190	216	367	928	236	692										
157	621	252	518	146	376	746	447	369	365									
391	410	171	437	78	165	925	285	548	285	222								
163	480	83	366	190	377	765	295	554	169	185	256							
934	1419	1050	1316	944	1174	478	1246	491	1164	840	1017	1086						
301	757	388	654	282	512	604	584	227	502	169	355	354	698					
258	539	170	436	69	294	806	365	429	283	109	108	257	900	229				
549	112	332	420	395	168	1151	138	871	362	544	333	416	1342	671	462			
444	410	227	58	314	376	1046	239	790	178	463	380	311	1261	590	381	366		
525	602	315	385	416	562	1127	431	891	199	565	481	307	1362	691	483	557	373	
362	438	152	221	252	399	964	267	728	36	401	318	143	1199	528	319	394	210	179
360	332	143	152	230	292	962	161	706	78	379	296	227	1177	506	297	287	98	273	110

SAFETY

For peace of mind, keep car doors locked while you are driving. In large cities, particularly in the south, keep windows shut.

Never leave anything visible in the car when you're not using it. Italians usually detach their radios and take them with them.

If you're taking your own car, lower the aerial and tuck in the wing mirrors when you leave the vehicle.

In the countryside watch out for APEs (three-wheeler all-purpose mini-pickups) as their drivers rarely signal their intentions. Be aware of animals, slow-moving agricultural vehicles, soft roadsides and unsurfaced roads, which can be lethal in long spells of drought or heavy rain.

PARKING

Parking in Italy is difficult as its ancient and picturesque towns and villages were not built to accommodate vehicles.

● Invest in a parking dial; these are used in permitted parking areas and are displayed in your windscreen to indicate when you arrived. Rental cars are normally equipped with one; they are also available at tourist offices.

● Many cities have parking zones: Blue zones (with blue lines) have a maximum stay of 1–2 hours. Pay the attendant or at the meter. White zones (with white lines) are free and unlimited in some cities, but reserved for residents in others. Yellow zones (with yellow lines)

are generally for residents only.
● Pedestrianized historic towns allow cars in to deposit luggage—you may have to obtain a permit first from your hotel.
● Parking areas in the heart of cities are expensive.
● If you arrive at night, check that your chosen parking street does not have a market the following day. If it does, your car will be towed away well before dawn.
● A *zona di rimozione* is a tow-away zone.

BUYING FUEL

Italian service stations may not be self-service. If there is an attendant, he will fill your tank, check water, oil and tyre pressures and clean the windscreen if requested. Pay him direct; you will have to ask for a receipt *(una ricevuta)*. If they check the tyres it's customary to give a small tip (50c–€1).There are two grades of unleaded petrol *(senza piombo)*, 95 and 98 octane, diesel *(gasolio)* and LPG. Leaded petrol is virtually nonexistent and you will have to buy lead-substitute additive. Fuel prices are generally similar to UK prices and

A scooter—the fastest way to get around Rome's congested streets

considerably higher than US prices. Motorway service areas and filling stations in major towns accept credit cards.

If you need fuel at night, you will need to find a filling station with a 24-hour *(24 ore)* automatic pump. These take €5, €10 and €20 notes. Feed the money into the slot in the machine. The fuel stops automatically when the money runs out. These can be temperamental and often reject old notes.

SCOOTERS

In the land of the Vespa, it's tempting to rent a scooter *(motorino)*—ask at a tourist office for details. To rent a scooter you must be over 21 and hold a full driver's licence. You need to leave your passport and/or a credit card as a deposit. Crash helmets are compulsory.

Scooters are not for the faint-hearted, and if you've never ridden one in a big city Italy is not the place to start. But if you're having a seaside holiday or staying in a quiet rural area, they're economical, fun and easier to park than a car. Italian scooter drivers weave in and out of the traffic. Unless you are experienced, do not be tempted to emulate them.

TRANSLATIONS OF ITALIAN ROAD SIGNS

Accendere Switch on lights	**Parcheggio** Parking
Accendere i fari Switch on headlights	**Parcheggio autorizzato** Parking allowed
Banchina non Keep off hard shoulder	**Passaggio a livello** Level crossing
Caduta massi Falling rocks	**Pericolo** Danger
Crocevia Crossroads (intersection)	**Rallentare** Slow down
Curva pericolosa Dangerous bend	**Senso unico** One way
Discesa pericolosa Dangerous downhill	**Senso vietato** No entry
Divieto di accesso No entry	**Sosta autorizzata** Parking permitted
Divieto di sorpasso No overtaking	**Svolta** Bend
Divieto di sosta No parking	**Uscita** Exit
Entrata Entry	**Vietata ingresso veicoli** No entry for vehicles
Incrocio Crossroads (intersection)	

BICYCLING

Bicycling is popular both as a sport and as a way of getting around, particularly in the northern plains. Tourist offices will be able to give you details of local rental companies and maps of routes in and around towns. If you rent a bicycle you will need to leave your passport or credit card as a deposit. There are few bicycle paths, so you will need to keep your wits about you. Although wearing a helmet is not compulsory, it is recommended that you do so.

Buses

Italy has no national long-distance bus company. Buses are operated by myriad different companies, mainly running services within their own region, though there are a few that operate outside their own immediate area. With the low cost of rail travel, longer journeys are more efficient and cheaper by train (▷ 56–57). Smoking is not permitted on public transport.

If you are planning to use buses to get around a particular region, you can get **timetables and information** from the company office or the tourist information office.
● **Bus stations** are often next to the railway station. In small towns and villages, buses stop in the main piazza. Bus stations in larger towns tend to have toilets, a newsstand, bar and lost-property office.
● **Tickets** must normally be purchased before boarding the

bus, from newsstands, shops or *tabacchi* (tobacconists).

RURAL BUSES
Rural buses link outlying small towns and villages with the main regional centres or the larger local towns.
● **Timetables and information** are available from the bus company office (normally in the major towns of the region) or from tourist information offices.
● **Tickets** are available from the bus office, tobacconists,

newsstands and sometimes from the driver on board.
● Buses stop at **designated stops**, both at points along the route and in the main piazzas of the villages.
● Services are geared to the local population's needs. Many buses operate to suit working and school hours and are drastically reduced at weekends, during school holidays and at night. So if using rural buses you may need to adapt your plans accordingly.

Taxis

Taxis are available in all towns and cities. Government-regulated vehicles are either white or yellow. Always check that the taxi is registered and that the meter is running—avoid taxis without a meter, as they may not be insured. All charges should be listed on a rate card displayed inside the vehicle. It can be difficult to hail a cab, so it is often better to go to a rank or reserve over the phone. Supplements are added for telephone reservations, luggage and additional passengers. Rates are higher at night and on Sundays and public holidays. Many city taxis have set rates from the airport to the city. Confirm the price before you begin your journey.

TAXIS					
	ROME	**MILAN**	**FLORENCE**	**VENICE**	**NAPLES**
COLOUR	Yellow or white	Yellow	White with yellow graphics	A boat with a white cabin	White with yellow Neapolitan emblem
RANKS	Termini, Piazza Venezia, Piazza San Silvestro, Piazza di Spagna, Piazza Sonnino (Trastevere)	Stazione Centrale, Piazza Duomo, Largo Cairoli, Piazza San Babile	Piazza della Repubblica, Santa Maria Novella, Piazza della Stazione, Piazza del Duomo, Piazza San Marco, Piazza Santa Croce, Piazza della Santa Trinità	San Marco, Piazzale Roma, Aeroporto Venezia Marco Polo, Ferrovia (Santa Lucia train station)	Piazza Garibaldi, Piazza Plebiscito, Piazza Municipio, Piazza della Repubblica, Piazza de Nicola, Piazza Dante
RADIO TAXI TELEPHONE NUMBERS	06 3570 06 4157 06 4994 06 88177 06 5551 06 6645 06 8822	02 6969 02 4040 02 4000 02 8585	055 4390 055 4798 055 4242 055 4386	041 522 2303	081 552 5252 081 551 5151 081 556 4444 081 570 7070
NUMBER OF PASSENGERS	4	4	4/5	6/8	4
PRICE	Moderate	Moderate	Expensive	Extremely expensive	Moderate

Trains

Italy has an extensive rail system and a variety of train types. Fares are the cheapest in Europe and train travel can be a great way to tour the country and enjoy an ever-changing view of the landscape. Trenitalia, the State railway company, covers the whole country, though there are also some privately operated lines and services. Italian trains have a poor record of punctuality, which doesn't seem to bother Italians but which can be of critical importance if your journey involves several changes of trains. So be patient and allow plenty of time between arrivals and departures to make your connections.

FARES

Train fares are calculated by distance but vary depending on whether you take a local, regional, InterCity or night train. New Eurostar Italia trains are the most expensive but offer the best service and use modern carriages of the type used on Eurostar services. Premium fares apply on Eurostar Italia trains and you must pay a €12 supplement if travelling with an InterRail, EurRail or Trenitalia freedom pass.

The easiest, and quickest, way to find the price of a train journey is to use the touch-screen ticket machines installed in most stations. They have an English-language option and you can buy tickets and reserve seats.

Return (round-trip) fares are simply double the single ticket price, and first-class fares are only a little more than second class, and may be a good option for extra comfort, quiet and reliability

of air-conditioning. Local trains are usually second class only.

Point-to-point fares are so cheap that the freedom passes such as the Trenitalia Pass or Eurodomino ticket may not be the best value calculated on the daily average unless you plan to do a lot of train travel each day of the ticket's validity. You may be better off paying for an ordinary ticket for a short trip on some days and save your pass for longer journeys on a tour.

When selecting the train for your destination, bear in mind

Passengers boarding at Stazione Termini in Rome

that while Eurostar Italia trains can reach speeds of 250–300 kph (155–185 mph), they only reach anything like their top speeds when they run on new high-speed track between Rome and Florence, Milan and Turin. Where they run on old track their speed is restricted, but journey times are shorter than InterCity services on the same route because Eurostar trains make fewer intermediate stops.

WHERE TO BUY TRENITALIA PASSES	
Trenitalia agents in your country or in Italy	
At the following stations in Italy:	
● Bari	● Napoli Centrale
● Bologna Centrale	● Palermo Centrale
● Brindisi	● Fiumicino Aeroporto
● Firenze SMN	● Roma Termini
● Genova PP	● Torino Porta Nuova
● Milano Centrale	● Venezia Santa Lucia
	● Venezia Mestre
	● Verona

TICKETS

Ask for either *andata* (one way) or *andata e tornata* (return or round-trip) and tell the ticket clerk which train you want to take, as there may be a supplement to pay. It is cheaper to pay supplements at the time you buy the tickets, as upgrading on board the train involves an additional charge. On long journeys with changes of train at different stations, you may be issued with several tickets, representing the different legs of your journey. Keep them together as onboard inspectors may want to see them all. On the other hand, if two of you are travelling together, you may be issued with only one ticket printed with an indication of two travellers.

Children aged 4–12 travel at half the normal fare; children under 4 not occupying a seat travel free.

VALIDATING TICKETS

Just buying a ticket is not enough for travelling on Italian trains. Whichever train you take you must validate your ticket by punching it in a yellow or red slot machine in the station booking hall before you board the train. This applies even if your ticket is for a reserved seat on a specified train. The ticket inspector may ask

you to pay a surcharge of €20 if your ticket does not have the pre-boarding validation mark on it.

For information about rail passes that give you the freedom of the Italian rail network, ▷ 46–47.

TIMETABLES

All stations have timetable posters, one for Arrivals *(Arrivi)* and one for Departures *(Partenze)*. These show every train stopping at the station and all the intermediate stations on the journey. They also show the platform number that the train is expected to use, but also confirm this by listening to announcements or asking a member of staff. If you use the self-service touch-screen ticket machines, they will give you details of the timing of your train and offer choices for different parts of the day. If you are touring Italy, it is wise to carry a train timetable such as the latest edition of the Thomas Cook European Rail Timetable, which is updated every month.

Trenitalia now offers a searchable train timetable in English on its website (www. trenitalia.com/en/index.html).

*A timetable information board on a platform (*binario*) at Termini station in Rome*

GETTING ON BOARD

Station platforms throughout Italy are very low, and passenger carriages have three steps to negotiate, which can be a nuisance with large suitcases or other heavy baggage. Passengers with a disability should seek help from Trenitalia station staff in advance, to arrange for a lifting machine to help you get on board. Larger stations have a dedicated assistance office for people with disabilities, and it is wise to give 24 hours' notice of your travel arrangements.

Some long-distance InterCity trains, and most international services, are composed of carriages heading to different destinations down the line, so make sure you are in the right section of the train for your journey. Trains to Sicily, for example, are loaded on to a ferry for the short sea crossing between Villa San Giovanni and Messina, and the carriages are reassembled into separate trains heading west for Palermo and south for Taormina, Catania and Siracusa.

NIGHT TRAINS

Night trains are particularly good value for covering long distances, such as to and from Sicily. You have the choice of cabins fitted with beds *(classe)* or couchettes (comfort) and advance reservations are strongly recommended as these trains get full, especially in July and August. Reservations can be made through services such as Rail Europe or your travel agent, or at main stations in Italy.

AIRPORT TRAIN SERVICES
Most major airports have good train connections to city centres, and trains are a much more economical option than taxis (▷ 42–43). The notable exception is Ancona, where plans to build a rail line to the airport have been delayed by protests from local taxi drivers concerned about losing lucrative business. At Turin airport a state-of-the-art station was built as part of the modernization leading up to the 2006 Winter Olympic Games.

TRAIN CATERING
InterCity and Eurostar Italia trains usually have a restaurant car serving coffee, cold drinks, and some pre-packed convenience snacks, and at certain times full meals. Be aware that train catering is very basic and pricey, and not all that it could be, given Italy's resources and tradition for fine food.

Biglietteria/Tickets

A train ticket machine

You may prefer to stock up with food before joining the train.

SECURITY
Train stations are a fertile ground for thieves and confidence tricksters, so take special care over your possessions. Don't leave bags unattended and only accept help from uniformed employees of Trenitalia. Be alert for gangs of children and women who create a commotion to distract attention while attempting to steal from travellers' bags or pockets.

LEFT LUGGAGE
Most stations have a left-luggage (deposit) storage facility. Bear in mind that the one at Rome Termini station is often very busy, especially in the early morning when night trains from all over Italy and the rest of Europe pull in. The service is very slow and the staffing arrangements never seem to match these peak periods of demand, so allow plenty of time to deposit your bags before going around the city.

POINTS TO REMEMBER
● Smoking is not permitted inside station buildings or on

The chart on the left gives the duration in hours and minutes of a train journey between major towns in Italy by the fastest route. It is a general guide and does not allow for delays.

	Ancona	Bari (Centrale)	Bologna (Centrale)	Bolzano (Novarese)	Firenze (S.M.N.)	Genova (Piazza Principe)	Milano (Centrale)	Napoli (Centrale)	Padova	Perugia	Piacenza	Pisa (Centrale)	Ravenna	Reggio di Calabria	Roma (Termini)	Siena	Trento	Torino (Porta Suza)	Venezia (Santa Lucia)	Verona (Porta Nuova)
Bari (Centrale)	403																			
Bologna (Centrale)	152	601																		
Bolzano (Novarese)	653	1250	444																	
Firenze (S.M.N.)	316	647	053	447																
Genova (Piazza Principe)	455	906	302	343	231															
Milano (Centrale)	344	753	146	141	247	131														
Napoli (Centrale)	508	403	432	831	326	717	620													
Padova	341	753	115	433	217	413	207	613												
Perugia	230	652	304	721	148	608	507	414	410											
Piacenza	308	719	116	253	219	128	039	623	252	411										
Pisa (Centrale)	453	817	222	607	049	146	341	457	357	303	317									
Ravenna	209	618	100	456	217	422	255	619	207	423	243	357								
Reggio di Calabria	951	640	915	1315	809	1202	1219	421	1058	907	1109	935	1125							
Roma (Termini)	308	439	241	631	135	418	430	134	400	204	418	247	406	615						
Siena	518	811	246	723	119	358	434	506	430	319	423	143	424	955	301					
Trento	435	845	221	445	319	424	235	708	158	553	331	502	408	1142	505	543				
Torino (Porta Suza)	502	913	324	202	420	137	123	817	403	604	152	328	435	1347	602	545	436			
Venezia (Santa Lucia)	414	825	147	507	249	447	240	645	029	441	326	409	242	1126	432	449	230	148		
Verona (Porta Nuova)	332	814	118	336	216	316	118	605	046	450	214	359	255	1039	402	434	053	314	119	
Trieste	609	1021	337	717	441	646	424	843	230	719	518	606	425	1318	624	648	431	631	203	303

ITALY'S MAJOR RAIL ROUTES

CH

FL

A

Bolzano
(Bozen)

Trento

SLO

MILANO

PADOVA

TRIESTE

VERONA

VENEZIA

HR

TORINO

Piacenza

F

GENOVA

BOLOGNA

Ravenna

MC

Pisa

FIRENZE

Siena

Ancona

Isola
d'Elba

Perugia

F

ROMA

BARI

NAPOLI

Sardegna

Reggio di Calabria

Sicilia

board any train, even if old window stickers indicate a 'smoking' carriage. Smoking is allowed only in the open air on station platforms.
● For **lost property** call the station at either your departure or arrival point.
● Except for the smallest, all Italian stations have a ticket office, bookstall, bar, toilets and left luggage.

● Station bars sell **food** to take away; in larger stations there are also trolleys selling drinks and snacks. Ask for what you want … *da portare via* (to take away).
● **Luggage trolleys (baggage carts)** are few and far between. There are **porters** at Rome, Milan, Venice, Turin, Naples, Genoa and Bologna.
● There are occasional **platform changes**—check the departure

board before boarding. Boards at the end of the platforms show the next train to leave.
● Train doors automatically close 30–60 seconds before departure.
● Intercity, Eurostar and Espressi trains have **on-board catering** and **air-conditioning**.
● Eurostar and Intercity have **telephones**.
● All trains have **toilets**.

Domestic Flights

The main Italian cities and regional capitals all have their own airports, with daily connecting flights between the Italian airports and international gateways.

Italy's national carrier, Alitalia, runs regular flights between all the major cities. In addition, there are a number of regional airlines, useful for accessing more out-of-the-way places. Internal flights within Italy make sense if you want to see a lot quickly, and are particularly useful for travelling to Sicily and Sardinia.

● You can use the web to reserve and purchase tickets on Italy's regional airlines, as well as with Alitalia. If you don't have access to the internet, your travel agent can do this for you.

● Tickets for flights within Italy are relatively expensive (eg Naples–Milan costs around €160, Rome–Venice around €135), but advance reservations may secure you one of the

Air One livery

INTERNAL AIRLINES			
AIRLINE	**BASE**	**WEBSITE**	**DESTINATIONS**
AIR DOLOMITI	Trieste	www.airdolomiti.it	Alghero, Ancona, Bari, Bologna, Cagliari, Genoa, Milan, Olbia, Naples, Rimini, Pisa, Trieste, Verona, Venice
AIR EUROPE	Milan	www.aireurope.it	Bari , Milan, Naples, Palermo, Rome, Verona, Venice
AIR ONE	Pescara	www.air-one.it	Alghero, Bari, Bologna, Brindisi, Cagliari, Catania, Crotone, Florence, Genoa, Lamezia Terme, Milan, Naples, Olbia, Palermo, Pescara, Pisa, Reggio di Calabria, Rome, Turin, Venice (seasonal: Lampedusa, Pantelleria)
AIR VALLEE	Aosta	www.airvallee.com	Ancona, Bari, Bologna, Brindisi, Catania, Cagliari, Florence, Genoa
ALITALIA	Rome	www.alitalia.it	Lamezia Terme, Milan, Naples, Palermo, Perugia, Pisa, Reggio di Calabria, Rome, Trieste, Turin, Venice, Verona
ALPIEAGLES	Venice	www.alpieagles.com	Cagliari, Catania, Lamezia Terme, Milan, Naples, Olbia, Palermo, Rome, Verona, Venice
AZZURRA AIR	Bergamo	www.azzurraair.it	Bergamo, Rome
GANDALF	Milan	www.gandalf.it	Brescia, Milan, Pisa, Rome, Verona
MERIDIANA	Olbia	www.meridiana.it	Bergamo, Bologna, Cagliari, Catania, Florence, Milan, Naples, Olbia, Palermo, Pisa, Rome, Turin, Venice, Verona
VOLARE	Vicenza	www.volare-airlines.com	Bari, Catania, Milan, Naples, Palermo, Rome, Venice

limited number of cheap seats available on each flight. The popular routes tend to sell out more quickly. If you fly to Italy with Alitalia, you are eligible for its Visit Italy Pass, which allows you to take three internal flights for around €125, useful if you're going south.

● Check-in times vary from 1 to 2 hours. Security can be very slow, so allow plenty of time for this.

● You will need personal identification; a passport will serve this purpose.

● Most domestic flights have no first- or business-class seats.

● Smoking is not allowed at airports except outside in the open air. There are stiff fines for smoking inside public buildings, and these can be increased on a scale from €27.50 to €275 if children or pregnant women are present. Smoking is not allowed on the tarmac or on board any aircraft.

● On short hops you are offered a drink; on longer flights a light snack is served.

● Regional airports are generally well equipped with the usual range of facilities and services, albeit on a small scale.

AIRPORTS NEAR POPULAR AREAS

Below is a list of popular sightseeing and holiday destinations and the airports that best serve them:

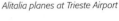
Alitalia planes at Trieste Airport

Adriatic Riviera—Ancona Raffaello Sanzio (AOI).
Calabria—Lamezia Terme (SUF).
Cinque Terre—Genova Cristoforo Colombo (GOA).
Dolomites—Verona Valerio Catullo (VRN) or Venice Marco Polo (VCE).
Florence—Firenze Amerigo Vespucci (FLR) is 4km (2.5 miles) northwest of the city, and Pisa Galileo Galilei (PSA) is 80km (50 miles) west of the city.
Lake Como—Bergamo Orio al Serio (BGY).
Lake Garda—Verona Valerio Catullo (VRN), Brescia (Verona) (VBS), Milan Linate (LIN), Milan Malpensa (MXP), Milano Orio al Serio (BGY).

Inside the light and spacious terminal building at Venice Marco Polo Airport

Lampedusa island—Lampedusa (LMP).
Milan—Milano Linate (LIN), Milano Malpensa (MXP).
Naples, Sorrento and the Amalfi coast—Naples Capodichino (NAP) is 6km (3.8 miles) north of the city of Naples.
The Northeast and Emilia-Romagna—Bologna Guglielmo Marconi (BLQ), Trieste International (TRS).
Pantelleria island—Pantelleria (PNL).
Puglia—Bari Palese (BRI).
Riviera di Levante—Genova Cristoforo Colombo (GOA).
Riviera di Ponente—Genova Cristoforo Colombo (GOA).
Rome—Rome Ciampino (CIA) is 16km (10 miles) southeast of the city, and Rome Leonardo da Vinci Fiumicino (FCO) is 36km (22 miles) southwest of the city.
Sardinia—Cagliari Mario Mameli (CAG) in the south and Alghero Fertilia (AHO) in the northwest.
Sicily—Catania (CTA) in the east and Palermo Punta Raisi (PMO) in the northwest.
Turin and the Alps—Torino Caselle (TRN) is 16km (10 miles) north of Turin and (48km) 30 miles from the Alps.
Tuscany—Pisa Galileo Galilei (PSA).
Umbria—Perugia International (PEG).
Venice—Venice Marco Polo (VCE) is 13km (8 miles) from the city.

Domestic Ferries

ISLAND FERRIES

Besides the main islands of Sardinia and Sicily, Italy has a number of smaller islands. Italians have gone to these destinations for years, but now foreign visitors are beginning to discover their charms and the pleasures of their laid-back, low-key resorts. All are regularly served by ferries from the mainland, often with a choice of departure ports. Caremar is the main operator providing services to Ischia and Capri, but there are several others, all operating from the Molo Beverello in Naples. It is essential to reserve ferries and accommodation in advance in peak season (July and August). Out-of-season services are drastically reduced, or even, in the case of the more remote islands, nonexistent.

Sicily—See page 46
www.traghettionline.net
Sardinia—See page 46
www.traghettionline.net

VENICE

ACTV runs a comprehensive service between the lagoon islands and the city (▷ 50).

The Garda Express carries passengers across Lake Garda

FERRIES TO ITALY'S ISLANDS					
	ELBA	**GIGLIO**	**ISOLE PONZIANE**	**ISCHIA**	**CAPRI**
MAINLAND PORT	Piombino	Porto Santo Stefano	Anzio, Formia and others (Terracina, Naples)	Naples, Pozzuoli, Procida	Naples, Sorrento
ARRIVAL PORT	Portoferraio	Giglio Porto	Ponza	Ischia Porto	Marina Grande
JOURNEY TIME	1 hour	1 hour	From Anzio 2 hours, Formia 2 hours 30 min, Terracina 2 hours 30 min	From Naples 1 hour 20 min; from Pozzuoli 1 hour 40 min	From Naples 1 hour 15 min, from Sorrento 50 min
FERRY COMPANY	**Moby** Nuova Stazione Marittima, Piombino tel 0565 225211 Via Ninci 1, Portoferraio tel 0565 9361 www.mobylines.it **Toremar** Nuova Stazione Marittima, Piombino tel 0565 31100 Calata Italia 23, Portoferraio tel 0565 918080 www.toremar-elba.it	**Maregiglio** Porto Santo Stefano tel 0564 812920 www.maregiglio.it **Toremar** Porto Santo Stefano tel 0564 810803 www.toremar.it	**Caremar** Via Ardeatina 114, Anzio tel 06 9860 0083 Molo Musco, Ponza tel 0771 80565/081 317 2999 (overseas callers)/199 123199 (call centre from Italy) www.caremar.it **Caremar** Banchina Azzurra, Formia tel 0771 22710/0771 23800	**Caremar** Molo Beverello, Napoli tel 081 551 3882 Banchina Redentore e Olimpia, Ischia tel 081 984818 Banchina Emporio Pozzuoli tel 081 5262711/199 123199 (call centre from Italy) www.caremar.it	**Caremar** Molo Beverello, Napoli tel 081 5513882 Angelina srl, Marina Grande Capri tel 081 8370700 Dott Raniero Morelli, Piazza Marinai d'Italia, Sorrento tel 081 8073077/199 123199 (call centre from Italy)
ADVANCE RESERVATIONS	Yes	Yes	Yes	Foot passengers no, cars yes	No

LAKE FERRIES

Italy's most scenically beautiful lakes are in the north, and are one of the country's most popular holiday destinations. The big names—Como, Garda and Maggiore—draw crowds throughout the summer, the majority of whom use the lake ferries to enjoy waterborne views. Ferries link the lakeside towns and are as much a useful form of transport as excursion boats. Further south, the two central Italian lakes of Bolsena and Trasimeno have pleasure boats to their islands.

THE NORTHERN LAKES

Services on Lakes Como, Garda, Maggiore and smaller Iseo are all run by Navigazione Laghi. The service on Lake Como links Cadenabbia, Menaggio, Varenna and Bellagio, a cluster of attractive resort villages in the central part of the lake. Maggiore and Garda have a comprehensive service, with boats making stops at numerous villages on either side of the length of the lakes. The boats

People boarding at Orta San Giulio on Lake Orta

on Lake Maggiore cross the border and run into Switzerland. In addition, there are many cruises (including night-time) and excursions to the islands. Tickets are sold in the villages or on board; timetable information is displayed at the landing stages.

Contact:
Navigazione Laghi
Via L. Ariosto 21, 20145 Milano
800 551801/02 467 6101
www.navigazionelaghi.it

LAGO TRASIMENO
Excursions run from Castiglione del Lago and Passignano to Isola Maggiore.

LAGO DI BOLSENA
Excursions run from Capodimonte and Bolsena to Isola Bizantina.

FERRIES TO ITALY'S ISLANDS

ISOLE EOLIE	ISOLE EGADI	PANTELLERIA	ISOLE PELAGIE	ISOLE TREMITI
Milazzo	Trápani	Trápani	Porto Empédocle	Vieste (Jun–Sep)
Porto di Levante, Vulcano	Favignana	Pantelleria	Linosa, Lampedusa	San Nicola
1 hour 30 min	1 hour	5 hours 30 min	To Linosa 5 hours 45 min, to Lampedusa 7 hours 30 min	From Manfredonia 2 hours (hydrofoil); from Vieste 1 hour (hydrofoil)
Siremar Allia srl, Via dei Mille (Palazzo Sta Rita), Milazzo tel 090 928 3424 Vulcano Viaggi srl, Piazza Vulcano Levante 3, Porto di Levante tel 090 985 2149/199 123199 (call centre from Italy) tel 0039 081 317 2999 (from UK) www.siremar.it **N.G.I.** tel 090 928 4091 www.cormorano.net/ngil	**Siremar** Terminal Aliscafo, Stazione Marittima Molo Dogana, Trápani tel 0923 545455 Catalano Viaggi, Molo S Leonardo, Favignana tel 0923 921363/199 123199 (call centre from Italy) tel 0039 081 317 2999 (from UK) www.siremar.it	**Siremar** Terminal Aliscafo, Stazione Marittima Molo Dogana, Trápani tel 0923 545455 Agenzia Rizzo, Via Borgo Italia 22, Pantelleria tel 0923 911120/199 123199 (call centre from Italy) tel 0039 081 317 2999 (from UK) www.siremar.it	**Siremar** Tricoli e Nuara, Via Molo 13 tel 0922 636683 Porto Empédocle Gaetano Cavallaro, Via Principe Umberto tel 0922 972062 Linosa, Sebastiano Strazzera, Longomare L Rizzo, Lampedusa tel 0922 970003/199 123199 (call centre from Italy) tel 0039 081 317 2999 (from UK) www.siremar.it	**Adriatica** Gargano Viaggi, Piazza Roma 7, Vieste tel 0884 708501 Dita Cafiero Emilio, Via degli Abbati 10, Tremiti tel 0882 463008/199 123199 (call centre from Italy) tel 081 317 2999 (from abroad) www.adriatica.it
Foot passengers no, cars yes	Foot passengers no, cars yes	Yes	Yes	Yes

VISITORS WITH A DISABILITY

As in so many other countries, the overall picture of facilities for people with disabilities in Italy is mixed. The major problems are often not with transport, accommodation or public buildings, but in the layout and nature of the cities and towns themselves. The historic interest and architectural beauty of many of the main tourist attractions in Italy inevitably make disabled access a challenge. Things are progressing, particularly with regard to public transport and access to museums and galleries, but visitors with disabilities will often find that it's not easy getting there in the first place. Italians are generally helpful, but, with some key exceptions, facilities for disabled people have not yet caught up with those in northern European countries and North America.
● If you have a disability, plan carefully, aim to travel with able-bodied friends or consider reserving your holiday with a specialist tour operator.
● You should contact your airline in advance of your date of travel They will let the airports know what assistance you will need.

An electric stairlift organized by Regency San Marino Travel Agency

● Trains sometimes have wheelchair access, and this is indicated on the timetable by a wheelchair symbol. If you need assistance at the station, contact them 24 hours in advance.
● Taxis can take wheelchairs folded and stored in the boot (trunk), but Italian taxis are saloon (sedan)-type cars and getting in and out may be difficult.
● If you are driving, you can use your blue Disabled Person's Parking Badge in Italy.
● Be aware that many streets in historic towns are cobbled and can be very steep.
● Major pedestrian crossings in cities have a sound signal for the visually impaired.
● An increasing number of public places and some museums have information in braille.
● Reserve well in advance and be specific about your requirements when reserving accommodation.

USEFUL CONTACTS

ATAC DISABLED SERVICES
tel 06 4695 4887/06 4695 4286
open daily 8–2.30
ATAC manages and provides information on Rome's public transport system.

INFORMAHANDICAP
Viale Garibaldi 155, 30174 Venezia Mestre
tel 041 534 1700, fax 041 534 2257, email informahandicap@comune.venezia.it
Informahandicap can give you help and advice if you are planning to visit Venice.

**CO.IN SOCIALE
(COOPERATIVE INTEGRATE ONLUS)**
Via Enrico Giglioli 54, Roma
tel 06 232 69231
www.coinsociale.it
CO.IN plans and promotes the building of accessible public spaces in Rome and produces a list of sights that have disabled access.

**UNIONE ITALIANA DEI CIECHI
(ITALIAN SOCIETY FOR THE BLIND)**
Unione Italiana dei Ciechi, Via Borgognona 38, 00187 Roma
tel 06 699881, fax 06 678 6815
www.uiciechi.it (in Italian only)

SATH (SOCIETY FOR ACCESSIBLE TRAVEL AND HOSPITALITY)
www.sath.org
Lots of useful travel tips for American holidaymakers who are visually impaired or have a disability.

ACCESSIBLE ITALY (REGENCY SAN MARINO SRL)
Via C. Manetti 34, 47891 Dogana Borgomaggiore
Repubblica di San Marino 47031
tel 0549 941108, fax 0549 907189
www.accessibleitaly.com
An Italian travel company that run tours for visitors with disabilities. Local contacts give the company the edge over many foreign operators.

● For a more relaxed Italian holiday, steer clear of the major cities and use a car to explore rural areas and the smaller picturesque towns and villages.

VENICE

Venice poses particular problems for wheelchair users, but, with judicious planning, you will be able to see plenty. *Vaporetti* (▷ 50) can take wheelchairs, and some of the major sights are accessible from the *vaporetto* stops without having to negotiate bridges. Facilities inside some museums and galleries are good, and there are hotels and restaurants where you will have no problems. The tourist office publishes a map with routes suitable for wheelchairs, and four main bridges in the *sestiere* (district) of San Marco have automated ramps; access keys are available from the tourist office. For more information contact Informahandicap (see above for contact information).

This chapter is divided geographically into nine sections. Places of interest are listed alphabetically within each area. The major sights are listed at the front of each regional section.

The Sights

THE NORTHWEST

This is an area of diversity, from the scenic splendour of Lago di Como, Lago Maggiore and the towering Alps to stylish Milan, Italy's economic powerhouse. The smaller historic cities, such as Mantova and Cremona, are crammed with artistic treasures, while the coast has beaches, picturesque villages and the vibrant port of Genoa.

MAJOR SIGHTS

Towers surrounding the central Piazza del Risorgimento in Alba

Children enjoying the cool water in the Piazza del Duomo, Bergamo

ALBA

✚ 432 C5 ℹ Piazza del Risorgimento 2, 12051 Alba, tel 0173 35833 🚆 Alba
www.langheroero.it

Prized for its wines and white truffles *(tartufi bianchi),* the medieval town of Alba, 62km (39 miles) from Turin, is the main town in the Langhe, a beautiful region of vine-clad slopes and hills crowned by ancient castles. Here gastronomy reigns supreme: Delicatessens are piled high with hams, wild boar, homemade pastas, *funghi* and bottles of Barolo and Barbaresco.

The old town is compact and its cobbled streets, arcades, red-brick medieval towers and historic monuments have been well preserved. The Piazza del Risorgimento, or Piazza del Duomo as it is known, is overlooked by the town hall and the red-brick Duomo di San Lorenzo (Mon–Sat 9–12, 3–5.30, Sun and holidays 9–1, 3–5.30). The 15th-century duomo has beautifully carved and inlaid choir stalls. From the square you can see the tallest and best-preserved of Alba's medieval towers; there were originally 100 in the town.

ASTI

✚ 432 C5 ℹ Piazza Alfieri 34, 14100 Asti, tel 0141 530357 🚆 Asti

Asti is the home of, and synonymous with, spumante, the sweet sparkling wine. This large town, 60km (37 miles) east of Turin, is predominantly industrial, but its medieval past is evident in the historic buildings and churches that are scattered throughout the old centre.

In medieval times Asti was the largest town in Piedmont and a rival city to Milan. The town's *palio,* a horse-race, similar to Siena's (▷ 259), is the oldest in Italy, dating from the late 13th

century. Asti once had 125 towers, but only 12 survive.

The main cultural attraction is the medieval complex of the 15th-century church of San Pietro in Consavia, a Gothic cloister with a small circular baptistery dating from the 10th to 12th centuries and an archaeology museum (summer Tue–Sat 9–12, 4–7, Sun 10–12; rest of year Tue–Sat 9–12, 3–6, Sun 10–12). The large Gothic church of San Secondo on the piazza of the same name has a Romanesque bell tower and an altarpiece by Gaudenzio Ferrari (1475–1546) (Mon–Sat 8–12, 3.30–6, Sun 3.30–5.30).

BERGAMO

✚ 431 E3 ℹ (Lower Town) Viale Vittorio Emanuele 20, 24100 Bergamo, tel 035 210204 ℹ (Upper Town) Vicolo dell'Aquila Nera 2, 24100 Bergamo, tel 035 232730 🚆 Bergamo

Northeast of Milan in the southern foothills of the Alps, Bergamo could not be more different from Italy's business capital. The city is divided into the medieval Città Alta (Upper Town) and the relatively dull, modern Città Bassa (Lower Town).

The arches of the Palazzo della Ragione lead to the glorious Piazza del Duomo and the Cappella Colleoni (1470–76). Built as a mausoleum for Bartolomeo Colleoni, the famous Venetian *condottiere* (▷ 33), it has a pink and white marble façade covered with statues, reliefs and stuccowork, with a large rose window above the portal (daily 9–12.30, 2–6.30). To the right of the chapel is a copy of the 14th-century octagonal baptistery, complete with a red marble gallery. Inside are Flemish and Florentine tapestries, 15th- to 17th-century frescoes, the tomb of Gaetano Donizetti, the composer, and a

splendid wooden choir stall (1522–55) with inlaid panels designed depicting scenes from the Old Testament (Sun 3–6 or on request, tel 035 210223).

BRESCIA

✚ 434 F4 ℹ Corso Zanardelli 34, 25121 Brescia, tel 030 43418 🚆 Brescia
www.bresciaholiday.com

Brescia may lack the charm of nearby Bergamo, but it is an ancient city with a strong cultural heritage. The most appealing of its three squares is the Venetian-style Piazza Loggia, where you will find the richly decorated Palazzo della Loggia (the town hall), with its arcade and cupola. An archway on the south side leads to the controversial Piazza della Vittoria (Victory Square), built in a Fascist style during Mussolini's rule (▷ 38–39). The archway brings you to Piazza Paolo VI, the religious heart of the city, overlooked by the great green cupola of the Duomo Nuovo (daily 8–1, 4–7.30). This towering, modern baroque cathedral dwarfs its older and more interesting neighbour, the Duomo Vecchio, a rare example of a Romanesque cathedral with a circular plan—hence its nickname, La Rotonda (Apr–end Oct Tue–Sun 9–12, 3–7; Nov–end Mar Tues–Sun 9–12, 3–6).

The remains of the Capitoline Temple around Piazza del Foro are a legacy of the Roman colony of Brixia, established here in AD73 by Emperor Vespasian. Archaeological remains from the site are housed in the Museo della Città, in the nearby 16th-century Monastery of Santa Giulia. The highlight is a bronze *Winged Victory* discovered in 1826 (Tue–Sun 10–1, 2–5 free entry).
Don't Miss The Capitoline Temple.

The white houses of Vernazza clinging to the coast

Genoa, Italy's most important commercial port

CINQUE TERRE

🚩 433 E6 ℹ️ Viale Mazzini 47, 19100 La Spezia, tel 0187 770900 🚊 La Spezia–Monterosso line 🚢 Apr–end Oct Navigazione Golfo dei Poeti operates a regular boat service linking all the villages except Corniglia. Summer ferries and catamarans from Genoa to the Cinque Terre www.aptcinqueterre.sp.it

The ravishing coastline of the Cinque Terre (Five Lands) is named after the five little fishing villages that cling precariously to the cliffs northwest of La Spezia. From here to Levanto the landscape is characterized by mountains cloaked in woods, terraces of vines and cliffs, which provide spectacular views over the turquoise sea. Tourism is growing rapidly here, but the area is a protected national park and the locals are encouraged to maintain their traditional occupations of fishing and viticulture. Grapes grown on the steep slopes produce the fragrant and fruity white Cinque Terre wine and the rarer, stronger and sweeter Sciacchetri. The villages most easily reached by road, and hence the best-equipped and least charming, are Monterossa and Riomaggiore. Vernazza is arguably the most beautiful of the five villages, a huddle of painted houses, narrow alleys and arcades. Genoese fortifications here include medieval bastions and a watchtower. Manarola is another highly photogenic village, with a cluster of pastel-washed houses, steep cobbled streets, a quaint harbour and the only sandy beach in the Cinque Terre. Corniglia, the smallest of the villages, clings to a ridge, with steps leading down to the sea. The clear blue waters and rocky coastline are home to a huge variety of fish and thriving underwater gardens, making this a popular destination for divers.

CREMONA

🚩 433 E4 ℹ️ Piazza del Comune 5, 26100 Cremona, tel 0372 21722 🚊 Cremona www.aptcremona.it

This is the birthplace of the Stradivarius. The first modern violin, as opposed to the medieval fiddle, was made here by Andrea Amati in 1566, and Antonio Stradivarius, the great violin-maker, was born here in 1644. His life and work are commemorated in the Museo Stradivariano, where many of his tools are on display (Tue–Sat 9–6, Sun and holidays 10–6). The Sala dei Violini in the Palazzo Comune also has a collection of historic violins, including examples by Amati and Stradivarius.

This little market town on the north banks of the River Po, 95km (59 miles) southeast of Milan, revolves around the Piazza del Comune, with its ensemble of medieval monuments. The Romanesque and Gothic cathedral (1107–1332) has an ornately sculpted marble façade with a fine rose window. The frescoes inside by the Cremona school are the highlight. Particularly notable is Pordenone's *Crucifixion* (1520–21), prized for its bold spatial effects (Mon–Sat 10.30–12, 3.30–6, Sun and holidays 10.30–11, 3.30–5.30). The 14th-century Lombard-Gothic church of Sant'Agostino (1339–45) is also worth visiting to see its serene altarpiece by Perugino, *The Madonna and Saints,* in the fifth chapel on the south side (daily 9.30–12, 3.30–6).

Don't miss The Romanesque and Gothic cathedral.

GENOVA (GENOA)

🚩 433 D5 ℹ️ Piazza Acqua Verde–Statione Porta Principe, 16126 Genova, tel 010 246 2633 🚊 Genova www.apt.genova.it

Its outskirts are unattractive, but Genoa has a rich heritage and a wealth of historical palaces, churches and museums to explore. It was, and still is, Italy's principal seaport and was famously the birthplace of Christopher Columbus in 1451. Genoa enjoyed a major facelift when Renzo Piano revamped the harbour in preparation for EXPO 92. Its *carruggi* (narrow alleys) and lavishly decorated mansions and palazzi, especially along Via Garibaldi and Via Balbi, further soften its rough exterior.

The Galleria Nazionale di Palazzo Spinola on Via San Luca, an opulent 16th- to 18th-century palace, has original furnishings, frescoed ceilings and an art collection that includes works by Van Dyck, Antonello da Messina, Rubens and Pisano (Tue–Sat 8.30–7.30, Sun 1.30–7.30). The Museo Civico di Palazzo Bianco, housed in a 16th-century palace on Via Garibaldi, also has an exceptional collection of paintings by Genoese and other European artists, including works by Rubens, Van Dyck, Antonello da Messina, Caravaggio and Murillo. The early 13th-century Cattedrale di San Lorenzo in the piazza of the same name has a Gothic black-and-white striped marble façade (Mon–Sat 9–11.30, 3–5.30). Opened for EXPO 92, the Acquario di Genova is the second-largest aquarium in Europe. It was built to commemorate the fifth centenary of Columbus' discovery of the New World (Mon–Fri 9.30–7.30, Sat–Sun and holidays 9.30–8.30).

Don't miss The Galleria Nazionale di Palazzo Spinola; the Museo Civico di Palazzo Bianco; the Cattedrale di San Lorenzo; the Acquario di Genova.

LAGO DI COMO

Its temperate climate and lavish villas make Como the most romantic of the three major Italian lakes. Enjoy boat trips, walks in the mountains, visits to lakeshore villas and gardens and the wonderful panoramas.

Surrounded by high mountains and rugged hills, Lake Como has inspired writers, artists and musicians from Pliny the Younger in Roman times to 19th-century Romantics such as French novelists Stendhal and Flaubert and the Italian composer Rossini. The first steamboat was launched from here in 1826 and visitors have been taking boat trips to enjoy the views of the lakeside ever since.

Como is smaller than lakes Maggiore and Garda but it has the longest perimeter (over 170km/106 miles). Between Argegno and Nesso, it reaches a maximum depth of 410m (1,345ft), making it the deepest lake in Italy.

THE THREE LAKES
The sunny and gentle west coast of the Como branch of the lake is typified by patrician villas, elegant hotels, harbours and villages often presided over by an ancient campanile. The shadier Lecco branch, between the High Brianza to the west and the Grigna to the east, is less accessible, with fewer villages and harbours. At the southern tip, Lecco developed into a large industrial centre in the 19th century. The northern section of the lake, often referred to as Alto Lario, is different again. Here the lake widens and campsites dot both shores. In the north, Monte Legnone (2,609m/8,560ft) towers above Culico, south of which lies the main attraction along the coast—Piona's ancient abbey, on the tip of a peninsula. The 'three lakes' meet at the Punta Sparivento (the Point That Divides the Wind).

LAKESIDE TOWNS AND VILLAS
At this central headland is Bellagio, known as the pearl of the lake for its charming setting and beautiful villas. Geographically isolated, it has excellent boat connections, which make it popular for day trips. Against a backdrop of high mountains, the lively resort of Menaggio has some excellent walking, windsurfing, swimming, trekking and rock-climbing opportunities. Villa d'Este at Cernobbio (▷ 285) is the most famous of Como's villas. Built in the 16th century, it is now a sumptuous hotel. In a glorious wooded peninsula, Villa del Balbianello, in Lenno, is full of unusual treasures, including mementoes collected by the eccentric explorer who lived here.

RATINGS				
Good for food	●	●	●	●
Good for kids	●	●	●	● ●
Historic interest	●	●	●	
Photo stops	●	●	●	● ●

BASICS

✚ 431 D3

🛈 Piazza Cavour 17, 22100 Como, tel 031 269712; Mon–Sat 9–1, 2–6

🚉 Como town

🚢 Car ferry service linking Menaggio, Varenna, Bellagio and Cadenabbia

www.lakecomo.com
A stylish website providing ferry information and links to tour guides and hotels. English version.

TIP

● Spring and autumn are the best times to visit as in peak season the main resorts and the narrow winding coastal roads are uncomfortably crowded.

A view of Varenna on the shores of Lago di Como (top)

LAGO MAGGIORE

An area of natural beauty that is best admired from the water. Famous for its gardens, Borromean Islands and elegant resorts.

Maggiore is the second-largest and the most westerly of the three main lakes. Piedmont in the west, Lombardy in the east and the Ticon canton in Switzerland, in the north, all converge on its shores. With its southern tip approximately 55km (35 miles) northwest of Milan, the lake is 65km (40 miles) long, averages 2km (1.3 miles) across and has a perimeter of 170km (106 miles). The surface area is 212sq km (82sq miles) and the deepest point, in the Gulf of Borromeo, is 372m (1,220ft). The scenery ranges from wild, mountainous landscapes in the north to gentle Mediterranean views further south. Gardens flourish in the spring, when camellias, rhododendrons and azaleas brighten up the shores.

RATINGS

Good for food	● ● ●
Good for kids	● ● ● ● ●
Historic interest	● ● ● ● ●
Photo stops	● ● ● ● ●

BASICS

⊞ 431 D3

🛈 Viale Mazzini 47, 19100 La Spezia, tel 0187 770900

www.borromeoturismo.it

🚆 From Milan

🚆 From Verona

🛥 Boats run to the Borromean Islands every 30 minutes in high season. There are ferries to and from other lakeside destinations (Angera, Stresa, Pallanza, Intra)

TIP

● The best places to stay are Stresa, Baveno and Pallanza. The resorts further north are quiet but unexciting and, in comparison to the western shore, the eastern shore is scenically dull.

Statues overlooking the coast of Isola Bella on Lago Maggiore (top)

EARLY TOURISM

Maggiore has long been a popular holiday destination. In the 17th century, the illustrious Borromeo family of Milan built opulent palaces and gardens on Isola Bella and Isola Madre. The Lombard aristocracy followed in the 18th and 19th centuries with their splendid villas between Stresa and Arona and, thanks to the mild climate and fertile soil, their gardens flourished. Grand hotels were opened to accommodate wealthy Europeans, and Stresa became a stop on the Grand Tour. The shores also provided inspiration for musicians such as the Italian conductor Arturo Toscanini, and literati, including John Ruskin, Charles Dickens, Lord Byron and Percy Bysshe Shelley from Britain, and Gustave Flaubert and Stendhal from France. Queen Victoria and Sir Winston Churchill stayed in Baveno, and the Hôtel des Îles Borromées in Stresa was a popular choice with royalty.

STRESA AND THE BORROMEAN ISLANDS

In Stresa, Baveno and Pallanza, flower-filled promenades have delightful views of the Borromean Islands (Isola Bella, Isola Madre and Isola dei Pescatori). Rising above Stresa and accessible by cable car or toll road, the snowcapped peak of Monte Mottarone commands stunning views, while from the west-shore road between Arona and Stresa, known as The Riviera, you can see across to the eastern shore.

Don't miss The towering fortress of the Rocca Borromeo in Angera; the islands and majestic mountains of the Gulf of Borromeo.

View overlooking the town of Malcesine on Lago di Garda

Boats moored on Lago d'Iseo

People enjoying refreshment in Orta San Giulio

LAGO DI GARDA

✚ 434 F4 🛈 Lungolago Regina Adelaide 13, 37016 Garda, tel 045 6270384 ▦ Mar–Oct
www.aptgardaveneto.com

The largest and most visited of the Italian lakes, Garda stretches between the Dolomites and the Lombardy plain, with the regions of Trentino Alto-Adige, the Veneto and Lombardy meeting here. The landscape is remarkably diverse: In the north, narrow and fjord-like with dramatic rocks dropping sheer into the deep water; in the south, sea-like, with beaches lining the huge expanse of water. From the early Middle Ages, ruling dynasties identified the strategic importance of the lake, building splendid defences that are visible along its shores today. Although picturesque villages still dot the shorelines and medieval castles rise from the waters, the south in particular has become commercialized.

Lake Garda is 51km (32 miles) long and 17km (11 miles) across at its widest point. Its waters are renowned for their clarity and are warm enough for summer swimming. The daily Ora del Garda wind ensures superb windsurfing and sailing conditions, particularly in the north. Mediterranean flora, including olive and citrus trees, flourishes in the warm climate and the lakeside promenades are lined with palms and pines. A cable car runs up to Monte Baldo. Rising above the eastern shore, the mountain is known as the Garden of Europe.

LAGO D'ISEO

✚ 431 E3 🛈 Lungolago Marconi 2C/D, 25049 Iseo, tel 030 980209; closed Sat pm and Sun winter 🚊 Iseo ▦ Seasonal ferry linking Sarnico with Lovere, calling at towns, villages and Monte Isola
www.bresciaholiday.com

With its wild, mountainous scenery and peaceful villages, Lago d'Iseo—or Sebino, as it is sometimes still called—is a quiet alternative to the larger, more commercialized lakes. Between the provinces of Bergamo to the east and Brescia to the west, Iseo is the seventh-largest Italian lake. It is 24km (15 miles) long, averages 2.4km (1.5 miles) across and has the largest lake island (Monte Isola) in Italy. An Ice Age glacier created the lake's characteristic S shape, and the River Oglio feeds it from its source at Passo Gavia in the Camonica Valley.

The attractive hilly region of Franciacorta in the south, renowned for its champagne-style wines, lies between the lake and Brescia. The main town of Iseo, in the south, has a medieval centre, a long, pleasant, tree-shaded promenade, a lido with good sports facilities and the best choice of shops, hotels and campsites on the lake. Clusane, to the west, is a fishing village famous for *tinca ripiena* (stuffed tench), while Sarnico is popular for sports. Lovere, in the north, is the most appealing town and Pisogne, across the lake, is also worth a detour for the 16th-century frescoes of Girolamo Romanino in the Church of Santa Maria della Neve.

At the hamlet of Zone (turn off the eastern shore road at Marone) is the Riserva Naturale Piramidi di Zone, an amazing landscape of erosion pillars, created by weather-beaten debris from glaciers. Tapering at the top, these strange natural formations look like pinnacles, some spectacularly high and others with huge boulders on top. Cislano is the best place from which to admire them.
Don't miss The Riserva Naturale Piramidi di Zone.

LAGO D'ORTA

✚ 430 C3 🛈 Via Panoramica, Orta San Giulio, 28016, tel 0322 905614 🚊 Orta San Giulio ▦ Ferry service links the main towns: Easter to mid-Oct; rest of year weekends only
www.orta.net

Separated from Lago Maggiore by the Mottarone peak, Orta is the westernmost lake in the northwest. With its island and beautifully preserved medieval village of Orta San Giulio, it is arguably the most enchanting of all the pre-Alpine lakes. Legend has it that in the fourth century St. Julius drove away the dragons and serpents from the island in the middle of the lake and founded a church there. From here he preached to the fishermen and the island became the religious heart of the lake, a role that it maintains today.

Measuring 14km (9 miles) in length and around 3km (2 miles) at its broadest point, Orta is tiny compared to the lakes further east. The largest town on the lake is Omegna, in the north. Known chiefly for manufacturing, it still preserves some of its old quarter around Piazza XXIV Aprile. The village of Quarno Sotto, 7km (4 miles) west of Omegna, stands 809m (2,654ft) above sea level and has spectacular views of the lake. In the 19th century the village was renowned worldwide for making wind instruments, some of which can be seen in the local Museo Etnografico e dello Strumento Musicale a Fiato. 20km (12 miles) west is Varallo, a predominantly industrial town dominated by the Sacro Monte, the prototype for the Orta San Giulio's Sacro Monte. This huge complex consists of 45 chapels, over 800 statues and 4,000 paintings of scenes from the life of Christ.
Don't miss The Orta San Giulio's Sacro Monte.

Milano (Milan)

Italy's most dynamic city, the powerhouse of the country's economy.
One of Europe's richest cities, with chic shopping and cutting-edge style in its
galleries, shops and restaurants.
An abundance of historical and artistic heritage and a thriving
contemporary cultural scene.

The magnificent marble façade of Milan's Duomo

A close-up view of the Duomo's exterior (above) and the glass-roofed shopping complex of the Galleria Vittorio Emanuele II (right)

RATINGS	
Historic interest	●●●○
Shopping	●●●●●
Specialist shopping	●●●●●
Value for money	●●●

BASICS

✚ 431 D4

ℹ Via Marconi 1, 20123 Milano, tel 02 72524301/2/3; Mon–Sat 8.45–1, 2–6, Sun 9–1, 2–5

🚆 Milano Centrale, Milano Garibaldi, Milano Lambrate, Milano Porta Genova, Milano Nord

✈ Milano Malpensa and Milano Linate

www.milanoinfotourist.com
Crammed with information: extensive accommodation, restaurant, entertainment and shopping listings; full information on museums and public monuments; transport details; up-to-date information on what's going on and how to get the most out of your visit; in English and Italian.

One of the Duomo's many statues

SEEING MILAN

Booming Milan lies in the flat country 48km (30 miles) south of the Alps and 3 hours 30 minutes by fast train northwest of Rome. It is a northern, grey city, with a fast pace of life and efficient infrastructure. Milan is not immediately beguiling, but its architecture reflects its diversity. There are a few medieval and Renaissance buildings, but the style is predominantly neoclassical, art nouveau and modern, and the streets are wide and busy. The historic core lies within three concentric ring roads, and most of the major sights are within the Cerchia dei Navigli, which follows the path of the medieval walls. The Piazza del Duomo is the heart of Milan: it's a good place to get your initial bearings, and most sights are within walking distance. For farther-flung sights, simply hop on a bus or tram or take the metro (▷ 50).

HIGHLIGHTS

DUOMO

✚ 74 C2 • Piazza del Duomo, 20123 Milano ☎ 02 86463456 🕐 Daily 9–6 www.duomomilano.com

Milan's Duomo is the hub of the city, the world's largest Gothic cathedral and the third-largest church in Europe. Building began in 1386 under Duke Gian Galeazzo Visconti and finally finished nearly 500 years later. The façade, built of marble from the Lake Maggiore area, is a strange mix of Gothic and baroque. The brass strip on the pavement near the entrance is part of Europe's largest sundial, laid out in 1786. Above the chancel, the crucifix has a nail from Christ's cross, while the nearby crypt contains the remains of St. Charles Borromeo, who worked with Milan's poor in the 16th century. The highlight is the roof itself, a forest of pinnacles and statues with views as far as the Alps.

PINACOTECA DI BRERA

✚ 74 C1 • Via Brera 28, 20121 Milano ☎ 02 722631 🕐 Tue–Sat 8.30–7.30 🎟 €5
www.breara.beniculturali.it

La Scala and Museo la Scala

✚ 74 C2 • Corso Magenta, 20123 Milano ☎ 02 4691528 ◷ Daily 9–4 💷 €5

La Scala is one of the world's most famous opera houses, designed in 1778, with an opulent gilt and velvet interior that can seat over 2,000 people. It remains the social and cultural focus for the city's rich. Backstage tours Tue and Thu (tel 02 433 53521 for reservations).

Sant'Ambrogio

✚ 74 A3 • Piazza Sant'Ambrogio 15, 20123 Milano ☎ 02 86450895 ◷ Daily 7–12, 2.30–7 www.santambrogio-basilica.it

An outstanding Lombard-Romanesque church, founded in the fourth century by St. Ambrose, patron saint of Milan, whose remains lie in the crypt. The simple church, with relics, carving and mosaics, is reached through a colonnaded courtyard; outside is Bramante's Cortile della Canonica.

Right in the heart of the smart Brera district, the Pinacoteca di Brera is Milan's most prestigious art gallery, originally founded by Napoleon to display loot from churches, convents and displaced aristocrats. The collection is huge, with over 600 works exhibited in 40 rooms. The emphasis is on Italian Renaissance painting, and in particular the Venetian school. Early Renaissance Venetian works include pictures by Carpaccio and Giovanni and Gentile Bellini, and there is a striking *Dead Christ* by Andrea Mantegna, viewed from the soles of Jesus' feet. There is a lively Veronese *Supper in the House of Simon*, and a more spiritual *Deposition* by Tintoretto, painted in the 1560s. For a serene contrast to Venetian drama, don't miss Piero della Francesca's *Madonna with Saints and Federigo di Montefeltro*, all harmony and pellucid greys, and Raphael's sumptuously languid *Marriage of the Virgin.* For something different again, there is the 17th-century realism of Caravaggio and Il Pitochetto, a Lombard artist who specialized in depicting the poor.

SANTA MARIA DELLE GRAZIE

✚ 74 A2 • Piazza Santa Maria delle Grazie, Corso Magenta, 20123 Milano ☎ 02 89421146 ◷ Tue–Sun 8–7.30; reserve at least 2 days in advance; visits restricted to 25 people and for 15 minutes 💷 €8

The church of Santa Maria delle Grazie was begun in Gothic style in the mid-15th century, and altered considerably by Bramante in 1492 when he added the beautiful tribune, serene cloister and massive dome. What draws the crowds, however, is Leonardo da Vinci's fragile fresco of the *Last Supper* on one wall of the Old Refectory in the adjoining monastery. This huge work portrays the moment when Christ announces that one of his disciples will betray him. Da Vinci applied the tempera and oil to dry plaster, rather than using the more stable, wet-plaster technique, so his work began to deteriorate five years after it was completed. Napoleonic troops used the fresco for target practice and the building was bombed in 1943, but amazingly the fresco survived. The work is fading fast despite continuous restoration, but against the odds, the brilliance of the artist's hand continues to shine through.

CASTELLO SFORZESCO
⊞ 74 B1 • Piazza Castello, Milano ☎ 02 6208 3940; Museo 02 88463701 🕐 Tue–Sun 9–5.30 🎫 Free
The Castello Sforzesco, built originally by the ruling Visconti family in the 15th century, is one of Milan's major landmarks. Destroyed in the 1440s, it was rebuilt by the Sforzas and, under their patronage, became the heart of one of Europe's most powerful and cultured courts. It was used as a barracks from the 15th century, when the Sforzas fell, until it was converted into a museum complex in the

Galleria Vittorio Emanuele II
⊞ 74 C2 • Piazza del Duomo, 20123 Milano
A monumental glass-roofed shopping arcade, built in 1867, which links the Piazza del Duomo with the Piazza della Scala. The central mosaic shows the symbols of the cities of the newly united Italy. It is considered good luck to stand on the testicles of Turin's bull. Lined with expensive bars, cafés and shops, its is a great place for people-watching.

The Museo Nazionale della Scienza e della Tecnica (left) and outside La Scala opera house (right)

19th century. Artistic highlights include Michelangelo's unfinished *Rondanini Pietà*, sculpted at the end of his life, works by Bellini and Mantegna, and Arcimboldo's 16th-century surrealistic portrait of *Primavera* (Spring), an image composed entirely of flowers.

BACKGROUND
Mediolanum, the Roman precursor of modern-day Milan, became the seat of the rulers of the Western Empire in AD286, and it was here that Constantine gave his approval to Christianity in AD313. From the 13th to the 16th century, Milan was ruled by dynastic families. Under the rule of the Viscontis, the city became powerful through marriage with other European royal houses, and under the Sforzas, art and culture flourished, enriching the city with some of its finest monuments. The late 16th century saw the start of 300 years of foreign rule by the French, Spanish and Austrians, an era when Milan developed into Italy's economic capital. The city was bombed extensively during World War II, and much of the city has been rebuilt since 1945.

Pinacoteca Ambrosiana
⊞ 74 B3 • Piazza Pio XI 2, 20123 Milano ☎ 02 806921 🕐 Tue–Sun 10–5.30 🎫 €7.50
www.ambrosiana.it
Cardinal Federico Borromeo founded this art gallery in the early 17th century. Highlights include Leonardo da Vinci's *Portrait of a Musician,* Raphael's cartoon for the *School of Athens* in the Vatican and Caravaggio's *Basket of Fruit*—purportedly Italy's first still life. The adjoining library also has exhibitions, and is Italy's oldest public library, founded in 1609.

Museo Poldi Pezzoli
⊞ 74 C2 • Via Alessandro Manzoni 12, 20123 Milano ☎ 02 794889 🕐 Tue–Sun 10–6 🎫 €6.20 🚇 Montenapoleone
The museum has a fine collection of paintings, jewellery, clocks and *objets d'art*, bequeathed to the city by the 19th-century collector Gian Giacomo Poldo Pezzoli. There are some good Renaissance pictures here, including Pollaiuolo's *Portrait of a Young Woman* and *San Nicola da Tolentino* by Piero della Francesca. The building itself contains many original features and is a good example of a late 19th-century aristocratic residence in Milan.

RATINGS

Value for money	● ● ●
Good for kids	● ●
Historic interest	● ● ● ● ●
Photo stops	● ● ● ● ●

BASICS

✚ 430 B3
ℹ Via Umberto I, 100080 Noasca
Near the town hall, tel 0124 901070;
daily 9–12.30, 2–7
🚉 Aosta and Pont Canavese
🎫 For guided tours tel 0124 901070

www.parks.it/parco.nazionale.gran.
paradiso
The English version of this website picks
out points of interest in the park and
places to stay and provides itineraries
and information on the park's visitor
centres, up-coming events and
environmental education schemes.

TIPS

● In summer the visitor centres
organize activities, show films
and run trips for children.
● The park offers many winter
activities, including cross-
country skiing, snow trekking
and walking tours to see
frozen waterfalls. Information
is on the park website (above).

*A view of the Gran Paradiso
mountains*

PARCO NAZIONALE DEL
GRAN PARADISO

**Once a hunting reserve of the house of Savoy, now Italy's
premier national park.
Spectacular panoramas of mountains and glaciers.**

The Parco Nazionale del Gran Paradiso was established in 1922, the
first national park in Italy. Surrounding the Gran Paradiso massif, the
park extends over some 70,000ha (173,000 acres), shared between
the Valle d'Aosta and Piedmont and linked to the Vanoise National
Park across the French border. At the heart of the park, the Gran
Paradiso massif rises to 4,084m (13,400ft). The scenery is extremely
varied: snowcapped mountain peaks and glaciers, flower-filled slopes,
high pastures, waterfalls, fast-flowing streams, and forests of larch,
pine and fir in the valleys.

THE PARK'S RESORTS

Two of the most popular resorts are Valsavarenche, the main village
in the valley of the same name and a starting point for the climb of
Gran Paradiso and Grivola (3,969m/13,022ft), and Cogne, the main
resort on the Aosta side of the park and another good base for
excursions. The park has 450km (280 miles) of tracks. The most
popular takes you from Valnontey, near Cogne, up a steep path to
the Rifugio Vittorio Sella (2,599m/8,527ft), then on to the Rifugio
Sella Herbetet and the head of the valley (full day).

FLORA AND FAUNA

The number of ibex in the park declined drastically in the 1940s, but
careful protection has seen numbers rise to around 3,500, and they
have now been reintroduced to other parts of the Alps. They are
normally seen well above the tree line; one of the best places to
observe them is from the pastureland of the Gran Piano di Noasca in
the Piedmont section of the park (a beautiful path, with fine views of
the Orco Valley, connects Nivolet and the Gran Piano). There are
around 6,000 chamois in the park, as well as Alpine marmot and rare
birds such as the bearded vulture, which disappeared from here in
1912 and is now returning, thanks to a reintroduction project. Many
rare species of Alpine flora can be seen in the Giardino Alpino
Paradiso at Valnontey near Cogne. Established in 1955, this garden
now supports around 2,000 species of Alpine flora, including the
mountain lily *(Paradisea liliastrum)*. Late spring is the best time to
visit to see the flowers, while winter is ideal for cross-country skiing.

The colonnaded portico of the Palazzo Ducale in Mantova

The compact rows of tall, brightly painted houses that line the waterfront of the ancient fortified coastal town of Portovenere

LERICI

✚ 433 E6 ⓘ Via Biaggini 6, 19033 Lerici, tel 0187 967346

Surrounded by steep terraced slopes, Lerici is an attractive resort with a seafront lined with elegant villas, gardens, pines, palms and pebble beaches. A former fishing village, its sheltered cove and bay, in the Golfo dei Poeti, was immortalized by the 19th-century English Romantic poets Lord Byron and Percy Bysshe Shelley. Byron famously swam from Portovenere across the gulf to visit Shelley, who rented a house in the village of San Terenzo, 2km (1.3 miles) north of Lerici. In 1822, while returning from Livorno to his home on San Terenzo, Shelley drowned (aged 30) when his yacht capsized in a storm near Viareggio.

MANTOVA (MANTUA)

✚ 434 F4 ⓘ Piazza Mantegna 6, 46100 Mantova, tel 0376 363292 🚆 Mantova www.aptmantova.it

In the heart of the featureless Lombard plain, Mantua's uninspiring outskirts belie a beautifully preserved medieval city which, under the Gonzaga family (1328–1708), grew to be centre of one of the greatest Renaissance courts in Europe.

Life here revolves around three squares. The spacious cobbled Piazza Sordello is flanked on one side by the formidable red-brick walls of the Palazzo Ducale. Once home of the Gonzagas, this is a vast complex of buildings, courtyards and gardens between Piazza Sordello and Lake Inferiore. The palace's history spans four centuries, from the end of the 13th century to the early 17th century. The oldest parts are the Palazzo del Capitano and the adjacent

Magna Domus, founded by the Bonacolsi family, who ruled Mantua from 1271 to 1328. There are over 500 rooms, the most famous being the Camera degli Sposi (Bridal Chamber), decorated with a cycle of frescoes (1474) by Mantegna, glorifying the Gonzaga family (Tue–Sun 8.45–7.15; ticket office closes 6.30). Opposite the Palazzo Ducale stand the Palazzo Bianchi (Archbishop's Palace) and the Cattedrale di San Pietro, whose Romanesque tower is all that remains of the original church (daily 7–12, 3–7). The interior was rebuilt by Giulio Romano in 1545 after a fire and was richly decorated with 16th- and 17th-century works of art.

PAVIA

✚ 433 D4 ⓘ Via Fabio Filzi 2, 27100, tel 0382 22156 🚆 Pavia and Certosa di Pavia www.provincia.it

Fine Romanesque and medieval buildings grace Pavia, but it is the nearby Certosa di Pavia, one of the most extravagant religious complexes in northern Italy, that draws the crowds. In medieval times Charlemagne and Frederick Barbarossa were crowned here and in the 14th century it was taken by the Viscontis of Milan, who built the castle and founded both the university and the Certosa. Pavia's rich heritage of art and architecture is reflected in its Renaissance cathedral, whose architects include Leonardo da Vinci, Bramante and Amadeo, several fine medieval churches and the Visconti castle.

The Certosa lies 8km (5 miles) north of Pavia, set in former hunting grounds. This monastery was originally founded as a mausoleum by Gian Galeazzo Visconti in 1396. The church's exuberant marble façade (1400s–1560) has a profusion

of sculpture. Notable works include the frescoes by Bergognone in the transept, chapels and vaulting and the polyptych by Perugino (1499) in the second chapel on the left (Tue–Sun 9–11.30, 2.30–4.30; later in summer).

PORTOVENERE

✚ 433 E6 ⓘ Piazza Bastreri 7, 19025 Portovenere, tel 0187 790691 🚢 Catamarans link Genoa and Portovenere (summer) www.aptcinqueterre.sp.it

Almost as picturesque as Portofino on the Riviera di Levante (▷ 80), and very much cheaper, Portovenere has an old town and magnificent views to the offshore islets. Its tall, pastel-painted houses, built in defensive form, are wedged along the seafront and main street. The steep narrow stairways lead up from the port to the cobbled streets and alleys of the old town, home to the Romanesque church of San Lorenzo. Its prized possession is a revered Madonna Bianca (White Madonna), reputedly washed up on the shores of Lerici.

On the cliff top are the ruins of the Genoese 12th-century Castello di San Lorenzo, worth visiting if only for the magnificent views across the Cinque Terre (▷ 68). San Pietro, the windswept sanctuary on the tip of the promontory, is said to stand on the site of an ancient temple dedicated to Venus. It was built in 1277 in the local style with black and white marble.

Boat trips run from Portovenere to the Cinque Terre and the offshore islands: Isola Palmaria, visited for its Blue Grotto; Isola del Tino, with ruins of a Romanesque abbey; and the tiny Isola del Tinetto, home to the remains of an ancient monastery.

Torino (Turin)

Splendid baroque architecture, elegant shops and excellent museums. An important cultural hub with many contemporary art museums and commercial galleries hosting major exhibitions.

The racetrack on top of the Lingotto Fiat factory   *The rooftops of Torino*   *The Caffè Torino*

RATINGS

Cultural interest	●●●●○
Shopping	●●●●○
Historic interest	●●●●●
Photo stops	●●●○○

BASICS

✚ 432 C4

ℹ Atrium, Piazza Solferino, tel 011 535181; daily 9.30–7
Also at Torino Caselle airport and Porta Nuova train station

🚇 Torino's new metro (underground) line uses state-of-the-art technology and is adapted for people with limited mobility.

🚌 The city is served by buses, trams and a funicular. Tickets are sold at stations, *tabacchi*, etc. A tourist bus takes visitors around the city with a guide (departs from Piazza Castello)

🚆 The city is a major rail terminus. Regular trains run to and from Milan (1 hour 15 minutes)

✈ Torino Caselle Airport is 16km (10 miles) north of the city, accessible by regular bus and train services.

🛍 Guided tours for individuals or groups tel 011 535181/535901
www.turismotorino.org

www.comune.torino.it
This website has a great deal of information in English.

SEEING TURIN

Turin has had a rebirth. The 2006 Winter Olympics have put Turin firmly on the world map for winter sports and as an all-year place to visit. The city and its locality in the foothills of the Alps have benefited from huge investment, including Europe's most modern metro (subway) system. A new ice skating complex has changed the city's landscape and become a modern ice palace. More than any other city in Italy, Torino has made great strides in improving its hospitality to visitors, whether they are drawn by the upgraded winter sports facilities or the historic assets and cultural life that it offers all year round. The Duomo or Cathedral is renowned as the location of the Turin Shroud, the Mole is a grand domed tower in the city centre and there is a rich nightlife in the Murazzi and Docks Dora areas and on the streets of the Roman Quarter. Nestling in the shopping arcades of Via Po, off Piazza Castello, are numerous historic cafés and restaurants serving traditional Piedmont dishes and wines. Be sure to take time for a cocktail or *aperitivo* beside the River Po: Turin is the home of Martini.

HIGHLIGHTS

MUSEO EGIZIO AND GALLERIA SABAUDA

Palazzo dell'Accademia, Via Accademia delle Scienze 6, 10100 Torino
☎ 011 5617776 🕐 Tue–Sun 8.30–7.30 💶 Museo Egizio €6.50; Galleria Sabauda €4; combined ticket €8
www.museoegizio.org, www.museitorino.it/galleriasabauda

Housed in a vast baroque palace, this is the world's third most important collection of Egyptian antiquities after those in Cairo and London. Among the great treasures are a black granite statue of Ramses II, the tomb of the architect Kha, and the reconstructed temple of Ellesija. The Galleria Sabauda, in the same building, has an exceptional collection of paintings, begun by the Dukes of Savoy, with works of art by Piedmontese, Tuscan, Lombard and Venetian masters, and a major Flemish and Dutch collection (Van Eyck, Memling, Rembrandt). The museum adjoins Piazza San Carlo, known as the 'the drawing room of Turin'—a baroque square flanked at the far end by the twin churches of San Carlo and Santa Cristina.

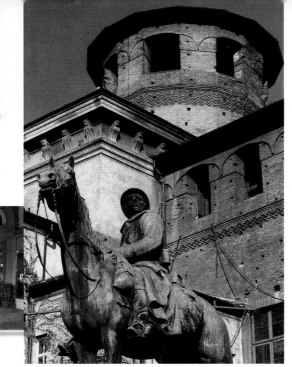

A statue of the Cavaliere d'Italia in Piazza Castello

PALAZZO CARIGNANO
Via Accademia delle Scienze 5, 10123 Torino ☎ 011 5621147 🕐 Museum: Tue–Sun 9–7.30 📖 €5
www.regione.piemonte.it/cultura/risorgimento/iindex.htm
The nearby Palazzo Carignano, designed by Guarino Guarini (1679), was the birthplace of Vittorio Emanuele II in 1820 and the seat of the Subalpine parliament. The Unification of Italy was proclaimed here in 1861. It is now home to the Museo del Risorgimento. You can visit the royal apartments and the Royal Armoury (separate entrance) of the Palazzo Reale (apartments Tue–Sun 8.30–9.30; garden daily 9–7).

GALLERIA CIVICA D'ARTE MODERNA E CONTEMPORANEA
Via Magenta 31, 20100 Torino ☎ 011 442 9518 🕐 Tue–Sun 9–7 📖 Adult €7.50, child/youth/students (10–25) €4, free all day Tue
www.gamtorino.it
If you like modern art, seek out the Galleria Civica d'Arte Moderna e Contemporanea (GAM), northwest of the station. It has 15,000 works of art including pieces by Modigliani, De Chirico, Klee and Warhol.

MOLE ANTONELLIANA
Via Montebello 20, 10124 Torino ☎ 011 8125658 🕐 Tue–Sun 9–8, Sat 9–11 📖 Museum: Adult €5.20, child (under 10) free. Panoramic lift: Adult €3.62, child (under 10) free. Combined ticket: Adult €6.80, child (10–16) €5.20, child (under 10) free
Turin's answer to Paris's Eiffel Tower is 167m (548ft) high. Built between 1798 and 1888, it now houses an outstanding museum tracing the history of cinema.

BACKGROUND
In 1574, the house of Savoy made Turin its capital and remained here for the next eight centuries. After Unification, Turin-born Vittorio Emanuele II was proclaimed the first king of Italy in 1861 and ruled until 1865. Giovanni Agnelli founded Fiat here in 1899, and the Lingotto, the ex-Fiat car factory designed in 1914–16, has been transformed by Renzo Piano into a vast conference, exhibition and shopping space.

TIPS

● The Turin card (€15 for 48 hours, €17 for 72 hours) covers 120 museums, monuments, castles and palaces in Turin and Piedmont, plus urban and suburban transport and river trips. It also gives reductions on services such as guided tours, car rental and theatre tickets.

● TurismoBus Torino is a hop-on hop-off tour bus with live commentary on the sights, culture and history of Torino. A ticket lasting all day costs €5 for adults and €3 for children under 12. You can buy the tickets at tourist information offices in Piazza Solferino and the Porta Nuova train station, at Torino Caselle airport, in hotels or on board the bus. TurismoBus Torino is free if you hold a Torino Card.

● The ChocoPass entitles you to sample the range of tastes and products around the city. It costs €10 for ten tastings in 24 hours or €15 for 15 tastings in 48 hours, from Turismo Torino information points.

● Just outside the city at Pessione di Chieri you can visit the premises of Martini & Rossi, makers of the famous aperitif since the mid-1800s. At the end of the visit you can relax on the Martini Terrace and savour a tasting of the four types of the famous drink. Visits daily 9.30–7. Via Piazza Luigi Rossi 1, Pessione di Chieri, tel 011 941 9217.

Rapallo's palm-fringed bay

The Romanesque bell tower (1113) of the Santa Orso rising up above the Collegiata (collegiate church) in Aosta

RAPALLO

➕ 433 D6 ℹ️ Lungomare Via Veneto 7, 16034 Rapallo, tel 0185 230346; summer daily 9.30–12.30, 3–7.30 🚉 Rapallo

Rapallo's bay overlooks the Gulf of Tigullio and is protected by the surrounding mountains. Its temperate climate and natural beauty attracted the wealthy here in the early part of the last century, and in the 1920s it became a haunt of literati. Authors D. H. Lawrence and Ernest Hemingway stayed here briefly and the American poet Ezra Pound lived here for 20 years.

At the end of a promenade, lined with palm trees, orange trees and open-air cafés, stands the 16th-century castle. Built to protect the town against the Saracens, it is now an exhibition venue. In the hills behind Rapallo, overlooking the valley and bay, the Santuario di Montallegro was built in the 16th century to protect a Byzantine icon of the Madonna that miraculously appeared here in 1557 (daily 7–12.30, 2.30–6; until 8 in summer).

RIVIERA DI LEVANTE

➕ 433 D6 ℹ️ Via XXV Aprile 2B, Santa Margherita Ligure, tel 0185 287485; Via Roma 35, Portofino, tel 0185 269024 🚉 Santa Margherita Ligure www.turismo.liguriainrete.it

This stretch of coastline between Genoa and La Spezia is bordered by rugged mountains and hills cloaked in pine, olives and vines. Subtropical trees and flowers form a lush backdrop to the resorts and tiny fishing villages that cling to the cliffs.

The most attractive section of the Riviera is the Cinque Terre (▷ 68), whose fishing villages have kept their picturesque charm. East of Genoa most of the rugged Portofino promontory

is a national park. A retreat for the rich and famous, Portofino has an idyllic natural harbour, with pastel-washed houses and a piazza overlooked by chic but notoriously pricey cafés, restaurants and designer boutiques. Down the road from Portofino is Santa Margherita Ligure, a fashionable, but slightly more affordable resort. La Spezia in the far east, the largest naval base in the country, is worth a visit for its Pinacoteca Civica Amedeo Lia, a Franciscan convent converted into an art gallery with works by Bellini, Titian, Tintoretto, Veronese and other great Italian masters (Tue–Sun 10–6).

SACRA DI SAN MICHELE

➕ 432 B4 • Abbazia Sacra di San Michele, 10651 Avigliana ☎ 011 939130 🕐 Mon–Fri 9.30–12.30, 3–6, Sat and Sun 12–1, 2–7 💵 Adult €4, child (under 14) €3 🚉 Avigliana (26km/16 miles west of Turin; 30 minutes' journey time) www.sacradisanmichele.com

This ancient monastery perches spectacularly on a spur halfway up Monte Pirchiriano at 962m (3,156ft), 18km (11 miles) from the ancient town of Avigliana. Founded as a small church in 983–986 by Hugues de Montboissier from the Auvergne, the monastery was entrusted to five Benedictine monks. It was enlarged in the 12th century with the addition of a five-apsed church and soon became a pilgrimage church for worshippers en route to Rome. The complex began to decline in the 14th century and suffered French attacks in the 17th century, but it has undergone major renovations since. The fortress-like church is accessed via 154 steps cut into the rock, gruesomely named Scalone dei Morti (Stairway of the Dead) after restorers discovered skeletons of

monks in the walls. Inside, the church has a high altar by the Piedmontese artist Defendente Ferrari and a fresco of *The Assumption* (1505) in the north aisle, painted mainly by Secondo del Bosco di Poirino.

TORINO (TURIN)

See pages 78–79.

VALLE D'AOSTA

➕ 430 B3 ℹ️ Piazza Chanoux 2, 11100 Aosta, tel 0165 33352 www.regione.vda.it/turismo

The Aosta Valley, dominated by Alpine peaks, is a region of finely preserved medieval castles, traditional villages and monumental Roman remains. In 1948 it was granted semi-autonomous status in recognition of its French culture and language. The region encompasses the towering peaks of the French and Swiss Alps, Mont Blanc, Monte Rosa, the Matterhorn and Gran Paradiso, whose snow-covered slopes are ideal for winter sports. The most popular resort is Courmayeur, both for winter sports and as a summer base for excursions by car, foot or cable car. The south-eastern part of the valley is famous for its castles, built in the Middle Ages by ruling families both as military outposts and palatial residences. The finest are Fenis, Issogne and Verres.

Aosta, capital of the Valle d'Aosta, is an industrial town and popular with visitors. The town, enhanced by its mountain setting, makes a good base for trips to the Parco Nazionale del Gran Paradiso (▷ 76) and Valle del Gran San Bernardo. It is often called the Rome of the Alps, and its long stretches of city walls, Porta Pretoria (Main Gate), Roman theatre, Arch of Augustus and Roman forum all impressively illustrate its ancient past.

VENICE

Arguably Italy's most compellingly beautiful city, Venice is unique, a city built on water in the midst of a lagoon, with a plethora of churches and museums to experience. Its heart is Piazza San Marco and the great Basilica di San Marco, while elsewhere stately palaces line the canals and tantalizing streets and squares invite exploration.

MAJOR SIGHTS

Venice

🅿 Piazza San Marco, San Marco 71f, 30124 Venezia, tel 041 529 8711; daily 9.30–3.30
www.turismovenezia.it • Official tourist board site with English option, packed with information
www.comune.venezia.it • City council site with excellent practical information and English-language option

THE SIGHTS

HOW TO GET THERE

✈ Airports
Venezia Marco Polo
At Tessera, 7km (4 miles) north of the city centre by water
Tel 041 260 6111
Treviso Sant'Angelo
Treviso, 26km (16 miles) north of Venice
Tel 042 231 5111

🚆 Railway stations
Venezia Santa Lucia
Trains cross the causeway linking Venice with the mainland to terminate at Venezia Santa Lucia, situated on the Grand Canal; automated train information on 041 258 0136 (Italian only)

Gondola jam!

TIPS
● If possible, avoid visiting Venice between late June and the end of September, when the city is swamped by crowds.
● Reserve accommodation well ahead and, as all luggage has to be carried, consider the hotel's distance from a *vaporetto* stop.
● If visiting the lagoon islands, use the *vaporetti* rather than taking a tour—more time, more flexibility and less cost.
● For an inexpensive gondola experience, take one of the *traghetto* gondolas that cross the Grand Canal at fixed points.
● Bring comfortable shoes and be prepared to walk, bearing in mind that you will be crossing numerous steep bridges during your stay.

SEEING VENICE

Venice is a surprisingly small city, but also a confusing maze, and first-time visitors should follow the yellow signs, painted above head height on buildings throughout the city. These mark the routes to the main attractions and other key points, such as the railway station. Longer distances will entail travelling by water, and all parts of the city and the lagoon islands are served by *vaporetti* (water buses). A journey down the Grand Canal is an excellent way to start your sightseeing, taking you under the iconic Rialto Bridge and past some of Venice's loveliest palaces, before depositing you amid the glories of the Piazza San Marco. It's worth investing in a tourist *vaporetto* pass for transport, which is available for 90 minutes, 24 or 72 hours, and gives unlimited travel on all services. It costs €5, €10.50 and €22 respectively, and is available from the ticket offices at main *vaporetto* stops. If you plan to do a lot of sightseeing you can buy various museum passes, ranging in price from €11 to €15.50; these are available at the museums. The APT also issues the Venice Card, which is valid for all transport and entrance to the civic museums. Prices range from €26 for one day to €58 for seven days. It must be reserved at least two days in advance, either online at www.venicecard.it or by calling 899 90 90 90 within Italy or (39) 041 271 4747 from abroad. Try to walk as much as possible during your visit; it's the best way to see the city, make serendipitous discoveries and soak up its unique atmosphere, though even with a good map you can expect to get lost—an essential part of the Venetian experience.

BACKGROUND

For centuries, Venice has been welcoming visitors and remains one of the world's ultimate travel destinations. This unique city, built on water, was founded in the fifth century by mainland dwellers fleeing the barbarian invaders and, by the 12th century, had established itself as a world trading and commercial hub. A republic was established, headed by a doge (chief magistrate) and ruled by councils, which acquired a vast overseas empire that made Venice both feared and envied by every major power. Wealth poured into the city to fund the building of its great churches and palaces, adorned with paintings and sculpture, and Venice was renowned for its marvels and sybaritic way of life. Its power declined as other trade routes to the East were opened, and in 1797 the Republic fell, the city becoming part of newly unified Italy in 1866 (▷ 38). Today, Venice faces huge problems associated with a falling population and the effects of pollution and climate change, but steps are being taken to counteract these, and this superb city, a dream-like harmony of water, light and stone, continues to enchant millions of visitors.

DON'T MISS

CANAL GRANDE
Take a trip down one of the world's most breathtaking waterways (▷ 86–87)
PALAZZO DUCALE
An airy Gothic palace with a sumptuous interior (▷ 93–95)
BASILICA DI SAN MARCO
Domed 11th-century basilica glittering with interior mosaics (▷ 84–85)
GALLERIA DELL'ACCADEMIA
Superlative collection with paintings from every period of Venetian art (▷ 90–91)
RIALTO
With vibrant markets and a famous bridge over the Canal Grande, this is one of Italy's most colourful urban districts (▷ 97)

Bright houses reflected in the waters of Burano's canal

Gothic arches under the staircase leading up from the courtyard at the Ca' d'Oro, a flamboyant Gothic palazzo

BURANO

🔲 423 off F1 ℹ️ Piazza San Marco 71f, San Marco, 30120 Venezia, tel 041 529 8711; daily 9.30–3.30 🚤 *Vaporetto*: Burano
www.comune.venezia.it

For a change of pace, Burano is an island tucked away in the northern part of the lagoon, whose brilliantly painted houses and miniature canals provide some of Venice's best photographic opportunities. Burano, and Mazzorbo next door, were among the first settlements in the lagoon. As Venice proper boomed, Mazzorbo declined, but Burano thrived as a fishing community, where the men went to sea and the women stayed home to make gossamer-fine lace, once famous all over Europe. The *rii* (canals) are still busy with boats and all the paraphernalia of fishing, and the *fondamente* (streets along the canals) are lined with houses of varying shades. Lace is still on offer everywhere, although few women make the real thing now; you can see it at the Scuola di Merletti (Lace-making School). **Don't miss** The morning fish market; the fish restaurants along Via Galuppi, the main street.

CA' D'ORO

🔲 422 C2 • Calle Ca' d'Oro, Cannaregio, 30121 Venezia 🕿 041 523 8790 🕒 Mon 8.15–2, Tue–Sun 8.15–7.15 💶 Adult €5, students (18–25) €2.50, under 18 and over 65 free (EU citizens) 🚤 *Vaporetto*: Line 1 Ca' d'Oro 🔲 Overlooking the sculpture garden 🏛️
www.cadoro.org

One of the city's finest and most flamboyant examples of a Gothic palazzo, the Ca' d'Oro (Golden House) stands on the Canal Grande just above the Rialto. It was built for the Contarini family in the early 15th century, but

changed hands repeatedly until it was heavily (and badly) restored in the 1850s by the Russian Prince Troubetskoy. Forty years later, Baron Franchetti bought and restored it, filling it with his painting, sculpture and coin collections. As a result, the ground floor regained its medieval layout, with a courtyard, tiny pleasure garden and main door opening onto the water. An exterior staircase leads to the upper floors, where the family lived. These floors, imaginatively converted into light and airy galleries, now house the collections, and have beautiful Gothic loggias overlooking the canal. Artistic highlights include Andrea Mantegna's powerful *St. Sebastian* and the ghostly fragments of frescoes by Giorgione that once decorated the nearby Fondaco dei Tedeschi. **Don't miss** Views of the water traffic on the Canal Grande from the upper loggias; the 15th- and 16th-century Flemish tapestries.

CA' REZZONICO

🔲 422 B4 ℹ️ Fondamenta Rezzonico, Dorsoduro 3136, Venezia 30123 🕿 041 241 0100 🕒 Apr–end Oct Wed–Mon 10–6; rest of year Tue–Sun 10–5 💶 €6.50, students (15–29) €4.50 🚤 *Vaporetto*: Ca' Rezzonico
www.museiciviciveneziani.it

This grandiose palazzo on the Canal Grande is now a museum devoted to the hedonistic, dying days of the Republic. Emerging from a lengthy restoration in 2001, the Ca' Rezzonico, with its huge rooms, gilded stuccowork, frescoed ceilings and opulent textiles, is a fabulous expression of patrician wealth.

As you glimpse the façade from the canal or walk through the courtyard you can see why the palazzo's construction costs virtually bankrupted the Bons, who commissioned Baldassare

Longhena to design the building in 1667. Seventy years later, the unfinished palazzo was acquired by the Rezzonicos, who poured money into the building and decor. Its most original architectural feature is the ballroom. Two floors high, this immense space was the scene of some of the 18th century's most prestigious events. From here, a series of ornately decorated, interconnecting rooms fans out, each furnished with fine contemporary pieces. Highlights include the Tiepolo ceiling panels in the Throne Room and Nuptial Room, the flower-decorated Murano glass chandeliers, and furniture designed by Andrea Brustolon. In the gallery look for the quirky genre paintings by Pietro Longhi and the superb Tiepolo panels from Villa Zianigo, the painter's home. The Pulcinella (Carnival Clown) scenes will charm, but it is the surreal Mondo Novo (New World) panels that will linger in the memory.

CAMPO SANTA MARGHERITA

🔲 422 B3–4 ℹ️ Campo Santa Margherita, Dorsoduro, Venezia 30123 🚤 *Vaporetto*: Ca' Rezzonico

At the heart of the *sestiere* (district) of Dorsoduro, Campo Santa Margherita is one of Venice's liveliest squares. Browse the morning market stands, sit in the cafés, eat one of the best ice creams in the city (at Causin), eavesdrop on raucous local housewives and mingle with the university crowd—all in all, a slice of Venetian life.

The square is surrounded by old Gothic houses, many dating from the 14th century. The central expanse is broken by market stands, trees and benches, while in the middle there is an oddly

Continued on page 88

Basilica di San Marco

●

The great Byzantine-Venetian basilica—a reflection of Venice's historic role as a bridge between East and West.
The spiritual heart of Venice and the focal point of Piazza San Marco.
One of the world's finest medieval buildings, filled with mosaics and precious objects.

Visitors sit on passarelle *(walkways for* aqua alta, *Venice's high water)*

The main cupola with a detailed mosaic depicting the Ascension

A view of the five domes from the Campanile

BASICS

✛ 422 C3 • Piazza San Marco, San Marco, 30124 Venezia
☎ 041 522 5205
⊙ Basilica, Tesoro and Pala d'Oro May–end Sep Mon–Sat 9.45–5.30, Sun 2–4; Oct–end Apr Mon–Sat 9.45–4.30, Sun 2–4
💶 Basilica, Tesoro and Pala d'Oro €1.50. Loggia €1.20 (no concessions). Tickets can be reserved at www.alata.it
🚤 *Vaporetto*: San Marco (Vallaresso)/San Zaccaria
📖 Wide range at various prices. *Electra* is the best of those published in Italy; it covers various specific sights in Venice (available at the Palazzo Ducale)
🎫 Stands in atrium and Loggia selling postcards, religious souvenirs and tourist guides to Venice

SEEING THE BASILICA DI SAN MARCO

The best approach is on foot from the west end of the piazza (*vaporetto* stop San Marco (Vallaresso)). Aim to arrive early before the queues build up, and be prepared to wait. There's a fixed route around the interior. Allow your eyes to accustom to the low light levels, and take your time; this is an overwhelming building.

HIGHLIGHTS

THE LOGGIA

For a superb overview of the basilica, climb the steep stairs from the atrium to the gallery, where you'll find yourself at eye level with the mosaics (▷ below). From here you can gain access out onto the Loggia, a splendid vantage point from which to view the piazza.

THE BRONZE HORSES

Also here are replicas of the famous bronze horses (the originals are inside). These powerfully evocative creatures were looted from Constantinople in 1204 and are the only surviving four-horse chariot group from antiquity. They were thought to have been made for the Hippodrome in the third century, but they could be as much as 500 years older. Apart from a brief spell in Paris in the Napoleonic years, they have stood at San Marco for 800 years.

THE MOSAICS

The Sant'Alipio doorway, one of five leading to the atrium, is the only door with an original 13th-century mosaic. In the glittering darkness, shafts of light and slanting sunbeams illuminate more than 4,000sq m (43,000sq ft) of mosaics illustrating stories from the Bible. The early Byzantine-Venetian examples are the finest and include the Pentecost dome, nearest the entrance, the Ascension in the central dome, and Christ Emmanuel in the eastern dome. Old as it looks, the great Christ Pantocrator above the apse is actually a faithful 16th-century copy of the 11th-century original.

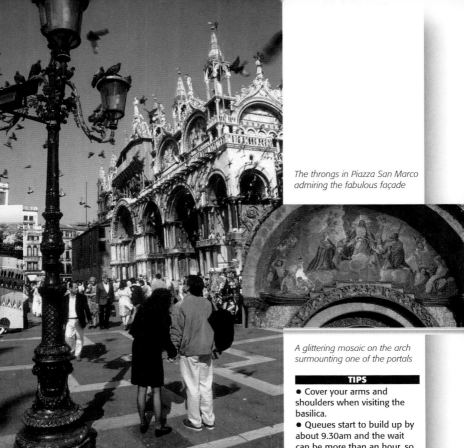

The throngs in Piazza San Marco admiring the fabulous façade

A glittering mosaic on the arch surmounting one of the portals

TIPS
● Cover your arms and shoulders when visiting the basilica.
● Queues start to build up by about 9.30am and the wait can be more than an hour, so get there early. It tends to get quieter just before closing time.
● You can gain access to the basilica for prayers from 8am via the side door (off Piazzetta dei Leoncini).

THE PALA D'ORO

The focal point at ground level is the iconostasis, a Byzantine marble screen that hides the chancel and high altar. The remains of St. Mark lie beneath the altar, which is backed by the Pala d'Oro, an opulent gold and silver altarpiece. Made by a Sienese master in 1342, it is covered with more than 3,000 precious stones and 80 enamel plaques, many of which date from the 10th to 12th centuries.

CHAPEL OF THE MADONNA NICOPEIA AND THE TREASURY

To the left of the Pala d'Oro is the Chapel of the Madonna Nicopeia, a tiny, much-revered 12th-century Byzantine icon, and there is more Byzantine work in the Treasury (Tesoro). Look out for the 12th-century censer in the shape of a domed church.

BACKGROUND

The present basilica, built between 1063 and 1094, is the third to occupy this site. The original was built in 832 to house the remains of St. Mark the Evangelist, brought by merchants from Alexandria to become the city's patron saint. During the 11th century, Venice was culturally influenced by Byzantium, hence the centralized Greek cross plan and multiple domes of the newer church. The interior also owes much to the East, while the façade was altered between the 11th and 15th centuries with the addition of Gothic-style marble columns and carved stonework.

The upper portion of the red-brick Campanile, 99m (325ft) high, viewed from Piazza San Marco (far left). Begun in 912, it also doubled as a lighthouse. It had to be totally rebuilt after collapsing in 1902, and was reopened to the public in 1912

Canal Grande

Take a boat ride along one of the world's most mesmerizing waterways.
A host of magnificent palazzi and churches line its famous banks.
Sit back and watch the water traffic that keeps Venice alive and on the move.

The Canal Grande—a waterway for traditional and modern boats

The Ponte di Rialto is illuminated at night

Gondolas on the Canal Grande near San Marco

RATINGS				
Good for kids	●	●	●	● ○
Historic interest	●	●	●	● ●
Cultural interest	●	●	●	● ○
Photo stops	●	●	●	● ○

TIPS

● The *vaporetto* is the cheapest and probably most entertaining way of seeing the Canal Grande. A gondola or water taxi is a more expensive option.
● It is best to begin at the station end and keep San Marco for the end of the trip.
● For the best chance of getting a good vantage point (and a seat) get on at Piazzale Roma.
● *Vaporetti* can be very crowded, particularly during the morning and evening rush hours. The best time is between 12.30 and 3 (siesta time), along with very early or late in the day.
● Few palazzi along the Canal Grande are floodlit, but a night ride is still a great experience.

SEEING THE CANAL GRANDE

Bisecting the city, the Canal Grande is Venice's main thoroughfare, a sinuous waterway lined with a succession of glorious buildings. It is 4km (2.5 miles) long and varies in width from 30m to 70m (100ft to 230ft), with an average depth of around 5m (16ft). Three *sestiere* (city districts)—Cannaregio, San Marco and Castello—lie to the east of the canal, with three more—San Polo, Santa Croce and Dorsoduro—to the west. Along its length are *traghetti* stations, from where gondolas ply back and forth. There are few places where you can walk or sit beside the canal; the best are at the railway station, at San Marcuola and Santa Sofia, by the Ponte di Rialto, on Campo San Vio, in front of Santa Maria della Salute and at San Marco. The best way to appreciate it is to board the No. 1 *vaporetto* at Piazzale Roma or Ferrovia and relax as far as San Marco (Vallaresso) or San Zaccaria. The whole trip takes 45 minutes.

HIGHLIGHTS

FERROVIA TO RIALTO

The present 1950s railway station *(ferrovia)* replaced the original 1846 construction, built when the causeway to the mainland was created; the stone-built Ponte dei Scalzi went up in 1934. On the right is the domed church of San Simeone Piccolo (1738); on the left is the ornate façade of the Scalzi (1656) and the entrance to the wide Canale di Cannaregio, the gateway to Venice in its pre-causeway days. The brick church soon after this is San Marcuola, unfinished since funds ran out in the 18th century; the two impressive buildings opposite are the Fondaco dei Turchi, trading headquarters for the Turks in Republican days, and the Deposito dei Megio, once a granary. In winter, the Casino moves to the Renaissance Palazzo Vendramin Calergi, where Richard Wagner died in 1883. Opposite, to the left, is the white baroque façade of San Stae. Two highlights are Longhena's Ca' Pesaro on the right (1652), now housing the Museo d'Arte Moderna (Apr–end Oct Tue–Sun 10–6; rest of year Tue–Sun 10–5; tel 041 524 0662), and the Gothic Ca' d'Oro (▷ 83). Across the water lie the *pescheria* (fish market) and Rialto market stands; the long building beside them is the Tribunale Nuove (1555), now

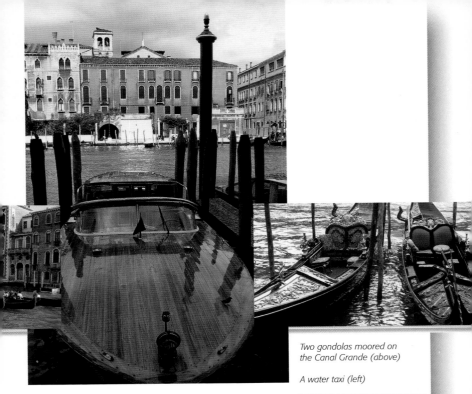

Two gondolas moored on the Canal Grande (above)

A water taxi (left)

the Assize Court. Opposite is the Fondaco dei Tedeschi, once home to German merchants, and overhead is the graceful Ponte di Rialto.

RIALTO TO ACCADEMIA

Highlights on the next stretch are the Gothic 13th-century Palazzo Barzizza (on the right), and the Palazzo Mocenigo (on the left), where Byron lived in 1818. Beyond a sweeping bend known as La Volta, are the huge Palazzo Giustinian and Ca' Rezzonico (▷ 83) on the right, along with the 18th-century Palazzo Grassi, one of Venice's prime exhibition venues. More Gothic façades follow before the Galleria dell'Accademia and its bridge (1932) come into view (▷ 90–91).

ACCADEMIA TO SAN MARCO

Below the bridge, Campo San Vio fronts the water on the right, followed by Palazzo Barbarigo, decorated with 19th-century mosaics, and the Palazzo Venier dei Leoni, home to the Peggy Guggenheim Collection (▷ 88). Opposite is Ca' Grande, designed by Sansovino in 1545, followed by some of Venice's grandest hotels. Look for the tiny Gothic Palazzo Dario on the right as the great plague church of Santa Maria della Salute approaches. The canal ends at the Dogana di Mare (customs), opposite which are the Giardini Reali, laid out by Napoleon, and the glories of San Marco.

BACKGROUND

Running northwest to southeast, the Canal Grande was originally the main thoroughfare for merchants approaching the Rialto. An uninterrupted sequence of palazzi and churches lines the canal, their façades lapped by water. Built across four centuries, these superlative buildings cover the whole span of Venetian styles of architecture.

BASICS

☩ 422 C3

🚢 *Vaporetti*: Piazzale Roma, Ferrovia, Riva di Biasio, San Marcuola, San Stae, Ca' d'Oro, Rialto, San Silvestro, Sant' Angelo, San Tomà, San Samuele, Ca' Rezzonico, Accademia, Giglio, Salute

A statue in the Peggy Guggenheim Collection, housed in the 18th-century Palazzo Venier dei Leoni on the Canal Grande

The palace of Ca' Rezzonico from the Canal Grande

Market stands in Campo Santa Margherita, the heart of the Dorsoduro district

Continued from page 83

shaped small building, the Scuola dei Varoteri, once the headquarters of the tanners' guild. At the north end stands the church of Santa Margherita, which has been beautifully restored and now forms part of the university. Look for the St. Margaret's dragon on the campanile and, on the façade of a house at the same end of the square, the saint standing on the beast. At the opposite end, past the vegetable and fish stands and the interesting shops, you will find the entrance to the Scuola Grande dei Carmini (▷ 102).

CANAL GRANDE

See pages 86–87.

COLLEZIONE PEGGY GUGGENHEIM

✚ 422 B4 • Palazzo Venier dei Leoni (entrance on Fondamenta Venier), Dorsoduro 701, 30123 Venezia ☎ 041 240 5411 🕑 Wed–Mon 10–6 💷 Adult €10, over 65 €8, students with card €5, under 12s free 🚢 Vaporetto: 1 Salute 🍴 Snacks and lunches overlooking the sculpture garden 🏛 www.guggenheim-venice.it

The Palazzo Venier is one of the Canal Grande's most eccentric buildings, an oddity whose construction began in 1759 but had progressed only as far as the first storey before the Venier money ran out. Its bizarre appearance appealed to the rich American millionairess Peggy Guggenheim (1898–1979), who realized its potential as a showcase for her collection. She began collecting contemporary art in the 1920s, buying from and dealing in the works of a whole generation of innovative abstract and surrealist artists. She married Max Ernst, one of the greatest exponents of Surrealism, in 1941, but divorced him in 1946

and moved to Venice. Now administered by the Guggenheim Foundation, the collection is one of Venice's top attractions, its works the perfect antidote to an excess of Byzantine, Gothic and Renaissance art.

The light-filled rooms are approached through a garden court, scattered with sculptures by such artists as Alberto Giacometti (1901–66) and Henry Moore (1898–1986), all shaded by trees and greenery. Examples of work by all the big names of the early and mid-20th-century movements of cubism, surrealism, abstract expressionism and constructivism adorn the walls. Look for works by Marc Chagall, Jackson Pollock, Paul Klee, Max Ernst, Alexander Calder, Joseph Cornell and Marino Marini.

GALLERIA DELL'ACCADEMIA

See pages 90–91.

GESUITI

✚ 422 C2 • Campo dei Gesuiti, Cannaregio, 30121 Venezia ☎ 041 528 6579 🕑 Daily 10–12, 3–6 🚢 Vaporetto: Fondamenta Nove

Fans of baroque architecture must not miss the Jesuit Church of Santa Maria Assunta, known as the Gesuiti. The Jesuits, with their close ties to the papacy, were never popular in Venice and it was not until 1715 that they commissioned Domenico Rossi to build a church. He made up for the delay by going for maximum impact—a church with a vast façade and a mind-bogglingly ornate interior.

Inside you are struck by the baldachin over the altar, modelled on Bernini's version in St. Peter's in Rome (▷ 160–161), and festoons of drapery that billow from every corner and decorate every inch of

wall space. What appear to be swags and drapes of figured damask and brocaded velvet are actually intricately carved and polished pieces of green and white marble. With scarcely a corner unadorned, it all adds up to a visual feast that is far more memorable than the comparatively pedestrian paintings by Palma il Giovane in the sacristy. The best painting, though badly lit and hard to see, is a night scene by Titian, the *Martyrdom of St. Laurence,* over the first altar on the left.

LA GIUDECCA

✚ 422 B5 🚢 Vaporetto: Palanca, Redentore, Zitelle

Take a boat across the Canale della Giudecca to escape the crowds, explore a unique part of the city and visit one of Palladio's finest churches. During the ninth century the Giudecca, an island, began to develop as a location for the richly decorated summer palazzi of the aristocracy. By the 19th century it had become the city's industrial area, filled with boatyards and factories. Over the past 50 years, industry has declined and the Giudecca is today largely a residential area, with a distinctive way of life.

A broad *fondamenta* runs along the canal on the north side of the island, which is where you will find the main sights: the churches of the Redentore (Mon–Sat 10–5, Sun 1–5), built by Palladio in 1577 in thanks for Venice's deliverance from the bubonic plague, and the Zittelle and Santa Eufemia. You will also find rows of local food shops, bars and restaurants, modest houses and grand 14th-century palazzi.

MADONNA DELL'ORTO

See page 92.

Detail of mosaic floor, Basilica di Santa Maria e Donato, Murano

A traditional gondola on display in the Museo Storico Navale

MURANO

➕ 423 E1 ℹ Piazza San Marco 71f, San Marco, 30120 Venezia, tel 041 5298740; daily 9–3.30
🚤 Vaporetto: Murano
www.comune.venezia.it

Murano, 10 minutes by boat from Fondamenta Nuove, is a self-contained community of around 5,000 people, with a miniature Canal Grande, an excellent museum, old *palazzi* and fine churches. It has been the focus of the famous Venetian glass industry since the 13th century. There are many glass showrooms in the city proper, but if you want to buy glass or see it being made, Murano is the place to go.

Five or six main canals thread their way through the island, lined with shops and houses and crossed by bridges—a miniature version of Venice. You can leave the boat at the Colonna or Faro, explore the island and re-embark at Venier, at the other end of the main canal.

The main attraction is the glass, and there are workshops all over the island where you can see master craftsmen demonstrate the skills of flamework, twisting and blowing. Learn more in the Museo di Vetro (Glass Museum), in the splendid 17th-century Palazzo Giustinian, where the history and production of Murano's glass are explained (Thu–Tue 10–5). Don't overlook the 12th-century Basilica di Santa Maria e Donato, Murano's main church, with a colonnaded portico, a lively floor mosaic from

A pair of Venetian glass parrots made on the island of Murano

1140 and a grave Byzantine *Madonna* above the altar.
Don't miss The master craftsmen at work; the Museo di Vetro; the Basilica di Santa Maria e Donato.

MUSEO CORRER

➕ 422 C4 • Ala Napoleonica, Piazza San Marco 52, San Marco, 30124 Venezia ☎ 041 520 9070 🕐 Apr–end Oct daily 9–7; rest of year daily 9–5 💶 €11 for combined ticket to Museo Correr and Palazzo Ducale (▷ 93)
🚤 Vaporetto: San Marco (Vallaresso)
www.museicivicivenezianii.it

The Museo Correr bills itself as the Museum of Venetian Civilization, focusing on city life during the great days of the Republic. Set in a series of grand and elaborate rooms, many overlooking the piazza, it is now directly linked with the Museo Archeologico and the Biblioteca Marciana, so you can easily explore the whole complex (it occupies the upper floors of the Ala Napoleonica, the Procuratie Nuove and Sansovino's library).

At the museum's core are the 16th-, 17th- and 18th-century collections of Teodoro Correr, given to the city in 1830. Tours take you through halls devoted to the accomplished sculpture of Antonio Canova (1757–1822). Next is a series of princely rooms that provides an insight into the ducal elections, the workings of the Arsenale and everyday life and entertainment. Upstairs the Quadreria contains some fine works, notably *Two Venetian Noblewomen* by Vittore Carpaccio (1472–1526), erroneously known for years as *The Courtesans*. The route then leads through the Museo Archeologico

(Greek and Roman art strictly for enthusiasts) before reaching the opulent state rooms of the Biblioteca Marciana. Here there is a huge variety of manuscripts and early books displayed beneath an impressive ceiling covered in allegorical painting.
Don't miss The Museo Archeologico; the sculptures by Antonio Canova; Carpaccio's *Two Venetian Noblewomen*.

MUSEO STORICO NAVALE

➕ 423 E4 • Campo San Biagio, Castello, 2148 Venezia ☎ 041 520 0276 🕐 Mon–Fri 8.45–1.30, Sat 8.45–1 💶 €1.55 🚤 Vaporetto: Arsenale
www.regione.veneto.it/cultura/musei

Venice's power and wealth came from the sea, and few places better demonstrate this than the Museo Storico Navale, a child-friendly museum devoted to the history of sailing. Four floors are crammed with model ships, uniforms, weaponry, navigational instruments and more.

The museum occupies an old granary building on the water's edge, beside the Rio dell'Arsenale, a stone's throw from the entrance to the Arsenale. Highlights are the richly gilded Bucintoro, a model of the Doge's state barge, the huge 16th-century *galleass* (a large galley) and the last surviving private gondola, which once belonged to Peggy Guggenheim (▷ 88). There are vessels from all over the world, cannons and torpedoes, dress uniforms, sextants and astrolabes—more than 25,000 exhibits in total. Keep an eye out for the superb scale model of the *cammello*, a device used to lift ships from low water in the lagoon, and the naïve votive paintings, given in thanks for salvation from storm and shipwreck.
Don't miss The Bucintoro; the *cammello*.

Galleria dell'Accademia

**One of the world's great specialist collections.
Comprehensive overview of the very best of Venetian painting.
Well displayed in three historic buildings.**

A painter at the bottom of the Ponte dell'Accademia   Part of the St. Ursula Cycle *by Vittore Carpaccio*

RATINGS	
Historic interest	● ● ●
Cultural interest	● ● ● ●
Specialist shopping	● ● ● ●
Value for money	● ● ● ●

TIPS

● Staffing shortages mean that sometimes certain rooms are closed, so if there is something specific that you want to see, ask before you buy your ticket.
● The €11 combined ticket for the Galleria dell'Accademia, Ca' d'Oro (▷ 83) and Museo Orientale is a good bargain.
● You can reserve timed tickets if you don't want to stand in line (Mon–Fri 9–6, Sat 9–2, tel 041 520 0345).

SEEING THE GALLERIA DELL'ACCADEMIA

The Accademia's 24 rooms take a couple of hours to see properly. Pick up a plan from the entrance desk and, if you wish, an audioguide. Visit early or late to avoid the crowds—it is particularly busy on Sundays.

HIGHLIGHTS

THE SAN GIOBBE ALTARPIECE BY GIOVANNI BELLINI—ROOM 3

By the mid-15th century, the Bellini family had developed the concept of the *sacra conversazione*, a unified composition of the Madonna and saints. This superb altarpiece, all architectural detail, balance and warmth, is a prime example, painted at the time of the 1478 plague.

LA TEMPESTA BY GIORGIONE—ROOM 5

Giorgione's contribution to the development of Venetian painting was huge. In this, his most enigmatic work, its iconography still unsolved, we see the growing importance of realistic landscape and light—a far cry from the rigid gold used just over a century before.

CHRIST IN THE HOUSE OF LEVI BY VERONESE—ROOM 10

Figures stand out against a background of classical architecture in this stupendous set piece. The painting was originally titled *The Last Supper*, but was judged so secular by its patrons that Veronese faced heresy charges if he failed to change it; cleverly, he simply changed the name.

MIRACLE OF ST. MARK FREEING THE SLAVE BY TINTORETTO

Tintoretto's technical wizardry still shocks in this picture of the hurtling figure of St. Mark swooping down to help a persecuted slave, painted for the Scuola Grande di San Marco in 1547.

A further part of the St. Ursula Cycle *by Vittore Carpaccio*

DISCOVERY OF THE TRUE CROSS BY GIAMBATTISTA TIEPOLO—ROOM 11

Painted for a church in Castello, now destroyed, this ceiling panel perfectly embodies Tiepolo's style—dizzying perspective, startling light and sugary, light-hearted hues.

PROCESSION IN THE PIAZZA DI SAN MARCO BY GENTILE BELLINI—ROOM 20

Created in 1496, this work shows the Piazza di San Marco as it was more than 500 years ago, with St. Mark's and the Doge's Palace much as they appear today. Carpaccio's painting of the Rialto nearby makes a good contrast, as there is little that's recognizable in the 21st century.

ST. URSULA CYCLE BY VITTORE CARPACCIO—ROOM 22

Crammed with charming anecdotes and details, the *St. Ursula Cycle* was painted in around 1498. It's the complicated tale, mixing reality and imagination, of a princess who, accompanied by her fiancé and 11,000 virgins, attempted to cross Europe to Rome, only to be massacred in Cologne.

PRESENTATION OF THE VIRGIN BY TITIAN—ROOM 24

This beautiful picture, painted between 1534 and 1539 for the Scuola della Carità, still hangs in its original position. The composition balances landscape, architecture and figures, with the small figure of the Virgin ascending the stairway.

BACKGROUND

The Accademia di Belle Arti, which houses the Galleria dell'Accademia, was founded in 1807 under Napoleon, who had suppressed dozens of churches and monasteries and needed somewhere to house their artworks. The art school still exists, but today the Accademia is primarily known as one of Europe's finest specialized art collections. It takes over three connected former religious buildings, the Scuola Grande della Carità, its adjacent church of Santa Maria, and the monastery of the Lateran Canons.

GALLERY GUIDE

The rooms are arranged chronologically except for 19–24, which are specific collections.

Room 1: The Primitives—Byzantine and international Gothic gold-ground paintings, typified by Paolo Veneziano.
Rooms 2–3: 15th-century altarpieces and works by the Bellini family, Sebastiano del Piombo, Cima de Conegliano and Carpaccio.
Rooms 4–5: Giovanni Bellini, Mantegna, Piero della Francesca, Cosmè Tura and Giorgione.
Rooms 6 and 10: Titian, Jacopo Tintoretto and Paolo Veronese—the Venetian superstars.
Rooms 7–8: Lorenzo Lotto, Romanino and Jacopo Palma il Vecchio.
Room 11: Veronese and Tiepolo.
Rooms 14–18: The 17th and 18th centuries: pictures and genre paintings by Tiepolo, Canaletto, Bellotto, Guardi, Pietro Longhi and Rosalba Carriera.
Rooms 19–20: Stories of the Relic of the Cross by Vittore Carpaccio, Gentile Bellini and others.
Room 21: *St. Ursula Cycle* by Vittore Carpaccio.
Room 23: Former church of Santa Maria della Carità with 15th-century paintings by the Bellini and Vivarini families.
Room 24: Former Albergo Room of Santa Maria della Carità.

BASICS

✚ 422 B4 • Campo Carità, Dorsoduro, 1050 30123 Venezia ☎ 041 520 0345
🕐 Mon 8.15–2, Tue–Sun 8.15–7.15
💶 Adult €6.50, EU citizens (18–25) €3.25, under 18 and over 65 free
🚤 *Vaporetto*: Line 1 and 82 to Accademia
🛈 Tours in English and Italian, Mon–Sat 11–1, 3.30–5, Sun 10–2, tel 041 520 0345. Audiotours in English, Italian, French and German, €4
📖 Full and short illustrated guides in Italian, English, French, Spanish, German and Japanese, €15.50 and €8.20
🏪 One shop and a stand selling good postcards, prints, good-quality gifts and art books (mainly on Renaissance art and artists)
🚻 ♿

www.gallerieaccademia.org

THE SIGHTS

The roof and dome of the church of Madonna dell'Orto (above) and a close-up view of the statues on the façade of the church (left)

MADONNA DELL'ORTO

One of Venice's most unspoiled churches.
Contains some of Tintoretto's most compelling work.

The original church was founded at the end of the 14th century. It was dedicated to St. Christopher, the patron saint of voyagers, in the hope that he would keep an eye on the ferry service to the northern islands and the gondolas that ran from the jetty. He was demoted in 1377 when a statue of the Madonna and Child, which was said to have miraculous powers and which had been attracting a following in a nearby vegetable garden *(orto)*, was moved here. This Madonna still stands in the Chapel of San Mauro, while St. Christopher presides over the main door. The church was rebuilt between 1399 and 1473. Tintoretto's 16th-century paintings in the choir and apse and on the side walls represent 30 years of his working life. After the 1966 floods, this church was the first major restoration project funded by the British Venice in Peril Fund, and its first chairman, Sir Ashley Clarke, is commemorated by a plaque in the chapel near the main altar.

THE FAÇADE
Overlooking its own square and a canal, the beautiful Gothic façade has similarities to those of the Frari (▷ 101) and Santi Giovanni e Paolo (▷ 99), but the false gallery at the top is unique. The figure of St. Christopher is by Nicolò di Giovanni and the portal by Bartolomeo Bon. Rising behind is a splendid onion-shaped cupola, balanced by a slender campanile, one of the prominent landmarks of the lagoon.

THE PAINTINGS
The three naves draw the eye towards the chancel, site of two huge canvases by Tintoretto, the *Making of the Golden Calf* and the *Last Judgement*. In the apse are the *Beheading of St. Christopher* and *St. Peter's Vision of the Cross,* both full of swooping angels, while the south aisle's mystical *Presentation of the Virgin in the Temple* provides a peaceful contrast. Radiant blues shine in *St. Agnes* in the Contarini Chapel, and there is a superb Cima da Conegliano over the first altar on the right. Be sure to find *Saints John the Baptist, Mark, Jerome and Paul* by Cima da Conegliano (1494) and Tintoretto's tomb in the chapel to the right of the chancel.
Don't miss *Last Judgement; Presentation of the Virgin in the Temple.*

Palazzo Ducale

The political and judicial hub of the Venetian government.
The biggest, grandest and most opulent civic building in Venice.
A dream-like Gothic palace—one of the architectural highlights of the city.

A close-up of the Palazzo Ducale's balcony

The delicate tracery and elegantly regular columns of the façade viewed from the water

SEEING THE PALAZZO DUCALE

The Palazzo Ducale (Doge's Palace), seat of Venice's temporal power, is connected to the Basilica di San Marco at the east end of the Piazza di San Marco, a 45-minute walk or half-hour ride by *vaporetto* from the railway station. The meeting place of the councils that ruled Venice, the home to the Doge, the law courts, the civil service and the prisons, the palazzo overlooks both the piazzetta and the waters of the Bacino di San Marco. Founded as a castle in the ninth century, its present appearance as a masterpiece of Venetian Gothic architecture dates from the 14th century, a magnificent reminder of the city's past glories. Whether you approach it via the water or by strolling through the piazza, the first impressions of this fairy-tale palace are unforgettable.

HIGHLIGHTS

THE EXTERIOR, THE PORTA DELLA CARTA AND THE COURTYARD

One of the world's finest examples of Gothic architecture, the exterior of the Palazzo Ducale runs along the water's edge and the piazzetta. The waterfront façade was finished in 1419 and the side on the piazzetta was built in the 15th century. The beautiful pink-and-white frontage has an airy arcade topped by a gallery supporting the mass of the upper storeys; the play of light and shade over the masonry enhances the impression of harmony. The columns and pillars at ground level are mainly copies of the 14th- to 15th-century originals, now housed in the Museo dell'Opera, off the interior courtyard.

The main entrance into the palazzo is the Porta della Carta, a grand piece of florid Gothic architecture, built by Bartolomeo and Giovanni Bon between 1438 and 1442. This provides access through a portico to the courtyard, an enclosed space with a first-floor loggia. The most imposing approach to the loggia is undoubtedly via Sansovino's 1485 Scala dei Giganti (Giant's Staircase), used by the Doge at his inauguration. There is another flamboyant Sansovino stairway, the stucco-and-gilt Scala d'Oro (Golden Stairway), leading from the loggia to the upper floors.

RATINGS	
Historic interest	● ● ● ●
Cultural interest	● ● ● ●
Photo stops	● ● ● ●
Value for money	● ● ●

BASICS

✚ 422 C4 • Piazza San Marco 1, San Marco, 30124 Venezia ☎ 041 271 5911
🕐 Apr–end Oct daily 9–7; rest of year daily 9–5. Itinerari Segreti (Secret Itineraries) tour must be reserved in advance
💶 Adult €11, child (6–14) free
🚢 *Vaporetto*: San Zaccaria, San Marco (Vallaresso)
✈ Guided tours in English Tue–Thu, Sat 11.30, €6; audioguides in Italian, English, French, German and Spanish, €6
📖 Good Electra guidebooks available from bookshops in several languages
☕ Bar on ground floor serving drinks, coffee and snacks
📚 Excellent bookshop, with good range of guidebooks, art books, posters, postcards and souvenirs
🚻

● Expect parts of the Palazzo Ducale to be closed; a building of this age requires constant restoration.
● The Museum Card for the Musei della Piazza San Marco (€11) provides entrance to all the museums in Piazza San Marco (Palazzo Ducale, Museo Correr, Museo Archeologico Nazionale, Biblioteca Nazionale Marciana).
● A Museum Pass (€15.50) is available for all Venice's civic

The Sala della Bussola

museums in the Musei della Piazza San Marco (Palazzo Ducale, Museo Correr, Museo Archeologico Nazionale, Biblioteca Nazionale Marciana), the Musei del Settecento (Ca' Rezzonico (▷ 83), Palazzo Mocenigo, Casa di Carlo Goldini, Ca' Pesara) and the Musei delle Isole (Museo del Vetro and Museo del Merletto).

THE DOGE'S APARTMENTS

The Doge, elected from Venice's patrician families, was the one politician to sit on all the major councils and the only one elected for life—a position of such potential power that it was hedged about with endless restrictions to prevent abuse of power. After his election, the Doge gave his entire life over to the service of the State, and his apartments reflect this lack of privacy. They comprise a series of surprisingly intimate rooms, magnificently if austerely decorated, with splendid ceilings and superb fireplaces. Here, the Doge received deputations and ambassadors and oversaw council deliberations. The finest and biggest chamber is the Sala delle Mappe (Map Room), painted with maps of the whole of the 16th-century known world, with Venice firmly as the central focus.

THE ANTICOLLEGIO, THE COLLEGIO AND THE SALA DEL SENATO

The extraordinarily rich decoration of the state rooms in the Palazzo Ducale is intended to illustrate the history of Venice and was painted by some of the greatest 16th-century Venetian artists. The aim was to impress visiting emissaries, many of whom passed through the palace on official business. The Anticollegio served as a waiting room for ambassadors hoping to see the Doge; four mythological paintings, created in 1577–78 by Tintoretto (1518–94), hang on the walls, while facing the window is Veronese's *Rape of Europa*. From here, the ambassadors moved to the adjoining Collegio to be received. This was also the room where the inner cabinet met. The ceiling panels are by Veronese (1528–88), pure propaganda showing Justice and Peace as mere sidekicks to Venice herself. Venice triumphs yet again in Tintoretto's painting in the middle of the ceiling in the next-door Sala del Senato, where the 300-strong senate met to receive reports from returning ambassadors and debate questions of commerce, war and foreign policy.

THE SALA DEL MAGGIOR CONSIGLIO

The first-floor Sala del Maggior Consiglio is the largest room in the palazzo, stretching almost the entire length of the waterfront side of the building. This lavishly decorated room was the great council chamber where the 2,600 patricians met. The paintings in this room were commissioned to replace those lost in a fire in 1577. *Paradiso* on the far wall was begun by Tintoretto, then aged 70, who was responsible for its complex iconography. It was completed after his death by his son, Domenico (1562–1637). The *Apotheosis of Venice* on the ceiling is by Veronese. Devoted to the concept of Venice the superpower, its meaning is more straightforward. Around the walls are portraits of the first 76 doges. Look for the gap, where there is a black veil instead of a doge; this space should have commemorated Doge Marin Falier, but he was executed for conspiring against the State in 1355. If the windows are open on the left side of the hall, step out onto the balcony for lovely views across St. Mark's Basin.

Displays of weaponry, armour and a cannon in the Palazzo Ducale

Gilded, painted ceilings in the largest room in the palazzo, the Sala del Maggior Consiglio

THE PONTE DEI SOSPIRI AND THE PRIGIONI NUOVE

Until the 16th century, all Venetian criminals served their sentences in either the attics or the waterlogged basement of the Palazzo Ducale. This changed after the construction of the Prigioni Nuove (New Prisons) in 1598; from then on petty villains enjoyed the comforts of what was considered to be Europe's most sophisticated prison accommodation. The prisons are separated from the main palace by a canal, which is crossed by the world-famous Ponte dei Sospiri (Bridge of Sighs). Designed by the aptly named Antonio da Ponte, it is probably Venice's (if not the world's) most photographed bridge. By the 19th century the romantic legend was firmly established that once prisoners crossed this enclosed first-floor bridge they would never return. In the prison block, steep stairs lead down to the warren of cells, some of which have their number and capacity painted over the door. At the bottom there is a small courtyard for exercise, once home to an unofficial tavern.

BACKGROUND

The Palazzo Ducale was designed not only to provide a home for the Doge, but also to house the machinery of the State—the councils, committees and officials who administered the government of the city. From the 14th century only those noble families listed in the so-called *Libro d'Oro (Golden Book)* sat on the councils, and the building reflects their power, wealth and prestige as well as that of Venice itself. The Palazzo Ducale began to assume its present shape in 1340 when a new hall for the Maggior Consiglio (Great Council) was built. Much of the rest of what we see today dates from the mid-15th century. There were devastating fires in 1574 and again in 1577, but it was decided to restore the building rather than replace it with something new, leaving the magical Gothic exterior unaltered. The block across the Canale della Paglia, which is approached via the Ponte dei Sospiri (Bridge of Sighs), went up in the late 16th century. Since the fall of the Republic in 1797, the Palazzo Ducale has had many different functions; today, as well as being open to the public, it houses various city offices.

GALLERY GUIDE

Itinerari Segreti: A guided tour behind the scenes, taking in the warren of offices and small chambers that links the public rooms of the palazzo, as well as the old prisons in the basement (must be reserved in advance).
Museo dell'Opera: A ground-floor museum displaying, among other exhibits, the best of the palazzo's exterior arcade capitals.
Arco dei Foscari: A late Gothic arch in the courtyard, commissioned by Doge Francesco Foscari in 1438, designed and built by Antonio Bregno and Antonio Rizzo.
Sala del Magistrato: A small room housing some outstandingly bizarre paintings by the Flemish artist Hieronymus Bosch (c1450–1516), collected by the Grimani family.
Armoury: A huge and somewhat daunting collection of armour, weapons and instruments of war, mostly captured from Venice's enemies.
Bocche di Leone: 'Postboxes' adorned with lion's heads—in various parts of the palazzo, notably the loggia, the Sala della Bussola and the Sala della Quarantia Criminal—which served as delivery boxes for anonymous accusations made by Venetian citizens against each other.

PIAZZA SAN MARCO AND THE CAMPANILE

**The historic heart of Venice.
Some of the city's finest Byzantine, Gothic and
Renaissance architecture.
Bordered by compelling museums, chic shops and cafés.**

*Bustling Piazza San Marco
(above)*

*The clockface of the Torre
dell'Orologio (inset)*

As you emerge from the narrow surrounding streets into the piazza,
its sheer scale is breathtaking—not for nothing did Napoleon describe
it as 'the biggest drawing room in Europe'. Within the arcades that line
three sides of the piazza are Florian's and Quadri's, two historic cafés
with plush interiors, impeccable service and tables outside on the
piazza. They are very expensive, but a drink here is quite an
experience, often accompanied by an orchestra.

THE PIAZZETTA AND THE TORRE DELL'OROLOGIO

At the east end of the piazza's wide expanse stands the Basilica di San
Marco (▷ 84–85). The open space runs down to the water's edge, St.
Mark's Basin, and is flanked on the right by the Biblioteca Marciana and
the Zecca, designed by Sansovino between 1527 and 1537, and the
Palazzo Ducale (▷ 93–95) on the left. A winged lion, the symbol of
Venice, and St. Theodore, the city's first patron saint, top its two
columns. On the other side of the basilica, the tiny space fronted by
ancient marble lions, known as the Piazzetta dei Leoncini, is overlooked
by the Torre dell'Orologio. This clocktower has a zodiacal clock with
mechanical figures and is crowned with a golden lion. It was designed
by Mauro Coducci and built between 1406 and 1506.

THE ARCADES AND THE CAMPANILE

The arcaded buildings that run down the long sides of the piazza
are the offices of the Procurators of San Marco; the 16th-century
Procuratie Vecchie, to the north, and the Procuratie Nuove, built a
century later, to the south. After the fall of Venice in 1797, the two
were linked by another arcaded building, the Ala Napoleonica, now
home to the Museo Correr (▷ 89). In front of San Marco, the
campanile (bell tower), a great place for city and lagoon views, was
designed in 1514. What you see is a copy, as in 1902 the entire
tower collapsed. No other buildings were damaged but the
custodian's cat was killed. It was rebuilt *'Com'era, dov'era'* ('Like it
was, where it was') and Sansovino's Loggetta at the foot of the tower
was pieced together from the fragments.
Don't miss The Piazzetta; the Torre dell'Orologio.

RIALTO

**The traditional setting of one of Italy's most vibrant markets.
A place to jostle with the locals and experience
a slice of Venetian life.**

The Rialto was one of the earliest parts of the lagoon to be settled: the word *Rialto* is a corruption of *Rivoaltus*, the upper bank, the highest area and thus less likely to be flooded. By the 10th and 11th centuries, the Rialto was Venice's commercial heart and one of Europe's most important trading areas. In 1097 the market became a permanent fixture. A pontoon of boats linked the two banks, but in the 12th and 13th centuries the first of five wooden bridges was built across the canal. Venetian merchants controlled trade between Europe and the Far East, while Europe's major banks and international trading companies set up offices here. The name Rialto was as familiar to medieval moneymen as that of Wall Street or the City of London is today.

PONTE DI RIALTO
The idea of a stone bridge at the Rialto was first mooted in 1557 and a competition was held to choose the best design, with big names such as Michelangelo, Palladio and Sansovino all submitting their plans. The prize went to the aptly named Venetian, Antonio da Ponte, for his revolutionary single-span suggestion. Two *fondamente* (canalside streets) stretch along either side of the water, one of the few places in Venice where you can actually stroll along the edge of the Canal Grande (▷ 86–87). The San Marco side is the Riva del Ferro, named after the iron that was once unloaded here, while opposite, the Riva del Vin is a reminder that this was originally the discharge point for wine barrels.

THE MARKET
Behind the Riva del Vin is a labyrinthine maze of narrow streets, many named after the goods sold during the great days of the Republic: Ruga de'Orefici (Goldsmiths' Row), Ruga Speziali (Spicemakers' Street), Riva dell'Olio (Oil Quay) and Campo della Pescheria (Fish Market Square). Nearby is the Rialto market and its surrounding specialist shops, the city's main place for food shopping, where people bargain for meat, fruit, vegetables and, above all, fresh fish and seafood.

The little church of San Giacomo, on the San Polo side of the bridge, is said to be Venice's oldest, founded, according to legend, on the same day as the city itself, 26 March 421. The clock above the church is famous for its inaccuracy; it has been incorrect since its installation in the 15th century.

RATINGS			
Good for kids	● ● ● ○		
Specialist shopping	● ● ● ●		
Photo stops	● ● ● ○		
Good for food	● ● ● ○		

BASICS
✚ 422 C3
🚤 *Vaporetto*: Rialto

TIP
● The fish market is closed on Mondays.

Traffic criss-crossing the Canal Grande in front of the Ponte di Rialto (top) and the Campo della Pescheria, where you can buy fresh fish and seafood, the staples of Venetian cuisine (above)

The view over Venice from the top of San Giorgio Maggiore

A silhouette of Santa Maria della Salute seen from San Marco

SAN GIORGIO DEI GRECI

➕ 423 D3 • Fondamenta dei Greci, Castello, 30122 Venezia ☎ 041 523 9569 🕐 Wed–Mon 9–11, 2.30–4.30 🚤 *Vaporetto*: San Zaccaria

San Giorgio dei Greci is a tangible reminder of the foreign communities that lived and settled in Venice. Renaissance Venice had a large Greek population, particularly after Constantinople fell to the Turks in 1453, and the Greek community received permission to build their own church in 1539. The church was designed by Sante Lombardo, with an interior that is completely Orthodox in layout and design. Look for the *matroneo* (women's gallery) above the main door and the iconostasis (screen) that separates the high altar from the body of the church. The icons on the screen are a mixture of dates and styles, the oldest dating back as far as the 12th century. The campanile, drunkenly leaning towards the canal, is one of the landmarks in this part of the city.

SAN GIORGIO MAGGIORE

➕ 423 D4 • Isola di San Giorgio Maggiore, 30124 Venezia ☎ 041 522 7827 🕐 May–end Sep 9.30–12.30, 2.30–6.30; Oct–end Apr 9.30–12.30, 2.30–4.30 🚤 *Vaporetto*: San Giorgio

The open waters of St. Mark's Basin frame the great Palladian church of San Giorgio Maggiore. The island of San Giorgio was home to a Benedictine monastery from the 10th century to 1806, and in 1565 Andrea Palladio was commissioned to design a church for the monks. He united two temple fronts in the façade: four central columns that rise to the full height of the nave are flanked by shorter, Corinthian columns, which match the height

of the aisles—an arrangement echoed in the luminous interior and emphasized by the use of white marble and stucco. This is a triumphantly light and airy building, full of soaring space decorated with fine pictures by Tintoretto and his school. Stop to admire the works on either side of the chancel, *The Fall of Manna* and the *The Last Supper*, both of which emphasize the importance of the Eucharist, before taking the lift up the campanile for views over the city and lagoon.

Don't miss Tintoretto's paintings; the campanile.

SANTA MARIA DEGLI MIRACOLI

➕ 422 C3 • Campo Santa Maria Nuova, Cannaregio, 30121 Venezia ☎ 041 275 0462 🕐 Mon–Sat 9–6, Sun 1–6 💶 €2.50. Santa Maria degli Miracoli is one of the CHORUS group of 15 artistically important churches; a pass covering entry to all 15 costs €8 🚤 *Vaporetto*: Rialto www.chorusvenezia.it

The exquisite Church of Santa Maria degli Miracoli is tucked away in Cannaregio. It was built between 1481 and 1489 to house a miraculous image of the Madonna by Nicolò di Pietro, which still hangs over the altar. The church is entirely covered inside and out with polychrome marble, creating a jewel-casket effect, with one side of this perfect Renaissance church running along a quiet canal.

Begin by looking closely at the exterior, built, like the inside, by the Lombardo brothers, stoneworkers who uniquely fused architecture, decoration and sculpture. Marble in subtly different shades covers every surface, while graceful pilasters make the church appear longer. The interior has some of the most intricate carving in Venice, seen at its best when the sun

streams in, illuminating the rose, white and silver-grey marble. The altar steps and balustrade leading to the raised choir are beautifully carved with figures, while fine filigree stonework covers the columns below the nuns' choir and a carved frieze runs right around the church.

SANTA MARIA DELLA SALUTE

➕ 422 C4 • Campo della Salute, Dorsoduro, 30123 Venezia ☎ 041 522 5558 🕐 Church: Apr–end Sep daily 9–12, 3–6.30, Sacristy: Apr–end Sep daily 3–5.30 💶 Sacristy €1.50 🚤 *Vaporetto*: Salute

An unmistakable feature of the Venetian cityscape, the gleaming white bulk of the great baroque 17th-century church of Santa Maria della Salute looms over the San Marco entrance to the Canal Grande. Built in thanksgiving for the end of the disastrous plague of 1630, which wiped out a third of the city's population, the church has outstanding paintings by Titian (c1490–1576). Baldassare Longhena designed the huge, domed, octagonal construction, his first commission.

From the canal-side, a flight of steps leads up to the Palladian façade, with huge half-columns. The main dome is buttressed by circular volutes, affectionately known to Venetians as *orecchini* (little ears), surrounded by more than 120 exuberant statues and ornate decoration. By contrast, the interior is austere, with six chapels around the central space. On the high altar, the marble Virgin and Child are shown rescuing Venice from the plague.

Don't miss There are eight Titians in the sacristy, including *The Sacrifice of Abraham* and *David and Goliath,* and Tintoretto's *Marriage Feast at Cana;* the church is illuminated at night.

SANTI GIOVANNI E PAOLO

Dubbed the 'Pantheon of Venice', this is the final resting place of Venice's doges and heroes.

Northern Castello is home to the huge Gothic church of Santi Giovanni e Paolo or, in Venetian dialect, San Zanipolo. The L-shaped *campo* (square) that fronts the church is a good vantage point from which to appreciate the impressively large exterior: the church is 100m (330ft) long, 38m (125ft) wide and 33m (108ft) high. Constructed between 1246 and 1430, of red brick with stone ornamentation, Santi Giovanni e Paolo is among the most ambitious expressions of Gothic architecture in Venice, complete with a soaring façade and five apses at the east end.

The main portal has Byzantine reliefs and marble columns from an abandoned church on the island of Torcello (▷ 102). The most ornate of four tombs built into the façade is that of Doge Giacomo Tiepolo, who in 1234 reputedly dreamed that he should found a church here, on what was then a swamp.

THE INTERIOR

The vast, shadowy interior is a single spatial unit punctuated by simple columns. The walls are lined with tombs and monuments by some of Venice's most famous Renaissance artists and sculptors. They include some of the best pieces by the Lombardo family of sculptors. No fewer than 25 doges are buried here. Particularly striking are the Morosini, Vendramin, Nicolò Marcello and Corner monuments, and the Lombardo Mocenigo monuments on the rear entrance wall. Paintings to look for are the superb polyptych *St. Vincent Ferrer* by Giovanni Bellini, *St. Antonius Pierozzi Giving Alms to the Poor* by Lorenzo Lotto, in the south transept, and the ceiling paintings by Veronese in the Cappella del Rosario. There is some good stained glass in the transept, designed by Bartolomeo Vivarini and made at Murano (▷ 89).

THE COLLEONI STATUE AND SCUOLA GRANDE DI SAN MARCO

The Lombardo family were also responsible for the elaborate façade of the Scuola Grande di San Marco, which stands at right angles to the front of the church. Completed in 1495 with stunning marble *trompe l'oeil* panels, it was one of the major Venetian *scuole* (confraternities) and today houses Venice's main civic hospital. Opposite the entrance, and the focal point of the *campo*, is Andrea del Verrocchio's powerful equestrian statue of the *condottiere* Bartolomeo Colleoni (▷ 33).

BASICS

✚ 423 D3 • Campo Santi Giovanni e Paolo, Castello, 30122 Venezia
☎ 041 523 5913
🕐 Mon–Sat 7.30–7; Sun 3–6
💶 €2.50
🚢 *Vaporetto*: Ospedale
📖 In Italian, English, French, German, €3.60
📅

The statue of condottiere *Bartolomeo Colleoni (top) and a close-up of the heavily armoured figure on top of the tomb of Doge Michele Steno, one of the many important monuments inside the church (above)*

The flower-filled cemetery on the island of San Michele

Inside the church of San Polo

The altarpiece inside the church of San Zaccaria

THE SIGHTS

SANTA MARIA FORMOSA

✚ 423 D3 • Campo Santa Maria Formosa, Castello, 30122 Venezia ☎ 041 523 4645 🕐 Mon–Sat 10–5, Sun 1–5; Jul, Aug closed Sun 🖳 €2 🚤 *Vaporetto*: San Zaccaria, Rialto www.chorusvenezia.org

The church of Santa Maria Formosa gives its name to the surrounding *campo*, a typically Venetian square that is constantly busy with the comings and goings of both Venetians and visitors, a great place to experience life in Castello. This irregular space is bordered by a fine range of *palazzi*. The ancient church got its name from a seventh-century vision that appeared to St. Magnus, where he saw the Virgin as a buxom and shapely matron—*formosa*.

The present church was designed by Mauro Coducci in 1492; he retained the original 11th-century Greek-cross plan, threading a Renaissance design around a typically Byzantine layout. The campanile is baroque. The church has two façades, one on the canal (1542) and one on the *campo* (1604), both added after Coducci's death. The harmonious grey-and-white interior has three naves and barrel-vaulted side chapels. Look for the triptych in the first chapel on the right, showing the Virgin in her role as Our Lady of Mercy by Bartolomeo Vivarini, with scenes from her life on either side.

SAN MICHELE IN ISOLA

✚ 423 D1 • Isola di San Michele, 30121 Venezia 🕐 Cemetery: daily 7.30–4. Church: daily 7.30–12.15, 3–4 🖳 Free 🚤 *Vaporetto*: San Michele (from Fondamente Nuove)

The island of San Michele, a few minutes' journey across the lagoon from the Fondamente Nuove, is the final resting place for Venetians. But the cemetery

is by no means a morbid place. Infused with a gentle and romantic melancholy, it is busy with Venetians bringing flowers for their loved ones. Today it is only a temporary resting place as it became full years ago. Bones are now removed after 10 years or so and taken to an ossuary.

Begin by pausing at Venice's first Renaissance church, the beautiful San Michele in Isola, designed by Mauro Coducci in the 1460s. From here a walkway leads through the cloisters of the monastery; the brothers look after the church and cemetery. It is covered in an array of stacked tombs, dramatic sculpture, photographs and flowers. Most tourists head for the Protestant section to visit the tomb of American poet Ezra Pound (1885–1972), before tracking down the graves of Russian composer Igor Stravinsky (1882–1971) and Russian ballet impresario Sergei Diaghilev (1872–1929) in the Greek Orthodox section. The children's area is poignant, and there is a corner dedicated to gondoliers, whose graves are decorated with stone gondolas.

SAN POLO

✚ 422 B3 • Campo San Polo, San Polo, 30125 Venezia ☎ 041 275 0462 🕐 Mon–Sat 9–6, Sun 1–6 🖳 €2 🚤 *Vaporetto*: San Tomà, San Silvestro www.chorusvenezia.org

The district of San Polo, the Venetian version of San Paolo (St. Paul), gets its name from this church, a ninth-century foundation. Tucked into a corner of the square of the same name, the church faces the canal, though it has lost its waterfront façade and entrance. The original building was Byzantine, but Gothic elements such as the side portal, the rose window and the wooden ceiling were added in

the 14th and 15th centuries. In 1804 there were more alterations in an attempt to impose a neoclassical look; some were removed in the 1930s. The campanile, detached from the church, has suffered less since its construction in 1362; look for the pair of stone lions at the base. Inside, the main draw is Tiepolo's cycle of the Crucifix in the oratory behind the main church. These dazzling paintings show scenes from *The Stations of the Cross*.

SAN ZACCARIA

✚ 423 D3 • Campo San Zaccaria, Castello, 30122 Venezia ☎ 041 522 1257 🕐 Mon–Sat 10–12, 4–6, Sun 4–6 🖳 Church: free. Chapels of St. Athanasius and St. Tarasius, sacristy and crypt: €1.50 🚤 *Vaporetto*: San Zaccaria

San Zaccaria, dedicated to the father of John the Baptist (said to be buried here), is the only Venetian church with an ambulatory and crypt. On a square off the Riva degli Schiavone, it is a Venetian mix of Gothic and Renaissance styles.

The ambulatory is instantly striking, an elegant ring of elliptical cupolas lit by long windows. The church is stuffed with 17th- and 18th-century paintings, of distinctly variable quality. Standing artistically apart from this mass is Giovanni Bellini's luminously stunning and serene *Madonna and Four Saints*, in the second chapel on the left. The Chapel of St. Tarasius was once part of the original church and houses three ornate *ancone* (volutes supporting a cornice) by Antonio Vivarini and Giovanni d'Alemagna, wonderfully hieratic pictures in sumptuous gold Gothic frames. This chapel also gives access to the permanently waterlogged crypt, the burial place of eight of the early doges. It is confirmation that the water continues to rise in Venice.

SANTA MARIA GLORIOSA DEI FRARI

**The Franciscans' Venetian power base and the city's second-largest church.
The perfect setting for some of Venice's famous works of art and monumental tombs.**

The Franciscans, *frari* in Venetian dialect, came to Venice around 1222 and built their first church on the site in the 1270s. As the order developed, they outgrew it, and work started on a new church and bell tower in 1340. The latter was finished in 1396, but it was not until the 1430s that the church was completed. The adjoining cloisters, chapter house and convent (now housing the Archivio di Stato) were built at the same time. The convent was suppressed under Napoleon, but today the Frari is a parish church still in the care of the Franciscans.

GREAT PAINTINGS
Built of terracotta brick with a typical Gothic stone exterior and architectural details, the Frari is huge—102m (335ft) long, 48m (158ft) wide and 28m (92ft) high—and has one of the tallest bell towers in Venice. Enter the vast nave (the 12 pillars represent the Apostles) and you will be immediately drawn to Titian's famously radiant and dynamic *Assumption* (1518) over the high altar, one of the most important and innovative paintings of the Venetian High Renaissance. To the left of the main altar is Titian's *Madonna di Ca' Pesaro* (1526), commissioned by Bishop Pesaro and showing members of his family. In the sacristy, the inspiring and tranquil triptych *Madonna and Child* (1488) by Giovanni Bellini is noted for its skilful use of perspective; it is still in its original frame. Immediately to the right of the high altar is Donatello's sculpture of *St. John the Baptist,* the only work by the Florentine master in Venice. In the Monks' Choir *(Coro dei Frati)*, the 124 wooden choir stalls were carved by Marco Cozzi in 1468.

MONUMENTAL TOMBS
Less immediately appealing than the paintings but of equal interest are the monumental tombs. The rear section of the nave has a 19th-century monument to Titian and opposite there is a large neoclassical marble pyramid containing the heart of the sculptor Antonio Canova (1757–1822). Look for the late Gothic monument to Doge Foscari (1457) near the high altar, and the Renaissance monument to Doge Tron (1476) nearby. The composer Claudio Monteverdi (1567–1643) is buried in a chapel to the left of the high altar.

RATINGS
Historic interest	●●●●●
Cultural interest	●●●●
Photo stops	●●●●
Value for money	●●●●

BASICS
✚ 422 B3 • Campo dei Frari, San Polo, 30125 Venezia ☎ 041 522 2637
🕐 Mon–Sat 9–6, Sun 1–5
💶 €2.50. The Frari is one of the CHORUS group of 15 artistically important churches; a pass covering entry to all 15 costs €8
🚤 *Vaporetto*: San Tomà
🎧 Audioguides
📖 Several versions, with differing levels of information, in English, Italian, French, German, Spanish, €4–€9
📮
www.basilicadeifrari.it
www.chorusvenezia.org

TIPS
● Enter via the north transept but once inside start your visit from the back of the church.
● If you are visiting between Christmas and the end of January, don't miss the *presepio* (crib), one of the city's best, with sound and light effects and moving figures.

The wooden cross beams accentuate the height of the Frari's fine Gothic ceiling

The façade of the Scuola Grande di San Rocco

The Ponte del Diavolo on Torcello's main canal

SCUOLA GRANDE DI SAN ROCCO

⊕ 422 B3 • Campo San Rocco, San Polo, 30123 Venezia ☎ 041 523 4864 ⊙ Apr–end Oct daily 9–5.30; Nov–end Mar daily 10–4; Dec–end Feb Mon–Fri 10–1, Sat–Sun 10–4 💷 €5.50 🚤 *Vaporetto*: San Tomà 📖 In Italian, English, French, German and Spanish, €4.50–€15 🎧 Audiotours in Italian, French, English included in ticket

There is little in Venice so powerful as the colossal picture cycle by Tintoretto in the Scuola Grande di San Rocco. These 54 compelling and moving paintings, produced by the artist in three bursts of creativity over a period of 23 years, cover the walls and ceilings of the headquarters of the richest of the 15th-century *scuole* (confraternities).

The building was designed by Bartolomeo Bon in the early 16th century and was decorated between 1564 and 1587. Chronologically, the panels begin upstairs, in the Sala dell'Albergo, where there is the portrayal of *St. Roch in Glory*, the painting that won Tintoretto the commission. One wall is dominated by the *Crucifixion*, a powerful synthesis of narrative and devotion. The Main Hall has Old Testament scenes on the ceiling and a Life of Christ cycle on the walls, all set off by sumptuous woodcarving and gilding. At the peak of his stylistic development Tintoretto's use of light and form lends an almost impressionistic feel to his works *Annunciation, Flight to Egypt* and *Massacre of the Innocents.*

SCUOLA GRANDE DEI CARMINI

⊕ 422 A4 • Campo dei Carmini, Dorsoduro 2617, 30123 Venezia ☎ 041 528 9420 ⊙ Apr–end Sep Mon–Sat 9–6, Sun 9–4; Oct–end Mar daily 9–4 💷 Adult €5, child (under 10) €2 🚤 *Vaporetto*: Ca' Rezzonico, San Basilio

The Scuola Grande dei Carmini was the only one to escape the maraudings of Napoleon's troops, and is thus the only surviving *scuola* with an 18th-century appearance. Tucked away just off the atmospheric Campo Santa Margherita, this Carmelite confraternity base has flamboyant interior decoration.

Pause before you go in to admire the formal symmetry of the façade, designed by Longhena between 1668 and 1670. This was the Venetian headquarters of the Carmelites, a religious order devoted to the Virgin Mary. From here they practised their charitable works. In 1739 they employed the artist Giambattista Tiepolo (1696–1770) to decorate the upper hall, a task that occupied him for 10 years. Access upstairs is via an ornate staircase, and the hall itself is dominated by Tiepolo's nine audacious panels. Incomprehensible iconography aside, they can be appreciated for their swirling figures and off-beat composition and the extraordinary accomplishment of trompe-l'oeil perspective.

SCUOLA DI SAN GIORGIO DEGLI SCHIAVONI

⊕ 423 D3 • Fondamenta dei Furlani, Castello, 30122 Venezia ☎ 041 522 8828 ⊙ Apr–end Oct Tue–Sat 9.30–12.30, 3.30–6.30, Sun 9.30–12.30; Nov–end Mar Tue–Sat 10–12.30, 3–6, Sun 10–12.30 💷 €3 🚤 *Vaporetto*: San Zaccaria

This intimate little building on a side canal houses one of the most appealing of all Venetian Renaissance picture cycles. After the splendours of the great set pieces, the low-key charm of Vittore Carpaccio's paintings is a great contrast. By the 15th century, the Slavs had established an important community in Venice, and obtained permission to found their own *scuola* here. In 1502 they commissioned Carpaccio (*c*1460–*c*1525) to decorate the interior with scenes from the lives of three special saints revered by the Slavs, St. George, St. Tryphon and St. Jerome.

The Carpaccio cycles occupy a dimly lit, wood-panelled chamber entered directly from the street. Much of their appeal stems from their meticulous detail. The iconography is confusing, but it is easy to spot St. George killing the dragon, while the princess looks on in rapture.

TORCELLO

⊕ 423 off F1 ℹ Piazza San Marco 71f, San Marco 30124, tel 041 529 8740; Mon–Sat 9.30–3.30 🚤 *Vaporetto*: Torcello www.comune.venezia.it

On the marshy, neglected island of Torcello, 9km (5 miles) northeast of Venice in the northern part of the lagoon, you will find a handful of working Venetians, a single muddy canal and the oldest building in the lagoon, the superb ninth-century Basilica di Santa Maria Assunta.

Established in the fifth century, this was Venice's earliest settlement; by the 1300s the population numbered over 20,000. But the rise of the Rialto (▷ 97) and the mosquito-fed fevers took their toll in the 14th century, forcing the inhabitants to flee. All that remains is a few houses, an 11th-century church and the basilica.

The interior of Santa Maria Assunta, first built in 638, is serene and cool, with a superb marble pavement and a series of outstanding mosaics, dating from the ninth to the 12th centuries, including a melancholy *Madonna* in the apse and a magnificently detailed *Last Judgement* on the back wall.

THE NORTHEAST AND EMILIA-ROMAGNA

Prosperous and thriving since ancient times, this area includes some of the country's loveliest cities—Bologna, Parma, Padua and Vicenza. Europe's finest Byzantine mosaics are found at Ravenna, while the soaring and dramatic peaks of the Dolomites are perfect for summer walking and winter sports.

MAJOR SIGHTS

The Romanesque basilica in Aquileia

Karneid Castle at the end of the Eggental, a spectacular valley road through Trentino Alto-Adige, with Bolzano in the distance

THE SIGHTS

AQUILEIA

435 J3 Via Julia Augusta, Piazzale Terminal, 33051 Aquileia, tel 0431 919491; Viale Dante Alighieri 72, Grado, tel 0431 877111, fax 0431 83509 www.turismo.fvg.it

Most great Roman cities were transformed into settlements that survive as modern cities, but Aquileia (33km/20 miles south of Udine), once the fourth most important centre in Italy, is little more than a tangle of ruins, a few houses and a superb Romanesque basilica. Founded in 181BC as a defensive and trading hub, it is now a peaceful hamlet.

In AD314, a Christian patriarchate was founded here and Theodore, the first patriarch, built a basilica. Sacked by Attila and then by the Lombards, it was rebuilt in the early 11th century by Poppo, the patriarch at the time. The basilica's chief treasure is the mosaic floor, its Christian and pagan scenes as fresh as when they were laid by Theodore in 320. The basilica and bell tower, visible for miles around, are the focus today, while around them lie the grassy ruins of the Roman city, much of whose stone was stolen by the Venetians for their buildings. Climb the bell tower, see Roman finds in the Museo Archeologico and the Museo Paleocristiano, and maybe visit Grado, one of the Adriatic's least-known resorts, 12km (7 miles) away.
Don't miss The mosaics in the basilica.

BOLZANO (BOZEN)

434 G2 Waltherplatz/Piazza Walther 8, 39100 Bolzano, tel 0471 307000 Bolzano/Bozen www.bolzano-bozen.it

Residents of Bolzano enjoy one of the highest standards of living in Italy. The town is a good starting point for a trip into the Dolomites (▷ 107, 290–291). It is strongly Tyrolean—it was only after World War I that it became part of Italy. It lies at the heart of an excellent wine-producing region, and is relaxed, with a handful of sights, plenty of cafés and one of the best museums in the Alto-Adige (Südtirol).

The town stands at the confluence of the rivers Talfer (Talvera) and Eisack (Isarco), 86km (53 miles) northeast of Trento and surrounded by mountains whose lower slopes are planted with vines and apple trees. West of the Talfer sprawls the 'Italian' town, laid out by Mussolini in the late 1920s. Most visitors concentrate on the old town to the east, where arcaded streets spread out from the central Waltherplatz (Piazza Walther). The duomo stands on one side, a distinctive building whose tower is a local landmark.
Don't miss Ötzi, the body of a man 5,000 years old in the Museo Archeologico.

BRESSANONE (BRIXEN)

434 G2 Viale Stazione/ Bahnhofstrasse 9, 39042 Bressanone, tel 0472 836401 Bressanone/Brixen www.brixen.org

Bressanone makes a good stopping-off point en route to or from the Brenner Pass. It is a popular year-round resort, with winter access to miles of pistes and excellent summer walking in the surrounding mountains.

Founded in 901 as the seat of an important bishopric, the town stands on the River Eisack, 47km (29 miles) northeast of Bolzano. The heart of the town is focused on the duomo, with porticoed streets and frescoed medieval buildings. The duomo was ruthlessly modernized in the 18th century, but the Romanesque cloisters are intact. Local artists created the frescoes in the 1390s and there are more examples in the 11th-century baptistery. The duomo's treasure is kept in the Museo Diocesano, in the 13th-century Bishop's Palace.

You can sample a local wine at the Abbazia di Novacella, just north of town.
Don't miss The collection of crib figures in the duomo's crypt.

CIVIDALE DEL FRIULI

435 J3 Piazza Paolo Diacono 10, 33043 Cividale del Friuli, tel 0432 710460; Mon–Fri 9–1, 3–6 Cividale del Friuli

A few miles from the Slovenian border, delightful Cividale (7km/10 miles east of Udine), founded by Julius Caesar in 50BC, is little known to visitors. Its medieval streets and squares line the banks of the River Natisone, and it is one of the few places in Italy with tangible reminders of the Lombards (▷ 31). This Teutonic race invaded in the sixth century, embraced Christianity and left behind some of the finest Lombard carvings in Italy.

Simply walking around Cividale is a pleasure; it is small enough to get your bearings but big enough to have some great architecture. The river, spanned by the Ponte del Diavolo (Devil's Bridge), is particularly pretty. Cividale's sights lie west of the river; the pearl is the Tempietto Longobardo (Lombard Temple), whose eighth-century stucco arch, with gently smiling saints, is a peerless example of Lombard art. There is more Lombard carving in the Museo Cristiano (in the precincts of the 15th-century duomo), notably the baptismal font of Callisto and the altar of Ratchis, a haunting masterpiece. The main museum is the Museo Archeologico Nazionale, where finds from Lombard tombs include stunning examples of carving and intricate jewellery.

The illuminated Fontana del Nettuno in Piazza Maggiore

BOLOGNA

Capital of Emilia-Romagna, known for its beauty, wealth and fine cuisine, as well as for its left-wing politics. An ancient settlement full of history.

Bologna is endowed with beautiful streetscapes—arcades of mellow brick and stone, juxtaposed with the stark shapes characteristic of the high-tech industry that generates the money that sustains the expensive restaurants and elegant shops. Bologna is a classic Roman city that, after the Dark Ages, became a free *comune* and subsequently, in the 15th century, gave way to rule by an individual family, the Bentivoglio, until annexed by the Papal States. Its university is one of Europe's oldest and is of great importance.

THE MEDIEVAL CORE

The compact historic core is medieval in plan, scattered with churches, monuments, civic buildings and museums. Elegant porticoed streets radiate from two main squares, Piazza Maggiore and Piazza del Nettuno, with most of interest to visitors on the eastern side of the city. Around Piazza del Nettuno, named after Giambologna's Fontana del Nettuno, rise medieval civic palaces. Behind it, Piazza Maggiore is dominated by the late Gothic church of San Petronio, the Palazzo dei Notai, home to 14th-century lawyers, and the Museo Civico Archeologico (Tue–Sat 9–6.30, Sun 10–6.30). Farther east are some of the loveliest streets and buildings—a series of porticoes punctuated by attractive squares. Head for Via Clavatura, with its tempting food stands, before exploring the Archiginnasio complex, the oldest part of the university. More arcades lead south to the church of San Domenico, built in 1251 to house the relics of the saint, enclosed in the superb Arca di San Domenico, sculpted by Pisano and the young Michelangelo. Only two of the dozens of towers from the Middle Ages survive; climb Torre degli Asinelli (Apr–end Oct daily 9–6; rest of year daily 9–5) for great views. From here the university quarter is within striking distance.

THE UNIVERSITY

Via Zamboni leads to the heart of the university, in the medieval palaces. Palazzo Poggi has two quirky museums (summer daily 10–3; rest of year Tue–Fri 10–5, tel 051 209 9398): an idiosyncratic assemblage of anatomical waxworks, and the Specola, an observatory.

BASICS

✚ 436 G5

ℹ Piazza Maggiore 1, 40124 Bologna tel 051 246541; daily 9–8

🚩 Bologna

www.bolognaturismo.info
The tourist office has a range of books, gifts and quality souvenirs for sale.

TIPS

● Bologna makes few concessions to tourists, so don't expect cheap accommodation or restaurants, other than in the university area. It is vital to reserve a hotel in advance as rooms are in constant demand during trade fairs.
● Two organizations provide 2-hour guided walks (in English) from the tourist office in Piazza Maggiore. No reservations required.
● There are 40-minute tours of the Museo della Specola at the university. For information about tours in English, tel 051 209 9398.

Bicycles are a common sight in the medieval town of Ferrara

Castel Tirolo (Schloss Tirol) in Merano was built in the 12th century for the Counts of Tyrol and is now the museum of Tyrolean history

THE SIGHTS

CONEGLIANO

✚ 435 H3 ℹ Via XX Settembre 61, 31015 Conegliano, tel 0438 21230
🚂 Conegliano
www.conegliano2000.it/inglese/index.htm
www.marcatreviso.it

Low-key but prosperous, Conegliano is a beguiling mix of simple buildings and expensive antique shops. It's an excellent stop en route north through the Veneto. The town perches on the edge of the hilly area, 33km (20 miles) north of Treviso, surrounded by vineyards that produce the best *prosecco*, a light, dry, sparkling wine. You can follow the Strada del Prosecco west to Valdobbiadene.

Conegliano neatly splits into a medieval and Renaissance old town and a grander, neoclassical quarter. In the old section, the Contrada Grande/Via XX Settembre, is an arcaded street lined with palazzi, restaurants and shops. The duomo, with a 14th-century frescoed portico, lies west of the main square, Piazza Cima. Farther uphill is the birthplace of Conegliano's most famous resident, the High Renaissance painter Giambattista Cima (c1459–1517). Look for his *Sacra Conversazione* in the duomo. Above town looms the *castello* (castle), now the town's museum. The collection is unexciting, but the views enjoyed while strolling uphill are superb.

FERRARA

✚ 434 G5 ℹ Castello Estense, 44100 Ferrara, tel 0532 299303 🚂 Ferrara
www.ferrarainfo.com

A major player on the Renaissance political scene, Ferrara was ruled by the dynamic d'Este family. Their court was one of Europe's most prosperous, and their money paid for the palaces and artistic treasures that are scattered around. Beautiful Romanesque façades, excellent museums, medieval streets and gracious piazzas make up the city.

Ferrara stands on the banks of the Po di Volano, an offshoot of the River Po, 55km (35 miles) northeast of Bologna. Within the walls, which can be explored on foot or by bicycle, the city is divided by the Viale Cavour/Corso Giovacca. Most sights of interest lie in the *centro storico* to the south. Start at Castello Estense, a bulky, moated 14th-century fortification with sumptuous state apartments and spooky dungeons. Nearby, the cathedral has a beautiful Romanesque-Gothic façade and an interior of 18th-century ornate gold. Follow the vaulted Via delle Volte south to the Palazzo Schifanoia, a former Este summer palace, or cross the Viale Cavour to the Palazzo dei Diamanti, where there are four museums, including the Pinacoteca Nazionale, tracing the history of painting in Ferrara.

MERANO (MERAN)

✚ 434 G2 ℹ Corso Libertà 45, 39012 Merano, tel 0473 272000
🚂 Merano/Meran
www.meraninfo.it

If you plan to explore the Alto-Adige (Südtirol) and want a base with a touch of sophistication, Merano is a good choice. It has chic shops (with an Austrian accent), restaurants and hotels, a lively cultural scene, gracious architecture and pretty gardens. This mountain-ringed town, with an unexpected Mediterranean-type micro-climate, found a new role for itself in the 1800s as a major spa resort. Elegant thermal buildings, solid villas and civic buildings were built around its medieval heart, and parks and promenades were laid out.

The town lies on the banks of the Passirio River, 30km (19 miles) northwest of Bolzano (▷ 104). The buildings of the medieval core cluster around the 14th-century duomo, while 13th- and 14th-century arcaded streets run parallel to the river. Passeggiata d'Estate and Passeggiata d'Inverno are two beautiful garden walks laid out in the 1860s and the 1870s, while the 4km (2.5-mile) Tappeiner promenade runs north above the town. The terraced Trautmansdorff Botanical Gardens are planted with shrubs and trees from all over the world.

MODENA

✚ 436 F5 ℹ Via Scudari 12, 41100 Modena, tel 0592 032660 🚂 Modena
www.comune.modena.it/infoturismo

Modena, a quietly prosperous town along the Via Emilia, makes a good outing from Bologna, 55km (35 miles) southeast (▷ 105), or a pleasant stopping point en route to Lombardy. Historically Modena is a rival to Bologna, but it has an entirely different atmosphere. It has a splendid Romanesque cathedral, tranquil arcaded squares, baroque palaces and an excellent museum complex. Today's money comes from the knitwear, ceramics and Ferrari car factories on its outskirts. Modena's most famous modern citizen, the opera singer Luciano Pavarotti, gives the occasional summer concert here. It is good for shopping and there are some excellent restaurants and bars.

The town's historic core is split by the Via Emilia. To the south is Piazza Grande, with arcades and elegant cafés. Alongside is the magnificent 12th-century Romanesque duomo, with a leaning tower and fine carving. The web of medieval streets and pleasant squares makes Modena a serendipitous place to explore.

Cortina d'Ampezzo is surrounded by splendid peaks. It is well served by cable cars and is great for skiing, but it comes at a price

DOLOMITES

Europe's most dramatic and beautiful mountains. Jagged pinnacles and needle-sharp rock formations. Skiing in winter, high-altitude hiking and rock-climbing in summer.

Fertile green valleys, villages of wooden houses with window boxes dripping with geraniums, swathes of mountain flowers and air like champagne make the Dolomites an outdoor feast. Geologically different from the rest of the Alps, the Dolomites are composed of ancient coral reefs, formed beneath the seabed 250 million years ago and uplifted 190 million years later. Wind, ice and storms acted on the relatively soft, pinky-orange limestone, creating the astounding shapes that are so distinctive. The lower slopes are wooded or covered in alpine pasture, and vines and apples are cultivated in the fertile valley.

YEAR-ROUND ACTIVITIES

In the 20th century the massifs developed into a year-round recreational area. There are ski resorts and a good network of cable cars and lifts. There are pistes to suit all levels and there is cross-country skiing, sledging and tobogganing in the valleys. The walking is some of the best in Europe, with a network of scenic trails. Accessed by cable cars and lifts, they are linked by *rifugi alpini* (mountain refuges, end Jun–end Sep). By using the refuges, you can walk the *alte vie*, eight long-distance trails.

THE DIFFERENT REGIONS

The Italian-speaking Cadore Dolomites lie north of Belluno in the Veneto. The main resort is the glitzy Cortina d'Ampezzo, venue for the 1956 Winter Olympics.

In the western Dolomites, Trento (▷ 111) and Bolzano (▷ 104) are two beautiful main towns. The Val di Fassa is the heart of the old Ladino region. An exhibition at the Castel de Tor Museum is dedicated to this unique culture; the Ladino language is still alive, and each valley has its own dialect. To the west rises the Catinaccio/Rosengarten Massif, one of the most dramatic ranges. The main areas of the Brenta group are Madonna di Campiglio and Molveno. Dramatic rock formations, summer walking and winter sports make the area very popular. The most important valleys are the Val di Sole, with meadows and pretty villages, and the wooded Val di Non.

RATINGS				
Good for kids	●	●	●	○
Outdoor pursuits	●	●	●	●
Photo stops	●	●	●	●

BASICS

✚ 434 G2

ℹ Piazza Duomo 2, 32100 Beluno, tel 0437 940083; Piazzetta San Francesco 8, 32043 Cortina d'Ampezzo, tel 0436 3231; daily 9–12.30, 3.30–6.30

🚉 Trento, Bolzano/Bolzen, Merano/Meran

www.infodolomiti.it
A multilingual site helping you to pick an area in the Dolomites that best suits you. They have photographs of all the different areas and provide good information on ski resorts, road, air and rail links and visitor itineraries.

www.fassa.it
www.sunrise.it/dolomiti
www.dolomitimolveno.it
www.vinschgau.suedtirol.com
www.dolomitipark.it

TIPS

● If you plan some serious walking, invest in good maps (available in most villages—Kompass maps are excellent) and take proper equipment and provisions.
● Remember that even over short distances driving can take time as the roads are twisty.
● It is worth learning a few basic German phrases.

RATINGS

Historic interest	● ● ● ●
Cultural interest	● ● ● ●
Photo stops	● ● ●
Walkability	● ● ●

BASICS

✚ 434 G4

🚉 **Railway station:** Stazione Ferroviaria, 35100 Padova, tel 049 875 2077; Galleria Pedrocchi, Padova, tel 049 876 7927; Mon–Sat 9–7, 3–6, Sun 9–12

🚃 Padova

www.turismopadova.it

TIPS

● Driving in Padua is confusing and parking a problem, so come by train. The station is about 10 minutes' walk from the centre and there are buses.
● The main tourist office is in the station, so pick up a map as soon as you arrive.
● Access to the Cappella degli Scrovegni is limited to 25 people at a time; advance reservations are vital during the high season and advisable all year round (tel 049 820 4550).

MAKE A DAY OF IT

Venice: ▷ 81–102
Vicenza: ▷ 114

The Basilica di Sant'Antonio (above) was dedicated to St. Anthony, a preacher who modelled himself on Francis of Assisi

PADOVA (PADUA)

Famous for Giotto's frescoes in the Scrovegni Chapel and its Byzantine basilica, a historic pilgrimage site. A university city with the most vibrant nightlife in the area and some of the best markets in Italy.

Historic Padua, the Veneto's most important economic hub and an ancient university city, combines lively, spacious squares and narrow, medieval streets with important works of art and monuments, elegant shops, buzzing markets and green spaces. With its efficient transport connections, it is also a good base for exploring the region.

WHERE TO GO

Padua's overlords were the Da Carrara family from 1337 until the capture of the city by the Venetian Republic in 1405. Great cultural patrons, they attracted stars such as Giotto, Dante and Petrarch, and Padua remained a cultural focus even after the fall of the city. Many people come only to see Giotto's frescoes in the Cappella degli Scrovegni and the Venetian art collections in the Musei Civici; others head straight for the attractive squares, Piazza della Frutta and Piazza dell'Erbe. The two are divided by the bulk of the 13th-century Palazzo della Ragione or Il Salone (Tue–Sun 9–7), ringed with cafés, bars and shops. The eclectic Caffè Pedrocchi on Via VIII Febbraio was once Padua's main intellectual salon (Tue–Fri 9.30–12.30, 3.30–6, Sat–Sun 9.30–12.30, 3.30–7; bar: daily 8am–11pm).

BASILICA DI SANT'ANTONIO

The Basilica di Sant'Antonio (or Il Santo) is one of Italy's main pilgrim shrines (Apr–end Oct daily 6.30am–7.45pm; Nov–end Mar daily 6.30am–7pm, tel 049 824 2811), begun after the death in 1232 of St. Anthony of Padua. In the square is Donatello's equestrian bronze of mercenary Erasmo de Narni, known as *Gattamelata (Honey Cat)*.

GIOTTO AND THE VENETIAN SCHOOL

Padua's most precious jewels are in Cappella degli Scrovegni (daily 9–7, tel 049 201 0020) and the adjoining Museo Civico on Piazza Eremitani (daily 9am–7pm). Between 1303 and 1309 Giotto painted a series of scenes in the chapel from the life of Christ and the Virgin. Like his Assisi cycle (▷ 137) this marked a turning point in Western art, introducing a naturalism not seen in the stylized art of the Middle Ages. The museum's excellent collection of works by Paduan and Venetian artists includes a Giotto crucifix and two exquisite Giorgione paintings.

Detail of the Byzantine frescoes in the baptistery in Parma

Sun worship on one of Rimini's many beaches

PARCO NAZIONALE DELLO STELVIO

✚ 434 F2 ℹ Comitato di Gestione per la Provincia Autonoma di Bolzano, Piazza Municipio 1, 39020 Glorenza, tel 0473 830430
www.stelviopark.it

The Parco Nazionale dello Stelvio embraces the entire Ortles range, sprawling across Lombardy, Trentino and the Alto-Adige (Südtirol). It is one of Italy's most important and largest national parks, ideal for winter sports and spectacular summer walking. The landscape includes high peaks, fertile valleys, woodland, more than 50 lakes and 100 glaciers. There is a great deal of diversity in the animal and plantlife here. The park is criss-crossed with superb hiking trails, and many visitors head away from the roads, spending nights in *rifugi alpini* (mountain refuges).

The Ortles (3,950m/12,960ft) are south of the Val Venosta (Vinschgau), a broad valley east of Merano (▷ 106). Three roads thread through the foothills from the valley into the massif: Val Martello, Val d'Ultimo and Val di Solda. These are jumping-off points for the park. In summer drivers can cross the park via Passo dello Stelvio (2,758m/ 9,050ft), the second-highest pass in the Alps (early Jul to mid-Sep). Begin your explorations at the park's main information office in Glorenza, a miniature walled city. The whole area is very Austrian and, away from the tourist areas, it helps to speak some German.

PARMA

✚ 434 F5 ℹ Via Melloni 1, 43100 Parma, tel 0521 218889 🚉 Parma
www.turismo.comune.parma.it/turismo

Parma's name is synonymous with *prosciutto* (Parma ham) and *parmigiano* (Parmesan cheese).

But this rich, cultured provincial city also has artistic treasures and a strong musical tradition. The old city has a beautiful cathedral, Renaissance palaces, and a famous opera house. It also has good designer shops.

Parma's three most famous residents are the artists Corregio (c1490–1534) and Parmigianino (1503–40) and the musician Artur Toscanini (1867–1957).

The elegant, pedestrianized streets at the heart of the city are on the east of the River Parma. The three main piazzas—della Pace, Duomo and Garibaldi—are as different in themselves as Parma's most important monuments. Most notable are the 11th-century duomo (daily 9–12.30, 3–7), a lovely Lombard-Romanesque church with interior frescoes by Corregio, and the beautiful octagonal 12th-century baptistery, built of pink Verona marble with sculpted friezes. This simple ensemble contrasts with the Renaissance magnificence of Santa Maria della Steccata and its frescoes by Parmigianino (daily 9–12, 3–6). Also important are the well-displayed artistic pieces in the Palazzo della Pilotta, the perfectly restored Renaissance Teatro Farnese and, across the river, in verdant parkland, the Palazzo Ducale (Mon–Sat 9–12). The Casa Natale e Musei di Arturo Toscanini, the birthplace of Tocanini, is not far from here on Via Rodolfo Tanzi.

PIACENZA

✚ 433 E4 ℹ Piazza Cavalli, 29100 Piacenza, tel 0523 329324 🚉 Piacenza
www.comune.piacenza.it
www.provincia.piacenza.it

Piacenza is a perfect example of Emilia-Romagna's unostentatious, prosperous provincial towns. It is off the main tourist trail, near the Lombardy border. The Roman town marked the end of the Via

Emilia, a major military road. In the Middle Ages it flourished as a free city, then came under the control of the Farnese and the Bourbons, and was the first town to join the embryonic Italian state in 1848 (▷ 38). With fine medieval buildings and churches, a couple of museums and good shops, it is a great place to stop and sample the local cooking.

Piacenza, in the flat Po Valley, is misty and raw in winter and baking hot in summer. The Lombard-Gothic, red brick Palazzo del Comune dates from 1280, as does the church of San Francesco. From the piazza, Via XX Settembre leads to Piazza del Duomo, scene of a weekly market.

RAVENNA

See page 110.

RIMINI

✚ 437 H6 ℹ Piazza Federico Fellini 3, 47900 Rimini, tel 0541 56902 🚉 Rimini
www.riminiturismo.it

Rimini's beaches, 51km (32 miles) south of Ravenna, stretch for more than 16km (10 miles), a strip of hotels, arcades, shops, restaurants and clubs. In peak season the resort heaves with noisy crowds day and night; off-season, it is dead. The beach has very few free areas but many privately owned *stabilimenti*, fenced-off areas that you pay to use. The hotels are good, but there is virtually no accommodation available in August, as Italian families pour in. Some parts of town have a bad reputation after dark.

If hedonism doesn't appeal, explore the amphitheatre, palazzi and the Renaissance Tempio Malatestiano, an unusual building that served as a chapel and a monument to Sigismondo Malatesta, a 15th-century mercenary of the worst kind.

A mosaic dating from AD450 in the Mausoleum of Galla Placidia

RATINGS

Historic interest	●●●○
Cultural interest	●●●○
Walkability	●●○

BASICS

✚ 437 H6

🛈 Via Salara 8–12, tel 0544 35404;
Mon–Sat 8.30–7, Sun 10–4

🚉 Ravenna

www.turismo.ravenna.it
A bright website in Italian and English
with all you need to know about
Ravenna; the city and mosaics, the
coast, the flora and fauna, the latest
events, accommodation and tourist
information services.

TIPS

● Reserve tickets in advance
if you want to visit the
Mausoleum of Galla Placidia
between 1 March and 15 June
(tel 0544 219938). At busy
times you will only have a few
minutes inside.
● The Ravenna Visitcard is a
combined ticket for all the
main sights. Buy it at any of
the sights in low season or
reserve in advance.
● To see the mosaics at
Sant'Apollinare in Classe, take
bus 4 or 44 (hourly) from
outside the railway station.
● The main sights are floodlit
and open on Friday evenings
throughout July and August.

RAVENNA

**Capital of the Roman Empire, later ruled by Byzantine
Constantinople.
The world's most accomplished Byzantine mosaics, decorating
fifth- and sixth-century churches and monuments.**

In AD402, with the imperial court installed at Milan and the Roman
Empire threatened by invaders from the north, Emperor Honorius
decided to move his capital to Ravenna, an easily defensible marshland
town near the important naval base of Classis, on the Adriatic coast.
After the fall of Rome in AD410, Ravenna became the imperial capital,
fittingly ornamented with lavish monuments. The city fell to the Goths
in AD476, but they, too, were Christian and pursued the building
design, a process continued by the Byzantines after their annexation of
Ravenna in the sixth century. The city later came under Venetian
control, but was sacked in the 16th century and absorbed into the
Papal States, becoming part of Italy after 1870. Ravenna was heavily
bombed in World War II and it has been extensively rebuilt, but it still
has an important port, 12km (8 miles) from the old city.

THE MOSAICS

The most important sites date from fifth- and sixth-century Roman,
Ostrogoth and Byzantine eras, and are UNESCO World Heritage Sites.
They are scattered around the Piazza del Popolo, where shoppers on
bicycles weave in front of outdoor cafés. A few minutes' walk south is
the complex of the Basilica of San Vitale, the Mausoleum of Galla
Placidia (▶ 31) and the Museo Nazionale.

San Vitale (daily 9–7) was begun in 525 under the Roman
emperor Theodoric and completed by the Byzantine ruler Justinian in
548. It is typically Byzantine, with a central dome supported by eight
columns. The apse is covered with glowing mosaics showing Christ,
the Apostles, and biblical scenes in the choir, while the side walls are
covered in processional scenes. Across the grass is the Mausoleum of
Galla Placidia, half-sister of Honorius. Tiny and jewel-like, it is richly
ornamented with blue and gold mosaics. Also important is the
Basilica of Sant'Apollinare Nuovo (daily 9–7), built in the sixth century
by Theodoric; mosaics high above the nave show martyrs bearing
gifts for Christ and the Virgin. There are more mosaics in the
baptisteries, and a short bus ride away, at Classe, in the evocative
Basilica di Sant'Apollinare (Mon–Sat 8.30–7.30, Sun 1–7.30).

The copper cupolas of Treviso's duomo, originally built in the Middle Ages and rebuilt between the 15th and 18th centuries

Modern architecture and funky stained glass in Trieste Airport

TRENTO

✚ 434 G3 ℹ️ Via Alfieri 4, 38100 Trento, tel 0461 983880 🚉 Trento
www.apt.trento.it
www.provincia.tn.it/turismo

Capital of Trentino, and 150km (93 miles) north of Verona, Trento stands on the River Adige, surrounded by green hills. Ruled for centuries by prince-bishops, the town rose to prominence when Bishop Bernardo Cles made it the meeting place for the 16th-century Council of Trent, the Counter-Reformation movement. He opened up the old medieval town with the construction of Via Belenzani, which cuts a straight line through to Piazza Duomo, site of the Romanesque duomo.

At the foot of the hills is Castello del Buonconsiglio, the prince-bishops' residence and one of the first castle-palaces in Italy. Its courtyards, loggias and sumptuous state apartments form the perfect setting for Trento's greatest artistic work, the ravishing fresco cycle *The Months of the Year* (c1400), full of flirting nobility and working peasants.

For a change of pace, take the cable car up Monte Bondone to see the alpine plants in the botanical garden at Viotte.

TREVISO

✚ 435 H4 ℹ️ Piazza Monte di Pietà 8, tel 0422 547632 🚉 Treviso
www.provincia.treviso.it
www.marcatreviso.it

With frescoed façades, porticoed streets and shimmering waterways, historic Treviso is quite different from nearby towns. Modern money comes from knitwear—Treviso is home to Benetton (▷ 17)—while past glories are reflected in fine early Gothic buildings and Renaissance churches. The city was painstakingly rebuilt after bombing in World War II, and there is a

great sense of the new Italy here, with relics of the past co-existing happily with casual, stylish wealth. The excellent shops include tempting delicatessens, and the nightlife buzzes.

Treviso is ringed by Venetian-built walls, bordered by the River Sile. Willow-fringed branches of the river weave through the old town, at the heart of which is the Piazza dei Signori. Here is the Palazzo dei Trecento, first built in 1217, and behind are the churches of San Vito and Santa Lucia, with superb frescoes by the 14th-century Tommaso da Modena, considered the finest artist of his age after Giotto. To the east is a maze of streets and waterways around the bustling market (don't miss the *pescheria*, fish market). Calmaggiore is an attractive arcaded street with fine shops. At the far end, the duomo has a Titian *Annunciation*, but more interesting artistically is the Dominican church of San Nicolò, rich with frescoes.

TRIESTE

✚ 435 K4 ℹ️ Piazza Unità d'Italia 4B, 34121 Trieste, tel 040 347 8312; daily 9.30–7 🚉 Trieste ✈️ Trieste R dei Legionari (TRS)
www.triestetourism.it

Trieste was built by the Austrians as a port. Its slightly battered neoclassical streets and buildings contrast with a clutch of Roman remains and a dramatic medieval castle and cathedral. With its café culture, literary associations (writer James Joyce lived here) and contrasting socialist and right-wing politics, Trieste is border territory—a mix of cultures, languages and allegiances that straddles the bridge between the Mediterranean world and that of Teutonic and Slavic central Europe. With exceptionally friendly people and great food, it is an ideal base for

exploring the Carso, a plateau that stretches into Slovenia.

Trieste's position is stunning, with a grid of 18th-century streets, the Borgo Teresiano, nestling between the sea and a limestone plateau. Piazza Unità d'Italia is a splendid square, open on one side to the sea. Behind rises the hill of San Giusto, where you find the city's oldest buildings with the best sea views. Highlights are the Romanesque Cattedrale di San Giusto, Venetian mosaics and a 13th-century fresco cycle in the Capella di San Giusto, and the Risiera di San Sabba, a thought-provoking museum in a World War II concentration camp.

UDINE

✚ 435 J3 ℹ️ Piazza I Maggio 7, 33100 Udine, tel 0432 295972 🚉 Udine
www.udine-turismo.it

More Italian in spirit than Trieste, Udine is the second city of Friuli-Venezia Giulia. It is a provincial town with more than a touch of Venetian style—arcaded streets, canals, restaurants and a relaxed pace make it worth exploring. It is also a stronghold of Friulian nationalism—listen for Slovenian influences in the dialect.

The sprawling outskirts might put you off, but the *centro storico* is unspoiled. It is overshadowed by the *castello*, said to have been built with soil carried in the helmets of Attila's invading Huns (▷ 30). Reach it from Piazza della Libertà, described as the most beautiful Venetian square on *terra firma*: The striped Loggia del Lionello echoes the Doge's Palace (▷ 93–95); there is a lion of St. Mark, and a fine Palladio gateway leading past a Venetian Gothic gallery to the castle.
Don't miss Tiepolo's *Abraham and the Sacrifice of Isaac*, in the Palazzo.

Verona

●

**Impressive Roman remains, medieval castles and Romanesque and Renaissance churches and palaces.
A beautiful city, the setting of Shakespeare's *Romeo and Juliet*.
Streets lined with expensive shops and fashionable restaurants.**

Verona's Roman amphitheatre has capacity for 22,000 people

SEEING VERONA

Beautiful Verona—Roman ruins, rose-red medieval buildings and romantic dreams of young love—is the largest city in mainland Veneto, a quietly prosperous, cultured place where tourism plays second fiddle to the rest of the economy. Most of its historic heart is enclosed by a loop of the River Adige, with a few other important sights on the north bank. Wonderful churches and buildings are scattered throughout the pleasant streets, which are themselves punctuated by lovely squares.

RATINGS

Historic interest	●	●	●	●
Specialist shopping	●	●	●	●
Walkability	●	●	●	●
Good for food	●	●	●	●

BASICS

✚ 434 F4

🛈 Via degli Alpini 9 (Piazza Brà), 37121 Verona, tel 045 806 8680; Mon–Sat 9–5, Sun 9–3

🚉 Verona

www.tourism.verona.it
You can send e-cards, get the latest weather forecast or get the latest view over Piazza Brà via the webcam at this website dedicated to Verona and Lake Garda. It also has a guide for visitors and information on accommodation, regional food and wine, events and sport. Italian, English and German versions.

HGHLIGHTS

THE ARENA

Piazza Brà, 37121 Verona ☎ 045 800 3204 ⏱ Sep–end Jun Mon 1.45–6.30, Tue–Sun 8.30–6.30; Jul, Aug (opera season) daily 9–3.30; closed to visitors during performances 🎫 Adult €4, child €1
Piazza Brà should be your first stop, an irregular open space dominated by one of the city's best-known monuments, the great Roman amphitheatre. Built in the first century AD, it is the third-largest of the surviving Roman amphitheatres in Italy. A 13th-century earthquake destroyed most of the exterior arcade, but the interior is intact, with steeply pitched tiers of pink marble seats and dizzying views from the top. Since 1913 people have flocked to Verona to catch a performance during its summer opera season.

BASILICA DI SAN ZENO MAGGIORE

Piazza San Zeno, 37121 Verona ⏱ Mon–Sat 8.30–5, Sun 1–6 🎫 €2.10
Farther west from Castelvecchio stands San Zeno Maggiore, a Romanesque church founded in the fourth century that attained its present form around 1398; a set of superb 11th-century bronze doors open into a lofty interior with Roman columns and an altarpiece by Andrea Mantegna (c1431–1506). The church is the burial place of Pepin the Short, king of the Franks. Father of Charlemagne and founder of the Frankish dynasty of the Carolingians, he led his army into Italy to defeat the Lombards in AD754.

PIAZZA DELLE ERBE

From Piazza Brà, Via Mazzini, an elegant and tempting pedestrian-only shopping street, leads north to Piazza delle Erbe, the setting for a lively daily market, and Piazza dei Signori, the heart of medieval Verona. Piazza delle Erbe is surrounded by exquisite buildings: The Torre dei Lamberti soars above the brightly frescoed Casa Mazzanti, and there is a loggia, a 14th-century fountain and a fine Lion of St. Mark.

PIAZZA DEI SIGNORI

From Piazza delle Erbe an arch leads to the old civic area, the Piazza dei Signori, the focus of which is a statue of the Renaissance poet

Dante Alighieri (1265–1321). The candy-striped Palazzo della Ragione has a fine Romanesque-Gothic courtyard. The building behind Dante is the Renaissance Loggia del Consiglio dating from 1493, with the Tribunale next to it. Don't overlook the Scaligeri tombs, next to the Tribunale, covered with statuary and Scaligeri emblems, dogs and ladders.

Cangrande II's Ponte Scaligero on the River Adige near Castelvecchio (below left)

CASA DI GIULIETTA
Via Capello 23, 37121 Verona ⏰ Tue–Sun 9–7, Mon 1.30–7.30 💰 €3.10

The ivy-clad walls and balcony of the Casa di Giulietta (below)

From Piazza delle Erbe, Via Cappello leads southeast to the so-called Casa di Giulietta (House of Juliet), a graffiti-adorned mecca for love-sick teenagers and bus tours; the balcony was added in 1935.

LA CATTEDRALE
⏰ Mon–Sat 10–6, Sun 1–6 💰 €2.10
On the northern point of the promontory is the Romanesque cathedral, which has a beautiful apse and a fine *Assumption* by Titian in the first chapel of the north aisle.

BACKGROUND

Verona is on the River Adige, 50km (30 miles) west of Vicenza, at the bottom of an Alpine pass, and was first colonized by the Romans in 89BC. It became a regional capital and survived the Ostrogoth and Frankish invasions of AD489 and AD754, becoming a free *comune* in 1107. Feuds and vendettas between the city's noble families dominated the next century or so and provided the basis for William Shakespeare's tale of doomed love, *Romeo and Juliet*, set in Verona. By the late 1200s one family had emerged as top dogs, the Scaligeris, a terrifyingly successful mercenary clan who named themselves after dogs. They were ousted in their turn by the Milanese Viscontis in 1387. In 1402, having had their fill of lords, Verona turned to republican Venice, and remained part of *La Serenissima* (the Venetian Republic) until 1797, after which the city passed to the Austrians, who retained control until 1866, when Verona and Venice became part of the new Kingdom of Italy. The city was badly bombed during World War II, but quickly recovered to become one of Italy's outstanding economic success stories.

TIPS
● The historic heart is closed to traffic for most of the day, so come by train or use the parking area near the station.
● You can rent a bicycle in Piazza Brà (tel 333 536 7770).
● The Verona Card, valid for a day or a week, includes unlimited travel and museum admissions and is available from the tourist office. Pick up a free copy of *Passport Verona* for up-to-date listings.
● Verona is the venue for plays and musical events all year round, including great jazz and rock concerts, often in historic monuments and in open spaces outdoors. In July and August there is opera in the amphitheatre.
● Verona has a great café scene and is much livelier in the evenings than Venice. It is also a better bet for buying clothes.

RATINGS

Historic interest	● ● ●
Cultural interest	● ● ● ●
Photo stops	● ● ●
Walkability	● ● ●

BASICS

✚ 434 G4

🛈 Piazza Matteoti 12, 36100 Vicenza, tel 0444 320854; Piazza dei Signori 8, 36100 Vicenza, tel 0444 544122; daily 9–1, 2–6

🚉 Vicenza

www.vicenzae.org

TIPS

● Reserve hotels in advance—Vicenza has surprisingly few and it is a big conference city.
● A Vicenza Card, a combined ticket, costs €7 and gives entrance to all the main attractions at big reductions.
● There are parking areas at the east and west ends of town—catch the shuttle bus into town.
● Touring Club Italiano has produced a guidebook to the villas of Andrea Palladio in Vicenza and its province. It is available from tourist information offices, bookshops or direct from the TCI (www.touringclub.it).

MAKE A DAY OF IT

Padua: ▷ 108

Relief work on the pediment of a building topped with statues, with a copper spire behind, in the Piazza dei Signori

VICENZA

A UNESCO World Heritage Site, home to some of the finest examples of Palladio's neoclassical architecture.

In 1404, under threat from stronger forces in Padua, Verona and Milan, the free *comune* of Vicenza offered itself to Venice and became a satellite city. As a Venetian possession, the city was given Gothic palaces, but its big architectural makeover came in the 16th century, when Andrea Palladio (1508–80) started to develop his own classical style. Palladio was born in Padua, but found his major patron, the humanist nobleman Trissino, in Vicenza. Between 1549 and his death in 1580 he transformed the face of the city.

PALLADIO'S CLASSICAL MASTERPIECES

Corso Andrea Palladio, lined with superb palazzi, ends at Piazza Matteoti. Palazzo Chiericati, designed by Palladio in 1550, now contains the Museo Civico, with paintings by Tintoretto, Tiepolo and Veronese (Tue–Sun 9–5). Across the piazza is the Teatro Olimpico, Europe's oldest indoor theatre, opened in 1585 (Tue–Sun 9–5). Palladio died before it was complete, but his designs inspired the astonishing *trompe l'oeil* backdrop—it appears to be hundreds of metres deep, but it only stretches back 15m (50ft).

PALLADIO'S BASILICA

At the heart of the *centro storico* is Piazza dei Signori, site of Palladio's dazzling basilica, his first major project and the one that made his reputation, and the stunning double-tiered Loggia del Capitaniato.

PALAZZI

Fruit and vegetables have been sold in the Piazza dell'Erbe since medieval times. Near here on Contrà Porti and Contrà Riale are several palaces, the finest of which are the Palazzo Thiene, Palazzo Barbaran (Museo Palladiano, Tue–Sun 10–6) and Palazzo Colleoni Porto. The fine baroque Palazzo Montanari contains the other main museum, exhibiting Longhi genre paintings (Tue–Sun 10–6). Notable churches include the reconstructed duomo (the original was destroyed in World War II), 13th-century Santa Corona, notable for its paintings by Bellini and Veronese, and Santo Stefano. The hill to the south is Monte Bérico, an important plague shrine topped by a 17th-century basilica. Nearby, is Andrea Palladio's famous Villa Capra (1567), also known as the Villa Rotonda because of its symmetrical plan with a central circular hall.

FLORENCE

Florence was the birthplace of the Renaissance and the focal point of creative activity for some of the world's greatest artistic talents. The city's churches and museums contain familiar masterpieces, while the narrow streets are lined with splendid palaces and elegant shops. Highlights are the Duomo, the Piazza della Signoria and the Galleria degli Uffizi.

MAJOR SIGHTS

Florence

ℹ Piazza Stazione 4 (opposite the railway station), 50123 Firenze, tel 055 212 245; Mon–Sat 8.30–7, Sun, public holidays 8.30–2. Borgo Santa Croce 29, 50122 Firenze, tel 055 234 4044; Mon–Sat 9–5, Sun, public holidays 9–2
www.firenzeturismo.it • Helpful English-language site

THE SIGHTS

HOW TO GET THERE

✈ Airports
Amerigo Vespucci (Peretola)
10km (6 miles) northwest of the city
Galileo Galilei, Pisa
80km (50 miles) west of the city (most international flights)

🚆 Railway stations
Stazione Centrale di Santa Maria Novella
The main station, centrally located, is adjacent to the city's public transit terminal.
www.trenitalia.com

The Duomo is an icon of the city

SEEING FLORENCE

The historic heart, *centro storico*, of Florence is compact and walkable. In fact, walking is often the only way to navigate the narrow pedestrian streets between its major landmarks. While a few are a bit farther—hop on a bus for the views from Piazale Michelangelo, and to visit San Miniato beyond it—most major sights are within a 0.5km (500-yard) radius of Piazza della Signoria. San Marco, the Accademia and Santa Maria Novella lie just outside this circle. Although these sights are close, do not underestimate the time it will take to see them. Most are multi-faceted, with many attractions within. And the lines for the most popular ones can add up to long hours of waiting unless you reserve ahead (locking you into a schedule) or arrive very early. Florence has become Italy's—perhaps Europe's—most popular destination for students and the very young, despite the fact that it offers few after-dark youth venues, lacking the lively club and music scene of Milan or Turin. These milling throngs of the under-20 set can fill and block an entire street or piazza; in the summer, simply picking a pathway up the few steps of the Duomo can be daunting.

BACKGROUND

Florence was a magnet for the brightest and best of Italy's artists, and it is the birthplace of the Italian Renaissance. Brunelleschi's brilliantly conceived dome changed the way domes were built ever after; Michelangelo coaxed hitherto unimagined power from marble; Ghiberti's baptistery doors opened a whole world of perspective in relief metalwork; and da Vinci painted the Mona Lisa here. Donatello, Giotto, Fra Angelica, Pisano, della Robbia and fellow artists created masterpiece after masterpiece in Florence.

The family that encouraged—and financed much of—this artistic flowering was the Medici, who began their rise in the 12th century. By the 13th, their acuity in banking and commerce had made them both rich and powerful, so by the 14th they were able to lead a revolt that made them virtual dictators, setting the stage for Cosimo il Vecchio. Popular and known for his largesse on the city's behalf, he set the standard that later generations would uphold, and Florence became Europe's cultural capital. Under grandson Lorenzo, the city reached even greater artistic heights, and by 1569, Cosimo I was the ruler of all Tuscany, with Florence as his capital. The Medici ruled Florence until the 1700s, although the city's prominence, both political and economical, had dwindled by then. Today, the city seems like one grand museum of that artistic legacy.

TIPS

● Be at the door when the most popular attractions open, before lines begin to form. For example, you can walk right into the Galleria dell'Accademia at 8.15 am.
● To avoid coach tours at major sights, arrive just after 12, when they schedule lunch.
● Have your hotel or restaurant phone a taxi for you; it is almost impossible to find one at a stand and they will not respond to telephone calls from individuals.

DON'T MISS

BRUNELLESCHI'S DOME
Even if you don't climb to the top, stand beneath its lantern and look up (▷ 118–121)

MUSEO DELL'OPERA DEL DUOMO
Michelangelo's most moving *pietà* and the original baptistery doors (▷ 120)

PIAZZALE MICHELANGELO
The classic view of the city (▷ 132)

GALLERIA DEGLI UFFIZI
Just the Florentine Renaissance artists can take all day (▷ 122–123)

GIARDINO DI BOBOLI
A peaceful respite, where the Medici played (▷ 124)

Detail of frescoes on the ceiling of the Badia Fiorentina

The Crucifixion before the Proconsul *in the Cappella Brancacci*

Funerary figures by Michelangelo in San Lorenzo

BADIA FIORENTINA

✚ 425 D3 • Via del Proconsolo, 50122 Firenze, tel 055 264402
🕐 Mon 5–6

The Benedictine abbey of Badia Fiorentina was founded by Willa, the widow of the Margrave of Tuscany, at the end of the 10th century to commemorate her husband. The church bell, mentioned by Dante in the *Paradiso*, sits inside the beautiful tower. The church opens for limited periods and it is undergoing restoration, but the art makes it worth a visit.

On the left of the entrance is Filippino Lippi's enchanting *Madonna Appearing to St. Bernard*. On the opposite wall is a sculpted marble altarpiece by Mino da Fiesole, the artist also responsible for the marble monument to Ugo, Willa's son and the benefactor of the church, in the left transept. A door to the right of the choir leads to the upper loggia of the Chiostro degli Aranci (Cloister of Oranges), a reminder that monks once grew orange trees in this peaceful setting. Designed by Bernardo Rossellino between 1432 and 1438, it has a well-preserved series of frescoes of scenes from the life of St. Benedict.

CAPPELLA BRANCACCI

✚ 424 A3 • Piazza del Carmine, 50125 Firenze, tel 055 238 2195 🕐 Mon–Sat 10–5, Sun and public holidays 1–5; last entrance 4.30
🎟 Adult €3.10, under 18s €1.50
www.museoragazzi.it

This small chapel at the end of the right transept of the church of Santa Maria del Carmine has some of the most significant works of Florentine Renaissance painting—the Cappella Brancacci frescoes. The church's exterior is dull—a rough stone façade rebuilt after a fire in 1771. The frescoes survived the fire and, thanks to restoration in the 1980s, are vibrant once again.

The chapel, so small that only 30 people can enter at one time, is covered with paintings by Masolino, Masaccio and Filippino Lippi. Certain sections date back to 1425. In particular, look for Masolino's *Temptation of Adam* and *Healing of the Cripple*, and Masaccio's *Expulsion of Adam and Eve*. The depiction of Adam and Eve being expelled from the Garden of Eden, and their consequent anguish, is particularly emotive.

CAPPELLE MEDICEE

✚ 424 C2 • Piazza Madonna degli Aldobrandini 2, 50123 Firenze, tel 055 294883 🕐 Daily 8.15–5; closed 2nd and 4th Sun and 1st, 3rd and 5th Mon of each month, 1 Jan, 1 May 🎟 Adult €6, under 18s free 🎫 🅿 Under Santa Maria Novella Station (5-minute walk) www.firenzemusei.it

The Medici's main monument, the Cappella dei Principi, is awesome in its dimensions and kitsch opulence, and provides ample proof of their wealthy egotism. This gloomy monstrosity can be appreciated for its sheer size. The other chapel, Sagrestia Nuova, is modest in comparison and has statues by Michelangelo.

The chapels are at the eastern end of the church of San Lorenzo, where most of the Medici family are buried. Glass cases display gold and silver objects from the church treasury, including beautifully crafted reliquaries and a 16th-century pearl-encrusted mitre. Stone steps lead to the entrance to the Cappella di Principi; the Grand Duke's octagonal mausoleum was begun in 1604, and is lined with marble and gems.

The Sagrestia Nuova has some superb examples of tombs and statues by Michelangelo. The tomb of Lorenzo, Duke of Urbino, is decorated with the famous reclining figures of *Dawn* and *Dusk*. The statues on the tomb opposite, that of Giuliano, Duke of Nemours, of *Day* and *Night* are considered by some to be Michelangelo's finest. The beautiful *Madonna and Child* is also by Michelangelo, along with the two candelabra on the altar.

CASA BUONAROTTI

A425 E3 • Via Ghibellina 70, 50122 Firenze, tel 055 241752 🕐 Fri–Wed 9.30–2 🎟 €6.50 🎫
www.casabuonarotti.it

The Casa Buonarotti is a typical Renaissance town house. Now the Michelangelo museum, it provides an interesting insight into the life and times of one of the world's most famous artists.

Michelangelo Buonarotti (1475–1564) bought the house in 1508. On his death he left the property and several works of art to his nephew Leonardo, who in turn left it to his son, also named Michelangelo. He was an art collector and in 1612 he turned part of the house into a gallery dedicated to his great-uncle. The last direct descendant of the family founded the present museum in 1858. Three of Michelangelo's sculptures and a few of his drawings are displayed, along with works of art collected and created by his descendants.

There are several portraits of Michelangelo and the marble bas-relief of *The Madonna of the Steps*, his earliest known work. Particularly charming are the Camera degli Angeli, a chapel, and the library with a frieze portraying famous Florentines.

THE SIGHTS

Duomo and Museo dell' Opera del Duomo

One of the most important early-Renaissance architectural complexes in Italy. The first free-standing dome to be constructed in the post-Roman period.

THE SIGHTS

RATINGS					
Good for kids	●	●	●	●	●
Historic interest	●	●	●	●	●
Cultural interest	●	●	●	●	●
Value for money	●	●	●	●	●

TIP

● Skimpy shorts and sleeveless tops are frowned upon.

Detail of Michelangelo's Pietà in the Museo dell'Opera del Duomo (top)

A souvenir umbrella in the style of the Duomo (above left)

The octagonal Battistero di San Giovanni decorated with marble geometric motifs (above middle)

Detail of one of the bronze panels of the Door of Paradise of the Battistero di San Giovanni (above right)

View over the Duomo (right)

SEEING THE DUOMO, BATTISTERO AND CAMPANILE

The sublime, if somewhat grimy, complex of the Duomo, Campanile and Battistero lies a few blocks north of the Piazza della Signoria and the River Arno and less than 20 minutes' walk east from the railway station. The three buildings stand in their own piazza, a clear space that is constantly busy with visitors. The best way to tackle the Duomo is to start early in the day to beat the tour groups. Many of the best artworks are displayed in the Museo dell'Opera del Duomo, behind the east end of the Duomo.

HIGHLIGHTS

THE DUOMO

The Duomo of Santa Maria del Fiore is huge—there is room inside for 20,000 people. It is worth walking right around its green-and-white striped marble exterior to appreciate the vast proportions. Several doors punctuate the walls, the most elaborate being the Porta della Mandoria with its relief of the Assumption sculpted by Nanni di Banco in 1420. By contrast, the ornate Gothic façade dates from the 19th century; the original was destroyed in the late 1500s.

Compared with the outside, the interior is remarkably austere. Over the years many of the finest artworks have been moved to the Museo dell'Opera del Duomo, leaving the Duomo relatively bare. This enables you to appreciate the soaring space beneath the Gothic arches, the patterned marble pavements, the scale of the dome itself, and the superb mid-15th-century stained-glass windows, some of Italy's best.

There are two equestrian memorials dedicated to two of Florence's most famous *condottieri*: A monument to Niccolò da Tolentino (1456) by Andrea del Castagno, and a far sharper-edged portrait (1436) of Sir John Hawkwood, an English mercenary, by Paolo Uccello. Terracotta reliefs by Luca della Robbia decorate both north and south sacristy doors, and a superb bronze reliquary urn by Ghiberti stands in the central apse.

Steps to the ancient church of Santa Reparata lead down from the south aisle; excavated in the 1960s, this ancient and confusing space has archaeological finds and, more inspiring, the tomb of Filippo Brunelleschi, architect of the dome.

Climbing the rather claustrophobic 463 steps of the dome is a must; it is the high point of this great building, rewarded with sweeping views.

Duomo

✚ 425 D2 • Piazza del Duomo, 50122 Firenze ☎ 055 230 2885
www.opera.duomo.firenze.it
🕐 Mon–Wed, Fri 10–5, Thu 10–3.30, Sat 10–4.45, Sun and holidays 1.30–4.45; Easter 3.30–4.45; closed 1 Jan, Easter Day, 15 Aug and 25 Dec
🎫 Free ☛ Free guided tours. Fixed audioguide points in the Duomo, €1
📖 Guidebooks cover the whole complex, in Italian, English, French, German and Spanish, €10 🚇 Duomo

Museo dell'Opera del Duomo

bookshop sells guidebooks, art books, postcards, gifts and posters 🛍
🅿 Underground parking at Santa Maria Novella; parking for visitors with disabilities in Piazza del Duomo

KEY

A   Portale Maggiore with relief Maria in Gloria by A. Passaglia
B   Porta dell Mandoria
C   Crypt, with remains of old cathedral
D   Chancel and High Altar
1. L'Assunta window by Ghiberti Incoronazione di Maria
2. Equestrian portrait of Niccoló da Tolentino, by A. del Castagno
3. Equestrian statue of Giovanni Acuto (John Hawkwood) painted by P. Uccello
4. 14th-century window, and below, Dante and the Divine Comedy by D. di Michelino
5. Marble altar (Buggiano)
6. In the door, lunette, Risurrezione, by Luca della Robbia
7. Sagrestia Nuova o della Messe
8. Above the altar, two angels (Luca della Robbia), below the altar reliquary of St. Zenobius by Ghiberti
9. Lunette, Risurrezione, terracotta by della Robbia
10. Sagrestia Vecchia o dei Canonici
11. Altar by Michelozzo
12. Entrance to the dome
13. Bust of Brunelleschi, by A. Cavalcanti
14. Stairs to the Crypt

MUSEO DELL'OPERA DEL DUOMO

The Museo dell'Opera del Duomo contains the sculptures and paintings of the Duomo complex, too precious to be left to the mercy of modern pollution. Ghiberti's *Gates of Paradise* (see below) probably steals the show, but there is a *Pietà* by Michelangelo that many see as equally exquisite. The sculptor was 80 when he created it, his last work, and intended it to be for his own tomb, but never finished it; the figure of Nicodemus is said to be a self-portrait. Donatello, the greatest of Michelangelo's precursors, is represented by two works: A gaunt and bedraggled *Mary Magdalene* and the powerful figure of the prophet *Habbakuk*. Donatello carved this for the campanile and it is so realistic he is said to have seized it, crying 'Speak, speak'. His lighter side emerges in the choir loft from the Duomo, carved with capering *putti* (children), the perfect contrast to Luca della Robbia's version, ornamented with earnest angels.

GHIBERTI'S BAPTISTERY DOORS IN THE MUSEO DELL'OPERA

Having finished the north doors in the baptistery in 1425, Ghiberti set to work on the doors for the east side, a work of such beauty that Michelangelo named them the 'Gates of Paradise'. Completed in 1452, they are made up of 10 relief panels of biblical subjects, exquisitely carved in low relief. Their artistic importance is in their use of perspective, extending the scenes far into the background–a totally new concept at the time that became typical of the Renaissance. The composition is far more naturalistic than the earlier baptistery doors, with figures grouped off-centre to intensify the drama of each scene. The baptistery doors are Ghiberti's finest achievement. On the frame of the left-hand door is his self-portrait–the smug-looking gentleman with a bald head.

THE BATTISTERO

The octagonal baptistery, entirely encased in green and white marble, is one of Florence's oldest buildings, probably dating from around the sixth to seventh century, and remodelled in the 11th century. It is most famous for its three sets of bronze doors, the south set dating from the 1330s by Andrea Pisano, and the north and east by Lorenzo Ghiberti. Ghiberti, aged 20, won the commission for the north doors in a competition and worked on them from 1403 to 1424, embarking on his finest achievement, the east set (see above), immediately afterwards. The panels in the doors you see are reproductions; the originals are kept away from 21st-century pollution in the Museo dell'Opera del Duomo.

INSIDE THE DOME

The interior of the dome glitters with Florence's only mosaic cycle, the earliest dating from 1225. Begin by looking above the entrance door and follow the history of the world from the Creation to John the Baptist, before taking in the main image of Christ and the Last Judgement, together with the Apostles and the Virgin.

THE CAMPANILE

Giotto designed the campanile in 1334, but he died in 1337, before it was completed. Both Andrea Pisano, who took over after Giotto's death, and Talenti altered the original design considerably, strengthening the walls and adding large windows. The building is covered with bands of green, white and pink marble and is decorated with copies of sculptures and reliefs showing prophets, patriarchs and scenes from the Old Testament; the originals are in the Museo dell'Opera del Duomo. There are 414 steps to the top of the campanile, well worth it for the views of Florence and the hills.

BACKGROUND

The sixth- to seventh-century baptistery was originally Florence's cathedral, later replaced by the church of Santa Reparata, whose remains lie beneath the present building. In the 13th century, the city fathers decided to replace it, largely to flaunt the city's political clout and growing wealth and size. In 1294 the project was entrusted to Arnolfo di Cambio, and work continued throughout the 14th century, with various architects realizing his plan. The campanile was finished by 1334 and by 1418 the nave and tribunes were complete. The building awaited the massive dome planned for the crossing—the only drawback being that nobody had yet worked out how it would be built. The architect Filippo Brunelleschi offered his services, refusing to explain his solution, but exuding confidence. The building committee finally gave him the job, insisting that he work with his rival Lorenzo Ghiberti, who had been responsible for the baptistery doors. In 1436 the dome was completed, and the cathedral consecrated. The lantern was finally completed in the 1460s.

The mosaic ceiling inside the Battistero

Battistero
✚ 424 C2 • Piazza del Duomo, 50122 Firenze ☎ 055 230 2885 ◔ Mon–Sat 12–6.30, Sun and holidays 8.30–1.30; closed 1 Jan, Easter Day, 8 Sep, 24 and 25 Dec ▮ €3 ▰ Audioguide

Museo dell'Opera del Duomo
✚ 425 D2 • Piazza del Duomo 9, 50122 Firenze ☎ 055 230 2885 ◔ Mon–Sat 9–7.30, Sun and holidays 8.30–1.30; closed 1 Jan, Easter Day, 8 Sep, 25 Dec ▮ Adult €6, under 6s free ▤ ▮▮ �&

Campanile
✚ 425 D2 • Piazza del Duomo 9, 50122 Firenze ☎ 055 230 2885 ◔ Daily 8.30–7.30; closed 1 Jan, Easter Day, 8 Sep, 25 Dec ▮ Adult €6, under 6s free

Santa Reparata (crypt)
◔ Mon–Wed, Fri 10–5, Thu 10–3.30, Sat 10–4.45, Sun and holidays 1.30–4.45; Easter 3.30–4.45; closed 1 Jan, Easter Day, 15 Aug and 25 Dec ▮ €3

Dome
◔ Sun–Fri 8.30–7, Sat 8.30–5.40 (last admission 40 min before closing) ▮ €6

Galleria degli Uffizi

Priceless paintings and sculptures from the world's most important collection of Renaissance art.
Giotto's *Maestà*, Botticelli's *The Birth of Venus* and Titian's *Venus of Urbino*.
Superb collection of Roman and Hellenistic sculpture.

RATINGS	
Good for kids	● ● ● ●
Cultural interest	● ● ● ●
Specialist shopping	● ● ●
Value for money	● ● ● ●

GALLERY GUIDE

Rooms 2–6: Giotto, 14th-century Florentine, International Gothic
Rooms 7–9: Early Renaissance
Rooms 10–14: Botticelli
Room 15: Leonardo da Vinci
Rooms 16–24: Perugino, Signorelli, Giorgione, Corregio
Rooms 25–26: Michelangelo, Raphael and Andrea del Sarto
Rooms 27–29: Mannerism
Room 30: Emilian painting
Room 31: Veronese
Room 32: Tintoretto
Rooms 33–45: 16th- to 18th-century—Rubens, Caravaggio and Rembrandt

The Holy Family *by Michelangelo*

SEEING THE GALLERIA DEGLI UFFIZI

Set aside plenty of time to see the Uffizi—there is so much art of such importance that a flying visit is out of the question. Do not attempt to see the entire collection in one day, though. In a first visit concentrate on Rooms 1 through 15, which present major Florentine works, Tuscan Gothic and Early Renaissance in the East Corridor, and 16th-century artists in the West Corridor. You can avoid a wait by reserving tickets in advance.

HIGHLIGHTS

MAESTÀ: GIOTTO—ROOM 2

A painting of the Madonna enthroned, combining Byzantine tradition with the first crucial steps towards the realism of Renaissance painting.

ADORATION OF THE MAGI: GENTILE DA FABRIANO—ROOM 6

This intricate picture (1423), with its sumptuously portrayed fabrics, epitomizes the zenith of the International Gothic movement.

PORTRAIT OF THE DUKE AND DUCHESS OF URBINO: PIERO DELLA FRANCESCA—ROOM 7

A double portrait showing the sitters in profile; the Duke lost his right eye in battle and was always portrayed from the left.

MADONNA AND CHILD WITH ANGELS: FILIPPO LIPPI—ROOM 8

Painted in 1465; the beautiful model for the Virgin was Lucrezia Buti, a nun, with whom the painter eloped.

THE BOTTICELLI WORKS—ROOMS 10–14

The Uffizi's most famous paintings are *Primavera* and *The Birth of Venus*. *Primavera* symbolizes spring, with a Zephyr chasing Flora, transforming her into spring and covering her with flowers. *The Birth of Venus* is inspired by Politia's poem and shows Zephyrus and Chloris blowing Venus ashore on the edge of a scallop shell.

LEONARDO DA VINCI—ROOM 15

Early works painted by Leonardo when he was living in Florence. See his large *Annunciation* (1475), along with the *Adoration of the*

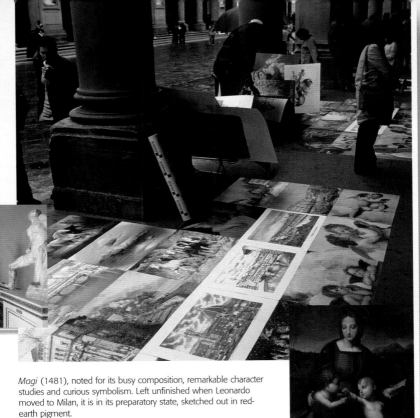

Magi (1481), noted for its busy composition, remarkable character studies and curious symbolism. Left unfinished when Leonardo moved to Milan, it is in its preparatory state, sketched out in red-earth pigment.

THE HOLY FAMILY: MICHELANGELO—ROOM 25
Also known as the *Doni Tondo*, this painting was created between 1504 and 1505 for the marriage of Agnolo Doni and Maddalena Strozzi. It's Michelangelo's only completed work in tempera, a precursor to the Sistine Chapel frescoes.

THE RAPHAEL PAINTINGS—ROOM 26
Several important works hang here, including the luminous *Madonna of the Goldfinch*, a self-portrait, and the portrait group *Leo X with Giulio de' Medici*, painted shortly before the artist's death.

SALA DI PONTORMO E DEL ROSSO FIORENTINO—ROOM 27
Mannerism at its most startling, with attenuated forms and vivid shades.

VENUS OF URBINO: TITIAN—ROOM 28
This sensuous nude with a wistful and chaste gaze was painted in 1538 and described by Lord Byron as 'the definitive Venus'.

BACKGROUND
The gallery in the vast Palazzo degli Uffizi extends from Piazza della Signoria to the River Arno. Originally intended to be government offices *(uffizi)*, the U-shaped building was constructed between 1560 and 1574 by Giorgio Vasari, under the orders of Cosimo I de' Medici. Succeeding Medici dukes added to the collections, which were bequeathed to the people of Florence by the last member of the family, Anna Maria Lodovica, in 1737, on the condition that the works never leave the city. The museum continues to acquire paintings and drawings. In 1993 a terrorist bomb caused great damage, and the gallery has undergone major reorganization.

Prints for sale outside the gallery (top); Raphael's Madonna of the Goldfinch *(above)*

BASICS
✚ 424 C3 • Piazzale degli Uffizi, 50122 Firenze ☎ 055 238 8651, 294 883 (reservations)

🕐 Tue–Sun 8.15–6.50 (hours usually extended in summer); reservations in advance Mon–Fri 8.30–6.30, Sat 8.30–12.30, tel 055 294883, www.firenzemusei.it

💳 Adult €6.50, reservations €3, under 18s free

🎧 Audio tours in English, French, Spanish, German, Japanese, Italian, from €6.50

📖 Official guidebook from €4.50

☕ Café overlooking Piazza della Signoria

🚌 🅿 Limited parking on Lungarno Serristori (10-minute walk); underground parking at Santa Maria Novella station (15-minute walk); parking for visitors with disabilities in Piazza della Signoria

One of several fountains in the Giardino di Boboli

A painted mummy case in the Museo Archeologico

Michelangelo's David at the Galleria dell'Accademia

GALLERIA DELL'ACCADEMIA

✚ 425 D1 • Via Ricasoli 60, 50122 Firenze ☎ 055 294 883 (reservations) 🕐 Tue–Sun 8.15–6.50 (hours often extended in summer); Easter Sun and Mon 8.15am–10pm; closed 1 Jan, 1 May, 25 Dec 🎫 Adult €6.50, under 18s free 🎫 🅿 Ample parking at the Parterre, Piazza della Libertà (10-minute walk); parking for visitors with disabilities outside www.firenzemusei.it

Michelangelo's powerful *David* is the main draw of this gallery of the art school. Transferred here from Piazza della Signoria (▷ 131), where it was replaced with a full-scale marble replica, this depiction of David in a pensive mood before his battle with Goliath, is a symbol of liberty to the Italians. Completed in 1504, when the sculptor was only 29, *David* immediately established Michelangelo as the leading sculptor of his day.

In the adjoining corridor stand five other remarkable Michelangelo sculptures. The four celebrated *Slaves*, created between 1519 and 1536, intended for the tomb of Pope Julius II in Rome, appear to be unfinished, hence their alternative name of *Nonfiniti*. The fifth is a statue of St. Matthew.

Elsewhere in the gallery are early Florentine paintings, including works by Botticelli and Lippi. Also here is the Medici family's collection of musical instruments, as well as the plaster cast for *Rape of the Sabine Women*, in the Loggia dei Lanzi at Piazza della Signoria.

GIARDINO DI BOBOLI

✚ 424 B5 • Palazzo Pitti, Piazza Pitti, 50125 Firenze ☎ 055 265 1838 🕐 Jun–end Aug daily 8.15–8; Apr, May, Sept daily 8.15–7; Mar, Oct daily 8.15–6; Nov–end Feb daily 8.15–5; closed 1st and last Mon of each month 🎫 Adult €4, under 18s free. Tickets are also valid for 3 days for the Museo delle Porcellane and the Museo degli Argenti in the Palazzo Pitti (▷ 128–129) 📷 🎫

This green space in the middle of Florence, a cool oasis on a hot summer's day, is the perfect fresh-air antidote to the many indoor sights in the city. Even at the height of summer, the warren of small lanes and pathways provides a welcome refuge from the tourist crowds. Elaborate fountains, grottoes, elegant buildings and formal gardens sit happily alongside lichen-covered statues and secluded glades, a playground for local cats.

The gardens are laid out on a hillside behind the Palazzo Pitti (▷ 128–129) and stretch from the palace up to Forte Belvedere. They were designed by Niccolò Tribolo (1500–50) for Cosimo I de Medici and were opened to the public in 1766. Near the main courtyard of the Palazzo Pitti is the magnificent Grotta Grande. In each of the four corners are copies of Michelangelo's unfinished *Slaves* (the originals are in the Galleria dell'Accademia). Walk up the terraces to the Neptune Fountain (1571), where you can either take a detour to the elegant, frescoed Kaffehaus for wonderful views and refreshments, or continue up to the top of the garden to the large statue, *Abundance*.

Off the beaten track, follow the magnificent Viottolone, a wide, steep path lined by cypress trees and statues leading to the lower part of the garden. At the bottom is the magical Isolotto, an island surrounded by a moat, adorned with statues, lemon trees and the Oceanus Fountain.

Don't miss Before you leave, pass by the Bacchus Fountain, a comic sculpture of Cosimo I's pot-bellied dwarf riding a turtle.

MUSEO ARCHEOLOGICO NAZIONALE

✚ 425 E2 • Via della Colonna 38, 50121 Firenze ☎ 055 23575 🕐 Mon 2–7, Tue, Thu 8.30–7, Wed, Sat–Sun 8.30–2 🎫 €4, 18–26 years (EU nationals) €2, under 18s, over 65s (EU nationals) free 🎫 www.comune.firenze.it

The Museo Archeologico Nazionale has an excellent collection of art and ancient items, including the most important Etruscan and Egyptian collections in Italy—a welcome relief from the potential overload of Renaissance art in the city.

The museum is in the elegant, 17th-century Palazzo della Crocetta on a busy street east of Piazza della Santissima Annunziata. One of the most important pieces in the museum, the restored bronze *Idolino*, is exhibited in a room on the ground floor. The torso of this statue of a young man, probably once used as a lampstand, is thought to date from the first century BC.

The Etruscan collection includes the famous bronze *Chimera*, part lion, part goat and part snake, dating from the late fifth to the early fourth century BC. Here also is the monumental *Arringatore*, or *Orator*, dating from the Hellenistic period, and a statue of Minerva.

The Egyptian collection includes mummies, statuettes, sarcophagi and vases, along with a 14th-century Hittite chariot made of bone and wood. On the second floor is a collection of Attic vases dating from the sixth and fifth centuries BC. Outstanding among these is the famous François Vase. Made in Athens around 570BC, this huge, highly decorative piece is one of the earliest examples of its kind.

MUSEO DI SAN MARCO

A shrine to Fra Angelico, little changed since the 1400s. See his paintings in their original context, the Dominican Convent of San Marco. Ethereal images full of endlessly fascinating detail.

The Annunciation *by Fra Angelico*

The Convent of San Marco, within which the museum resides, is next to the church of the same name. The original convent on the site was of the Silvestrine Order, but it was given to the Dominicans by Cosimo il Vecchio, who commissioned the architect Michelozzo to enlarge the existing buildings. Fra Angelico (*c*1400–55), also known as Beato Angelico, lived here from 1436 to 1447. The museum was founded in 1869 and in 1921 most of Fra Angelico's panel paintings were transferred here from other museums in Florence.

THE CLOISTERS AND THE PILGRIMS' HOSPICE

A visit starts in Michelozzo's peaceful Cloister of Sant'Antonio. In the middle is an ancient cedar of Lebanon and at each corner is a small lunette fresco by Fra Angelico. Off this cloister is the Pilgrims' Hospice, a long room full of beautiful paintings by Fra Angelico, glowing in bright jewel shades and gold leaf. At one end of the room is the superb *Deposition from the Cross* (*c*1435–40), while at the other is the famous *Linaiouli Tabernacle* (1433) with its *Madonna Enthroned and Saints.* The border consists of musical angels, often reproduced on Christmas cards. In this room is also the great *Last Judgement* altarpiece (1431) and a series of charming reliquary tabernacles in gold frames featuring 35 tiny scenes from the life of Christ.

Other paintings here are by Fra Bartolomeo, Giovanni Sogliani, Lorenzo Lippi and others. Before climbing the stairs to the monks' quarters, visit two more frescoes: Fra Angelico's large *Crucifixion and Saints* (1441–42) in the Chapter House and Domenico Ghirlandaio's *Last Supper* in the small refectory.

THE MONKS' CELLS

At the top of the stairs to the dormitory is one of Fra Angelico's most famous frescoes, the *Annunciation* (1442). The 44 tiny cells where the monks lived each has a shuttered window and a small fresco by Fra Angelico or his assistants. Those by the master himself are in cells 1 to 9. Note the beautiful angel in Cell 3 and the Nativity scene in Cell 5. Girolamo Savonarola, the rebel priest who was prior in 1491, occupied the Prior's Cell. Other famous inhabitants include the Florentine painter Fra Bartolommeo, who was a friar.

RATINGS			
Historic interest	●	●	● ●
Cultural interest	●	●	● ●
Value for money	●	●	● ●

BASICS

✚ 425 D1 • Piazza San Marco 1, 50121 Firenze ☎ 055 238 8608, 055 294883 (reservations)

🕐 Tue–Fri 8.15–1.50, Sat–Sun 8.15–7; closed 1st, 3rd and 5th Sun and 2nd and 4th Mon of each month and 25 Dec, 1 Jan, 1 May 💶 Adults €4, 18–26 years (EU nationals) €2, under 18s, over 65s (EU nationals) free

📖 Official guidebook €7.50

🚻 ♿ Includes toilets for visitors with disabilities

🅿 Parking at the Parterre (10-minute walk); parking for visitors with disabilities in Piazza San Marco

www.polomuseale.firenze.it
An Italian site bringing together the major museums and galleries in Florence. Site plans of the major collections and pictures of the highlights.

TIPS

● **The museum can be busy; a visit out of peak season allows you to experience the spirituality of the place, which may be compromised by the crowds.**

● **Only 120 people are allowed up to the dormitories at one time, so reserve your visit in advance (tel 055 294 883), arrive early in the morning or be prepared to wait.**

Detail of the stone carvings of patron saints on the walls of the church of Orsanmichele

The stylish courtyard at the Palazzo Medici-Riccardi

MUSEO NAZIONALE DEL BARGELLO

See page 127.

MUSEO DI STORIA DELLA SCIENZA

⊞ 425 D3 • Piazza dei Giudici 1, 50122 Firenze ☎ 055 265311 ⏰ Jun–Sep Mon, Wed–Fri 9.30–5, Tue, Sat 9.30–1; Oct–May Mon, Wed–Sat 9.30–5, Tue 9.30–1 ✋ Adult €7.50, child (7–18) €4, under 7s free
www.imss.fi.it

This fascinating and informative museum explores the history of physics, chemistry, astronomy and medicine through several examples of mathematical and scientific instruments, many of which, besides being practical, are beautifully decorated.

As you look at the exhibits, the significant contribution Florence and Tuscany have made to the history of science becomes clear. Room IV is dedicated to Galileo Galilei (1564–1642), one of Tuscany's famous sons, who was born in Pisa and died in Florence, having spent years in the service of the Medici family. One of his many achievements was the perfection of the telescope, and here you can see the one through which he observed Jupiter's four satellites for the first time. Another room charts the progressive improvement of the telescope from Galileo's first examples, perfected in 1610 (▷ 35).

There's a room dedicated to the development of the mechanical clock, with beautiful examples of pocket watches. Room XVIII has some gruesome anatomical waxworks and terracotta models that demonstrate possible complications of childbirth, along with sets of 18th-century surgical instruments, including one for amputation.

ORSANMICHELE

⊞ 424 C3 • Via Arte della Lana, 50122 Firenze ☎ 055 284944 ⏰ Mon–Sat 9–12, 4–6, Sat–Sun and holidays 9–1, 4–6; closed 1st and last Mon of each month

The unique Orsanmichele was built as a market in 1337, and the original building had a granary on the upper floor. When the market was moved in 1380, the ground floor became a church. The city's guilds commissioned some of the best artists of the day to make statues of patron saints to sit in the canopied niches, and so created a permanent outdoor exhibition of 15th-century Florentine sculpture. Some of the original statues are still here, including Ghiberti's bronzes of St. Matthew (1419–22) and St. Stephen (1427–28).

Inside, faded frescoes of patron saints decorate the walls. The jewel here is Andrea Orcagna's Gothic tabernacle, a large decorative work commissioned by the survivors of the Black Death in 1349.

OSPEDALE DEGLI INNOCENTI

⊞ 425 E2 • Piazza della SS Annunziata, 50122 Florence ☎ 055 249 1708 ⏰ Thu–Tue 8.30–2; last entrance 1.30 ✋ Adult €2.60, child (6–18) €1.50

The Ospedale degli Innocenti opened as a foundling hospital in 1445. It was the first of its kind in Europe and remained open as an orphanage until 2000. The building is an important architectural landmark—its beautiful loggia by Filippo Brunelleschi is an early Renaissance masterpiece.

A portico with nine arches borders Piazza della Santissima Annunziata, one of the loveliest squares in Florence. The spandrels are adorned with the familiar blue and white tondi

(glazed terracotta medallions) of babes in swaddling clothes by Andrea della Robbia, while at one end of the loggia is the window-wheel where babies were left by their mothers. In the Museo dello Spedale are fine paintings, including Domenico Ghirlandaio's vivid Adoration of the Magi (1488). At one end of the room is a poignant collection of identification tags left by mothers in the hope that one day they might see their children again.

PALAZZO MEDICI-RICCARDI

⊞ 425 D2 • Via Cavour 3, 50129 Florence ☎ 055 276 0340 ⏰ Mon, Tue, Thur, Fri 9–7; last entrance 6.30 ✋ Adult €4, child (6–12) €2.50, under 6s free 🏛

The massive Palazzo Medici-Riccardi was built by Michelozzo some time after 1444 as a town mansion for Cosimo il Vecchio, and was the residence of the Medici until 1540. The Riccardi family bought the palace in 1659 and enlarged it. It is now the headquarters of the provincial government.

The main, columned courtyard is suitably impressive, and the adjacent gardens are filled with lemon trees in huge terracotta pots. The main staircase off the courtyard leads to the chapel, which is covered by Benozzo Gozzoli's beautifully restored frescoes of the Procession of the Magi to Bethlehem (1459–63). Gozzoli also dotted the scene with members of the Medici family and other celebrities of the day. The gallery is a large and elaborate baroque room decorated with mirrors, plasterwork and ceiling frescoes by Luca Giordano (1683). Look out for the restored Madonna and Child by Filippo Lippi in the smaller adjoining room.

MUSEO NAZIONALE DEL BARGELLO

A superb collection of sculpture by stars such as Michelangelo and Donatello—and yet rarely crowded. Wonderful terracotta pieces by the della Robbia family and an unusual collection of miniature mannerist bronzes.

The crenellated Palazzo del Bargello, home to the Bargello Museum, was built in 1255 as the Palazzo del Popolo, the seat of the city's government. In the 16th century the police headquarters was here, along with a prison, which was in use until 1858. The museum was first opened to the public in 1865.

GROUND FLOOR

Begin in the Gothic courtyard with its fine statues and sculptures. Until 1786, executions were carried out here, and condemned prisoners would spend their last night in the chapel on the first floor.

Off the courtyard, the spacious hall has the most celebrated sculptures, by Michelangelo and his contemporaries. Michelangelo's works include an early *Bacchus Drunk* (c1497), a humorous portrayal of the god of wine, and the marble tondo of the Madonna and Child with the infant St. John, known as the *Pitti Tondo* (c1503). Important works by Benvenuto Cellini include *Narcissus*, carved from a block of Greek marble, and *Apollo and Hyacinth*, once in the Boboli Gardens (▷ 124). There is also a life-size bronze cast of his famous *Perseus*.

FIRST FLOOR

The loggia has a group of bronze birds by Giambologna, made for the Villa di Castello. The Gothic Salone del Consiglio Generale contains works by Donatello and his contemporaries. His *Marzocco Lion*, the symbol of Florence carved in *pietra serena*, is the focus of the room. On the walls hang two of the trial bronze panels made by Ghiberti and Brunelleschi for the baptistery doors (▷ 121), a marble relief of the *Madonna and Child with Angels* by Duccio and a number of delightful glazed terracotta Madonnas by Luca della Robbia.

DECORATIVE ARTS

There are several rooms dedicated to European and Middle Eastern decorative art, including fabrics, carpets, ceramics, jewellery and clocks, and a large room filled with characteristically lively glazed terracottas by Giovanni della Robbia. Also worth seeing are the Renaissance bronzes, the most important collection of its kind in Italy.

RATINGS	
Historic interest	●●●●
Cultural interest	●●●●
Value for money	●●●●●

BASICS

✚ 425 D3 • Via del Proconsolo 4, 50122 Firenze

☎ 055 238 8606

🕐 Daily 8.15–1.50; closed 1st, 3rd and 5th Sun, and 2nd and 4th Mon of every month, 1 Jan, 1 May and 25 Dec

💶 Adults €4, 18–26 (EU nationals) €2, under 18s, over 65s (EU nationals) and art history students free

📖 Official guide €7.50

🅿 Limited parking on Lungarno della Zecca Vecchia (10-minute walk); ample parking under the station (15- to 20-minute walk). Parking for visitors with disabilities in Piazza San Firenze ♿

www.firenzemusei.it

The courtyard of the Museo Nazionale del Bargello (top) and Andrea della Robbia's Ritratto d'Ignota *(above)*

Palazzo Pitti

●

A building of immense proportions with extensive grounds. Florence's largest and most opulent palazzo, once the main seat of the Medicis. Home to the Galleria Palatina, Florence's most important picture collection after the Uffizi, and seven other collections.

The vast 205m (673ft) façade of the Palazzo Pitti

SEEING THE PALAZZO PITTI

The Pitti collections are huge, so it makes sense to concentrate on the Galleria Palatina, a suite of 26 rooms covered with paintings. The works are displayed much as they were in the 17th century, adorning the walls from floor to ceiling in no discernible order. Allow 2–3 hours to fully appreciate the paintings before moving on to another gallery that takes your fancy. Be prepared for crowds, and also for sections or collections that are closed; you can reserve ahead to avoid disappointment (tel 055 294883). There is much to see, but make sure you leave time to relax afterwards in the Giardino di Boboli (▷ 124).

HIGHLIGHTS

THE COURTYARD

The main entrance to the palace leads you through to Ammanati's splendid courtyard (1560–70), an excellent example of Florentine mannerist architecture. It was used as a stage for lavish spectacles between the 16th and 18th centuries, and is still the venue for concerts and ballet in the summer.

GALLERIA PALATINA
MADONNA AND CHILD: FILIPPO LIPPI–SALA DI PROMOTEO

Painted in 1452 and known as the *Pitti Tondo*, Lippi's famous work perfectly combines exquisite painting and intense spirituality. The eye is drawn to the pure face of the Virgin, the central point, surrounded by scenes from the life of her mother, St. Anne, and the Christ Child lying on her knee.

MADONNA DELLA SEGGIOLA: RAPHAEL–SALA DI SATURNO

Raphael painted this tondo in Rome in 1514, and it has been at the Pitti since the 18th century. Although heavily influenced by Venetian painting, evident in its use of light and shade, the painting follows a strictly Florentine form, its shape emphasizing the tender curves of the Virgin and Child.

PIETRO ARETINO: TITIAN–SALA DI APOLLO

Portraiture gained importance during the High Renaissance, as the Church lost its total control on subject matter, and new money brought self-made men to prominence. Titian painted this portrait of the satirical poet Pietro Aretino in 1545, after Aretino had moved from Mantova to Venice, Titian's native city.

SLEEPING CUPID: CARAVAGGIO–SALA DELL'EDUCAZIONE DI GIOVE

This plump little sleeping Cupid is full of allegorical references to passion and lost love. Caravaggio painted it when he was in Malta in 1608. By this time he had already lived in Rome, where he had studied and grasped the fine details of human anatomy and was beginning to concentrate on the development of *chiaroscuro*, the contrast of light and dark, a technique expertly employed in his work later on in his life.

Inside the Grotto del Buontalenti (1583–88) in the Giardino di Boboli, the formal gardens of the Palazzo Pitti

APPARTAMENTI REALI

These royal apartments have been expertly and sensitively restored to their 19th-century condition. From the 17th century onwards they were the residence of the Medici, the dukes of Lorraine, and members of the house of Savoy, including Italy's first monarch, King Umberto I. They are hard to beat in terms of extravagance; gilding and stucco, rich damask hangings, vast chandeliers, gilt mirrors, period furnishings, paintings and sculptures are impressive.

MUSEO DEGLI ARGENTI

In a series of sumptuous state rooms, this museum concentrates on luxury *objets d'art* amassed by the Medici dukes. There is a huge range of items, from antique vases collected by Lorenzo Il Magnifico to stunningly worked, but aesthetically banal, figurines, and a vast array of inlaid pieces.

BACKGROUND

Construction began on the Palazzo Pitti in 1457, supposedly to a design by Brunelleschi. It was originally the private residence of the banker Luca Pitti, a rival of the Medici family, and his descendants, but in 1549 the family funds dried up and it was purchased by Cosimo I's wife, the Grand Duchess Eleonora. It became the official residence of the Grand Dukes and was occupied by ruling families until 1919, when it was presented to the state by Vittorio Emanuele III. Under Medici ownership it was repeatedly enlarged, notably in the 16th century, when Bartolomeo Ammanati (1511–92) lengthened the façade and built the courtyard, while the side wings were added in the 18th and 19th centuries. The Medici family began decorating and amassing the collections in the 17th century. The main galleries opened to the public in 1833 and the Galleria d'Arte Moderna, Florence's modern art museum, joined the gallery complex in 1924.

GALLERY GUIDE

Galleria Palatina: The main collection, strong on 16th-century works, particularly Raphael, Titian and Andrea del Sarto. In a wing of the main palace.

Galleria d'Arte Moderna: Works spanning the mid-18th to mid-20th centuries. In the main building on the floor above the Galleria Palatina.

Museo degli Argenti: *Objets d'art*, gold and jewellery from the Medici collections. Accessed from the main courtyard.

Museo del Costume: Rotating exhibitions of historic clothes from the early 18th to mid-20th centuries. In Palazzina Meridiana in the south wing.

Museo delle Porcellane: French, Italian, German and Viennese porcelain and ceramics. In a pavilion at the top of the Boboli Gardens.

Appartamenti Reali: Lavishly decorated state apartments following on from the Palatina.

Collezione Contini Bonacossi: A picture collection on long-term loan, strong on Spanish painting. Next to the Museo del Costume in the Palazzina Meridiana.

Museo delle Carozze: Carriage collection—currently closed.

Statue in the Sala di Venere (Room 4) in the Galleria Palatina

PALAZZO VECCHIO

Florence's town hall, an outstanding example of Florentine civic purpose, with superb rooftop views from the loggia. Vast, elaborately decorated public rooms and intimate private apartments.
Fine sculptures, including *Victory* by Michelangelo.

The palace stands on the site of the medieval Palazzo dei Priori, rebuilt to Arnolfo di Cambio's design. Designers of *palazzi comunali* throughout Tuscany based their designs on its battlemented structure. Cosimo il Vecchio was imprisoned in the asymmetrically placed tower before his exile in 1433. Savonarola was also imprisoned here in 1498, but went on to be burned at the stake in Piazza della Signoria.

THE COURTYARD

Past the main entrance is the courtyard, reconstructed by Michelozzo in 1453. It was elaborately decorated by Giorgio Vasari in 1565 to celebrate the marriage of the son of Cosimo I to Joanna of Austria.

FIRST FLOOR

The largest room is the Salone del Cinquecento, a meeting room for the 500-member Consiglio Maggiore. Vasari painted the frescoes to celebrate Cosimo I's triumphs over Pisa and Siena. The most notable sculpture is Michelangelo's *Victory*.

Next door, the tiny, windowless Studiolo di Francesco I has allegorical paintings by Vasari and small bronze statues by Giambologna and Ammanati. It was here that the melancholic son of Cosimo I pursued his interest in alchemy. On the same floor, Vasari and Cosimo I's assistants decorated the Quartiere di Leone X with ornate illustrations of the history of the Medici family.

SECOND FLOOR

Access to the Quartiere di Eleonora di Toledo, the private apartments of Cosimo I's wife, is via a balcony across the end of the Salone del Cinquecento, providing a close-up view of the ceiling. The chapel, decorated with frescoes of various saints, is one of Bronzino's most important works. The Sala dei Gigli owes its name to the lily *(gigli)* motif, a symbol of the city. Here also is Donatello's bronze statue, *Judith and Holofernes* (1455). Niccolò Machiavelli used the Cancellaria next door as an office from 1498 to 1512, when he was a government secretary. The *guardaroba*, or wardrobe, contains a fascinating collection of 57 detailed maps of the world as it was then known.

RATINGS

Historic interest	●●●○
Cultural interest	●●●○
Value for money	●●○

BASICS

✚ 425 D3 • Piazza della Signoria, 50122 Firenze ☎ 055 276 8465
🕐 Mon–Fri 9–7, Sun, holidays 8–1
💶 Adult €5.70, under 12s free
🎧 Audiotours in Italian, English, French, German, Japanese, €4.10
📖 From €4.65
🏛 🚻
🅿 Nearest parking under Santa Maria Novella Station (15-minute walk). Parking for visitors with disabilities in Piazza della Signoria

www.comune.fi.it
www.museoragazzi.it

A copy of Verrochio's Pluttino Fountain in the courtyard (top)
A marble bust on the façade (above)

PIAZZA DELLA SIGNORIA

Florence's most noble and famous piazza—the place to get a real feel for the city. A vast open-air, traffic-free sculpture gallery with elegant cafés and restaurants.

This wide, open square marks the heart of the *centro storico* and is next to the Galleria degli Uffizi (▷ 122–123). The Piazza della Signoria has been the political focus of Florence since the Middle Ages. Surrounded by tall buildings, notably the vast, sombre Palazzo Vecchio (▷ opposite), this is where the ruling city fathers called open-air public assemblies in times of crisis. The crowd was often provoked by speeches on the *arringhiera* (oration terrace), a raised platform, and the gatherings frequently degenerated into violence. The area in front of the Palazzo Vecchio was named Piazza del Popolo (People's Square) in 1307.

THE SCULPTURES

The enormous Loggia dei Lanzi (also known as the Loggia della Signoria) was designed to be used by dignitaries for formal meetings and ceremonies. It was completed in 1382 and has been used as an open-air sculpture museum since the late 18th century. Dominating the front is Cellini's mannerist bronze *Perseus* (1545). Considered his greatest work, it shows Perseus triumphantly holding aloft the severed head of Medusa. Near it is Giambologna's last work, the *Rape of the Sabine Women*, completed in 1583. Donatello's *Judith and Holofernes* was the first of the statues to be placed in the piazza (this is a copy—the original is in the Palazzo Vecchio).

In front of the main entrance to the Palazzo Vecchio stands a copy of Michelangelo's *David* (the original is in the Galleria dell'Accademia, ▷ 124). The other large statue nearby is Bandinelli's *Hercules and Cacus* (1534), described by his rival Cellini as an 'old sack full of melons'. At the corner of the Palazzo Vecchio is Ammanati's massive fountain (1575), with the undignified figure of Neptune. The large equestrian bronze, Giambologna's monument to Cosimo (1595), shows detailed scenes of Cosimo's coronation and victory over the Sienese. The plaque in the pavement in front of the fountain marks the spot where Girolamo Savonarola was burned at the stake as a traitor on 23 May 1498.

Ammanati's statue of Neptune (above); the Calcio Storico, a football match held here each year in medieval costume (top)

RATINGS	
Good for kids	● ● ●
Historic interest	● ● ● ● ●
Cultural interest	● ● ● ●
Walkability	● ● ● ●

BASICS

✚ 424 C3 • Piazza della Signoria, 50122 Firenze 🅿 Parking at Lungarno Torrigiani (10-minute walk) 🏛 In Palazzo Vecchio

TIPS

● An elegant, expensive, table at the Café Rivoire is a good place to people-watch. Or perch on a stone bench under the Loggia dei Lanzi.

● Free open-air concerts are held here in summer.

Rape of the Sabine Women

Two of the *Four Seasons* statues on *Ponte Santa Trinità*

Ponte Vecchio—one of the most famous bridges in the world—has survived against the odds

PIAZZALE MICHELANGELO

✚ 425 E5 • Piazzale Michelangelo, 50125 Firenze

It is worth making the climb, or taking a bus, to Piazzale Michelangelo, for the unrivalled views over Florence. Here you can marvel at the full-scale replica of Michelangelo's *David* in the middle of the square or enjoy the panoramic view and a drink at one of the terraced bars. On a clear day, views extend way beyond the city to the surrounding hills, and the sunsets are fantastic. On Sunday afternoons the place is heaving with everyone taking advantage of the city's best photo opportunity.

Up on a hillside south of the Arno, Piazzale Michelangelo's wide, open space is bordered by a stone balustrade on the northern side overlooking the city. It is about halfway along the broad, leafy *viale* that winds through this part of the city, so traffic can be heavy at peak times.

PONTE SANTA TRINITÀ

✚ 424 C3 • Piazza Santa Trinità, 50123 Firenze

The Santa Trinità bridge has the best view of the Ponte Vecchio and is a fine monument in itself. It is also remarkable, for in 1944 it was destroyed—along with all the other bridges in Florence except the Ponte Vecchio—by bombing, and was carefully reconstructed using stone from the original quarries. What you see today is a faithful replica of Ammanati's 1567 bridge.

Three wide, graceful arches make up the bridge, which links elegant Via Tornabuoni to the north and the characterful Oltrarno to the south. In each of the four corners stands a statue, the original *Four Seasons*. They

fell into the river during the World War II bombing, but were salvaged and reassembled (the last piece, the head of *Spring*, was fished out in 1961).

PONTE VECCHIO

✚ 424 C3 • Ponte Vecchio 50123 Firenze 🅿 Limited meter parking on Lungarno Serristori (5-minute walk); underground parking at Santa Maria Novella station (15-minute walk); parking for visitors with disabilities in Via Guicciardini (100m/110 yards)

If you can ignore the crowds and the modern gold shops, the Ponte Vecchio gives you a taste of what the medieval city was like—as well as a good view of the River Arno, its palaces and the adjacent Ponte Santa Trinità.

The present bridge was built in 1345, a reconstruction of an earlier structure washed away by a flood. Until 1218 this had been the only access across the river. At the end of the 16th century, Grand Duke Ferdinand I replaced the evil-smelling hog-butchers' shops that lined the bridge with gold- and silversmiths' shops, and they have remained here ever since. The bridge has survived two major traumas in recent history: In 1945, while all the other bridges in Florence were destroyed by bombing, the Ponte Vecchio was saved on Hitler's orders; then in 1966 the waters of the Arno rose so high that a fortune in gold was washed away in the floods.

Small shops and houses line the bridge on both sides, supported by brackets that overhang the river. They are painted in mellow shades of ochre, and with their wooden shutters, ancient wrought-ironwork and awnings they have retained their medieval appearance. Vasari's 1565 corridor is clearly visible running over the top of the eastern

shops. Originally designed to be a secret passageway for Cosimo I, it joins the Galleria degli Uffizi (▷ 122–123) and the Palazzo Pitti (▷ 128–129).

SANTISSIMA ANNUNZIATA

✚ 425 E1 • Piazza Santissima Annunziata, 50123 Firenze ☎ 055 239 8034 🕐 Daily 7–12.45, 4–6.30 🎟 Free www.ss-annunziata.it

In the mid-15th century this grand church was one of the most important in Florence. It was founded in 1250 to protect a miraculous picture of the Virgin, and it was expanded between 1444 and 1481 by Michelozzo, who also designed the Chiostrino dei Voti in front of the church, an unusual glass-roofed atrium decorated with frescoes by Andrea del Sarto (1486–1531) and some of his contemporaries.

The church's façade is made up of a graceful portico that leads into the Chiostro dei Voti. On the right are frescoes by Rosso Fiorentino of the Assumption and to the left is Jacopo Pontormo's *Visitation*. The interior is dark, yet lavishly decorated with marble and gold leaf. The tabernacle commissioned by the Medici in the 15th century contains the miraculous painting of the Virgin, said to have been painted by a monk with help from an angel. Unusually, entry to the large apse behind the main altar is through a triumphal arch.

More notable works of art in the main body of the church include, in the north aisle, an *Assumption* by Perugino (c1450–1523) and *The Holy Trinity with St. Jerome* by Andrea del Castagno (c1421–57). The splendid organ in the nave, built between 1509 and 1521, is the oldest in the city and the second-oldest in Italy.

SANTA CROCE

**The largest Franciscan church in Italy, reputedly founded by St. Francis.
Cappella dei Pazzi—one of Brunelleschi's most important works and a masterpiece of the early Renaissance.
Several important Florentines are buried here.**

In the heart of one of Florence's most attractive areas, the present Santa Croce was begun in 1294 and completed in the 1450s. The original plain front was replaced in the 19th century with an elaborate neo-Gothic one. The interior is vast, with a wide nave and superb stained-glass windows by Agnolo Gaddi. Although some frescoes were damaged in the 1966 flood, there are some exceptional works.

THE NORTH AISLE
Lorenzo Ghiberti (1378–1455) is buried under the tomb-slab with the eagle on it. There is also a monument to Galileo Galilei (1564–1642), the great scientist who spent his latter years in Florence (▷ 35).

THE EAST END
The polygonal sanctuary in the east end is covered with vivid frescoes by Gaddi. On either side are small chapels, each dedicated to an eminent Florentine family of the day, with frescoes by Giotto. The Bardi di Libertà Chapel has frescoes by Bernardo Daddi and an altarpiece by Giovanni della Robbia. The Bardi di Vernio Chapel has frescoes by Masi di Banco, while Donatello's wooden crucifix hangs in the Bardi Chapel in the north transept. The frescoes in the Castellani Chapel are by Gaddi, whose father Taddeo was responsible for the beautiful paintings in the Baroncelli Chapel. Next to the Baroncelli Chapel a corridor leads to the Medici Chapel by Brunelleschi.

THE SOUTH AISLE
In the south aisle are the tombs of Michelangelo (designed by Vasari), the poet Dante, and Niccolò Machiavelli (▷ 35).

CAPPELLA DEI PAZZI
From the south aisle there is access to Brunelleschi's Cappella dei Pazzi. He was still working on this masterpiece of tranquillity when he died in 1446. Inside, in contrast to the elaborate Gothic tendencies of the age, grey *pietra serena* stone, simply carved in classical lines, is set against a white background. At the base of the elegant dome, 12 terracotta roundels by Della Robbia depict the Apostles.

RATINGS	
Historic interest	● ● ● ○
Cultural interest	● ● ● ○
Value for money	● ● ● ○

BASICS

✚ 425 E3 • Piazza Santa Croce, 50122 Firenze
☎ 055 244619
🕐 Thu–Tue 10–6 🎫 Adult €3 (also covers museum); child (11–18) €2; child (under 11) free
🎧 Free tours in English, French, German, Spanish, Italian Mon–Sat 10–12.30, 3–5, Sun 3–5 (tours given by volunteers, so times and availability of languages may vary). Audioguides at fixed points: English, French, Spanish, Italian, €1
📕 €8
🚉 🅿 Lungarno della Zecca Vecchia (10-minute walk); parking for visitors with disabilities in Piazza Santa Croce

www.firenzeturismo.it

TIP

● The Calcio Storico, an established football (soccer) match, is played in medieval costume in Piazza Santa Croce or Piazza della Signoria on St. John's Day, 24 June (St. John is the patron saint of Florence). Other dates are picked from a hat on Easter Sunday (▷ 251).

The decorative floor tombs of illustrious Italians in the Basilica di Santa Croce

Neat hedges and lawns within the cloisters of San Lorenzo

A bronze turtle in Piazza Santa Maria Novella

The column-framed window of San Miniato al Monte

SAN LORENZO

🔲 424 C2 • Piazza San Lorenzo, 50123 Firenze ☎ 055 216634 🕐 Church: Mon–Sat 10–5.30. Cloister: Mon–Sat 10–6, Sun 9–1 🎫 Adult €2.50; child (under 6) free

The principal members of the Medici dynasty from Cosimo Il to Cosimo il Vecchio III are buried in this church. The basilica that once stood on the site was consecrated in 393 and is thought to have been the oldest church in Florence. The Medici commissioned Brunelleschi to rebuild it in 1425, enlisting Michelangelo's expertise for certain projects. There are fewer important works of art here than elsewhere in Florence, but the church is a shining example of archetypal Renaissance architecture.

The basilica dominates the bustling market area of San Lorenzo, rising above the lively and sometimes tawdry stands that attract bargain-hunters. The interior is dominated by the grey shades of *pietra serena* stone columns and the grey-white marble floor designed by Brunelleschi. Donatello's massive rectangular pulpits in the nave were his last work. Off the north transept is the Sagrestia Vecchia by Brunelleschi, featuring vaulting with terracotta tondi by Donatello, who also made the bronze doors. The small dome above the altar is decorated with frescoes of the zodiac in midnight blue and gold. You can wander out of the main door on the left into the graceful two-tiered cloisters that frame the garden planted with orange trees.

SANTA MARIA NOVELLA

🔲 424 B2 • Piazza Santa Maria Novella, 50123 Firenze ☎ Church: 055 215918; museum: 055 282187 🕐 Church: Mon–Thu, Sat 9.30–4.30, Fri, Sun 1–4.30. Museum: Mon–Sat 9–4.30, Sun 9–1.30 🎫 Church: adult €2.50, under 18s free. Museum: adult €2.60, under 12s free 🖥 www.smn.it

This Gothic church has numerous works of art but it attracts significantly fewer visitors than San Lorenzo and Santa Croce (▷ 133). It is a beautiful building, with outstanding stained-glass windows, chapels with important frescoes and calm cloisters.

The church stands on Piazza Santa Maria Novella, and has a striking black-and-white marble façade. Its lofty interior, with high stone vaulting decorated with stripes, is calm and uncluttered. The church's most famous fresco, Masaccio's *Trinità* (c1425), is remarkable for its use of perspective. The sanctuary is decorated with delightful frescoes by Domenico Ghirlandaio (1485–90), showing the lives of the Virgin Mary, John the Baptist and the Dominican saints. Next to it is the Filippo Strozzi Chapel in which there are some frescoes by Filippino Lippi illustrating the lives of St. Philip and St. John.

There are more important frescoes in the Museo di Santa Maria Novella, in the convent.

SAN MINIATO AL MONTE

🔲 425 E5 • Via Monte alle Croci, 50125 Firenze ☎ 055 234 2731 🕐 Summer daily 8–7.30; rest of year daily 8–12.30, 2.30–7.30 🎫 Free

The church of San Miniato al Monte, on a hill to the south of the city, is the finest example of a Romanesque church in Tuscany. Apart from being a beautiful church in itself, the site provides wonderful views across the Arno and the *centro storico* as far as Fiesole and the hills. A visit requires an uphill walk from town or a bus ride.

Built in 1013, the famous façade can be seen all over the city. White-and-green geometrical marble designs surround a glittering 13th-century mosaic of Christ between the Virgin and St. Minias. Little has changed inside the church since the 11th century. In the middle of the nave the 1207 marble floor is made up of intarsia panels decorated with animals and signs of the zodiac. The Cappella del Crocifisso has a freestanding tabernacle carved by Michelozzo (1396–1472) and terracotta pieces by Luca della Robbia (1400–82). At 5.30pm (4.30pm in winter) you can hear the Benedictine monks, who inhabit the convent next door, singing Gregorian chants.

SANTO SPIRITO

🔲 424 B4 • Piazza Santo Spirito, 50125 Firenze ☎ 055 287043 🕐 Church: Mon–Tue, Thu–Sat 10–12, 4–5.30, Wed 10–12, Sun 4–5.30. Cenacolo: summer Tue–Sun 9–2; winter 10.30–1.30 🎫 Church: free. Cenacolo: adult €2.10, child (under 20) €1.60 🖥 www.firenzeturismo.it

The massive Santo Spirito was the last church designed by Filippo Brunelleschi (1377–1446). Its most notable feature is the simple 18th-century façade, now an emblem for the Oltrarno district of Florence. This is a great place to escape the crowds and discover artistic gems.

Brunelleschi began designing the church in 1444 and the work was finished in 1481. The huge structure, with its strange, blank façade, dominates pretty Piazza Santo Spirito. In spite of its grandeur, it is still a parish church and its broad steps provide a convenient outdoor sitting room for the local residents.

Inside, grey *pietra serena* stone dominates, with massive columns, arches and vaults creating a harmonious space. The walls are lined with 38 chapels.

TUSCANY AND UMBRIA

With their rolling hills, vines, olives and cypresses, Tuscany and Umbria are synonymous with the Italian idyll. Both regions are rich in hilltop villages and historic towns, while cities such as medieval Siena, fortified Lucca, Perugia and Orvieto hold artistic treasures. The east, dominated by the Apennines, has some of Italy's finest upland landscapes, with boundless opportunities for enjoying the great outdoors.

MAJOR SIGHTS

Basilica di Santa Chiara (above) and the fountain in Piazza del Comune

ASSISI

Medieval treasures associated with the lives of San Francesco (St. Francis) and Santa Chiara (St. Clare).

Assisi, the birthplace of St. Francis (1182–1226), stands on the whalebacked slopes of Monte Subasio, above the Vale of Spoleto. Founded by the Umbrians, it became an important Roman *municipium*, and in the Middle Ages fell into the hands of the Baglioni family of Perugia. Plague, famine and tight ecclesiastical control later turned Assisi into a moribund backwater. Its economic decline was reversed when St. Francis was made patron saint of Italy in 1939. As a result, Assisi became one of the most prosperous towns in the region.

BASILICA DI SAN FRANCESCO

Combining Umbrian Romanesque with French-inspired Gothic architecture, the complex consists of two churches, one above the other. The dimly lit lower church (1228–30) has frescoes by Cimabue and Giotto. The four frescoes over the main altar depict St. Francis in glory and the virtues of the Franciscan order—poverty, chastity and obedience. Don't miss Cimabue's simple portrait of St. Francis in the right transept. St. Francis is buried in the crypt.

By contrast, the upper church, superbly restored after the 1997 earthquake, is drenched with light, its soaring arches the perfect backdrop for Giotto's fresco *Scenes from the Life of St Francis*.

BASILICA DI SANTA CHIARA

St. Clare (1193–1253), founder of the Order of the Poor Clares, dedicated her life to the Franciscan movement. The Romanesque basilica, with its pink and white striped stonework and huge flying buttresses, was built between 1257 and 1265. The highlight is the iconic painting of *St. Clare and Eight Scenes from Her Life* behind the altar, painted in 1283 by an unknown Umbrian artist. St. Clare's remains are in the crypt.

PIAZZA DEL COMUNE

At the heart of Assisi is the Piazza del Comune, the site of the Roman forum. Here the imposing Torre del Popolo stands next to the Temple of Minerva, intact with its elegant Corinthian columns. Erected in the first century BC, it has been a church since 1539. Overlooking the town is Rocca Maggiore, a fearsome 14th-century fortress (daily 9–8).

RATINGS

Historic interest	●●●○
Cultural interest	●●●●●
Photo stops	●●●○
Walkability	●●●○

BASICS

🖫 437 H8

🛈 Piazza del Comune 22, 06082 Assisi, tel 075 812534; Mon–Fri 8–2, 3–6, Sat 9–1, 3–6, Sun 10–1

❓ Tickets for Rocca Maggiore, Pinacoteca and Foro Romano from €2, www.sistemamuseo.it 🖢 Official guides can be hired in English, French Spanish, German, Russian and Swedish (tel 075 815228, www.umbria.org./tourguides)

🚉 Assisi, Santa Maria degli Angeli www.ambria2000.it

TIPS

● **Shorts, miniskirts, sleeveless tops, mobile phones and flash photography are not permitted in the churches.**

● *Calendimaggio*, **a medieval costume festival with street parades and music, takes place on the first Thursday, Friday and Saturday in May. The Festa di San Francesco is on 3 or 4 October.**

St Francis' wooded retreat, the Eremo delle Carceri, to the east of Assisi; the convent there dates from 1426 (left)

The Abbazia di Monte Oliveto Maggiore

The Piazza Grande in Arezzo, the venue for the Giostra del Saracino (medieval jousting) in late August and a monthly antiques fair

THE SIGHTS

ABBAZIA DI MONTE OLIVETO MAGGIORE

✚ 436 G8 ☎ 0577 707611
🕐 May–end Sep daily 9.15–12, 3.15–5.45; Oct–end Apr daily 9.15–12, 3.15–5 💲 Free ⬛ 🍴 ⊞

Near Chiusure, 9km (6 miles) northeast of Buonconvento, the isolated and beautiful medieval monastery of Monte Oliveto Maggiore is still home to a thriving monastic community. Set on a tree-covered hillside, the abbey draws numerous visitors who come to see the fresco cycle, one of the finest in Tuscany, in the Chiostro Grande (Grand Cloister). The abbey was founded by Bernardo Tolomei, a member of a wealthy Sienese family, and the delightful old buildings date from 1272. The Chiostro Grande has a fresco cycle on the life of St. Benedict, founder of the Benedictine order. It was created by Luca Signorelli, who began the work in 1498, and by the Milanese artist, Sodoma, who completed the majority of the work between 1505 and 1508. The church has a 15th-century layout. The monks have a library of 40,000 books and other documents, along with a workshop where they restore old books.

ABBAZIA DI SAN PIETRO IN VALLE

✚ 438 H–J9 ☎ 0744 780316 🕐 Daily 10–5; closed occasionally 1–2 💲 Free 📖 ❓ Custodian in the village will show you around (her family has been providing the service free for 100 years)—in Italian only, but she speaks very slowly

Set in idyllic surroundings, with its tall campanile rising above woods, San Pietro in Valle is steeped in history. Founded by Faroaldo II, the Lombard Duke of Spoleto, in 720, this abbey has some exceptional frescoes and beautiful cloisters. The restored fresco cycle in the nave depicts Bible scenes, and is considered to be one of Italy's most important examples of Romanesque art for the variety of scenes depicted and the complexity of the work (late 12th to early 13th century). Look for the lively images of Noah being called to Eternity and Adam naming the animals. More frescoes cover the apses—those in the right-hand apse are by followers of Giotto. A small fresco in the left aisle illustrates the *Dream of Faroaldo*; it shows Faroaldo being visited by St. Peter, who is instructing him to build a monastery on this holy spot in his honour.

Also to be found in the open nave are a rare seventh-century Lombard altar showing the signature of the original craftsman (Ursus), and Roman sarcophagi carved with mythological scenes and reused as tombs for Faroaldo and his family.

AREZZO

✚ 437 G7 ℹ Piazza della Repubblica 28, 52100 Arezzo, tel 0575 377678 🚇 Arezzo

Arezzo thrived during the Middle Ages as a major hub of goldwork and jewellery manufacture and its historic old town still survives. About 80km (50 miles) southeast of Florence, it sits on a hilltop overlooking a fertile plain near the Arno, dominated by its cathedral and fortress. Many people come simply to enjoy Piero della Francesca's famous fresco cycle, *The Legend of the True Cross*, in the Church of San Francesco (Apr–end Sep Mon–Fri 9–7, Sat 9–6, Sun 9.45–10.45; Oct–end Mar Mon–Fri 9–6, Sat 9–5.30, Sun 9.45–10.45. Reserve in advance on tel 0575 24001).

One of Italy's most famous paintings, painted on the walls around the high altar in the Cappella Bacci (Apr–end Sep Mon–Fri 9–7, Sat 9–6, Sun 9.45–10.45; Oct–end Mar Mon–Fri 9–6, Sat 9–5.30, Sun 9.45–10.45) between 1453 and 1466, illustrates the legend of the cross on which Christ was crucified. There is another fresco by Piero della Francesca in the duomo (daily 6.30–12.30, 3–7). A short stroll away is the Passeggio del Prato, an attractive park overlooked by the Fortezzo Medicea (1538–60), a castle built by the town's Medici rulers. The Museo Archeologico (daily 8.30–7.30), in the Roman amphitheatre, has some priceless collections of local pottery.

The alleys around the main square, Piazza Grande, are full of dark workshops smelling of wood, where artisans restore antique furniture. On the first Sunday of the month the town is taken over by an excellent antiques fair.

BAGNO VIGNONI

✚ 436 G8 ℹ Strada di Bagno Vignoni, 53027 S. Quirico d'Orcia, tel 0577 888975

Bagno Vignoni is one of Tuscany's most fascinating sights, a village whose old stone buildings cluster around a large, open-air pool filled with water from a natural hot spring. When the air is cool, a mist rises from the warm water and drifts over the village square. The spring was known in Etruscan times, and the waters were enjoyed over the years by the Romans, along with popes and saints, including Catherine of Siena. In medieval times the baths became a resting place for pilgrims going along the Via Francigena, the pilgrims' route over the St. Bernard Pass and through Italy to Rome. Today this is still a great place to stop and rest, with plenty of restaurants. There's a children's playground near the parking area.

Bevagna's Teatro Torti is an example of the many theatres that once graced numerous Italian towns

Statue at the Abbazia di Monte Oliveto Maggiore, Buonconvento

BARGA

✚ 436 F6 🚹 Piazza Salvo Salvi, 55051 Barga, tel 0583 72471 🚉 Fornacci di Barga or Barga Gallicano (nearer to town); long uphill climb from both
www.barganews.com
www.commune.barga.lu.it

Off the beaten track, yet easily accessible, Barga makes an ideal trip into the country for anyone staying in Lucca (▷ 142) or Pisa (▷ 149). Stroll through its attractive, winding streets, shop for local produce, or simply enjoy a drink in one of its historic cafés.

Barga sits on a hill above the Serchio Valley, 28km (17 miles) north of Lucca, with lovely views of the Alpi Apuane. The town has strong links with Scotland, as many of its residents emigrated to Glasgow. The town even has its own fish-and-chip fair in August.

It has kept much of its medieval appearance and layout, with remnants of the old walls and narrow, steep streets stretching down from the imposing duomo. It is a steep climb to the duomo, but worth it for the views.
Don't miss Caffè Capretz, a historic and atmospheric café established in 1870; for local produce, visit Mazzolini Andrea, a delectable shop on Via di Mezzo that sells a wide range of foods, from chestnut flour to mountain pecorino cheese.

BEVAGNA

✚ 437 H8 🚹 Pro Loco I.A.T Bevagna, Piazza Filippo Silvestri 1, 06031 Bevagna, tel 0742 360 031
🕘 Guided tours of the town, theatre and Roman remains: daily 10.30–1, 2.30–5 💶 Adults €3.50, child (6–14) €1, under 6s free. Reserve by telephone or fax on 0742 360 031

The serenely beautiful walled town of Bevagna, lying 8km (5 miles) southwest of Foligno on the edge of the Vale of Spoleto, is

an ancient settlement that once straddled the Roman Via Flaminia. Five gates pierce the walls, from which a warren of medieval streets converges on the irregular Piazza Filippo Silvestri, home to two of Umbria's finest Romanesque churches, San Michele and San Silvestro (daily 10–1, 3–6). Both were built in 1195 by an architect known as Maestro Binello, who also worked in Spello (▷ 155), and have a similar interior layout, with a raised presbytery and sunken crypt. The naves are lined with sturdy columns, whose Egyptian-style capitals were perhaps copied from those of a Roman temple, and both churches are faced with pink stone from Monte Subasio across the plain. These splendid buildings are balanced by the 12th-century Palazzo dei Consoli. In the 19th century its interior was adapted to house the charming Teatro Torti, a minuscule theatre complete with balconies and boxes. East of here, down the Corso Matteoti, Bevagna's Roman past is still present in the shape of a magnificent black-and-white Roman mosaic, the remains of a Roman temple and the tunnels that once lay beneath the stage of the amphitheatre.

BUONCONVENTO

✚ 436 G8 🚹 Museo di Arte Sacra della Val d'Arbia, Via Soccini 18, 53020 Buonconvento, tel 0577 807181
🚉 Buonconvento

Buonconvento is a small historic town, an important trading post in the mid-13th century and a prominent stopping-off point for pilgrims along the Via Francigena.

The town is at the confluence of the Arbia and Ombrone rivers, between Siena and Montalcino. Its outskirts are unattractive but well-preserved medieval parts are surrounded by walls built between 1371 and 1381.

The Museo d'Arte Sacra (summer Tue–Sun 10.30–1; winter Sat–Sun 10–1, 2–5) is a museum of religious art displaying Sienese paintings from the 14th to the 17th century. It also has displays of jewellery, wood and marble sculptures.
Don't miss The 14th-century Church of Santi Pietro e Paulo has an early 15th-century fresco by an unknown Sienese artist and a *Madonna and Child* (1450) by Matteo di Giovanni.

CHIANTI

✚ 436 G7 🚹 Via Ferruccio 40, 53011 Castellina in Chianti (Siena), tel 0577 742311
www.chiantinet.it

The Chianti region, between Florence and Siena, is generally explored by driving down the Chiantigiana (SS222), a designated scenic wine road that runs through the heart of the district. This seductive area of rolling hills, has produced wine since Etruscan times. The landscape is often wild, characterized by rich farmland, heavily wooded slopes, isolated villas and numerous vineyards. Visit some of the region's towns, such as Castellina in Chianti, Greve in Chianti (the unofficial capital) and Radda in Chianti.

Castellina in Chianti was once of great strategic importance as it sits on the border between the territories of Siena and Florence. You can still see its ancient fortress and walk along the Via delle Volte, a tunnel-like road that runs around the walls.

Radda in Chianti (tel 0577 738494) is a hilltop town offering great views over the region, with fine buildings dating from the 15th and 16th centuries.

The lovely town of Greve in Chianti (tel 055 854 6287) has plenty of wine shops, cobbled streets and alleyways to explore.

The Renaissance church of the Madonna del Calcinaio on the hillside a few miles from the Tuscan town of Cortona

A woman decorating ceramics, a common sight in Deruta

CITTÀ DI CASTELLO

✠ 437 H7 ℹ Logge Bufalini, Piazza Matteoti, 06012 Città di Castello, Perugia, tel 075 855 4922
❓ CartaMusei (€5), valid for one week, gives reduced entry to certain museums (including Pinacoteca Comunale, Collezione Burri, Museo del Duomo and Centro Documentazione Tradizioni Popolari)
www.umbria2000.it
www.guideinumbria.com

Città di Castello has an interesting range of ancient and modern art housed in its elegant palazzi and former tobacco-drying sheds, where traditional crafts continue to thrive. Surrounded by medieval walls, the town occupies a central position in the Upper Tiber Valley. The Pinacoteca Comunale, in the Palazzo Vitelli alla Cannoniera, is an important gallery in Umbria. The oldest painting here is a large altarpiece by Maestro di Città de Castello, *Madonna in Trono col Bambino*, surrounded by six angels (13th century). In Room 6 is the only painting by Raphael to remain in the Pinacoteca, the *Gonfalon of the Holy Trinity*, one of his first works. It has been used for hundreds of years as a *gonfalone* (banner) during religious festivals and has suffered wear and tear. In Piazza Gabriotti, the newly restored ecclesiastical museum, the Museo del Duomo (Oct–end Mar Tue–Sun 10–1, 2.30–6.30; Apr–end Sep Tue–Sun 9.30–1, 2.30–7), houses the Treasure of Canoscio from the palaeo-Christian period (sixth century), a rare collection of embossed silver ceremonial objects used during Mass.

CORTONA

✠ 437 H7 ℹ Via Nazionale 42, 52044 Cortona, tel 0575 630352

Perched on a steep hillside overlooking the Valdichiana and Lake Trasimeno, beguiling

Cortona, with its medieval streets and good hotels and restaurants, makes a perfect overnight stopping point heading from southern Tuscany into Umbria. Substantial parts of the town's Etruscan walls are incorporated into the medieval structure, and churches and fine museums grace the precipitous cobbled streets.

From the focal point, Piazza della Repubblica, it is a short stroll to Piazza del Duomo, the setting for the Museo Diocesano (daily 10–5, tel 0575 62830). The highlights include two masterpieces by Fra Angelico, an *Annunciation* and a *Madonna and Child with Saints*, along with works by Sassetta, Bartolomeo della Gatta and Luca Signorelli. The archaeological star is a second-century Roman sarcophagus carved with scenes depicting Dionysus's battle with the Amazons, a work much admired by the Renaissance sculptors Donatello and Filippo Brunelleschi. The town's Etruscan past is recalled in the Museo dell'Accademia Etrusca (daily 10–5), which has a huge fifth-century bronze lamp, some exquisite jewellery, urns and vases, and an impressive, if incongruous, ancient Egyptian collection.

DERUTA

✠ 437 H8 ℹ Piazza dei Consoli 4, 0653 Deruta, tel 075 971 1559; Mar–end Jun only

Deruta has been famous for its ceramics and majolica since the 14th century. Shops selling pottery abound, and in the old town you can visit the Museo Regionale della Ceramica (Apr–end Jun daily 10.30–1, 3–6; Jul–end Sep daily 10.30–1, 3.30–6.30; Oct–end Mar Wed–Mon 10.30–1, 2.30–5, tel 075 971 1000). This restored

museum building traces the history of ceramics from the earliest examples of terracotta to lavish Renaissance majolica. Among the fascinating exhibits is a display of plates presented as wedding gifts, devotional plaques, spouted drug jars and even a shoe-shaped handwarmer. The museum also contains fragments of floor from Perugia's Rocca Paolina and Priors' Chapel. The old town has a fountain by its main street, and many of the façades of the shops and buildings are covered in ceramic tiles. Next to the museum is the 14th-century church of San Francesco, which has Umbrian frescoes.

ISOLA D'ELBA

✠ 436 E8 ℹ Calata Italia 43, 193 Portoferraio, tel 0565 914671 🚢 From Piombino

Most people visit the mountainous island of Elba to explore the place where Napoleon lived in exile from May 1814 to February 1815, but others come to enjoy the delightful scenery, unspoiled beaches and bustling resort towns. There are plenty of historic sites to visit, including Napoleon's former villa and ancient, abandoned mines. The island is also an excellent place for walking.

About 10km (6 miles) west of the mainland and an hour's ferry ride from Piombino, Elba is a natural mosaic made up of gulfs, headlands, a precipitous coastline, peaceful bays, maquis scrub, wooded mountains and terraced vineyards. It is the largest island in the Tuscan archipelago, a group of islands once described as the 'necklace that slid from the neck of Venus'. There are several walking trails as well as a cable car to the top of Mount Capanne, from where you can enjoy excellent views of the archipelago.

Bridge crossing the River Serchio in Castelnuovo di Garfagnana

The waterfront at Passignano on Lago Trasimeno, from where you can get to Isola Maggiore

In Portoferraio, the Palazzina dei Mulini, Napoleon's home while he was exiled, is now a museum (Wed–Mon 9–7, Sun and holidays 9–1) housing period furniture and Napoleon's library.

Porto Azzurro, the island's Spanish capital, is a busy resort dominated by a huge fortress that was once used as a prison.

FIESOLE

✚ 436 G7 ℹ Piazza Mino da Fiesole 36, 50014 Fiesole, tel 055 598720 www.commune.fiesole.fi.it

On a hilltop 7km (4 miles) northeast of Florence, Fiesole offers sweeping views.

Originally an Etruscan settlement, Fiesole grew in importance under the Romans; in the Area Archeologica east of the main square, Piazza Mino da Fiesole, there is a Roman amphitheatre, baths and temple and sixth-century Etruscan ruins.

Piazza Mino da Fiesole is where you'll find the duomo, shops and restaurants. From here you can climb Via San Francesco for views of Florence. The Museo Bandini (daily 9.30–7) has ivories, ceramics and paintings on display, while the church of San Domenico has Fra Angelico's *Madonna with Saints and Angels*.

GARFAGNANA

✚ 436 F6 ℹ Centro Visite Parco Alpi Apuane, Piazza delle Erbe 1, 55032 Castelnuovo di Garfagnana, tel 0583 65169 ℝ Castelnuovo di Garfagnana www.garfagnanavacanze.it www.pacapuane.toscana.it

This delightful, undiscovered area north of Lucca is dotted with historic little towns and laced with a range of walking trails. If you have a car, you can visit the spa town of Bagni di Lucca, visited by Lord Byron, the area's main hub of Castelnuovo di Gafagnana, and the remote hamlet of San

Pellegrino in Alpe. Even without a car, you can reach towns such as Barga (▷ 139). The area is perfect for wildlife-lovers, as the surrounding Alps are home to many species of bird, including the golden eagle.

The Garfagnana is on the eastern side of the River Serchio, which forges a path between the rugged Alpi Apuane and the gentler, more rounded slopes of the Garfagnana. The most rugged part of the Garfagnana is the nature reserve of Orecchiella, near Castelnuovo.

Castelnuovo di Garfagnana is a pleasant, bustling town at the heart of the Garfagnana. It has an open-air market every Thursday.

San Pellegrino in Alpe is an ancient pilgrimage area, and has a good folk museum. The winding roads mean that the area cannot be explored quickly, but it is easily accessible from Lucca (▷ 142) and Pisa (▷ 149).

GUBBIO

✚ 437 H7 ℹ Piazza Odersi 6 (off Corso Garibaldi), 06024 Gubbio, tel 075 922 0790 www.umbria2000.it

Gubbio's grey limestone medieval buildings are built on a series of terraces against the backdrop of Mount Ingino, 40km (25 miles) from Perugia (▷ 148).

The spectacular Palazzo dei Consoli (town hall) is home to the Museo Civico (daily 10–1, 3–6, tel 075 927 4298) and its unique treasure, the *Tavole Iguine* (Eugubine Tablets). The seven bronze plaques (second- to first-century BC) are written in the ancient Umbrian language, using the Etruscan and Latin alphabets. Discovered in 1444, they are the most important sacred texts in the whole of Italian classical antiquity, comparable in importance to the Rosetta Stone. They provide

information about worship, legal systems, the city-state structure and the religious ceremonies of the ancient Gubbian community.

A centuries-old ritual, *Corsa dei Ceri*, takes place here on 15 May, the eve of the feast of St. Ubaldo (Gubbio's patron saint) (▷ 258). The *ceri* are three 4m (13ft) wooden structures, each weighing about 200kg (440lb), made of two octagonal prisms joined by a central mast and crowned with statues of St. Ubaldo, St. George and St. Anthony. The *ceri* bearers race up through the streets to Basilica di Sant'Ubaldo on Mount Ingino. Near the Roman theatre is the 13th-century church of San Francesco, where St. Francis once took refuge.

LAGO TRASIMENO

✚ 437 H8 ℹ Piazza Giuseppe Mazzini, 06061 Castiglione del Lago, tel 075 965 2484 ℝ Castiglione del Lago www.umbria2000.it

Lake Trasimeno is the largest inland lake on the Italian peninsula, but it is also one of the shallowest, with an average depth of 6m (20ft). Its bays, capes and islands are surrounded by fertile hillsides dotted with castles and olive groves. There are beaches, a wild nature reserve, jetties for boating, fishing and day trips by ferry to its two main islands, Isola Polvese and Isola Maggiore. Isola Maggiore is small, with a pretty 14th- to 15th-century village. It is inhabited by fishermen, and the women still make traditional 'Irish stitch' lace. St. Francis spent Lent here in 1211, and Castello Guglielmi (Villa Isabella), on the southern tip is built over a former Franciscan convent. On the eastern shore of the lake, San Feliciano is a pretty fishing village. From here take a summer ferry to Isola Polvese, the lake's largest island, which is being made into a nature reserve.

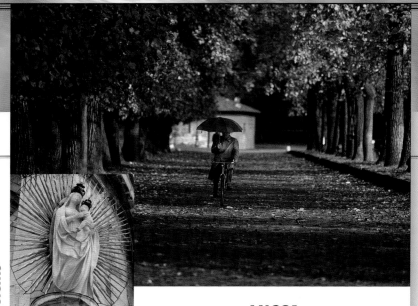

LUCCA

A well-preserved medieval town—the birthplace of Puccini. Completely encircled by 17th-century walls.

RATINGS				
Value for money	●	●	●	
Good for kids	●	●		
Historic interest	●	●	●	●	●
Photo stops	●	●	●	●	●

BASICS

✚ 436 F6
ℹ Main office: Piazza Santa Maria,
tel 0583 919931; daily 9–7; Piazzale
Verdi, 55100 Lucca, tel 0583 583150;
summer daily 9–7; rest of year 9–5
🚃 Lucca

www.commune.lucca.it

TIPS

● Lucca is easily explored on foot. The station is only 10 minutes' walk away and parking is not easy, so it is worth visiting by train.
● Do as the locals and get around by bicycle; they can be hired from the tourist office or numerous places around town (look for *noleggio de bici*).
● Walk along the famous encircling walls (4km/2.5 miles).
● For great views over the city, climb the Torre Guinigi, easily recognized by the tree sprouting improbably out of the top.

Mature trees line sections of the broad town wall (top); a Virgin and Child by Civitali in San Michele church (above)

Lucca lies in the heart of a fertile plain in northwest Tuscany, an hour's drive from Florence (▷ 115–134) and 22km (14 miles) northeast of Pisa (▷ 149). Piazza San Michele is the site of the old Roman forum, hence the name of the Romanesque church here, San Michele in Foro. The church (daily 7.30–12, 3–6) dates from 1070 and has a dazzling exterior of striped marble walls and an intricate medley of tiny loggias, decorated columns and lavish carvings. A few minutes' walk away is the Casa di Puccini (daily 10–6), the birthplace of Giacomo Puccini, composer of operas such as *Tosca* and *Madame Butterfly*. His former home is now a museum where you can see the piano at which he composed his last work.

THE CATHEDRAL

Lucca's cathedral, the Duomo di San Martino (mid-Mar to end Oct daily 7–7; rest of year daily 7–5), has 13th-century reliefs on and around the three principal doors, including some by Nicola Pisano, a noted 13th-century Pisan sculptor. Inside is Lucca's most important artwork, the *Volto Santo (Holy Face)*. A cedarwood crucifix, it is said to be an exact likeness of Christ, carved by Nicodemus. In the sacristy (mid-Mar to end Oct Mon 9.30–5.45, Sat 9–6.45, Sun 11.20–11.50, 1–4.45; rest of year Mon 9.30–4.45, Sat 9.30–6.45, Sun 11.20–11.50, 1–4.45) is the tomb of Ilaria del Carretto, a sublime funerary monument by the Sienese sculptor Jacopo della Quercia, depicting the wife of Paolo Guinigi, a medieval ruler of the city.

Next to the cathedral is the Museo della Cattedrale (mid-Mar to end Oct daily 10–6; rest of year Sat–Sun 10–2), which displays paintings and various religious objects.

ARTISTIC TREASURES

The Museo Nazionale di Villa Guinigi (Tue–Sat 9–7, Sun 9–2, tel 0583 496033) has an eclectic collection of paintings, sculpture, textiles, Roman and Etruscan archaeological finds, silverware and important works by the painter Fra Bartolommeo and the sculptor Matteo Civitali. The Museo Nazionale di Palazzo Mansi (Tue–Sat 9–7, Sun 9–2), also in a former palace, is worth visiting to see the sumptuous apartments, tapestries, precious *objets d'art* and fine furniture. Particularly impressive is the 18th-century bridal chamber, richly decked with gold.

Montalcino's timeless streets are a pleasure to wander around

Fishing boats in Porto Santo Stefano near Monte Argentario

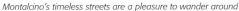

MAREMMA

⊞ 438 G8 ⓘ Parco Regionale della Maremma, Via Besagliari 7–9, 58010 Alberese, tel 0564 407098; summer only
www.parcomaremma.it

Cowboys on horseback herd long-horned bulls in this area of empty, often melancholy countryside, often referred to as the Wild West of Tuscany. The Maremma is the name given to the coastal plain that stretches from Cecina (south of Pisa) to Civitavecchia in Lazio. It includes the Monte Amiata range. Unspoiled coastal areas with wide, sandy beaches dominate the western part, while the landscape inland has been covered for centuries in wild, marshy tracts of maquis—fragrant scrub containing a variety of herbs (such as thyme), wildflowers and low bushes. The Etruscans started draining the region, but it reverted to malarial swamp until it was finally drained by Mussolini.

The area between Principina a Mare and Talamone on the Tyrrhenian coast is a nature reserve, where you might spot porcupines, wild boar and deer, as well as migratory birds. The park visitor centre is in Alberese, about 14km (9 miles) south of Grosseto, capital of the Maremma.

Don't miss Grosseto, a walled town with a 13th-century red and white cathedral and an archaeological museum.

MASSA MARITTIMA

⊞ 438 F8 ⓘ Via Paneati 2, 58024 Massa Marittima, tel 0566 902756

A former mining town might not have much to offer the visitor in most countries, but this ancient city has some fascinating artworks, a fine 12th-century cathedral, an archaeological museum and a museum

commemorating the town's mining history.

South of Volterra, 66km (41 miles) east of Centro Carapax, Massa Marittima overlooks the valley of the River Pecora. The town is divided in two: the lower, Città Vecchia (Old Town), and the upper, Città Nuova (New Town), the sense of which is debatable, as it dates from 1228.

There is a fortress between the two, built after the area was conquered by Siena in 1335. The old town has a striking, sloping medieval square, dominated by the cathedral, while the new town has a 13th-century tower with far-reaching views over the surrounding metal-rich hills.

The duomo was initially built in Romanesque style and later enlarged in the Gothic style. Dedicated to St. Cerbone, it has a baptismal font dating from 1267 and a sculpture carved in 1324 by Giraldo da Como. The Palazzo Podestà (Tue–Sun 10–1, 4–7), a 13th-century palazzo housing the museum of archaeology, has many not very interesting Etruscan finds and a small collection of medieval works of art, including a superb *Maestà (Majesty)* by Ambrogio Lorenzetti.

MONTALCINO

⊞ 436 G8 ⓘ Via Costa del Municipio 8, 53024 Montalcino, tel 0577 849331
www.prolocomontalcino.it

Montalcino is one of Tuscany's most important wine-producing towns, the home of the excellent rich red Brunello, the lighter Rosso di Montalcino and the fragrant Moscadello di Montalcino. The streets are liberally scattered with wine shops (*enoteche*), where you can often taste before purchasing.

High on a hilltop 40km (25 miles) south of Siena, the town is dominated by its *rocca* (fortress), a picture-perfect 14th-century

castle (daily 9–8). From the battlements you can look out over southern Tuscany. The Palazzo Comunale, a fine civic palace built in 1292, dominates Piazza del Popolo, the main square. The Fiaschetteria Italiana (daily 7.30–midnight) here is a bustling café established in 1888 with an ornate mirrored interior.

The Museo Civico (Apr–end Oct Tue–Sun 10–6; Nov–end Mar Tue–Sun 10–1, 2–6), the town's principal museum, is in the former convent of Sant'Agostino; with medieval and late Gothic artworks, and wood sculptures from the 14th and 15th centuries.

Montalcino is a good place from where to explore the abbey of Sant'Antimo and the villages of the Val d'Orcia.

MONTE ARGENTARIO

⊞ 438 F9 ⓘ Corso Umberto 55, Archetto del Paliol, 58019 Porto Santo Stefano, tel 0564 814208 ⓡ Orbetello

If you would like to see where the Italian jet set hides out, this is one place worth visiting. Southwest of Grosseto, Monte Argentario was once an island, but the shallow waters silted up and it is now a promontory linked to the mainland by causeways. It was on one of the beaches here that the painter Caravaggio died in 1609.

At one time owned by the Spanish, it became part of Tuscany in the 19th century. Its Spanish heritage can be seen in Porto Santo Stefano, where a Spanish fortress still stands, and in Porto Ercole, where there are three Spanish forts.

The harbours of the nearby villages are filled with expensive yachts, while the southern tip of the promontory is less developed and sophisticated. The highest point is Monte Telegrafo, from where there are good views over the Maremma.

Montefalco's Piazza del Comune is the highest point in town

The classical church of San Biagio outside Montepulciano

The medieval town of Narni with its rustic ochre buildings

THE SIGHTS

MONTEFALCO

438 H8 🛈 Museo Civico de San Francesco, Via Ringhiera Umbra 6, 06037 Montefalco, tel 0742 379598
www.montefalcodoc.it

High up in rolling countryside, Montefalco is known as *La Ringhiere dell'Umbria* (Balcony of Umbria). Extensive views of the green Valle Umbra unfold from its majestic circular piazza. The medieval walls form a solid circle around the town.

Enter via the second-century gate of Sant'Agostino and climb the Corso to Piazza del Comune. Streets branch off downwards from this irregular-shaped square. The Museo Pinacoteca di San Francesco, in the former 14th-century church, has paintings dating from the 13th to the 17th century, including works by Perugino. The highlights are the world-famous 15th-century frescoes by Benozzo Gozzoli in the central apse, illustrating scenes from the life of St. Francis.

Montefalco is famous for traditional linen crafts, red wine (particularly Sagrantino) and gastronomy. The excellent wine shop Enoteca di Benozzo, in the main square, specializes in wine, truffles and oil.

MONTEPULCIANO

437 G8 🛈 Piazza Don Minzoni, 53045 Montepulciano, tel 0578 757341; summer daily 9–12.30, 2.30–7; rest of year 9.30–12.30, 3–6
🚉 Chiusi-Chianciano Terme (24km/ 15 miles away)
www.prolocomontepulciano.it

On a narrow ridge, with medieval streets, Montepulciano attracts lovers of art and culture, who come to admire the cathedral, palaces and Renaissance architecture. Wine buffs also enjoy the local Vino Nobile. When the town sided with Florence in 1511, it underwent a Renaissance

overhaul, a vast building project that involved leading architects, including Antonio Sangallo and the mannerist master Vignola. Today Montepulciano plays host to various cultural events, including an International Arts Workshop every summer.

The Museo Civico (Apr–end Sep daily 10–1, 3–7; Oct–end Mar daily 10–1, 3–6, tel 0579 717 300) has an impressive collection of ancient pottery, medieval sculpture, Etruscan tombs and cinerary urns, along with paintings by Sienese artists. The main square, Piazza Grande, is dominated by the duomo (daily 9–12, 3–6), whose altarpiece is an *Assumption* by Taddeo di Bartolo. In the baptistery are numerous reliefs, terracottas and other sculptures by an array of medieval and Renaissance artists, including Andrea della Robbia. There are plenty of wine shops and restaurants in town, including the elegant Caffé Poliziano, with its art nouveau interior.

On the outskirts is the superb Renaissance church of San Biagio, built by Sangallo in the mid-16th century.

MONTERIGGIONI

436 G7 🛈 Largo Fontebranda 5, 53035 Castello di Monteriggioni, tel 0577 304810
www.monteriggionicastello.it

It is impossible to miss Monte-riggioni. Set on a hill with grey walls punctuated with towers, it has the appearance of a granite crown. This perfectly preserved Tuscan village is in better condition than popular San Gimignano (▷ 151) and, although there is not much to visit inside the walls—just a little church and a shop—the defensive walls are remarkable.

The town was founded by the Sienese in 1203 to defend the northern approach to Siena from

the Florentines. The enclosing walls were built between 1213 and 1219, destroyed in 1244 by invading Florentines and rebuilt between 1260 and 1270. Its 14 grim towers were described in Dante's *Inferno* as resembling giants.

NARNI

438 H9 🛈 Piazza dei Priori, 05035 Narni, tel 0744 715362 🚉 Narni
www.comune.narni.tr.it

The ancient hill town of Narni is built on a rocky spur overlooking the Nera gorge. From the grid of ancient Roman streets, a road climbs up to two labyrinthine medieval districts and the spectacular *rocca* (fortress), a papal stronghold built in 1370.

From Piazza Garibaldi, past the bronze fountain and the medieval tower, is the cathedral of San Giovenale (1145), entered through an arch to Piazza Cavour. The main doorway has a graceful Renaissance portico with a frieze of garlands above the arcade, and the interior is a fusion of Romanesque and baroque styles. From here on, Via Garibaldi, which has been the main street since Roman times, becomes Piazza dei Priori, once the Roman forum. The square was narrowed in medieval times with the construction of two tower-houses, the Palazzo della Podestà and Palazzo dei Priori. The latter has a fine 14th-century loggia attributed to Gattapone.

NORCIA

439 J8 🛈 Viaile Lubani, Palazzo Comunale, Piazza San Benedetto, Norcia, tel 0743 816090
www.norcia.net

Norcia, in a fertile valley at the foot of the Sibillini Mountains on the Marche border, is a town of wide streets and low stucco-fronted buildings—many built after

An elegant arcade and a stone carving of a lion at the bottom of the steps in Piazza San Benedetto, Norcia

Looking out over the Tuscan countryside from Pienza's walls

the 1859 tremors, when a maximum height of 12.5m (41ft) was set. In Piazza San Benedetto, the main square, you can see a statue of St. Benedict, the father of Western monasticism, who was born here in 480. The Basilica di San Benedetto, the Palazzo Comunale and the Castellina are all on the piazza.

The Castellina houses Norcia's Civic Museum (summer daily 10–1, 5–7.30; rest of year daily 10–1, 3–5), and was built in 1554 as a cross between a fortress and a government palace. There are archaeological displays and a diocesan collection with a fine 13th-century *Deposition from the Cross*, a *Risen Christ* by Nicola da Siena, a *Madonna and Child* by Antonio da Faenza and a glazed terracotta *Annunciation* by Luca della Robbia.

Well known for their expert knifework, Norcia's butchers were often empolyed as surgeons in the Middle Ages. Today, Norcia is still famous for its *norcinerie* (pork butchers' shops). Around the square there are food shops bursting with local delicacies like wild boar sausages, black truffles and cheese.

ORVIETO

See page 146.

PARCO NAZIONALE DEI MONTI SIBILLINI

See page 147.

PARCO REGIONALE MONTE SUBASIO

☩ 437 H8 ☎ 0742 301144 ◎ Closed to traffic 8pm–6am ⊠ Spello or Assisi

Monte Subasio rises behind Assisi (▷ 136–137), overlooking the Valle Umbra, and has played a part in the town's history and culture. It was from here that the timber and rose-pink Subasio stone, so characteristic of the area, was taken to construct the

city. St. Francis, who had a passion for nature, is said to have walked here.

The Subasio mountain range is a protected area, reaching heights of 1,290m (4,232ft), and extending over 7,500ha (18,532 acres). Monte Subasio was once entirely covered by a forest of tall holm oaks. Today a splendid group of these oaks remains around the Franciscan hermitage, the Eremo delle Carceri.

From the Porta Cappuccini on the edge of Assisi you can drive over the broad, flat mountain beyond Spello to Collepino, densely covered with olive trees. The unsurfaced road over the top has potholes; it is not recommended in winter, but in spring there are huge spreads of narcissi, wild orchids, fritillary and wild peonies.

PERUGIA

See page 148.

PIANO GRANDE

☩ 439 J8 ⓘ Via Solferino 22, 06047 Norcia, tel 0743 816090

Remote, wild and beautiful, the Piano Grande (Great Plain) is a high plateau in eastern Umbria, overshadowed by Monte Vettore, at 2,476m (8,127ft) the highest summit in this stretch of the Apennines, the Monti Sibillini (▷ 147). The plain is ringed with whaleback hills, which still support a unique agricultural and pastoral way of life, with sheep, cattle and wild horses constantly moving across the grassland, and strip fields where lentils, one of Italy's most renowned products, are grown. In spring and early summer, the plain and surrounding hills are covered in a thick carpet of wildflowers; numerous types of orchid, wild peony, wild tulip, fritillary, narcissus and spreads of thyme and globularia are among the

many species. In July these give way to drifts of poppies, cornflowers and marigolds, drawing visitors from miles around to admire the Fioritura dei Piani (Blossoming of the Plains).

At the far end of the plain is the weather-beaten village of Castelluccio. At about 1,450m (4,757ft) above sea level, it is the highest village in Umbria and the last outpost of the region. Castelluccio is a good base from which to explore Sibillini Mountains National Park. There is also a hang-gliding and para-sailing school here.

PIENZA

☩ 437 G8 ⓘ Piazza Pio II 59, 53026 Pienza, tel 0578 748852 www.turisimo.toscano.it

Pienza lies in ravishing, rolling countryside in the southeast corner of Tuscany, close to the hilltop town of Montepulciano and 55km (34 miles) southeast of Siena. Barely more than a village, it consists of a maze of small lanes that runs parallel with the main square. You will be enchanted by its timeless atmosphere and crisp beauty, qualities recognized by UNESCO, which has ensured that Pienza will be preserved for future generations.

The cathedral (daily 7–1, 2.30–7) has paintings by five prominent Sienese painters, commissioned by Pope Pius II. Behind it, from the lanes and alleyways that run along the top of the walls, there are beautiful views towards Monte Amiata. The Museo Diocesano (Wed–Mon 10–1, 3–7), in Corso Rossellino, brings together paintings, sculptures, tapestries and other medieval and Renaissance pieces of art from various churches in the area, including a 14th-century cope (priest's cloak-like vestment) embroidered by English monks.

RATINGS

Historic interest	● ● ● ● ●
Cultural interest	● ● ●
Specialist shopping	● ● ● ●

BASICS

✚ 438 H8

🛈 Piazza Duomo 24, 05018 Orvieto, tel 0763 341772; Mon–Fri 8.15–1.50, 4–7, Sat 10–7, Sun and holidays 10–6

🎫 Carta Orvieto Unica, €12.50/€10.50, includes entrance to Cappella di San Brizio in the duomo, Museo Claudio Faina, Orvieto Underground and the Torre del Moro; it also covers up to 5 hours' free parking and free city transport. Available from above sites and the tourist information office

🚉 Orvieto

TIPS

● The Orvieto Underground takes you on a guided journey through the tunnels and caves under the city (www.orvieto underground.it).

● The centuries-old *Festa La Palombella* (Festival of Doves) takes place at Pentecost each year in and around the cathedral square.

A view across the rich volcanic vineyards to Orvieto

ORVIETO

Surrounded by vineyards that produce the renowned wine. One of the Italy's great art cities, with a cathedral that's the best of its period in Italy and exciting archaeological sites.

Orvieto is one of the oldest settlements in Umbria, already in existence when the Etruscans arrived in the eighth century BC. Corso Cavour winds up from Piazza Cahen to Piazza della Repubblica, where it runs over the Roman *decumanus* (the main east–west thoroughfare) and the site of the Etruscan, and later Roman, forum. The Museo Claudio Faina (Apr–end Sep daily 9.30–6; Oct–end Mar Tue–Sun 10–5), in the Palazzo Faina, has an impressive collection of Etruscan finds.

THE DUOMO

The duomo (Mar–end Oct daily 7.30–12.45, 2.30–6.15; rest of year daily 7.30–12.45, 2.30–5.15) was built to commemorate the miracle of Bolsena. In 1264 a priest from Prague visiting Bolsena on his way to a pilgrimage to Rome witnessed blood dripping from the communion host on to the altar cloth. Pope Urban IV was so impressed that he ordered the blood-stained linen to be brought to a shrine built to house the holy cloth, the Cappella del Corporale. The cathedral's striking façade was begun by Lorenzo Maitani in 1304 but not completed for 300 years. At the top of the steps, bas-reliefs depict biblical scenes. In the right transept is the Cappella di San Brizio (separate ticket required); its cycle of frescoes, unique in Renaissance Italy, was worked on first by Fra Angelico, with help from Benozzo Gozzoli, and then by Luca Signorelli.

CURIOSITIES

Near the funicular station and the Rocca dell'Albornoz, in Piazza Cahen, is the Pozzo di San Patrizio (daily 10–6.45), a vast well with a shaft dropping 62m (203ft) constructed to guarantee a supply of water during a siege. Spendthrifts in Italy are said to have 'pockets as limitless as the Pozzo di San Patrizio'. The Necropoli Etrusca del Crocifisso del Tufo (daily 8.30–7) is a necropolis that dates back to the sixth century BC. The alleys are lined with chamber tombs made from blocks of tufa.

ORVIETO WINE

Well known since Etruscan times, Orvieto is one of the most ancient wines of Italy. The vines benefit from the mild climate and the mixture of clay and sandy soil full of volcanic minerals. The Enoteca Regionale (Mon–Fri 11–1, 5–7, Sat–Sun by appointment) in Piazza San Giovanni run guided tours and wine tastings.

PARCO NAZIONALE DEI MONTI SIBILLINI

An area of outstanding natural beauty, perfect for driving, walking, mountain-bicycling and skiing. A haven for some very rare species of birds and wildflowers.

The Sibillini Mountains National Park extends across 70,000ha (173,000 acres) of protected land in Umbria and the Marche, with more than 20 summits higher than 2,000m (6,562ft). The highest, Monte Vettore, rises to 2,476m (8,123ft). As can be seen in the massive limestone outcrops, sheer slopes, steep cliffs and deep escarpments scored by springs and waterfalls, this is a karstic landscape—limestone with cavities, passages and underground drainage, created by the dissolution of the rock.

ANIMAL AND PLANTLIFE

The wild, open spaces make the park a winner with wildflowers. To date, around 1,800 botanical species have been recorded. Above the tree line extremely rare species of plants, such as the Apennine edelweiss (*Leontopodium nivale*) and gentians grow in the grazing areas. Wildcats, wolves, deer and porcupine are just some of the wildlife that roam the park, but you are more likely to see flocks of grazing sheep, known as the white gold of the Sibillini Mountains, or shaggy white cattle. Eagles, peregrine falcons, goshawks and Alpine chough all nest in the park and there is a very wide range of butterflies, moths and insects.

FACT OR FICTION?

The Saracens came up from Sicily and raided the Valnerina region around the end of the ninth century. In the Upper Nera Valley there are many castles and watchtowers from where the inhabitants of the valley defended themselves against the raids. In the 15th and 16th centuries, the Sibillini Mountains were known all over Europe as a land of myth and legend. The rugged, magical landscape has inspired many popular romance tales, including the story of Sibyl, a divine soothsayer who lived in the caves in the mountain of the same name near Montemonaco and was thought to be able to foresee the future.

Another legend concerns Pontius Pilate: Buffaloes are said to have pulled the lifeless body of the Roman procurator into the waters of a demoniac lake, which turned red. In reality, the reddish waters of the circular Lago di Pilato come from a tiny crustacean—*Chircephalus marchesonii*—that inhabits the lake.

RATINGS				
Good for kids	●	●	●	●
Outdoor pursuits	●	●	●	●
Photo stops	●	●	●	●	●
Walkability	●	●	●	●	●

BASICS

➕ 439 J8

ℹ Main park office: Piazza P Capuzi 55, Visso tel 0737 95262; Apr–end Sep Mon–Fri 9.30–1, 3.30–6, Sat and Sun 10–1; Oct–end Mar Mon–Fri 9.30–1, 3–5, Sat and Sun 10–1
Other offices at Norcia and Preci; Opening hours erratic

❓ Mountain refuges at Forca Canapine and at ski resorts, tel 0743 823012; (Rifugio Perugia), tel 0743 8323015; (Monti del Sole), tel 0743 823002

www.sibillini.net
The official website of the Parco Nazionale dei Monti Sibillini has more information on the park's geography and plant and animal life and the projects that are protecting them. There is also information on the best way to visit the park, with practical information on hiking and mountain-bicycling.

TIPS

● Pick up a map of the area at any of the park's offices or tourist information points.
● The park's noticeboards and literature carry a characteristic blue and green emblem.
● There are many refuge points, ideal for picnic stops.

Monte Vettore and the Piano Grande in the Parco Nazionale

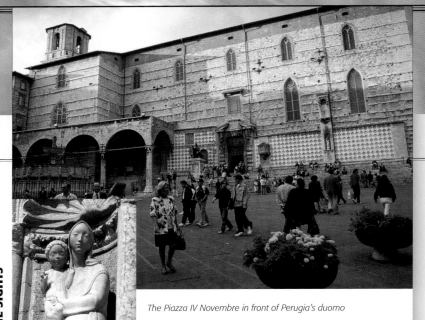

The Piazza IV Novembre in front of Perugia's duomo

THE SIGHTS

RATINGS

Historic interest	●●●○
Cultural interest	●●●○
Walkability	●●●○

BASICS

➕ 437 H8

🏠 Palazzo dei Priori, Piazza IV Novembre 3, Perugia, tel 075 573 6458; daily 8.30–1.30, 3.30–6.30 (holidays 9–1)

🚌 Perugia

TIPS

● The legendary Bar Pasticceria Sandri (Corso Vannucci 32) serves mouth-watering pastries and was recently voted one of the top 10 *pasticcerias* in Italy.
● An antiques market is held in the Giardini Carducci on the last Sunday of the month.

PERUGIA

**The cosmopolitan capital of Umbria, a city of immense cultural vitality and diversity.
Home to two universities, a world-famous jazz festival and a rich heritage.**

A settlement from the ninth century BC, Perugia became part of the Roman state under Emperor Augustus in the first century BC. A series of monastic complexes developed in the 13th and 14th centuries, and during the Renaissance and baroque period the new nobility built showy palaces. Today you can make a journey into the bowels of medieval Perugia by escalator: It takes you from Piazza Partigiani to Piazza Italia via a network of underground streets. Or take respite in the Orto Botanico Medievale, the old monastic garden behind San Pietro Convent, laid out with medicinal plants and herbs.

HEART OF THE CITY

The hub of Perugia is Piazza IV Novembre. The duomo, on the square, was begun in 1300 by Fra Bevignate and has an exterior pulpit from where San Bernardino preached. Inside, the chapel of St. Bernardino contains Federico Barocci's *Deposition* (1567), and the Cappella del Santo Annello has the Virgin Mary's prized wedding ring.

HIGHLIGHTS

The top floors of the Palazzo dei Priori, just off Piazza IV Novembre, house the Galleria Nazionale dell'Umbria (daily 8.30–7.30, closed 1st Mon of the month). It traces the development of Umbrian painting from its Byzantine-influenced roots through the Renaissance, which is particularly strongly represented by Umbria's two great masters, Perugino and Pinturicchio. Perugino was also responsible in 1496 for the superb fresco cycle in the Collegio del Cambio (Mar–end Oct Tue–Sat 9–12.30, 2.30–5.30, Sun 9–12.30; Nov–end Feb Tue–Sat 8–2), headquarters of Perugia's banking fraternity in Corso Vanucci, the city's classy main street. From here, steep and narrow streets lead to other churches and museums; the best include San Severo, which contains one of Raphael's earliest works, the simple fifth-century church of Sant'Angelo, the ornate San Pietro, and San Domenico, whose cloisters house the Museo Archeologico Nazionale dell'Umbria (Mon 2.30–7, Tue–Sun 8.30–7.30).

A detail of one of the duomo's statues (above)

Pisa's duomo, crowned by an elliptical dome, stands in front of the famous Leaning Tower

PISA

Campo dei Miracoli—home of the famous Leaning Tower, a striking cathedral and Italy's largest baptistery. A lively university city with attractive old churches, excellent museums and bustling streets lined with shops.

Pisa reached the peak of its power in the 11th and 12th centuries, but this golden age was followed by naval defeats, the collapse of its commercial empire and the silting up of the harbour. In 1406 it was taken over by Florence, and the Medici embarked on major rebuilding while turning Pisa into a focus for science and learning. Little of the city's former glory remains, as much of it was destroyed during World War II.

THE LEANING TOWER OF PISA

Pisa's most important treasures stand on the Campo dei Miracoli and include the Torre Pendente (Leaning Tower) (Apr–end Sep daily 8–7.50; Mar, Oct daily 9–7.10; Nov–end Feb daily 9–4.40), the duomo, the baptistery and the Camposanto, a medieval cemetery. Begun in 1173, the Leaning Tower was intended as the cathedral's bell tower. As it was built on sandy soil, it began to lean before it had been completed. By 1284 the lean was 90cm (35in) from the vertical, and medieval engineers were attempting to correct it. By 1350, when the tower was completed, the lean was 1.45m (4.75ft). In 1990 the tower was closed to allow scientists to stabilize it—it was now 4.5m (14.75ft) from the vertical, and getting worse. Tons of lead were attached to the northern side, steel cables were attached to hold it in place, and a wedge of soil was removed. Gradually the structure began to settle into the cavity and within five months had returned to the position it held in 1890.

OTHER HIGHLIGHTS

The duomo (1064) (Apr–end Sep Mon–Sat 10–7.30, Sun 1–7.30; Mar and Oct Mon–Sat 10–5.30, Sun 1–5.30; Nov–end Feb Mon–Sat 10–12.30, 3–4.30, Sun 3–4) has an ornate marble-striped exterior and carvings depicting New Testament stories. Inside, note the carved pulpit by Giovanni Pisano. Begun in 1152, the baptistery is the work of Giovanni and Nicola Pisano, with a pulpit carved with scenes from the life of Christ. The Camposanto (Apr–end Sep daily 8–7.30; Mar and Oct daily 9–5.30; Nov–end Feb daily 9–4.30), a medieval cemetery within a Gothic cloister, was decorated with some of Tuscany's most important frescoes, but only a few survived a World War II bomb.

RATINGS	
Good for kids	●●●●●
Historic interest	●●●
Cultural interest	●●●●
Photo stops	●●●●●

BASICS

✚ 436 F7

🛈 Campo dei Miracoli (behind Leaning Tower), 56100 Pisa, tel 050 560 464; Apr–end Sep Mon–Sat 9–7, Sun 10.30–4.30; Oct–end Mar Mon–Sat 9–5.30. Piazza della Stazione (left on exiting the railway station), 56100 Pisa tel 050 42291; Apr–end Sep Mon–Sat 9–7, Sun 9.30–3.30; Oct–end Mar Mon–Sat 9.30–1, 3–5.30

🎫 Joint ticket (Duomo, Baptistery, Camposanto, Museo delle Sinopie): €10.50. Duomo: €2 but free Nov–end Mar. Duomo plus any two other sites: €8. Duomo plus any four sites: €8.50

🎟 Leaning Tower guided tour (35 min). Timed tickets should be reserved in advance at the ticket office or online at www.opapisa.it (€15)

🚉 Pisa Centrale

www.pisa.turismo.toscana.it

TIPS

● It is much cheaper to buy a combined ticket to all sights in the Campo dei Miracoli.
● Public transport to the city is excellent, so leave the car.
● Children under 8 are not allowed up the Leaning Tower.

MAKE A DAY OF IT

Florence: ▷ 115–134.
Lucca: ▷ 142.

The Church of the Baptistery of San Giovanni, Pistoia

Pitigliano's medieval skyline, on a volcanic ridge

A detail of the Bacchus Fountain in the central square at Prato

THE SIGHTS

PISTOIA

✚ 436 F6 🛈 Palazzo dei Vescovi, Piazza Duomo 4, 51100 Pistoia, tel 0573 21622 🚇 Pistoia
www.tourismo.toscana.it

The heart of Pistoia is Piazza del Duomo, with its 14th-century baptistery and sumptuous cathedral. The town has several other churches worth visiting, a museum and the historic Caffè Valiani. Every Wednesday and Saturday morning one of Italy's largest markets is held on Piazza del Duomo.

Pistoia's surroundings are uninspiring, but the town has a Renaissance heart. It sits at the foot of the Apennine Mountains, 47km (29 miles) east of Lucca, and its name probably derives from the Latin *pistores*, meaning 'bakers'—it was a town that supplied provisions to the Roman troops. The opulent cathedral has a striking silver altarpiece, the *Dossale di San Jacopo*, made between 1287 and 1456, with figures by Filippo Brunelleschi. The 14th-century Church of the Baptistery of San Giovanni has a font made in 1226 and a 16th-century, gold-painted wooden altar. The Church of San Giovanni Fuorcivitas is proud of its *Visitation* by Luca della Robbia. The Museo Civico's collection includes paintings that chronicle Pistoia's art, ranging from Romanesque to 19th-century works.

PITIGLIANO

✚ 438 G9 🛈 Piazza Garibaldi 51, 58017 Pitigliano, tel 0564 617111
www.collidimaremma.it

Pitigliano, 8km (5 miles) south of Sovana, is a medieval town that was once an Etruscan settlement. Its main attraction is the 16th-century Palazzo Orsini, which displays an impressive collection of Etruscan finds in its beautifully decorated rooms.

Elsewhere you can see the remains of a large 14th-century aqueduct.

Pitigliano's jumble of mellow buildings is delightfully set on a volcanic ridge that rises dramatically from the countryside. The village was once owned by the powerful Orsini family and was home to a thriving Jewish community until World War II. The synagogue is a poignant reminder of the town's Jewish heritage. Explore the many cobbled streets and interesting alleyways that surround the Palazzo Orsini on the main square inside the fortress, and enjoy the views of Monte Amiata. The cathedral has a lovely 18th-century baroque façade and a medieval belfry.

PRATO

✚ 436 G6 🛈 Piazza delle Carceri, 59100 Prato, tel 0574 24112 🚇 Prato
www.comune.prato.it

Prato, nestling between Pistoia and Florence, has several good museums and galleries and some interesting churches. Romantics might also be attracted by the news that Prato is where the monk and artist Filippo Lippi met and fell in love with a nun, Lucrezia Buti, whom he married.

Prato means 'meadow', but today the town is surrounded by industry. It has a long association with textile manufacturing and has been famous for its fabrics since the 13th century. Most of the sights are within the medieval walls that enclose the old part of town. The mighty turreted walls of the Castello dell'Imperatore, built by Frederick II between 1217 and 1248, are reminiscent of castles of the Swabian period, when Frederick II, King of Sicily, controlled Puglia and Sicily, at which time there were huge developments in literature, then science and poetry.

The duomo, at the heart of the city, was built in the 12th century. The *Pulpit of the Sacred Girdle* by Michelozzo and Donatello graces its exterior, while the interior contains frescoes by Filippo Lippi, including a famous depiction of Salome dancing at Herod's feast. You can see more works from the duomo in the Museo dell'Opera del Duomo.

The church of Santa Maria delle Carceri, built in the form of a Greek cross, is a masterpiece of Renaissance architecture and contains terracotta works by Andrea della Robbia.

SAN QUIRICO D'ORCIA

✚ 436 G8 🛈 Via Dante Alighieri 33, 53027 San Quirico d'Orcia, tel 0577 897211; Apr–end Oct, 19 Dec–6 Jan only

San Quirico, 15km (9 miles) east of Montalcino and 10km (6 miles) west of Pienza, is a strange mixture of the enchanting and the banal, with bland, post-World War II housing next to exquisite medieval churches and 16th-century gardens. It stood on Via Francigena, the pilgrim route to Rome, and fine medieval houses line Via Poliziano.

The main attraction is the Collegiata, a 12th-century church off Piazza Chigi, built on the ruins of an eighth-century church. Of note are the Lombard-influenced carvings around the doors. Highlights inside include inlaid Renaissance choir stalls and a *Virgin and Child Enthroned with Four Saints* by Sano di Pietro. The Church of Santa Maria di Vitaleta features a terracotta *Madonna* by Bartolomeo della Robbia. The Horti Leoni were laid out in 1580 and are made up of a flower garden and a natural woodland area. If you have time to wander around this partly walled village, you can also take a look at the Palazzo Chigi, decorated with Baroque frescoes.

SAN GIMIGNANO

**A visual spectacle that cannot fail to delight.
Nicknamed 'the medieval Manhattan' for its ancient towers
that spear the skyline.**

San Gimignano flourished throughout the Middle Ages, largely due to
its position on the Via Francigena pilgrim route. The town split into
factions over allegiance to the papacy and the empire—those
supporting the pope were known as Guelphs, those supporting the
emperor, Ghibellines—and during these years of conflict, the wealthy
families in the town built 72 protective towers, 14 of which still stand.

THE COLLEGIATA

From the Porta San Giovanni, the main gate, Via San Giovanni runs up
to the town's two main squares, the Piazza della Cisterna and Piazza
del Duomo. In the latter is the Collegiata, a church. The interior is
covered with dazzling frescoes (Mar–end Oct Mon–Fri 9.30–7.30, Sat
9.30–5, Sun 1–5; Nov–20 Jan Mon–Sat 9.30–5, Sun 1–5; 21 Jan–28
Feb open for Mass only). On the rear wall is a *Last Judgement* by
Taddeo di Bartolo, alongside an *Inferno*, a *Paradiso* and a *St. Sebastian*.
The second cycle on the right wall is now attributed to Lippo Memmi
and the Old Testament cycle opposite is by Bartolo di Fredi.

PALAZZO DEL POPOLO

To the left of the Collegiata stands the Palazzo del Popolo, the main
museum (Mar–end Oct daily 9.30–7.20; rest of year daily 10–5.50).
Within are paintings by Florentine, Umbrian and Sienese artists
such as Filippino Lippi. The Sala del Consiglio (or Sala di Dante,
because it was here that Dante, as a Florentine diplomat, met
members of San Gimignano's council) is dominated by Lippo
Memmi's *Maestà* (1317).

MUSEO D'ARTE SACRA AND MUSEO ARCHEOLOGICO

The Museo d'Arte Sacra (Apr–end Oct daily 9.30–7.30; Nov–end Dec
and Mar 9.30–5; closed Jan–end Feb) is a museum of religious art in
the old Rectai Palace, while the Museo Archeologico (Mar–end Oct
daily 11–6; Nov–end Dec Sat–Thu 11–6; Jan–end Feb Fri–Mon 11–6)
houses a small collection of Etruscan objects in a former convent.

Don't miss Torre Grossa, the only tower you can climb; the Cappella
di Santa Fina in the Collegiata, with frescoes by Domenico
Ghirlandaio; the frescoes by Benozzo Gozzoli in Sant'Agostino.

RATINGS	
Historic interest	●●●
Cultural interest	●●●
Photo stops	●●●●●
Walkability	●●●●

BASICS

🔲 436 F7

ℹ️ Piazza Duomo 1, 53037 San
Gimignano, tel 0577 940008; Mar–end
Oct daily 9–1, 3–7; rest of year 9–1, 2–6

✋ Combined tickets for the Museo
Civico, Museo Archeologico and Torre
Grossa, Spezeria di Santa Fina, Museo
Ornitologico and Galleria d'Arte
Moderna: adult €7.50; child (6–18) and
over 65s €5.50

www.sangimignano.com

TIP

● Do not try to park in town.

MAKE A DAY OF IT

Siena: (▷ 152–153)
Florence: (▷ 115–134)
Volterra: (▷ 156)

*Just some of San Gimignano's
14 medieval towers (top)*

Siena

**One of the most beautiful medieval cities in Italy, second only to Florence for its artistic and architectural treasures.
The Campo, a piazza surrounded by medieval palaces, is the venue for Siena's world-famous horse-race, the Palio.**

The shell-shaped Campo, first laid out in the 12th century

A typical Sienese street scene

Inside the Museo dell'Opera del Duomo

RATINGS

Historic interest	●●●●●
Cultural interest	●●●●●
Photo stops	●●●●
Walkability	●●●●

BASICS

✚ 436 G7

🛈 Piazza del Campo 56, tel 0577 280551; Mar–end Nov Mon–Sat 9.30–7.30; rest of year Mon–Fri 8.30–1, 3–7, Sat 8.30–1

🎟 Combined tickets for: Museo Civico and Torre del Mangia (€9.50); Ospedale di Santa Maria della Scala, Centro di Arte Contemporanea (€9); Museo dell'Opera del Duomo (Metropolitana), Libreria Piccolomini, Battistero di San Giovanni (€7.50), Museo dell'Opera del Duomo (Metropolitana), Libreria Piccolomini, Battistero di San Giovanni, Oratorio di San Bernardino, Museo Diocesano (€9.50)

🌐 Siena

Romulus, Remus and the she-wolf atop a plinth at the duomo

SEEING SIENA

The beautifully preserved, homogeneous medieval city of Siena is a magical mix of narrow streets, open spaces and superb buildings focused around the great central square of the Campo. This lies at the convergence of the city's three main streets, each of which runs along a ridge through Siena's three medieval *terzi* (districts), which are divided into 17 *contrade* (wards). The best way to explore Siena is to start at the Campo, and from there, head west to the Duomo and the complex of the medieval Ospedale di Santa Maria della Scala, now a major exhibition space. The heart of the city is surprisingly small; you'll be able to walk to all the main sights in well under half an hour.

HIGHLIGHTS

THE CAMPO

Every year, on 2 July and 16 August, the Campo fills up for the Palio, a vital part of Siena life since the Middle Ages. The three-lap horse-race is ridden by 10 jockeys in medieval costume, representing 10 of the city's 17 *contrade* (wards). The race is preceded by spectactular parades and flag-throwing (▷ 259).

Whatever the time of year, it is hard to tear yourself away from the scene in the Campo, but the Museo Civico (daily 10–7) in the Palazzo Pubblico, on the Campo, demands attention. Many of its rooms are richly decorated with frescoes by some of Siena's finest artists, including one of the best examples of an early medieval secular fresco cycle in Europe, Ambrogio Lorenzetti's *Allegories of Good and Bad Government* (1338). Entrance to the museum also allows access to the Torre del Mangia, the imposing tower rising above the Campo. Climb the 503 steps for rewarding views.

THE DUOMO

Piazza del Duomo ☎ 0577 283048 🕐 Mar–end Oct daily 7.30–7.30; rest of year daily 7.30–5 🎟 Free

Piazza del Duomo cannot rival the Campo for scale or spectacle, but it is here you'll find the city's most interesting buildings, and many artistic treasures. The duomo's magnificent black-and-white and richly decorated façade was overseen by the sculptor Giovanni Pisano, who also carved the lavish pulpit. Some 40 Sienese artists worked on the marble floor, a series of 57 inlaid pictures. The Umbrian artist Pinturicchio painted the vivid frescoes (1509) in the entrancing Libreria Piccolomini, a tiny room on the left of the nave.

MUSEO DELL'OPERA DEL DUOMO
Piazza del Duomo 8 ☎ 0577 283048 🕓 Mar–end Oct daily 9–7.30; rest of year daily 9–1.30 💵 €5.50
Treasures in the Museo dell'Opera del Duomo (or Museo dell'Opera Metropolitana) include a relief of the *Madonna and Child* by Donatello and Duccio's vast *Maestà*. In the Battistero di San Giovanni the font has bronze panels by Jacopo della Quercia, Donatello and Ghiberti.

PINACOTECA NAZIONALE
Via San Pietro 29, 53100 Siena ☎ 0577 281161 🕓 Mon 8.30–1.30, Tue–Sat 8.15–7.15, Sun 8.15–1.15 💵 €4.15
Siena produced some of the greatest Italian painters of the 13th and 14th centuries, and the Pinacoteca Nazionale has the city's best collection of paintings by this influential school. Artists represented include Duccio di Buoninsegna, the first to move painting on from the austere traditions of Byzantine art, Simone Martini, and brothers Pietro and Ambrogio Lorenzetti.

BACKGROUND
Siena was reputedly founded by Senius, son of Remus, brother of Romulus, the founder of Rome. By 1125 Siena was a free commune, despite the rivalry with Florence that was to dominate its medieval history. The old enemy was defeated in 1260 at the Battle of Montaperti, the high point of a century during which Siena was one of Europe's wealthiest cities. The Black Death of 1348 scarred the city, but two charismatic saints emerged and dominated the ensuing period of spiritual uncertainty: St. Catherine of Siena and St. Bernardino. Siena struggled against a succession of papal, imperial and autocratic rulers; she owed allegiance to Charles V, suffered a devastating siege at the hands of Florence and eventually, in 1559, succumbed to the military might of the Grand Duchy of Tuscany. Today Siena is a bustling provincial city grown rich on banking, agriculture and tourism.

The Romanesque-Gothic façade of the duomo

www.terresiena.it
This sleek and informative website run by Siena's tourist authority won the Interactive Key Award in 2003. It has information in Italian, English and Japanese about Siena's accommodation, food and museums and an excellent selection of e-postcards with scenes of Siena that you can send to friends for free while you are away.

TIPS
● Buy one of the combined tickets to save money.
● For a great view of the Campo and excellent ice cream, head for Gelateria La Costerella on Via di Città (corner of Costa dei Barbieri and Via di Fontebranda).
● Tickets for seats for the Palio are hard to come by and expensive, but you can, like most Sienese, watch free from the Campo. It can be very hot and crowded. The event is televised live on RAI 1. Palio tickets sell out months ahead but can be reserved through Palio Viaggi, Piazza Gramsci 7, tel 0577 280 828 (€150–€300).

Spoleto offers many charming views

RATINGS

Historic interest	●●● ○
Cultural interest	●●● ○
Photo stops	●●● ○
Walkability	●●● ○

BASICS

⊕ 438 H8

ℹ Piazza della Libertà 7, 06049 Spoleto, tel 0743 220 311; Apr–end Sep Mon–Fri 9–1, 4–7, Sat–Sun 10–1, 4–7; Oct–end Mar Mon–Fri 9–1, 3.30–6.30, Sat 10–1, 3.30–6.30, Sun 10–1

🚉 Terni, Perugia, Roma. Buses run from station to city. Tickets can be bought at newsstands and *tabacchi*

www.conspoleto.co
An Italian/English website promoting tourism in Spoleto with information on accommodation in the area.

TIPS

● The Basilica di San Salvatore has no lights, so try to visit before sundown.
● Have an ice cream or coffee at Bar La Portella, on a little promontory with views down the valley.
● The annual Festival dei Due Mondi, founded in 1958, usually takes place at the end of June (www.spoletofestival.it).
● There is an antiques fair in Piazza della Libertà on the morning of the second Sunday of the month.

SPOLETO

Graceful hilltop town with a rich Roman heritage and some of central Italy's finest early churches. The setting for the famous summer *Festival dei Due Mondi.*

ROMAN HERITAGE

Roman Spoletium was founded in 241BC, and the upper town's main square, the beautiful Piazza del Mercato, stands on the site of the forum, its entrance still straddled by the Arco di Druso, built in AD23. Nearby is the much-restored Roman theatre, used for performances during the summer festival, with an adjoining archeological museum (daily 8.30–7.30; €2). In the lower town are the remains of the amphitheatre and a Roman bridge.

SANTA MARIA ASSUNTA

Up the hill in the old town, a sloping piazza fronts the elegant façade of the cathedral of Santa Maria Assunta (consecrated 1189). The exterior is a sublime blend of Romanesque and Renaissance elements, while the interior is dominated by glowing frescoes showing scenes from the life of the Virgin, painted by Filippo Lippi.

THE REST OF THE TOWN

Near the cathedral is Spoleto's most famous church, Sant'Eufemia, built in the 12th century and unique in Umbria for its *matroneum*, a high gallery above the nave where women heard mass. Beside the church is the Museo Diocesano d'Arte Sacra (Apr–end Sep Mon, Wed–Sat 10–1.30, 4–7; Oct–end Mar Mon, Wed–Sat 10.30–1, 3–6; €3), a fine collection of paintings and *objets d'art* from churches across the diocese. From here, an uphill walk leads to the Rocca, a postcard-perfect fortress complete with crenellations, towers and soaring walls, which was built from the late 14th century. Below the Rocca's walls, a leafy lane leads to the Ponte delle Torri, a magnificent medieval aqueduct, whose ten arches span the Tessino gorge; it was designed by Gattapone and built towards the end of the 13th century.

Don't miss San Salvatore, an ancient church built from Roman stone in the style of a temple; the 12th-century church of San Ponziano; the Romanesque church of San Gregorio; the walk across the Ponte delle Torri through olive groves to the 12th-century church of San Pietro.

Looking up towards Spello from the surrounding vineyards

Piazza del Popolo in Todi during a rally

SANSEPOLCRO

✚ 437 H7 ℹ️ Piazza Garibaldi 2, 52037 San Sepolcro, tel 0575 740536
www.sansepolcro.net

This small and delightful town is filled with Renaissance buildings and churches. Along with its artistic heritage, the town is noted for its lace-making and jewellery. It is also the setting for the Palio of the Crossbow, a famous crossbow shooting event.

At the foot of the Apennines in the Tiber Valley, 8km (5 miles) northeast of Anghiari, Sansepolcro is said to have been founded by two 10th-century monks returning from the Holy Land with relics of Christ's sepulchre. It is packed with medieval palazzi and stone-built towers surrounded by ancient walls. The town's major claim to fame is as the birthplace and home of the Renaissanace artist Piero della Francesca (1416–92). The Museo Civico (Jun–end Sep daily 9–1.30, 2.30–7.30; rest of year daily 9.30–1, 2.30–6) has a collection of works by him, including *The Resurrection*, *The Madonna della Misericordia* and *San Giuliano*. It also has works by Raffaellino del Colle and Santi di Tito, who were also local artists. The church of San Lorenzo has a *Deposition* by Rosso Fiorentino.

SIENA

See pages 152–153.

SOVANA

✚ 438 G8 ℹ️ Pitigliano (▷ 150)

Sleepy Sovana might be small but it has several striking reminders of its illustrious past. On the border with Lazio, 80km (50 miles) southeast of Grosseto, the village consists of little more than a single street, Via di Mezzo, with the ruins of a fortress at one end. There are Etruscan, Roman and medieval relics scattered about,

and the limestone cliffs are dotted with ancient tombs.

The birthplace of Hildebrand, who became Pope Gregory VII in 1073, Sovana has a fine cathedral. A highlight is the church of Santa Maria, a 13th-century church with a Romanesque exterior, frescoes by the Sienese school, and a carved ciborium (altar canopy)—a rare palaeo-Christian work dating from the eighth or ninth century. There is an Etruscan graveyard on the outskirts of the village dating from the seventh century BC.

SPELLO

✚ 437 H8 ℹ️ Piazza Matteotti 3, 06038 Spello, tel 0742 651408 🚊 Spello
www.comune.spello.pg.it

The enchanting town of Spello (Roman Hispellum) lies under the slopes of Monte Subasio (▷ 145). It is a smaller version of Assisi (▷ 136–137), and its cobbled streets and medieval houses of pinkish stone offer superb photographic opportunities from just about every angle.

The town's Roman origins are immediately visible as you approach Porta Consolare, one of five remaining gates. The town was founded at the beginning of the first century BC and enjoyed prosperity right through the imperial period.

Climb up to Via San Angelo and you pass the tiny Cappella Tega, which houses, behind glass, a Crucifixion fresco by Nicolò Alunno. From Via Consolare the street becomes Via Cavour, and in a small square to the right is the town's main church, Santa Maria Maggiore (13th to 17th century). It was built over the ruins of a Roman temple and is decorated with a sequence of three delightful frescoes by Pinturicchio, telling the story of the early life of Jesus.

The Pinacoteca Comunale (town art gallery) is in the Palazzo dei Canonici, next to Santa Maria Maggiore (summer Tue–Sat 10.30–1, 3–6.30; rest of year Tue–Sat 10.30–12.30, 3–5). Among the works on display are a mid-13th-century Umbrian sculpture of the *Madonna and Child Enthroned*, an enamelled silver processional cross by Paolo Vanni and a diptych by Cola Petruccioli, both late 14th century.

TODI

✚ 438 H8 ℹ️ Piazza Umberto 1, 06059 Todi, tel 075 894 3395
www.apmperugia.it
www.umbria2000.it
www.comune.todi.pg.it

Todi's museum, churches and palaces make it a popular hilltop town, but it has managed to remain unspoiled.

The main square, the Piazza del Popolo, is bordered by magnificent buildings. On the south side is the battlemented Palazzo dei Priori, opposite the sweeping steps of the cathedral, whose Gothic façade features an early 14th-century rose window above carved wooden doors. The interior is fairly simple, with a 14th-century altarpiece and choir stalls of inlaid wood. In the crypt are three sculptures by Pisano, originally part of the façade.

On the east side of the piazza, the Palazzo del Popolo, built in 1213, stands next to the Palazzo del Capitano, built in 1293. The two are connected by a broad external stairway and the top floors house the Museo Pinacoteca (Tue–Sun 10.30–1, 2.30–6). Exhibits trace the history of Todi; in the grand hall is an outstanding altarpiece by Lo Spagna, *The Coronation of Mary with Choir of Angels and Saints*, painted in 1511.

Continued on page 156

THE SIGHTS

One of the narrow cobbled lanes in Trevi

Umbria's famous truffles

Prancing horses carved out of alabaster, on display in Volterra

THE SIGHTS

Continued from page 155

The Tempio di San Fortunato (Tue–Sun 10.30–1, 3–6.30, Mon 3–6.30) sits grandly on Piazza Umberto. Frescoes by Umbrian painters from the 13th and 14th centuries decorate its chapels, and the crypt houses the tomb of the poet St. Jacopone, who died in Todi in 1306. There is a bronze sculpture of him at the foot of the steps of San Fortunato. You can climb the 153 steps of the Campanile di San Fortunato, accessed from the interior of the church, for views over the city and the surrounding countryside.

TREVI

✚ 438 H8 🛈 Piazza Mazzini 5, 06039 Trevi, tel 0742 781150 🚇 Trevi www.protrevi.com

Halfway between Assisi (▷ 136–137) and Spoleto (▷ 154), Trevi is known as the City of the Olive. This warm-stoned hilltop town is surrounded by olive groves—there are about 200,000 trees on the slopes. The town celebrates the new season's oil with a festival every autumn.

Trevi has Roman origins and its heart is enclosed by medieval walls and gates. The former convent adjoining the church of San Francesco makes an interesting museum space, comprising the Museo della Civiltà dell'Ulivo di Trevi (Museum of Olive Oil Cultivation) and the Raccolta d'Arte di San Francesco di Trevi (San Francesco Collection) (summer Tue–Sun 10.30–1, 2.30–6; rest of year 10.30–1, 2.30–5). The vaulted area downstairs has olive presses and huge antique storage jars. The museum also runs a cookery school. Upstairs, the San Francesco art collection includes an altarpiece by Lo Spagna, *The Coronation of the Virgin*,

which was formerly in the 14th-century church of San Martino.

Facing Sant'Emiliano in Palazzo Lucarini is the Trevi Flash Art Museum (Tue–Fri 3–7, Sat–Sun 10–1, 3–7), which has an internationally renowned contemporary art collection.

Also worth visiting is the church of the Madonna delle Lacrime, which has an *Adoration of the Magi* by Perugino and a painted altarpiece by Lo Spagna.

VALNERINA

✚ 439 J8 🛈 Via Cesare Battista 7, 05100 Terni, tel 0744 423047; Mon–Fri www.comune.terni.it

The Valnerina, the Valley of the River Nera, begins in Visso, in the north of the Marche, and winds its way down to Terni, in the southern reaches of the region. Against a backdrop of rugged mountains, the river has carved deep ravines through the countryside, providing views around every bend. Fortress villages, towers and churches perch either side of the river, underlining the importance of this ancient route that has for centuries connected the Tyrrhenian Sea with the Adriatic.

Syrian monks fleeing persecution during the early period of Christianity hid in the caves and woods. The monks set up hermitages in the Valnerina and Castoriana valleys, and these became the nucleus of the abbeys and monasteries that were founded later, including Sant' Eustizio and San Pietro in Valle.

The Nera River Park protects the area around the river's lower reaches, along with its tributary, the Velino. The region is famous for its black truffles, herbs, wild asparagus, river trout and crayfish. At various points along the valley, there are opportunities for river sports such as canoeing and

rafting, rock-climbing and even bungee-jumping, and as you travel along the SS209, the road that follows the river, you can easily visit any of a string of historic villages and hamlets.

The clear, cold waters of the river feed the 165m (540ft) Cascata delle Marmore waterfalls. The highest waterfalls in Europe, they are, surprisingly, a man-made phenomenon: They were created in 271 BC by a Roman consul, Manius Curius Dentatus, who diverted the River Velino into the Nera.

VOLTERRA

✚ 436 F7 🛈 Piazza dei Priori 20, 56048 Volterra, tel 0588 87257 www.volterratur.it

Volterra lies high in the volcanic hills, 50km (31 miles) west of Siena, in the triangle formed by Siena, Pisa and Florence. On a clear day you can see the islands of Corsica and Elba (▷ 140) off the Tuscan coast.

The town was founded by the Etruscans as an important stronghold and its medieval heart is Piazza dei Priori, with its 12th-century duomo and 13th-century octagonal baptistery. Volterra also has a good art gallery housing a *Deposition* by Rosso Fiorentino and a very well-preserved Roman theatre. This was built in the first century BC and unearthed only in the 1950s.

The Parco Archeologico is the site of an Etruscan and Roman acropolis, while the Museo Guarnacci (summer daily 9–7; rest of year daily 9–2) exhibits one of the most important collections of Etruscan works in the world.

Other highlights in the town include the Porta all'Arco, a rare Etruscan arch dating from the fourth century BC, and the Palazzo dei Priori, the first town hall built in Italy (1208–54).

ROME

Capital of modern Italy and home to the Vatican, the historic city of Rome has reminders of its past at every turn. Its history can be traced through its superb Roman monuments, great medieval churches, Renaissance palaces and rich museums, all set against a backdrop of bustling streets and bubbling fountains.

MAJOR SIGHTS

Rome

🏢 Visitor Centre, Via Parigi 5, tel 06 488991; Mon–Sat 9–7
www.romaturismo.com • Excellent, informative English-language website

THE SIGHTS

HOW TO GET THERE

✈ Airports

Roma Fiumicino, the main international airport 32km (20 miles) from the city with fast train links to Termini station

Ciampino, a smaller airport, located 15km (10 miles) southeast of the city, used by budget airlines, charters and internal flights. Connected to the Rome metro system and regular bus services into the city centre

🚆 Railway stations

Termini station is the main rail terminal, centrally located, served by international trains from all over Europe and routes to all Italy's main cities. Rome also has numerous suburban stations and an efficient metro (subway) train network

TIPS

• For a change from admiring ancient architecture, take a look at Renzo Piano's ultra-modern concert hall complex, the Auditorium, also known as Parco della Musica.

• Queuing for train tickets at Termini station can be time-consuming. It's quicker and easier to use self-service machines in the station concourse. You can select English-language touch screens to buy tickets and reserve seats.

• Go early in the morning to visit St. Peter's Basilica and the Vatican Museums, and avoid carrying big bags. The queues and security checks can take up a lot of your sightseeing time if you go later in the day.

• Take time to escape the city centre and visit Rome's seaside. There are regular trains from Termini to Ostia, which has modern beaches, and you can visit the remains of the ancient Roman port at Ostia Antica.

SEEING ROME

Rome is a city of 3,000 years of living history. Monuments, museums, galleries and ancient churches make it a treasure house of art, architecture and culture. At the same time it is a thriving modern capital city with a social life that positively buzzes. Rome is a patchwork of ancient, medieval and modern sights, and just as it was not built in a day, you need more than a day to explore it fully. The Forum and Colosseo (Colosseum) occupy sites of prime real estate in the historic centre *(centro storico)*, and the Vatican, dominated by St. Peter's Square, the Basilica and the Vatican Museums, is one of Rome's main attractions both as a piece of history and as the administrative centre of the modern Catholic Church. Former aristocratic villas are much in use today as offices, museums and galleries. For example, the Quirinale, once a papal residence, is now the Palace of the President of the Republic and also a concert venue. Monumental squares such as Piazza di Spagna, Piazza Navona and Piazza Venezia are places to take a break amid fabulous architecture and stylish coffee bars and restaurants. Rome is also renowned for its public fountains. Many of Rome's attractions can be seen on foot, but to get around quickly there is an efficient and cheap metro system and an extensive network of bus routes.

BACKGROUND

Tribes had colonized the seven hills of Rome as early as 1000BC, and Julius Caesar took control around 49BC, making it a hub of learning and civilization from which the Roman Empire grew throughout Europe and north Africa. In the Middle Ages the city was dominated by the popes, who were not only spiritual leaders but temporal lords of vast tracts of territory. It was the wealth of the Church and the artistic aspirations of successive popes that were the driving force behind Rome's artistic and architectural heritage. The city became the capital of Italy only relatively recently, with the Unification of the country in 1870. Italy was but a collection of autonomous city-states, kingdoms and the remnants of the Holy Roman Empire, until Napoleon intervened and took over the Papal States and Garibaldi occupied Rome. The Pope was confined to the Vatican, which today is recognized internationally as an independent sovereign state marooned like an island surrounded by the swirl and bustle of modern Rome. In spite of political upheavals, Rome has bloomed as a wealthy capital city amid relics of its rich and glorious past.

DON'T MISS

ST. PETER'S BASILICA AND VATICAN MUSEUMS
Admire the Colonnade in St. Peter's Square and the magnificent works of art in the Basilica and the Sistine Chapel (▷ 160–161)

COLOSSEUM
The most famous Roman amphitheatre and site of gladiatorial contests and other imperial entertainment (▷ 162–163)

FONTANA DI TREVI
Decorated with gloriously over-the-top sculpture and set in a central square that has become a popular meeting place (▷ 159)

QUIRINALE HILL
One of the best viewpoints from which to look over the city (▷ 174)

PIAZZA DI SPAGNA
Location of the famous Spanish Steps (▷ 171)

VIA CONDOTTI
A shopper's paradise if you have the money for buying Prada, Gucci, Bulgari, Louis Vuitton, Cartier and the rest (▷ 262–263)

The Fontana di Trevi is even more charismatic at night

A giant foot in the Palazzo dei Conservatori at the Musei Capitolini

ARCO DI COSTANTINO

✚ 427 F5 • Piazza del Colosseo, Roma
🚇 Colosseo 🚊 Tram 3, 117

Rome's best-preserved and largest Roman arch, the Arco di Costantino stands proudly alongside the old Roman triumphal way. Highly decorated and nearly 25m (82ft) high, it was built by the Senate and people of Rome in AD315 to commemorate Emperor Constantine's victory over the tyrant Maxentius, after which he granted freedom of worship to the Christians. An inscription on each side celebrates his coming to power, and scenes show combat against the Dacians and the triumphs of Constantine and his son. When first carved, the bas-reliefs between the statues of the four Dacian prisoners showed episodes in the life of Marcus Aurelius, but his features were later altered to resemble those of Constantine.

BASILICA DI SAN PIETRO

See pages 160–161.

CASTEL SANT'ANGELO

✚ 426 C3 • Lungotevere del Castello 50, 00120 Roma ☎ 06 681 9111
🕐 Tue–Sun 9–8. Prison: Sun by guided tour 💶 Adult €5, under 18s free
🚇 Ottaviano–San Pietro 🔲 ♿

Mausoleum, fortress and papal stronghold, this imposing ancient monument is now home to the Museo Nazionale's collection of ceramics, weapons, furnishings and Renaissance paintings. As you approach over the Ponte Sant'Angelo, pause to share with the ten stone angels their view of the Tiber and San Pietro. Commissioned in AD135 by Hadrian to be the resting place for himself and his family, the castle remained a mausoleum until Caracalla's death in AD217. Aurelian later

converted it into a fortress.

Legend has it that when Rome was struck by the plague in 590 Pope Gregory the Great organized a procession to pray for the city. As the people approached the mausoleum, the statue of the Archangel Michael rose into the air holding aloft a flaming sword, signalling the end of the plague. From then on it was called Castel Sant'Angelo. In the ninth century, Leo IV linked it to the Vatican with a high defensive wall topped by the Passetto, a covered walkway.

Castel Sant'Angelo has also served as a prison.

Don't miss The frescoes in the papal apartments.

COLOSSEO

See pages 162–163.

FONTANA DI TREVI

✚ 427 E3 • Piazza Trevi, 00187 Roma
🚇 Barberini

Immortalized in Federico Fellini's 1960 film *La Dolce Vita*, this is the most photographed fountain in Rome, and has stood here, at the junction of three roads *(tre vie)*, since 1762.

In the middle, Neptune rides a shell-shaped chariot drawn by seahorses steered by giant tritons. Behind is a baroque façade with statues of Plenty, Health and the Four Seasons. In 19BC, General Agrippa built a 19km (12-mile) aqueduct to bring water to the baths near the Pantheon (▷ 172). The story is told in bas-reliefs: On the right a young girl leads Agrippa's soldiers to a spring; on the left he approves plans for the aqueduct. Today the water, called Acqua Virgo, runs underground in one of the few Roman canals still in use.

Toss two coins over your shoulder into the fountain, make a wish and, it is said, you will return to Rome and your wish will come true.

FORO ROMANO

See pages 164–165.

GALLERIA BORGHESE

See page 166.

IL GESÙ

✚ 427 E4 • Piazza del Gesù/Via degli Astalli 16, 00186 Roma ☎ 06 697001
🕐 Daily 6.30–12.30, 4–7.15 🚊 Tram 8

For fans of the baroque, the highlight of this church, dedicated to the Holy Name of Jesus and completed in 1584, is the chapel of St. Ignatius of Loyola. He lived, died and founded his Jesuit order here, and this chapel is the work of the architect Andrea Pozzo.

MUSEI CAPITOLINI

✚ 427 E4 • Piazza del Campidoglio, 00186 Roma ☎ 06 6710 2475
🕐 Tue–Sun 9–7 💶 Adult €6.20, under 18s free 🚇 Colosseo ♿
www.museicapitolini.org

The Palazzo dei Conservatori and the Palazzo Nuovo make up the Musei Capitolini, home to one of Rome's richest collection of sculptures, mosaics, frescoes and paintings. In 1450 the Palazzo dei Conservatori became the world's first public museum when it began to show bronze statues given to the Romans by Pope Sixtus IV. In the courtyard are fragments of a colossal statue of Constantine. Inside, highlights include the delightful *Spinario*, a first-century Greek bronze of a boy extracting a thorn from his foot, and the famous sixth-century Etruscan bronze of the Capitoline Wolf. The art gallery has a collection of 16th- and 18th-century paintings. The Palazzo Nuovo has more excellent pieces, including energetically carved sarcophagi, the headless *Capitoline Venus* and a bronze of Marcus Aurelius.

Basilica di San Pietro

The most famous church in Christendom.
The spiritual capital of the Roman Catholic faith and the focus of Vatican City,
the independent Papal State.
Testament to the genius of Michelangelo, architect and sculptor.

A bird's-eye view of Piazza San Pietro and Bernini's colonnade

Looking towards the basilica from Piazza San Pietro (below)

The South Wind depicted on a plaque in the square (bottom)

SEEING SAN PIETRO

It is the monumental scale of the Basilica di San Pietro (St. Peter's), the largest Roman Catholic building in the world, that is mesmerizing. The proportions are huge—it is 218m (715ft) long, 137m (450ft) high, and covers a total of 22,067sq m (237,535sq ft). It can accommodate 60,000 people. With 778 columns, 44 altars, 135 mosaics and 395 statues, the interior is overwhelming. Concentrate on the highlights: the view of and from Michelangelo's soaring dome, one of his earliest and most moving sculptures, and Bernini's contributions to the interior.

HIGHLIGHTS

THE PORTICO
The approach to the basilica is impressively grand, through the embrace of Bernini's colonnade (284 columns and 140 statues). The obelisk in the middle of the square was brought here by Caligula from Alexandria in Egypt. As you reach Bernini's broad staircase, note the central balcony above the portico, the Loggia delle Benedizioni, where the Pope stands to bless the people gathered in the square below. Inside the portico, the last bronze door on the right is the Holy Door, opened only every 25 years, in a Holy Year (the last was 2000). Over the central door is what remains of Giotto's *Navicella* mosaic (1298).

MICHELANGELO'S LA PIETÀ
The most famous of all the statues in San Pietro, now protected by bulletproof glass, is in the first chapel in the south aisle. Michelangelo's *Pietà* was begun in 1498, when he was 24 years old. It is his only signed work; he engraved his name on a band across the Virgin's breast, and an M inside her right hand. Look up to see his other contribution to the building, the vast dome, covered in mosaics.

BERNINI'S SCULPTURES
Directly under Michelangelo's dome is Bernini's *baldacchino*, an amazing bronze canopy 29m (50ft) high. Its twisted columns are decorated with golden olive and laurel branches and bees, the emblem of the Barberini, the family from which Pope Urban VIII came. It stands over the Altar of the Confession, where only the Pope may celebrate Mass. Beneath this is St. Peter's tomb, lit by 99 lamps, and to the right sits a statue of St. Peter (attributed to Arnolfo di Cambio from the late 1220s), his right foot worn by the touch of pilgrims. Behind the *baldacchino*, in the end apse, are Bernini's baroque monument to Pope Urban VIII and his extraordinary *cattedra*, which encases a chair that was supposedly used by St. Peter.

The rooftop statues and the dome (far left)

The bronze canopy over the altar inside (left)

Michelangelo's Pietà (1498–99) in the Cappella della Pietà (bottom)

Nuns ascend the wide flight of steps up to the basilica (above)

At the top of the north aisle, past the Cappella della Colonna—dedicated to St. Leo, who persuaded Attila the Hun to spare Rome—is a chapel containing the monument to Alexander VII, by Bernini, portraying Death as a skeleton. Past many more papal monuments, and almost back at the portico, is the baptistery. The basin is made from an ancient porphyry sarcophagus taken from the tomb of Hadrian.

THE GROTTOES AND THE DOME

Under one of the dome's great supporting pillars is the entrance to the Vatican grottoes, which are lined with tombs of emperors and popes. To climb the dome, take the elevator to the cupola and terrace, then climb the 330 steps for a closer look at the mosaics. The final ascent, via a spiral staircase, takes you to the top of the lantern, from where you can marvel at the panoramic views of Rome.

BACKGROUND

It was here, in about AD67, that Nero had the Apostle Peter crucified, and it was over his tomb that Constantine built the first basilica, in 324. By 1452 it had started to crumble and Nicholas V began restoring it. In 1547, Pope Paul III appointed Michelangelo to control the project. Michelangelo refused all payment, insisting that he work for the glory of God. He began rebuilding the church in the form of a Greek cross. Then, in 1606, Pope Paul V decided to make some alterations. He chose a Latin cruciform, and employed Carlo Maderno to extend the complex, making a nave and a new portico, while Bernini transformed the interior with baroque touches. San Pietro was finally consecrated in 1626.

BASICS

🞐 426 B3 • Piazza San Pietro, 00120 Roma

☎ 06 6988 2019/1662

🕐 Basilica: Apr–end Sep daily 7–7; Oct–end Mar daily 7–6. Cupola: Apr–end Sep daily 8–6; Oct–end Mar daily 8–5 (1 hour before closing, access by elevator only). Museo del Tesoro: Apr–end Sep daily 9–6.30; Oct–end Mar daily 9–5.30. Grottoes: Apr–end Sep daily 9–5; Oct–end Mar daily 8–5. Necropoli: Mon–Sat 9–3.30. Visits must be requested 2 weeks in advance in writing to Officio Scavi di San Pietro, tel 06 6988 5318, fax 06 6987 3017. Basilica closed during papal celebrations

🞐 Basilica: free. Dome: from €6. Museo del Tesoro: €6. Grottoes: free. Necropolis: €10. Free tickets for papal ceremony at main entrance.

🚇 Ottaviano–San Pietro

🚌 Tours: Groups with reservation. No private tours before 10.30am (tel 06 6988 4466)

📖 €5

🞐 Via della Conciliazione, Borgo Pio

♿ 🞐 With disabled access

www.vatican.va

Colosseo

The largest monument of imperial Rome in existence, an amphitheatre where gladiators fought to the death with wild beasts. Rome's number one landmark and symbol of classical times. Superbly designed sports arena that is the model for modern stadia.

Archways inside the Colosseo

The Colosseo, illuminated, viewed from Via dei Fori Imperiali

The four levels of the Colosseo

TIPS

● Buy your entrance ticket at the Palatine, as there is often a very long wait at the Colosseo.
● If you want a clearer idea of what the interior of the stadium was like, take a guided tour. The service provided by the Italian Sovrintendenza dei Beni Culturali is very good.

SEEING THE COLOSSEO

The Colosseo (Colosseum) stands just to the east of the Foro Romano, encircled by the Caelian, Palatine and Esquiline hills. The best approach is from Via dei Fori Imperiali, where you'll get a good sense of its scale and size. Walk around the outside before tackling the damaged and confusing interior. Take a guided tour or rent an audioguide to help you visualize the arena's past glory.

HIGHLIGHTS

THE EXTERIOR

The elliptical structure covers about 2.4ha (6 acres), and enough survives of the exterior to give a good idea of its original appearance, though the marble facings, painted stucco and statues have all gone. Externally, the Colosseo measures 188m by 156m (617ft by 512ft) and rises to 48m (159ft), with a façade of three tiers of arches and an attic. The tiers are faced with three-quarter Doric, Ionic and Corinthian columns, and the attic has square window openings. At the top were 240 brackets and sockets that anchored the *velarium*, a shade and bad-weather canopy that could be pulled across the interior. The holes you see on the walls once held the metal clamps that pinned the massive blocks together; they were pillaged, together with tons of stone, for later building.

THE ARCADES AND SEATING

Inside, arcades run right around the outer edge of the building on each level, linking the stairways that connect the different floors. Passages from the arcades accessed, via 80 doorways, the tiers of marble benches, some still complete. The spectators were arranged by rank, with humble citizens and women at the top, a special box, closest to

The Colosseo is the largest surviving structure of the Roman Empire

the action, naturally, for the emperor, and ringside seats for the senators and Vestal Virgins (▷ 29). The tickets, which were wooden plaques, carved with the entrance numbers, are still visible above the exterior arches. The system was very efficient, and the organizers could move up to 70,000 people in or out in a matter of minutes.

THE ARENA

The middle of the Colosseo is a jumble of ruins, all that's left of the labyrinthine passages beneath the arena itself. In Roman times, this area had wooden flooring covered with canvas and sand—the word 'arena' comes from the Latin word for sand. The four principal entrances were used by the gladiators, stagehands and corpse removers. Far more dramatic entrances were made through trapdoors in the floor—you can still see their outlines. These opened into the passages and lifts from where men and wild animals emerged—tens of thousands of animals, sent to Rome from all over the Empire, were slaughtered at the Colosseo. Other passages were water conduits, and the arena was regularly flooded for water battles.

Gladiatorial games began in the morning with an elaborate procession, the prelude to staged hunts when wild animals were pitted against each other or pursued by *bestiarii*, gladiators specializing in animal slaughter. The lunch break was accompanied by executions, a taster for the day's climax—the individual gladiatorial combats.

BACKGROUND

Known since the eighth century as the Colosseo, the arena was built by the three Flavian emperors, Vespasian, Titus and Domitian. Construction started in AD72, and the inaugural games were held in AD80. It was the first permanent amphitheatre built in Rome, brilliantly combining grandiose design with practicality. Games and fights were held here right up to the end of the Empire in the sixth century. During the Middle Ages the Colosseo was used as a fortress, and from the 15th century as a source of building materials for some of Rome's finest palazzi. By the late 1700s the crumbling structure was a romantic and overgrown ruin, and since 1750 it has been dedicated to the Christians killed in its arena. Conservation began in the 19th century and is ongoing.

BASICS

⊞ 428 F4–5 • Piazza del Colosseo, 00184 Roma

☎ 06 700 5469

🕐 Apr–end Sep Mon 9–2, Tue–Sun 9–7.15; Oct–end Mar daily 9–sunset

🎟 Adult €10, under 18s free. Timed tickets: Palatine and Colosseum valid 24 hours. Roma Archaeologia Card valid 7 days for Colosseum, Palatine, Baths of Caracalla, Palazzo Altemps, Palazzo Massimo, Baths of Diocletian, Crypta Balbi, Tomb of Cecilia Metella and Villa dei Quintili, €20

Ⓜ Colosseo (line B)

🚋 Tram 3, 8

🎧 Tours €3.50: Apr–end Oct daily on the hour 9–5; rest of year daily on the hour 9–3. Audiotours, €4

📖 Official guide published by the Sovrintendenza dei Beni Culturali

🏧

🚻 Outside on south side (open until 6pm) and inside the Colosseum.

www.archeorm.arti.beniculturali.it
An Italian website bringing together the key archaeological sites in Rome, with photos, site maps and information on the Collosseo, the Domus Aurea, the Museo Nazionale Romano, the Terme di Caracalla, the Mausoleo di Cecilia Metella and the Villa dei Quintili.

www.ticketclic.it

Foro Romano

•

The political, commercial, economic and religious focal point of Republican Rome.
One of the city's most important archaeological sites, with many famous monuments spanning more than 900 years.

THE SIGHTS

The broad Via Sacra links two triumphal arches

A section of the right aisle of the ruins of the formerly lavish Basilica di Massenzio (AD308)

RATINGS	
Historic interest	●●●○
Cultural interest	●●●●○
Photo stops	●●●○
Walkability	●●●●

TIPS

• The Forum can be confusing, so before you enter, get an overview of the general layout from Via del Campidoglio, the northern side of Piazza del Campidoglio (▷ 173) or the Orti Farnesiani (▷ 167) gardens.
• Take something to drink, as there are no bars or cafés in the immediate area.

Detail of the Arco di Settimio Severo

SEEING THE FORO ROMANO

The Roman Forum was the hub of daily life in the days of ancient Rome, and its ruins lie in what is still the heart of the city, between the Colosseum and Piazza Campidoglio and the great Victor Emmanuel monument. There are several points of entry, but the main entrance, and the best one, is from Via dei Fori Imperiali. This leads immediately onto Via Sacra, the most ancient road, which runs through the heart of the Roman Forum, linking two triumphal arches, the Arco di Settimio Severo and the Arco di Tito. The most important sights lie between these arches. At first the Forum seems nothing more than a jumbled collection of ruins with one or two intact buildings—you'll need a plan to get your bearings.

HIGHLIGHTS

VIA SACRA, TEMPIO DI ANTONINO E FAUSTINA, BASILICA AEMILIA

Via Sacra, which bisects the Forum, linked the Palatine to the Capitoline hills. Holy sanctuaries lined the way, and victorious generals led processions along the route to give thanks to Jupiter in the Temple of Jupiter Capitolinus. Near the main entrance are the remains of the Temple of Antoninus and Faustina, the best-preserved temple in the Forum, chiefly because it was converted into a Christian church in the seventh century. To the right is a large area of broken columns, the Basilica Aemilia, built in the second century AD to house the law courts.

TEMPIO DI VESTA AND TEMPIO DEI CASTORI

Back near the main entrance, by the Via Sacra, is the circular white Temple of Vesta, where the six Vestal Virgins, priestesses to the goddess of fire, kept the sacred fire alight (▷ 29). The women lived in the House of the Vestal Virgins next door (the central courtyard with its three pools survives), dedicating most of their lives to the service of the goddess and receiving social privileges in return.

Nearby are the three Corinthian columns that remain of the Tempio dei Castori (Temple of Castor and Pollux), built to commemorate the Battle of Lacus Regillus, during which the two divine figures helped the Romans defeat the Latins.

BASILICA JULIA, CURIA, ARCO DI SETTIMIO SEVERO

Via Sacra runs westwards beside the steps of the ruined Basilica Julia, built by Julius Caesar after he returned from the Gallic Wars. Across the Forum proper from here is the remarkably intact, red-coloured Curia (senate house), politically the Roman Republic's most important building. It was here that famous orators and statesmen made their speeches.

At the western end of the complex, the triumphal Arch of Septimius Severus was built in AD203 by his sons, Caracalla and Galba, to

commemorate the 10th anniversary of the emperor's reign and his victory over the Parthians between AD197 and 202. Statues of Septimius Severus and Caracalla stand on top of the arch.

BASILICA DI MASSENZIO AND ARCO DI TITO

East of the main entrance to the Foro Romano, Via Sacra passes the Basilica di Massenzio (Basilica of Maxentius), the largest and most impressive of all the ruins, built by Constantine and Maxentius in the fourth century. Note its arches, constructed of poured cement.

At the far end of the Foro, Via Sacra is spanned by the Arco di Tito, built on the Palatine after Titus's death in AD70 to commemorate his victory over the Jews and the capture of Jerusalem.

BACKGROUND

In the eighth century BC the site of the Foro Romano was a marshy area between the Capitoline and Palatine hills, used as a burial ground and a meeting place for the leaders of the nearby agricultural settlements. The area then came under the rule of the Etruscans, who drained the land. In 497BC one of the first temples to be built here was dedicated to the Etruscan god of crops. The area developed as the hub of social, civic and political life. As Rome grew in wealth and power, triumphal arches and monuments were erected to celebrate the victories of the Roman Republic, and the area became the city's financial focus. With its *comitium*, a square in front of the Curia, and the *rostra*, where the tribunes met, the Forum became the focal point for the men who planned the future of the empire.

By 44BC, however, the Forum had become overcrowded, and Julius Caesar moved the Curia and *rostra* to the Fori Imperiali. The Mercati Traianei (Trajan's Market) became the city's commercial hub, and in AD391, with Christianity spreading, Theodosius closed the pagan temples. From then the Foro gradually fell into ruin, its buildings became a quarry for building stone, and what had been the power behind a mighty empire reverted to pasture for cattle.

The Forum began life as a market

BASICS

✚ 427 F4 • Via dei Fori Imperiali, Via Sacra, Via di San Teodoro, Via di San Gregorio (entrance to the Palatine), 00186 Roma

☎ 06 3996 7700

🕐 Foro: daily 9–7.30 (ticket office closes at 6.30). Groups with reservations may enter at any time. Palatine: Mar–end Oct daily 9–6.30; Nov–end Feb daily 9–3.30.

💶 Foro: free. Palatine: €8; 18–24 years (EU nationals) €4; under 18s (EU nationals) free. Timed tickets: Palatine and Colosseum valid 24 hours

🚇 Colosseo

🚊 Tram 3 💶 Foro: €3.50; daily at 10.30 in English

www.capitolium.org
www.comune.roma.it

Detail of the remains of an architrave surmounting a solitary Corinthian column in the Foro Romano

Canova's reclining statue of Paolina Borghese, sister of Napoleon

RATINGS

Historic interest	● ● ●
Cultural interest	● ● ● ●
Specialist shopping	● ● ●

BASICS

✚ 428 F1 • Piazzale Scipione Borghese 5, 00197 Roma (entrance in Via Pinciana)

☎ 06 854 8577

🕐 Daily 9–7 (last entry 6.30)

💶 Adult €8.50, under 18s €2. Advance reservations required, tel 06 328101

🚇 Spagna or Flaminio

👕 2-hour tour with an art historian in English (9.10am, 11.10am) and Italian (11.10am, 1.10pm, 5.10pm), €5. Advance reservations required (through website or fax 063 265 1329). Audiotours in Italian, English, Spanish, French and German, €2

🖥️ 💻 ♿ 🚻 🅿 On Via Pinciana

www.ticketeria.it
You can make advance reservations for the Galleria Borghese via this website, along with many other famous museums and galleries in Italy that require reservation.

www.galleriaborghese.it
This site has pictures of some of the highlights in the collection.

TIPS

● If possible, reserve in advance as only 360 people are admitted every 2 hours.
● There is a free guided tour of the Secret Garden on Saturday at 10.30 and Sunday at 9.30 and 10.30. Arrive early, as the tours are limited to 20 people (tel 06 8207 7304).

GALLERIA BORGHESE

A remarkable and much-loved collection of art in the peaceful setting of the Villa Borghese.
Masterpieces include famous sculptures by Bernini and Canova, and paintings by Caravaggio, Titian and Raphael.

Cardinal Scipione, Ortensia Borghese's son, was passionate about art and founded this outstanding collection of sculpture and painting. He was also a man without scruples, however. For example, he arranged for Raphael's *Deposition* to be stolen from a church in Perugia and put the painter Domenichino in jail for refusing to give him his *Diana*. In 1620 his collection was moved to the Villa Pinciana. At the end of the 19th century the villa was sold to the Italian State to settle debts, and in 1903 the once-secret gardens were given to the municipality of Rome.

ROOM I

The main draw is Canova's sensuous sculpture of Paolina Borghese, Napoleon Bonaparte's sister, controversial in its day for its naked depiction of a wealthy subject.

ROOMS II, III AND IV

These rooms display sculptures by Bernini. First is *David,* preparing to fight the giant Goliath. The piece is thought to be a self-portrait. In homage to Bernini's patron, Scipione Borghese, his harp features an eagle's head, a Borghese family emblem. Note how the facial expression changes as you move around the statue. Next is *Apollo and Daphne*, showing Daphne changing into a laurel tree as she escapes Apollo's advances. Bernini's energetic statue *The Rape of Proserpina*, shows Pluto, god of the underworld, attempting to rape Demeter's daughter.

ROOM VIII

The six Caravaggio paintings here are noted for their use of *chiaroscuro*. This technique of highlighting figures with a shaft of light from the surrounding darkness is used beautifully in the *Madonna dei Palafreni*.

OTHER HIGHLIGHTS

Paintings by Raphael, Pinturicchio and Perugino are exhibited in Room IX. Correggio's *Danaë* illustrates Jupiter's love for the eponymous heroine. In Room XVIII is the stolen *Deposition* by Raphael (1507).

Ancient ruins and tranquil gardens on the Palatino

Exterior of the Palazzo Barberini by Borromini and Bernini

Painted ceilings and elegant statues in the Palazzo Doria

MUSEI VATICANI

See pages 168–170.

ORTI FARNESIANI

✚ 427 E–F5 • Via dei Fori Imperiali/Via Sacra/Via di San Teodoro/Via di San Gregorio, 00186 Roma ☎ 06 3996 7700 🕓 Apr–end Sep daily 9–7; rest of year daily 9–3.30 💷 Adult €8; 18–24 €4; under 18s free. Ticket valid for Palatino and Colosseo 🚇 Colosseo

A cool retreat, the Orti Farnesiani (Farnese Gardens) are worth climbing the Palatino for. The gardens were laid out in the 16th century by Vignola at the behest of Cardinal Farnese. Shady paths meander through scented orange groves and cypresses.

PALATINO

✚ 427 E5 • Via dei Fori Imperiali/Via Sacra/Via di San Teodoro/Via di San Gregorio, 00186 Roma ☎ 06 3996 7700 🕓 Apr–end Sep daily 9–7; Oct–end Mar daily 9–3.30 💷 Adults €8, under 18s free. Tickets valid for Palatino and Colosseo 🚇 Colosseo

One of Rome's seven hills, the Palatino is considered the cradle of the city. Romulus, legendary founder of Rome, is said to have ploughed a deep furrow around the foot of the hill to define the original city boundary. Take a walk through the shady Orti Farnesiani (see above) or sit and enjoy the views of the Forum (▷ 164–165). In Republican times the hill was an élite residential area. Augustus lived here, and it became the preferred site for imperial palaces. There are temples dedicated to Apollo and Cybele, goddess of fertility, the frescoed Casa di Livia (Augustus' wife), Domitian's Domus Flavia, Domus Augustana and stadium, and the baths of Septimius Severus. Look for the House of the Griffons, where frescoes depict mythological animals, and the Loggia Mattei, a noble

15th-century palace. The museum has archaeological finds from excavations on the hill.

PALAZZO ALTEMPS

✚ 427 D3 • Piazza Sant'Apollinare 44, 00186 Roma ☎ 06 3996 7700 🕓 Tue–Sun 9–7.45 💷 Adult €5, under 18s free 🎧 Audiotours, €4 🏛 www.pierreci.it

Part of the Museo Nazionale Romano complex and home to a remarkable collection of classical sculpture, the Palazzo Altemps is one of Rome's finest Renaissance buildings. Girolamo Riario, nephew of Pope Sixtus IV, commissioned the palace in 1477 and it was completed by the Altemps family a century later. The Italian State acquired the building in 1982 to accommodate classical masterpieces that had belonged to the Mattei, Altemps and Ludovisi families. The courtyard is the handsomest feature, with marble and frescoes. Subjects in the Hall of Portraits include Julius Caesar and Marcus Aurelius. The highlight is The Room of Moses, which houses one of the most important sculptures in the Ludovisi collection, the *Ludovisi Throne*. The fifth-century, bas-relief sculpture depicts Aphrodite rising from the waves.

PALAZZO BARBERINI

✚ 427 F3 • Via Barberini 18, 00184 Roma ☎ 06 3263 2810 🕓 Gallery: Tue–Sun 9–7. Apartments: Tue–Sun 9.30–1.15, 2.15–6.45 💷 Gallery: free. Apartments: Adults €6.30, under 18s €1.30 🚇 Barberini 🛒 🏛 www.ticketeria.it

This imposing baroque palace was commissioned in 1623 by Pope Urban VIII, and completed in 1633 by Bernini and Borromini. It houses the national collection of 12th- to 18th-century works once owned by Rome's

aristocratic families, but the interior is also a sumptuous expression of high baroque style. In the entrance hall are two remarkable staircases, the wide monumental one on the left by Bernini, and the smaller, spiral one on the right by Borromini. Pietro da Cortona's *The Triumph of Divine Providence*, on the ceiling of the Gran Salone, is considered one of the masterpieces of baroque painting. Other highlights include Caravaggio's *Narcissus* and *Judith and Holofernes*, Titian's *Venus and Adonis*, Raphael's *La Fornarina* and a Holbein portrait of Henry VIII.

PALAZZO DORIA PAMPHILJ

✚ 427 E4 • Piazza del Collegio Romano 2, 00186 Roma ☎ 06 679 7323 🕓 Daily 10–5 💷 Adult €8, under 18s €5.70. Reserve concert tickets 10 days in advance Fri–Wed 10–4 and on concert days from 7.30pm (tel 800 907080) 🎧 Informative audiotours 🛒 🏛 👥 www.doriapamphilj.it

Overlooking Via del Corso, this is one of the largest palaces in Rome, with a good collection of paintings displayed in four resplendent galleries.

Gallery 1 has several important paintings by Titian, Coreggio, Raphael, Caravaggio and Paolo Veronese. Caravaggio's *Flight into Egypt* is controversial as he used the same model for the Virgin Mary in this painting as for Mary Magdalen in another painting in this gallery. Gallery 2 is dedicated to Flemish artists. In Gallery 3 a portrait of Pope Innocent X by Velàzquez, the highlight of the collection, hangs next to a bust of the same pope by Bernini. Gallery 4 has 17th-century landscapes by Claude Lorrain. There are guided tours of some of the private apartments and the ballroom.

Musei Vaticani

The largest and richest museum complex in the world—at least 1,400 rooms. Sculpture, paintings and *objets d'art* spanning more than 3,000 years, from every corner of the Classical and modern world. The Sistine Chapel and Michelangelo's famous frescoes.

SEEING THE MUSEI VATICANI

The vast complex includes the museum, galleries and parts of the papal palace, richly decorated by the world's greatest artists. The galleries, themselves of great architectural interest, have a diverse collection of art, with a particular emphasis on Western art and sculpture.

The complex fills a large space in the city

RATINGS	
Good for kids	●●
Historic interest	●●●●●
Value for money	●●●●
Walkability	●●●

TIPS

● Dress respectfully—shorts and bare upper arms are unacceptable.
● To avoid crowds, arrive as the museum opens, or late in the morning. Wednesday morning can be peaceful as people go to the Piazza di San Pietro for the papal blessing.

The Vatican Gardens (above right)

Ancient sculpture (below)

HIGHLIGHTS

CAPPELLA SISTINA

The Cappella Sistina (Sistine Chapel) was built by Pope Sixtus IV between 1473 and 1481, both as the pontiff's private chapel and as a venue for the conclave of cardinals that gathers to elect each new pope. It is a huge, cavernous structure, with an intricate cosmatesque mosaic floor and a marble screen by Mino da Fiesole. But, above all, it is the frescoes, entirely covering the walls and ceiling, that attract up to 20,000 visitors a day.

Even during the construction of the chapel, Sixtus was planning the interior decoration, settling on scenes from the Old and New Testaments as the subject matter, with an emphasis on the parallels between the lives of Moses and Christ. From Florence, he summoned Sandro Botticelli, together with Domenico Ghirlandaio, Cosimo Rosselli and Perugino. These artists, joined by Pinturicchio, Luca Signorelli and Piero di Cosimo, worked for 11 months, producing a series of glowing works. The two most important scenes are Perugino's *Christ Giving the Keys to Peter* and Botticelli's *The Punishment of Korah,* each showing the Arco di Costantino in the background (▷ 159).

Though undoubtedly masterpieces, they tend to be overshadowed by Michelangelo's frescoes on the ceiling and altar wall, arguably Western art's finest achievement and certainly the largest work ever planned and carried out by one man. Julius II commissioned the ceiling in 1508, and Michelangelo completed it in 1512, an artistic *tour-de-force* combining narrative scenes, architectural *trompe l'oeil* effects and statuesque figures of immense beauty. The central panels illustrate the Creation and tell the story of Noah, surrounded by a decorative scheme dominated by the figures of the Prophets and Sibyls and containing wonderful details, including the famous *ignudi* (nude youths).

Years later, in 1535, Michelangelo was again summoned to the chapel, this time by Paul III, to decorate the altar wall with scenes of the Last Judgement, a task that occupied him until 1541. Even before it was finished, the amount of nudity offended many, not least the pope's master of ceremonies. Furious, Michelangelo depicted him in the bottom right-hand corner of Hell as Minos, the doorkeeper, complete with ass's ears. Later, Pius IV commissioned Daniele da Volterra to

One of several massive sculpted heads on the terrace

BASICS

✚ 426 B3 • Viale Vaticano, 00165 Roma

☎ 06 6988 4676

🕐 Mar–end Nov Mon–Fri 8.45–4.45 (last entrance 3.20), Sat 8.45–1.45 (last entrance 12.20); Dec–end Feb Mon–Sat 8.45–1.45. Open last Sun of month (free); closed for public holidays

💰 Adult €12, child (under 15) €8

🎧 2-hour guided tour, €4; reserve at information point or tel 06 6988 4466. Audiotours in Italian, English, French, German, Spanish, Japanese, €5.50

📷 €7.50 ⬛ 🏧 🚻

🅿 Gianicolo underground parking

Ⓜ Cipro Musei Vaticani, Ottaviano-Vaticano

www.vatican.va

This website dedicated to Vatican City is very stylish and informative. Under the section on the Vatican Museums you can view the collection online, read about the artworks and zoom in on individual paintings for a closer look. There are also online tours and up-to-date practical information, such as opening times and prices.

paint over the genitals—an exercise that earned him the name Braghettone, the trouser-maker. This alteration was reversed during the restoration of the chapel frescoes of the 1980s and 1990s, a project said to have cost more than $3 million.

One of the Pope's Swiss Guards

STANZE DI RAFFAELLO

In 1508 Julius II embarked on a major project to decorate his private apartments, today known as the Stanze di Raffaello (Raphael Rooms). The Stanza della Segnatura, the pope's study, is deservedly the most famous room and was Raphael's first major Roman commission, painted between 1508 and 1511.

The four frescoes, compositions imbued with balance and harmony, are allegories representing the humanist ideals of theology, philosophy, poetry and justice. The *School of Athens* emphasizes truth acquired through reason, with all the great Classical thinkers represented and the central figures of Plato—probably a portrait of Leonardo da Vinci—and Aristotle dominating the scene. The figure on the left is said to be Michelangelo, added after Raphael had a sneak preview of his work in the Cappella Sistina. Opposite is the *Disputation of the Holy Sacrament*, while the side walls show *Parnassus*, home to the Muses, and the *Cardinal Virtues*.

Chronologically, the next room to be painted was the Stanza di Eliodoro, with its energy-charged *Expulsion of Heliodorus* and serene *Miracle of Bolsena*. The latter tells the story of the medieval miracle that occurred in that town, when a priest who doubted the doctrine of transubstantiation saw the wafer bleed during Mass. The window wall has a superb night scene, showing the *Deliverance of St. Peter from Prison*.

The Stanza di Costantino depicts the life of Constantine, the first Christian emperor, while the main focus in the Stanza dell'Incendio, commissioned by Leo X, is the miraculous quenching of a *Fire in the Borgo*, which occurred when Leo IV made the sign of the cross.

LOWER FLOOR

Museo Pio Clementino: The cream of the classical sculpture collection is in this museum's octagonal courtyard. Two statues here influenced Renaissance sculptors more than any others, the *Laocöon* and the *Apollo Belvedere*. Highlights within include a beautiful Hellenistic *Sleeping Ariadne*, candelabra from the Villa Adriana at Tivoli, and Roman portrait busts, including a splendid Julius Caesar.

Museo Gregoriano Egizio: Founded in the 19th century by Gregory XVI, this museum displays a reconstruction of the Temple of Serapis from the Villa Adriana at Tivoli, mummy cases, mummies and tomb treasures.

Museo Gregoriano Profano: Built in 1963 and opened in 1970, a museum with a collection of antique and Christian art moved here from the Lateran Palace.

Museo Pio Cristiano: A collection of documents and objects illustrating religions of the world.

Museo Storico Vaticano: An unusual collection of papal transportation, including carriages.

Museo Chiaramonti: Another collection of Roman sculpture, in particular portrait busts.

Braccio Nuovo: A beautiful collection in a superb architectural setting.

Biblioteca Vaticana: A huge, brilliantly frescoed hall with letters from Petrarch, Michelangelo and Martin Luther, and King Henry VIII's love letters to Anne Boleyn.

UPPER FLOOR

Museo Gregoriano Etrusco: Founded in 1837, this is a major collection of Etruscan sculpture and funerary art.

Galleria delle Carte Geographiche: This upper-floor gallery links the museums with the papal palace. It was painted in 1580 by Ignazio Danti with maps of Italy, Mediterranean islands, papal possessions in France, the Siege of Malta and Venice. **Cappella di Nicolò V:** Serene and delicate frescoes (1446–49) by Fra Angelico in the pope's private chapel.

A map of Sardinia in the Galleria delle Carte Geographiche, painted by Ignazio Danti, a Dominican monk

PINACOTECA VATICANA

The Pinacoteca, founded in 1816 by Pius VI, occupies a separate building (1932) within the museum complex. It is widely considered to be Rome's best picture gallery, with works from the early and High Renaissance to the 19th century. Among these are some of the most remarkable early paintings in Rome, with Giotto's *Stefaneschi Triptych* stealing the show (Room II). Painted in the early 1300s it shows the *Martyrdom of St. Peter and St. Paul.* St. Peter is shown being crucified, at his own request, upside down, as he felt unworthy to die the same way as Christ. The next rooms are devoted to 15th-century Italian art; look for Fra Angelico's lovely *Madonna and Child with Saints* in Room III and the serene Umbrian pictures in Room VII, particularly Perugino's luminous *Madonna and Child.* Room VIII is the Pinacoteca's finest, with a collection of Raphael's work, including

Maps of the papal lands in the Galleria delle Carte Geographiche

tapestries, woven in Brussels from his cartoons, that once hung in the Cappella Sistina. Dominating the room, however, is the *Transfiguration*, a sublime work that was hung above the artist's coffin and completed by his pupils later. The triumphant figure of the ascending Christ pulses with energy amid piercing light and lowering cloud formations, a superb contrast to the artist's first major composition, the *Coronation of the Virgin*, painted when he was only 20. The gentle *Madonna of Foligno* was commissioned in 1512 as a votive offering.

In Room IX is Leonardo da Vinci's unfinished and curiously monochrome *St. Jerome*, one of only a few of Leonardo's works whose authorship has never been disputed. Here, too, is the exquisite *Pietà* by Bellini. Venetian painting is featured heavily in Room X in two canvases by Titian, a glowing *Madonna with Saints* and the subtle *Portrait of Doge Nicolò Marcello*. There are further psychological insights in Caravaggio's despairing *Deposition* in Room XII, all muted tones and intense *chiaroscuro*.

BACKGROUND

Pope Innocent III (1179–81) began building a palace near the Basilica San Pietro, and his successors enlarged and embellished

it. Major work was carried out under Nicolò V in the mid-15th century, and in the 1470s Sixtus IV added the Cappella Sistina. Both Julius II (1503–13) and Leo X (1513–22) built and decorated further buildings—Julius commissioned Michelangelo to paint the Cappella Sistina and Raphael to decorate his private rooms. In the 18th century the collections were arranged into a museum, with galleries built to display sculpture, paintings, and *objets d'art*—a huge project that continued into the 20th century.

THE SIGHTS

The cafés around Piazza Campo dei Fiori at night

Piazza Navona is a good place to come at night

The Spanish Steps, a popular meeting place for centuries

PALAZZO MASSIMO ALLE TERME

🚩 428 G3 • Largo di Villa Peretti 1, 00185 Roma ☎ 06 3996 7700
🕐 Tue–Sun 9–7 🎫 Adult €6, child (under 18) free 🚇 Repubblica, Termini 📷
www.pierreci.it (online reservations)

The Palazzo Massimo alle Terme, an imposing building, houses the Museo Nazionale Romano and its collection of sculptures, mosaics, frescoes and coins from the end of the Republican Age (second century BC) to the late Imperial Age (fourth century AD).

The ground floor displays portraits from the Republican period and an interesting collection of coins. In Room V are a statue of Augustus and a marble altar from Ostia showing the wedding of Mars and Venus, along with a sculpture of Apollo and the sleeping Aphrodite from the Villa Adriana in Tivoli. In Room VII is the magnificent statue of Niobe's daughter trying to extract an arrow from her back.

Other rooms display portraits, bas-reliefs and sarcophagi, and remarkable mosaic floors and beautiful frescoes discovered in the Villa Farnesina in Trastevere and the Villa Livia on the Palatino. The second floor can be visited only as part of a group or with a guide so reserve in advance or wait for a group or a guide to come along.

PIAZZA CAMPO DEI FIORI

🚩 427 D4 • Piazza Campo dei Fiori, 00186 Roma 🚋 Tram 8

Piazza Campo dei Fiori bustles with *trattorie*, bookshops and a famous market. Relax with a drink at one of the famous *vinerie* and delight in one of the most attractive and lively squares

in Rome. In ancient times it was used as grazing land for cattle—hence the name, which means field of flowers. Many of the nearby streets and squares are named after the various artisan workshops in the area.

It was also the venue for executions. In 1600 the philosopher Giordano Bruno, who advocated the separation of political and religious power, was burned alive on the spot where his statue stands. The statue, by Ettore Ferrari (1887), and the Cinema Farnesen are traditional meeting places for Rome's intellectuals and anti-establishment thinkers.
Don't miss The Il Forno bakery sells some of the best pizzas in Rome

PIAZZA NAVONA

🚩 427 D3 • Piazza Navona, 00186 Roma 🚌 23, 30, 62, 64, 70, 81

Piazza Navona is a lively, crowded place at the heart of the city, a popular meeting place for both Romans and visitors. You can go to an exhibition at Palazzo Braschi, watch street performers or have your portrait painted. Alternatively, sit and enjoy a drink at one of the outdoor cafés.

The piazza was laid out in the late 15th century on the ruins of a stadium. From 1650 to the late 19th century the square was flooded in summer and used for aquatic games. Brightly painted carriages floated on the water like boats while people freshened up in the temporary 'lake'.

Today the real attraction is the famous Fontana dei Quattro Fiumi (Fountain of the Four Rivers), created by Bernini in about 1651, in the middle of the square. It represents the Danube, the Ganges, the Nile and the Rio de la Plata.

At the southern end of the piazza the Fontana del Moro, designed by Giacomo della Porta in 1576, features dragons and dolphins. The central figure of the so-called Moor—actually a marine divinity—was added in the mid-17th century. The Fontana del Nettuno, at the northern end, dates from the 19th century.

PIAZZA DI SPAGNA E SCALINATA DI TRINITÀ DEI MONTI

🚩 427 E2 • Piazza di Spagna, 00187 Roma 🚇 Spagna

Piazza di Spagna and the Scalinata di Trinità dei Monti (the Spanish Steps) are famous as a meeting place for visitors from all over the world. The steps are also a popular place to pose, people-watch or just sit and enjoy life carrying on all around you. The view of Rome from the top is unequalled.

The square was called Platea Trinitatis, in honour of its church, until the 17th century, when the Spanish ambassador took up residence here and changed the name to Piazza di Spagna. Francesco de Sanctis built the elegant flight of 138 steps in the 1720s. With the 16th-century Franciscan church of Trinità dei Monti at the top, they form the perfect backdrop for the annual fashion show *Donne sotto le Stelle* (Women in Starlight).

At the top of the steps is an obelisk found in the Horti Sallustiani, while at the bottom is the Barcaccia, a boat-shaped fountain created by the Berninis, father and son. Built in 1629 to commemorate the Great Flood of 1598, it shows a boat sinking under the floodwaters. Low water pressure means the fountain is sluggish and the boat is often full of water.

RATINGS

Historic interest	◕ ◕ ◕ ◕
Cultural interest	◕ ◕ ◕
Walkability	◕ ◕ ◕

BASICS

✚ 427 D3 • Piazza della Rotonda, 00186 Roma ☎ 06 6830 0230
🕐 Mon–Sat 8.30–7.30, Sun 9–6.30, public holidays 9–1. No visits during celebration of the Sun 10.30am Mass
💶 Free
🚋 Tram 8 to Argentina
🍴 In the Square
🏨 On Piazza della Rotonda

TIPS

• There is not much information to help visitors on site, so have your guidebook handy.
• Have a drink in one of the cafés or sit around the central fountain of the piazza to enjoy the view of the Pantheon.
• The Pantheon is often very crowded, especially at the weekend. To make the most of a visit, go on a weekday or early in the morning.

Shafts of sunlight shine through the oculus, illuminating the porphyry, granite and yellow marble walls and floors

PANTHEON

**Simple, solid and austere, an architectural *tour de force* by the engineers of ancient Rome.
Pagan temple turned Christian church—now Italy's best-preserved building from antiquity.**

The original Pantheon was built by Agrippa, according to the inscription on the façade. It was erected in 27BC in honour of the heavenly gods and was also dedicated to the Julia family, thought to be direct descendants of gods. Agrippa's building was destroyed in the great fire of AD80 and the Pantheon was rebuilt in the early second century by Emperor Hadrian. In the sixth century, Emperor Phocas gave the Pantheon to Pope Boniface IV, who turned it into a Christian church. The building was then covered in bronze and lead, and despite being pillaged over the years, the covering helped to preserve the dome and other surfaces. The portico of Egyptian granite columns was once a fishmarket. Pope Urban VIII had the bronze on the ceiling removed in the 17th century for use on Bernini's *baldacchino* in San Pietro (▷ 160–161), but the bronze doors survive from ancient Rome.

THE DOME

The design is superbly simple: a dome on a circular base attached to a rectangular portico. With a diameter wider than the dome of San Pietro, this is the largest dome ever built before the introduction of reinforced concrete, testimony to the amazing ingenuity of the Roman engineers. The height of the dome from the floor is identical to its diameter, 43.3m (142ft). The walls supporting the dome are 7m (23ft) across, and the thickness of the dome itself diminishes from base to apex. The unglazed oculus, the circular hole in the middle of the dome (9m/29.5ft across), is the only source of natural light. A statue of Jove Ultor, the Avenger, who punished the murderers of Caesar, once stood directly under the oculus, and shrines and niches once held statues of the 12 Olympian gods, along with emperors Hadrian and Augustus. The tombs of Italy's first two kings and the artist Raphael are the only tombs you can see today.

PIAZZA DELLA ROTONDA

The Pantheon faces Piazza della Rotonda, a pretty square with cafés, a fountain, and a 13th-century BC Egyptian obelisk built by Ramses II, brought to Rome and used in the Temple of Isis and Serapis in Campo Marzio, then moved here by Pope Clement XI. In the evening this is a lively place with people dining or enjoying coffee and ice cream.

PIAZZA DEL CAMPIDOGLIO

A grand piazza on the Capitolino, the most famous of Rome's seven hills and the hub of the Roman Empire. A showplace for Michelangelo's majestic work.

Michelangelo was called upon to redesign this piazza as part of Pope Paul III's plan to restore the city to its ancient splendour after the Sack of Rome in 1527. The magnificent buildings that stand on three sides of the square—the Palazzo Senatorio, the Palazzo Nuovo and the Palazzo dei Conservatori, built on the site of the great Temple of Jupiter Capitolinus—were part of his scheme.

THE CORDONATA
The new piazza was designed for Emperor Charles V's triumphal entry into Rome in 1536, and the best approach is via the Cordonata, Michelangelo's elegant ramp intended for the emperor. The top of the Cordonata is flanked by two large statues of Castor and Pollux, the mythical sons of Jupiter, standing by their horses. To their left and right is a display of captured enemy arms from the reign of Domitian. The balustrade is embellished with columns from the Via Appia and statues of Constantine the Great and his son Constantine II in full military dress.

THE PIAZZA
The floor of the piazza is inlaid with a star-shaped pattern, in the middle of which Michelangelo placed a plinth for the equestrian statue of Marcus Aurelius. This escaped the fate of the many statues of pagan emperors that were melted down and reused during the Middle Ages. The original is in the Musei Capitolini (▷ 159, 167); this is a copy.

PALAZZO SENATORIO
The Palazzo Senatorio (Senate House) was built during a period when the people of Rome demanded an end to the power of the papacy and re-established a republic. Michelangelo designed a new façade, subsequently built by Giacomo della Porta, and the palazzo became the hub of political activity in the 16th and 17th centuries. A fountain near the steps is flanked by two huge bearded statues representing the Nile, and the Sphinx, the Tiber, Romulus and Remus and the she-wolf.

MUSEI CAPITOLINI
Note the twin balconies of the Palazzo dei Conservatori and Palazzo Nuovo, designed by Michelangelo, with statues looking across at each other. These buildings house the Musei Capitolini (▷ 159, 167).

RATINGS	
Historical interest	● ● ● ●
Cultural interest	● ● ● ●
Photo stops	● ● ●
Walkability	● ● ● ●

BASICS
✚ 427 E4 • Piazza del Campidoglio, 00186 Roma
Ⓜ Colosseo
🚊 Tram 8 to Argentina
📖 In the museum shops (Libreria Capitolina)
♿ First floor of Palazzo Caffarelli
🍴 In the museums

www.museicapitolini.org

A silhouette of the statues of Castor and Pollux guarding the Cordonata by the Palazzo Senatorio (top)

A reclining statue at the Palazzo Nuovo (above)

Sant'Andrea al Quirinale's ornate ceiling

The statue of Santa Cecilia in Santa Cecilia in Trastevere

A bridal couple at the church of Santi Cosma e Damiano

SANT'ANDREA AL QUIRINALE

➕ 427 F3 • Via del Quirinale 29, 00184 Roma ☎ 06 4890 3187 🕐 Wed–Mon 8–12, 4–7 💶 Free 🚇 Barberini

Known as 'the Baroque Pearl', this elegant little oval church, designed by Bernini, has a very peaceful atmosphere. Bernini himself often came and sat here. It was commissioned by Cardinal Camillo Pamphili in 1658 as the church of the Jesuit novitiate in Rome, and employed the most talented workers, decorators and sculptors of the time. An elegant flight of steps leads to the semi-elliptical portico. Inside is another oval space, with eight deep rectangular chapels ranged around it, linked by the elliptical cornice. The pillars are made of red Sicilian marble. The dome above the altar is richly decorated with gold and stucco cherubs by Antonio Raggi. In the first chapel on the right paintings by Gianbattista Gaulli depict the death of St. Francis Xavier, while the relics of St. Stanislaus, a young Jesuit novice who died here, are in the third chapel on the left. Look for the coats of arms of the Pallavicini, Spinola and Melzi families in the marble floor.
Don't miss The beautiful frescoed vaulting in the sacristy.

SAN CARLO ALLE QUATTRO FONTANE

➕ 427 F3 • Via del Quirinale 23, 00184 Roma ☎ 06 488 3261 🕐 Daily 10–1, 3–5 💶 Free 🚇 Barberini www.sancarlino-borromini.it

This extremely small church is said to be no larger than one of the columns supporting the dome of San Pietro (▷ 160–161). Known as San Carlino, it was designed in 1638 by the great baroque artist Francesco Borromini and is opposite his rival Bernini's Sant'

Andrea al Quirinale. This was Borromini's first work, but also his last—he committed suicide after adding the façade in 1667. The architecture reflects the tormented and contradictory state of mind of its creator.

Overall, the interior is simple—an elliptical plan with stuccoed niches—but every concave section is mirrored by its convex opposite, forming strange shapes and visual effects. The intricately designed coffered ceiling, with sunken ornamental panels, exemplifies the bizarre yet elegant effect that Borromini managed to create in such a small space.
Don't miss Borromini's beautifully proportioned cloister, with two rows of Doric columns and convex corners.

SAN GIOVANNI IN LATERANO

See page 176.

SANTA CECILIA IN TRASTEVERE

➕ 427 D5 • Piazza di Santa Cecilia 22, 00153 Roma ☎ 06 589 9289 🕐 Daily 9.30–12.30, 5–6.30. Cavallini fresco: Tue, Thu 10–12, Sun 11–12 💶 Free 🚋 Tram 8; Bus 23, 44

The approach to this basilica is through a courtyard garden where flowers surround a fountain. Ahead are the ancient columns of the 12th-century portico and the Romanesque campanile. Pope Paschal I built the church in the ninth century, on the site of the home in which Cecilia was killed by Emperor Marcus Aurelius. In the much restored baroque interior is Stefano Maderno's beautiful sculpture of St. Cecilia, modelled on the body that, miraculously, was found intact inside her tomb when it was opened in 1599.

Other treasures include the Gothic altar canopy by Arnolfo di Cambio and early ninth-century

apse mosaics depicting Jesus with saints Paul, Agatha, Peter, Paschal, Valeriano and Cecilia. Of interest, too, are the remains of the 13th-century fresco the *Last Judgement* by Pietro Cavallini that once covered the walls of the central nave.

The Chapel of the Bath, at the end of the south aisle, is said to contain the bath in which St. Cecilia was martyred, and a painting by Guido Reni depicts her beheading.

SANTI COSMA E DAMIANO

➕ 427 F4 • Via dei Fori Imperiali 1, 00186 Roma ☎ 06 699 1540 🕐 Daily 9–1, 3–6. 💶 Free 🚇 Colosseo

Consecrated in 526 by Pope Felix IV in honour of twin Arab physicians, this was the first Christian church to reuse a building in the Roman Forum (▷ 164–165). It was formed by joining the library of the Foro della Pace to part of the round temple dedicated to Romulus, the remains of which are still visible inside. In the 16th century, Pope Urban VIII Barberini, a Franciscan, commissioned the architect Arrigucci to restore the building. The present-day façade of the church and the cloister were built at this time, and the original Roman church was hidden underground in a crypt. The highlight is the sixth-century mosaics in the apse showing the Apostles Peter and Paul presenting the saints Cosmas and Damian to Christ. The baroque high altar partially hides the detail of Christ as the Lamb surrounded by the 12 Apostles. The 17th-century ceiling is decorated with sunken panels, with paintings depicting the triumph of the saintly brothers along with the Barberini family emblem, bees.

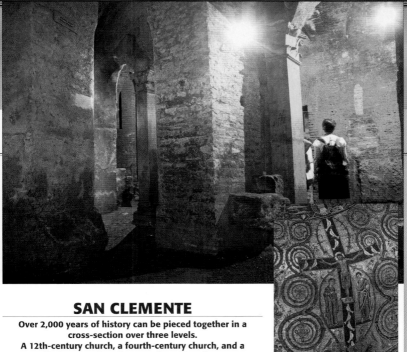

SAN CLEMENTE

Over 2,000 years of history can be pieced together in a cross-section over three levels.
A 12th-century church, a fourth-century church, and a first-century temple—one above the other.
Magnificent mosaics and a temple to Mithras.

The present church was built in the 12th century after its predecessor was damaged in a Norman attack in 1084. The lower church has a similar layout, but was wider, and very little of the original walls of this fourth-century building survive. According to legend, St. Cyril, evangelizer of the Slavs, brought St. Clement's relics to Rome and laid them here in 869. On the lowest level are buildings from imperial Rome, including a well-preserved Mithraic temple.

THE MITHRAIC TEMPLE
Head straight for the underground level by taking the steps in the sacristy down through the first church (second level). Here are two buildings dating from Roman days. One is thought to have been Rome's mint; the second was the house of a rich family, built of brick with an underground courtyard and later converted into a temple to the Persian god, Mithras. Mithraism was a pre-Christian, all-male cult, popular with soldiers, and this is the best-preserved of a dozen Mithraic temples found in the city. The temple was used until the fourth century, when Christians probably destroyed it. From the temple, walk along a narrow passage, at the end of which you can hear the sound of water running in an underground watercourse.

THE LOWER CHURCH—THE FIRST SAN CLEMENTE
Go back up the steps to the lower San Clemente basilica, built in 375, consisting of a nave and two aisles. Pillars and walls added in the 11th and 12th centuries support the church above. Frescoes date from the 8th to 11th centuries; the one depicting St. Sisinius is remarkable for the inscriptions below, perhaps the oldest in the Italian language.

THE UPPER CHURCH—THE SECOND SAN CLEMENTE
Little altered since it was built, San Clemente is dominated by a choir screen and the golden 12th-century mosaic of the Crucifixion in the apse. Birds and animals are entwined in foliage, the Virgin and St. John stand alongside the cross represented as the Tree of Life, and the four rivers of Paradise spring from the foot of the cross. The cosmatesque inlaid floor is one of the best-preserved in Rome.

RATINGS	
Good for kids	●●
Historic interest	●●●●●
Specialist shopping	●●
Value for money	●●●●

BASICS
✚ 428 G5 • Piazza San Clemente/Via San Giovanni in Laterano, 00184 Roma
☎ 06 7045 1018
🕐 2nd and 3rd level: Mon–Sat 9–12.30, 3–6, Sun 10–12.30, 3–6. Upper Basilica: all day
💶 2nd and 3rd level, €3. Upper Basilica, free
🚇 Colosseo, San Giovanni
🏫 👬

TIPS
● Buy a plan before you start, as in the underground and second-level basilicas there is no defined route and you may miss points of interest.
● Start with the underground church.

The underground Mithraic temple below the church of San Clemente (top)

One of the mosaics in the apse (above)

The nave of San Giovanni in Laterano

RATINGS

Value for money	● ● ●
Good for kids	● ●
Historic interest	● ● ● ● ●
Photo stops	● ● ● ● ●

BASICS

✚ 428 H5 • Piazza di San Giovanni in Laterano 4, 00184 Roma ☎ 06 6988 6433

🕐 Basilica: daily 7–7. Cloister: daily 9–6. Baptistery: daily 7–12.30, 4–7.30. Scala Santa: daily 9–12, 3–6. Museo Storico del Vaticano: Sat 9–12

💶 Basilica, Scala Santa, baptistery: free. Cloister: €2. Cappella Sancta Sanctorum: €3.50. Museo Storico del Vaticano: €4

🚇 San Giovanni

🎫 Tours: basilica, cloister, baptistery, Scala Santa (reserve in advance; tel as above, Mon–Fri 9–1, or email), in all languages, €5.50. Guided tour of Museo Storico del Vatticano. Audiotours: basilica and cloister, in all languages, €2. *Mater et caput* guided tour: tel 06 6988 6392 or email mater.caput@org.va

TIP

● If you go in the morning and have time, walk around Via Sagno, the famous flea market.

SAN GIOVANNI IN LATERANO

The cathedral church of Rome, the papal residence for hundreds of years, up to the 14th century.

The first basilica, named after the family that owned the property on which it was founded, was built by Constantine between AD313 and 318. At the time, it represented the victory of Christianity over paganism. In 314 Pope Sylvester I took up residence in the Lateran buildings and it was the official papal residence until the papacy moved to Avignon in the 14th century, though popes were crowned here until the 19th century. San Giovanni has been rebuilt many times—damaged by vandals, an earthquake and two fires, it was finally restored by Borromini in the 17th century in the baroque style.

The basilica's 1735 baroque façade by Alessandro Galilei (modelled on San Pietro) is crowned with 15 gigantic statues of Christ, the Apostles and the Church Fathers. The portico has bronze doors taken from the Foro Romano's *curia*, and a huge statue of the first Christian emperor, Constantine. The last door on the right, the Holy Door, is opened only during the Jubilee or Holy Year, every 25 years.

Inside, the central nave is flanked with niches containing statues of the 12 Apostles. The dove from the coat of arms of Innocent X, who commissioned Borromini, is set over each recess, with bas-reliefs depicting stories from the Old and New Testaments. To the right of the entrance a restored fragment of a fresco by Giotto shows Boniface VIII declaring the first Holy Year in 1300. In contrast to the unadorned nave, the transept is a fine example of mannerist ornamentation. A 14th-century tabernacle above the altar contains relics of St. Peter and St. Paul. Several frescoes depict the Good Shepherd, the Crucifixion, the Virgin Mary and various saints. In the apse is a mosaic of the figure of Christ, a 19th-century restoration of a 13th-century copy of a fourth-century original by Jacopo da Camerino and Jacopo Torriti. Notice the small figure of St. Francis on the left, included because da Camerino and Torriti were Franciscan monks.

The most beautiful part of the cathedral is the cloister—a peaceful refuge, with slim columns, and inlaid marble and gold mosaics.

THE BAPTISTERY AND SCALA SANTA

In Piazza San Giovanni, the octagonal baptistery, the first in Christendom, survives from Constantine's era. The Scala Santa (Holy Staircase), a flight of 28 steps with glass sheets covering what is thought to be a trail of Christ's blood, leads to the Sancta Sanctorum, a chapel with frescoes by the great 13th-century painters Cimabue and Pietro Cavallini.

The Bocca della Verità in Santa Maria in Cosmedin

The sixth-century BC obelisk on the back of Bernini's marble elephant in the square outside the Church of Santa Maria Sopra Minerva

SANTA MARIA IN ARACOELI

427 E4 • Via dell'Aracoeli, 00186 Roma ☎ 06 679 8155 ⏰ Daily 9–12.30, 2.30–6.30 💶 Free 🚇 Colosseo

The church of Santa Maria in Aracoeli stands on the Capitoline Hill at the top of a wide, steep flight of steps. Today's church dates largely from the end of the 13th century, when Franciscan monks took over a Benedictine monastery church. The steps, traditionally climbed by newly married couples, offer a splendid view of the city, and lead to an austere brick frontage lightened only by doors and tiny rose windows. Inside, a gilded ceiling commemorates the Battle of Lepanto in 1571. Other highlights are the marble floor and the pulpit, good examples of cosmatesque inlay work, and Pinturicchio's frescoes in the first chapel on the right, depicting the life and death of St. Bernardino of Siena. The left transept leads to a little chapel dedicated to the Holy Child; its wooden statue is celebrated for its miraculous healing powers.

SANTA MARIA DELLA CONCEZIONE

427 F3 • Via Vittorio Veneto 27, 00187 Roma ☎ 06 487 1185 ⏰ Fri–Wed 9–12, 3–6 💶 Free/ contribution to the cemetery 🚇 Barberini www.cappucciniviaveneto.it

Also known as the Church of the Capuchins, this austere Counter-Reformation church is famous for its ghoulish ossuary. It contains the bones of about 4,000 Capuchin monks who lived and died in the once-adjacent convent between 1528 and 1870. The macabre display in the crypt includes chandeliers made from human bones.

There are separate chapels for femurs and tibias, pelvises, skulls and skeletons (some still dressed). The floor is scattered with soil from Palestine. The church was built in 1624 by Cardinal Antonio Barberini, a Capuchin monk whose tombstone in front of the main altar is inscribed *Hic jacet pulvis, cinis et nihil* (Here lies dust, ashes, nothing). This brother of Pope Urban VIII clearly did not share the Barberini love of grandeur. Look also for Guido Reni's painting *St. Michael Trampling the Devil*.

SANTA MARIA IN COSMEDIN

427 E5 • Via Bocca della Verità, 00186 Roma (Piazza Venezia/Circo Massimo) ☎ 06 678 1419 ⏰ Daily 9–6.30 💶 Free 🚇 Circo Massimo

By 772 the church built here in the sixth century on the site of a pagan temple had become the church of the local Greek community, and it was they who called it Cosmedin (lovely) because of its décor. It is also known as Santa Maria in Scuola Greca because people still come to Greek Orthodox Mass here.

It is most famous for the Bocca della Verità (Mouth of Truth), a large stone that was used as a drain cover by the ancient Romans. It's said that if a person places their hand inside its gaping mouth and tells a lie, the mouth clamps shut, severing the liar's fingers.

Between 1118 and 1123 the church was rebuilt and the elegant Romanesque bell tower was added. Inside, the nave and two aisles are divided by ancient Roman columns. There is fine cosmatesque marble-inlaid work in the floor, pulpits, screen and paschal candlestick. There is also a fragment of an eighth-century mosaic in the sacristy.

SANTA MARIA MAGGIORE

See page 178.

SANTA MARIA SOPRA MINERVA

427 E3 • Piazza della Minerva 42, 00186 Roma ☎ 06 679 3926 ⏰ Mon–Sat 8–7, Sun 8–12; no visits during Mass 💶 Free 🚇 Tram 8 www.basilicaminerva.it

In 1280 two Dominican friars, Sisto and Ristoro, who designed Santa Maria Novella in Florence (▷ 134), began building a church here on the site of a pagan temple to Minerva. The baroque-style refurbishment of the interior in the 16th and 17th centuries masked the church's medieval Gothic structure, a rarity in Rome, and the church was further embellished in the 19th century when the Dominican architect Girolamo Bianchedi added frescoes to its walls and vaults. Kept by Dominican friars, the Minerva offers a peaceful escape from the crowds.

St. Catherine of Siena is buried beneath the high altar. Frescoes in the Capranica Chapel illustrate her life. More famous are the frescoes by Filippino Lippi in the Carafa Chapel, depicting the life of the Dominican St. Thomas Aquinas and the Assumption. Other works of art include the statue of *Christ Risen* by Michelangelo. To the left of the altar is the tomb of the great Florentine artist and Dominican monk Fra Angelico, who died here in 1455.

Other noteworthy funerary monuments include tombs of the Medici popes, Leo X and Clement VII, sculpted by Antonio da Sangallo, and that of Maria Raggi, by Bernini. To the rear are the cloisters and the Dominican convent. It was here that Galileo was condemned for insisting that the earth moves around the sun (▷ 35).

The interior of the church, the finest example of an early Christian basilica in Rome

RATINGS

Good for kids	●●
Historic interest	●●●
Cultural interest	●●●●●
Value for money	●●●

BASICS

✚ 428 G4 • Piazza Santa Maria Maggiore, 00184 Roma ☎ 06 483195
🅒 Basilica: daily 7–7. Cappella Sforza: Mon–Fri 9–5. Museum: daily 9.30–6.30. Sacristy: daily 7–12.30, 3–6.30
🅦 Basilica and Cappella Sforza: free. Museum: adult €4, child (under 18) €2
🅠 Cavour or Termini, Vittorio Emanuele
🔲 Guided tours, tel 06 483058. Loggia delle Benedizioni: daily 4–6, €2.60; Presepe di Arnolfo di Cambio: Mon–Sat 9.30–1, €1.50. Audiotours, €1
🔲 🔲
🚻 Access for visitors with disabilities
🅿 On the square, €1 per hour

www.prtour.it

TIPS

● Start in the Loggia delle Benedizioni, where a mosaic tells the story of the basilica.
● There is little information on site and parts of the basilica are closed to the public or can be seen only with a guide.
● The basilica is badly lit, so bring a torch (flashlight) to get a better view.

SANTA MARIA MAGGIORE

Shares with San Pietro, San Giovanni in Laterano and San Paolo fuori le Mura the privilege of papal sovereignty. Sumptuously decorated with bright mosaics, the only one of the four to have kept its early Christian structure.

In the fourth century, the story goes, Pope Liberius had a dream in which the Virgin Mary told him it would snow that night and that he was to build a church in her honour where the snow settled. That night, 5 August 356, it snowed on the Esquiline Hill, and Santa Maria Maggiore was constructed on top of it. It was probably commissioned by Sixtus III in AD432—the first basilica to be built by a pope rather than an emperor.

THE BASILICAN NAVE

The interior of this immense church has kept its original medieval structure. Above the Roman columns in the nave, 36 fifth-century mosaic panels illustrate Old Testament stories. Easier to see are the mosaics depicting scenes of Christ's life on the arch at the entrance to the Cappella Paolina. The nave's 16th-century coffered ceiling by Giuliano da Sangallo is said to be decorated with some of the first gold brought from America. The floor has 12th-century inlay work.

THE BALDACCHINO AND MOSAICS

The *baldacchino* (altar canopy) by Ferdinando Fuga is made of porphyry columns with bronze foliage. It stands over the Confession (crypt), where a silver urn is believed to contain fragments of Christ's wooden cradle. The chancel arch is decorated with a fifth-century, Byzantine-style mosaic showing Jerusalem and Bethlehem, and Jesus as a child at the Feast of the Epiphany. The apse has a fine mosaic depicting the *Coronation of the Virgin Mary* (1295) by Jacopo Torriti. To the right of the apse is the humble tomb of the sculptor Gian Lorenzo Bernini.

THE CHAPELS

The Cappella Paolina is also known as the Cappella Borghese after the family of Pope Paul V, who commissioned the bejewelled surround to the altar and whose elaborate tomb is here. Next to this is the Cappella Sforza, designed by Michelangelo. Across the nave, the Cappella Sistina, commissioned by Pope Sixtus V and built by Domenico Fontana in 1585, is almost a church in its own right, with a dome, frescoes and papal tombs. The highlight is the *Presepe* (Nativity crib) by Anolfo di Cambio, which stood outside from the sixth century but was moved on Sixtus' orders, during the process of which much of it was broken.

Inside the Church of Santa Maria del Popolo

Statues outside the Basilica di Santa Maria in Trastevere

Detail of one of the beautiful mosaics in Santa Prassede

THE SIGHTS

SANTA MARIA DEL POPOLO

✚ 427 D2 • Piazza del Popolo 12, 00186 Roma ☎ 06 361 0836 ⊙ Mon–Sat 7–12, 4–7, Sun 8–1.30, 4.30–7.30 ⏱ Free ⊕ Flaminio, Spagna

Tucked into a corner of the Piazza del Popolo, Santa Maria del Popolo is famed for its collection of Renaissance art. Replacing an 11th-century chapel on the traditional site of Nero's grave, St. Mary of the People was built by Andrea Bregno in simple Renaissance style and paid for by the people of Rome, in 1472. The baroque embellishments to the interior were added later. In the della Rovere chapel the altar painting *The Adoration of the Child* is by Pinturicchio, and frescoes of the life of San Girolamo are the work of his pupil Tiberio d'Assisi. In the choir are masterpieces by Andrea Sansovino, monuments to Cardinal Ascanio Sforza (1505) and Cardinal Girolamo Basso della Rovere (1507). The early stained glass is by the French artist Guillaume de Marcillat. In the little Cappella Cerasi are Caravaggio's two magnificent works of 1601, *The Conversion of St. Paul* and *The Crucifixion of St. Peter*. The Cappella Chigi was built in 1516 as a mausoleum for the Chigi family, with sculpture, paintings and mosaics all designed by Raphael.

SANTA MARIA IN TRASTEVERE

✚ 427 D5 • Piazza di Santa Maria in Trastevere, 00153 Roma ☎ 06 589 7332 ⊙ Daily 7.30–9 ⏱ Free ☐ Tram 8 ⊞ 9–5

The picturesque quarter of Traste-vere, in which the medieval gem of Santa Maria stands, lies on the right bank of the Tiber. Legend has it that in 38BC a fountain of oil suddenly started flowing here,

heralding the birth of Jesus Christ, and Pope Callixtus (217–22) built a sanctuary to commemorate the miracle. The present-day basilica was built in the 12th century, using materials from the Terme di Caracalla (▷ 180). The mosaics on the façade, probably 12th-century, have survived as Rome's only example of what all the city's medieval church façades once looked like. Inside, the mosaics in the apse are beautiful above all else. In the half-dome, 12th-century mosaics show Mary embraced by her son and flanked by popes and saints. Below this, Pietro Cavallini's masterpiece depicts scenes from the life of the Virgin (1290). More 12th-century mosaics on the chancel arch depict the prophets Isaiah and Jeremiah. The central panel of the 17th-century coffered ceiling has an *Assumption* by Domenichino. Try to visit after dark, when the basilica's golden façade is floodlit and you can sit at one of the outdoor cafés in the piazza.

SAN PIETRO IN VINCOLI

✚ 428 F4 • Piazza San Pietro in Vincoli, 00184 Roma ☎ 06 488 2865 ⊙ Daily 7–12.30, 3.30–7; no visits during Mass Sun 11am ⏱ Free ⊕ Colosseo

The main tourist attraction in San Pietro in Vincoli is the chains that bound St. Peter. The church is in a charming square of the same name, and is always crowded. Initially erected in the third century and consecrated in 439 by Sixtus III, this early church was largely rebuilt, with the addition of a Renaissance portico, in the 15th century. Tradition holds that two sets of chains were used to bind St. Peter—one in Jerusalem, the other in the Mamertine prison—and when placed side by side they miraculously fused together. The ceiling fresco illustrates the event. The chains are in an urn under the high altar.

The church's other attraction is Michelangelo's *Moses*, one of 40 statues commissioned to adorn a mausoleum for Julius II intended for San Pietro, but never completed. The huge seated figure of Moses, sculpted from Carrara marble, is shown with the Ten Commandments tablets under his arm.

SANTA PRASSEDE

✚ 428 G4 • Via di Santa Prassede 9/A, 00184 Roma ☎ 06 488 2456 ⊙ Daily 7.30–12, 3–6.30; closed Aug ⏱ Free ⊕ Cavour, Termini, Vittorio Emanuele ☐ 16, 70, 71

Santa Prassede is home to one of Rome's most important Byzantine treasures, the San Zeno chapel, built by Paschal I as a mausoleum for his mother, Theodora, and known as the Garden of Paradise because of the unique beauty and richness of its gold mosaics. A house of worship has stood on this spot since AD489, rebuilt and restored many times before it was enlarged in 822 by Paschal I to house relics of martyrs taken from the catacombs. The jewel in Santa Prassede's crown are the ninth-century mosaics by artists brought from Byzantium in the San Zeno chapel, depicting Christ Pantocrator, the saints and Virgin Mary, but the apse and the triumphal arch are also covered with beautiful mosaics. These show St. Peter and St. Paul introducing St. Prassede and her sister, St. Pudenziana, to Christ and, in the arch, New Jerusalem, Christ and the saints. The Chapel of San Zeno also has an excellent example of ornamental *opus sectile* paving in multihued marble. In a corner stands the Column of the Flagellation, brought from Jerusalem in 1223.

Outside the chapel is Bernini's first work, a memorial to Bishop Giovanni Battista Santoni.

The remains of the Terme di Caracalla

The Via Appia Antica, still partly paved with Roman cobbles

The fake Greek temple in the Villa Borghese gardens

TERME DI CARACALLA

428 off F5 • Viale delle Terme di Caracalla 52, 00153 Roma ☎ 06 575 8626 ◷ Tue–Sun 9–6, Mon 9–2 €5; 18–24 years €2.50; under 18s free Circo Massimo www.beniculturali.it

The Terme di Caracalla (Baths of Caracalla) in Celio are one of the most impressive ancient Roman complexes. Designed primarily to care for the body, the baths were also a cultural meeting place. Begun by Septimius Severus in AD206 and opened by Emperor Caracalla in AD217, they were functional until AD537, when the Goths destroyed the aqueducts that supplied the water. There was an immense pool for cooling the body called a *frigidarium*, a large, hot, circular room known as a *caldarium*, rooms for hot and warm baths, porticoes, halls, gymnasia, statues, libraries, gardens and a stadium. Up to 600 people were able to bathe at one time. All the rooms were decorated with alabaster, granite and mosaics, most of which are intact. Recent excavations have uncovered an underground Mithraic temple. Open-air opera is staged here in summer.

VIA APPIA ANTICA

428 off F5 • Via Appia Antica, 00178 Roma Circo Massimo 118, 160, 628

The Via Appia (Appian Way), also known as the Regina Viarum (Queen of Roads), was the first road built by the Romans. The magistrate Appius Claudius began building it in 312BC, and by the second century BC it reached Brindisi, a distance of 589km (366 miles). Now 212km (132 miles) long, running between Rome and Capua, it is closed to cars, and a green park lines the route—a popular spot with Romans at weekends. It is paved with *basoli*, basalt rock stones of polygonal shape, many of which are intact. You can walk on these ancient stones, passing venerable busts and statues, churches, catacombs and ancient villas.

In Rome, the road begins at Porta San Sebastiano. Look for the ancient column inserted in a modern wall marking the first mile. At the corner with Via Ardeatina is the Church of Domine Quo Vadis, Latin for 'Lord, where are you going?' It was here that St. Peter, escaping Nero's persecutions, was stopped by Jesus, who asked him to return to Rome and face his destiny. On the other side of the Via Appia are the ruins of Maxentius's circus and imperial residence. The tomb of Cecilia Metella, wife of Marcus Crassus, son of the Republican Roman ruler, stands at a crossing with a road of the same name. From here pine and cypress trees, statues and funerary monuments flank the way. Farther along are the remains of a nymphaeum, the pleasure house of Villa dei Quintili, the largest villa in ancient Rome's suburbs. Along the way, look for the catacombs of St. Priscilla, St. Callisto and St. Sebastian.

VILLA BORGHESE

427 F1–2 • Villa Borghese, 00187 Roma ◷ Sunrise–sunset Flaminio, Spagna

The Villa Borghese's beautiful avenues and paths, embellished with ancient statues and fountains, make it one of the grandest parks in Rome. Cardinal Borghese created both it and the imposing Villa Pinciana, or Casino Borghese, in the early 17th century to house his rich art collection. Highlights of the gardens are the Casino della Meridiana, the aviary and the artificial lake with its little island, in the middle of which stands an 18th-century Ionian-style temple to Aesculapius, the Greek god of medicine. At the heart of the park is Piazza di Siena, a popular venue for international horse-races. There is also a zoo.

VILLA GIULIA AND MUSEO NAZIONALE ETRUSCO

427 E1 • Piazzale Villa Giulia 9, 00196 Roma ☎ 06 322 6571 ◷ Daily 8.30–7.30 Adult €4, child (under 18) free Flaminio www.ticketeria.it www.beniculturali.it

The national museum of Etruscan art and relics is in the splendid 16th-century Villa Giulia, near Piazza del Popolo. The way of life, and death, of this mysterious civilization is displayed in this quiet corner of Rome, once Julius III's country villa. Surrounded by a series of courtyards, the villa has a loggia by Ammanati, sumptuous interiors and a nymphaeum with caryatids, rockeries, false grottoes and a Vasari fountain.

The Etruscan museum houses the pre-Roman heritage of Latium, Umbria and southern Etruria, found in the necropolises of Cerveteri (▷ 183) and Veio. It contains treasures and objects from the Etruscan, Faliscan and Greek civilizations. Hall 7 houses statues from Veio made of polychrome terracotta, including one depicting Heracles in combat with Apollo for the doe, a masterpiece. These statues all come from one temple in Veio and are thought be the work of Vulca, who carved the statues for the Temple of Jupiter on the Capitol in 509BC. The most celebrated piece of Etruscan art is the Sarcophagus of the Spouses, found in the Cerveteri halls. It dates from the end of the sixth century BC and indicates that the Etruscans believed in an afterlife. A vase decorated with the Etruscan alphabet is displayed in Hall 15.

LAZIO AND THE MARCHE

Low-key Lazio and the remote Marche have some of Italy's best-kept secrets, with undiscovered cities such as Urbino, great gardens and villas like those of Tivoli, and 4,000-year-old Etruscan treasures at Tarquinia. There is also a great deal of variety—the inland lakes and the mountain town of Ascoli Piceno contrasting with the summer resorts on the east and west coasts.

MAJOR SIGHTS

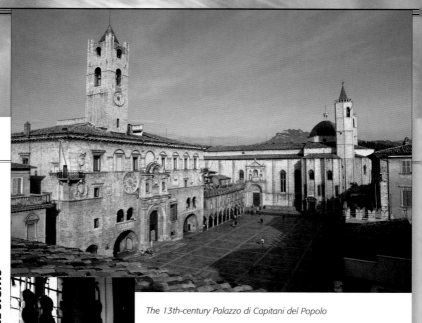

THE SIGHTS

The 13th-century Palazzo di Capitani del Popolo

ASCOLI PICENO

**Romanesque churches, medieval towers, baroque palaces and busy cafés.
An ancient town of white travertine marble, with narrow streets and porticoed piazzas.**

Some 65km (40 miles) southwest of Fermo, Ascoli is today a prosperous town relatively untouched by tourism. It began as a strategic Roman settlement founded after the defeat of the local Piceni tribe. During medieval times rich families living in the town, like those in San Gimignano (▷ 151), built defensive towers as a symbol of their wealth and dominance. At one time there were around 200 spearing the skyline; many were destroyed on the orders of Frederick II, but about 50 remain.

THE WHITE CITY
Architecturally, Ascoli is striking, built largely from white travertine stone. At its heart is Piazza del Popolo, lined with an elegant Renaissance portico, reminiscent of those in Bolgona (▷ 105). It is dominated by the 13th-century Palazzo dei Capitani, once the seat of the *comune* (town council), and the Church of San Francesco. Visitors and locals are also drawn to this square by the delightful Caffè Meletti, an art deco café decorated with huge mirrors, and having wooden floors and marble tables. Various famous people have sought refreshment here over the years since it opened in 1903, including novelist Ernest Hemingway; try the local liqueur, the aniseed-tasting Anisetta Meletti. Piazza Arringo, built over the Roman forum, is home to the 15th-century duomo, dedicated to St. Emidius, whose relics are kept in the crypt. In a chapel on the right of the nave is a polyptych considered to be one of Carlo Crivelli's finest works.

MUSEUMS
The Diocesan Museum (Mon–Fri 9.30–1, Sat 9.30–1, 3.30–7), in the Palazzo Panichi, displays a collection of prehistoric and Roman archaeological finds, while the Pinacoteca Civica (daily 9–1, 3–7), an art gallery in the Palazzo Comunale, also on the square, is worth visiting just to see the palace's rich red drapes, marble floors and chandeliers. Among the pieces on show are an *Annunciation* by Guido Reni and Titian's *St. Francis Receiving the Stigmata*, along with works by Carlo Crivelli and Pietro Alemanno.

A violin-maker measures the thickness of a fiddle front

RATINGS	
Good for kids	●●●
Historic interest	●●●●
Cultural interest	●●●
Specialist shopping	●●●

BASICS

✚ 439 J8

🛈 Piazza Arringo 7, 63100 Ascoli Piceno, tel 0736 298204; daily 9–1, 3–7

🚉 Ascoli Piceno

www.le-marche.com
You can get up-to-date tourist information by phoning the region's freephone service on 800 222111. There are English-speaking operators but this number only works when dialled in Italy.

MAKE A DAY OF IT
Urbino: ▷ 190
Offida: ▷ 185

The restored Abazzia di Montecassino

An Etruscan tomb in the necropolis near Cerveteri

Crenellations crown the Augustan walls of Fano

ABBAZIA DI MONTECASSINO

⊞ 440 K10 • Via G. di Biasco 54, 03043 Cassino ☎ 0776 21296
◉ Mon–Sat 8–8. Abbey: daily 8.30–12.30, 3.30–6 🚌 Cassino, then bus to the abbey
www.montecassino.it

St. Benedict, supposedly guided by three ravens, chose this dramatic site to found a monastery in 529. High on a mountaintop, 200km (125 miles) south of Rome, the huge white bulwarks of the abbey of Montecassino can be seen for miles around. This strategic position meant that the abbey was frequently involved in conflict, and it has been destroyed and rebuilt many times. During World War II the Nazis made the abbey their regional headquarters, and on 15 February 1944 it was destroyed by Allied bombing. The rest of the abbey was faithfully reconstructed in a medieval style. It has a slightly sterile appearance, but the views from here are superb (much of the abbey is closed to the public).

Large parts of the town of Cassino were also destroyed during World War II. The ruins of the Roman town of Casinum, however, can still be seen.
Don't miss The crypt is the only original part of the abbey building that remains.

CASTEL GANDOLFO AND LAGO ALBANO

⊞ 438 H10 🛈 Piazza Libertà 5, Castel Gandolfo, tel 06 932 4081

Castel Gandolfo, 24km (15 miles) south of Rome, is named after the powerful Genoese Gandolfi family, who originally built a castle here in the 12th century. The palace, built over the ruined castle in 1624 and later remodelled by Pope Pius XI, comes into its own in July, August

and September, when the papal court transfers here from the Vatican. The palace can be seen only from the outside, but large numbers of visitors flock here just for a sight of it. The Pope generally appears in the palace's courtyard at noon on Sundays during this period to address the public.

The palace is the dominant feature of the town, but don't overlook the Church of San Tommaso di Villanova, designed by Bernini, with frescoes by Pietro da Cortona.

Castel Gandolfo looks out over the waters of Lake Albano, the largest of the lakes in this region. Along the Via Appia, which runs down the length of the lake's west shore, are ancient towns such as Albano Laziale, founded as a Roman camp, as well as a number of restaurants and cafés.

CERVETERI

⊞ 438 H10 • Necropoli della Banditaccia, Piazza Libertà 5, 00052 Cerveteri ☎ 06 995 51971
◉ May–end Sep Tue–Sun 9–7; rest of year Tue–Sun 9–4

Cerveteri was one of the wealthiest Etruscan towns in Italy and dates back to the 7th century BC. Known as Kysry (Roman *Caere*) in ancient times, it accumulated its wealth by trading the rich mineral deposits found in the Tolfa hills nearby.

Today the heart of the town is largely medieval in appearance and the Etruscan remains for which it is famous are found 3km (2 miles) to the west.

The Necropoli della Banditaccia were laid out to create a 'city of the dead', providing space for 5,000 tombs dating from the seventh to first century BC. With streets and houses like a town, this extraordinary burial site and the archaeological finds here give a fascinating insight into Etruscan culture. The tombs are

carved into the rock or covered by earth, and several are elaborately constructed, including the Tomba degli Scudi e delle Sedie, in the form of an Etruscan house. Slaves were cremated and their ashes put in with their masters.
Don't miss The Museo Nazionale di Cerveteri (Tue–Sun 9–7) displays some of the many Etruscan objects that were buried with the dead. Other finds from these tombs are on display in Rome's Villa Giulia (▷ 180).

FANO

⊞ 437 J7 🛈 Via Battisti 10, 61032 Fano, tel 0721 803534 🚌 Fano
www.turismofano.com

Fano's beaches make it a popular, but not overcrowded, resort, with a good choice of either sandy beaches sprinkled with sun umbrellas, or pebbly stretches with promenades.

Fano is 11km (7 miles) south of Pesaro on the Adriatic coast, and was once a Roman port on the Via Flaminia, but little of its Roman heritage remains visible. Today it is split by the railway, with the modern resort on one side and the old town on the other. In addition to some imposing palaces, Fano has a museum and art gallery, the Museo Civico and Pinacoteca, in the 15th-century Palazzo Malatesta. It has a collection of Roman mosaics, medieval coins and paintings by artists such as Michele Giambono, Giovanni Santi and Guido Reni, along with some 19th- and 20th-century works.

The impressive Biblioteca Federiciana has on display more than 200,000 volumes and two 17th-century globes, one of the earth and one of the skies.
Don't miss The highlight of the historic heart is the Arco di Augusto, a triumphal arch built by Emperor Augustus in AD2 to mark the city's foundation.

One of the huge statues at the Villa Aldobrandini in Frascati

The distant promontory of Capodimonte, viewed from across Lago di Bolsena

FRASCATI AND COLLI ALBANI

⊞ 438 H10 🛈 Piazza G. Marconi, 00044 Frascati, tel 06 942 0331 🚉 Frascati

A popular destination with both Romans and tourists, Frascati has been a retreat for the rich for centuries and is still dominated by one of their villas, Villa Aldobrandini, begun by Giacomo della Porta in 1598 but not completed until 100 years later. You can't go inside the villa as it is still lived in by the family, but the grounds are worth a visit. They are adorned with large water features and sculptures; you can visit them free with a permit obtained at the visitor centre at Piazza G. Marconi (grounds: Apr–end Sep Mon–Fri 9–1, 3–6; rest of year Mon–Fri 9–1, 3–5; visitor centre: closed Sat afternoon and all Sun).

The Colli Albani, the hills to the south of Frascati, 21km (13 miles) southeast of Rome, form a backbone to the Castelli Romani towns, so called because they grew up around the feudal castles of Rome's wealthy families. The soil of this 60km (37-mile) chain of volcanic hills is very fertile and produces many good wines, the best-known being, naturally, Frascati. Give it a try in one of the local bars, where it is often available from huge wooden barrels.

There are a number of little towns to visit in the area besides Frascati, including Nemi and Rocca di Papa—the most dramatically positioned town in the Collini Albani.

GROTTE DI FRASASSI

⊞ 437 J7 • Genga ☎ 0732 90080 or 90090 ⏰ Guided tours: Mar–end Jul, Sep, Oct daily 9.30, 11, 12.30, 3, 4.30, 6; continuous tours Aug daily 8–6.30; Nov–end Feb Mon–Fri 11.15, Sat 11, 12.30, 3, 4.30, Sun 9.30, 11, 12.30, 3, 4.30, 6 🎟 Adult €12, child (6–14) €11, under 6s free 🚉 Genga, then shuttle bus in summer
www.frasassi.com

This is one of the most interesting cave complexes in Italy, situated next to the Church of San Vittore delle Chiuse, near Genga. The intriguing underground world of silent lakes and countless stalactites and stalagmites, 61km (38 miles) from Ancona, provides an arresting contrast to the surrounding countryside.

Discovered in 1971, the caves opened to the public in 1974. So far, 13km (8 miles) of limestone caves have been explored, and the complex is thought to extend a further 35km (22 miles). Less than 2km (1.3 miles) is open to the public, but it is sure to impress.

The Grotta Grande del Vento (Great Cave of the Wind) is possibly the largest cave of its kind in Europe, so huge that Milan Cathedral could fit inside. The warrens of other caves bear such evocative names as the Hall of the Candles, the Hall of the Bear and the Hall of Infinity. Theatrically lit walkways lead through them all.

LAGO DI BOLSENA AND BOLSENA

⊞ 438 G9 🛈 Piazza Matteotti 9, 01223 Bolsena, tel 0761 799923
www.lagodibolsena.org

Lago di Bolsena, 112km (70 miles) north of Rome, is the largest volcanic lake in Italy and the fifth-largest in the country. It is lined with busy towns such as Capodimonte, where the waters lap the edge of the town, Gradoli, which lies at the heart of a large wine region, Etruscan Montefiascone and medieval Bolsena. Guided tours by boat run from Capodimonte and Bolsena to Isola Bisentina (daily 11 and 5, Sun 11, 3 and 5), an island in the middle of the lake where you can visit Etruscan tombs and the Farnese family gardens.

On the hillside overlooking the lake, Bolsena's medieval castle dates back to the 13th century and today contains a museum displaying archaeological finds from the lake and objects from the Roman city of Volsinii (Roman Bolsena). On Piazza Santa Cristina stands the collegiate Romanesque Church of Santa Cristina. The oldest part of this church is the grotto, where the miracle of Corpus Christi is said to have taken place in 1236; blood supposedly dropped from the Host on to the altar cloth, and the priest who witnessed it felt it proved the real presence of Christ. The grotto contains a 15th-century polyptych attributed to Sano di Pietro and Benvenuto di Giovanni, along with frescoes by painters from the Umbrian-Sienese school.

LORETO

⊞ 439 J7 🛈 Via Solari 3, 60025 Loreto, tel 071 970276 🚉 Loreto
www.loreto.it

Loreto, 22km (14 miles) southwest of Portonovo, is a place of pilgrimage—thousands make the journey every year to see the Virgin Mary's house. It was transported here from Nazareth by the Angeli family during the 13th century. In the 16th century an enormous church, the Santuario della Santa Casa, was built over the house to protect it.

The Santa Casa (Holy House) is directly beneath the dome and protected by an ornate marble screen by the Italian Renaissance architect Bramante. Around the Santa Casa are the sacristies of San Marco, San Giovanni and

The remains of the Capitolium at Ostia Antica

Take time to sunbathe or shelter under the parasols on one of the white, sandy beaches near Portonovo in Parco del Conero

San Luca, which contain works by Melozzo da Forli and Luca Signorelli. Outside in the Piazza della Madonna is the Fontana della Madonna, a fountain designed by Giovanni Fontana and Carlo Maderno, one of the architects who worked on San Pietro in Rome (▷ 160–161).

Opposite the church is the Palazzo Apostolico, begun by Bramante in 1509 and now occupied by the town's museum and art gallery. The collection includes notable paintings by Lorenzo Lotto.

OFFIDA

✚ 439 K8 🛈 Museo di Offida, Corso Serpente Aureo 66, 63035 Offida, tel 0736 888609; summer only

Easily reached from Ascoli Piceno and the coastal towns of the region, Offida is famous in the Marche for its fine lace, which has been produced by the women of the town for generations. There are plenty of places to purchase their craftwork, and the Lace Museum has examples of local lace, including a 19th-century tablecloth, dainty bridal shoes and an exquisite dress modelled by Naomi Campbell in 1997 for Antonio Beraddi.

Offida is surrounded by vineyards and the gently rolling hills to the west of San Benedetto del Tronto. It has a pleasant, unhurried atmosphere, with streets that invite exploration. The town's main focus is the square, which is flanked by the 14th-century Palazzo Comunale, home to the archaeological museum, a small art gallery and the Teatro Serpente Aureo.

From here it is about five minutes' walk to the Church of Santa Maria della Rocca, up on an exposed hillside overlooking the surrounding countryside. The monks used its crypt as a hospital from the 12th century.

During restoration in the 1980s, it was discovered that wide cavities in the walls had been used to bury the dead.

OSTIA ANTICA

✚ 438 H10 • Via Romanogli 717, 000125 Ostia ☎ Mon–Fri 06 5635 2830; Sat–Sun 06 5635 2830 🕔 Apr to mid-Oct Tue–Sun 8.30–6; Nov–end Feb Tue–Sun 8.30–4; Mar Tue–Sun 8.30–5 💷 Adults €4, under 18s free 🔲 Ostia Antica 🔲 🔲
www.itnw.roma.it/ostia/scavi
www.ostia-antica.org

Ostia Antica is Italy's best-preserved Roman settlement after Pompei (▷ 204–207). The sprawling remnants of this once-bustling town include shops and workshops, Mithraic shrines, barracks, tombs, grain warehouses (horrea), baths, inns and domestic dwellings.

In about 335BC a small fishing community settled on this site 23km (14 miles) west of Rome. The settlement grew to become Rome's principal port, trading commodities from all over the empire. With the outbreak of the First Punic War, the port also became an important naval base and by the second century it had a population of nearly 500,000. Excavations of the site began in the 19th century and have so far revealed about one half of the town.

The Terme di Nettuno (Baths of Neptune), the first main building on the right after the Porta Romana, was built by Hadrian and preserves a series of elaborate mosaics depicting Neptune and Amphitrite. The mill is equally well preserved, with millstones, basins and kneading machines on view. The amphitheatre was built in the age of Augustus, with capacity for 3,000 people. At the end of the second century its capacity was extended to 4,000, and later it

was adapted for the staging of aquatic shows. The Thermopolium in Via di Diana was once a bar; you can still see the marble counter, washbasins, stove, benches for the customers and wall paintings illustrating the menu.

PARCO DEL CONERO

✚ 439 J7 🛈 Centro Visite Parco del Conero, Via Peschiera 30/a, 60020 Sirolo, tel 0719 331879; Jun–end Sep daily 9–1, 4–7; rest of year Mon–Sat 9–1 📅
www.parcoconero.it

This is one of the most beautiful areas on the Adriatic and a good destination for those wanting to enjoy the outdoors. There are numerous coastal resorts where you can swim, sail, scuba dive and windsurf, and for walkers there are 18 waymarked tracks around Monte Conero. There are many rare plants and excellent birdwatching opportunities, as well as some sites of cultural and geological interest to explore.

The park covers 5,800 hectares (14,300 acres) and is dominated by Monte Conero (572m/ 1,877ft). At the top of the mountain are the remains of a Palaeolithic settlement dating back 100,000 years.

To its north is Portonovo, a pretty bay that is home to the 11th-century church of Santa Maria di Portonovo, mentioned by Dante in La Divina Commedia. To the south is Sirolo, the area's main resort, with good beaches that are safe for children. Close by is Numana, where you can visit the Santuario della Croce, a shrine containing a wooden crucifix dating from the 12th to 13th century that is said to have miraculous powers.

On the road to Numana, Sirolo is home to the Villa Vetta Marina, the site of a convent founded by St. Francis in 1215.

The quiet main square of the small hillside town of San Severino Marche, founded by refugees who were fleeing raiding barbarians in the sixth century

THE SIGHTS

PESARO

⊞ 437 J6 ⓘ Viale Trieste 164, 61100 Pesaro, tel 0721 69341 ▣ Pesaro
www.comune.pesaro.ps.it

Founded by the Romans in 184BC, Pesaro is a busy provincial town characterized by a pleasant old town, elegant, broad streets and a waterfront lined with white-stucco hotels overlooking soft, sandy beaches. The hub is Piazza del Popolo, where you'll find the most impressive building, the 15th-century Palazzo Ducale.

Pesaro's beaches make it a great place for anyone simply wanting to relax in the sun. It also attracts opera-lovers, as it was the birthplace of the composer Rossini (1792–1868), and is the venue for a festival celebrating his works every August. His birthplace, Casa di Rossini, is a small museum, which preserves the original furnishings and memorabilia of the composer. Heavy bombing in World War II destroyed much of the town, so it lacks the charm of other Italian towns, but it still has its art treasures.

Paintings in the Museo Civico include Giovanni Bellini's masterpiece, The Coronation of the Virgin. The ceramic collection includes a terracotta work by Andrea della Robbia.

SAN LEO

⊞ 437 H6 ⓘ Piazza Dante 10, 91018 San Leo, tel 0541 916306

Some 12.5km (8 miles) east of Novafeltria, San Leo sits precariously on top of a tall cliff and is reached by a single-track road cut into the rock. Named after a Dalmatian saint, who was said to have converted the area to Christianity in the fourth century, the town was originally a defensive fortress.

The dramatic beauty of the landscape was the inspiration for Dante's Purgatorio, and it still attracts visitors.

San Leo is dominated by its castle, which Machiavelli considered to be the greatest fortress in Italy. It also served as a prison, notably to Count Alessandro di Cagliostro, a leading freemason, alchemist and medium who was sentenced to death during the Inquisition. The little village sits in the shadow of the fortress, on the remarkably preserved cobbled square, Piazza Dante. Here—in addition to several good restaurants and cafés—is the 12th-century Roman-esque duomo, erected in honour of St. Leo, and La Pieve, the town's oldest church, founded in the eighth century.

SAN MARINO

⊞ 437 H6 ⓘ Palazzo del Turismo, Contrada Omagnano 20, 47031 San Marino, tel 0549 882410
www.omniway.sm

Marino, a stonemason fleeing religious persecution, supposedly founded this autonomous town in AD301. Between Romagna and the Marche, 14km (9 miles) southwest of Rimini, the town has a commanding position on a hilltop, with impressive battlements on the highest ridges. It covers an area of just 61sq km (24sq miles) and still declares itself an independent republic, with its own mint, postage stamps and international soccer team. This makes it the longest-surviving republic in Europe.

San Marino is something of a tourist trap, so you have to fight your way past numerous souvenir shops to enjoy its main attraction—the views from the fortress on Mount Titan. This mountain is said to have been used by the Titans, mythological gods of ancient Greece, to help them reach the sky and defeat Jupiter.

SAN SEVERINO MARCHE

⊞ 439 J8 ⓘ Pro Loco, Piazza del Popolo 43, 62027 San Severino, tel 0733 638414 ▣ San Severino

A town with a rich artistic heritage, San Severino Marche was the birthplace of the Salimbeni brothers, whose works adorn the local churches and art gallery. The town's past is revealed further in the archaeological museum, which also has remains from the Roman town of Septempeda.

There are two parts to the town: The Borgo, which focuses on the medieval Piazza del Popolo, and the ancient castello (castle) on Montenero Hill, the heart of the old town. The Pinacoteca Civica (art gallery), just above the piazza in the lower part of town, has works by Lorenzo and Jacopo Salimbeni, paintings by Alunno, and the great Mannerist artist Pinturicchio's painted wood masterpiece, the Madonna della Pace. In the sixth-century Church of San Lorenzo in Doliolo, at the top of Via Salimbini, are the remains of a pagan temple and frescoes by the Salimbeni brothers. The 10th-century Duomo Vecchio is also decorated with frescoes by the brothers. The Duomo Nuovo, with a Madonna by Pinturicchio, is also worth visiting.

SPERLONGA

⊞ 439 J11 ⓘ Via Emanuele Filiberto 5, 04024 Gaeta, tel 0771 461165; summer only ▣ Fondi Sperlonga

Sperlonga is Lazio's most fashionable resort, 98km (61 miles) southeast of Castel Gandolfo. Like the town of Gaeta, Sperlonga juts into the Tyrrhenian Sea, on the region's prettiest stretch of coastline, shaped by little coves and promontories and several attractive beaches. The houses are whitewashed, and the narrow streets make the town an

The Convento di San Benedetto clings to the rockface in the small medieval town of Subiaco

A section of the Roman aqueduct at Tarquinia

appealing place to explore, although it can get very busy in summer. Combine time on the beach and a leisurely meal in a restaurant with a visit to nearby historical sites—perhaps the Grotta di Tiberio (Cave of Tiberius) and its museum, with works of art and several classical sculptures.

At Gaeta you can also visit the tomb of Cicero, the great Roman orator and writer, killed in 43BC.

SUBIACO

➕ 439 J10 ℹ️ Via Cadorna 59, 00028 Subiaco, tel 0774 822013

Subiaco is an isolated town on the edge of the Simbruini Mountains, 28km (17 miles) south of Anticoli Corrado. There were once 12 monasteries around the town, but now only two remain, both a short distance from the town. It was here in the fifth century that St. Benedict wrote the famous *Benedictine Rule*, the cornerstone of Western monasticism. He lived in a nearby cave, the Sacro Speco, now part of the Convento di San Benedetto. The cave is in a lower part of the monastery; steps lead down to an early 13th-century fresco of St. Francis. It is this monastery and the Monastery of Santa Scolastica that attract most visitors to the town. Reached by a 25-minute walk from town, the Convento di Santa Scholastica has three painstakingly restored cloisters. The first, from 1580, is decorated with columns from Nero's villa, the second (1052) is one of the oldest in Italy, and the third dates from the 13th century.

TARQUINIA

➕ 438 G9 ℹ️ Piazza Cavour 1, 01016 Tarquinia, tel 0766 856384
🚊 Tarquinia, then bus

The cultural and political capital of Etruscan Italy, Tarquinia is famous for its necropolis, 6,000 original

Etruscan tombs that honeycomb the Monterozzi plateau to the east of the town. There are a handful that can be visited within the ancient town. The Hellenistic-style wall paintings inside span about 500 years, depicting mythical scenes, banquets, games and horse-races. The tombs with the most fascinating paintings are *The Augurs* (530BC), *The Lionesses* (late sixth century BC) and *The Leopards* (470BC).

The modern town overlooks the Tyrrhenian Sea, and here are more reminders of the past in a museum that has a wide variety of Etruscan objects. On display are tomb paintings, jewellery, coins and vases, but the highlight is a pair of Etruscan terracotta winged horses from the fourth century BC. There are also some medieval sites worth visiting here, including the 12th-century Church of Santa Maria in Castello.

TIVOLI

See pages 188–189.

TOLENTINO

➕ 437 J8 ℹ️ Piazza della Libertà, 62029, Tolentino 0733 972937 🚊 Tolentino

Tolentino is one of Italy's lesser-known towns but it has plenty to attract history-lovers, including frescoes in the Basilica di San Nicola, several Romanesque churches, and a fine 18th-century theatre.

Its position in the Chienti River Valley, 100km (62 miles) north of Ascoli Piceno, made it an important industrial focus in the Middle Ages, the river water being used to drive mills. Today Tolentino has kept its industrial tradition, and the historic heart is surrounded by a sprawl of uninspiring modern buildings.

An ancient bridge, the Ponte di Diavolo (Devil's Bridge), leads to the 13th-century Basilica di San Nicola da Tolentino, the home of

St. Nicholas until he died in 1305. Inside is a fresco cycle by Pietro da Rimini, painted early in the 14th century in the style of Giotto.

Tolentino also has some interesting museums: the Museo dell'Opera del Santuario has paintings, frescoes and rich religious objects, while the slightly more unusual Museo della Caricatura e dell'Umorismo nell'Arte displays a collection of caricatures by Italian and foreign artists.

URBINO

See page 190.

VITERBO

➕ 438 H9 ℹ️ Piazza San Carluccio 5, 01100 Viterbo, tel 0761 304795
🚊 Viterbo Porta Romana

Viterbo is the largest town in northern Lazio, 81km (51 miles) north of Rome. Originally an Etruscan town, it was colonized by the Romans in 310BC. The outskirts are uninspiring, but the walled centre is lively, with plenty of good bars and restaurants, as well as a number of cultural sites.

It is worth visiting simply to soak up the atmosphere of the ancient medieval quarter, San Pellegrino—an intriguing maze of narrow streets lined with romantic-looking houses, enticing archways, balconies and external staircases. The town was home to artists such as Lorenzo da Viterbo (1440–76), and it was the official papal residence for many years.

The heart of town is Piazza del Plebiscito, from where you can walk along Via San Lorenzo to Piazza San Lorenzo, an airy square built on the site of an Etruscan acropolis. The 13th-century Palazzo Papale and the striking Romanesque duomo are both found here. At the Villa Lante at nearby Bagnaia, you can walk in the Renaissance garden and enjoy its open-air thermal pools.

TIVOLI

Fountains and aquatic displays in the beautiful gardens at the Villa d'Este.
Romantic remains of Emperor Hadrian's luxurious Villa Adria, the largest ever built in the Roman Empire.

Tivoli's scenery and cool hilltop location 40km (25 miles) east of Rome made it a popular spot for wealthy Romans to build their country villas.

VILLA ADRIANA

Via di Villa Adriana, 00010 Tivoli ☎ 06 399 67900 🕐 Summer daily 9–6; rest of year daily 9–5 🎫 Adult €6.50, under 18s free 📷 🏛 👫
www.villa-adriana.net

The Villa Adriana's ruins sprawl lazily away from Tivoli through peaceful olive groves. Begun in AD125 and completed 10 years later, the Villa Adriana was so vast that it covered an area as great as the heart of imperial Rome. It was the most costly palace ever built in the empire, with two bathhouses, libraries, temples and a Greek theatre, as well as apartments. It even had a beach heated by steam pipes buried under the sand, and a series of underground service passages big enough to accommodate horses and carts. The parkland is dotted with pools and buildings connected by covered walkways. The Teatro Marittimo is a small palace built on a private island in an artificial lagoon; it is thought to have been Hadrian's private retreat.

VILLA D'ESTE

Piazza Trento, 00010 Tivoli ☎ 0774 332920 🕐 May–end Aug Tue–Sun 8.30–6.45; Sep Tue–Sun 8.30–6.15; Oct Tue–Sun 8.30–5.30; Nov–end Jan Tue–Sun 8.30–4; Feb Tue–Sun 8.30–4.30; Mar Tue–Sun 8.30–5.15; Apr Tue–Sun 8.30–6.30. Closes one hour after last entry 🎫 Adult €6.50, under 18s €3.25 📷 🏛 👫
www.villadestetivoli.info

The Villa d'Este is in Tivoli itself, next to the main square, Largo Garibaldi. Pirro Ligorio adapted the former convent into a country retreat for Cardinal Ippolito d'Este, son of Lucrezia Borgia and the Duke of Ferrara, in 1550. The gardens are both theatrical and elegant, with water spouting from all corners and cascading down every surface. Particularly impressive are the Viale delle Cento Fontane (Avenue of a Hundred Fountains) and the Fontana dei Draghi (Fountain of the Dragons), built in honour of Pope Gregory XIII, whose emblem was a short-tailed dragon. But the most visually striking aquatic display is the Fontana di Biccierone (Fountain of Glass) by Bernini. A curious addition is the Rometta, with scale models of Rome's major buildings.

RATINGS				
Good for kids	●	●	●	
Historic interest	●	●	●	
Photo stops	●	●	●	●
Walkability	●	●	●	●

BASICS

✚ 438 H–J10
ℹ Largo Garibaldi, 00019 Tivoli, tel 0774 334522; Wed–Fri 9–1, 3–6, Mon–Tue, Sat 9–1
🚂 Tivoli
❓ Both villas are so popular that many companies run bus tours from Rome.

www.tivoli.it/turismo

TIP

● Spring and autumn are the best times to visit to avoid the biggest crowds.

The Fontana dei Draghi at the Villa d'Este (top); one of the more unusual water features (above); statues among the ruins of the Villa Adriana (opposite)

URBINO

**One of Italy's best-preserved Renaissance cities.
The home town of Raphael and Bramante, a city with an
unmistakable artistic legacy.**

In the 15th century the court of Duke Federico da Montefeltro was
one of the most civilized in Europe, and the city of Urbino is still an
elegant and urbane place to explore. The town was important during
the Romans' time, but there is little visible evidence of this period
except for the Teatro Romano. Urbino was extensively redesigned in
the 15th century by Federico da Montefeltro, and this medieval layout
is the one you see today. The artist and architect Raphael
(1483–1520) was born in the city and the architect Donato Bramante
(1444–1514) was born in nearby Fermignano. A number of other
great artists worked here, including the Salimbeni brothers, Luca della
Robbia, Pisanello and Piero della Francesca. The Casa di Raffaello,
Raphael's birthplace, is now a small museum displaying reproductions
of his paintings and works by his father.

RATINGS

Good for kids	●●
Historic interest	●●●●
Cultural interest	●●●
Photo stops	●●●●

BASICS

✚ 437 H7
🛈 Piazza del Rinascimento 1
61029 Urbino, tel 0722 2613;
Mon–Sat 9–1, 3–7, Sun 9–1

www.urbino.com

PALAZZO DUCALE

The great Palazzo Ducale (Tue–Sun 8.30–7.45, Mon 8.30–2) is
Urbino's largest edifice, almost a city within a city. Described as
'wondrous' by Giorgio Vasari, the Italian painter and art historian, the
palace was designed by Luciano Laurana in the 15th century,
exemplifying elegant, geometric discipline. The heart of the palace is
the Cortile d'Onore (Main Courtyard), said to be one of the most
beautifully proportioned Renaissance courtyards ever built. Inside you
can explore the Duke's study, noted for its inlaid wood, his audience
room, in which hang two masterpieces by Piero della Francesca—a
Flagellation and *The Madonna of Senigallia*—and the Duchess's
apartments (open by prior arrangement), where you will find Raphael's
The Mute and a *Last Supper* by Titian. From Piazza del Mercatale, an
unusual spiral staircase leads to Corso Garibaldi and the main square.

THE DUOMO

The duomo (daily 7.30–1, 2–7) dates from the 15th century and
was rebuilt by Giuseppe Valadier after it collapsed in an earthquake in
1789. The Museo Diocesano Gianfrancesco Albani (daily 9–1, 2–7),
within the cathedral, contains 14th-century frescoes from a local
church and paintings by Andrea da Bologna and Iacopo Barocci. The
late 14th-century Oratorio di San Giovanni Battista is decorated with a
dazzling fresco cycle by Lorenzo and Jacopo Salimbeni.

*The 15th-century Palazzo
Ducale, housing the major
museum and galleries of Urbino
(top).*
*Typically quiet road through the
rolling, cultivated countryside
around Urbino (above)*

THE SOUTH

There are some major highlights in this area—noisy Naples, the preserved ancient Roman city of Pompei and volcanic Vesuvio are the stars. From here the coast-line leads to the laid-back deep south, with dramatic mountains, sun-baked inland plains and historic towns. East lies more prosperous Puglia, worth exploring for towns like Lecce and the untouched coastline.

MAJOR SIGHTS

A mythical beast on the façade of the Basilica di San Nicola in Bari

Inside the Reggia di Caserta

An entrance portico at Castel del Monte in Puglia

ALBEROBELLO

➕ 443 P12 ℹ️ Piazza Sacramento 10, 70011 Alberobello, tel 080 432 6030
🚂 Alberobello
www.alberobellonline.it

Trulli are strange-looking whitewashed limestone houses of a style that may date back to prehistoric times. They have a few tiny windows and cone-shaped roofs formed from spirals of grey limestone slabs. With more than 1,000 of them, Alberobello is the *trullo* capital and looks quite unlike any other town. Built mainly in the 18th century, this unique community is a UNESCO World Heritage Site. Enjoy the other-worldly atmosphere of the streets—ignoring the souvenir shops. Some of these bizarre dwellings have been converted into art galleries, craft shops and cafés with rooftop panoramas. The oldest *trulli* are in the Aia Piccola area, north of Via Indipendenza. Other highlights include Trullo Sovrano, a rare two-storey *trullo* built in the 18th century and now a museum-house (summer daily 10–8; winter daily 10–5), and Rione Monti, where hundreds of *trulli* are home to the best of the galleries and craft shops. Visit too the *trullo*-style parish church, Chiesa di Sant'Antonio (1926).

L'AQUILA

➕ 439 J9 ℹ️ Via XX Settembre 8, 67100 L'Aquila, tel 0862 22306, fax 0862 27486 🚂 L'Aquila
www.abruzzoturismo.it

This cultured university city is uninviting at first glance and is sedate and insular. However, once inside the old town, art-lovers will find plenty to appreciate in its churches, squares and fountains. Frederick II of Hohenstaufen founded L'Aquila ('the eagle') in about 1245. The 15th-century moated fortress that dominates the old town houses the Museo Nazionale d'Abruzzo (Tue–Sun 8am–9pm). Icons, sculptures and works of art from the 16th to 18th centuries are displayed, along with archaeological finds.

Walk along the steep cobbled path into Piazza San Vito to the extraordinary Fontana delle 99 Cannelle, a fountain with 99 gargoyle heads. The Tre Marie Restaurant, one of the best in the Abruzzo, dates from the 18th century. Kings and statesmen may have dined here, but the excellent food is still affordable.

BARI

➕ 443 P11 ℹ️ Piazza Aldo Moro 33a, 70122 Bari, tel 080 524 2361 🚂 Bari
www.pugliaturismo.com/aptbari

Puglia's rival to Naples is the biggest town on the long heel of Italy's boot, and most visitors use it as a ferry port for Greece, Croatia and Turkey, or as a gateway to the southeast coast. The modern city is brash and smart, but the old town is a delightfully confusing warren of narrow streets, courtyards and archways— deliberately designed to confuse invading pirates and armies. Fine Romanesque churches can be found before emerging in front of the reassuring fortifications of the massive *castello* (castle). The Basilica di San Nicola (daily 7–1, 4–7) is a beautiful example of 11th-century Romanesque architecture, with relics of the original Santa Claus, Bishop Nicholas. The modern town, south of Corso Vittorio Emanuele II, has luxury boutiques that rival any in Milan, Florence or Rome.

CASERTA

➕ 440 K11 ℹ️ Via Nazionale Appia Caserta, tel 082 327 7111 🚂 Caserta
www.casertaweb.com

The magnificent Reggia di Caserta, in the middle of this little-known southern corner, is a compulsory stop for lovers of formal gardens and royal palaces. Built at the foot of Mount Tifitani, this impressive white palace was commissioned by the Bourbon King Carlos II in 1752, and took almost 100 years to complete.

There are 1,000 elaborately decorated rooms within the royal apartments, but they are now almost empty. It is the external grandeur that is so striking, and the extensive gardens, both formal Italian and English in style, are on a par with those of the Palace of Versailles in France. A cascading waterfall flows through one part of the gardens, flanked by manicured lawns and trees. Stroll and discover other water features in the 18th-century English garden, a paradise in spring and early summer. The guided tours through the English garden are recommended.

CASTEL DEL MONTE

➕ 442 N11 • SS 170, 70031 Andria
☎ 0883 569997 🕐 Mar–end Sep daily 10–7.30; rest of year daily 9–6
🎫 Adult €3, under 18s free
www.proloco.andria.ba.it

Of Emperor Frederick II's many south Italian fortresses, Castel del Monte is by far the most impressive and handsome. Cresting a peak with views of the low hills of the surrounding Murge, 18km (11 miles) south of Andria, this octagonal, crown-like fortress has an austere Gothic exterior. A slim octagonal tower stands at each of the eight corners, and the eight rooms on each of the castle's two floors are set around an octagonal courtyard. Frederick's refined tastes are reflected in the finely sculpted columns and arches of pink, green and white cipollin marble—inspiration for the monks' monumental library in the 1986 film *The Name of the Rose*, based on Umberto Eco's book and starring Sean Connery.

CAPRI

A miniature kingdom, an island with an enchanting quality, untarnished by the influx of mass tourism. Take in bird's-eye views, nose around imperial gardens and villas and marvel at the famous Blue Grotto.

RATINGS	
Good for kids	●●●
Historic interest	●●●
Outdoor pursuits	●●●●●
Photo stops	●●●●●

BASICS

✚ 440 K12

🛈 Piazza Umberto 1, 80070 Capri, tel 081 8370686; Easter–end Oct daily 8.30–8.30; Nov–through Easter daily 9–1, 3.30–6.30; Via G. Orlando 59, 80071 Anacapri, tel 081 8371524; Mon–Sat 9–3

⛴ Regular ferry or hydrofoil services from Sorrento and Naples on the mainland

www.capritourism.com/en/index.php

www.capri.it
Caprionline has extensive hotel and restaurant listings with contact details, descriptions, photos and prices. There is also basic information available on what you can see and do on the island and on the boat trip operators. Italian and English versions.

Capri is at the mouth of the Gulf of Naples, where the Faraglioni, two great jagged rocks, rise sentry-like out of the sea. Capri town's heart is the Piazzetta, where the baroque cathedral watches over the café scene. An infinite list of royals, stars, politicians and other VIPs, including Graham Greene and D. H. Lawrence, have lost their hearts to Capri, either acquiring homes here or anchoring their yachts in the bay.

Caesar Augustus fell under Capri's spell in about 29BC, when he traded the bigger and richer island of Ischia to Naples in exchange for Capri. The Villa Jovis, built for Emperor Tiberius in AD1, is an imposing example of the Roman love affair with the island. Tiberius moved his court here and lived here until his death in AD37. A 45-minute walk from Capri town, the villa overlooks the Gulf of Naples. Stand and admire the views on the spot where unfortunate enemies of the emperor were flung to their death, so creating the saying 'See Naples and die'.

MONTE SOLARO

Mount Solaro, the highest peak on the island at 589m (1,932ft), surveys the streets of terraced houses winding their way uphill, brushing past olive groves and fragrant rosemary bushes. A trip to Capri is worth it just for the chairlift ride to the top of Monte Solaro; it skims the tops of the pine trees and provides fantastic views over the Bay of Naples and the Amalfi coast. At the top is Anacapri, a charming village where you can visit the Villa San Michele, built by the Swedish author Axel Munthe (1857–1949), in a superb panoramic setting. Here small terraced houses sit alongside immaculate white villas immersed in Mediterranean and subtropical vegetation.

GROTTA AZZURRA

If you are staying longer than a day or so, consider a boat trip to the Grotta Azzurra (Blue Grotto). Experience the unique blue glow of the cave, caused by the reflection of natural sunlight passing through its underwater cavity. Little rowing boats carry passengers through the opening of the grotto, so small that you have to lie flat on the bottom of the boat. Boats leave regularly from the Marina Grande, the main harbour.

The Faraglioni Rocks characterize Capri's coastline

At the lively town of Ischia Ponte, on the island of Ischia, a causeway stretches across to the mid-15th-century Castello Aragonese (right of photo)

ERCOLANO (HERCULANEUM)

✚ 440 K12 • Ercolano Scavi, 80056 Ercolano ☎ 081 777 7008
◷ Nov–end Mar daily 8.30–5; Apr–end Oct daily 8.30–7.30
💰 Adults €10, under 14s €5; 3-day combined ticket valid for Pompei €18
🚉 Circumvesuviana railway connects Ercolano to Sorrento and Naples
www.pompeiisites.org

This interesting archaeological site is often bypassed for the more glamorous Pompei, but the eruption of Vesuvio in AD79 that buried Pompei also submerged Ercolano, preserving both settlements.

Probably the most famous of the well-preserved houses is Villa dei Papiri, the home of a rich and powerful Roman statesman, thought to be either Lucio Pisone, Julius Caesar's father-in-law, or his son. More than 50 marble and 20 bronze sculptures were found in the villa, together with an amazing collection of 1,700 Greek and Roman papyri. The villa and Roman theatre can only be visited by advance reservation (fax 081 861 3183).

Other highlights include the Casa del Atrio Mosaico, with its beautifully preserved mosaic flooring. Most of the objects found in excavations are in the Archaeological Museum in Naples (▷ 198–200).

FORESTA UMBRA

✚ 441 N10 ❑ Ufficio Amministrazione Foreste Demaniali del Gargano, 71030 Foresta Umbra, tel 0881 560967; Mar–end Sep daily 8–2, 4–8; Oct–end Feb, phone for opening times (0884 991104) 🚉 Gargano railway runs along forest periphery between San Severo and Peschici
www.parks.it/parco.nazionale.gargano

Take a break from the summer heat in the cool of this rich and varied forest at the heart of the Gargano Peninsula (▷ opposite). Signposted trails lead through a protected nature reserve, with picnic areas along the way.

The Foresta Umbra's 5,500 ha (13,600 acres) account for half of the Gargano promontory's woodlands. After the Aleppo pines of the coast, the dominant trees are maple, hornbeam, birch and beech. The Valle del Tesoro is where you will find the forest's biggest beech tree *(faggio)*, a giant 40m (131ft) specimen with a 5m (16.5ft) circumference (signposted *Colosso del foresto*). The forest also has 65 species of orchid. Animals to look for include deer, curly-horned moufflon (wild sheep), boar and Italy's largest colony of badgers, while birdwatchers can spot the Dalmatian woodpecker, sparrow-hawk, buzzard and royal or tawny owl. With only a couple of hills rising above 1,000m (3,300ft), the forest is a mixture of dense vegetation and clearings created by the karst limestone formation of caves and sinkholes that provide waterholes for wildlife.

GALLIPOLI

✚ 443 Q13 ❑ Piazza Aldo Moro, 73014 Gallipoli, tel 0833 262529; summer only, plus Tue and Thu, Oct and Mar 🚉 Gallipoli

Gallipoli is built on an extended headland, 37km (23 miles) south of Lecce, with the old town standing on an island linked to the modern town by a seven-span bridge. While the new town may seem unprepossessing, the old town has the mysterious charm of a labyrinthine Arab city.

Not to be confused with the World War I battlefield in Turkey, Gallipoli is Greek in origin (the ancient Greek name, *Kalé polis*, means beautiful city). The old town is full of white-painted houses along narrow, winding streets and alleys and has a fine 17th-century baroque cathedral. The handsome carved friezes of the honey-coloured façade are influenced by the cathedral of its sister city, Lecce (▷ 196), where Gallipoli-born painter Giovanni Andrea Coppola went on to make his name.

From the waterfront Riviera road, which encircles the old town, there are views of the fishing port and the nearby beaches.

ISCHIA

✚ 440 K12 ❑ Piazza Trieste e Trento 9, 80077 Ischia, tel 081 333 4747
🚢 Hourly ferries from Naples; 55-minute journey on the fast service
www.ischia.it

About 10km (6 miles) long and 7km (4 miles) wide, the island of Ischia is surrounded by soft golden sands and enjoys a temperate climate almost all year round. It is famous for its spa facilities, ranging from mud-bath treatments to natural hot springs. Safe family beaches and summer nightlife make this a popular holiday destination.

The gardens of the beautiful villa of La Mortella (Apr–end Oct Tue, Thu, Sat–Sun 9–7), created by British composer William Walton and his widow Susana, have more than 1,000 different species of plants. Forio is an attractive town with a sunny beach, backed by the magnificent Poseidon Gardens. The village of Sant'Angelo can be reached only on foot and is connected by a causeway to the Rocca di Sant' Angelo, a green lava rock rising out of the sea.

Villa Arbusto (Tue–Sun 9.30–12.30, 3–6), at Lacco Ameno, documents the history of the island from prehistoric to Roman times. The fragrant gardens, planted with magnolias, hibiscus, pomegranates and fig trees, are also open to the public.

Limestone arches and promontories along the Gargano Peninsula

GARGANO PENINSULA

Rugged rocks, caves and cliffs, broad sandy beaches, neat whitewashed villages.
A great coastline for camping, watersports, picnics and hiking.

Cave paintings on the peninsula's southeast coast are evidence that there were Stone Age settlements in the Gargano some 20,000 years ago. In the 13th century, Emperor Frederick II and his son Manfred built castles and watchtowers along the coast to fend off pirates and Saracens. The following centuries saw invasions by the Normans, Angevins and Spanish, and in the 17th century the Turks. The area remained relatively neglected until the 20th century. In 1979 a campaign to save the peninsula from the threat of real estate development began, leading to the creation of the Gargano National Park in 1995.

WHAT TO SEE AND DO

Known as the *sperone d'Italia*, the 'spur' of the Italian boot is about 45km (28 miles) wide in the middle and juts out 65km (40 miles) into the Adriatic Sea. Citrus groves and umbrella pines on the coast give way to the national park's densely wooded hills of the cooler interior.

Manfredonia is a good starting point, with a visit to Emperor Manfred's Castello (1256), now an archaeological museum. Southwest of the town is Siponto and the lovely 11th-century Romanesque Church of Santa Maria. The eastern coast, beyond the Baia di Vignanotica, is rugged and lined with rocky coves and grottoes, notably the Grotta Smeralda and Grotta dei Marmi.

At the eastern tip of the peninsula, Vieste (▷ 210) is a popular resort with a castle, cathedral and sandy beaches at Pizzomunno and Castello. On the northern coast the fishing village of Peschici has preserved its picturesque medieval heart (▷ 203). At the green heart of the peninsula you will find the beech and hornbeam woodlands of the Foresta Umbra (▷ opposite) and the little town of San Giovanni Rotondo. Its monastery, which was home to the 20th-century miracle-worker Padre Pio da Petralcino, is one of the most revered sites in Italy.

East from here is the pilgrimage town of Monte Sant'Angelo, where a church was built in 1273 over the Santuario di San Michele, a cave where the archangel Michael had appeared in a vision some 800 years earlier. Steps inside the church lead down to the sanctuary past a pair of 11th-century sculpted bronze doors.

RATINGS

Good for kids	● ● ● ●
Outdoor pursuits	● ● ● ●
Walkability	● ● ● ●
Photo stops	● ● ●

BASICS

✚ 441 M–N10
🛈 Via S. Antonio Abate 121, 71037 Monte Sant'Angelo, tel 084 568911; Tue and Thu 9.30–12.30, 4–6
🚉 Peschici

www.parks.it/parco.nazionale.gargano
Weather forecasts, itineraries and information on points of interest and events in the park. Italian and English versions.

TIPS

● To swim in high summer, avoid the beaches and rent a boat to get to a secluded cove.
● Cool off in the inland forests.

MAKE A DAY OF IT

Foresta Umbra: ▷ 194
Isole Tremiti: ▷ 197
Peschici: ▷ 203
Vieste: ▷ 210

Small fishing boats at Peschici harbour (above)

LECCE

**The most beautiful town in southern Italy, fancifully ornamented in its own style of baroque.
An oasis of bright and airy refinement, with extravagant churches, elegant 18th-century palazzi and sandstone houses.**

BASICS

✚ 443 Q12

🏠 Via Monte San Michele 20, 73100 Lecce, tel 0832 314117, fax 0832 310238; May–end Sep Mon–Sat 9–1, 4–8; Oct–end Apr Mon–Sat 9–1

🚉 Lecce

www.pugliaturismo.com/aptlecce
The official site of the Azienda di Promozione Turistica in Lecce. It has some interesting articles with pictures outlining the history, handicrafts and architecture of Lecce. There is also information on the holy sites and the Uragano villages, part of the former Greek settlements. Italian, English, French and German versions.

TIP

● Don't even think of driving in Lecce's chaotic traffic; park outside the *centro storico* (old town).

MAKE A DAY OF IT

Gallipoli: ▷ 194
Otranto: ▷ 202
Taranto: ▷ 210

The detailed and ornate stonework on the façade of the baroque Basilica di Santa Croce

There are vestiges of early Hellenistic settlements (fifth and fourth century BC) in Lecce, the principal town in the Salentine Peninsula, but the town really entered history under Emperor Augustus as a Roman city named Lupiae (later Licea). An amphitheatre built during Hadrian's rule (first century AD) has been excavated in the main square, and Lecce's first bishop and patron, Sant'Oronzo, now honoured with a statue set on a Roman pillar, was one of Nero's Christian martyrs.

In the 11th century the Normans put Lecce back on the map, and the city expanded under the German emperors. Under Spanish rule in the 16th and 17th centuries the *centro storico* acquired its golden Renaissance and baroque glow (Emperor Charles V is celebrated by a triumphal arch). Prosperity attracted bankers and merchants from Florence, Venice, Milan and Genoa, who built grand palaces along Via Palmieri and Via Libertini.

BAROQUE LECCE

The city's characteristic baroque ornamentation is made from the area's fine-grained golden sandstone, known as *pietra di Lecce*. Typical of this is Giuseppe Zimbalo's intricately sculpted rose window for the Church of Santa Croce (1646). Gabriele Riccardi created the more subdued interior. Architectural ornament makes an elegant theatrical set of Piazza del Duomo, comprising the seminary, Bishop's Palace and cathedral. The five tapering levels of the campanile were completed in 1682. Other baroque buildings—both churches and, even more ornate, private palazzi—are on Via Palmieri (Palazzo Guarini, Teatro Paisiello, Palazzo Palmieri) and Via Libertini. In particular look for the exuberantly decorated Chiesa del Rosario (Rosary Church). Completed in 1691, it was the last and most elaborate of Zimbalo's architectural achievements.

Outside the old city walls, the Norman Church of Santi Niccolò e Cataldo (1180) is a rare combination of Romanesque austerity and baroque ornament added in 1716. The adjoining 12th-century monastery has an elegant Renaissance fountain in its first cloister.

A major attraction of Lecce is the local cuisine: It is renowned for its lamb and kid *(capretto)* dishes, oven-baked aubergine (eggplant), *puccia* black olive bread, and fine regional wines—Alezio, Copertino and Leverano.

A tiny bay overlooked by medieval Maratea

Sasso Caveoso in Matera, with ancient dwellings carved out of the rock and the Church of San Pietro Caveoso in the distance

ISOLE TREMITI

✚ 441 M9 ℹ Via E. Perrone 17, 71100 Foggia, tel 0881 723141/723650 ⛴ Adriatica hydrofoil (tel 08131 72999) operates Jun–end Sep from Manfredonia (2-hour journey, €42 round trip) or Vieste (1-hour journey, €27 round trip)
www.pugliaturismo.com/aptfoggia

The three tiny islands known as the Isole Tremiti lie in the Adriatic 22km (14 miles) north of the Gargano Peninsula. Consisting of limestone rocks and cliffs, with pine-wooded hills in the interior, they have a combined surface area of 3sq km (1.2sq miles).

They are the perfect place for a day trip from the mainland: You can swim in the clear waters of secluded coves, explore grottoes and walk along the rugged cliffs or through the interior's shady pine woods.

San Nicola is the smaller of the two inhabited islands, with a 15th-century monastic fortress and the small, 11th-century Church of Santa Maria a Mare. The island has no beaches, but there are some delightful rocky coves to swim in; there is nude bathing on the east coast.

The larger, more spectacular island of San Domino is 10 minutes by shuttle-boat (€1.25 each way). Its beaches are lovely—some accessible only by a climb down steep cliffs, and the caves—Grotta del Bue Marino, Grotta di Sale and Grotta delle Viole—are a major attraction.

MARATEA

✚ 442 M13 ℹ Piazza del Gesù 32, 85040 Maratea, tel 0973 876908 🚉 Marina di Maratea, then bus
www.costadimaratea.com

Here verdant mountains sweep down to a craggy coast characterized by numerous coves and small, secluded beaches. The little town of Maratea lies in the folds of the hills, connected to the sea by its pretty port. Confusingly Maratea has also given its name both to the port, which has very good fish restaurants, and to the main beach, Marina di Maratea, 5km (3 miles) away. The town itself is divided into Superiore and Inferiore. Superiore, the higher part, is largely in ruins after being deserted during the Middle Ages in favour of Inferiore, site of the present town of steps and narrow alleys. The Church of San Vito is the oldest church, built in the 11th and 12th centuries. At the summit, a sanctuary, Santuario di San Biagio, was built on the site of a Greek temple. There are fine views from the top of Mount Biagio, where you can also get a closer look at the enormous 22m (72ft) marble statue of Christ that overlooks the town, port and beach.

MATERA

✚ 442 N12 ℹ Via Spine Bianche 22, 75100 Matera, tel 0835 331817 🚉 Matera
www.materaturismo.it/english/index.htm

This is a startling troglodyte town of dwellings cut into the limestone *sassi* (rockfaces) of a deep ravine, 80km (50 miles) south of Bari. Some were inhabited up to 7,000 years ago. There are many *chiesi rupestri* (cave churches) in the area, carved out by monks and often decorated with Byzantine murals. The poverty and disease that held the town in the early half of the 20th century were eventually cleaned up and the town became a UNESCO World Heritage Site in 1993. Now a few of the houses have been converted into apartments and art galleries.

A *strada panoramica* (scenic route) on the east side of the ravine has views over the two *sassi* districts, Sasso Caveoso to the southeast, and Sasso Barisano to the northwest. Walks into the heart of the *sassi* begin from Via Duomo and lead down to Via Fiorentini, which runs along the bottom of the ravine.

Leave time to visit San Pietro Caveoso and the nearby Santa Maria de Idris churches, both of which have 14th-century Byzantine rock paintings.

METAPONTO

✚ 442 P12 ℹ Via de Viti de Marco 9, 75100 Matera, tel 0835 331983

Archaeology buffs can combine a visit to the region's most important ancient Greek settlement with some pleasant sunbathing or swimming at the nearby beach resort, Lido di Metaponto. Metaponto is 50km (31 miles) south of Matera; the sandy beaches of Lido di Metaponto are 2.5km (1.5 miles) southeast of the archaeological museum.

The ancient site that was home to the mathematician Pythagoras in the seventh century BC is best seen in conjunction with a visit to the town's excellent Archaeological Museum (Mon 2–7, Tue–Sun 9–7). It has a first-rate collection of ancient Greek jewellery and gold ornaments, ceramics and sculpture displayed in a handsome modern museum. At the archaeological site, signed 'Zona Archeologica', you can see the remains of a theatre, the marketplace *(agora)* and four temples, notably the Temple of Apollo Licius (sixth century BC).

Better preserved, 3km (2 miles) north of the main site, is the Temple of Hera (or Tempio delle Tavole Palatine), with 15 of its outer columns still standing (daily 8am–half an hour before sunset).

NAPOLI (NAPLES)

See pages 198–201.

Napoli (Naples)

A beautiful coastal setting for one of Italy's most vibrant cities.
The best place to experience southern Italian urban life.
A seemingly dilapidated city, packed with historical and artistic treasures.

A view over Naples from Castel San Elmo

A cart full of vegetables in the Porta Nolana market

Artichokes for sale

Easter celebrations in the Spanish Quarter (right)

SEEING NAPLES

Naples is southern Italy's great city, pulsing with life, full of wonderful buildings and museums and flanked by an idyllic bay. Capital of the region of Campania, on Italy's west coast, it is two hours by fast train from Rome. It is as famed for its citizens as its monuments, and there is nowhere else in Italy where you can find such a level of life lived on the streets. With more than a million inhabitants, Naples is a big, sprawling city, so be prepared to walk; the upshot will be some fascinating discoveries and fabulous views.

HIGHLIGHTS

SPACCANAPOLI

🕂 200 B1 • Via Capitelli, Piazza del Gesù Nuovo, Via Benedetto Croce, Via San Biagio dei Librai

The grid plan of streets that makes up the *centro storico* was the core of ancient Neapolis, and its three main streets—the ancient *decumani*—still slice relentlessly through the oldest part of the city. Spaccanapoli is one of these *decumani*; its name means 'split Naples' and it crosses the heart of the old city, a thoroughfare teeming with people and lined with churches, palazzi and idiosyncratic shops selling everything from books and musical instruments to religious objects and woodcarvings.

Spaccanapoli is made up of a string of streets, now mainly pedestrianized, from Piazza del Gesù Nuovo to Via Viccaria Vecchia. The heart of the university district, it has plenty of bars and restaurants, including Scaturchio, one of Naples' oldest and best *pasticcerie*. Along its length, highlights include the rococo obelisk, the Guglia dell'Immacolata in Piazza del Gesù, the Church and Convent of Santa Chiara (▷ 201), Piazza San Domenico with its obelisk and 13th-century castellated church, and some fine Renaissance palaces.

MUSEO ARCHEOLOGICO NAZIONALE

🕂 200 B1 • Piazza Museo 19, 80135 Napoli ☎ 081 440166 🕐 Wed–Mon 9–7.30 🎟 €6.50, under 18s free

The Museo Archeologico Nazionale houses one of the world's most important collections of classical Roman sculpture, mosaics, gems,

Duomo di Napoli

⊞ 200 B1 • Via Duomo 147, 80138
Naples ☎ 081 449097 🕐 Duomo:
daily 8.30–12, 4.30–6.30. Cappella di
San Gennaro: Sat 10–7 💰 €5.50,
under 18s €3.50

A 13th-century Gothic cathedral
dedicated to San Gennaro, patron
saint of Naples; the first chapel on
the right contains two phials of his
blood, said to liquefy three times
a year. Also part of the complex
are the fourth-century Basilica
Santa Restituta (the oldest church
in Naples), a baptistery and a
Renaissance crypt.

Palazzo Reale

⊞ 200 B3 • Piazza del Plebiscito 1
☎ 081 580811 🕐 Thu–Tue 8.30–7.30
💰 €7.50

The 17th-century palace of the
Spanish viceroys of Naples was
extended in the 18th century by
the Bourbons and altered in the
19th century by the French. It
houses the historic Biblioteca
Nazionale (National Library) and
a series of grandiose state rooms.

wall paintings, glass and silver, much of it plundered from the
excavations around and to the south of Naples. The museum is badly
labelled and confusingly laid out, with whole sections often closed, but
it is nevertheless outstanding, and the exhibits do much to enhance
visits to Pompei (▷ 204–207) and Ercolano (▷ 194).

The ground floor is devoted to sculpture, much of it from the 17th-
century Farnese collections, which were largely discovered in Rome.
Highlights are the muscular *Farnese Hercules* and the *Farnese Bull*
(200BC), the largest surviving classical sculptural group. There is a
wonderfully vivid mosaic collection and the Gabinetto Segreto
(Secret Chamber), a collection of Roman erotica from Pompei, which
ranges from sensual wall paintings to phallic charms. Upstairs, rooms
are filled with more finds from Pompei and Ercolano, including a
naturalistic wall painting of a graceful Flora scattering spring flowers,
and a *cave canem* (Beware of the Dog) mosaic from the entrance
to a house in Pompei.

CERTOSA DI SAN MARTINO

⊞ 200 A2 • Largo San Martino 5, 80129 Napoli ☎ 081 578 1769 🕐 Tue–Fri
8.30–7.30 💰 €6, under 18s free

The huge hilltop Carthusian complex of the Certosa di San Martino was
founded in 1325, but what you see today dates mainly from the 16th
to 18th centuries. The baroque church is crammed with the best of
Neapolitan painting and sculpture, and there are more riches in the
choir, sacristy and treasury. Explore the expertly restored, arcaded 16th-
century Chiostro Grande, the lavishly decorated Quarto del Priore and
the Pinacoteca in rooms set around the cloister with views over the city
and the bay. Don't miss the exhibition of *presepe*—people and animals
fashioned for 18th-century Christmas cribs. The Certosa is surrounded
by terraced gardens, with sweeping views.

THE SIGHTS

SANTA CHIARA

✚ 200 B2 • Via Benedetto Croce/Via Santa Chiara 49, 80134 Napoli ☎ 081 552 6209 🕓 Mon–Sat 9.30–1, 3.30–5.30, Sun and holidays 9.30–1

Santa Chiara is Naples' great Franciscan church, a simple and austere 14th-century Gothic conventual complex. Founded by King Robert of Anjou for his wife, Sancia, in 1310, it became a focal point for Naples' Angevin rulers, several of whom are buried here. The original church, greatly altered over the centuries, was catastrophically bombed in 1943. Rebuilding started almost at once, using whatever could be salvaged, and the church, restored to its original Gothic appearance, re-opened in 1953. Three Angevin royal tombs survive: that of Robert himself and those of his son, Carlo and daughter-in-law, Mary of Valois.

Behind the church is the 14th-century cloister, remodelled by Domenico Vaccaro in 1742. He decorated the central garden with

Castel Nuovo

✚ 200 B2 • Piazza Municipio, 80133 Napoli ☎ 081 795 5877 🕓 Mon–Sat 9–7

A huge castle erected in 1282 by the Angevins, converted into a royal residence by the Aragonese; now accommodates the council offices and the Museo Civico.

Mergellina

✚ 200 off A3

The waterfront area and ferry port, with its attractive harbour

72 octagonal pillars, interspersed with benches, each of which is covered with hand-painted majolica tiles. The church's Museo dell'Opera (Thu–Tue 9–1, 4–6) lies off the cloister, also providing access to a fascinating Christmas crib scene, complete with street life, flying angels and a variety of people and animals.

MUSEO E PARCO DI CAPODIMONTE

✚ 200 A1 • Via Miano 1, 80132 Napoli ☎ 081 749 9111 🕓 Tue–Sun 8.30–7.30 💶 €7.50, under 18s free

Built in 1738 as King Charles III's hunting lodge, and surrounded by a wooded park, the Palace of Capodimonte houses one of Italy's richest museums. The bulk of the collection is made up of works acquired by Charles from his mother, Elizabeth Farnese. You can wander freely through the opulent royal apartments on your way to the majolica and porcelain collection, much of it made by the Neapolitan Capodimonte factory and painted with local scenes. Upstairs is a picture gallery, a collection amassed by the Farnese and Bourbon rulers and spanning the 15th to 17th centuries, with the emphasis on Renaissance painting. Botticelli, Perugino and Pinturicchio are all represented, but it is the High Renaissance works that shine, particularly the portraits by Titian, Raphael and Sebastiano del Piombo. Leave time to wander through the shady avenues of the surrounding park.

BACKGROUND

Greek settlers founded Neapolis in 750BC, and the city prospered under both Greek and Roman rule before declaring itself independent in 763. The Normans took the city in 1139, and were soon followed by the Hohenstaufens, German rulers who held on until the Angevins took over in 1269. The Spanish moved in next in 1422 and remained in control for over 300 years. Bourbon and French rule followed before Naples became part of united Italy.

The city has a long history of foreign rule and neglect by government. Despite money pouring into the south under the Mezzogiorno scheme in the late 20th century, unemployment and social deprivation remain common, but the late 1990s, when Antonio Bassolino was mayor, saw a burgeoning civic pride and a burst of creative activity.

Castel dell'Ovo and Santa Lucia

✚ 200 A3 • Borgo Marinari, 80132 Napoli ☎ 081 764 0590 🕓 Mon–Sat 9–6, Sun 9–2

The oldest castle in Naples (ninth century) attained its present form in 1503. Restored in the 1970s after centuries of decline, it is now used for exhibitions and concerts. There are some excellent fish restaurants around the Santa Lucia district, close to the city's harbour.

Villa La Floridiana

✚ 200 A2 • Via Cimarosa 77, Napoli ☎ 081 459188 🕓 Mon–Sat 9 until 1 hour before sunset

A beautiful villa and park in the Vomero district, once the home of the Duchess of Floridia, morganatic wife of Ferdinand I. It now houses the Museo Nazionale della Ceramica, the porcelain museum (Tue–Sun 9.30–11), with a superb Limoges and Meissen collection.

Vespas are a common sight, zipping around the streets of Naples (above left)

The Capodimonte Gardens (above right)

The Doric Temple of Neptune (450BC) at Paestum

A river flows through the sparsely wooded lowlands of the Parco Nazionale d'Abruzzo

OTRANTO

443 R12 ℹ Piazza Castello, 73028 Otranto, tel 0836 801436 🚉 Otranto
www.comune.otranto.ie.it

This charming little fishing village has some splendid monuments to its Greek, Byzantine and Norman past—in the 11th century it was an important Crusader and pilgrim port. In the areas just outside the town people still speak a Greek patois rather than Italian, and in summer a car ferry runs from the port to Greece.

Many visitors come to Otranto for its convenient sandy beaches, which have good watersports facilities and fishing coves. The Normans' 11th-century Cattedrale di Santa Maria Annunziata (daily 8.30–12, 4–7) has some spectacular Byzantine floor mosaics depicting Adam and Eve, Noah and the Flood, the Queen of Sheba, Alexander the Great and King Arthur. In grim contrast, the Martyrs' Chapel contains the bones of 800 Christians massacred by the Turks in 1480. A hill covered with cypress trees on the southern edge of town marks the spot where the martyrs were beheaded. The massive castello (castle) (exhibitions Oct–end Mar Mon–Sat 9.30–12, Sun 10.30–12.30, 3.30–6.30) dominates the south side of the port, built after the Turkish attack. The best beaches, notably Torre dell'Orso, are north of town.

PAESTUM

441 L12 ℹ Via Magna Grecia 887, 84063 Paestum, tel 0828 811016
🌐 Ancient site of Paestum: daily 9 until 1 hour before sunset 🚉 Paestum (1km/0.5 mile from site)
www.infopaestum.it

Paestum, about 35km (22 miles) south of Salerno and about 3km (2 miles) from Capaccia Scalo, has some of the best-preserved

Greek temples outside Greece, standing with mountains on one side and a marine vista on the other.

The area includes a temple dedicated to Poseidon (the site was known as Poseidonia), the god of the sea, known to the Romans as Neptune (450BC), a temple to Athena, and the basilica, which historians believe to have been built in honour of Heres or Zeus. Stand in the fields, which in spring are filled with wildflowers, and contemplate the majesty of Neptune's temple. The site was created by the Greeks in the sixth century BC and was taken over by the Romans 200 years later, who changed the name. The structures are all built of a golden stone that glows richly in the afternoon sun. The site was deserted from the ninth century and rediscovered in the 18th.

The Museo Archeologico (daily except 1st and 3rd Mon of month, 8.45–7.45) illustrates the fascinating history of this exceptional site. Of particular interest is the *Tomba del Tuffatore* (Diver's Tomb), one of the few remaining and best-preserved Greek mural paintings from the fifth century BC.

The area a few kilometres south of Paestum is worth exploring for its emerald-green sea and deserted beaches.

PARCO NAZIONALE D'ABRUZZO

440 K10 ℹ Corso Vittorio Emanuele II 301, tel 085 429 00212
🚉 Avezzano, then bus to Pescasseroli
www.abruzzoturismo.it

The Parco Nazionale d'Abruzzo was set up in 1923 by conservationists to protect native species of animals and plantlife threatened with extinction—a small revolution for a predominantly agricultural region with a strong hunting tradition.

Particularly rare animals were the brown *marsicano* bear, the golden eagle and the chamois deer, all of which are now thriving again in their natural habitats. With more than 300 species of birds and 12,000 different species of wildflower, it is reputedly the oldest park of its kind in Europe.

This fertile wilderness covers an area of 44,000 hectares (108,720 acres) in the south of the Abruzzo region. The park's Visitor Centre in Pescasseroli has a small museum and rehabilitation centre for injured animals.

Steeped in tradition, Pescasseroli has managed to maintain its traditional sheep farming, woodcarving and stonework customs. The village is also the birthplace of Benedetto Croce (1866–1952), the Italian writer, philosopher and politician. Stay to sample the local way of life and benefit from the range of park facilities, including horseback riding, mountain-bicycling and guided tours along some 150 marked walks and trails.

Within driving distance of Pescasseroli, in the terraced white-stone village of Civitella Alfedena, is the Centro Lupo (Wolf Museum), where you can learn all about the wolf packs that live in the park (▷ 13).

PARCO NAZIONALE DEL GRAN SASSO

439 J9 ℹ Via XX Settembre, 67100 L'Aquila, tel 0862 22306
www.abruzzoturismo.it
www.parconazionalegransasso.it/eng/index.htm

The Parco Nazionale del Gran Sasso, nicknamed Little Tibet because of its 2,912m (9,551ft) Gran Sasso mountain peaks, was set up in 1991 to preserve the animals and plants unique to the area.

Tossica, in the hills of the Parco Nazionale del Gran Sasso, with the Gran Sasso ridge in the background

Three mountain ranges, a fertile, cultivated valley and the nearby Adriatic coastline are all visible. Well-signposted footpaths and trails throughout the park make this an ideal destination for walkers, while winter sports enthusiasts can choose from the many ski resorts in the area.

The Cima Alta, a rocky vista about 1km (0.5 mile) from Prati di Tivo, is easily accessible and a good place to begin any walk.

The soft rock characteristic of this section of the Apennines forms caves, gorges and impressive waterfalls, including those at Cento Fonti, Morricana and Volpara. In spring the flowers in the meadows and plains are a riot of different shades and at higher altitudes you can find edelweiss and wild orchids.

The Abruzzo chamois, an agile goat/antelope once threatened with extinction in this region, has recently been reintroduced and about 50 now live in the park. There are also small packs of the Apennine wolf, as well as polecats, beech-martens, badgers and wildcats.

PARCO NAZIONALE DEL POLLINO

🟦 442 N13 🛈 Park Centre (Sede Ente Parco), Via delle Frecce Tricolori 6, 85048 Rotonda (Potenza), tel 0973 669311
www.parcopollino.it

The Parco Nazionale del Pollino is the largest national park in Italy and one of the richest in terms of wildlife. Famous for the loricate pines (*Pinus leucodermis*), found only here and in the Balkans, the park is also home to eagles, ravens, pine martens, wildcats, roe deer and the very rare Italian wolf (*Canis lupus italicus*). Here, too, are over 1,700 species of wildflowers, including periwinkle, asphodels, gentians and peonies (*Paeonia peregrina*).

This vast national park covers about 196,000 hectares (484,000 acres) of mountainous terrain, equally divided between Basilicata and Calabria, with areas of woodland, rocky outcrops, alpine meadows and unpolluted streams. The highest peaks are Monte Pollino (2,248m/7,344ft) and Serra Dolcedorme (2,267m/7,436ft), in the middle of the park.

Along the park's eastern borders, towns such as San Costantino Albanese and San Paolo Albanese are home to Albanian (Arbresh) communities which have largely preserved their own language, traditions and religious festivals since their arrival in the 16th century.

Southwest, the wildest area of the park, the Monti di Orsomarso, is named after the brown bears (*orso*) that once roamed here. There are many interesting towns scattered through the park, including Rotonda, the park's capital, whose visitor centre organizes excellent excursions into the park.

PESCHICI

🟦 441 M10 🛈 Via E. Perrone, 71100 Foggia, tel 0881 723141 🚌 Calenella, then bus
www.peschici.it

At the northern tip of the Gargano Peninsula (▷ 195) and 80km (50 miles) north of Manfredonia, this tiny, walled medieval fishing village makes an ideal base for exploring the Gargano National Park—in particular the nearby grottoes just east along the coast at San Nicola and the Foresta Umbra in the interior (▷ 194).

Dependent on an abbey on the Isole Tremiti (▷ 197), built in the 10th century to fend off Saracen raids, its grey-domed houses and the maze of narrow winding streets are reminiscent

of an Arab village. The sandy bay at the foot of Peschici's promontory is where some of the Gargano's most attractive and popular beaches are to be found.

POMPEI AND VESUVIO

See pages 204–207.

REGGIO DI CALABRIA

🟦 444 M16 🛈 Via Roma 3, 89100 Reggio di Calabria, tel 0965 21171
🚆 Reggio di Calabria Centrale or Lido (fewer trains) 🚢 Napoli and Catania (Sicily)

Reggio di Calabria is noteworthy mainly for being the gateway to Sicily, but it is also worth visiting if only for the Museo Nazionale, which has some priceless treasures from Calabria and Basilicata. In particular, seek out the *Bronzi di Riace* (460–430BC), two magnificent bronze warriors, and two rare painted panels by Antonello da Messina (c1460).

A busy modern city and seaport, Reggio was largely rebuilt in an organized grid fashion after the devastating earthquake of 1908. This is the toe of Italy's boot, and the coast of Sicily can clearly be seen from here—by night, the lights on her shore twinkle invitingly.

The city may not be the brightest star in Calabria's firmament, but the gardens of the Villa Comunale and the tree-lined coastal promenade along Viale Matteotti, with a diversity of palms, trees and shrubs akin to a botanical garden, leaven the traffic pollution and noise. At the northern end of the promenade, almost hidden by a grove of pines, is a small museum of musical instruments.

Nearby are the unprepossessing remains of a Greek defensive wall, and some ruins of baths and mosaics from the later Roman period.

Pompei and Vesuvio

●

A virtually intact first-century AD Roman town, complete with houses, shops, temples and public buildings, a time capsule sealed on 26 August AD79.
Walk around the summit of one of the world's most famous volcanoes.

Ruins at Pompei (above) and the bronze statue in the House of the Faun at Pompei (below)

RATINGS	
Good for kids	● ● ●
Historic interest	● ● ● ●
Photo stops	● ● ●
Walkability	● ● ●

TIPS

● Signposts in Pompei are few and far between, so make sure you have a good map before you start.
● Remember that most of the important artistic finds are now in the Museo Archeologico Nazionale in Naples (▷ 198, 200). Visit it either before or after your Pompei trip.
● Wear comfortable, flat shoes and be prepared for rough walking at both Pompei and Vesuvio.
● Tackle Vesuvio in the early morning and avoid windy days, when conditions near the crater can be bad.
● Pompei is exposed and it can be very hot, so take plenty of drinking water.

SEEING POMPEI AND VESUVIO

Mount Vesuvio, half an hour by train and bus from Naples, rises to the south of the city, a peak of 1,281m (4,203ft) that forms the backdrop to the beautiful Bay of Naples. On the lower slopes, 13 communities house over 750,000 inhabitants, all of whom choose to ignore the threat that looms over them. The Roman town of Pompei, on the volcano's southern slopes, was caught unawares by a massive eruption in AD79, which smothered the town, its people and their goods and chattels. Preserved for centuries, the site has been, and continues to be, excavated, so as you walk up and down the streets you can peer into shops and private homes, read advertisements and graffiti—and generally get a unique picture of daily life in Roman times.

HIGHLIGHTS

VIA DELL'ABBONDANZA

Via dell'Abbondanza was Pompei's most important thoroughfare, running through the middle of the town from the Porta Marina in the west (the main harbour gate) to the Anfiteatro (amphitheatre) in the east. The Foro, the civic heart of the town, lies off the west end of Abbondanza, an elongated open space with a colonnade running along three sides and the remains of the Temple of Jupiter on the north side. To the left is the porticoed entrance to the *macellum*, the covered meat and fish market, while across the road from the entrance to the Foro stands the basilica, site of Pompei's law court and stock exchange. Farther along the street are the Terme Stabiana, a large public bath complex with an exercise court in the middle and some well-preserved wall paintings.
Via dell'Abbondanza carries on past shops and houses; look for the shop counters and

BASICS

POMPEI

440 L12 • Scavi di Pompei, Via dei Misteri 2, 80045 Pompei ☎ 081 857 5347

Apr–end Oct daily 8.30–7.30 (last entrance 6); rest of year daily 8.30–5 (last entrance 3.30)

€10

Circumvesuviana train from Naples to Pompei Scavi Villa dei Misteri

2-hour guided tours in Italian, English, French, German and Spanish, €90; audioguides in English, French, German, €5

€8–€15

Bar/restaurant with self service—expensive and usually very crowded; numerous restaurants just outside the site

300m (330 yards) from site entrance

www.pompeiisites.org

www.pompei.biz
A very basic site outlining the history of Pompei and what you can see today. Italian and English versions.

VESUVIO

440 L12 • EPT, Via IV Novembre 82, 80056 Ercolano ☎ 081 788 1243

Daily 9–6

€6, covers a brief explanatory talk

Circumvesuviano train from Naples to Ercolano, then bus

www.volcano.und.nodak.edu/vwdocs/volc_images/img_vesuvius.html
An excellent English-language site about the volcano, tracing the history of its eruptions through the centuries. Satellite photos and background information on the effects of the eruption that destroyed Pompei.

the symbols outside many of the commercial premises, which were aimed at drawing in the illiterate country people shopping in town.

VILLA DEI MISTERI

The Villa dei Misteri lies outside the main walls of Pompei, and was a working farm for much of its existence. It is probably the best-preserved of all Pompei's grand villas, a series of chambers and courtyards first built in the third century BC. Its name comes from the superb series of wall paintings in the *triclinium* (dining room)—a cycle of vibrant scenes showing a young woman's initiation rites into the Dionysiac mysteries, a popular cult in the early imperial era. The paintings, in vivid reds and ochres, are intensely clear and show sacrifice, dancing and flagellation. They are thought to have been copied by a local artist from third-century BC Hellenistic originals. Here you can also see a reconstruction of a wine press, with a decorative ram's head used for crushing grapes.

HOUSE OF THE VETTII

The House of the Vettii is named after its owners, the wealthy merchants Aulus Vettius Conviva and Aulus Vettius Restitutus, who spent their profits decorating their house with mythological paintings. It is one of Pompei's most beautiful houses, and gives an excellent picture of the domestic life of the town's upper-middle-class citizens. The house was altered in the first century AD and the atrium, complete with strongboxes, leads straight through into the peristyle. There are frescoed chambers all around, illustrating such scenes as Hercules struggling with serpents, Ixion tied to a wheel and tortured for daring to set eyes on Zeus's wife, and Dirce being dragged to her death. Even the servants' quarters are decorated with erotic wall paintings, including a more than potent Priapus (phallic symbols were believed to ward off the evil eye).

Terme del Foro

Via di Mercurio 🕔 Apr–end Oct daily 8.30–7.30 (last entrance 6); rest of year daily 8.30–5 (last entrance 3.30) These public baths, north of the Forum, still have much of their original stucco decoration. There is a fine fountain in the hot room with a bronze inscription that records the cost of the fountain and the names of those who donated money towards its construction.

THE HOUSE OF THE FAUN

A block away from the House of the Vettii, the House of the Faun is one of the largest and most sophisticated houses in Pompei. It gets its name from the copy of the charming second-century BC bronze statue in the middle of the *impluvium* (an opening in the roof of the atrium); the original is now in the Museo Nazionale in Naples (▷ 198, 200). The house, sprawling over almost 3,000sq m (32,300sq ft), probably belonged to a local dignitary. The floor mosaic at the entrance welcomes visitors with its inscription *'Ave'* ('Hail'). The front of the house is arranged around two atria (halls); behind is a peristyle and graceful portico, which led to a discussion hall for public meetings. This was decorated with a million-piece mosaic floor depicting the 300BC Battle of Issus (now in the museum in Naples). As in many of Pompei's grander houses, the gardens have been lovingly restored.

The remains of the Anfiteatro in Pompei

Detail of the ruins at Pompei

THE SIGHTS

House of the Tragic Poet

Via di Mercurio 🕔 Apr–end Oct daily 8.30–7.30 (last entrance 6); rest of year daily 8.30–5 (last entrance 3.30) One of the up-market houses on Via di Mercurio, named after its theatrical mosaics. The entrance mosaic of a fierce but welcoming dog bears the inscription *cave canem* (Beware of the Dog).

MOUNT VESUVIO

Mount Vesuvio's fertile volcanic soil has made it attractive to farmers for centuries, and even today the lower slopes are heavily planted with olives, vines and vegetable crops, while wild plants cover the scars of the lava flows left after the last eruption, in 1944, which caused widespread damage to the surrounding towns.

Vesuvio is now a designated national park and a UNESCO Biosphere Reserve, seen at its best in early summer, when the slopes are covered in wildflowers and bird life is at its liveliest and most interesting. It is only when you climb the slopes above the official

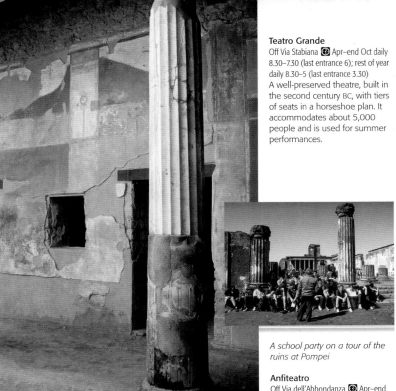

Teatro Grande
Off Via Stabiana ⊙ Apr–end Oct daily 8.30–7.30 (last entrance 6); rest of year daily 8.30–5 (last entrance 3.30)
A well-preserved theatre, built in the second century BC, with tiers of seats in a horseshoe plan. It accommodates about 5,000 people and is used for summer performances.

A school party on a tour of the ruins at Pompei

Anfiteatro
Off Via dell'Abbondanza ⊙ Apr–end Oct daily 8.30–7.30 (last entrance 6); Nov–end Mar daily 8.30–5 (last entrance 3.30)
This is one of Italy's oldest amphitheatres. Built in 80BC, it had capacity for between 12,000 and 14,000 people and was used for gladiatorial combats. It could hold about half of Pompei's population; much of the seating area is intact. It is used during summer for concerts and classical plays.

House of Meneander
Off Via dell'Abbondanza
⊙ Sat–Sun 2–4
One of the largest houses in Pompei, this probably belonged to the family of Nero's wife, Poppaea. It dates from the third century BC and has a central garden and peristyle with an intricate floor mosaic, a domestic shrine *(lararium)* in the atrium and a room painted with scenes from the Trojan War.

parking area that you first appreciate its rocky aridity. The stony zigzag path up to the rim of the crater winds through lava, gravel and cindery rock. At the top, you can peer down into the crater 200m (650ft) below and enjoy good views of steaming fumaroles and stratified pyroclastic deposits across the void.

The Museo dell'Osservatorio Vesuviano has interesting exhibits that outline the volcano's geology and the threat that future eruptions pose.

BACKGROUND
Pompei is the world's best-preserved Roman town, frozen in time by the catastrophic eruption of Vesuvio on 24 August AD79. Founded as a Greek colony, the town became part of Rome in about 200BC, thriving as a chic holiday resort for rich Romans and as a trading place exporting wine and fish products. It was severely damaged by an earthquake in AD63, and the volcanic eruption 16 years later was the final nail in the coffin. Of the 20,000 inhabitants it is thought that about 2,000 people died, including Pliny the Elder, the Roman naturalist, at Stabiae (Castellammare) nearby. His nephew, Pliny the Younger, recorded the events of the days in a letter to the historian Tacitus.

Excavations began in earnest in 1748, and continue today. Pompei has yielded more information about everyday Roman life than any other site, as well as artistic treasures.

Vesuvio, the cause of the disaster, is the only active volcano in mainland Europe. It last blew in 1944 and it is generally thought to be well overdue for another eruption—the longer the period of quiescence, the greater the risk. The mountain is constantly monitored. Scientists believe that the danger lies not in ash deposits and lava flows, but in a surge of super-heated, poisonous gas that could roll down the slopes at more than 80kmh (50mph)—much like the cloud that was responsible for so many deaths in AD79.

Fishing on the shores below the town of Scilla

Hills bordering a moutain lake in the Sila Grande, Calabria

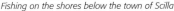

THE SIGHTS

RIVIERA CALABRESE

✚ 442 N14 ℹ Corso Mazzini 92, 87100 Cosenza, tel 0984 27271 🚆 Rail line runs right along the coastline

The Calabrian Riviera is a term used to describe a succession of beaches and resorts along the Tyrrhenian coast. The more popular resorts, such as Tropea (▷ 210), are busy in the summer, but away from these areas and out of season it should be possible to find a quiet spot to swim and relax.

For most of its length, the Tyrrhenian coast is a comparatively narrow strip of land flanked by the Appennino Lucano and Appennino Calabro mountains, where rocky, tree-lined shores give way to coves and long, sandy beaches. Worth visiting are the beaches of Praia Mare, close to the Basilicata border, and the nearby Isola di Dino. Diamante, an attractive town with narrow streets and good restaurants, also merits a visit. Amantea, another coastal resort, has a recently discovered sixth-century BC Greek sanctuary, while Pizzo is famous for its beach and curious little church, Chiesa di Piedigrotta, decorated with rock carvings of religious icons and famous people.

SCILLA

✚ 444 M16 ℹ Co/Pro Loco, Piazza San Rocco, 89058 Scilla, tel 0965 754003 🚆 Scilla

This pretty fishing town lies 20km (12 miles) north of Reggio di Calabria (▷ 203), with fine views across the Straits of Messina to the hills of Sicily. It has an interesting fishermen's quarter, a beautiful bay that is perfect for swimming and sunbathing, and plenty of cafés and restaurants.

The town of Scilla occupies a rocky crag and the shore on either side. To the east is the port and fishermen's quarter and to the west is a suburb built around the beach. The old houses of the Chianalea (fishermen's area), reach right down to the water's edge, with front doors opening directly onto the port.

The crag supporting the castle is allegedly the Scylla of Greek legend, and the swirling waters of the straits are its counterpart, Charybdis—the mythical sea monsters that were the personification of these hazards. There have been fortifications on the rock since the fourth century BC, but the present castle dates mainly from the 17th century and is now used for cultural events. During the Napoleonic Wars the castle was occupied by the French, then the English, and later by Garibaldi, who came here during his reunification campaign (▷ 38).

SIBARI

✚ 442 N13 ℹ Via Amendola 1, Cassanoionio, tel 0981 76352

The Sibari region is blessed with long stretches of beach, especially in Villapiana, 9km (6 miles) to the north, but it is most famous for the ancient site of Sybaris-Copia, founded on the banks of the River Crati almost 3,000 years ago. It grew to become an immensely rich city (the word *sybarite*, someone who enjoys luxury, comes from its name), but it was destroyed in the fourth century BC when Croton (modern Crotone) obliterated the city by diverting the River Crati over the remains. Today nothing is visible above ground, but the excavations can be viewed, and the nearby museum, the Museo Nazionale Archeologico della Sibaritide in Casa Bianca, has finds excavated from here and other sites.

Sibari is on the Ionian coast 70km (44 miles) southwest of Taranto. Ancient Sybaris gave its name to this fertile coastal plain between Cape Spulico and Cape Trionfo. The mouth of the River Crati is home to one of the few colonies of Mediterranean seals.

LA SILA

✚ 444 N14 ℹ Corso Mazzini 92, 87100 Cosenza, tel 0984 27271

This extensive, mountainous plateau lies at the heart of Calabria, east of Cosenza and north of Catanzaro, and supports some of southern Italy's most unusual plantlife and animals. It is wonderful walking territory, particularly in spring, and the winter snows provide ample opportunities for downhill and cross-country skiing, mostly around the towns of Camigliatello Silano and Lorica.

Since controls in tree felling and hunting have been introduced, forests of beech, oak and pine clothe much of the mountainsides, and are inhabited by foxes, badgers, black squirrels, otters and a few specimens of the rare Italian wolf (▷ 13).

A wild and unspoiled region, the plateau, which includes the small Parco Nazionale della Sila, is composed of three separate massifs: La Sila Grande to the north, La Sila Greca, and La Sila Piccola to the south. The average height is 1,000m (3,280ft).

The visitor centre at Cupone, close to Lago Cecita, has a display of the natural history of the park, a botanical garden and an arboretum. Head for Lago Arvo and Cecita for walking, good scenery and a chance to fish for trout in Lago Arvo.

Camigliatello Silano, the area's capital, is a great place to enjoy the local crafts and food. It is also the best place seek out hotels, restaurants and tourist information.

SORRENTO PENINSULA AND THE AMALFI COAST

The Sorrento Peninsula—a heady mix of cobalt-blue sea, plunging cliffs and orange and lemon groves. The perfect place to relax and soak up the sun and an ideal base from which to explore Pompei, Capri and Naples.

SORRENTO

Piazza Tasso, the main square, is a quintessential Italian square. Sit at one of the outdoor cafés and drink in the atmosphere around the maze of narrow streets and shops selling bottles of *limoncello*, the local liqueur. Decadent, grand hotels perch on the cliffs with splendid sea views on one side and lush gardens on the other.

Take time out from the beaches and cafés to visit the Palazzo Correale and its museum. This 15th-century villa has an impressive collection of porcelain, glass, china and paintings dating from the 17th to 19th centuries. The grand cathedral dates from the 14th century and has paintings by artists from the Neapolitan school, a marble archbishop's throne and wooden choir stalls.

Take the public ferry or one of the many well-publicized private boat trips from Sorrento along the coast and around the bay to Capri (▷ 193).

AMALFI COAST

From the southern side of the Sorrento Peninsula, the beautiful Amalfi Coast runs east to Salerno, with steeply terraced villages of stuccoed houses and seafood restaurants clinging to jagged cliffs. It is best-known for its thrilling coastal drive, the 80km (50-mile) stretch of hairpin bends that leads from Positano to Salerno with vistas over the shimmering Gulf of Salerno at every turn.

Amalfi itself, so the legend tells, was created by Hercules, who fell in love with a nymph called Amalfi. Their love was short-lived as she died young, but Hercules promised to bury her in the most beautiful spot in the world, and built the city of Amalfi in her honour. History books, on the other hand, tell us that it was founded after the death of Emperor Constantine, in AD447. Drive or take the blue SITA bus to the pretty villages of Praiano, Positano and Cetara. Praiano is 10km (6 miles) west of Amalfi. A further 6km (4 miles) from Praiano is Positano, popular with artists, stars and sophisticates, with an excellent if expensive array of restaurants and hotels. In spite of this, it has kept its fishing-village charm. East from Amalfi, Cetara, known as 'the tuna town', because of its tuna and anchovy festivals in May and June, has two lovely beaches.

RATINGS				
Good for kids	●	●	●	●
Specialist shopping		●	●	●
Outdoor pursuits	●	●	●	●
Photo stops	●	●	●	●

BASICS

➕ 440 K–L12

ℹ Corso Roma 19, 84011 Amalfi, tel 089 871107; Jul–end Oct Mon–Sat 8.30–1.30, 3.30–7.30; rest of year Mon–Sat 3.30–5

🚂 Sorrento; Circumvesuviana–light railway from Naples to Sorrento

🚢 Ferries from Sorrento to Capri hourly in summer; at least six times daily in low season

www.sorrentoweb.it
Mainly provides hotel and restaurant listings. Also has basic information on the main attractions, lists of museums, cinemas and shops, and links to ferry operators' websites.

TIP

● Petty theft is rife, particularly in crowded areas, so avoid carrying large amounts of money or valuables and keep a close eye on bags.

Positano (top).
A shop selling lemons in Amalfi (above)

An example of Greek statuary in the Museo Nazionale in Taranto

White houses in the old town of Vieste, perched on the rocks overlooking the Adriatic Sea

TARANTO

➕ 443 P12 🛈 Corso Umberto I, 74100 Taranto, tel 0994 532397 🚉 Taranto
www.comune.taranto.it
www.pugliaturismo.com

An ancient Greek colony, founded by the Spartans in 706BC, Taranto, has fine Greek sculpture, gold jewellery and Roman mosaics in its celebrated Museo Nazionale.

Vestiges of the Temple of Poseidon can be seen in the medieval quarter *(città vecchia)*. The commercial and industrial districts of the modern town *(borgo nuovo)*, on the mainland, joined to the old town by bridges, may put off casual visitors, but it is worth staying to see the Museo Nazionale di Taranto (daily 8.30–7.30), which is temporarily housed in the Palazzo Pantaleo. It has a collection of masterpieces, including a sixth-century BC bronze of Poseidon, two marble sculptures of Eros and Aphrodite (fourth century BC) and a beautiful collection of gold jewellery in the Sala degli Ori.

Taranto is also famous as the ancient home of the hairy tarantula spider that caused a disease traditionally cured by dancing the *tarantella*. The latter is not to be confused with *tarantello*, a local culinary delicacy (tuna fish pie) that is a good enough reason in itself for many gourmets to make the trip here.

TRANI

➕ 442 N11 🛈 Piazza Trieste 10, Palazzo Palmieri, 70059 Trani, tel 0883 588830 🚉 Trani

The region's finest Romanesque cathedral, a charming harbour, some first-rate art galleries and good seafood restaurants make Trani one of the most appealing towns on the coast of Puglia.

The town and its people enjoy an uncommon reputation for sophisticated elegance. The beauty of the 12th-century cathedral is enhanced by its isolated position on a promontory overlooking the Adriatic. The handsomely weathered limestone of this three-tiered church, at once graceful and massive, changes from pink to white to gold through the day. Grand bronze doors lead into the Norman interior, built over a crypt in which is housed the Ipogea di San Leucio, a sixth-century Palaeo-Christian tomb.

Around the sheltered harbour, beside the 15th-century Gothic Palazzo Caccetta, several good restaurants serve seafood brought in from the early morning fish market.

Street names in the medieval *centro storico* behind the harbour are evidence of the town's mercantile heyday and Jewish heritage, notably Via Cambio (Street of the Moneychangers) and Via Sinagoga. Today the narrow streets conceal attractive art galleries and antique shops. The view from the Spanish fort, Fortino di San Antonio, is outstanding.

TROPEA

➕ 444 M15 🛈 Pro Loco, Piazza Ercole, 89861 Tropea, tel 0963 61475 🚉 Tropea

Tropea's charms are self-evident. Built on a sandy cliff, the little town of narrow streets and pleasant squares overlooks the sea and its two sandy beaches, from where you can make out the island of Stromboli and the coast of Sicily. There are plenty of cafés, restaurants and pizzerias, as well as two small museums displaying Roman and medieval pottery and a collection of early Christian tombstones.

A short climb takes you to the most eye-catching feature of the town, the Benedictine Monastery of Santa Maria dell'Isola, up on a rock near the sea. Nearby is the town's port, recently enlarged to accommodate visiting yachts as well as fishing vessels.

Each year on 3 May, the Sagra del Cammello (Festival of the Camel) commemorates the defeat of the Saracens, when the vanquished Saracen commander was paraded on a camel before being burned at the stake. Today a symbolic burning of a straw camel and fireworks suffice.

VIESTE

➕ 441 N10 🛈 Piazza Kennedy, 71019 Vieste, tel 0884 708806 🚢 Ferries to Isole Tremiti
www.vieste.com

Quite simply Puglia's best beach resort, Vieste, 57km (35 miles) northeast of Manfredonia, has convenient sandy beaches, popular with families, secluded rocky coves and picturesque sea caves that can be explored from boat cruises.

The peninsula's easternmost town is also an ideal starting point for day trips by ferry to the Isole Tremiti (▷ 197) and a great base from which to explore the Gargano Peninsula (▷ 195).

The town's whitewashed houses sprawl over two promontories jutting into the Adriatic. At the edge of the *centro storico*, the cathedral is 11th-century Romanesque with 18th-century baroque embellishments. The *castello* (castle), built by Emperor Frederick II in 1240, is closed to the public, but you can enjoy a great view of the Gargano coast from the outside.

South of town are the long sandy beaches of Pizzomunno and Castello, along with Grotta Smeralda (Emerald Cave) and Grotta dei Marmi (Marble Cave).

SICILY AND SARDINIA

Sicily's history spans 5,000 years, and this beautiful island, home over the centuries to Greeks, Romans, Arabs and Normans, has everything from classical sites and cities, such as Palermo and Siracusa, to high inland mountains and dramatic coastline. Sardinia has its own charms—the internationally renowned resorts of the Costa Smeralda and the evocative town of Cagliari.

MAJOR SIGHTS

The Castello di Lombardia in Enna, Sicily

CEFALÙ

🔲 445 K16 ℹ️ Corso Ruggiero 77, 90015 Cefalù, tel 0921 421050
🚉 Cefalù
www.cefalu-tour.pa.it

As you approach Cefalù the view is unforgettable—the cathedral rising above the medieval streets, all squeezed onto a promontory between the sea and a towering crag, La Rocca. This lively, popular seaside town just about has it all, from scenery and sandy beaches to museums and historical monuments, plus shops, cafés and restaurants. Cefalù's most important treasure is the cathedral, founded in 1131 by Sicily's first king, Ruggiero II. Particularly precious is the Byzantine-style mosaic of Christ Pantocrator in the apse. For a view of the town and the second-century BC Temple of Diana, climb to the top of 278m (912ft) La Rocca.

ENNA

🔲 445 K17 ℹ️ Via Roma 411, 94100 Enna, tel 0935 528228 🚉 Enna

At 1,000m (3,280ft), Enna is Sicily's highest provincial capital and notable for its awe-inspiring views of the mountains, including, on a clear day, Mount Etna. The fortress town, inhabited before the arrival of colonists from Gela in 664BC, has an imposing ruined, 13th-century castle, Castello di Lombardia. Don't miss the view from the Torre Pisana (480BC) at the Rocca Cerere, site of the temple to Ceres, Greek goddess of agriculture. The Museo Alessi (daily 8–8) in Via Roma has treasures from the duomo. The Chiesa San Salvatore (1261) is an exquisite little baroque church; get the keys from Signore Armenio, owner of the barber shop in Via Salvatore.

AGRIGENTO

A spectacular complex of ancient Greek temples. The medieval town, often overshadowed by the temples, is a delight to explore.

Even if ancient Greek ruins are not usually part of your itinerary, make this group an exception. Most of the temples in Akragas, to use the name given to the site by the sixth-century BC Greek colonists, were built in the fifth century BC, a period of prosperity that ended with the Carthaginian invasion of 406BC. The city was successively reconquered—and its name changed—by Corinthians, Romans, Saracens and Normans. It was only in 1927, under Mussolini, that the name Agrigento came into use.

RATINGS	
Good for kids	●●
Historic interest	●●●●
Cultural interest	●●●●
Walkability	●●●

BASICS
🔲 445 J17
ℹ️ Viale della Vittoria 225, 92100, tel 0922 401352; Thu–Tue 9–1, Wed 9–1, 3–6
🚉 Agrigento
www.provincia.agrigento.it

Agrigento lies along a ridge on the southwest coast of Sicily. The medieval heart is west of the ridge, where Arab and Norman influences can still be seen and the steep streets are dominated by the cathedral. East of the medieval quarter, north of Via Atenea, is the beautiful 13th-century Cistercian Monastero di Santo Spirito and its museum (daily 10–1, 4–6).

Along the SS115 towards Porto Empedocle, the birthplace of Nobel Prize-winning dramatist Luigi Pirandello (1867–1936) is now a museum dedicated to his life.

THE VALLEY OF THE TEMPLES
The famous archaeological zone, Il Valle dei Templi (daily 8.30–1, 3–7), south of the city, is where the ruined temples rise from a plain dotted with almond, eucalyptus and pine trees. Three huge temples lie east of the entrance, the most spectacular being the Doric Il Tempio della Concordia (daily 8.30–10), built about 450BC and amazingly intact. Next are the vast Il Tempio di Giove Olimpico and a group of small buildings dedicated to Demeter and Persephone (daily 8.30–7). The Museo Archeologico (Tue–Sat 9–7.30, Mon 9–1.30) has finds from local sites, notably a giant stone *telamon* (male figure) and a fifth-century BC *krater* (bowl) depicting Perseus and Andromeda.

The cliff-top town of Erice (above); the Valle dei Templi (left)

The crater of famous Mount Etna in Sicily

A fountain splashes merrily in the sweet wine capital, Marsala

ERICE

➕ 445 H16 ℹ️ Viale Conte Agostino Pepoli II, 91016 Erice, tel 0923 869388

This medieval town, atop a 755m (2,476ft) mountain, is one of the most beautiful in Sicily, with impressive views of Trapani and the Egadi Islands. It has aged gracefully and from the time of the Elymian settlers, who came here around 1500–1250BC, through to the Roman era, Erice was venerated as a place where deities were honoured. The Museo Civico Antonello Cordici displays a fourth-century BC head of Aphrodite and an *Annunciation* by Antonello Gagini. Be sure to try some of Erice's famous pastries.

ETNA

➕ 445 L17 ℹ️ Via Garibaldi 63, 95030 Nicolosi, tel 095 911505 🚉 Nicolosi www.aast-nicolosi.it

Of all the sights in Sicily, Etna is the most extraordinary. Frequent eruptions may make a visit to the crater impossible, but if you have the chance, take it.

Etna stands at 3,350m (11,000ft). It is Europe's largest live volcano, and one of the world's most active. Believed by the ancient Greeks to be the forge of Hephaestus, god of fire, it usually trails a plume of smoke, visible from at least half the island. The wooded lower slopes provide scope for walking and wonderful scenery and views. Here you will find chestnut, oak and pine, while higher up, the crumbling lava fields (*sciara*), support the perfumed Etna broom.

ISOLE EGADI

➕ 445 H16 ℹ️ Piazza Saturno, 91100 Trapani, tel 0923 545511 🚢 Trapani

These islands provide what many visitors seek: a slower pace of life, idyllic scenery, country walks, the occasional sandy beach, rocky coves and crystal-clear water for diving and snorkelling. All this is only minutes by hydrofoil, or a bit longer by ferry, from Trapani. The islands can get busy, especially during May and June, when the brutal spectacle of La Mattanza (slaughter of tuna) takes place in Favignana.

The largest of the three islands is Favignana. The Grotta del Genovese, on Levanzo, has some of the oldest-known wall paintings in Sicily, dating from 10,000 to 6000BC. These can be visited overland via a footpath or, more easily, by sea. Marettimo has the highest peak of the three, Pizzo Falcone, at 884m (2,900ft).

ISOLE EOLIE

➕ 445 L15 ℹ️ Via Vittorio Emanuele 202, 98155 Lipari, tel 0909 880095 🚢 Milazzo or Naples

Each island in this fascinating archipelago has its attractions: Alicudi and Filicudi—remoteness and tranquillity; Panarea—beauty and sophistication; Salina (the movie *Il Postino* was filmed here)—Malvasia wine; Stromboli and Vulcano—the excitement of volcanic islands; and Lipari—encounters with the islands' ancient past. Most of the islands have beaches; all have rocky coves and inlets perfect for sunbathing, swimming and diving.

The islands were originally volcanic but now only Stromboli and, to a lesser extent, Vulcano show signs of activity. Lipari's Museo Archeologico Eoliano, near the duomo, houses an important collection of Greek theatrical masks, some beautiful fourth-century BC *kraters* (bowls) and carved obsidian, a type of volcanic glass that in the Neolithic period was traded for its sharp cutting edges and was the source of Lipari's wealth.

The islands become very busy in July and August. Lipari is the largest and most developed, while the more remote and less accessible Alicudi and Filicudi are comparatively untouched by the tourist trade.

MARSALA

➕ 445 H17 ℹ️ Via XI Maggio 100, 91025 Marsala, tel 0923 714097 🚉 Marsala www.antoniogenna.net/marsala

For wine-lovers, a visit to the heart of Sicily's famous wine-producing region is a must. The town has another claim to fame: It was here, in May 1860, that Garibaldi and the one thousand landed at the start of the campaign to unify Italy (▷ 38). It is also a good place from which to visit the island of Mozia, site of an important Phoenician colony.

Marsala, on Cape Lilibeo, Sicily's westernmost promontory, is surrounded by vineyards. Site of the ancient Carthaginian colony of Lilybaeum, the historic quarter is in the northwest of town, next to the Roman archaeological site. The Museo Archeologico (daily 9–2, 4–7) has finds from the site as well as the only Punic battleship ever found, dredged from the seabed north of Marsala and dating from third century BC.

The Museo Garibaldino (Tue–Sun 9–1, 4–8) displays items relating to the Risorgimento, including an important painting by Renato Guttuso, *La Battaglia di Ponte dell'Ammiraglio*. The Museo degli Arazzi Fiamminghi (Tue–Sat 9–1, 4–7, Sun 9–1) has 16th-century Flemish tapestries.

Marsala's reputation has been damaged by overproduction of inferior sweet wines, but the authentic Marsala wine can still be sampled in *enoteche* (wine shops).

If you have time, visit the Convento del Carmine, a 12th-century Carmelite monastery (Tue–Sun 10–1, 6–8).

Elaborate balconies on Via Corrado Nicolaci in Noto

Detail of a mosaic in the Villa Imperiale at Piazza Armerina

Ruins of an ancient temple at Selinunte

MONREALE

⊞ 445 J16 🛈 Salita Belmonte 1, Villa Igea, 90142 Palermo, tel 0916 398011

The hillside town of Monreale has treasures to equal those of the capital, Palermo. The city is set on the lower slopes of the hills that surround Palermo, with views to the sea beyond. There are some attractive piazzas and cafés and a massive 12th-century cathedral. The greatest Norman building in Sicily, it is an inspiring sight. Designed to impress, it was commissioned by William II in an attempt to undermine the influence of his rival, the Archbishop of Palermo, whose power base was the less impressive cathedral of Palermo. Glittering mosaics cover almost every surface of the interior, culminating in the main apse with Christ Pantocrator with angels and saints. Climb the stairs near the right aisle for a view of the Gulf of Palermo, Monreale and the beautiful, mesmerizing cloisters of the former 12th-century Benedictine abbey.

NOTO

⊞ 445 L18 🛈 Piazzale XVI Maggio, 96117 Noto, tel 0931 573779; May–end Sep daily 9–1, 3.30–6.30; Oct–end Mar Mon–Fri 8–2, 3.30–6.30 🚉 Noto

The golden façades of Noto's handsome buildings are masterpieces of Sicilian baroque architecture. The town is also known for its almond pastries and its wine, notably Moscato di Noto. In May, Via Corrado Nicolaci is carpeted with flowers for the Primavera Barocca (Baroque Spring) flower festival.

The town lies on the slope of Colle delle Meti, 32km (20 miles) south of Siracusa, and was designed and built from scratch by Giuseppe Lanza after the original town was destroyed by an earthquake in 1693. His

careful planning produced a neat and ordered town, with many magnificent buildings. The local stone, although attractive, is not durable; the collapse of the cathedral dome in 1996 was a wake-up call and now many buildings are shrouded in scaffolding while repairs are carried out. The baroque Palazzo Ducezio is wonderfully proportioned and has a beautiful portico; ask to see the Sala degli Specchi (Hall of Mirrors), which displays the text of a telegram from Garibaldi to the patriots of Noto, and a fresco by Antonio Mazza. Other highlights include the balconies of the Palazzo Villadorata, with carved angels, lions, horses and mythical creatures, the duomo, and the Church of San Domenico, by Rosario Gagliardi.

PIAZZA ARMERINA (VILLA DEL CASALE)

⊞ 445 L17 🛈 Via Cavour 15, 94015 Piazza Armerina, tel 0935 680201

Piazza Armerina, a small town in the Erei Mountains, is famous for the Roman mosaics in the third-century AD Villa del Casale, at the foot of Monte Mangone, 5km (3 miles) southwest of Piazza Armerina. Abandoned in about the year 1000 and engulfed by a landslide in the 12th century, it was not excavated until the early 1900s. Buildings discovered include a central courtyard, baths and a gymnasium. The mosaics depict animals and birds, and in the renowned Sala delle Dieci Ragazze (Room of the Ten Girls), lithe young gymnasts. The quantity and quality of the mosaics indicate that the villa belonged to someone of importance, perhaps Emperor Maximianus Herculius (AD286–305). It is a World Heritage Site.

SEGESTA

⊞ 445 H16 • Parco Archeologico, 91013 Segesta ☎ 0924 952356 🕘 Daily 9–7; closed 1 hour before sunset 🎫 €4.50, under 18s free 🚉 Segesta Tempio

For the sheer beauty of their setting, the ruins of Segesta are hard to beat. The jewel is the beautiful fifth-century BC Doric temple, one of the finest remaining examples of classical architecture. Segesta was founded in the 12th century BC by the Elymians, but subsequent alliances with the Carthaginians brought the city into conflict with the Greeks. In the third century BC Segesta capitulated to the Romans and the city began to decline. The ruins are spread across a low hill overlooking a wide fertile valley and surrounded by rolling hills. Built into the hillside, the theatre could seat some 4,000 spectators.

SELINUNTE

⊞ 445 H17 🛈 Parco Archeologico, 91022 Selinunte, tel 0924 46251 🕘 Mon–Sat 8–8, Sun 9–12, 3–6 🎫 €4.50, under 18s free 🚉 Castelvetrano www.apt.trapani.it

Selinunte was founded in about 650BC. For a long while the city maintained an alliance with the Carthaginians, and during this period, between about 550 and 480BC, most of its temples were built. The death knell sounded in 250BC, when its citizens razed it to the ground before fleeing ahead of the invading Romans.

This vast archaeological park occupies about 270ha (667 acres). Highlights include Temple E, built in the fifth century BC and reconstructed in the 1950s, and the Temples of the Acropolis—particularly the mid-sixth-century BC Temple C, the oldest on the site.

The cathedral (above); fish at the Piazza Ballaro market (right)

PALERMO

**A lively, vibrant city, encompassing some of Sicily's most beautiful and interesting historical monuments.
A reflection of the island's chequered history.
Peerless examples of the mosaics of Norman Sicily.**

Palermo lies on a coastal plain in northwest Sicily. Chaotic and noisy, it can be exhausting, but there are some incredible sights: Arabo-Norman and Byzantine architecture jostles with Spanish and baroque. There is excellent shopping on the elegant Viale della Libertà and Via Maqueda, while Via Roma has lively bars, cafés and markets. At the hub of the old city are the Quattro Canti, four 17th-century Spanish baroque façades forming gateways to the ancient quarters of the city.

Founded by the Phoenicians in the eighth century BC and subsequently occupied by the Romans and Byzantines, Palermo reached its zenith under the Saracens, becoming a major focus of Arab civilization. The Normans, too, left an extraordinary architectural legacy. There followed the Holy Roman Emperor Frederick II (Frederick I of Sicily), the French Angevins and, in the 18th century, the Spanish. Despite this being the period that introduced much of Palermo's best baroque architecture, the city began to slide into disrepair and only recently has restoration improved the situation.

NORMAN HERITAGE

Visit the Arabo-Norman Church of San Cataldo, with its red domes, and the Byzantine-Norman La Martorana (Mon–Sat 8–1, 3.30–7), with fine mosaics. Along Corso Vittorio Emanuele is Il Capo, the cathedral (Mon–Sat 7–7); the exterior is a masterpiece of Sicilian-Norman carving, while the baroque interior houses tombs of kings. Another red-domed gem is San Giovanni degli Eremiti, unsurpassed in its peaceful cloisters. A visit to the Capella Palatina (Mon–Fri 9–12, 3–5, Sat 9–10, 11–1) is compulsory for the sheer beauty of its mosaics—perhaps the most accomplished example of Arabo-Norman art.

OTHER HIGHLIGHTS

In Via Roma, the Museo Archeologico Regionale (Tue–Fri 8.30–7, Sat, Sun 8.30am–10pm) has a rich collection of Greek sculptures, including the fifth-century BC bronze *Youth of Selinunte* and carved friezes from Selinunte. On the outskirts, La Zisa and La Cuba are the bizarre and grisly Cappuchin catacombs (daily 9–12, 3–5).

RATINGS

Good for kids	●●●
Historic interest	●●●●
Specialist shopping	●●●●
Walkability	●●●

BASICS

✚ 445 J16

ℹ Piazza Castelnuovo 35, 90141 Palermo, tel 091 583847; Mon–Fri 8.30–2, 3–7, Sat, Sun and public holidays 9–1

🚉 Palermo Centrale

www.palermotourism.com

TIP

● Driving in Palermo is not fun, and parking is worse. If you can, come by train. The station is 15 minutes' walk and buses run regularly. If you have to drive, Sunday is best, when many Sicilians leave the city or lunch with their families.

MAKE A DAY OF IT

Monreale: ▷ 214
Cefalù: ▷ 212

RATINGS

Good for kids	● ● ●
Historic interest	● ● ●
Specialist shopping	● ● ● ●
Good for food	● ● ● ●

BASICS

✚ 445 M18

ℹ Via Sebastiano 45, Siracusa, tel 0931 67710; daily 8.30–1.30

🚉 Siracusa

www.apt/siracusa.it

MAKE A DAY OF IT

Noto: ▷ 214

The charming Piazza del Duomo with the cathedral and fifth-century BC Temple of Athena

SIRACUSA

The most formidable Greek power base in Sicily for 500 years. World-renowned classical ruins and a great Greek theatre. Fabulous finds from sites all over Sicily displayed in an impressive archaeological museum.

Siracusa lies on Sicily's southeast coast, 60km (37 miles) south of Catania, divided between the mainland and the island of Ortygia. The city's historic heart, Ortygia is a maze of small streets, shabby in parts but with much baroque charm, with shops, cafés and restaurants. The sixth-century BC Tempio di Apollo, in Piazza Pancali, is one of the oldest in Sicily, but more impressive is the fifth-century BC Temple of Athena, incorporated into the cathedral in Piazza del Duomo. Some of its Doric columns can be seen embedded in the walls. The façade was rebuilt in baroque style after a massive earthquake in 1693, along with many of the surrounding buildings, transforming the piazza into a beautiful square. In Via Capodieci, the Galleria Regionale di Palazzo Bellomo (Tue–Sat 9–1, 3–7, Sun 9–1) exhibits Sicilian and Arabic ceramics, sculpture and paintings.

In 734BC the Corinthians colonized the island of Ortygia, swiftly expanding onto the mainland. The colony continued to flourish under the first of Siracusa's 'tyrants', Gelon (540–478BC), and eventually grew to rival the power of Athens. In 415BC Athens invaded, but her fleet was annihilated and prisoners were confined in the quarries that are now the archaeological park. After falling to the Romans in 213BC, the city began to decline, a process unrelieved by Byzantine and Saracen occupations. Things improved under Norman, then Spanish rule. Extensive rebuilding followed the 1693 earthquake, and Ortygia has many fine examples of the period's baroque style. The industrial buildings of modern Siracusa may not appeal to everyone, but are evidence of ongoing prosperity.

CLASSICAL REMAINS

The Parco Archeologico Neapolis (9am to 2 hours before sunset) lies northwest of Siracusa's high-rise developments. Classical ruins stand in a pleasant, open setting dotted with pines. The great third-century BC Teatro Greco is cut into the white rock of the hillside. Not far away is the second-century AD Roman amphitheatre, while in the southern area is the Ara di Ierone II, an altar on which, at one feast, no fewer than 450 oxen were sacrificed. Other important sites include the Orecchio di Dionisio (Ear of Dionysius), a man-made grotto probably used as a sounding board for theatrical performances.

Cloisters in Trapani (above)
Taormina's Greek theatre (right)

TRAPANI

⊞ 445 H16 🛈 Piazza Saturno, 91100
Trapani, tel 0923 29000/545511
🚆 Trapani
www.apt.trapani.it

The town of Trapani occupies a
sickle-shaped peninsula on the
northwest coast of Sicily. At its
tip are the historic heart, with a
tangle of alleyways, and the port
and ferry terminal, while the
modern town lies at its base,
at the foot of Mount Erice.

Trapani is a perfect base from
which to visit Erice, Segesta,
Marsala, the Isole Egadi—which
can be reached from the ferry
terminal of La Stazione Marittima
di Trapani—and the salt pans
and salt museum at Nubia, 5km
(3 miles) south. Trapani itself has
some unusual works of art in its
churches and museums

In the western part of the old
town, the Chiesa del Purgatorio
houses the *Gruppi dei Misteri*,
20 tableaux of life-size figures
that tell the story of Christ's final
days. Each is owned by a specific
city guild, and on Good Friday
they are carried in procession
through the town during one of
the island's most important
festivals. In Via San Pietro, the
16th-century Gothic-Renaissance
Church of Santa Maria del Gesù
has a beautiful Andrea della
Robbia *Madonna degli Angeli*.

The 14th-century convent of
Santuario dell'Annunziata in Via
Conte Agostino Pepoli, in the
eastern part of the city, has a
delicate rose window and the
venerated sculpture of *Madonna
di Trapani*, possibly by Nino
Pisano. The adjacent Museo
Nazionale Pepoli (Tue–Sun
9–1.30, Sun and public holidays
9–12.30) houses historic items,
including an 18th-century
guillotine, works of art dating from
the 17th century and the flag of
the steamship that brought
Garibaldi to Sicily.

TAORMINA

**Sicily's most select and attractive holiday resort, not least
because of its stunning Greek theatre.
Exclusive shops that attract a chic clientele.**

The town's prominent position
on the slopes of Monte Tauro,
48km (30 miles) south of
Messina, provides views of the
coast and Mount Etna. Narrow
alleyways lead from the main
thoroughfare, Corso Umberto
I, on which are most places of
interest. In Piazza Vittorio
Emanuele, Palazzo Corvaja
houses the Museo Siciliano
d'Arte e Tradizione Popolari
(Tue–Sun 9–1, 4–8), with
fascinating collections from
religious paintings to domestic
utensils. Farther south are
Piazza IX Aprile and La Porta di
Mezzo, gateway to the oldest
part of town. Badia Vecchia
has an archaeological museum
(Tue–Sun 9–1, 4–8) whose
collection includes a Roman
child's sarcophagus that was
later used as a pig trough.

RATINGS				
Good for kids	●	●	●	
Historic interest	●	●		
Cultural interest	●	●	●	●	●
Specialist shopping	●	●	●	●	●

BASICS
⊞ 445 M16
🛈 Palazzo Corvaja, Corso Umberto 1, 98039 Taormina (Me), tel 0942 23243; Mon–Sat 8.30–2, 4–7
🚆 Taormina-Giardini, then bus or steep climb up to town

TIP
● During July and August Taormina is crowded and expensive. Don't drive—parking places will be scarce.

MAKE A DAY OF IT
Siracusa: ▷ 216
Etna: ▷ 213

Taormina became a city of high status after the Roman conquest
of 241BC. However, prosperity ended when the city allied itself
with Pompey rather than his rival Octavian, who wreaked his
revenge by deporting the entire population. When he became
emperor, Octavian repopulated the city, but the golden days were
over and under Saracen, Norman and Spanish occupations the city
sank into obscurity. Civil unrest after the death of Frederick II in
1250 all but destroyed the town, and it was not until the 18th
century and the advent of the Grand Tour, when the fashionable
toured the Mediterranean visiting ancient ruins, that Taormina's
fortunes improved.

THE GREEK THEATRE
Via Teatro Greco leads to Taormina's most famous monument, the
third-century Greek theatre (Apr–end Oct daily 9–7; Nov–end Mar
daily 9–5.30). With excellent views of Etna, it is thought to have
held up to 5,400 spectators. It was rebuilt in the second century BC
by the Romans to present gladiatorial shows rather than drama.

Marshland close to the coast at the resort town of Alghero

The sweeping sandy beaches and tree-lined shores of spectacular Cala Gonone

THE SIGHTS

SARDINIA

ALGHERO

🔲 445 C12 ℹ️ Piazza Porta Terra 9, 07041 Alghero, tel 079 979054 🚃 An open tourist train, the Trenino Catalano, tours Jun to early Sep. Departs from the port daily: Apr, Jun, Sep 10, 1, 3.30, 9; Jul, Aug 10, 1, 4.30, 11. Adults €5, children €3 🚉 Alghero
www.infoalghero.it

The coast around Alghero is known as the Coral Riviera for its production of beautiful coral jewellery in shades from pink to blood red. The province of Sassari is popular with the rich and famous, who moor their yachts or land their private jets here to enjoy the lovely beaches and emerald-green water. Most of them flock to Porto Cervo and the Spiaggia Rosa, an amazingly pink beach of protected status. Alghero's aquarium, the Mare Nostrum Aquarium (www. aquariumalghero.com), is the only exhibition of marine and fresh-water life in Sardinia, including sea-horses, piranhas and sharks.

Once under Aragonese rule, Alghero has a distinctly Spanish feel to it, and the local dialect is a mixture of Catalan and Sardinian. The highlight is the Necropolis of Anghelu Ruju (Apr–end Oct daily 9–7; Nov–end Mar daily 9.30–4). This burial complex, about 10km (6 miles) out of Alghero on the road to Porto Torres, has about 40 *ipogei* (funeral monuments), including sepulchres known as the *domus de Janas* (fairy or witch houses).

BARBAGIA

🔲 445 D13 ℹ️ Mandrolisai Via IV Novembre 23, 08038 Sorgono (Nu), tel 078 460099

The Barbagia area is on the west side of the Gennargentu Mountains. This isolated region was once a land of bandits,

infamous throughout the ages for feuds and vendettas. The largest town has little more than 3,200 inhabitants, and often the only life in this wild landscape are sheep and a shepherd or two. The hamlets and towns are not geared up for tourists. However, the people have a strong sense of hospitality and it is worth trying to overcome the language barrier to get an insight into local life, folklore, ancient traditions and crafts such as cheesemaking, woodcarving and copper and brass. Several roads wind through the region, and those who brave the tortuous bends are rewarded with views over the steep, harsh slopes and the beech and chestnut forests.

Aritzo has several hotels and restaurants and is famous for its delicious handmade *torrone* (nougat). On the last Sunday of October is the chestnut festival, when sweet and savoury chestnut concoctions are the attraction. Look for the *tacchi*, stone relics from the Mesozoic era found in several areas, including Belvì and Desulo. The most famous is the mushroom-shaped 'Texile', near Aritzo and visible from miles away.

CALA GONONE

🔲 445 D12 ℹ️ Piazza Italia 19, 08100 Nuoro, tel 078 432307/430083 www.enteturismo.nuoro.it

Cala Gonone is one of the most spectacular coastal areas on Sardinia. The rocky, barren cliffs that tower over the limpid Tyrrhenian Sea on this scenic east coast reach almost 1,000m (3,280ft). The coast of Orosei, in which Cala Gonone is located, is now a marine reserve, protecting seals and other species. Swim in the clear, emerald waters, sunbathe on the soft white sand or take a boat trip to the Grotta del Blu Marino, a natural limestone formation with wide

arches, to see monk seals.

Set in the province of Nuoro, Cala Gonone began life as a port for ships transporting wood, coal, wine and cheese, but as early as the 18th century it developed its present role as a tourist port. In the peak season it hums with chic yachts, boats and ferries going back and forth to the bays and coves. One of the most secluded but most popular coves, Cala Luna, can be reached only from the sea or by a long walk through the scenic mainland.

Dorgali, in the hills 9km (6 miles) above Cala Gonone and overlooking Lake Cedrino, is a large agricultural town with a flourishing craft industry. It also produces excellent sheep and goats' cheese, as well as some of the island's best wines.

CASTELSARDO

🔲 445 C11 ℹ️ Viale Caprera 36, 07100 Sassari, tel 079 299544

Ancient walls encircle the historic area of this little medieval town, clinging to a spear of rock on a promontory overlooking Asinara Bay. Every year the historic hub is taken over by the Feast of Luni Santi, which begins at dawn on the Monday before Easter. Members of the Confraternità dell'Oratorio di Santa Croce represent the 12 *apostoli* (apostles) and carry sacred objects—a chalice, chains, a crown of thorns, a cross, a hammer and other symbolic articles. Twelve other people form the *cantori* (choir) and sing polyphonic chants, the ancient form of the spiritual Sardinian music. The songs and processions go on for 24 hours and are rounded off with a Pantagruelian dinner.

In the Church of Santa Maria, seek out the 13th-century crucifix and, in the cathedral of Sant' Antonio Abate, the gilt-inlaid altar and pulpit.

The late 19th-century Bastione di San Remy built into the bastions

CAGLIARI

An ancient town with an interesting legacy of monuments, including a Roman amphitheatre.
Capital of Sardinia's southern province, a region of beautiful hills, hamlets, beaches—and some fiery liquors.

Cagliari is thought to date back to Phoenician days and has been invaded countless times over the centuries by the Carthaginians, the Romans, the Barbarians, the Pisans, the Spanish and, in 1718, the English, before surrendering to the Italian royals, the Savoia. Inevitably, all these civilizations and cultures have left their mark on the city.

The city is at the heart of the Gulf of Cagliari, also known as the Bay of Angels. Its medieval quarter sits on the hill of Colle di Castello. The most scenic of the access roads is Viale Regina Elena, from where you can admire the view of the cathedral and the Palazzo Reale. The Belvedere del Bastione di Santa Croce is a tranquil area that looks out over the city towards the Sulcis Mountains.

Cagliari is a large modern city, the biggest in Sardinia, but its *centro storico* (old town), overlooked by the remains of the *rocca* (fortress), is compact, and many hours can fruitfully be spent wandering around. The Castello, the attractive medieval quarter and home to many of the more interesting monuments, is isolated from the rest of the city by the walls and towers built by the Pisans. The Roman amphitheatre (Tue–Sun 10–4; occasionally closed for musical events), carved into the rock on the slopes of Buon Cammino Hill, dates from the second century AD. It is thought to have had a capacity for around 10,000 spectators, and the pits for the lions and other wild beasts are still visible. In the summer, concerts and operatic performances take place here. If you can obtain a ticket, the atmosphere is magical.

OTHER ATTRACTIONS

To get a feel for the wildlife and plants of the area, go to Monte Arcosu, an oasis of wildlife where Sardinian deer and other indigenous animals and plants are actively preserved.

Typical liquors of the province include Mirto, distilled from a type of blackcurrant, and Gennargentu and Filu di Ferro (iron wire) grappa, so called because when the farmers produced it in secret during World War II they buried the bottles under the ground and left a wire protruding a few inches to mark the spot.

RATINGS	
Good for kids	● ● ●
Historic interest	● ● ●
Cultural interest	● ● ● ●
Good for food	● ● ● ●

BASICS

✚ 445 D14
🛈 Piazza Matteotti 9, 09124 Cagliari, tel 070 669255; daily 8–2, 4–8
🚃 Cagliari

www.aast.ca.it

www.regione.sardegna.it
This is the official site of the Regione Autonoma della Sardegna. Here you can find out more about Sardinia's history, geography, economy, traditions, culture, crafts and food. There are Italian, English, French, German and Spanish versions.

TIP

● In August the area is particularly hot and humid, and the city loses some of its local shine as residents go on holiday.

Enjoy secluded coves lapped by deep azure waters on the Costa Smeralda near Cappricione

Cork oaks in the northern Gallura area

COSTA SMERALDA

🔲 445 E11 🛈 Arzachena, 07020 Cannigione, tel 078 982624
www.cannigione.com

The Costa Smeralda is widely known as a playground for the rich and famous. Celebrity-spotting is best in July and August. No stay would be complete without a boat trip to nearby islands such as Soffi, Bisce or Mortorio, part of the Parco Nazionale della Maddalena. The 55km (34-mile) Costa Smeralda has some lovely beaches, including Poltu di Li Cogghji and Spiaggia del Principe.

Karim Agha Khan, an Islamic prince, fell in love with the Costa Smeralda when he came here in 1962. He settled in the little fishing village of Porto Cervo and transformed it into a sophisticated resort. This part of Sardinia is stunningly beautiful, with pure white beaches and clear turquoise and emerald waters, but for those whose budget will not stretch to this, there are other areas that are just as lovely, with hotels a fraction of the price.

Some of the bends along the coastal roads are hair-raising, but a drive in any direction is rewarded with panoramic vistas. **Don't miss** The natural spectacle of Capo d'Orso, a granite sculpture above Palau with views as far as Punta Sardegna.

GIARA DI GESTURI

🔲 445 D13 🛈 Via G. B. Tuveri, 09029 Tuili (Ca), tel 070 936 4277
www.regione.sardegna.it

This plateau lies above Gesturi, an attractive village with an interesting history, ancient stone houses and a 15th-century Gothic church. Volcanic in origin, the plateau is about 500m (1,640ft) above sea level, approximately 4km (2.5 miles) wide and 12km (7.5 miles) long.

The Giara di Gesturi is the last place in Europe where wild horses—numbering 600 or 700—truly roam free. Other wildlife here includes boar, woodpeckers and foxes.

Not far away, on the main Giara road, the village of Bruncu Màdugui is famous for its prehistoric *nuraghi*. These towers, made from rough blocks of stone, were used as dwellings, fortresses or sacred sites and are thought to date from about 6000BC. They connected up with other *nuraghi* settlements, forming a defensive network that covered 45sq km (17sq miles).

NORA

🔲 445 D14 • Nora Sito Archeologico, 09010 Capo di Pula (CA) ☎ 070 920 9138 🕙 9am–dusk 💶 Adult €5.50, under 14s €2.50 📷 Guided visits every hour

This is Sardinia's most fascinating and best-known archaeological site. The Phoenicians settled here as early as the eighth century BC, but the ruins that survive are mainly Roman. These include a theatre, burial sites, baths, a temple and some beautiful mosaics. It is also known as the sunken city, because part of the sloping site is submerged under the sea.

Nora is on a narrow strip of land about 35km (22 miles) south of Cagliari. The *nuraghi* towers found in the area suggest that the site dates from the eighth century BC. During the third and fifth century AD the Sardi people rebelled against the Romans and Nora went into a decline. Malaria epidemics and attacks by pirates followed, and Nora succumbed to Vandal occupation from 456 to 466AD. People moved away to safer parts, and the city, which depended on marine trading for survival, declined further still. In the seventh century the city was turned into a defensive fortress, but bands of Arabs attacked it from the sea and the few inhabitants left could no longer resist.

Be sure to see the Roman mosaics in the Terme di Levante, dating from the fourth century AD, and the foundations of the Punic Temple of Tanit.

PARCO NAZIONALE DEL GENNARGENTU

🔲 445 D13 🛈 Piazza Italia 19, 08100 Nuoro, tel 0784 30083; summer only 🚆 Ferrovie Sardegna trains call at several stations (timetables for the Trenino Verde at FS rail offices or travel agents, tel 800 460220, www.trenino verde.com)
www.parcogennargentu.it

This park is one of the last great Mediterranean wildernesses, characterized by cropped, bare valleys and grazing animals. Explore cork, walnut, hazelnut and chestnut woods in the valleys. Wild boar, hares, foxes, mouflons (wild mountain sheep) and wild cats thrive here, and majestic golden eagles soar through the intense blue skies over the highest peak, Punta la Marmona (1,834m/6,017ft).

The inhabitants of the villages and hamlets maintain ancient crafts, such as embroidery and the making of *launeddas* (traditional bamboo instruments), and culinary traditions, such as cheese-making, aniseed, hazelnuts, honey and biscuits made with alcohol.

The Trenino Verde, a tourist train, links Mandax and Arbatax. The journey of 159km (99 miles) takes almost 5 hours and can be broken up with overnight stops.

A delightful 3- to 4-hour walk through woods and past caves and waterfalls leads to Cala Luna, a beautiful beach.

This chapter gives information on things to do in Italy other than sightseeing. Italy's best shops, arts venues, nightlife, activities and events are listed region by region.

What to Do

SHOPPING

Shopping is an essential part of *la bella figura* (▷ 17). It is taken seriously by both men and women in Italy, where quality is the focus, and personal service reigns supreme. It's seen at its best in the rich north of the country, particularly in Milan, Florence, Turin, Rome and Bologna, but every provincial capital has its fair share of stylish shops, and you'll find some nice surprises in even the smallest towns. In design and fashion, the big names have conquered the world, but there's more to retail therapy than *haute couture* and designer labels. Craftsmanship is highly valued and everything from furniture to underwear can still be made to order. You will certainly find a greater selection of the goods that Italy exports worldwide at better prices, but the back streets are the place to go to find the tiny stores and workshops selling souvenirs and self-indulgent purchases.

Out-of-town shopping arcades, outlet stores and factory shops are slowly making an appearance, while towns traditionally associated with a particular product—ceramics, silk, jewellery—have a huge choice at excellent prices. Wine, food and olive oil are sold direct and you'll be able to taste and buy other local food products at one of the many summertime *sagre*, food festivals (▷ 234).

MARKETS

There are daily food markets in provincial and regional capitals and other large towns throughout the country. They generally take place in a specially built market hall or in a specific piazza or street, selling meat, groceries, fish, dairy products, fruit and vegetables. Where there's a daily food market, the weekly market will be devoted to clothes, shoes, household goods, plants, flowers, toys, toiletries and fabrics. Rome's major markets are held around Piazza Vittorio, Piazza Testaccio, Porta Portese and Via Sannio. In Florence the most prominent are Mercato Centrale, Mercato di Sant'Ambrogio and Mercato Nuovo. In Venice, head for the Rialto, a famous focal point for trade since the 10th century, and still the best place in the city for stocking up on fresh

CHAIN STORES

NAME	Menswear	Womenswear	For children	Shoes	Cosmetics and toiletries	Sports equipment and clothes	Accessories	Household	Books, music and DVDs	Perfume	HEAD OFFICE
Beauty Point					✔					✔	06 904 0631
Benetton	✔	✔	✔								0422 519111
BluNauta	✔	✔					✔				06 696421
Cisalfa						✔					035 455 6111
Coin	✔	✔	✔	✔	✔	✔	✔	✔		✔	041 239 8000
Etam	✔	✔	✔				✔				33 1 5590 7070
Ethic		✔									06 41200621
Felrinelli									✔		02 7529151
Foot Locker				✔		✔					02 4528 1314
Furla				✔			✔				051 620 2711
Geox				✔							0423 2822
Intimissimi	✔	✔									06 6830 1784
Mandarina Duck							✔				051 764411
Mariella Burani		✔									0522 373131
Oviesse			✔								041 239 8000
Prénatal	✔	✔	✔								039 651638
Replay	✔	✔	✔	✔	✔		✔	✔		✔	0423 9251
Rinascente	✔	✔	✔	✔	✔	✔	✔	✔	✔	✔	02 57581
Stefanel		✔									0422 8191
Upim	✔	✔	✔	✔	✔	✔	✔	✔		✔	06 446 5579

produce, especially fish and seafood.

OUTLET SHOPPING
You can pick up bargains in big-name fashion and luxury goods at outlet shopping malls, usually located outside big cities. Fidenza Village, for example, is halfway between Milan and Bologna off the A1 motorway, and has Versace, Elena Miro, Phard, Nike, Bodum and Lindt, among many other top brands.

KEEP YOUR RECEIPT
Till receipts may seem a minor nuisance unless you've bought a major item and they are part of the guarantee or warranty. It's different in Italy. Keep a receipt for everything you buy, and ask for one—scontrino—if it is not volunteered by the shopkeeper. The authorities have tightened up on cash trading to cut down on tax abuse, and the Guardia di

Finanza patrols cities and towns like a police force. You could be asked by an officer, sometimes in plain clothes but carrying ID, to show a receipt as you leave a shop, to prove that the shop has declared the sale. Failure to produce a receipt can result in a fine of up to €155.

OPENING HOURS
These are fairly standard and apply for most of the year, but be prepared for erratic changes.
● Supermarkets, larger stores and tourist-oriented shops generally stay open all day (orario continuato).
● Shops are open from 8.30–1 and 5.30–7 Monday–Saturday.
● Clothes shops may not open until 10am.
● Hours may change from mid-June until the end of August; some shops close completely when their owners go on holiday, while others stay open later for visitors.

● Small shops may close for anything from a week to a month during July and August, when Italians are on holiday.
● A chemist/pharmacy (farmacia) somewhere around the area you are staying in will be open for prescriptions 24 hours a day; this is done on a rota system and chemists post addresses and opening times in their windows.

WHAT TO BUY
Handicrafts
Italy has a strong artisan tradition that continues to flourish. There is a huge range of regional handicrafts to seek out, such as olive-wood bowls and plates in Tuscany and Murano glass in Venice, with many products only available in the area they are made. Florence has an abundance of artisan workshops specializing in picture frames, soft furnishings, accessories and restored antique furniture.

WHAT TO DO

As well as individual designer boutiques and small specialist shops, Italy, like most other Western European countries, has its fair share of chain stores. The most renowned Italian export is Benetton, who have more than 300 stores in their home country. You will encounter branches of chain stores listed in the chart below in shopping districts and malls throughout Italy.

NUMBER OF SHOPS	DESCRIPTION	SHOP WEBSITE
70	Glossy cosmetics store, selling all the best-known brands at bargain prices.	www.beautypoint.it
300	Some of the best and most affordable casualwear in Italy.	www.benetton.com
80	Simple designs, good-quality fabrics and good all-round value.	www.blunauta.it
200	All the well-known brands of sportswear, sports equipment and trainers.	www.cisalfa.com
79	A department store selling mid-range to elegant stock.	www.coin.it
24	French version of H&M; less hip, but affordable and imaginative.	www.etam.com
29	Cool, cheap and original, with a focus on vintage looks and ethnic fabrics.	www.ethic.it
54	One of the best bookshops in Italy, with regular book launches by writers.	www.lafeltrinelli.it
99	All the trainers you could ever want under one roof.	www.footlocker-europe.com
83	Handcrafted leather bags and footwear with an ultra-modern twist.	www.furla.it
105	Modern styles with soles that keep water out, but let your feet breathe.	www.geox.com
447	Cute and indulgent underwear at affordable prices.	www.intimissimi.it
61	Functional, high-tech leather bags and leisurewear.	www.mandarinaduck.com
22	Well-tailored womenswear—from romantic and retro to sexy and revealing.	www.mariellaburani.it
222	Low-end to medium-priced clothes (including swimwear) and homeware.	www.oviesse.com
188	Everything your baby or toddler needs in one store.	www.prenatal.it
54	The place to go for jeans and funky accessories.	www.replay.it
16	Department store selling quality clothes, accessories and household items.	www.rinascente.it
336	Affordable, but up-to-date fashion for women.	www.stefanel.it
140	Department store selling cheap but sturdy fashions and household items.	www.upim.it

Paper

Beautiful handmade paper, often marbled or block-printed, is one of the top buys in Florence, Tuscany and Venice.

Ceramics

Ceramics and pottery are produced all over Italy with designs and glazes varying from region to region. The little town of Deruta in Umbria is overflowing with workshops. You can buy ceramics all over the country, but there's more choice and items are cheaper to buy in their hometown. Other top places for ceramics are Santo Stefano di Camastra on the north coast of Sicily,

the northern lakes and the Puglia region.

Fashion

You will find big names and chain stores in every major city and large town. Stores selling popular Italian exports generally carry a larger range than you'd find at home at more competitive prices. Smaller stores sell individual items with a distinct Italian twist.

Jewellery

Italy is one of the world's biggest jewellery manufacturers. Production is most prolific in Arezzo in Tuscany. Naples is famous for its coral and cameos, but there's a well-established tradition of in-house design across the country, and many jewellers will make pieces to order.

Shoes and Leather

You'll find shoes, belts, bags and accessories in Italy at both ends of the price range—don't neglect the markets, which are great trawling grounds for bargains.

Linens and Underwear

Italian women see luxurious underwear as their birthright, and you'll find plenty to choose from among the wisps of silk, satin and lace. Como is a major silk-producing town—a lot goes to Milan, but there's a huge amount on sale at source, too.

Food and Wine

Every region has its own unique food and wine, available in shops, markets and delicatessens. Buy such items when you see them—move on and you may find that you have unwittingly moved out of the production area.

DESIGNER LABELS			
DESIGNER	**LINES**	**MAJOR STORES**	**WEBSITE**
Giorgio Armani	Fashion, shoes, leather goods	Rome, Venice, Florence, Milan	www.armani.it
Benetton	Fashion	Venice, Florence, Milan	www.benetton.com
Bottega Veneta	Shoes, leather goods	Rome, Venice, Milan	www.bottegaveneta.com
Bulgari	Jewellery	Rome, Florence, Milan	www.bulgari.com
Dolce and Gabbana	Women's fashion	Rome, Milan	www.dolcegabbana.it
Emporio Armani	Fashion, shoes, leather goods	Rome, Venice, Florence, Milan	www.emporioarmani.com
Fendi	Shoes, leather goods	Rome, Venice, Florence, Milan	www.fendi.it
Ferrè	Women's fashion	Milan	www.gianfrancoferre.it
Gucci	Fashion, shoes, leather goods, jewellery	Rome, Venice, Florence, Milan.	www.gucci.com
Krizia	Women's fashion	Rome, Milan	www.krizia.net
Laura Biagiotti	Women's fashion	Rome, Venice, Florence, Milan	www.laurabiagiotti.it
La Perla	Fashion, children's fashion, shoes	Rome, Venice, Florence, Milan	www.laperla.com
Max Mara	Women's fashion	Rome, Venice, Florence, Milan	No website
Missoni	Women's fashion	Rome, Venice, Florence, Milan	www.missoni.com
Prada	Fashion, shoes, leather goods	Rome, Venice, Florence, Milan	www.prada.com
Pucci	Women's fashion	Florence, Milan	www.emiliopucci.com
Roberto Cavalli	Women's fashion	Rome, Milan	www.robertocavalli.net
Salvatore Ferragamo	Men's fashion, shoes, leather goods	Rome, Florence, Venice, Milan	www.salvatoreferragamo.it
Trussardi	Fashion, shoes, leather goods	Rome, Florence, Milan	www.trussardi.it
Valentino	Women's fashion	Rome, Florence, Milan	www.valentino.it
Versace	Fashion, shoes, leather goods, jewellery, linens, tableware	Rome, Milan	www.versace.it

ENTERTAINMENT

There is plenty to keep you entertained in Italy, from cinema and theatre to classical music and opera. This is the home of opera, and you should be able to catch something from the year-long schedule in a romantic or historic venue. The main concert and theatre seasons run throughout the winter, while festivals and outdoor spectacles take over in the summer.

CINEMA

Italy makes around 100 films a year, and the Cinecittà cinematic powerhouse near Rome is constantly busy producing foreign and Hollywood films and nurturing native talent. Given this, it's not surprising that cinema is thriving in Italy, and you can catch anything from the latest blockbuster to the most obscure art-house movie.

Saschell, Florence's major music venue

The main problem will be the language. It's acknowledged that Italian dubbing is the best in the world, so films are automatically dubbed rather than subtitled. In Rome, Milan, Florence and Naples, you should be able to find a cinema showing VO *(versione originale)* movies; elsewhere, outside film festivals, films are likely to be in Italian. In summer films may be screened outdoors, in piazzas and parks.

● City cinemas generally have four showings in the afternoon and evening; 4.30, 6.30, 8.30 and 10.30. Smaller cinemas show films at 8.30 and 10.30.

● Box offices usually open half an hour before the first showing.
● Arrive early on Fridays and Saturdays, when cinemas can be very busy.
● Tickets normally cost around €7, with reductions for the early shows on Monday, Tuesday, Thursday and Friday and all day Wednesday.
● Very few cinemas accept payment by credit card.
● At busy times, some cinemas sell *posto in piedi* (standing only) tickets; there is no discount for these.

CLASSICAL MUSIC, BALLET AND DANCE

The huge number of summer classical music festivals testifies to the Italian passion for the great composers. During the winter months, most cities and towns of any size will have a regular schedule of classical and orchestral music, though you're unlikely to hear anything avant-garde or contemporary.

As in so much else, when it comes to musical taste, Italians are staunchly conservative, happy with a diet of popular classics. Conscious of their funding, organizers, with the odd exception, stick to the tried and tested. Ballet and dance are in much the same position. Unlike theatre, ballet gets no official subsidies and little corporate sponsorship, and consequently standards, even in Rome, are low. Most major opera houses have a ballet season, but the best time to see ballet is during the summer festivals, the most famous being the International Ballet Festival held in Nevi, near Genoa, in July. Contemporary dance has little support and even less funding;

the best time to see something memorable is during the summer festivals.

MUSIC IN CHURCHES

Concerts are often staged in some of Italy's most beautiful churches, providing a chance to hear organ, orchestral and choral recitals in superb surroundings, often with acoustics to match. Look out for posters or ask at local tourist offices.

Italy has some magnificent opera houses

OPERA

There are hundreds of opera houses in Italy, mainly dating from the late 18th and 19th centuries. Many are still home to their own opera companies, or at the very least, in regular use throughout the season. Permanent companies pay their way by putting on classical music concerts and ballet for at least part of the season.

If you are an opera fan, don't miss the opportunity to see Italian opera performed on home soil—popular entertainment with a great deal of audience participation. Shows can be held up after arias for minutes at a time while the audience show their appreciation (or disapproval), and many houses still have unofficial cliques that attend every performance and control the crowd. It makes a refreshing change from the reverent hush that accompanies opera in other countries.

● The season runs from October to the end of March, with minor differences from city to city.

● Top names tend to sing for the first few nights of a production only, so keep an eye on cast-lists.

● Italian opera houses generally have stalls, three to four tiers of boxes around the house, and a gallery. Stall seats and middle- and lower-tier boxes

Florence's Teatro Communale

are the most expensive. Prices range from €20 to €70 depending on the venue and company.

● Top places for summer opera outdoors are the Roman sites of the Terme di Caracalla in Rome (**www**.opera.roma.it) and the Arena in Verona (**www**.arena.it).

FOLK AND REGIONAL MUSIC

If you're looking for the sounds of traditional Italy, head for the *festas* when local bands and groups will be out in force. In more remote areas, you may catch a glimpse of some national costumes and dances. Sardinia, Sicily, the Abruzzo, Puglia and the German-

speaking northern regions are good places to hear folk music.

The festivals organized by the political parties are also good for folk music, often accompanied by dancing. The Festa dell'Unità, child of the Democratici di sinistra, is the biggest of these, taking place in towns and villages all over the country. There's more folk and regional music at some of the city summer festivals, where lively Latin-American and Cuban music sets the tone.

ROCK AND JAZZ

International bands and stars tend to concentrate on Milan, Rome and other major cities, performing in the larger stadiums. Concerts are well advertised with posters. Local rock is performed all over the country—it's at its best and most innovative in central and northern Italy and in the university towns.

Jazz takes centre stage at a number of summer festivals, notably Umbria Jazz, held in July and August. Visit **www**.allaboutjazz.com/italy for the latest listings and jazz news.

THEATRE

Many of the most beautiful and historic provincial theatres are primarily opera houses, doubling up as venues for drama, music and dance, so it's worth checking the press to see what's on (▷ 412).

Apart from Rome and Milan, other cities with a thriving theatre scene include Turin, Bologna, Venice, Florence, Naples and Palermo.

In summer, there are open-air festivals throughout the country celebrating theatre, music and dance. These often take place in classical theatres and arenas, or the courtyards and gardens of historic buildings.

LISTINGS
Rome
Trovaroma—free on Thursdays with *La Repubblica*.

Roma C'è—Fridays from newsstands.
Zero6—free in shops and bars.

Venice
Leo Bussola—free from tourist offices.
Venezia News—from newsstands.

Florence
Firenze Oggi (Florence Today)—free in hotels and bars.
Firenze Spettacolo—Fridays from newsstands.

TICKETS
Rome
Available direct from venues or agencies, who charge a *diritti di pervendita* (supplement):

Checking what's on at the cinema

ORBIS
Piazza Esquilino, Roma
Tel 06 482 7403
RICORDI
Via Cesare Battista, Roma
Tel 06 679 8022

Florence
Available direct from venues or from:
BOX OFFICE
Via Alamanni 39, Firenze
Tel 055 210804

Venice
Available direct from venues or from ticket booths:
VELA
Piazzale Roma, Venezia
Tel 041 2424
www.hellovenezia.it

NIGHTLIFE

Rome and Milan are the big party cities, closely followed by university towns like Bologna, Florence and Perugia, and major provincial centres such as Turin, Genoa and Naples. Night-time activity moves to the coastal resorts during the summer, when the open-air bars and clubs attract huge crowds.

OPENING HOURS

Things start to hot up around midnight, but many bars have a prolonged happy hour from 7 to 9. In smaller towns and rural areas, the opposite's the case, and you may struggle to find a bar open after 11.

BARS

Bars are open from early till late and serve everything from breakfast, coffee and snacks to

The six-level Matilda Club in Sorrento

beer, wine and aperitifs, with no licensing hours to curtail your drinking. Evening-only bars often have live music nights and guest DJs. The main objective for most Italians is to be seen, so there's plenty of posing and little hard-core drinking going on.

CLUBS

● There is not much difference between music bars and small clubs in Italy.
● Many charge an entrance fee, which usually includes a free drink.
● Some clubs make you take out membership *(tessera)*. Prices vary and it may be free.
● If there is no entrance fee, you may receive a card, which

is stamped when you buy drinks or go to the toilet, and totalled up when you leave.

HOT SPOTS
Rome

The *centri sociali* have catapulted Rome's night scene into the 21st century. Emerging 20 years ago, the *centri* were originally squats, where young people occupied disused public buildings, turning them into art spaces and music venues. Rome's main clubs and bars are in Testaccio, the *centro storico* (around Piazza Navona and Campo dei Fiori), Trastevere and San Lorenzo.

Florence

Many central bars and clubs are underground and have no air-conditioning. Some shut in summer, when the action moves to the coast. As in Rome, there's a clutch of *centri sociali*, organizing live music and dance nights. Opening times are erratic and, as with everywhere, things can change without warning.

Venice

There's not much nightlife in Venice at first glance. For the pick of the live venues and clubs head for Mestre and Marghera, or take a boat to Jesolo or Cavallino in summer. The liveliest areas are Campo Santa Margherita in Dorsoduro and Fondamenta della Misericordia in Cannaregio.

Rimini

Italy's answer to Ibiza, Rimini has a frenetic summer club scene that stretches along the coast from Bellariva to Cattolica. The whole area is served by public transport that

runs through the night. There are more than 1,600 hotels, amusement parks, and a plethora of bars and restaurants: find current listings in *Chiamami Città* or *Guida d'Estate*, or visit **www.riminifiera.it** or **www.riminiturismo.it**

GAY AND LESBIAN SCENE

Over the last 10 years Italians have become far more tolerant

Out for the evening on the streets of Florence

towards gay and lesbian relationships, but there's still a long way to go in rural areas, and the gay scene remains low profile in the south. If you're looking for gay bars and clubs, head for the larger cities; Florence is particularly gay-friendly, and there's plenty going on in Rome and Milan.
● *Babilonia* is a monthly publication that includes gay listings for the whole of Italy (€5.20 at newsstands).
● Log on to **www.**arcigay.it, the official site of Italy's foremost gay and lesbian network, or **www.**mariomieli.org, a prominent Rome-based gay and lesbian group.

SPORTS AND ACTIVITIES

Italy's best-loved spectator sport is football (soccer), passionately followed by millions of fans. Hot on its heels is basketball, introduced after World War II and now hugely popular, with the national team ranked among the best in the world. Baseball and American football have also crept in from across the Atlantic, while the Italian passion for bicycling is totally homegrown.

A bit of exercise is often just the antidote to sightseeing or lazy days on the beach, and you'll find sports facilities all over Italy. Even the smallest towns have a *palestra* (gym), where you can work out. During the long, hot summers, swimming and watersports are popular, and there are plenty of pools and beaches. Classy resort hotels have pools and tennis courts, and some will fix you up with a round of golf. Many *agriturismo* enterprises organize activities such as horseback riding, mountain bicycling and walking—all great ways to explore the countryside.

ATHLETICS
International athletics meetings are held in both Rome and Milan.

San Siro Stadium, home of AC and Inter Milan

BASKETBALL
Find more information on Italy's seven major basketball leagues at www.basketball.it

BICYCLING
Bicycling is a way of life in Italy, and a hugely popular spectator sport. You can easily rent a bicycle to get around cities or venture out of town onto marked bicycle routes—tourist offices provide maps of the trails. Join the locals and rent a bicycle to get around the prosperous towns of Italy's flatlands. There are excellent bicycle routes throughout the Po Valley, with well-thought-out itineraries and general information provided by local

tourist boards. If you're in hilly country, think twice before embarking on what could be a tough day in high temperatures. Renting a bicycle is straightforward; ask at local tourist offices for further information, or consider an organized bicycling holiday.

Hundreds of local clubs take to the roads each weekend, and bicyclists out en masse and spectators lining the streets are a common sight all over the country. The main event is the Giro d'Italia, an annual around-Italy race, which takes place in the second half of May, attracting competitors from all over the world.

FOOTBALL (SOCCER)
● The season runs from the end of August until late June, with a two-week break from the end of December into January.
● The Italian League is divided into four main divisions; Serie A, Serie B, Serie C1 and C2. There are 18 teams in Serie A.
● Matches take place on Sunday afternoons. Home games are played virtually every Sunday from September to late June in cities with two major teams, such as Milan and Rome.
● Ticket prices range from €15 to €85. The cheapest seats are in the *curva* at each end of the pitch and the most expensive are along the side of the pitch, in the *tribuna*.

● Tickets can be purchased from venues, merchandise outlets or agencies.
● General information: www.lega-calcio.it

Horse-racing at the Ippodromo di Firenze

● Team sites:
www.asromacalcio.it
www.sslazio.it
www.juventus.it
www.inter.it
www.acmilan.it
www.acfiorentina.it
www.veneziacalcio.it

LISTINGS
Events are advertised in listings magazines, Italy's two daily sports newspapers, *La Gazzetta dello Sport* (the pink paper) and the *Corriere dello Sport*, and in Friday newspapers. Local tourist offices may be able to help you find out where you can buy tickets.

GOLF

Golf is still a prestigious game in Italy and fairly exclusive. The main Italian cities all have smart clubs on their outskirts and you'll find courses attached to some resort hotels in the northern regions.

Most clubs will want to see proof of membership of your home club and may also ask for handicap details before allowing you to play. Green fees normally cover the whole day, so there's always the chance to squeeze in a couple of rounds to get your money's worth. Expect to pay upwards of €65 and extra for club, trolley and electric cart rental. If you

Bicycling is hugely popular in Italy

want to play a lot of golf while you are in the country you could opt for an all-inclusive golf holiday such as those organized by The Holiday Group (www.golfingtrips.co.uk) in Britain, or USA Golf Holidays (www.usagolfingholidays.com) or Jerry Quinlan's Celtic Golf (www.celticgolf.com) in the US.

GRAND PRIX

Italy hosts two Formula 1 Grand Prix motor races annually; the San Marino Grand Prix at Imola in April (www.formula1.sm) and the Italian Grand Prix at Monza near Milan in September (www.monzanet.it).

GYMS

Italian gyms are mainly private, so you'll need to take out a temporary membership. Larger city gyms charge a daily rate ranging from €10 to €25.

Expect to find weights and machine rooms and a good choice of classes; the entrance fee sometimes includes a class—Tai chi, yoga or Pilates.

Bigger gyms may have a sauna, Turkish bath and solarium, and you can reserve a massage or some hydrotherapy; big city gyms may have squash or tennis courts.

HORSEBACK RIDING

This is becoming an increasingly popular holiday activity in Italy, and you'll find horseback riding establishments all over the country, with specialized tour operators organizing guided riding holidays through some of the most beautiful areas.

Things are better organized in central and northern Italy and information is available at APT offices. Many *agriturismo* enterprises offer riding as an activity.

If you intend to ride on holiday, bring your own riding hat and any safety equipment with you, as it may be of a low standard or not provided.

JOGGING

Italians are gradually coming around to the idea of running, though it's still largely a middle-class occupation and only popular in the more prosperous parts of the country. Rome, Milan, Florence and Venice all organize annual marathons, and running clubs are beginning to make their mark. If you just want to get out early and jog, avoiding ankle-twisting cobbled streets, try the suggestions below.

Rome

Villa Borghese: Rome's most prestigious park is home

to the Galleria Borghese and is only a few minutes from the Spanish Steps. It has wide paths lined with cool pines, but it can be crowded at weekends.

Villa Pamphilj: A lovely park on the slopes of the Gianicolo behind Trastevere; the park serves some of Rome's wealthier suburbs and has good paths and some workout stations.

Circo Massimo: Run around the pine-fringed expanse of the city's biggest chariot-racing venue near the Forum and Colosseum for a workout and a taste of ancient Rome.

Villa Ada: Out in the suburbs, this leafy park is near the Catacombe di Priscilla.

There are many excellent golf courses to choose from

Its lakes are lined with running paths, a green retreat at the heart of the modern Salaria residential area.

Florence

Giardino dei Semplici: Once a Medici physic garden, this oasis of greenery near the church of San Lorenzo has some good shady paths.

Giardino di Boboli: On a hill across the Arno, central Florence's only park has some testing wide paths.

Forte Belvedere: This area at the top of the Boboli Gardens is a great place to get away from the busy, crowded streets and run while enjoying the superb views over the city.

Venice

Zattere: Head for this wide waterfront area in Dorsoduro with views across Giudecca.

Giardini: Head east along the Fondamenta to Venice's public gardens, with great views over the lagoon, towards the residential area of Sant'Elena.

NATIONAL PARKS

Abruzzo, Lazio e Molise
www.parks.it
This is Italy's third-largest national park. The wild Apennine country is ideal for brown bears, wolves and chamois. Information offices in Pescasseroli (tel 0863 910097), Opi (tel 0863 910622), and Villetta Barrea (tel 0864 89333).

There are horseback riding establishments throughout Italy

Cinque Terre
Tel 0187 920633
www.parks.it/parco.nazionale.cinque. terre
A coastal park in Liguria that preserves agricultural and natural landscapes.

Gargano Peninsula
Tel 0884 568911
www.parcogargano.it
An extensive limestone promontory—the spur of the boot of Italy.

Gran Paradiso
www.parks.it
Italy's oldest national park covers three valleys, Cogne, Valsavarenche and Val de Rhêmes, in Val d'Aosta around the Gran Paradiso mountain range. Noted for chamois, ibex and mountain flora. Information offices at Noasca (tel 0124 901070) and Ceresole Reale (tel 0124 953186).

Gran Sasso e Monti Della Laga
www.parks.it
www.gransassolagapark.it
In the Abruzzo this park has the highest Apennine peaks flanking the Campo Imperatore. Information office at Amatrice (tel 0746 826344/9336609).

Monti Sibillini
www.parks.it
www.sibillini.net
Spread over eastern Umbria and the Marche, this park is famous for its wolves, excellent birdwatching and superb alpine flora. Information office at Norcia (tel 0743 817090).

Stelvio
www.parks.it
www.stelviopark.it
A spectacular Dolomite park stretching from Lombardy to Trentino-Alto Adige. Superb summer high-level walking, flora and fauna. Information offices at Bormio (tel 0342 910100), Fraches (tel 0473 830510), Cogolo di Peio (tel 0463 754186) and Rabbi Fonti (tel 0463 985190).

RUGBY
Rugby is beginning to make its mark, and interest has grown since Italy's inclusion in the Six Nations Championship in 2000. Home games are played at the Flaminio Stadium in Rome (www.sixnationsrugby.com).

SHOW JUMPING
The Concorso Ippico Internazionale di Piazza di Siena, a prestigious show-jumping event, takes place in Rome from the end of April to the first week in May (www.fise.it).

SWIMMING
During the searing heat of summer it's a relief to take to the water. In the main cities, where swimming pools, like gyms, are usually privately run, you may need to take out temporary membership to enjoy the facilities. Some pools offer day-tickets as well as weekly and monthly subscriptions.

Italian resort beaches are divided into sections, each run as a *stabilimento balneare* (bathing establishment). These are private, and you'll have to pay a fee to cover the use of a changing cabin, sun lounger and umbrella. Each *stabilimento* normally has

Hiking on the volcanic Mount Etna, Sicily

eating and drinking facilities, some of which are quite grand.

Beach standards are high, with sand cleaned and raked overnight, but water cleanliness can vary. Avoid swimming near major cities, ports or industrial coastal areas.

All Italian resorts have a legal obligation to allow free access to a section of the beach, so it is possible to avoid payment if you want a quick dip.

Lakes and rivers, particularly in mountain regions, are cool and refreshing choices for a swim on a hot day. Alternatively, splash out and sample the mineral-rich waters of one of Italy's many natural hot springs (▷ 232).

TENNIS

Most towns and cities have clubs where you can rent a court throughout the day, and some hotels have their own facilities—reserve in advance during the summer.

The Campionato Internazionale di Tennis (Italian Open) runs for 10 days in May in Rome (www.masters-series.com).

WALKING AND HIKING

Italy's mountainous north is the obvious place to go if you're looking for the best hiking and walking. From Val d'Aosta in the west across to Trentino-Alto Adige in the eastern Dolomites, there's

Sailing on Lago di Garda, Lombardy

superb walking to cater for all abilities.

Serious hikers and climbers can make for the hills and enjoy long-distance, high-altitude routes, sleeping at refuges overnight and not seeing a valley floor for days on end.

If you fancy something gentler, gondola cable cars provide easy access to well-marked paths and trails, or you could simply stroll through the quiet lanes that link the villages. The mountain regions are all keen to promote their walking opportunities, and tourist offices provide a variety of brochures and itineraries.

HIKING TIPS

- You'll find detailed maps of the more popular areas in bookshops and tourist shops; Kompass is a good series.
- If you are planning to go into the mountains or off the beaten track, take a map with a scale of no less than 1:50,000.
- Always wear suitable clothes and footwear, take plenty of water, something to eat, and leave word of where you're going and what time you expect to be back.

WATERSPORTS

With their country's long Mediterranean coastline, it's hardly surprising that Italians have embraced watersports. There's the choice of lake or sea if you're planning on joining in.

You can sail, water-ski and windsurf on the northern lakes and all around the coastline, while river canoeing and kayaking are extremely popular, particularly in Val d'Aosta, Piedmont, Lombardy and Trentino-Alto Adige.

Italians are keen scuba divers and Campania, Calabria and Sicily have the best underwater gardens to explore, but the less experienced can enjoy snorkelling along the rocky parts of the west coast. At many resorts you can sign up for a day's introductory course, or rent equipment if you're already experienced. Unfortunately few instructors for beginners speak fluent English. Local tourist offices have details of schools and there are plenty of advertisements around in seaside resorts.

WINTER SPORTS

The Italian Alps are a major European skiing destination, with many specialized tour operators offering all-in skiing packages to the main resorts. The Alps are accessible from

Milan, Turin, Bologna and Venice, while the Abruzzi Mountains are easily reached from Rome and Naples.

There are weekend, low-key resorts with a handful of lifts and a few runs virtually all over the country. Good options for a couple of days on the slopes include the Tuscan and Umbrian Apennines, the Abruzzo, the Sila in Calabria and inland Sicily.

If you want to arrange your own ski package, Settimane Bianche (White Weeks) are excellent value. They offer an all-inclusive accommodation package and hefty reductions on ski rental and lift passes—all you have to arrange is your

Rafting Umbria leads guided rafting excursions on the River Corno

transport to the resort. The regional tourist boards in Val d'Aosta and Trentino-Alto Adige have brochures, which give details of participating hotels, prices and contact details.

A.I.A.T AOSTA
Piazza Chanoux 42, 11100 Aosta (AO)
Tel 0165 236627
Fax 0165 40532
www.regione.vda.it/turismo

APT ALTO-ADIGE
Piazza Walther (Waltherplatz) 8, 39100 Bolzano (BZ)
Tel 0471 307000
Fax 0471 980128
www.bolzano-bozen.it

HEALTH AND BEAUTY

Italy is blessed with mineral-rich, naturally heated springs, and there are *terme* (spas) all over the country. There is a long, well-established tradition of using mineral waters to encourage better health, and to treat everything from allergies and skin problems to liver complaints, arthritis and rheumatism.

Many spas still function purely as therapeutic clinics, where doctors will work out a regime for different medical conditions, but an increasing number of *centri benessere* (health and beauty centres) are catering for those who want to be pampered in style.

Spa hotels now provide much more than the odd massage or dip in a pool, and you can check in for a few days of total relaxation and self-indulgence in a resort hotel.

To find out more visit www.hotelbenessere.it, with links to spas all over Italy.

ABANO TERME AND MONTEGROTTO TERME, VENETO
Consorzio Terme Euganee
Abano–Montegrotto
Largo Marconi 8, Abano Terme,

The warm thermal pools at Saturnia, Tuscany

35031 Padova
Tel 049 866 6609
Numero Verde 800 255161 (free number from within Italy)
Fax 049 866 6613
www.abanoterme.net
www.abanomontegrotto.it
Two spas in the Euganean hills of the Veneto in northeast Italy. Both specialize in water and mud treatments, which are considered to be beneficial in the treatment of rheumatic and arthritic conditions and skin disorders.

CHIANCIANO TERME, TUSCANY
Terme di Chianciano Spa
Via delle Rose 12, Chianciano Terme, 53042 Siena

Tel 0578 68292/3
Fax 0578 60622
www.chiancianoterme.com
www.termechianciano.it
This southern Tuscan spa specializes in treating liver and bladder complaints. There are three springs, and the emphasis is on medical rather than beauty treatments.

MERANO, TRENTINO-ALTO ADIGE
Terme di Merano
Via Piave 9, Merano, 39012 Bolzano
Tel 0473 24724
Fax 0473 237724
www.emmeti.it/Salute/TAA/Merano
A large spa resort in the eastern Dolomites, surrounded by mountains. The radioactive waters are used to treat a range of medical disorders.

SATURNIA, TUSCANY
Hotel Terme di Saturnia
Saturnia, 5805 Grosseto
Tel 0564 600800
Fax 0564 600111
www.termedisaturnia.com
Saturnia is popular with those seeking rest and relaxation. This long-established luxury spa resort hotel is more dedicated to pampering and beauty than to medical treatments, though the highly sulphurous waters have many beneficial qualities.

MONTECATINI TERME, TUSCANY
Viale Verdi 41, Montecatini Terme, 51506 Pistoia
Tel 0572 7781/0572 778487

Fax 0572 778444
www.montecatini-terme.com
www.termemontecatini.it
A huge spa, with nine springs and beautiful fin-de-siècle buildings. The emphasis is on

The Spa Tettuccio gardens at Montecatini Terme

health and rehabilitation rather than relaxation and pampering. They focus on the treatment of gastric disorders, heart conditions, and circulatory and respiratory problems.

LUIGIANE, COSENZA
Uffici Terme Luigiane, Località Terme Luigiane, 87020 Acquappesa (CS), tel 0982 94064
www.termeluigiane.it
The Luigiane thermal baths, in Cosenza province, Calabria, have a long history—the health benefits of their sulphur-rich waters were known 2,000 years ago. The water gushes from a spring at 37°C (99°F), and the baths offer a wide range of treatment therapies.

FOR CHILDREN

Children are considered part of mainstream society in Italy, so you'll find few child-specific facilities and amusements. There is still plenty to do, though, with the bonus that children are respected and integrated into whatever's going on.

BEACHES
The seaside holiday is a major part of Italian family life. Resorts all over the country are busy during the holiday period from July to late August. Small children will be happier at resorts along the Adriatic coast and in the flatter areas of the west coast (Tuscany, Lazio and Calabria), where there are plenty of sandy beaches with shallow bathing, beach games and playgrounds. Older

Take a ride on Rome's Time Elevator

children will probably prefer the more scenic areas such as the Cinque Terre or the Amalfi coast—underwater gardens that are great for snorkelling and spotting fish. Bear in mind that few *stabilimenti balneari* (▷ 230) have lifeguards, so children should not be left unattended.

CITIES
Tourist information offices will be able to recommend attractions that are likely to appeal to children. In Rome, Florence and Venice you can buy guidebooks aimed at children. Cities that older children may enjoy include Rome (lots of ruins and blood-

thirsty tales), Milan (some excellent child-oriented museums) and Florence (the Children's Museum of Florence, Museo Stibbert and the Museo di Storia della Scienza).

DISCOUNTS
In Italy, charges for museums, galleries and other attractions are nearly always reduced for children and some are free.

FAMILY-FRIENDLY AREAS
The northern lakes are great for watersports and boat trips, as well as walking and horseback riding. Tuscany and Umbria have plenty to keep most outdoor families occupied, from exploring tiny towns to bicycling, hiking and horseback riding. The mountain regions of the Veneto, Lombardy and the Alto Adige have hotels specializing in family activities.

PARKS
Although all the major cities have parks, only the biggest have grassy areas large enough for children to play games and run around in. However, many have playgrounds, with a selection of swings, slides and roundabouts, and they are good places for a picnic. Ask at tourist offices if there is a travelling funfair coming to town; fairs tend to visit on or around the community's major feast day.

THEME PARKS
There are several theme parks in Italy, so you should be able to find some amusements near your base. Some are very large, with exciting rides and roller-coasters for all ages and new attractions added every year.
Gardaland is Italy's biggest theme park, a Disney-style

complex with an Italian twist. The park's mascot is Prezzemolo (Parsley), a kindly green dinosaur. The park has everything from stomach-churning rollercoasters to scary space rides and water rapids.
Italians flock to The Flying Island, an orbiting space station, and The World of Barbie, dedicated to Italy's most popular doll. Most parks are open throughout the year and have long summer

Feeding the birds in Milan's Piazza Duomo

opening hours—many are open until midnight.

CONTACT DETAILS
FANTASY WORLD
Capriate San Gervasio (BG)
Tel 02 909 0169
www.fantasyworld.it
LUNEUR
Via delle Tre Fontane, Roma
Tel 06 592 5933
www.luneur.it
EDENLANDIA
Viale Kennedy 76, Napoli
Tel 081 239 4090
www.edenlandia.it
GARDALAND
Castelnuovo del Garda, 37014 Verona
Tel 0456 449777
www.gardaland.it

FESTIVALS AND EVENTS

There's no shortage of festivals in Italy celebrating religious holidays, the arts and gastronomic specialties—a great excuse for a local community to party. Celebrations are organized by Italians for Italians, but they are open to anyone who's willing to participate in the right spirit. That spirit differs enormously according to each festival's focus, so be prepared for everything from intense religious feeling to exuberant high sprits. Major festivals, such as Carnevale in Venice and Siena's Palio, attract visitors from all over the world, and if you're planning on attending, reserve your accommodation well in advance. You'll find low-key local events throughout the country during the summer. Keep an eye open for posters and ask at tourist offices for up-to-the-minute information. For an enthusiastic overview of Italian festivals, from the grandest to the quirkiest, visit www.hostetler.net

ARTS FESTIVALS
Italy has a lively arts festival scene, most active during the summer, when amphitheatres, arenas, churches and piazzas are transformed into venues for many of the cultural events. These festivals cover everything from Greek theatre to opera, dance, rock and jazz, and many run for well over a month. Some, such as Spoleto's Festival dei Due Mondi, Venice's Biennale and the Verona Opera Festival are world-class events, which need to be reserved in advance.

Central Italy is particularly prolific, and if you're in Tuscany or Umbria during the summer an evening dose of culture is easy to find. The main ones to look out for are Florence's Maggio Musicale Fiorentino, Umbria's Sagra Musicale Umbra and Umbria Jazz, all ranking high on the international circuit.

FOOD FESTIVALS
For a true taste of Italy seek out the *sagre* (food festivals), where you can sample many local products. Everything from truffles to trout is celebrated, with stands and long tables laid out with the local fare and handicrafts in all their guises. These are truly small-town festivities, providing a unique insight into rural Italian life. The eating and drinking is often accompanied by brass bands and dancing, all rounded off with a noisy fireworks display.

RELIGIOUS FESTIVALS
These festivals are closely linked to the church calendar. Holy Week, Christmas, which is celebrated by elaborate *presepi* (cribs) set up in churches, Corpus Domini, commemorating the cult of the Blessed Sacrament, and the August feast of the Assumption of the Virgin are celebrated across the country. The Day of the Dead (1 November) is when Italians return to their native towns and villages to tend their relatives' graves and reunite with their whole family.

At local levels, every town and village has its own patron saint, whose feast day is celebrated with processions and solemn church services, culminating in late-night partying. You'll find religious festivals everywhere, but the farther south you travel, the more fervent they become.

TRADITIONAL FESTIVALS
The Venetian festivals, celebrating the city's past grandeur, are superb, but for an adrenaline rush head for Siena and the passion and spectacle of the Palio, a hair-raising bareback horse race. Inhabitants of many small towns celebrate their history by dressing up in traditional costumes and processing through the streets, drumming and waving flags.

Opening ceremony of Gioco di Calcio, Florence

THE NORTHWEST

WHAT TO DO

As you would expect in this high-earning, high-spending region, there's plenty to spend your money on. Turin and Milan are the big consumer hotspots, with some of the country's chicest and most diverse shopping, but there is plenty on offer throughout the area—the wealth is apparent on the smartest streets of even the smaller towns. The strong northern work ethic has given birth to an equally strong let-your-hair-down-and-party philosophy, and the area has plenty of cultural entertainment, clubs and bars and some outstanding sporting opportunities. *Bambini* (children) are well-served too, with fun parks, child-friendly museums and summer-time attractions. Head for Milan, Turin and Genoa for serious shopping and the best of entertainment, the lakes and mountains for clear air and exercise, and the Ligurian coast for glitzy and luxurious beach life. If you like watching sport as the Italians do, you will be spoiled for choice. This region is famous for being home to the country's top soccer teams and a world-class Formula 1 motor-racing circuit. If you want to play, you will find some of the best summer-time golf and tennis facilities in the country here, while winter is the time for posing on the pistes.

KEY TO SYMBOLS
- 🌐 **Shopping**
- 🎭 **Entertainment**
- 🍸 **Nightlife**
- ⚽ **Sports**
- ⭐ **Activities**
- ♡ **Health and Beauty**
- 😊 **For Children**

BERGAMO

🎭 TEATRO DONIZETTI
Piazza Cavour 15, 24121 Bergamo
Tel 035 416 0602
www.teatrodonizetti.it
A wide range of music is performed at this old theatre, from productions of musicals such as *Grease* to hard-hitting Verdi. It's also home to three big international music festivals: jazz in February,

piano in May and opera every autumn.
🎭 8.30pm; some Sun shows from 3.30pm 💶 €35

COLA DI LAZISE

⭐ PARCO TERMALE DEL GARDA
Villa dei Cedri Spa, Piazza di Sopra 4, 37010 Cola di Lazise
Tel 045 759 0988
www.villadeicedri.com
This old-style manor house has indoor and outdoor thermal spas. Hydromassage and Jacuzzis inside—pools, caves, ponds and waterfalls in the elaborate grounds. Deluxe apartments are available for those wanting to stay. There's also water

polo and some good restaurants.
🕐 Sun–Thu 9–1am, Fri–Sat 9–2.30am
💶 €160 for 2 per night 🚗 On minor road between Castelnuovo, Peschiera and Lake Garda

COMO

🎭 TEATRO SOCIALE
Via Bellini 3, 22100 Como
Tel 031 270171
www.teatrosocialecomo.it
This 1,000-seat auditorium sits majestically in its own square, between the duomo and the Nord Lago rail station. The major theatre in town, the Sociale is the perfect venue for opera and classical music.
🎭 Weekly performances Oct–end May
💶 €15–€70

🅨 LUCA'S CAFÈ

Via Ugo Foscolo 7, 22100 Como
Tel 031 310 8672

Happy-go-lucky 20- to 40-
somethings live it up at this
intimate bar that provides a
warm welcome. Tasty
Warsteiner beer on tap and a
bar stuffed full of free nibbles
keep the clients satisfied. The
bar is right next to Como's
small train station.

🆗 Mon–Sat 8–1am 🚆 Nord Lago

GARDONE

🎭 IL VITTORIALE THEATRE

Piazza Vittorialle, 25083 Gardone Riviera
Tel 0365 296519
www.vittoriale.it

An open-air theatre operating
in summer in the grounds of
the magnificent Il Vittoriale
villa. Performances range from
ballets to classic musicals.
Tickets are available from the
box office outside the grand
manor.

🆗 Performances 7.30, Jun–end Aug
💶 €25–€30

GENOVA (GENOA)

🎭 TEATRO CARLO FELICE

Passo Eugenio Montale 4, 16121
Genova, tel 010 5381224
www.carlofelice.it

Unmissable premises on
Piazza dei Ferrari. Opera
dominates, but there are
plenty of other classical and
show performances woven
into the schedule. There are
some good cafés and bars
around the corner from the
theatre. Reserve tickets on the
website.

🆗 Performances 8pm 💶 €16 🚌 17,
18, 19, 20, 30, 32, 35, 37, 39, 40, 41 or
46 to Piazza dei Ferrari

✪ LA CITTÀ DEI BAMBINI

Area Porto Antico, 16128 Genova
Tel 010 247 5702
www.cittadeibambini.net

This is one of Genoa's few
places specifically aimed at
kids of all ages. The focus is
on learning about technology
and the world in a fun-fuelled
and fully interactive way.
Adults can leave their

children to entertain
themselves under the
supervision of trained staff,
and feel free to do some
shopping and explore Genoa's
premier tourist district.

🆗 Oct–end Jun Tue–Sun 10–6;
Jul–end Sep 11.30–7.30 💶 €5 🚌 1, 2,
3, 4, 7, 8, 12 or 15 to the Porto Antico
complex

MILANO (MILAN)

🛍 ARMANI

Via Manzoni 31, 20121 Milano
Tel 02 6231 2605
www.emporioarmani.it

This flagship Armani shop is a
veritable fashion megastore.
Children's clothes, lingerie,
accessories, and the latest

*The striking Teatro Carlo Felice
in Genoa*

fashions are spread across
eight floors.

🆗 Mon–Sat 10.30–7.30 🚇 Monte
Napoleone

🛍 DISCOVERY

Piazza dei Mercanti, 20123 Milano

As with many Milanese goods,
the records on this stand,
within striking distance of the
duomo, are exceptional.
Browse through rare LPs by
the Beatles, Lou Reed and
Jimi Hendrix, all priced around
€8. Picture discs cost slightly
more. You will find the stand
on Passaggio Santa
Margherita, just off Piazza dei
Mercanti.

🆗 Mon–Sat 9–6 🚇 Duomo

🛍 LE SAC FACTORY OUTLET

Via Carnevale 13, 20121 Milano
Tel 02 376 0399

You can find bargain bags,
belts and purses (leather and
snakeskin predominate) here.
Many items come with chic
labels, and prices range from
€50 to €500—reasonable
compared to some of the
other big stores nearby.

🆗 Tue–Fri 9.30–2, 3.30–7.30, Mon
3.30–7.30, Sat 9.30–1, 2.30–7.30
🚇 San Babila

🛍 LOUIS VUITTON

Via Monte Napoleone 2, 20121 Milano
Tel 02 777 1711
www.louisvuitton.com

Get your hands on the world's
most distinctive luggage.
Branded bags, purses and
cases for the international jet
set. The nearby branches of
Bruno Magli and Samsonite
are also useful if you need
extra luggage space to take
your shopping home.

🆗 Mon–Sat 9.30–7.30, Sun 11–7.30
🚇 San Babila

🛍 MANDARINA DUCK

Via Orefici 10, 20123 Milano
Tel 02 8646 2198
www.mandarinaduck.com

Mandarina Duck has two
floors of funky, functional
handbags and purses. The
shop is close to Milan's central
Piazza del Duomo, next door
to the British Abbey National
bank. Full sets of non-leather
luggage start at around €350.

🆗 Tue–Sat 10–7.30, Mon 3–7
🚇 Duomo

🛍 PRADA

Corso Sant Andrea 21, 20121 Milano
Tel 02 7600 1426
www.prada.it

The windows of this flagship
store, near Via Monte
Napoleone, are jam-packed—
purses, bags and shoes
beckon those with style and
money. Immaculately
turned-out staff are there to
help you choose from Prada's
reassuringly expensive range.

🆗 Daily 10–7.30 🚇 San Babila

WHAT TO DO

⊕ SISLEY
Via Dogana 4, 20123 Milano
Tel 02 86996191
www.sisley.com
This is very much a flagship fashion store for this smart-casual Italian label. In sight of the duomo, Sisley's huge window displays and moderately priced clothes draw the shoppers in droves. Quality Italian shirts for men are around €40. T-shirts for women start from around €12. This branch also stocks Sisley's latest lingerie collection.
🕓 Mon–Sat 10–7.30, Sun 11–7
🚇 Duomo

⊙ ODEON
Via Santa Radegonda 8, 20121 Milano
Tel 02 874547
Ten-screen multiplex cinema in the heart of town, showing all the latest blockbusters. Many are screened in their original language. Half of the theatres provide access for people with disabilities, and all have air-conditioning. Cheaper tickets available for daytime shows.
🕓 Most evenings (contact for details)
🎟 €6.50 🚇 Duomo

⊙ TEATRO ALLA SCALA
Piazza della Scala, 20121 Milano
Tel 02 7200 3744
www.lascala.milano.it
Milan's most famous playhouse is the venue for a huge variety of classical music and operatic performances. As well as entertainment this stunningly beautiful theatre has an on-site bookshop, bar and history museum to explore. You can reserve tickets and find details of up-and-coming events on their flash website.
🕓 Most evenings from 8pm
🎟 €10–€150 🚇 Monte Napoleone

⊙ ALCATRAZ
Via Valtellina 25, 20121 Milano
Tel 02 6901 6352
www.alcatrazmilano.com
This live music and disco venue is rock-oriented. One of the city's largest venues, it attracts more than 1,000 happy dancers at the weekend. It is frequented by the occasional famous face and the well dressed, so its best to dress to impress, as with most Milanese clubs. It only really gets going after midnight.
🕓 Fri–Sat 11pm–4am 🎟 €14
🚇 Garibaldi

⊙ ATM
15 Bastione di Volta, 20121 Milano
Tel 02 6552 2365
This wacky bar inside an old ATM Milano bus stop provides Milan's beautiful people with cocktails and dancing until late into the night. The Indian food served here is not of the best quality.
🕓 Mon–Sat 8pm–3am 🚇 Lanza

Milan's Teatro alla Scala is in a magnificent building

⊙ PLASTIC
120 Viale Umbria, 20123 Milano
Tel 02 733996
This buzzing disco for gay and straight revellers has a drag night on Tuesday. Even after 30 years it remains a popular and busy venue, but it's only open three nights a week.
🕓 Thu–Sat 11pm–4 am 🎟 €12
🚇 Duomo

⊙ POGUE MAHONE'S
1 Via Salmini, 20135 Milano
Tel 02 5830 9726
www.pogue.it
Lots of Brits, Irish and Australians hang out at this friendly Irish pub. Watch football matches on the big-screen TV while enjoying a €5 pint of Guinness and a bacon sandwich. They occasionally have Irish music and dancing.
🕓 Tue–Fri 11am–4pm, 6pm–11.30pm, Sat 6pm–2am, Sun 11am–1.30am
🚇 Porta Romana

⊙ ROLLING STONE
Corso XXII Marzo 32, 20135 Milano
Tel 02 733172
www.rollingstone.it
Listen to live rock, punk, indie and jazz at this hangout near the Porta Vittorio rail station. It is very relaxed and there is no dress code. Listings are in Milan's free newspapers.
🕓 Thu–Sun 7am–1pm, 8.30pm–4am
🎟 Free entry unless a live band is playing 🚇 Porta Vittorio

⊙ TOCQUEVILLE 13
Via de Tocqueville 13, 20121 Milano
Tel 02 2900 2973
www.tocqueville13.it
This posh club is popular with footballers and you might spot a few famous faces. Thursday and Sunday are the big nights. Entry is easier on other nights. Pricey nibbles available.
🕓 Daily 9pm–3am 🎟 €15
🚇 Garibaldi

⊙ AC MILAN AND INTER MILAN LIVE FOOTBALL
Via Piccolomini 5, 20151 Milano
Tel 02 4009 2175
www.acmilan.com, www.inter.it
Catch one of Italy's most illustrious clubs, AC Milan or Inter Milan, at the San Siro stadium. Tickets for a match with either sell out fast, so buy your tickets in advance from their club shop in Via Turati, from FNAC in Via Torino, online on their website or through TicketOne.
🕓 Sep–end Jun every other weekend
🎟 €14 (cheapest ticket) 🚇 Metro Lotto (free before matches)

⚑ ITALIAN GRAND PRIX
Parco di Monza, 20052 Monza
Tel 039 248 2212
www.monzanet.it
The Italian Grand Prix at
Monza is one of the highlights
of the Formula 1 calendar.
Phone for full details, or print
a reservations form from the
Monza website.
🕐 Mid-Sep 💶 €35–€500 🚆 Monza
is clearly signed 20km (12 miles)
northeast of Milan

✪ CENTRO SPORTIVO
MARIO SAINI
Via Corelli 136, 20134 Milano
Tel 02 756 1280
Hit a few tennis balls on an
open-air clay court or have a
game on one of the 12 indoor
synthetic courts. Quality
equipment is available to rent
at the club. Non-members are
welcome, but tennis whites
are appreciated.
🕐 Daily dawn–dusk 💶 €6.50 before
6, €10.50 after 6 🚌 38

PESCHIERA

✪ AQUAPARADISE
Via Fossalta 1, 37010 Peschiera
Tel 0457 590622
www.canevaworld.it
The biggest of all Lake Garda's
aquaparks, with water slides
and a wave machine. Float
down the rapids on blow-up
tubes, or dive-bomb hundreds
of feet down the Stuka slide.
The restaurants are tacky but
amusing—choose from the
salad bar, the pizzeria or one
of the fast-food outlets.
🕐 Mid-May to end Sep daily 10–7
💶 Adult €30, child (under 1m/3ft 4in)
free 🚆 Regular shuttle buses from train
station 🚆 2km (1.3 miles) from
Peschiera

✪ MEDIEVAL TIMES
Via Fossalta 1, 37010 Peschiera
Tel 0457 590622
www.canevaworld.it
A whole evening of medieval
fun and entertainment for all
the family awaits you here.
Walk around a Ruritanian
castle, watch the jousters, then
eat and drink all you can at the

king's feast. Crazy court jesters
and some serious sword
fighting make this unsuitable
for the very young.
🕐 Jul, Aug daily shows 7pm and
9.30pm; rest of year daily 7pm only
💶 €30 (discounts for additional entry
into other Canevaworld entertainment
sites, such as the adjoining aquapark)
🚆 Regular shuttle buses from train station 🚆 2km (1.3 miles) from Peschiera

STRESA

✪ MOUNTAIN BIKE HIRE
Piazzale Lido, 28838 Stresa
You can rent mountain
bicycles from the cable-car
station (next to Stresa's
Carciano harbour) and ride up
to Mount Mottarone

*The Teatro Regio Torino hosts a
range of performances*

(1,455m/4,772ft). The long,
slow descent is magnificent.
🕐 Mar–end Oct daily 8–8
💶 €20 for full day

TORINO (TURIN)

⚑ GERLA
Corso Vittorio Emanuele II 88, 10123
Torino
Tel 011 545422
Thousands of tiny chocolates
vie for customers' attention.
The ornate chocolate cakes
cost around €15. Piedmontese
savoury specials—as well as
fruit tarts, sweet breads
and pastries—complete the
spread.
🕐 Mon–Fri 9–7.30, Sat 8.30–1,
3.30–7.30, Sun 8.30–1 🚌 15

⚑ STICKY FINGERS
Via delle Orfane 24, 10122 Torino
Tel 011 521 7320
www.sticky-fingers.it
In the heart of the Roman
Quarter, Sticky Fingers brings
the 1960s and 1970s back into
fashion. Beautiful faux-vintage
trousers, shirts and dresses
from €50 fill this tasteful shop.
Check out the classy Simon
Kneen boutique next door, too.
🕐 Tue–Sat 11–2, 5–10
🚌 Buses to Piazza della Repubblica

⚑ TEATRO REGIO TORINO
Piazza Castello 215, 10122 Torino
Tel 011 881 5241
www.teatroregio.torino.it
You will find this unmissable
theatre on the corner of Piazza
Castello next to Via Guiseppe
Verdi. It hosts musicals, plays
and the occasional opera all
year round.
🕐 7.30pm 💶 €43.50 🚌 11, 12

⚑ JUVENTUS LIVE FOOTBALL
Piazza Crimea 7, 10131 Torino
Tel 011 65631
www.juventus.com
Italy's most decorated football
(soccer) club. Juve play
alternate weeks at the Stadio
delle Alpi. Tickets start from
€15 but you can pay up to
several hundred euros for the
best seats.
🕐 Sep–end Jun every other weekend
💶 €15 (cheapest ticket) 🚆 The Stadio
delle Alpi is clearly signed 4km (2.5
miles) southwest of the city centre

✪ CIRCOLO GOLF
Via Agnelli 40, Fiano, 10070 Torino
Tel 011 923 5440
www.circologolftorino.it
This is a classy 19-hole, 72-par
golf course. The club has a
practice field, swimming pool,
bar, fine restaurant, and
jewellery and fashion shops.
The summer heat tends to be
quite bearable up here too.
🕐 Mar–Dec 15 Tue–Sun 8–8
💶 A round of golf is €52 on a
weekday, €78 at the weekend.
Equipment rental extra 🚆 Take the
Venaria Reale exit from the Tangenziale
Nord from Milan

FESTIVALS AND EVENTS

JANUARY

FIERA DI SANT'ORSO
Aosta
www.fieradisantorso.it
Traditional street fair in honour of Sant Orso, a sixth-century Irish monk who lived in Aosta and was an expert woodworker, carving sandals for the poor. Today, more than 700 woodcarvers exhibit and sell their work, mostly traditional bowls and utensils, while artisan lace and fabrics are also on available. Local restaurants serve regional specialties throughout the two-day fair.
🕓 30–31 January

FEBRUARY

BATTLE OF THE ORANGES
Ivrea
www.carnevale.ivrea.it
Dating from the 12th century, this festival commemorates the assassination of the tyrannical Count Ranieri by a miller's daughter. Today, a girl is chosen annually to lead the festivities, which include historical processions and pageants. The high point is a series of 'battles' fought between rival factions, with more than 400 tons of oranges used as ammunition and thrown from wonderfully decorated horse-drawn carts.
🕓 21–24 February

JULY

WORLD FIREWORKS CHAMPIONSHIP
San Remo
www.sanremo.it/fuochi
Italians are world famous for their firework displays and the major companies operate worldwide. There's no better place to see what they can do than at San Remo, when incredible fireworks burst noisily and spectacularly over the port for a whole week. Look out for the pyrotechnics on the water.
🕓 1st week in July

AUGUST

FESTIVAL DEL MARE
Diano Marina
The feast of the Assumption is celebrated all over Italy with processions and general jollity, but pyrotechnic-lovers should head for Diano Marina on the Piedmont coast to see the superb firework displays over the sea.
🕓 15 August

San Remo's World Fireworks Championship

SEPTEMBER

SETTEMBRE MUSICA
Torino
www.comune.torino.it
Most of September is devoted to this music festival, which combines classical, modern, jazz and world music at various venues around the city. As befits the home of the RAI National Symphony Orchestra, standards are high; great venues include the Lingotto centre and the Teatro Regio opera house.
🕓 September

OCTOBER–NOVEMBER

GIOSTRA DELLE CENTO TORRI AND PALIO
Alba
www.langhe.com/
A donkey race that dates from the 12th century when troops from Asti chased the Albese inside their walls and ran a *palio* outside. The Albese promptly organized their own race inside the walls—but used donkeys. This is re-enacted to mark the opening of the National Truffle Fair, which runs for three weeks—the most famous celebration of the delicacy in Italy.
🕓 1st Sunday in October–1st weekend in November

NOVEMBER–JANUARY

ILLUMINAZIONE
Torino
www.comune.torino.it
For the six weeks around Christmas over 20km (12 miles) of Turin's streets are illuminated by lighting specialists from all over Europe. Areas on show include shopping streets, piazzas, and walkways beside the River Po—the perfect backdrop to Christmas shopping.
🕓 21 November–9 January

DECEMBER

MERCATO DI SANT'AMBROGIO
Milano
A festival in honour of Sant'Ambrogio, Milan's ninth-century patron saint and the city's first mayor. Stands selling a bit of everything appear around the church of Sant'Ambrogio, and thousands of people take the day off work to attend. Also called Oh Bej! Oh Bej! after the children's cries of delight in the 16th century.
🕓 7 December

VENICE

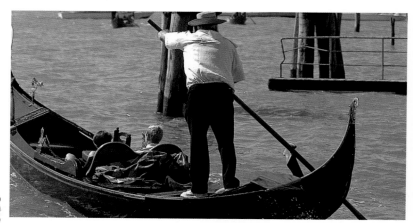

Still as irresistible to consumers as it was in its historic heyday, Venice lays out its wares in glittery style. This is a city that still specializes—in glass, fabrics, jewellery, handmade papers and carnival masks. Get off the beaten track and wander the side streets crammed with tiny specialist shops selling one-off pieces, or stick to the main routes and snap up designer clothes, soft leather and gossamer-fine lingerie. Browsing around antiques shops and bookshops is a pleasure and shopping for unique souvenirs is a delight.

Culture-seekers will find plenty of entertainment—Vivaldi's music played in his own church, opera in the beautiful Fenice (Phoenix) opera house. If you're looking for more 21st-century thrills, it's pretty low key, but there's a clutch of lively clubs. You'll get plenty of exercise walking the streets, but if you need more, there's tennis and golf nearby, or you could learn to row Venetian-style—standing up.

KEY TO SYMBOLS

- 🏬 Shopping
- 🎭 Entertainment
- 🍷 Nightlife
- 🏅 Sports
- ⚙ Activities
- ♡ Health and Beauty
- ✪ For Children

🏬 SHOPPING

ART, CRAFTS AND ANTIQUES

EBRÛ
Campo Santo Stefano, 3471 San Marco, 30124 Venezia
Tel 041 523 8830
www.albertovalese-ebru.com
Alberto Vallese's products are still the best—notebooks, photo frames, boxes and albums in marbled or stamped paper in a huge variety of colours. Superb value.
🕐 Tue–Sat 10–1 & 4–7; Mon 4–7
🚤 Accademia

GILBERTO PENZO
San Polo 2681, Calle Seconda dei Saoneri, 30125 Venezia
Tel 041 719372
www.veniceboats.com
Gilberto's practical approach to recreating Venetian boats in miniature, including gondolas, is respected the world over. His crowded workshop is fascinating and you can buy boats of all sizes, including inexpensive kits to build.
🕐 Mon–Sat 9.30–12.30, 3–7
🚤 San Toma

MONDONOVO
Rio Terà Canal, 3063 Dorsoduro, 30123 Venezia
Tel 041 528 7344
Venice's most famous *mascheraio* has been setting an example to other mask-makers for decades

with its enormous variety of masks, handmade on the premises from papier-mâché and beautifully gilded and painted.
🕐 Daily 10–1, 4.30–7
🚤 Ca' Rezzonico

VENINI
Murano 47–50, Fondamenta Vetrai, 30141 Venezia
Tel 041 273 7211
www.venini.com
If you're serious about buying some Murano glass, spend an afternoon seeing how it's made. The great thing about Venini is that it's not too packed, so you can appreciate the craftsmanship. A good balance of traditional designs and artier pieces.
🕐 Mon–Sat 9.30–7.30
🚤 Colonna, Murano

BOOKS

LIBRERIA LINEA D'ACQUA
San Marco 3717, Calle della Mandola (della Cortesia), 30124 Venezia
Tel 041 522 4030
www.librerialineadacqua.it
This welcoming bookshop has an interesting range of English-language guides to Venice, as well as some thoughtfully chosen coffee-table art books, popular fiction, poetry and plays. Sit down and take the weight off your feet as you leaf through whatever takes your fancy.
⊙ Mon–Sat 10.30–12.45, 3.30–7.15
🚢 Rialto

FABRICS

BEVILACQUA
Fondamenta della Canonica, 337/B San Marco, 30124 Venezia and Campo Santa Maria del Giglio 2520 San Marco, 30124 Venezia
Tel 041 528 7581 and 041 241 0662
www.luigi-bevilacqua.com
The big Italian fashion houses come to Bevilacqua for their Venetian brocades, velvets, taffetas and damasks, still produced on 17th-century looms. The curtain ties, swags and key tassels make wonderful souvenirs.
⊙ Tue–Sat 10–1, 4–7; Mon 4–7
🚢 San Zaccaria and Santa Maria del Giglio

FASHION AND LINGERIE

LA FENICE ATELIER
Calle dei Frati, 3537 San Marco, 30124 Venezia
Tel 041 523 0578
If you're looking for beautiful lingerie or table linen, this is a good place to start. Cristina Linassi has nightgowns and dressing gowns in gossamer-fine cotton and smooth linens, all exquisitely finished, while table linens come in rich damasks in white, cream and a rainbow of colours.
⊙ Mon–Sat 10–1, 4–7
🚢 Sant'Angelo

MANEKI–NEKO
Campo Sant'Angelo 3820 San Marco, 30124 Venezia
Tel 041 520 3340
Crisp cottons and linens are used here to make beautiful easy-to-wear shirts and blouses ranging from strictly tailored to casual. They also stock pretty nightgowns and bathrobes.
⊙ Apr–end Sep daily 10–6; Oct–end Mar Mon–Sat 10–6
🚢 Sant'Angelo

MISTERO
Castello 4755, Ruga Giuffa, 30122 Venezia
Tel 041 522 7797
Mistero is three shops next to one another: one sells items for the home, another sells

Hunting for unique souvenirs at the market

fashion for the young and the third sells ladies' clothes (including bigger sizes). The ladies' shop—Atelier—has tops, trousers, dresses and scarves imported from India, and there's a huge selection of vibrant styles to choose from.
⊙ Mon–Sat 9.30–12.30, 3.30–7.30
🚢 San Zaccaria

LA PERLA
San Marco 4828, Campo San Salvador, 30124 Venezia
Tel 041 522 6459
www.laperla.com
You can get some exquisite lingerie here, made from sumptuous materials. There is night- and swimwear on sale

too. The staff are helpful and very discreet.
⊙ Mon–Sat 9.30–7.30
🚢 Rialto

FOOD AND DRINK

CASA DEL PARMIGIANO
Erberia, 214 Rialto, 30125 Venezia
Tel 041 520 6525
www.aliani-casadelparmigiano.it
Next to the fish market, this little shop sells big cheeses and even bigger prosciutto. Locals shop here too—watch what they buy for inspiration. A number of cheeses and salamis are vacuum-packed, ideal for taking home.
⊙ Mon–Thu 8–1.30, Fri–Sat 8–1.30, 5–7.30; closed Sun
🚢 Rialto or San Silvestro

PANTAGRUELICA
Campo San Barnaba, Dorsoduro 2844
Tel 041 523 6766
Arguably the finest food shop in Venice, Pantagruelica offers the best produce from all over Italy, lovingly tracked down by the enthusiastic owner. The emphasis is on quality, so expect to find organic produce heavily featured. Highly recommended for cheese, *salumeria*, specialty oils, dried goods and fresh truffles in season.
⊙ Mon–Sat 9–6.30 🚢 Ca' Rezzonico

JEWELLERY

PERLE E DINTORNI
Calle della Mandola (Della Cortesia), 3740 San Marco, 30124 Venezia
Tel 041 520 5068
It's easy to spend hours in this shop, choosing beads for a necklace. However, benefit from the experience of the staff, who are on hand to help you combine colours and effects of which a novice would never have dreamed. There is also ready-made jewellery at a range of prices.
⊙ Mon–Sat 10–7
🚢 Sant'Angelo

MARKETS

RIALTO MARKET

Near the Rialto Bridge, on the San Polo side

Wander around the Rialto for fruit and vegetables or head down to the *pescheria*, or fish market, to see the strangest creatures in the lagoon.

A great experience that hasn't changed for centuries.

⏰ Mon–Sat 8am–12 🚉 Rialto

SHOES AND ACCESSORIES

BOTTEGA VENETA

San Marco 1337, Calle Vallaresso, 30124 Venezia

Tel 041 522 8489

www.bottegaveneta.com

An elegant shop, famed for its superior leather goods. This is an opportunity to get your hands on the new lines while staying in the Veneto region. Kit yourself out with belts, bags and wallets. A great place to buy classic gifts that are practical and enduring.

⏰ Mon–Sat 10–7.30, Sun 11–7

🚉 San Marco

🎭 ENTERTAINMENT

CLASSICAL MUSIC, DANCE AND OPERA

GRAN TEATRO LA FENICE

San Marco 1965, Calle del Fenice, 30124 Venezia

Tel 041 786611

www.teatrolafenice.it

The spiritual headquarters of 19th-century opera and classical ballet was ravaged by fire in 1996. After lengthy delays, the building reopened for the 2004–05 winter season. Tickets are available from the Cassa di Risparmio in Campo San Luca.

🎫 €40 🚉 Santa Maria del Giglio

SCUOLA GRANDE DI SAN ROCCO

Campo San Rocco, Santa Croce, 30135 Venezia

Tel 041 523 4864; 041 962999 for tickets

www.sanroccofestival.com

This famous 16th-century guild has a rich musical tradition. Its splendid interior contains famous Tintoretto paintings—

an ideal venue for the regular and popular baroque music concerts. You can reserve tickets online via their website or over the telephone.

🎫 €30 🚉 San Toma

SCUOLA GRANDE DI SAN TEODORO

Campo San Salvador, San Marco, 30124 Venezia

Tel 041 521 0294

www.imusiciveneziani.com

This magnificent guild building hosts baroque and operatic concerts all year round. Vivaldi's *The Four Seasons* is often performed, as is music by Mozart, Donizetti and Verdi, with the added bonus that the

Head to Rialto Market for fresh produce

orchestra and singers dress in 18th-century costume.

⏰ All year Tue–Sun. Contact for times

🎫 €21–€31

🚉 Rialto

TEATRO FONDAMENTE NUOVE

Cannaregio 5013, Fondamente Nuove, 30121 Venezia

Tel 041 522 4498

Venice's premier avant-garde dance and ballet theatre is not far from the Chiesa dei Gesuiti (▷ 88). Check out a modern production here, then head for Paradiso Perduto and the other night spots. It also stages alternative rock gigs.

🎫 €10

🚉 Fondamente Nuove

TEATRO MALIBRAN

Calle dei Milion, 5873 Cannaregio, 30121 Venezia

Tel 041 786 603; box office 041 899 909 090

This wonderful building stages well-known operas such as *La Traviata* and more modern works, as well as classical concerts and ballet. There is a full theatrical and musical programme.

🎫 €35

🚉 Rialto

CONTEMPORARY LIVE MUSIC

900 JAZZ CLUB

San Polo 900, Campiello dei Sansoni, 30125 Venezia

Tel 041 522 6565

www.jazz900.com

This is one of northeast Italy's premier jazz clubs, with a pretty decent pizzeria to boot. It attracts plenty of Italian and international artists.

⏰ Tue–Sun 12–2.30, 7–midnight

🎫 €10 🚉 San Silvestro

🌙 NIGHTLIFE

BARS AND CAFÉS

CASANOVA

Cannaregio 158A, Lista di Spagna, 30125 Venezia

Tel 041 275 0199

This internet café-cum-disco attracts a diverse group: students, tourists and the gay-and-lesbian crowd. This is one of Venice's truly wild night spots. In the early evening it shows live football on the TV.

⏰ Daily 9am–4am 🎫 €10 🚉 Ferrovia

IGUANA

Cannaregio 2515, Fondamenta della Misericordia, 30125 Venezia

Tel 041 713561

Mexican bar/restaurant drawing a crowd seeking songs and sangria. Happy hour is 6 to 7.30pm, but it's best to come later when the staff have warmed up.

⏰ Tue–Sun 10am–3pm, 6pm–1am

🚉 Madonna dell'Orto

WHAT TO DO

CLUBS

CASINO MUNICIPAL DI VENEZIA AND VENICE CASINO CA' NOGHERA
Ca' Vendramin Calergi, Palazzo
Vendramin Calergi, 2040 Cannaregio,
30123 Venezia
Tel 041 529 7111
Ca' Noghera, Via Pagliaga 2, near Mestre
Tel 041529 7111
www.casinovenezia.it

If you want a flutter in the opulent surroundings of a palazzo on the Grand Canal, Ca'Vendramin is the place to come—though the Casino at Ca' Noghera near Mestre is busier, flashier and more popular. Both offer table games such as roulette, baccarat and blackjack and banks of slot machines and electronic games. Wear a jacket and tie at the Ca' Vendramin Calergi.

🕐 Casino slot machines daily 11am–3am, tables daily 3pm–3am; Venice Casino Mon–Fri & Sun 10am–4am, Sat 10am–5am
💶 €5 entry or €10 for entry plus €8 token
🚤 San Marcuola or private boat (Naveta Casino) from Piazzale Roma every 10 min; ACTV 4 or shuttle service from Piazzale Roma

PICCOLO MONDO (EL SUK)
Accademia, Dorsoduro 1056,
30123 Venezia
Tel 041 520 0371

This is a small, elegant and intimate club with a dash of 1970s-style. It attracts a wide spectrum of people: from well-dressed Italians to student types from the nearby Università di Cà Foscari.
🕐 Daily 9pm–4am 💶 €10
🚤 Accademia

⊗ SPORTS AND ⊕ ACTIVITIES

BASKETBALL

REYER VENEZIA AND APG BEARS BASKETBALL
Via Vendramin 10, Mestre,
30173 Venezia
Tel 041 534 5250
www.reyervenezia.it and
www.bears.shineline.it

Basketball is very popular in Italy. The Reyer club is one of the leading female clubs and the APG Bears are the local men's team. Games are played at the Palasport Taliercio on Sundays.
🕐 Sun 6pm 💶 Free (usually) 🚌 To Mestre, then bus 12 to Via Vendramin

FOOTBALL

AC VENEZIA
Isola Sant'Elena, 30122 Venezia
Tel 041 238 0711
www.veneziacalcio.it

The open-air Stadio Penzo is on the island of Sant'Elena, to the east of San Marco. AC Venezia are a Serie B outfit who have also played in the top-flight

Circola Golf Venezia was designed in 1928

Serie A. Expect firecrackers, flag-waving, singing and a lot of gesticulating and moaning. Tickets are available from the ground, ACTV and Vela offices.
💶 *Curve* (behind the goal) €10, *distinti* (side of pitch) €20 🚤 Sant'Elena

GOLF

CIRCOLA GOLF VENEZIA
Via del Forte, Alberoni, 30011 Lido
di Venezia
Tel 041 731333

At the far end of the island, near the fortress, is the excellent, well-groomed 18-hole, par 72, Alberoni golf course. It has practice greens, a club house and a restaurant. Equipment rental is available.

🕐 Apr–end Sep Tue–Sun 8–8;
Oct–end Mar Tue–Sun 8.30–6 💶 €55
weekdays, €65 weekends 🚤 Santa
Maria Elisabetta (Lido), then bus B

GONDOLA RIDE
A gondola ride, the ultimate in Venetian romance, allows visitors to see the city at its most magical and is an unforgettable experience—even though the price may set you reeling. If you're planning a trip, you can discuss the itinerary beforehand with the gondolier; the route will depend on where you're boarding, but most gondola trips will cover either the Bacino di San Marco and some side canals, or a section of the Grand Canal and some smaller *rii*. Fares are set by the gondola board (tel 041 528 5075, www.gondolavenezia.it), and are based on six passengers, with no reductions for smaller numbers. Expect to pay between €65 and €80, depending on the time of day, for 50 minutes. If funds are short, you can ride in a gondola for just 50 centesimi by taking one of the *traghetti* (gondola ferries) across the Grand Canal. There are eight routes, each taking a couple of minutes, and using *traghetti* will often save a long hike to one of the bridges.

Gondola Stations
● Bacino Orseolo (behind Piazza San Marco)
● Campo San Moïse (in front of Grunwald hotel)
● Ferrovia (railway station)
● Piazzetta San Marco
● Piazzale Roma
● Riva degli Schiavoni (in front of Hotel Danieli)
● Riva del Carbon (south end of Rialto Bridge)
● San Marco (Vallaresso) (next to *vaporetto* stop)
● San Tomà (near *vaporetto* stop)
● Santa Maria del Giglio (next to *vaporetto* stop)

ROWING

REALE SOCIETÀ CANOTTIERI BUCINTORO
Fondamenta Dogana e Salute 15,
Dorsoduro, 30123 Venezia
Tel 041 522 2055
www.bucintoro.org
Experienced rowers as well as novices are welcomed by the famous Reale Società Canottieri Bucintoro. Try your hand at *voga veneta* (Venetian rowing standing up), *canotaggio* (ordinary rowing) or sailing. Lessons are also available for children.
◉ Tue–Sat 9–5, Sun 9–1
◉ Enrolment €42 then €52 for 8 lessons ◉ La Salute

SKYDIVING

AEROCLUB DI VENEZIA
Aeroporto G. Nicelli, San Nicolò,
30126 Venezia
Tel 041 526 0808
www.skydivevenice.com
Fancy flying over the lagoon and looking down on San Marco from above? This club has 20 years' experience. One-off jumps are available after a short but thorough introduction course. All equipment and qualified tuition are included in the price.
◉ By appointment only ◉ Phone for details of the latest courses (Signor Michele Zanella, tel 041 961154)
◉ Santa Maria Elisabetta (Lido), then bus A to San Nicolò

TENNIS

TENNIS CLUB CA' DEL MORO
Lido 6, Via Ferruccio Parri, 30126 Lido di Venezia
Tel 041 770 965
Bring your tennis kit and a supple wrist to this fantastic club on the Lido. Phone in advance to reserve one of the dozen or so floodlit clay courts and to rent rackets, balls, line officials, umpire and ballboys. Gym and pool also available.
◉ Mon–Sat 8.30–8.30, Sun 8.30–8
◉ €9 per hour ◉ Santa Maria Elisabetta (Lido) and then bus B

FESTIVALS AND EVENTS

FEBRUARY

CARNEVALE
Tel 041 522 5150 (tourist office)
Tel 041 717065 (Carnival Committee)
www.carnevale.venezia.it
www.meetingeurope.com (The Ball)
Carnevale was Republican Venice's ultimate anything-goes festival. It has been revived to become a hugely successful 10-day festival, with costumes, masks and fun and games all over the city. People flock to parade the streets in fancy dress and splendid masks. One of the hottest carnival tickets is for the official Baroque Ball (Il Ballo Tiepolo), which takes place at the splendid Palazzo Pisani-Moretta. If you can't afford this, there are four other balls to choose from and various other events.
◉ 10 days preceding Shrove Tuesday
◉ Ballo Tiepolo €390

JUNE–NOVEMBER

BIENNALE INTERNAZIONALE D'ARTE
Tel 041 521 8711
www.labiennale.org
Venice's Biennale began in 1895 as a showcase for the best in modern art, an aim it still pursues. It's based around a series of pavilions in Castello, in the east of the city, each designed and maintained by an exhibiting country and only open during the festival.
◉ In odd-numbered years

JULY

IL REDENTORE
www.comune.venezia.it/turismo/feste
A two-day festival celebrating Venice's deliverance from the plague of 1576, in honour of which the church of the Redentore was built on the Giudecca. A pontoon bridge spans the Giudecca canal so people can cross to the church, and there's a huge

party on the Saturday evening with a spectacular firework display.
◉ 3rd weekend of July

AUGUST

VENICE INTERNATIONAL FILM FESTIVAL
Lungomare Marconi, 30126 Lido di Venezia
Tel 041 272 6501
www.labiennale.org
A stylish film festival that attracts both big-budget movies and uncommercial art-house films. Held on the Lido, where the big stars occupy the ornate fin-de-siècle hotels, there's plenty of razzmatazz. The Palazzo del Cinema is the venue for the main-screen auditorium, but tickets get snapped up for the premières. During the festival the Arena Estiva di Campo San Polo becomes an open-air cinema.
◉ 1 week, late August
◉ €8 before 6pm, €25 for premières
◉ Casino 61 and San Silvestro

SEPTEMBER

REGATA STORICA
www.comune.venezia.it/turismo/feste
Venice's biggest water festival, which kicks off with a superb costumed procession in ornate boats down the Canal Grande. This is followed by big-money rowing races.
◉ 1st Sunday in September

NOVEMBER

FESTA DELLA SALUTE
www.comune.venezia.it/turismo/feste
A truly Venetian festival that commemorates the deliverance of the city from the plague of 1631, which triggered the construction of the great church of the Santa Maria della Salute. A pontoon bridge crosses the Grand Canal opposite the church, and people cross to light candles and attend mass.
◉ 21 November

THE NORTHEAST AND EMILIA-ROMAGNA

Busy, prosperous northeast Italy has lots going for it—great shopping, beautiful scenery from mountains to beaches, and historic towns that have glided seamlessly into the 21st century. Visitors on the cultural trail will find plenty to take their minds off art and history in the rich provincial cities of Bologna, Parma, Verona and Padua, where quality stores jostle for space. Designer wear, stylish home goods, antiques and jewellery are the focus, but the best finds, particularly in Emilia-Romagna, will indubitably involve excellent wine and food from some of Italy's best, and most famous, delicatessens. Up in the mountains, shopping has a distinctly Austrian feel, as do the cultural offerings throughout the autonomous Trentino-Alto Adige. The whole region is summer-festival land, where you can hear opera in a Roman arena, folk music at local celebrations or dance the night away at some of Italy's biggest and brashest clubs. Work it all off by day in the Dolomites, where you can enjoy the crisp air and some of Italy's finest scenery, or head for the coast and bask on the beach.

KEY TO SYMBOLS
- 🏬 Shopping
- 🎭 Entertainment
- 🍷 Nightlife
- ⚽ Sports
- ✪ Activities
- ♡ Health and Beauty
- ✪ For Children

BOLOGNA

🏬 TAMBURINI
Via Caprarie 1, 40124 Bologna
Tel 051 234726
www.tamburini.com
This is the finest delicatessen in what is considered the gastronomic capital of Italy. The large display of local produce includes fresh pasta (such as black pasta coloured with squid ink and tortelloni stuffed with pumpkin), cheeses, hams and salamis.

Make sure you sample the gourmet ingredients at the self-service café (open 12–2.30).
🕐 Mon–Wed, Fri–Sat 8–7, Thu 8–2

🎭 CANTINA BENTIVOGLIO
Via Mascarella 4b, 40126 Bologna
Tel 051 265416
www.cantinabentivoglio.it
Large, elegant bar (pictured above) in the university district. One of the top jazz venues in town, with music every night from 10. Good, cheap food. Music outdoors in July and August.
🕐 Daily 8pm–2am 🎫 €4

🎭 NOSADELLA
Via Nosadella 19/21, 40123 Bologna
Tel 051 331506
www.nosadella.it
A two-screen cinema about 10 minutes' walk southwest of the city's hub. It shows films in English on Mondays and in other languages on other days.
🕐 Four screenings daily, 4pm–midnight 🎫 Adult €7, child €4.50

🎭 TEATRO COMMUNALE
Largo Respighi 1, 40126 Bologna
Tel 051 529999
www.comunalebologna.it
Wagner preferred to premiere his operas here in Bologna's leading venue, an auditorium in the heart of the university district that first opened its doors in 1763.
🕐 Sep–end Jun 🎫 €30–€100

CLAURICAUNE
Via Zamboni 18, 40126 Bologna
Tel 051 263419
An Irish-themed bar on the edge of the university district, near the two towers. It is regularly packed to bursting with students and young townspeople.
Mon–Fri 12–2am, Sat 2pm–2am

ROSAROSE
Via Clavature 20, 40125 Bologna
Tel 051 225071
Lively, friendly bistro in the old market district in the heart of town. It serves drinks and good sandwiches—or you can graze on the food at the bar.
Wed–Mon 6–2

PADOVA (PADUA)

PRATO DELLA VALLE MARKET
Prato della Valle, 35137 Padova
Every Saturday the Prato della Valle—claimed to be the largest town square in Italy, and a marketplace since the 11th century—is turned into an open-air market selling clothes, kitchenware, shoes, woven baskets and more. An antique fair takes place on the third Sunday of the month.
Sat dawn–dusk

ROBERTO CALLEGARI
Via Davila 8, 35137 Padova
Tel 049 876 3131
Padua's top jewellery shop—in a town with a large number of jewellers—is less than 10 minutes' walk north of the middle of town. It sells watches, jewellery and antique silver.
Tue–Sat 9.30–12.30, 3.30–7.30

AUDITORIUM POLLINI
Via C. Cassan 15, 35121 Padova
Tel 049 875 6763
www.amicimusicapadova.org
One of the main concert venues in Padua, hosting performances by, among others, the Orchestra di Padova e del Veneto. It has capacity for 600 people.
Oct–end Mar €10–€22

VERONA

L'ENOTECA DELL'ISTITUTO ENOLOGICO ITALIANO
Via Sottoriva 7, 37100 Verona
Tel 045 590366
www.enotecaverona.com
Near the river on the east side of the old town, these old wine cellars lie beneath a 17th-century palace. Visitors have been tasting and buying top wines here for more than 40 years. There is an excellent selection, and afternoon wine-tasting sessions take place daily, with a different wine to sample every week. Pasta and jams on sale too.
Tue–Sat 9–12.30, 3.30–7.30, Mon 9–12.30

Verona's Arena is excellent for young gladiators

SALUMERIA G. ALBERTINI
Corso Sant'Anastasia 41, 37121 Verona
Tel 045 803 1074
This central shop is ideal for buying picnic food to take to the opera in the Arena. Sample the local prosciutto, wines and cheeses, or dive into the big barrel of olives.
Daily 8–8

STIMMATE
Via Montanari 1, 37121 Verona
Tel 045 800 4843
The only cinema in the city showing English-language films. Within walking distance of the piazza and the Arena.
English-language films Tue only
€5.20

ARENA
Piazza Brà, 37121 Verona
Tel 045 800 3204
This is one of the best-preserved Roman amphitheatres in Italy. When concerts are not taking place, kids can discover what it was like to be a gladiator in this ancient playground, running around the high-vaulted corridors and through the arches into the arena.
Sep–end Jun Mon 3.45–7.30, Tue–Sun 8.30–7; Jul, Aug Tue–Sun 9–3
Adult €4, child €1

GIARDINO GIUSTI
Via Giardino Giusti 2, 37129 Verona
Tel 045 803 4029
A magnificent garden, across the river from the heart of town. Get lost in the hedge maze or climb up to the grotto below a fearsome stone face and enjoy the view across the city.
Apr–end Sep daily 9–8; Oct–end Mar daily 9–dusk €5

FESTIVALS AND EVENTS

FEBRUARY

CARNEVALE
www.comune.cento.fe.it/carnevale
One of Italy's oldest carnivals (1615), twinned with Rio de Janeiro's extravaganza. More than 500 floats throw out 15,000kg (33,000lb) of sweets into the crowd lining the streets of Cento.
Shrove Tuesday

JUNE–AUGUST

INTERNATIONAL OPERA FESTIVAL
Piazza Brà, 37121 Verona
Tel 045 800 5151
www.arena.it
Opera in the Roman arena. There is a great choice of operas, which are very popular, so reserve well in advance—and take a cushion.
€16–€154

WHAT TO DO

FLORENCE

After cultural overdose in Florence, a bit of retail therapy is high on the agenda, and you'll find something to suit all tastes. Shopping is taken seriously in Tuscany's restrained capital—nothing flashy, just style, elegance and discreet ostentation. Designer labels are prevalent, but there are home-grown temptations too—look out for beautiful paper goods, leather of all sorts, funky street fashion and jewellery. Souvenir shoppers do well here, with beautiful art reproductions, calendars and cook books; museums are good trawling grounds for these, and you shouldn't neglect kitchen and homeware stores or the city markets either.

Spent out, you'll find year-round entertainment, from winter opera to summer-time classical music, when outdoor concerts are performed all over the city as part of Florence's famous Maggio Musicale festival. To keep you busy in the evening, there are contemporary clubs and laid-back bars, with everything from a pint of Guinness to the latest house music or sounds from Brazil, plus the occasional big-name acts. If you want some exercise, you can work out, swim, boat on the Arno or play tennis, or simply head for the Stadio Artemio Franchi and join the fans watching Florentia Viola, Florence's football heroes.

KEY TO SYMBOLS

- 🏬 **Shopping**
- 🎭 **Entertainment**
- 🎵 **Nightlife**
- 🏅 **Sports**
- ✪ **Activities**
- ♡ **Health and Beauty**
- ✿ **For Children**

🏬 SHOPPING

BOOKS

EDISON
Piazza della Repubblica 27r,
50123 Firenze
Tel 055 213110
Edison sells guides and books in English, but also maps, CDs, magazines and newspapers. The internet café is a good

place to sit, surf and watch the world news on huge screens.
🎭 Mon–Sat 9–midnight, Sun 10–midnight A, 6

FASHION AND LINGERIE

ZINI
Borgo San Lorenzo, 50123 Firenze
Tel 055 289850
Stocks Italy's most up-and-coming designers—and the future is looking bright and captivating. The tailoring and cut of the clothes are impressive, but the originality comes in the interesting and innovative use of prints and fabrics.
🚃 A

JEWELLERY

ARGENTERIA BRANDIMARTE
Via Lorenzo Bartolini 18r, 50124 Firenze
Tel 055 239381
www.brandimarte.it
The dedicated apprentices of the late Brandimarte Guscelli continue his unusual designs in silver, and you can see them at work here in the silver factory. Plates and goblets are decorated in relief with fruits, vines and leaves.
🎭 Mon–Fri 9–1, 2.30–6; closed Aug
🚃 D

FRATELLI PICCINI
Ponte Vecchio 23, 50125 Firenze
Tel 055 294768
www.fratellipiccini.com
If you want to go jewellery-shopping on the Ponte Vecchio, make sure you take in Piccini's. Their lovely gold charms make a nice gift.
🕐 Apr–end Oct daily 9.30–7.30; Nov–end Mar daily 9.30–1, 3.30–1
🚌 B, D

MARKETS
FLORENTINE MARKETS
Piazza San Lorenzo, Piazza Santo Spirito, Piazza dei Ciompi and Via dell'Ariento, Piazza Lorenzo Ghiberti, Piazza della Repubblica, Via Porta Rossa, Piazza del Mercato Centrale
Tel 055 234 0444 (tourist office)
Florence has a huge number of markets selling everything from food to antiques. There are also some superb flea markets. The most famous is in and around Piazza San Lorenzo, where you'll find leather and other assorted goods. There are stands daily at Santo Spirito, selling bedding, shoes, clothing and haberdashery. On the second Sunday of the month there is an ethnic flea market, and on the third Sunday there are organic foods, Tuscan clothing and herbal remedies on sale. On the last Sunday of each month there's an antiques market in Piazza dei Ciompi (9–7). Head towards Via dell'Ariento and the Mercatone delle Cascine (Tue 7–2) for a morning of browsing and bartering. Even though you can't take plants back home, a walk around the plant market on Thursday mornings around the Piazza della Repubblica is a memorable experience. Mercato Nuovo (Porcellino) on Via Porta Rossa (daily 9–7) is full of inexpensive reproductions of Florentine classics, which makes it a great place for souvenir-hunters. The leather bags and shoes are often a good buy, too. The Mercato Centrale is full of mouth-watering Florentine

delights—feast your eyes on the wonderful fruit and vegetable stands, and the *salumeria* counters brimming with meats and cheeses.
🕐 Mon–Sat 8.30–7, 8.30–2 in winter

MASKS
ALICE'S MASKS
Via Faenza 72, 50123 Firenze
Tel 055 287 370
www.alicemasks.com
Masks in exquisite detail and infinite numbers fill every corner of this shop/studio. Not only can you buy masks here, you can join in a workshop to learn the art of *papier mâché* mask-making.
🕐 Mon–Sat 9–1, 3.30–7.30

Don't miss Florence's famous markets

SHOES AND ACCESSORIES
CELLERINI
Via del Sole 37r, 50123 Firenze
Tel 055 282533
Drop in to view bags and purses that are wonderfully simple yet cleverly designed. Cellerini bags are *de rigueur* among fashionistas and will elicit envious glances once you get back home.
🚌 A, 6, 11, 36, 37

SCUOLA DEL CUOIO (LEATHER SCHOOL)
Piazza Santa Croce 16, 50122 Firenze
Tel 055 244533
www.leatherschool.it
This workshop, at the back of the famous church, was

once run by Franciscan monks. If you intend to shop for leather goods, come here first to learn how to spot quality and craftsmanship. If you make a purchase at the on-site shop, they'll personalize the goods for you with a stamp.
🕐 Mar–end Nov Mon–Sat 9.30–6, Sun 10–5 🚌 B, C, 23

STATIONERY
PINEIDER
Piazza della Signoria 13r, 50122 Firenze
Tel 055 284655
www.pineider.it
Pineider remains Italy's original and most prestigious stationer—the letters of Napoleon, Byron and Dietrich were scribed using Pineider's beautifully crafted tinted papers and inks. It also stocks exquisite leather-bound notebooks and accessories including seals.
🕐 Tue–Sat 10–7, Mon 3–7 🚌 23

🎵 ENTERTAINMENT
CINEMA
CINEMA GOLDONI
Via Serragli 109, 50124 Firenze
Tel 055 222437
The Goldoni is one of only three Florentine cinemas to show films in their original language.
🕐 Contact for latest details 💶 Adult €7, child €4.50 🚌 36, 37

CLASSICAL MUSIC, DANCE AND OPERA
ESTATE FIESOLANA (OPEN-AIR SUMMER CONCERTS IN FIESOLE)
Piazza del Mercato 5, Fiesole, 50014 Firenze
Tel 800 414240
www.estatefiesolana.com
Sunset concerts and operatic productions are held at the first-century Teatro Romano during the summer months. Reserve in advance and then head for the verdant, tranquil Fiesole hills, above the city. Tickets also available at Via Alamanni 39 (tel 055 210804).
🕐 Jun–end Sep 💶 €52 🚌 7
Fiesole central

TEATRO COMMUNALE
Corso Italia 16, 50123 Firenze
Tel 055 211158
Tel 199 109910
www.maggiofiorentino.com
Florence's major venue for all things orchestral, balletic and operatic. The winter concert season runs from January to end March, while opera and ballet is staged between September and end March. Expect old favourites like *Macbeth* and *Coppelia* as well as seminal composers' work from Bach to Wagner.
€10–€100 A, B

TEATRO GOLDONI
Via Santa Maria 12, 50125 Firenze
Tel 055 233 5518
Tel 199 109910
www.maggiofiorentino.com
This famous old theatre has a capacity for 1,500. It stages opera and ballet productions such as *Carmen* and *Barbablù*, as well as various classical concerts.
€15–€20 11, 36, 37

CONTEMPORARY LIVE MUSIC

PINOCCHIO LIVE JAZZ
Viale Giannotti 13, 50126 Firenze
Tel 055 683388
www.pinocchiojazz.it
Jazz musos will love this place as it attracts some of Italy's top artists, who can be heard during the club's annual two-season schedule. Members nod approvingly in this smoky venue while the musicians blow, brush and noodle their instruments into the night.
Membership fee plus €8 31, 32

SASCHALL
Lungarno Aldo Moro 3, 50136 Firenze
Tel 055 650 4112
www.saschall.it
Florence's leading music venue hosts big-name rock/pop acts and famous musicals. Expect to see international artists like Tori Amos and Italian stars such as Luca Carboni and PFM.
€27, €19 3, 14, 31, 32, 34

THEATRE

TEATRO PERGOLA
Via della Pergola 12–32, 50121 Firenze
Tel 055 226 4335
www.pergola.firenze.it
Well-known theatre productions are regularly held in the sumptuous main Sala and the elegant Saloncino. In addition to staging Italian classics by the likes of d'Annunzio and De Filippo, many English- and French-language playwrights, including Wilde, Berkoff, Hugo and Feydeau, are also showcased.
Theatre productions Wed–Sat, concerts Sat afternoons, Sun evenings
€14.50–€29 C, 14, 23

The Teatro Communale is one of Florence's main venues

NIGHTLIFE

BARS AND CAFÉS

FIDDLER'S ELBOW
Piazza Santa Maria Novella 7a, 50123 Firenze
Tel 055 215056
www.thefiddlerselbow.com
The original Florentine Irish pub in Campo Santa Maria Novella, popular with students and tourists. Enjoy a Guinness and catch up on the latest premiership football action on the wide-screen TVs.
Daily 11am–2am A, 1, 14, 17, 36, 37

LIDO
Lungarno Pecori Piraldi 1, 50122 Firenze
Tel 055 234 2726
This swanky gay-friendly bar along the River Arno has the feel of a colonial ship—you can even rent boats from here. Cocktails and innovative snacks are consumed to a sophisticated soundtrack of lounge, drum and bass and nu-jazz beats.
Tue–Sun 6pm–2am 8

CLUBS

CENTRAL PARK
Via del Fosso Macinate, 2, 50144 Firenze
Tel 055 353505
This is a true house music complex, complete with garden, eight bars, four dance floors, restaurant and a VIP terrace. Italian house dominates but there's also plenty of room for chilling out with loungecore and smooth piano-bar music.
Tue–Sun 10.30–4.30 €16 1, 9, 12, 80

CRISCO
Via Sant'Egidio 43r, 50122 Firenze
Tel 055 248 0580
www.crisco.it
One of Florence's leading gay clubs, near the Duomo in Santa Croce. In a city famed for its cross-dressing, expect to see the most glamorous of transvestites here.
Sun–Mon, Wed–Thu 10.30pm–3am, Fri–Sat 10.30pm–6am €12
A, 14, 23

JARAGUA
Via Erta Canina 12/r, 50125 Firenze
Tel 055 234 3600
www.jaragua.it
Italy's first exclusively Latino music club is bags of fun and free to get into. The spicy South American food also appeals to the 30-something crowd. For those who don't know how to dance salsa or merengue, there are lessons available as well as many willing tutors on the dance floor.
Daily 9.30pm–3am C, D

WHAT TO DO

MARACANA

Via Faenza 4, 50123 Firenze
Tel 055 210298
www.maracana.it
Six levels, a carnival stage and a party crowd make this club a winner with lovers of all things Brazilian. It's the place to watch carnival dancers, samba, sip *caipirinhas* (a cocktail made with lime juice and cachaça, Brazilian sugar cane liquor) and try some of the enormous *churrasco* (Brazilian barbequed meats). The bar staff juggle bottles while some of the crowd attempt dance-floor soccer acrobatics.
Tue–Sun 8pm–4am €12; free entry for women Tue, Thu and Sun
31, 32

TENAX

Via Pratese 46, 50127 Firenze
Tel 055 308160
www.tenax.org
Florence's premier house-music club, attracting big international names like Dimitri from Paris, Thievery Corporation, Grace Jones and Groove Armada. It has mind-blowing lighting and sound technology, as well as some very curious art installations. Also hosts live music acts.
Daily 11pm–4am €15
5, 29, 30, 56

YAB

Via Sassetti 5, 50122 Firenze
Tel 055 215160
www.yab.it
Theatrical décor and renowned DJs make this one of Florence's hippest clubs. House music dominates the schedule, with hard house on Fridays and happy house on Saturdays. Monday's Smoove Night sees electric boogaloo acrobatics on the dance floor and hip-hop tunes aplenty.
Mon–Tue, Thu–Sat 11pm–4am
€14 A, 1, 6, 14

SPORTS AND ACTIVITIES

BICYCLING

FLORENCE BY BIKE

Via San Zanobi 120, Firenze
Tel 055 488992
www.florencebybike.it
Florence by Bike has a good selection of bicycles and scooters to choose from should you wish to whizz around town or explore the countryside. Prices start at €2.70 an hour for a classic model, or €19 for a day's use of a standard mountain bicycle. Reserve a place on the daily 32km (20-mile) bicycle tour in advance.
Mon–Sat 9–1, 3.30–7.30 €2.70 per hour 20, 25, 31, 32, 33

Head to the Ippodromo della Mulina for horse racing

CANOEING

CANOTTIERI COMUNALI FIRENZE

Lungarno Ferrucci 4, 50126 Firenze
Tel 055 681 2151
www.canottiericomunalifirenze.it
Try your hand at kayaking at this club on the River Arno, where there are a number of courses available for all ages. There's also the chance to try dragon boating, Polynesian canoeing or even a game of canoe polo.
Mon–Sat 8.30–9, Sun 8.30–1
€95 joining fee (free for women)
8, 31, 32

FOOTBALL

FIORENTINA VIOLA

Sport - Santo Marte
Viale Manfredo Fanti 14, 50137 Firenze
Tel 055 262 5537
www.fiorentina.it
Watch the reborn Viola—complete with new name and owners—at the open-bowl, 47,000-capacity Stadio Communale Artemio Franchi. Expect fervent support for the club (formerly known as Fiorentina) who are still fighting back after bankruptcy and demotion in 2002.
Sep–end May alternate Sun €5
3, 10, 11, 17, 20, 34

HORSE RACING

LE CASCINE

Ippodromo della Mulina, Viale dell'Aeronautica/Viale del Pegaso 1, 50144 Firenze
Tel 055 411107
The Ippodromo della Mulina is the place to go for horse racing in Florence. If you fancy a flutter on a *galoppo* (flat race) or *trotto* (trotting race), many *tabbachi* (tobacco shops) have easy-to-use betting facilities.
Phone or check local press for upcoming meetings €15 17c

HOT-AIR BALLOONING

BALLOONING IN TUSCANY

Podere La Fratta, 53020 Montisi
Tel 0577 845211
www.ballooningintuscany.com
If you are feeling flush and have three companions, you can book a balloon ride over Tuscany. This small company, run by an English couple, organizes personalized balloon trips with a champagne breakfast. It is an hour's drive south of Florence, but the views are worth it.
Contact for details €200 (minimum 4 adults) A1 towards Siena, Montisi exit

ICE SKATING

PIAZZA SANTA CROCE

50122/ Fortezza da Basso, 50129 Firenze
Tel 055 2340444/226 4524 (tourist information)

In December and January each year, a temporary ice rink is constructed in Piazza Santa Croce or in the Fortezza da Basso. Glide around or just hold on to the edge and admire the surrounding architecture—either the magnificent Palazzi Cocchi-Serristori and dell'Antella or the imposing military structure.

C, 23/ 12, 14, 23, 28, 33, 80

MOTOR RACING

AUTODROMO DEL MUGELLO

Mugello
Tel 055 849 9111
www.mugellocircuit.it

Regular motor-sport events are held at this circuit owned by Ferrari. The biggest motorcycle races, including the Italian Grand Prix for 125cc and 250cc motorcycles, as well as the Superbike World Championship, draw large crowds, who fill the banks alongside the track.

€5–€25 including parking
Take the 302 Faentina road, passing Scarperia for Mugello or the A1 (Bologna–Firenze) motorway and exit at Barberino di Mugello

TENNIS

CIRCOLO DEL TENNIS

Viale del Visarno 1 (entrance on Viale degli Olmi), 50144 Firenze
Tel 055 332651/2
www.ctfirenze.org

Florence's oldest tennis club (1898) has excellent facilities including 10 clay courts, swimming pool, football pitches, gym, sauna, restaurant/bar and even a bridge room. Check the press for the latest details of upcoming tournaments and events.

Daily 10–10 1, 9, 12, 16, 26, 27, 80

VENUES

PALASPORT

Palazzetto dello Sport, Viale Pasquale Paoli 3, 50137 Firenze
Tel 055 678841

Various sports events are staged at this sports arena near the home of football club Fiorentina Viola. Check the local press for upcoming roller- and figure-skating, skateboarding, archery, water polo, volleyball and six-a-side football tournaments.

17

FESTIVALS AND EVENTS

MARCH/APRIL

SCOPPIO DEL CARRO

Florence's Scoppio del Carro (Explosion of the Cart) dates back to the 11th century when a carousel of fireworks was lit to spread the good news of Easter. Today, a ceremonial cart, stuffed with fireworks, arrives in the Piazza del Duomo, and a wire is run to the statue of the Virgin on top of the Duomo and into the cathedral itself. At about 11pm, the wire is lit and a mechanical dove slides down to the cart, causing a huge explosion and igniting all the fireworks.

Easter Sunday

MAY/JUNE

MAGGIO MUSICALE FIORENTINO

Biglietteria Teatro Communale, Via Solferino 15, 50123 Firenze
Tel 055 211 1158
Tel 199 109910
www.maggiofiorentino.it

Florence's major music festival, held in indoor and outdoor venues across the city. Founded in 1933, it's Italy's longest-running music festival, with a good mix of opera, ballet and classical music.

GB, D, 1, 9, 13

HEALTH AND BEAUTY

OFFICINA PROFUMO FARMACEUTICA DI SANTA MARIA NOVELLA

Via della Scala 16, 50123 Firenze
Tel 055 21 62 76
www.smnovella.com

One of the world's oldest pharmacies, this atmospheric apothecary is operated by Dominican friars, in a 14th-century chapel. Herbal compounds, from soothing eucalyptus cough drops to calendula hand creams, are sold in a fragrant environment.

Mon–Fri 9.30–7.30, Sun 10.30–6.30
A, 11, 36, 37

JUNE

GIOCO DI CALCIO

Ufficio Valorizzazione Tradizioni Popolari Fiorentine, Piazzetta di Parte Guelfa 1r, 50123 Firenze
Tel 055 261 6050/1/6
www.globeit.it/caf/storia.html

A no-holds-barred version of football that is played between the four city quarters, originally used to keep the city militia in fighting form and to weld the various factions into a united force. The final day is celebrated with a costumed procession and a flotilla of candle-lit boats and fireworks on the River Arno.

Sundays in June
€10–€25 C, 23

OCTOBER

MUSICA DEI POPOLI FESTIVAL

Via Maestri del Lavoro 24b, 50134 Firenze
Tel 055 422 0300
www.flog.it/mus_pope.htm

In October each year, artists from around the globe descend on Florence for this international folk music festival. Italy's finest world music event has been running for more than 25 years and attracts a friendly crowd to its main venue, the Auditorium Flog.

4, 8, 14

WHAT TO DO

TUSCANY AND UMBRIA

Tuscany and Umbria, central Italy's main tourist areas, have great shopping, traditional festivals and a plethora of sports. There's something to buy, or see, or do virtually 24 hours a day. Throughout the region, you'll find all the usual Italian specials—leather, fashion, jewellery, lingerie—along with some great local products. Look out for antique stores, wonderful ceramics and pottery and superb food. Wine and olive oil are sold direct from the growers, some of whom give vineyard and cellar tours and tastings.

If you're looking for entertainment, there is a huge variety of traditional *festas*. Siena's *Palio* tops the bill, but Arezzo, Pisa and Gubbio have their own unique celebrations, while towns like Lucca and Barga host cool summer music festivals. There are theme parks and zoos for the kids, or spend a family day horseback riding through the rolling hills, canoeing down Umbria's rivers, or watching the hang-gliders in the Sibillini mountains. Evening events range from classical concerts to club music, and there are plenty of cinemas showing original-language movies—some under the stars in summer.

KEY TO SYMBOLS

- Shopping
- Entertainment
- Nightlife
- Sports
- Activities
- Health and Beauty
- For Children

AREZZO

EMPORIO ARMANI
Corso Italia 306, 52100 Arezzo
Tel 0575 355262
www.emporioarmani.it
A branch of Emporio Armani offering 30 per cent discount off regular prices. Some of the fashion items are discounted by up to 70 per cent during the sales. Whatever time of year, you should find a bargain.
Apr–end Sep Mon 4–8, Tue–Sun 9–1, 4–8; Oct–end Mar Mon 9–1, Tue–Sun 9–1, 3.30–7.30; Jul, Aug Mon 9–1, Tue–Fri and Sun 9–1, 3.30–7.30, Sat 9–1

FIERA ANTIQUARIA
Piazza San Francesco, 52100 Arezzo
This leading antiques fair floods Piazza San Francesco, Piazza Grande and the Logge Vasari. Filled with more than 600 dealers, and with some items dating back to the Renaissance, the fair lures both serious collectors and browsing visitors.
1st Sun of the month Apr–end Sep 7.30–7; rest of year 7.30–3

PRADA FACTORY OUTLET
Località Levanella SS 69,
52025 Montevarchi
Tel 055 919 6528

Montevarchi, near Arezzo, is home to the Prada factory and its bargain outlet. You can get Prada bags, lingerie and shoes at up to 80 per cent discount. When you arrive, pull a ticket from the machine and wait your turn to enter. It also stocks Miu Miu, Helmut Lang and Jil Sander.
Mon–Sat 9.30–7.30, Sun 2–7.30
From Firenze to Montevarchi (about 1 hour), then taxi Take the A1. Turn off at Valdarno intersection and follow the signs

GRACE
Via Madonna del Prato 125, 52100 Arezzo
Tel 0575 403669
www.grace.it
This trendy club, discotheque and sushi restaurant, run by

three friends, verges on kitsch with its art deco seating and 1970s lighting.
🕐 Fri, Sat 12.30am–5am 💶 €16

✪ LFI LIGHT-GAUGE RAILWAY
Arezzo Train Station, Piazza della Repubblica 1/A, 52100 Arezzo
Tel 0575 39881
www.trenitalia.com
The LFI (La Ferrovia Italiana) railway linking Arezzo with Stia, Bibbiena and Sinalunga is a rolling train museum. Its antique fleet of electric locomotives and steam engines takes you through the surrounding countryside, past wonderful views. Reserve a seat on the steam train.

ASSISI

🏬 ENOTECA LOMBARDI
11 Via Borgo Aretino, 06081 Assisi
Tel 075 816697
A food store and *enoteca* (wine shop) selling more than 50 types of wine, priced €10 to €80. Truffle paste, roast peppers, artichoke pâté and dried porcini mushrooms also sold.
🕐 Daily 9–7 🚌 Linea C every half hour from Assisi's rail station to Piazza Unità d'Italia (3km/2 miles)

🎭 LYRICK THEATRE
Via Gabriele d'Annunzio, 06088 Assisi
Tel 075 812534 (tourist office)
A large theatre within walking distance of the rail station. Productions of anything from *Grease* to dance festivals take place here, but few are in English.
🕐 All year 💶 Contact for details

BEVAGNA

🏬 AZIENDA AGRARIA E FRANTOIO RONCI
Voc Sasso 14/A, 06031 Bevagna
Tel 0742 360 501
www.olioronci.it
Umbria's olive oils are internationally famous, and the Ronci family ranks among the best producers of high-quality, cold-pressed, extra-virgin, organically produced oils.

🕐 Mon–Fri 10–6, Sat 10–1; shout if no-one around
🚌 3km (2 miles) west of Bevagna on Gualdo Cattaneo road; follow yellow signs

COLLE VAL D'ELSA

🏬 TERRECOTTE TESI
Località Pian dell'Olmino, 53034 Colle Val d'Elsa
Tel 0577 928 130
Everything from giant terracotta garden urns to hand-painted plates produced at this small ceramics factory near Colle. Prices, compared with town-centre outlets, are excellent, and there are usually marked-down 'seconds' whose flaws are impossible to spot.

Traditionally made ceramics at Ceramisti d'Arte, Lucca

Shipment can be arranged for large orders.
🕐 Mon–Fri 9–6, Sat 12–4
🚌 3km (2 miles) south of Colle Val d'Elsa on the SS541

COLLODI

✪ PARCO DI PINOCCHIO
Via San Gennaro 3, 51014 Collodi
Tel 0572 429342
www.pinocchio.it
The Pinocchio Park brings the story of the famous wooden puppet alive with mosaics, statues and fountains incorporating all the story's characters. Watch the entertaining puppet shows or find amusement in the maze, playground or

exhibition centre. Children's restaurant.
🕐 Daily 8.30–dusk 💶 Adult €9, under 16s €7, under 3s free 🚌 From Lucca to Collodi 🚌 15km (9 miles) from Lucca on the SS 435

LUCCA

🏬 CERAMISTI D'ARTE
Via Mordini 74–78, 56100 Lucca
Tel 0583 492700
Tuscan artists Stefano Seardo and Fabrizio Falchi sculpt and paint at this workshop. Pick up hand-painted decorative tiles, terracotta sculptures and marble mosaics made from the prized Massa Carrara marble. Everything is produced using traditional techniques. Browsers are welcome.
🕐 Mon–Sat 9.30–1, 3.30–8

🏬 LUCCA BOOK FAIR
Off Via Beccheria, 56100 Lucca
Just behind the Chiesa di San Giusto and running towards Piazza Napoleone and Piazza San Michele, Lucca's old bookstalls sell anything and everything that is printed. Shoppers will find old prints of Lucca and other Italian cities, modern postcards and comic books in various languages.
🕐 Daily 10–6

🎭 NICOLAS
Viale S. Concordio 887, 55100 Lucca
Tel 0583 582378
Known for its live music concerts, Nicolas gives local musicians the chance to perform everything from jazz and blues to pop and reggae, as well as the odd traditional Italian song.
🕐 Tue–Sun 8pm–2am 💶 Free

🍸 THE GOLDEN FOX
Viale Regina Margherita 207, 55100 Lucca
Tel 0583 491619
www.thegoldenfox.it
The Golden Fox prides itself on being a real English pub, even to the point of importing all its furnishings from England. English, Scottish and Irish draught beers are on tap.
🕐 Tue–Sun 8pm–1am

🌀 MOPLEN
Via San Leonardo 19, 55100 Lucca
Tel 0339 645 6012
Aperitifs start at 7pm in Lucca's premier gay/lesbian-friendly lounge bar. The clientele is young and mixed. The music is also varied—resident DJs play everything from 1960s tracks to drum and bass tunes.
🕐 Wed–Mon 7pm–1am

MARINA DI PIETRASANTA
✪ TRENINO DELLE VACANZE
Fratelli Verona
Tel 0584 745737
With fantastic views of the Versilia coast, this *trenino delle vacanze* (little holiday train) runs from the middle of town along the coast of Marina di Pietrasanta during the summer season. The hour-long journey takes in several towns.
🕐 Jun–end Sep daily 5.30pm and 9pm
💶 Adult €5, child €3 🚆 Pietrasanta or Viareggio 🚗 Versilia exit off the A12

NORCIA
⊕ BRANCALEONE DA NORCIA
Corso Sertorio 17, 06046 Norcia
Tel 0743 828311
The town is famous for its black truffles and wild boar, hence the abundance of stores selling these delicacies. Brancaleone excels in *salse al tartufo* (truffle pastes) and loose truffles for sale. Local *pecorino di Norcia* (hard cheese) and Umbrian ricotta sit waiting to be popped into heavenly sandwiches.
🕐 Daily 8–8

⊕ GEOSTA
Via Foscolo 10, 06046 Norcia
Tel 0743 828 470
www.geosta.net
Hikers and outdoor enthusiasts exploring the Monti Sibillini will find everything they need in this specialist shop. There's a good selection of walking and climbing equipment, boots and clothing, an excellent range of local and other maps, guidebooks and picture books devoted to the great outdoors in both English and Italian, as

well as postcards and stationery.
🕐 Apr–end Sep Mon–Sat 10–7; Oct–end Mar Mon–Sat 10–1, 4–6
🏠 Inside city walls, down side street off right of main *corso*

✪ RAFTING UMBRIA
Serravalle di Norcia, 06040 Norcia
Tel 348 351 1798
www.rafting-umbria.it
Rafting Umbria offers 2-hour rafting expeditions on 7km (4 miles) of the River Corno, with all equipment provided and expert guides (pictured on page 252). The trip runs through gentle stretches interspersed with exciting, but safe, white-water rapids, and

Brancaleone da Norcia sells the town's celebrated wild boar

there are stops for swimming. The company can also arrange hang-gliding, paragliding, caving, climbing and high-altitude trekking, and many of the guides speak good English.
🕐 Mar–end Oct daily. Telephone to reserve
🚗 On SS396 6 km (4 miles) west of Norcia

✪ BALLA COI MULLI
Castelluccio di Norcia, 06040 Norcia
Tel 347 406 5269/320 172 3752
www.lamulattiera.it
Children and adults can enjoy the tranquillity and scenic grandeur of the Monti Sibillini from the back of a friendly donkey by joining one of the

treks organized by a local team based in the Parco Nazionale dei Monti Sibillini. Routes vary from a gentle morning's ramble across the Piano Grande to whole-day treks high into the mountains.
🕐 Apr–end Sep daily, but can arrange trips outside these months. Contact by phone or at info@lamulattiera.it for further information
🏠 Treks usually start from Castelluccio, on the Piano Grande east of Norcia

PERUGIA
⊕ PINKO UNDERGROUND
Via Oberdan 17, 06121 Perugia
Tel 075 572 3174
The sexy Italian label Pinko vies for space with the more practical US brand Converse at this offbeat women's fashion shop. The staff model some of the more bizarre items like plastic shirts. Men's shop at Via Baglioni 52.
🕐 Mon 4–8, Tue–Sat 9–1, 4–8 🚌 6, 7, 9, 11 to Piazza Italia

⊕ VIA OBERDAN FABRICS MARKET
Via Oberdan, 06121 Perugia
In between the stores on Via Oberdan, more than 20 stands sell a wide range of fabrics. Scarves, throws and ornamental pieces, in all shades, fabrics and sizes. Crystals and fairly cheap jewellery are also sold, as well as bags, incense and rugs.
🕐 Mon–Sat 4–8 🚌 6, 7, 9, 11 to Piazza Italia

🎵 AMICI DELLA MUSICA DI PERUGIA
Palazzo dei Priori, 06123 Perugia
Tel 075 572 2271
www.amicimusicapg.it
Weekly classical recitals at this theatre in the heart of Perugia. Violin and piano soloists as well as artists playing in small groups.
🕐 Oct–end Jun once a week
💶 €7–€26 🚌 6, 7, 9, 11 to Piazza Italia

WHAT TO DO

ST. ANDREWS
Via della Cupa 2, 06123 Perugia
Tel 075 609522
This disco has an international
clientele and a cave-like
interior.
Daily 9pm–2am €9

AC PERUGIA
Stadio Renato Curi, Pian di Massiano,
06125 Perugia
Tel 075 500 6641
www.perugiacalcio.it
Founded in 1905, Perugia's
football club has struggled in
recent years. Games are worth
watching if only to enjoy the
enthusiastic atmosphere.
Sep–end Jun Sun pm, and other
times €18–€118

GOLF PERUGIA
Località S. Sabina, Ellera Umbra,
06074 Perugia
Tel 075 517 2204
This is one of Perugia's most
beautiful, and tricky, 18-hole
golf courses.
Tue–Sun 8.30–6 €42 weekdays,
€52 weekends

NESTLÉ PERUGINA
Via Pievaiola, San Sisto, 20143 Perugia
Tel 075 527 6796 or 075 527 6635
Chocoholics can gorge
themselves at the Museo
Storico della Perugina. Antique
chocolate-making equipment
as well as packaging from the
20th century. Tours of the
factory can be reserved in
advance.
Mon–Fri 9–1, 2–5.30, Sat–Sun by
appointment. Factory tours 11–5 by
appointment Free

PIENZA

LA BOTTEGA DEL GHIOTTONE
Corso Rossellino, 53026 Pienza
Tel 0578 748 686
www.deliziavaldorciapienza.it
Pienza's food shops are
numerous, and the superb
selection here is the best in
town. Your senses will be
assaulted by the aroma of local
pecorino (sheep's cheese),
prosciutto and salami, while
the shelves are packed with

local oils, vinegars, jams and
honeys. There's also a good
range of spice mixes.
Mon–Sat 10–7, Sun 11–7
On right of main *corso* before the
Duomo

OLEIFICIO CHIANTI
Viale m Cappelli 33, 53020
Montichiello, Pienza
Tel 0578 755 075
www.oleificiochianti.it
If you're passionate about
olive oil, make a detour
from Pienza to buy direct
from the producers of some
of southern Tuscany's
smoothest cold-pressed
oils, still produced by stone-
grinding. Four varieties are

*Explore chocolate through the
ages at Nestlé Perugina*

on offer, and they also
sell locally sourced wines,
honeys, jams and dried
porcini mushrooms. Prices
are excellent and they will
make up a variety pack on
the spot.
Mon–Fri 9.30–1, 3.30–6
8km (5 miles) southeast of Pienza
off Acquapendente road

PIEVE SAN STEFANO

NAZIONALE TURISMO EQUESTRE
ANTE - Associazione Nazionale per il
Turismo Equestre e per l'Equitazione
di Campagna
Via Ponte Castel Giubileo 27/A,
00100 Roma
Tel 06 382 8060

Umbria's mountainous
environs provide some
impressive terrain for
horseback riding. The National
Equestrian Tourism bureau
can help you arrange a day's
ride with a recommended
establishment. There is also
an extensive choice of
horseback-riding schools,
stables and trails in Tuscany—
a great way to explore Mount
Amiata, Certaldo, Gambassi
Terme and the surrounding
landscape of vineyards, olive
groves and terracotta-roofed
farmhouses.
Contact individual establishments
for details Approximately €25
for half a day/€45 per day

PISA

PAUL DE BONDT
Via Turati 22, Corte San Domenico,
56125 Pisa
Tel 050 501 896
A Dutch-born pastry chef,
Paul de Bondt creates
handmade chocolates to
order with meticulous
attention to detail. De Bondt
won the Euro-chocolate
award in 1999 and the
tavoletta d'oro (the golden
bar) in 2003 for the best dark
chocolate and the best milk
chocolate bar in Italy. This
Pisa outlet has everything
from animal-shaped
chocolates filled with
almond paste to simple,
rich truffles. But the *ganascia*
chocolates, made with
fresh cream and butter,
are what de Bondt is most
famous for.
Tue–Sat 10–1, 4–8; closed Jun–end
Sep

ÀBSOLUT
Via Mossotti 10, 56100 Pisa
Tel 050 220 1262
www.absolut.gay.it
By day an internet café, by
night a laid-back gay-and-
lesbian pub with a young,
friendly atmosphere.
Entertainment is provided
by live music and cabaret.
Tue–Sun 10pm–2am

⊙ OFFSIDE
Ospedaletto, Uscita Pisa Nord Est,
Via Emilia, 56100 Pisa
Tel 340 496 4845
www.off-side.pisa.it
Themed evenings range from
Friday's gay-and-lesbian night
to live music gigs on
Wednesday and Saturday
nights and a cocktail and
dance club on Sundays.
Karaoke, the best night, is
on Thursday.
🕐 Mon–Thu 8pm–2am, Fri–Sat
8pm–4am, Sun 6pm–4am

✪ TENNIS CLUB PISA
Piazzale dello Sport 7, 56122 Pisa
Tel 050 530313
www.tennisclubpisa.it
Five outdoor clay courts
(three with lighting for night
games) and two indoor
courts can be rented at this
year-round tennis club. The
clubhouse has a bar, changing
facilities and a shop.
🕐 Daily 8am–10.30pm 🎫 €12 per
hour

POPPI

⊕ ZOO FAUNA EUROPA
52015 Poppi
Tel 0575 504541/2
www.parcozoopoppi.it
Opened in 1972 by vet Dr.
Roberto Mattoni, this zoo
preserves European species,
including deer, wolves, bears,
birds of prey, and species in
danger of extinction, such as
the Asinara donkey. There are
also a botanical garden, pony
rides and a children's play
area. Restaurant, bar, picnic
areas and free parking.
🕐 Daily 9–7 🎫 Adult €5, child (3–11)
€4.50 🚌 Regular service from Firenze
🚉 Trains to Poppi on the Arezzo–Stia
line 🚗 A 30-minute drive from Arezzo
along the SS71. Follow signs for
Bibbiena, then Parco Nazionale
Casentinese or Parco Zoo Poppi

RAPOLANO TERME

⊙ ANTICA QUERCIOLAIA THERMAL BATHS
Via Trieste 22, 53040 Rapolano Terme
Tel 0577 724091
www.termeaq.it

Antica Querciolaia has been a
spa resort since Etruscan and
Roman times. Its spring fills
the thermal baths and there is
an adjoining park with three
open-air pools. Try a mud
wrap or an inhalation
treatment. Water erupts from
the famous 'intermittent
fountain' every 10 minutes.
🕐 Oct–end Mar daily 10–6; May–end
Sep Sun–Fri 9–7, Sat 9–midnight
🎫 €52 for a 1-hour treatment.
Swimming pool €12 (child €6)
Mon–Thu, €13 Sat–Sun (child €8);
under 4s free 🚉 Rapolano Terme railway station is on the Siena–Chianciano
Terme line 🚗 Valdichiana exit on the
A1 or on the Firenze–Siena Valdichiana
SS 326

*Indulge yourself at Rapolano
Terme*

SAN GIMIGNANO

⊕ GELATERIA DI PIAZZA
Piazza della Cisterna, 53037 San
Gimignano
Tel 0577 942 244
www.gelateriadipiazza.com
Sergio Dondoli's marvellous
ice-cream emporium has
scooped just about every
award Italy has to offer and
made it into numerous
publications. You'll find all
the classic tastes on offer,
along with a changing range
of specialties that mark the
passing of the seasons;
popular options in summer
include pink grapefruit or
mango sorbet, bittersweet

cherry *amareno*, coconut
and three or four chocolate-
based ices.
🕐 Apr–end Sep daily 9.30–10pm;
Oct–end Mar daily 9.30–7
🚗 On the main square

⊕ PODERI DEL PARADISO
Località Strada 21/A, San Gimignano
53037
Tel 0577 941 500
If you're buying wine in San
Gimignano, head away from
the town's tourist outlets and
buy direct from the producers.
Paradiso wines, both *vernaccia*
(white) and full-bodied reds,
have won the coveted *Tre
Bicchiere* (Three Glasses)
award at major wine
exhibitions in Italy and abroad,
and you can see the state-of-
the-art production area
housed in a centuries-old
building. They also sell olive oil
and can arrange tasting
sessions.
🕐 Daily 10–1, 4–6
🚗 Take Certaldo road north out of
town and turn off onto side road at
Strada (2km/1.3 miles) then follow
signs

⊙ CINE ESTATE
Rocca di Montestaffoli, 53037 San
Gimignano
Tel 0577 940008
Every weekend, as well as
three nights during the week,
San Gimignano's public park is
transformed into an outdoor
cinema. Hollywood
blockbusters and European
art-house films are shown in
their original language.
🕐 Jun–end Aug 🎫 Adult €7, child €5

⊙ AVALON
Viale Roma 1, 53037 San Gimignano
Tel 0577 940023
www.avalon-pub.com
Avalon appeals to all tastes
with its *birreria* (pub), *enoteca*
(wine bar) and internet café
spread across three buildings
in the old town. Occasional
live music and karaoke nights.
Minimum age 18.
🕐 Jun–end Aug Tue–Sun noon–2am;
rest of year Tue–Sun 8pm–2am

WHAT TO DO

SAN GIULIANO TERME

⊙ SAN GIULIANO TERME
Largo Shelley 18, 56017 San Guiliano
Terme
Tel 050 818047
www.termesangiuliano.com
This 18th-century building,
once used by the Grand Dukes
of Tuscany, is in a beautiful
park of olive trees in the Pisan
foothills. The year-round spa
specializes in facial and body
treatments as well as sessions
to revitalize the respiratory and
immune systems. The hotel
has a bar and restaurant.
🕐 Daily Mon–Sat 8.30–1, 2.30–6.30,
Sun 8.30–1 💶 €35 for a 30-min
massage. Weekend packages start at
€135 🚆 The Pisa-to-Lucca line stops at
San Giuliano 7km (4 miles) from Pisa
on the Brennero Road (SS12) towards
Lucca

SIENA

⊕ BINACHI STAMPE E CORNICI
Via di Città 112, 53100 Siena
Tel 0577 282 152
www.siena-art.com
The wonderfully cluttered
interior of Bianchi, one of
Italy's oldest print and frame
shops, is a treasure trove of
prints, engravings, posters and
reproductions, where you can
be sure to find the perfect
image to take home as a
souvenir or gift. Designs range
from 18th-century engravings
and maps to vibrant posters
featuring Palio scenes and
architectural details, along
with modern prints and
postcards.
🕐 Mon–Sat 10–7
🚆 On right-hand side of Via di Città
heading from the Campo to the Duomo

⊕ CERAMICHE ARTISTICHE SANTA CATERINA
Via di Città 51, 74 and 76, 53100 Siena
Tel 0577 283098
www.ceramicart1.com
A family business run by the
founder, Marcello Neri, his wife
and son. The family works in
the traditional Sienese style
using only black, white, and
terra di Siena (burnt sienna).

Their art is inspired by the
local architecture, particularly
the duomo. Watch them at
work in the studio or take a
class.
🕐 Daily 10–8

⊕ DROGHERÍA MANGANELLI
Via di Città 61, 53100 Siena
Tel 0577 280002
A member of the Slow Food
Movement (▷ 24) and
something of a local
institution, the Drogheria
Manganelli has been selling
local produce since 1879.
Today it continues to sell
regional foods including cured
meats, cheese, vinegar, wine,
olive oil, homemade cakes,

*San Giuliano Terme is in a
historic setting*

ricciarelli (almond biscuits)
and pasta sauces.
🕐 Mon–Sat 9–8

⊕ BIRRERIA IL BARONE ROSSO
Via dei Termini 9, 53100 Siena
Tel 0577 286686
www.barone-rosso.com
Food, drink and live music in
the heart of Siena. Il Barone
Rosso is a regular haunt of
Sienese beer-drinkers.
🕐 Daily 9pm–3am

⊛ STADIO COMUNALE
Via Mille 3, 53100 Siena
Tel 0577 281084
Crowded with passionate and
vocal residents on match days,

this football ground is home to
AC Siena. The cheapest seating
is in the 'red curve' (▷ 228).
💶 €10

⊗ PISCINA COMUNALE
Via Coppi, Località Acquacalda, 53100
Siena
Tel 0577 47496
In the north of Siena, this
outdoor public swimming pool
has a number of diving
boards and ample space for
sunbathing.
🕐 Jun–end Aug daily 9.30–7; Oct–end
Jun daily dawn–dusk 💶 Adult €6, child
€4 🚌 10

⊗ VILLA CETINALE
Sovicille, 53018 Siena
Tel 0577 311 147
www.cetinale-manor.it
The gardens of the beautiful
15th–17th century Villa
Cetinale are acknowledged to
be among the finest in Italy,
where classic Italian garden
design goes hand in hand with
the English genius for planting.
Once the property of the Chigi
family, the villa has been
owned by Lord Lambton since
1977, and he and his wife are
responsible for the present
garden, which includes topiary,
a secluded walled garden in
the English style, magnolias,
wisteria pergolas, roses and
lemon and orange trees.
Mon–Fri 9.30–12; phone for
appointment 💶 €10
🚌 13 km (8 miles) southwest of Siena
off SS73; take turning to Sovicille

SPELLO

⊕ ARTE LEGNO
Via Fonte del Mastro II 2, 06038 Spello
Tel 0742 302028
www.artelegnospello.com
At this fantastic shop, close to
the Teatro Comunale Subasio
in the highest lanes of Spello,
most of the items are hand-
carved from olive wood.
Bowls, spoons, puppets, dolly
pegs and breadboards are all
on sale. Look upwards at the
wonderful old beams holding
up the roof.
🕐 Mon–Sat 10–1, 4–7

TIRRENIA

☉ PARCO GIOCHI FANTASILANDIA

Viale Tirreno, 42, 56018 Tirrenia
Tel 050 30326
Fantasilandia is brimming with attractions for kids. Split into two sections, the park has one free area with an electric car track, miniature train and mechanical bull. The other area has water slides and swings. There's also a park equipped for young children, with tricycles and pedal-cars. Bar and picnic tables.

🕐 May–end Sep daily; rest of the year Sun and public holidays 💶 Pay section: Adult €10.50, under 16s €8.50, under 3s free 🚌 Regular service between Pisa and Tirrenia 🚗 Take the Pisa Centro exit on the A12 motorway, then follow signs to Tirrenia

FESTIVALS AND EVENTS

FEBRUARY–MARCH

VIAREGGIO CARNEVALE

Piazza Mazzini, 22 c/o Palazzo delle Muse, 55049 Viareggio
Tel 0584 962568
www.viareggio.ilcarnevale.com
Viareggio's carnival is among Italy's biggest and best, with floats holding 200 people that wend their way along the waterfront. Gigantic moving puppets reflect current events and poke fun at famous people. It's all accompanied by music, dancing and food, and the national lottery awards a huge prize to the best float.

🕐 Four consecutive Sundays 💶 Free 🚌 Hourly from Pisa 🚗 Take the Versilia exit off the A12

MARCH–APRIL

HOLY WEEK

Assisi
Assisi, birthplace of St. Francis, celebrates Holy Week with religious processions throughout the town commemorating the passion and death of Christ. This is a serious religious occasion, and the atmosphere of piety in this holiest of Umbrian towns is almost tangible.

🕐 Week before Easter

MAY

FESTA DEI CERI

Gubbio
www.gubbio.com/ceri
A direct descendant of a pagan festival, Gubbio's Festa dei Ceri is unique. The three ceri (candles) are 66m (20ft) high, immensely heavy wooden constructions, which are paraded through the town's streets before being raced up the steep slopes of Monte Ingino behind the town. It's all in honour of Gubbio's patron saint, Sant'Ubaldo, but there are plenty of pagan phallic undertones surrounding this springtime celebration.

🕐 15 May

PALIO DELLA BALESTRA

Piazza Grande, 06024 Gubbio
Watch the medieval custom of the Eugubian (from Gubbio) and Sansepolcran (from Sansepolcro) battling it out to be crossbow champions. Don't miss the flag-throwing that precedes it.

🕐 Last Sunday in May

MAY–JUNE

CHIANTI WINE FESTIVAL

Montespertoli
One of the wine capitals of Tuscany, Montespertoli is the perfect place to taste the best of the year's vintage. Piazza San Pietro in the heart of the town is taken over by wine-lovers and professional buyers alike who flock to this well-established event.

🕐 Last Sun in May–1st Sun in June

JUNE

CORPUS DOMINI

Orvieto
www.cittadiorvieto.com
The feast of Corpus Christi (known as Corpus Domini in Italy) is marked in Orvieto by superbly costumed processions through the town's streets, many of which are decorated with elaborate carpets of flower petals. A deeply moving experience.

🕐 Mid-June

LUMINARIA AND GIOCO DEL PONTE

Pisa
Pisa's main festival focuses on tug-of-war games between 12 teams from the north and south banks of the River Arno, who attempt to push a 7-ton carriage over the Ponte di Mezzo—while dressed in Renaissance costumes. The highlight of the Luminaria are the blazing torches that light the houses and streets on either side of the river.

🕐 Last Sunday in June

PALIO DI SAN RANIERI

Pisa
Tel 050 560464 (Pisa tourist board)
www.comune.pisa.it
In celebration of Pisa's patron saint, this festival features eight oarsmen, a steersman and a climber who races to the top of a 10m (33ft) mast to grasp the winning banner at the finish. The race can be seen along the River Arno between the railway bridge and the Palazzo Medici. Try to get a spot at the Palazzo Medici to watch the mast-climbing finale.

🕐 17 June 💶 Free

JUNE–JULY

FESTIVAL DEI DUE MONDI
Spoleto
Tel 0743 44700
www.spoletofestival.it
A major performing arts festival encompassing music, dance and theatre, founded in 1958 by the composer Carlo Menotti. It attracts world-class Italian and international companies who perform in settings both indoors and out. Also has a lively fringe, with some alternative performances.
⊙ End June to mid-July

OPERA THEATRE OF LUCCA FESTIVAL
Vecchia Porta San Donato, 55100 Lucca
Tel 0583 583150
In summer Lucca's piazzas are filled with some of the world's best amateur and semi-professional singers and musicians. Sponsored by the Opera Theatre of Lucca and the Music College of the University of Cincinnati this is a great event and a showcase for new talent.
⊙ 15 June–15 July 🎭 Free

JUNE–AUGUST

ESTATE FIESOLANA
Fiesole
www.estatefiesolana.com
A summer festival of music, dance and theatre in the spectacular surroundings of Fiesole's Roman amphitheatre. There is a huge variety of music including classical, pop, contemporary jazz and gospel.
⊙ Mid-June to end August

ESTATE SAN GIMIGNANO
Piazza del Duomo 1, 53037 San Gimignano
Tel 0577 940008
A summer arts festival with a strong musical element, including open-air opera recitals, classical concerts and film screenings in the ruins of the Rocca fortress.
⊙ Mid-June to August 🎭 €14–€40

JULY

AREZZO WAVE
Corso Italia 236, 52100 Arezzo
Tel 0575 911005
www.arezzowave.com
Arezzo rocks for a week when Arezzo Wave comes to town. It's a huge rock festival that attracts nearly 250,000 people. Around 150 events take place over the week. Noisy and fun, with a good range of bands.
⊙ 1st week in July
🎭 Free

ESTATE MUSICAL LUCCHESE
Piazza Napoleone and Piazza Anfiteatro, 55100 Lucca
Tel 0584 46477
www.summer-festival.com
The Lucca Summer Music Festival is one of Tuscany's best-attended music festivals, and attracts major international artists. Plenty of Italian bands, too.
🎭 Adult €5–€20, child €3–€15

SETTIMANE MUSICALE
Siena
Tel 0577 22091
www.chigiana.it
A prestigious classical music festival run by the Accademia Chigiana, Siena's renowned *conservatoire*. Concerts take place all over the city, and the festival usually includes a major opera production.

UMBRIA JAZZ
Perugia
www.umbriajazz.com
Jazz is big in Italy and Perugia's been staging a major international festival since 1973, with a huge diversity of styles and top arists. Events take place all over the city—a must for serious jazz-lovers.

VOLTERRA TEATRO
La Fortezza, 56048 Volterra
Tel 0588 80392
www.volterrateatro.it
Held in Volterra and the surrounding towns, this is Italy's leading avant-garde theatre festival. The schedule includes experimental drama, dance and film, with a good variety of international acts performing in English.
⊙ 12–20 July
🎭 Adult €10, child €8

JULY–AUGUST

IL PALIO
Il Campo, 53100 Siena
Headquarters: Piazza Gramsci 7, 53100 Siena
Tel 0577 280551
www.comune.siena.it/contenuti/palio
www.ilpaliodisiena.com
The Palio—a bareback horse race around the Campo in Siena in honour of the Virgin Mary—is probably Italy's most famous festival. The high speed, confined space and lack of rules make it hazardous for horse and rider alike, if exhilarating for spectators. The race is over in a moment, but it takes weeks to prepare the accompanying pageantry, feasting and drama. This is a festival that the Sienese are immensely proud of, evoking passion on an extraordinary scale.
⊙ 2 July and 16 August
🎭 Free

PUCCINI FESTIVAL
Teatro all'Aperto,
55048 Torre del Lago Puccini
Tel 0584 359322
www.puccinifestival.it
Close to Villa Puccini (where Puccini wrote his most famous works), Torre del Lago's opera festival draws 40,000 spectators every year to its performances of Puccini classics.
🎭 €35–€100 🚗 A20—a minute drive from Lucca on the A11/SS1

WHAT TO DO

FESTIVALS AND EVENTS

WHAT TO DO

SIENA JAZZ FESTIVAL
Fortezza Medicea Anfiteatro, 53100 Siena
Tel 0577 271401
www.sienajazz.it
Since 1977, Siena Jazz has presented jazz performances and held seminars and master classes. Concerts are held in Piazza del Campo, Enoteca Italiana and Piazza Jacopo della Quercia.
🕐 24 July–7 August 🎫 Free

AUGUST

BARGA JAZZ FESTIVAL
Lucca and Barga
Tel 0583 711044
www.bargajazz.com
This international festival revolves around a jazz orchestra competition. Performances are held in the Teatro dei Differenti and on Piazza Angelio in Barga, as well as in Lucca's Palazzo Ducale and in Castelnuovo di Garfagnana's Piazza Umberto.
🕐 Last week in August
🎫 Adult €10, child €7.50 🚌 Barga
🚗 A40—1 minute's drive from Lucca (SS439 onto SS12, then onto SP2 and SP7)

BRAVIO DELLE BOTTE
Montepulciano
www.valdichiana.it/montepulciano
This bizarre race sees a two-man team from each of Montepulciano's eight *contrade* (districts) rolling 80kg (176lb) wine barrels, mainly uphill, through the town's streets to Piazza Grande. There is plenty of dancing and drinking in the crowd as well as plenty of encouragement for the rollers.
🕐 Last Sunday in August

AUGUST–SEPTEMBER

FESTIVAL DELLE NAZIONE DELLA MUSICA DA CAMERA
Città di Castello
Tucked away in northeast Umbria, Città di Castello plays host each year to a splendid chamber music festival. The town's churches and palazzi are used to showcase Italian and international groups playing intimate music that spans the centuries.

GIOSTRA DEL SARACINO
Piazza Grande, 52100 Arezzo
Tel 0575 377262
www.giostradelsaracino.arezzo.it
A vibrant medieval celebration of chivalry and jousting, which dates back to the Crusades combat training in the 14th century. The four teams, from the four quarters of Arezzo (Crucifera, Foro, Sant'Andrea and Santo Spirito), compete for the Lancia d'Oro (Golden Lance) trophy.
🕐 Last Sunday in August and 1st Sunday in September
🎫 Free

SEPTEMBER

EUROCINEMA FESTIVAL
Via A. Pucci 138/A, 55049 Viareggio
Tel 0584 30750
www.europacinema.it
A film awards festival including film premieres, European TV and animated short films. Screenings are in a variety of languages with Italian subtitles.
🕐 3rd week in September
🎫 Free 🚆 Trains run from Pisa to Viareggio every hour 🚗 Take the Versilia exit off the A12

LUMINARIA DI SANTA CROCE
Lucca
Lucca's treasured Volto Santo (Holy Face) is carried in procession through the torch- and candle-lit streets of the town. The statue is adorned with silver slippers and a diamond-studded crown, and the whole town turns out in homage to the effigy.
🕐 13 September

RENAISSANCE DAY
Scarperia in Mugello
Scenes from the 16th century come to life as music, archers, artisans, serfs, guards, and noblemen and women take over the streets for the day. Renaissance food can be sampled and paid for in florins.
🕐 1st Sunday in September

SAGRA MUSICALE UMBRA
Perugia
www.sagramusicaleumbra.com
Umbria's summer season culminates in the Sagra Musicale, a prestigious music festival based in Perugia, with performances taking place in venues throughout the region. Orchestras and soloists come from all over Europe, and it's worth asking what's on if you're anywhere in Umbria during the Sagra—you are bound to see something unique.
🕐 Middle 2 weeks of September

SIENA INTERNATIONAL FILM FESTIVAL
Cinema Nuovo Pendola
Via San Quirico 13, 53016 Siena
Tel 0577 43012
www.sienafilmfestival.it
This film festival screens two films per night for three nights at the end of September. The schedule includes mostly art-house films, some of which are in English.
🕐 26–29 September
🎫 Adult €6.20, child €4.65 🚌 3

OCTOBER

CHESTNUT FESTIVAL
The inhabitants of Marradi in Mugello celebrate the annual chestnut harvest. Sample some delicacies made with the nut and you are sure to go home with bags full of fresh chestnuts and homemade treats.

ROME

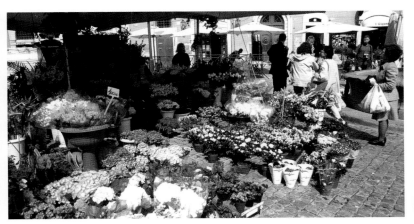

WHAT TO DO

Even if you don't go near a classical site or collection, there's enough in Rome to keep you busy for weeks. This is a consumer's paradise, where shopaholics can spend with consummate success. Shops and markets are scattered all over the city, but head for the area around Piazza di Spagna for the big names and bespoke tailoring. Via Nazionale has more cutting-edge temptations, but it is worth going across the river and into the *centro storico* for quirkier stuff and some great food shops. Rome's music scene is on the rise, with year-round opera, both in and out of doors, while the specially built Parco della Musica has at last given the city a world-class concert hall for music of all kinds. Palaeur, a huge stadium-turned-concert venue that hosts top international gigs, is its only rival. If you're in the mood for dancing, there are clubs and bars galore; Rome has great jazz and Latin music scenes. For the energetic there's swimming, tennis and golf, or sit back and watch a football or rugby match. Kids might enjoy this, but the child-friendly museums, fun parks and multimedia experiences are likely to be more appealing.

KEY TO SYMBOLS

- ⊕ **Shopping**
- ⊕ **Entertainment**
- ⊕ **Nightlife**
- ⊕ **Sports**
- ⊕ **Activities**
- ⊕ **Health and Beauty**
- ⊕ **For Children**

⊕ SHOPPING

ART, CRAFT AND ANTIQUES

COMIC'S BAZAR

Via dei Banchi Vecchi 127–128, 00186 Roma

Tel 06 6880 2923

This is a topsy-turvy Aladdin's cave of furniture, lamps and objects. Its niche is Viennese Thonet lamps from the early 20th century (late art deco) and furniture from the 1800s to the 1920s. The owners have

a more contemporary store close by at Via Giulia 140/e.

🕐 Tue–Sat 9.30–7.30, Mon 3–7.30

🚌 46, 62, 64, 116, 492, 571 or any bus to Corso Vittorio Emanuele II

MATHERIA FARNESE

Via G. Garibaldi 53–55/a, 00153 Roma

Tel 06 581 7566

www.farnese.it

The owners of this shop create bright, handcrafted ceramic floor tiles inspired by Roman villas and 18th-century patrician houses. The group of architects and artisans also restore beautiful antique tiles, plates and jugs. This kind of craftsmanship comes at a price though.

🕐 Mon–Fri 10–7, Sat by appointment

🚌 23, 280: stop closest to Via Garibaldi

BOOKS

ANGLO AMERICAN BOOK CO.

Via della Vite 102, 00187 Roma

Tel 06 679 5222

www.aab.it

A short distance from the Scalinata di Triniti dei Monti, this is one of the better English bookshops in town, housed in a 19th-century building. The excellent selection includes music, cinema, philosophy, religion, science, fiction and children's books. They also stock visitors' guidebooks to Rome, Italy and most world destinations.

🕐 Tue–Sat 10–7.30, Mon 3.30–7.30

🚌 40, 62, 64, 116

FASHION AND LINGERIE

BRIONI
Via Barberini 79, 00187 Roma
Tel 06 484517
www.brioniroma.com
Brioni has dressed royalty and
celebrities since 1945, earning
a well-deserved reputation as
one of Italy's top tailors. Leave
your measurements here and
you can call up for a suit
anytime, anywhere. This, the
oldest and largest of their
stores, also stocks women's
ready-to-wear items. Others
can be found at Via Condotti
21a and Via Veneto 129.
Mon–Sat 10–1.30, 3.30–7.30
Barberini 63, 116, 175, 492, 590,
630

FIORUCCI
Via Nazionale 236, 00184 Roma
Tel 06 488 3175
Fiorucci's signature angels
printed on T-shirts are
everywhere in this store, to the
delight of all teenagers and the
young at heart. Downstairs are
dresses, skirts and blouses by
the likes of Fiorucci, Kenzo,
Gaultier, Soleil, Kookai and
Dolce & Gabbana, as well as
jeans. Upstairs are kitsch
shoes, Hello Kitty gadgets and
more T-shirts.
Mon–Sat 10–8 Repubblica H,
40, 60, 64, 70, 117, 170

LEAM
Via Appia Nuova 26, 30, 32, 00183
Roma
Tel 06 7720 7204
www.leam.com
Three stores within a few
doors of each other, with top
designer fashion and
accessories for men and
women. The best of Italian
design under one roof. There
are Armani, Gucci, Dolce &
Gabbana, Prada and even
Philippe Stark dresses. The
shop assistants can be over-
attentive (not uncommon in
Rome). There is a roof terrace
and bar in the women's store.
Mon 4–8, Tue–Sat 9.30–8 San
Giovanni 87, 360

LEI
Via Nazionale 88, 00184 Roma
Tel 06 482 1700
Though the name on the shop
window is understated in small
letters, hip young women come
here for their Dolce & Gabbana
staples, Romeo Gigli ready-to-
wear, and a dazzling array of
party dresses and delicate slip-
on shoes by French designers
like Stéphane Kélian.
Tue–Sat 10–7.30, Mon 3.30–7.30
H, 40, 60, 64, 70, 117, 170

VALENTINO
Via Condotti 12, Roma
Tel 06 67391
One of the few Italian fashion
designers to be based in Rome

*Valentino's fashions have been
turning heads for decades*

rather than Milan. Valentino
has been dressing the rich and
famous since the late 1950s.
Further branches are in Piazza
Mignanelli (haute couture)
and Via Bocca di Leone.
Mon 3–7, Tue–Sat 10–7 Spagna

FOOD AND DRINK

LA DOLCEROMA
Via del Portico d'Ottavia 20/b,
00186 Roma
Tel 06 689 2196
This Viennese patisserie is an
unobtrusive little shop in the
heart of the Jewish quarter.
Once inside you'll understand
why people make detours for
it. Aside from the excellent
Sacher cake (also available by

the slice), you can buy
cheesecakes of all sizes and
with different fillings—from
yoghurt to Austrian cream
cheese—and various other
mouth-watering Austrian
specialties. There are also
cookies and brownies to
munch on to keep you going
while you sightsee. Not the
cheapest bakery in town, but
the most memorable.
Tue–Sat 8–1.30, 3.30–8, Sun 10–1.30
H, 23, 63, 280, 630, 780 to
Lungotevere dei Cenci, or walk from
Largo di Torre Argentina or Piazza
Venezia

VOLPETTI
Via Marmorata 47, 00153 Roma
Tel 06 574 2352
www.volpetti.com
One of the best (though not
the cheapest) delis in Rome.
An astounding variety of
breads, cheeses, hams,
salamis, fresh pasta and
ready-made dishes. Service is
professional and cheerful and
you can sample the cheese to
help you decide. Whatever
happens, you won't come
away empty-handed. Good for
gifts. There's another, more
expensive branch in Via della
Scrofa in the city centre.
Mon–Sat 8–2, 5–8.15 Piramide
23, 30, 60, 75, 280, 716 (or any to
Piramide or Via Marmorata); tram 3

GIFTS AND SOUVENIRS

FABRIANO
Via del Babuino 173, 00187 Roma
Tel 06 32600361
Minimalist in design, this store
sells stacks of paper goods and
stationery such as notepads
and address books, enticingly
arranged by colour. Shades run
the gamut from yellows, greens
and blues to whites, browns
and blacks. The paper is of the
highest quality and made by an
800-year-old firm; prices are
predictably high. They sell
briefcases, too.
Mon–Sat 10–7.30 Spagna or
Flaminio 81, 117, 119, 590, 628

HEALTH AND BEAUTY

ROMA STORE

Via della Lungaretta 63, 00153 Roma
Tel 06 581 8789
Despite the unimpressive name, this shop stocks a tantalizing selection of hard-to-find and sophisticated British and French perfumes, including L'Artisan Parfumeur, Creed, Etro, Penhaligon's, L'Occitane, Vetiver and Comptoir Sud Pacifique, to name but a few. Creams, imported US and UK brands of soap and toothpaste complete the range.
Daily 10–2, 3–8 H, 780; tram 8

JEWELLERY

BULGARI

Via Condotti 10, Roma
Tel 06 696261
www.bulgari.com
This is the most splendid jewellery shop in Rome, but it's also fantastically expensive. Andy Warhol called it the most important museum of art in the Western world. It specializes in glittering Renaissance-inspired pieces and a complete lack of refined taste.
Daily 10–7 Spagna

MARKETS

CAMPO DEI FIORI

Piazza Campo dei Fiori, 00186 Roma
Probably the most expensive, and without doubt the liveliest market in Rome. Hawkers collect their wares from the nearby medieval storage vaults and set up shop in this charismatic location. There was a time when heretics were burned here, and traitors hanged. These days the only things hanging are the flowers and food.
Mon–Sat 8–2 46, 62, 64, 116

PORTA PORTESE

Porta Portese, 00153 Roma
Rome's most famous flea market stretches all the way from Porta Portese to Trastevere station. It also branches off down the side streets. From trendy clothes and antiques to junk, you can find all sorts here. Arrive early for the best buys, and beware of pickpockets.
Sun 6.30–1 Tram 3

UNDERGROUND

Via Francesco Crispi 96, 00187 Roma
Tel 06 3600 5345
Flea markets have sprung up all over Rome in the past few years. One of the best-established is this antiques and collector's market in the Ludovisi underground car park, held once a month in the winter. More than 100 stands sell prints, small antiques, frames, comics, lace and old

Giorgio Sermoneta's is a glove cornucopia

vases. There are also children's stands where toys are sold and exchanged.
Oct–end Apr 1st Sun of the month 9–7; closed Feb Spagna 116, 119, 204, 630, 910 or any bus to Via Veneto

MUSIC

RICORDI MEDIA STORE

Via Cesari Battisti 120, 00187 Roma
Tel 06 6798022/3
www.lafeltrinelli.it
Rome's popular music store, in a nicely designed building that once housed the Verdi archives. It has the largest classical DVD/CD collection in Rome. There is a large Italian music section and sheet music and musical instruments are also sold. They have four other outlets: Termini, Viale Giulio Cesare, Piazza della Repubblica and Via del Corso.
Mon–Sat 9.30–8, Sun 3.30–8; closed Jul, Aug Sun 40, 62, 64, 117 to Piazza Venezia

SHOES AND ACCESSORIES

FURLA

Piazza di Spagna 22, 00187 Roma
Tel 06 6920 0363
www.furla.it
Purveyors of chic bags and practical totes in bright shades, along with scarves, shoes and jewellery. Some wild style combinations and original touches. Prices are moderate compared with other big-name accessory designers. The company has a fleet of branches all over the world, and several more in Rome.
Daily 10–8 Spagna 116, 117, 119, 590

GIORGIO SERMONETA

Piazza di Spagna 61, 00187 Roma
Tel 06 6791960
www.sermonetagloves.com
The shop is fairly small and may feel cramped, but don't be fooled—just look up! Top-quality gloves—thousands of them—decorate this shop, and come in bright shades and styles to fit every hand. Prices range from €23 to €100.
Mon–Sat 9.30–8 Spagna 116, 117

TOYS

LA CITTÀ DEL SOLE

Via della Scrofa 65, 00186 Roma
Tel 06 6880 3805
www.cittadelsole.it
A toy store for the progressive parent. Crammed with educational toys, puzzles, games and books divided up into sections for children aged 0 to 14, with a focus on creative playing and learning. All the best toys from big and small producers alike. Not a Playstation in sight!
Mon–Sat 10–7.30, Sun 11–7.30
116

🎭 ENTERTAINMENT

CINEMA

PASQUINO

Piazza Sant'Egidio 10, 00158 Roma
Tel 06 581 5208

This is something of a Roman institution. All films (about four per day on three screens) are shown in English, so there are many English-speakers in the audience. The crowded espresso bar is open before screenings.

🎬 Daily screenings at 5, 8 and 10.30 💶 €7 🚌 Bus or tram to Viale Trastevere

CLASSICAL MUSIC, DANCE AND OPERA

AUDITORIUM

Parco della Musica
Viale Pietro de Coubertin 30,
00197 Roma
Tel 06 808 2058
www.musicaperroma.it

Architect Renzo Piano has finally given Rome the concert hall it deserves. Opened in 2002, this year-round, three-auditorium complex is the city's biggest music venue, with a capacity of 4,600. Find it between Lungotevere Flaminio and Viale Tiziano.

🎬 Performances: Mon–Fri 7–9, 9–11; Box office: daily 11–6; Hello Ticket (credit card reservations): Mon–Fri 10–5 💶 €8 🚇 Piazzale Flaminio, and then tram 🚌 Bus to Auditorio

TEATRO OLIMPICO

Piazza Gentile da Fabriano 17,
00196 Roma
Tel 06 326 5991, 0800 907 080 (toll-free)
www.teatroolimpico.it

This Accademia Filarmonica-owned venue is very comfortable, although it has recently been upstaged by the new Auditorium. The main season runs from September to the end of May and the acoustics and range of productions are always excellent.

🎬 Daily 10–1, 3–5.30; after 8pm for same-day tickets 💶 €20–€35 🚌 Bus or tram to Piazza Mancini or Stadio Olimpico

TEATRO DELL'OPERA DI ROMA

Via Firenze 72, 00186 Roma
Tel 06 481 7517
www.opera.roma.it

A hidden gem, too often overlooked by the locals. The interior is adorned with all the trimmings of a true opera house complete with velvet boxes. Not to be missed by those who love classical dance. The theatre is beautiful and attracts first-rate dance troupes from all over the world. You are certain to see the cream of Roman society.

🎬 Performances: Nov–end May 9pm; Box office: Tue–Sat 9–5, Sun 9–1.30 💶 €8–€120 🚌 Bus to Via Nazionale

There is a great atmosphere at the Big Mama jazz club

CONTEMPORARY LIVE MUSIC

ALEXANDERPLATZ

Via Ostia 9, 00193 Roma
Tel 06 3974 2171

Rome's most famous jazz venue holds jazz festivals all year round, and organizes outdoor concerts at Villa Celimontana in summer. American bands are often on the bill. Creole cuisine is served in the restaurant.

🎬 Mon–Sat 9pm–1.30am; closed first 2 weeks of Aug 💶 €6.50 🚌 Bus to Piazza Risorgimento or Clodio

BIG MAMA

Vicolo San Francesco a Ripa 18,
00153 Roma
Tel 06 581 2551
www.bigmama.it

A famous Trastevere jazz club, where local and international bands play in the cavernous, smoke-filled underground hideaway. The audience sits close to the band, and it is not uncommon to see dancing on the table tops.

🎬 Daily 9pm–1.30am; closed Jul–end Oct 💶 €6–€13 🚌 75 or 170 to Viale Trastevere or Piazza Mastai

CARUSO

Via di Monte Testaccio 36, 00153 Roma
Tel 06 574 5019

The best bet for Latin beats, ranging from salsa to hip-hop. A mix of live bands and Rome's best DJs. It is always packed, especially on Sunday, which is disco night. There are Arabic music nights, too.

🎬 Tue–Sun 10.30pm–3am 💶 €8–€10 🚇 Piramide 🚌 Bus to Testaccio

PALALOTTOMATICA

Piazzale dello Sport
Viale dell'Umanesimo, 00144 Roma
www.palalottomatica.it

The biggest venue in the city, a huge sports stadium-turned-concert hall in EUR. It hosts all the top international acts—everyone from Sting to the Rolling Stones has played here at some time.

🎬 8pm (usually) 💶 Varies 🚇 Metro to EUR Palaeur and bus to Palazzo dello Sport

VILLAGGIO GLOBALE

Lungotevere Testaccio, 00153 Roma
Tel 06 5757 2333

This former slaughterhouse (the Mattatoio) is Rome's best-loved music venue. There's a huge outdoor courtyard for concerts and dancing. During larger events, food stands are set up inside.

🎬 6pm–3am (variable) 💶 €10 🚌 Bus to Testaccio or Lungotevere Testaccio

WHAT TO DO

PALAZZO DELLE ESPOSIZIONI
Via Nazionale 194, 00184 Roma
Tel 06 489411
www.palazzoesposizioni.it
This is Rome's all-round cultural centre where theatre, film showings and art exhibitions take place under one roof. If all of the city's artistic juices could be captured in a single space, this would be it. It can be found near the huge tunnel that connects Via Nazionale to Via del Tritone. The complex is at the mouth of the tunnel, on the left side of Via Nazionale.
🕐 9pm (usually). Box office: Wed–Mon 10–9 🚌 Bus to Via Nazionale

TEATRO DI ROMA
Largo di Torre Argentina 52, 00186 Roma
Tel 06 6880 4601/800 013390
www.teatrodiroma.net
A leading year-round venue for beautifully staged productions in one of Rome's oldest theatres. A performance here is a night to remember. Dress to impress. There is a bar serving cocktails at the intermission. The theatre is on the Campo de Fiori side of the square.
🕐 9pm. Box office: Mon–Sat 10–2, 3–7 💶 €12–€27 🚌 Bus or tram to Largo Argentina

🎵 NIGHTLIFE
BARS AND CAFÉS
ANIMA
Via di Santa Maria dell'Anima 57, 00186 Roma
Tel 06 6889 2806
At the heart of Roman nightlife, west of piazza Navona, this bar is a beloved hangout for foreigners and English-speakers. Excellent fresh-fruit cocktails, ultra-modern decoration and highly respectable resident DJs.
🕐 Tue–Sun 9.30pm–2am 🚌 46, 62, 64, 116, 81, 87, 492

CUL DE SAC
Piazza Pasquino 73, 00186 Roma
Tel 06 6880 1094
In a little piazza off Piazza Navona, this is one of the oldest wine bars in town and still one of the best. They have an excellent wine list, mouth-watering cheeses, meats and unusual dishes. Friendly service and frequent tastings.
🕐 Daily 12–4, 7–12.30 🚌 46, 62, 64, 492 to Corso Vittorio Emanuele II (get off near Sant'Andrea della Valle); 70, 81, 87 to Corso Rinascimento; 116 to Campo de' Fiori

THE GALLERY
Via della Maddalena 12, 00186 Roma
Tel 06 687 2316
www.thegallery.it
An enegetic, modern and elegant bar behind the Pantheon. Music from hip-hop to R&B to 1970s and 1980s

Cul de Sac is one of Rome's finest wine bars

revival draws a crowd that's young and ready to party.
🕐 Tue–Fri 8pm–3am, Sat–Sun 8pm–4am 💶 €10 🚌 116

MAX'S BAR
Via A. Grandi 7a, 00185 Roma
Tel 06 7030 1599
www.maxsbar.net
Very busy gay bar for men of all ages. Being underground, it can become quite hot when it gets crowded. Consists of two bars, a dance floor, and large sitting/socializing area.
🕐 Thu–Tue 10.30am–3.30am 💶 €8–€11, Mon free 🚇 Manzoni

QUBE
Via di Portonaccio 212, 00159 Roma
Tel 06 438 5445
www.muccassassina.com
The young crowd dance till they drop in Rome's biggest underground disco. Friday night is 'Muccassassina' night, once gay and transgressive, now more straight and mainstream than alternative.
🕐 Thu–Sat 11pm–4am 💶 Variable cover charge 🚇 Tiburtina 🚌 71, 168, 204, 409, 492, 545, 649

SIDE MEETING POINT
Via Labicana 50, 00184 Roma
Tel 0348 692 9472
Gay, retro-kitsch bar. One of the few exclusively gay nightspots in Rome, partying spills out onto the pavement and road in the summer. This club has stood the test of time.
🕐 Daily 4pm–2am 🚇 Colosseo 🚌 Various buses

🏃 SPORTS AND ACTIVITIES
FOOTBALL
STADIO OLIMPICO
Viale dello Stadio Olimpico, 00194 Roma
Tel 06 3237333
www.stadioolimpico.it
Football, football, football—no spectator sport is more important to Romans. The city has two rival teams: Roma fans sit on the south side of the stadium and Lazio fans on the north side.
🕐 Sun throughout season 💶 €15–€100 🚌 Bus to Lungotevere Maresciallo Cadorna 🚇 Line A to Otaviano then Bus 32

GOLF
CIRCOLO DEL GOLF DI ROMA
Via Appia Nuova 716/a, 00178 Roma
Tel 06 780 3407
www.golfroma.it
Excellent 18-hole golf course surrounded by umbrella pines and Roman ruins. There is a great on-site restaurant.
🕐 Tue–Sun 8–dusk 💶 €64 weekdays, €76 weekends 🚇 Colli Albani, then a taxi ride

WHAT TO DO

RUGBY

STADIO FLAMINIO

Viale Tiziano, 00196 Roma
Tel 06 3685 7832
www.federugby.it
Don't be fooled into thinking
Italians only go mad for *calcio*
(soccer). The country is home
to 24 rugby clubs, and the best
games are in the capital when
club RDS Roma hits the field.
€10–€30 Bus or tram to
Viale Tiziano

SPECTACLES

CINECITTÀ

Via Tuscolana, 00173 Roma
www.cinecitta.it
On warm summer nights,
Rome's celebrated film studio
opens to the public. Among the
attractions are chariot races à la
Ben Hur, when gladiators and
their horses are dressed in the
appropriate Roman attire.
Sat evenings, summer only €10
Cinecittà

SWIMMING

PISCINA DELLE ROSE

Viale America 20, 00144 Roma
Tel 06 592 6717
www.piscinadellerose.it
Rome's largest open-air pool
and a great place to bring the
kids at weekends. It's at the
ultra-sleek Palasport sports
facility built by Mussolini.
Daily 9am–10pm €10
Palasport, EUR

TENNIS

CIRCOLO DELLA STAMPA

Piazza Mancini 19, 00196 Roma
Tel 06 323 2452
This friendly tennis club has
both clay and synthetic-grass
courts at reasonable prices.
There are tennis lessons for all
levels.
Daily 8am–11pm €10–€30 per
hour Bus to Piazza Mancini

♥ HEALTH AND BEAUTY

AVEDA SALON

Rampa Mignanelli 9, 00187 Roma
Tel 06 6992 4257
www.aveda.com
Pampering at its finest by
Aveda, one of Europe's
leading potions-and-lotions
brands. Energize yourself
with plant steam inhalation,
skin hydration or mild
aromatherapy. Renew yourself
with a manicure, pedicure or
a quick wax.
Mon 3.30–8, Tue–Sat 10–8
€25 manicure, €31 plant steam
inhalation Spagna

✪ FOR CHILDREN

BIOPARCO DI ROMA

Piazzale del Giardino Zoologico 1, Villa
Borghese, Roma
www.bioparco.it
Bioparco is one of the oldest
zoos in Europe but is modern
and aims to promote the
conservation of endangered

*You can stock up on beauty
products at Aveda Salon*

species. It also hopes to
educate visitors about the
animals, some of which have
been rescued from illegal
trading in rare species. The zoo
is set in botanical gardens and
contains over 1,000 animals.
Apr–end Oct daily 9.30–6 (7 on Sat,
Sun, holidays); Nov–end Mar daily
9.30–5 Adult €8.50, child 3–12
€6.50 Flaminio 52, 53, 926;
tram 13,19

EXPLORA—IL MUSEO DEI BAMBINI

Via Flaminia 82, 00192 Roma
Tel 06 361 3776
www.mdbr.it
Rome's first and only
children's museum, opened in
2001. Four sections dedicated
to the human body, the
environment, communications
and society. Plenty of signs
and material in English. Kids
can star in their own TV show,
work in a supermarket and
find out about living
ecologically. Best for under
eights. Advance reservations
required at the weekend.
Tue–Sun 9.30–7 Adult €6, child
€7, under 3s free Flaminio 95,
117, 119, 204, 231, 490, 495, 618, 916;
tram 2, 3, 19

LUNEUR PARK

Via delle Tre Fontane, 00144 Roma
Tel 06 592 5933
www.luneur.it
Built in 1953, the oldest fun
park in Italy has kept up with
the times. Activities and rides
are both traditional and
adrenalin-pumping, with a
puppet theatre, several
haunted houses, bumper
cars, a lake with motor boats,
and rides called Flipper,
Thriller and Space Kickers.
The park is a lot bigger than
it seems. Suitable for kids
and teenagers.
Mon–Fri 4–midnight, Sat 3–2am,
Sun 10–1, 3–midnight Individual
rides €1–€6; half-day visit €15–€25
Magliana, Palasport or EUR Fermi
706, 707, 714, 717, 765, 771

TIME ELEVATOR

Via S.S. Apostoli 20, 00186 Roma
Tel 06 699 0053
www.time-elevator.it
A multimedia experience
illustrating the history of Rome
from its founding to the
present day. With headphones,
a screen, a moving platform
and other surprise special
effects, this is a genuinely fun
(if slightly cheesy and
occasionally factually weak)
introduction to the city. Watch
Rome burn and see Caesar's
assassination: worth the rather
high entrance fee.
Daily screenings 10am–10.30pm
Adult €11, under 12s €9.20 40,
62, 63, 64, 916 or any bus to Via del
Corso or Piazza Venezia

WHAT TO DO

FESTIVALS AND EVENTS

DECEMBER–JANUARY

BEFANA
According to legend, the Befana was an old woman who refused the Magi shelter on their journey to Bethlehem. Befana is associated with the Christmas period, as is the wise old woman who flies from house to house delivering the good children's presents on 6 January—bad children get coal. A lively fair runs in Piazza Navona during Christmas time. Toys and sweets are the main attraction: Look out for the sweet called *carbone*, which looks like lumps of coal.
🕒 December–6 January

MARCH

ROME CITY MARATHON
Via dei Fori Imperiali, 00186 Roma
Tel 06 3018 3022, 06 3018 3016
www.maratonadiroma.it
Each spring runners flock to Rome and, like gladiators, they come down the avenue that cuts right through the Forum. This event is slowly gaining the equivalent status of the marathons held in London and New York.
🕒 3rd Sunday in March
🚌 Bus to Piazza Venezia

APRIL–MAY

CONCORSO IPPICO INTERNAZIONALE DI PIAZZA DI SIENA
Villa Borghese, Piazza di Siena, 00186 Roma
Tel 06 327 9939
www.piazzadisiena.com
Few know it, but Rome plays host to an important annual equestrian event that has all the trimmings of the big horse shows around the world. Show jumping is the main event.
🕒 Late April–early May
🎟 Adult €10–€44, child €6–€7
🚌 Bus to Via Veneto

MAY

CAMPIONATO INTERNAZIONALE DI TENNIS
Foro Italico, Viale dei Gladiatori, 00194 Roma
Tel 06 323 3807
Every May, Rome hosts the Italian Open tennis tournament. This is Europe's most competitive non-grand slam tennis event.
🕒 1st two weeks in May
🎟 €8–€55
🚌 Bus to Lungotevere Maresciallo Cadorna

JULY

OPERA FESTIVAL AT THE BATHS OF CARACALLA
Terme di Caracalla
Box office: Teatro dell'Opera, Via Firenze 72, 00184 Roma
Tel 06 481601
This is what grand opera and ballet are all about. Big productions such as Verdi's *Aida* are staged—complete with horses and elephants—inside the ruins of the ancient Roman Baths of Caracalla. Shows are staged in the largest area of the baths, not the smaller indoor ones. Bring a cushion to sit on.
🕒 Performances 8pm; booking office: Tue–Sat 9–5, Sun 9–1.30
🎟 €20–€50
🚇 FAO 🚌 Bus to Terme di Caracalla

SEPTEMBER

NOTTE BIANCA
www.lanottebianca.it
An annual event at the end of the summer season when theatres, palaces, art galleries and other venues open all night in a city-wide party celebrating Rome's art and cultural heritage. From 8pm to 8am the next morning, over 500 events go on at various locations and in the streets of central Rome and some suburbs. Municipal, state and private museums, historic squares, villas and gardens, cultural institutes, theatres, libraries, churches and other places of worship, cinemas, art galleries and sports centres remain open, all night. Restaurants and food shops remain open and there is cheap public transport to get you around.
🕒 Saturday in mid-September

SEPTEMBER–NOVEMBER

ROMAEUROPA FESTIVAL
Tel 06 422 96300
www.romaeuroa.net
A major annual arts festival of classical and contemporary theatre, music and dance, held in different venues across the city.
🕒 20 September–30 November
🎟 €5–€30, festival pass €135

OCTOBER–NOVEMBER

ROME JAZZ FESTIVAL
Tel 06 5630 5015
www.romajazzfestival.it
A major festival that attracts international artists. Events take place at some of Rome's top music venues, including La Palma Club and The Auditorium, Parco della Musica.
🕒 Last week in October, 1st week in November
🎟 €10–€12

NOVEMBER

INTERNATIONAL FESTIVAL OF SACRED MUSIC
www.festivalmusicaeartesacra.net
A festival of church music and art in which some outstanding musical events take place in some of the most beautiful basilicas in Rome. In previous years the London Philharmonic Orchestra has taken part. The festival opens with the Holy Mass, complete with Gregorian chant performed by the choir of the Cappella Giulia at St. Peter's Basilica.
🕒 November (dates vary)

WHAT TO DO

LAZIO AND THE MARCHE

The tranquil provincial towns of the Marche and Lazio are a world away from the buzz of Italy's more frenetic regions. Despite its proximity to Rome, Lazio is a quiet area, with shops geared up to everyday needs. Lovers of luxury will be more attracted to the wine towns around Rome, and you'll find good weekly markets in places like Viterbo.

The same is true in the Marche. Urbino is the best place for shopping, with the usual chain-store fashion names, and the bonus of a couple of splendid weekly markets. Don't neglect Ascoli Piceno, famed for its ceramics and antiques. Both Urbino and Ascoli Piceno have a good cultural scene, with the emphasis on summer festivals, along with Lazio's larger towns, particularly Tivoli and Frascati. There's clubbing along the Marche coast, while children are catered for with waterparks and safe, sandy beaches.

KEY TO SYMBOLS

- ⊕ **Shopping**
- 🎭 **Entertainment**
- ▼ **Nightlife**
- ⚽ **Sports**
- ✪ **Activities**
- ♡ **Health and Beauty**
- ✤ **For Children**

ASCOLI PICENO

⊕ FIERA DELL'ANTIQUARIATO
Via del Trivio, Ascoli Piceno
Every Italian town has its flea market, but few could be described as antiques fairs. However, at Ascoli Piceno's monthly antiques market—against the backdrop of the Chiesa di San Francesco—you can find real treasures. Look out for the glazed ceramics.
🕐 9–dusk, third weekend of every month

⊕ LAUDI SAVINA CERAMICS
Via Pisa 4, 63100 Ascoli Piceno
Tel 0736 44024
In past times Ascoli Piceno's local economy was fuelled by its ceramics industry. Take a walk up Via del Trivio to the oldest and prettiest district and see today's artisans working in dimly lit studios. One of the most talented is Laudi Savina, whose floral and geometric designs are reminiscent of Renaissance pieces.
🕐 Mon–Sat 9–1, 3–8

🎭 COTTON JAZZ CLUB
Largo Cattaneo 4, 63100 Ascoli Piceno
Tel 348 6056390 or 0861 80401
With so many good jazz festivals in the vicinity (Ancona, Urbino, Umbria), it's no surprise that a jazz scene has evolved in Ascoli Piceno. Big-name performers drop by to jam in informal surroundings.
🕐 Tue–Sun 8pm–1.30am

🎭 TEATRO VENTIDIO BASSO
Via del Trivio 44, 63100 Ascoli Piceno
Tel 0736 298305, 0736 298306 (information). Box office: Via del Trivio 50: 0736 244970
Named after a local military hero, this mighty 1846 opera house has wedding-cake layers of balconies, glittering chandeliers and a neoclassical façade. The playbill is eclectic, from Puccini to *The Full Monty*.
🕐 Thu–Sat 8.30, Sun 5.30, 8.30. Box office daily 9–1, 3–8.30 💰 €8–€22

FRASCATI

⊕ ENOTECA SAN MARCO
Piazza San Pietro 8, 00044 Frascati
Tel 06 941 9519
The bottles of wine are stacked right up to the ceiling,

but the friendly assistants will help you choose the right one. Ample list of wines from Italy and abroad, including the celebrated local Frascati. Vintage and dated wines for the more demanding, plus grappa, champagne and calvados.

🕐 Mon–Thu 10–1, 4.30–8, Fri–Sun 9.30–1, 4.30–8

GABICCE MARE

🎵 BAIA IMPERIALE

Via Panoramica, 61011 Gabicce Mare
Tel 0541 950312, 0541 952135
www.baiaimperiale.net
Must be seen to be believed. Baia Imperiale claims to be the biggest nightclub in the world—and the most photographed. Imperial Roman decor, complete with a column-lined amphitheatre and Caesar statues for theme park appeal. Dance to the live bands, DJs and Latin grooves by the outdoor pool.

🕐 Jul, Aug daily 9pm–3.30am ✋ €15; free tickets can be requested at www.out4fun.it 🚗 From Urbino, drive 15km (9 miles) to the Adriatic Coast at Gabicce Mare, near Pesaro. Via Panoramica is the coastal road. Look for signs before the town

GUIDONIA MONTECELIO

❋ AQUAPIPER

Via Maremmana Inferiore km 29.300, 00012 Guidonia Montecelio
Tel 0774 3265 3839
www.aquapiper.it
Aquatic theme park with children's pools, water slides, wave machines and a hydro-massage lagoon—perfect for hot summer days. There is an ice-cream kiosk, a fast-food restaurant and a picnic area.

🕐 Jun to mid-Sep daily 9–7 ✋ Adult €9–€14, under 10s €6, one child free when accompanied by an adult

URBINO

🌐 MERCATO SETTIMANALE DI URBINO

Viale B. Buozzi, 61029 Urbino
Tel 0722 2631 (tourist office)
Arrive early Sunday morning for the best finds: World War I

helmets, 1950s chrome lamps and 16th-century dressers.

🕐 Sun 7–12.30

🎵 CAPPELLA MUSICALE DEL SS SACRAMENTO

Via Valerio 7, 61029 Urbino
Tel 0722 4120
Music students and visiting ensembles perform at this frescoed music venue (in the Sala Vecchiotti), which has existed for centuries. Everything classical from string quartets to church choirs.

🕐 Sat–Sun 9pm (usually) ✋ Free

🎵 SALA MANISCALCO, RAMPA DI GIORGIO MARTINI

Corso Garibaldi, 61029 Urbino
Tel 0722 2613
Next to the Teatro Sanzio is a curious music and theatre venue built inside what looks like a giant staircase. Events include everything from jazz to experimental theatre.

🕐 8.30pm (usually) ✋ From €8

🎵 TEATRO SANZIO

Via Matteotti, 61029 Urbino
Tel 0722 2281
When this theatre was built in 1845, local citizens thought it an eyesore that clashed with Urbino's Renaissance harmony. Today the Sanzio is considered one of the city's most important architectural sights and music venues.

🕐 Thu–Sun 8.30 ✋ Box office daily 9–1, 3–8.30 ✋ €10–€70

VITERBO

TERME DEI PAPI

12 Strada Bagni, 01100 Viterbo
Tel 0761 3501
www.termedeipapi.it
Beautiful grounds and a sumptuous wooden-decked swimming pool greet visitors to the Terme dei Papi in northern Lazio, 75km (47 miles) north of Rome. Mud baths, herbal inhalations, facials and organic treatments are all available.

🕐 Wed–Mon 9–9 ✋ €60 mud bath
🚗 The Terme dei Papi is 5km (3 miles) outside the town

FESTIVALS AND EVENTS

JUNE–SEPTEMBER

FRASCATI SUMMER FESTIVALS

Villa Torlonia, Frascati
Tel 06 941 7195 (Frascati Cultural Office)
Throughout the summer, festivals are organized in Frascati's parks and villas, with open-air shows, dance, cinema, fireworks and night markets.

AUGUST

INCHINATA

Piazza Trento and nearby streets, Tivoli
Tel 0774 311249, 0774 319051
In this religious festival celebrating the Assumption of the Virgin, images of Christ and his mother bow (inchinare) to each other in Piazza Trento at the end of the procession. Live music and fireworks follow.

🕐 14–15 August

TORNEO DELLA QUINTANA

Ascoli Piceno
One of the Marche's loveliest towns is the setting for this summer festival of parades and jousting. More than 1,200 people participate in the processions, with bands, drums and flag-waving. A totally authentic and passionate spectacle.

🕐 1st weekend in August

OCTOBER

SAGRA DELL'UVA

Piazza dei Quattro Mori, 00047 Marino
Tel 06 938 5555
This famous festival celebrates the new wine vintage with a parade in the afternoon. Later, the main fountain, Fontana dei Quattro Mori, bubbles and overflows with wine.

🕐 1st Sunday in October
🚗 From Frascati take S.S. n.216 following signs for Marino

THE SOUTH

Good shopping in southern Italy, the country's poorest part, is something of a rarity, and if you're in the spending mood, do your purchasing in and around Naples or along the lovely coastline to the south of the city. The Sorrento peninsula and its tiny villages are among Italy's chicest holiday areas, a great hunting ground for beachwear and cool, elegant, evening resort clothes. In Naples itself, head for Santa Lucia for designer stores, while the area around Via Toledo will fit the bill at the lower end of the price range.

Other towns worth browsing around include Puglia's Bari and Lecce; towns in Calabria and Basilicata have chain-store fashion and weekly markets. For live entertainment, Naples is your best bet—there's classical music, opera and high-standard ballet, as well as cinema and some crazy clubs. The action spreads farther south in the summer, down the coast and out to the islands of Capri and Ischia, where you'll find great music venues and clubs in fabulous waterside venues.

The south is great for outdoor activities, with sailing, windsurfing and swimming, plus some of the best scuba diving in the world. The walking in the southern hills is superb.

KEY TO SYMBOLS	
⊕	Shopping
⊙	Entertainment
⊙	Nightlife
⊗	Sports
⊗	Activities
♡	Health and Beauty
⊗	For Children

ARCO FELICE

⊗ CIRCOLO GOLF NAPOLI CARNEY PARK

Via Campiglione 11, 0078 Arco Felice, Napoli
Tel 081 660772
This golf course is right next to Lago d'Averno, an eerie lake that is the entrance to Hell according to the ancient Greeks. The nine-hole Circolo Golf Napoli has equipment hire, putting greens, a bar and restaurant.

🕐 Wed–Mon 8–dusk, Tue afternoon only 🅿 €17 🚇 Pozzuoli 🚋 Cumana train 🚗 Take the Tangenziale (Naples Circular) and exit at Pozzuoli for Via Campana

BAIA

⊗ SEA POINT ITALY

Via Molo di Baia 14, 80070 Baia
Tel 081 868 8868
www.seapointitaly.it
A wonderful place to go diving, the Baia is rich in aquatic wildlife and submerged Greek and Roman sites. Sea Point Italy has qualified instructors and a range of diving courses.
🕐 May–end Sep Tue–Sun 9–7; rest of year Tue–Sun 9–1, 3–7
🅿 Open-water diving course €190, snorkelling course €140 🚋 Cumana train to Baia

CAPRI

⊕ LIMONCELLO DI CAPRI

Via Listrieri 25A, 80073 Capri
Tel 081 837 1073
www.limoncello.com
Limoncello liqueur may be abundant in these parts, but there's no denying this shop is one of the best of its kind on the island. The lemon-based spirit is great mixed with champagne or *prosecco*, and as an after-dinner *digestivo*.
🕐 Daily 9–7

LECCE

⊙ TEATRO PAISELLO

Via Giuseppe Palmieri, 73100 Lecce
Tel 0832 245499
Expect neo-Renaissance architecture, classical Greek

motifs on a handsome 1872 façade and sumptuous interiors. Jazz, cabaret, classical and pop, plus Italian and international drama and dance productions.

🎫 Box office: Mon–Sat 10.30–1, 4.30–7
💶 €8–€30

☯ SUN S.A.S.
Via Orsini del Balzo 70, 73100 Lecce
Tel 0832 349444

Relieve those weary limbs after sightseeing and strolling the Salento sand with a visit to this health and beauty parlour. Facial and body treatments are reasonably priced. They have a team of masseurs, and a great range of beauty products to take home.

🕐 Mon–Sat 9–9 💶 Massage €30

NAPOLI (NAPLES)

⊕ IL CANTUCCIO DELLA CERAMICA
Via Benedetto Croce 38, 80134 Napoli
Tel 081 5525857

You'll find this ceramics studio down a small street between Piazza del Gesù Nuovo and Piazza San Domenico Maggiore. Ceramics in a multitude of hues are for sale, but you can also take classes here and make your own.

🕐 Mon–Fri 10–6 🚇 Piazza Cavour

⊕ ENOTECA PARTENOPEA
Viale Augusto 2, 80100 Napoli
Tel 081 593 7982

Don't leave Naples without tasting some of the region's fine wines. The rich volcanic soil gives the wine a remarkable richness; ask the staff for an introduction to the region's offerings and grab a few bargain bottles to take home.

🕐 Fri–Wed 9–1.30, 4.30–7.30, Thu 9–1.30 🚇 Campi Flegrei

⊕ ERNESTO BOWINKEL
Piazza Martiri 24, 80121 Napoli
Tel 081 764 4344

A smartly coiffed Neapolitan gentleman will guide you through the fabulous antiques and artworks here. There are many smaller pieces that would

make a worthy investment or great presents. Take time to ask about the history behind the paintings, historic prints, frames and elegant statues that fill this shop.

🕐 Mon–Sat 10–1.30, 4–7.30 🚇 Piazza Amedeo 🚌 102, 108, 122

⊕ MARINELLA
Riviera di Chiaia 287, 80122 Napoli
Tel 081 764 4214
www.marinellanapoli.it

If formal style is what you're after, then Marinella should be right up your street. This well-respected Neapolitan haunt has been patronized by the likes of Kennedy, Gorbachev and Caruso. The shop is famed

Track down some eclectic sounds at the Murat, Naples

for made-to-measure ties in silk, wool and other fabrics.

🕐 Mon–Sat 9.30–1.30, 3.30–8
🚇 Piazza Amedeo 🚌 102, 108, 122

⊕ MERCATO DI SANT'ANTONIO
Via Sant'Antonio Abate, 80139 Napoli

This market is always a feast for the senses and a little bewildering to the uninitiated. It's crammed with local produce, and traders use the local dialect. Try the fantastic tomatoes grown in the foothills of Vesuvio. If you would like a small amount of something, ask for *un etto, per favore* (100g, please).

🕐 Daily 9–8 🚌 14, 135, 254

♪ FONDAZIONE NUOVA ORCHESTRA ALESSANDRO SCARLATTI
Salita Betlemme 13, 80132 Napoli (headquarters)
Tel 081 410175
www.nuovaorchestrascarlatti.it

The Orchestra Scarlatti stages concerts at San Severo al Pendino and other historical sites and theatres around Naples. Well-known classical works and Neapolitan music through the ages.

💶 €5–€20 🚌 C4, 102, 128

♪ GRAN CAFFÈ GAMBRINUS
Via Chiaia 1 & 2, Napoli
Tel 081 417582
www.caffegambrinus.com/ing/home.htm

Sit out in Piazza Trieste e Trento or inside in the beautiful old-fashioned tea room of this Naples institution for a cocktail or to enjoy a pot of tea and exquisite Neapolitan cakes. Then you can buy their fine china cups and saucers, gift-wrapped in a rich blue box. The china is designed by Richard Ginori exclusively for this historic café. They also sell fine chocolates and fragrant fruit pastries *(sfogliate)* to take away. The tea room is decorated with the works of 13 artists and priceless sculptures, making it the most prestigious snack bar in Naples.

🕐 Daily 8.30–9pm

♪ MURAT LIVE CLUB
Via Bellini 8, 80135 Napoli
Tel 081 544 5919

This club on Piazza Dante has an adventurous music policy—the eclectic schedule includes lots of jazz and funk, all imbued with a touch of Neapolitan style. It also has the occasional world music night.

🕐 Daily 10pm–late 🚇 Montesanto
🚌 137, 160, 161

TEATRO POLITEAMA
Via Monte di Dio 80, 80132 Napoli
Tel 081 764 5001
This theatre often has lavish productions by the Scuola di Ballo del Teatro di San Carlo in conjunction with illustrious international companies, including the Birmingham Royal Ballet and the Conservatorio di San Pietro a Majella.
Box office: Tue–Sat 10–1, 4.30–6.30
€12–€45 102, 128

TEATRO SAN CARLO
Via San Carlo 98F, 80132 Napoli
Tel 081 797330
www.teatrosancarlo.it
The oldest opera house in Italy stages ballet as well as opera, classical concerts and short comic operas. It was here that some of the first ballet productions were performed, in the intermission between opera acts. Reserve tickets in advance.
Box office: Tue–Sun 10–1, 4.30–6.30
€20–€90 C4, 140, 149

SOLO
Via Ferrigni 19, 80121 Napoli
Tel 081 764 7420
Two floors of modern, cool furnishings set the mood in this trendy club. They serve superb aperitifs and have a fine menu. Mainstream dance and house music.
Tue–Sun 10pm–3.30am €15 membership Piazza Amedeo
1, 140, 152

VELVET ZONE
Via Cisterna dell'Olio 11, 80134 Napoli
Tel 339 670 0234
www.velvetnapoli.it
This long-established club attracts a discerning crowd with its eclectic, alternative music policy. Live bands and respected international DJs often play here.
Tue–Sun midnight–dawn €12 membership Montesanto

VIRGILIO
Via Tito Lucrezio Caro 6, 80123 Napoli
Tel 338 345 9007, 328 376 1518
Drag queens and a camp crowd flock to this open-air club to dance to classic hits and house on summer Saturday nights. It's a great place to people-watch.
Jun–end Sep Sat 11.30pm–4am
€13 Mergellina

YES BRAZIL
Via Posillipo 405/c, 80123 Napoli
Tel 349806 2385, 333 299 9332
www.yes-brazil.it
Join the fun-loving crowd at this tropical club with Brazilian beats. Dancers in skimpy outfits shake their tassels

Get up close to some volcanic mud at Solfatara

to the accomplished percussionists and the bubbly staff will keep you topped up with Brazilian drinks and fare all night long.
Daily 8pm–2am Mergellina

CIRCOLO DEL REMO E DELLA VELA 'ITALIA'
Banchina Santa Lucia, 80132 Napoli
Tel 081 764 6393
www.crvitalia.it
For those interested in sailing, this club has something to suit all abilities. Lessons and courses are available.
Daily 8.30–midnight 102, 140, 150

CLUB ALPINO ITALIANO
Via Trinità degli Spagnoli 41, 80132 Napoli
Tel 348 053 6215
If you fancy exploring the hills in the Campania region, the local branch of the Club Alpino should be your first port of call. They run trekking and climbing excursions to the summits of Vesuvio and Cervati.
Information Tue, Fri 7pm–9pm
Adult €51, child €18 102, 140, 150

EDENLANDIA
Viale Kennedy, Campi Flegrei, 80125 Napoli
Tel 081 239 0090
www.edenlandia.it
This theme park is just a short train ride away from the city. There are lots of attractions for all ages, including a fantasy castle, a 3-D cinema, variety shows, water rides and the exciting Star Wars ride.
Jun–end Aug daily 10.30am–midnight; check hours for rest of year
€2 152 Cumana train to Campi Flegrei

SOLFATARA
Via Solfatara 161, Pozzuoli, 80078 Napoli
Tel 081 526 2341
www.solfatara.it
Get closer to the volcanic rumblings of the earth's crust at Solfatara, a dormant volcano. Sulphurous fumes hang over the site, but the bubbling mud, fumaroles, and hot waters are the real spectacle to see.
Daily 8.30am to 1 hour before sunset €5 Pozzuoli–Solfatara and then bus P9 or 152

POSITANO

MUSIC ON THE ROCKS
Via Grotte dell'Incanto 51, 84017 Positano
Tel 089 875874
www.musicontherocks.it
Elegant club hewn out of the rocks serving fine cocktails. Italian-style piano bar most evenings and frequent appearances by well-known international DJs who spin house music.
Apr–end Sep daily 8pm–late
€10

CENTRO SUB
Via Fornillo, 84011 Positano
Tel 089 812148, 089 812884
www.centrosub.it
Discover fauna and archaeological wonders with Centro Sub. Dives visit the Grotte dello Smeraldo and Isola Li Galli, where you can learn about underwater photography and marine biology. They welcome all, from beginners to pros.
Daily 10–6 Courses €40

PRAIANO

L'AFRICANA
Vettica Maggiore, 84010 Praiano
Tel 089 874042
The most celebrated nightclub on this stretch of the Amalfi coast. A walkway hewn out of the rock leads to a network of caves that sit above the sea. Commercial dance and house music.
Thu–Sun 10–5 €12

RAVELLO

GIARDINI DI VILLA RUFOLO
Piazza Vescovado 1, 84010 Ravello
Tel 199 109910
www.ravellofestival.it
A Moorish-style villa and gardens that are a magnet for classical music fans. Wagner lived and composed at the nearby Palazzo Sasso. Ravello is a music capital, especially during the annual Festival Musicale di Ravello held from early June to late August.
Apr–end Sep daily 9–8; Oct–end Mar 9–6 €4

SALERNO

WIND'S AMICI DI GUIDO
Via Rocco Cocchia 181–185, Salerno
Tel 089 339316
www.flysurfsalerno.it
This windy spot is the best place to windsurf and fly power kites on the Amalfi coast. Equipment rental and lessons are available.
Daily 10–8 Lessons from €40 per day A3 Napoli–Salerno, exit Vietri sul Mare

SORRENTO

ENOTECA BACCHUS
Piazza San Antonio 20, 80067 Sorrento
Tel 081 807 4610
www.enotecabacchus.com
Sommelier Paolo Schiattarella selects the vintages here. There are more than 1,000 labels to choose from, as well as grappa, cognac, whisky, brandy, calvados, rum and various liqueurs.
Jun–end Sep daily 9–1, 4.30–10; rest of year 8.30–10pm

ARTIS DOMUS
Via San Nicolà, 80067 Sorrento
Tel 081 8772073
www.artisdomus.com
This elegant 19th-century villa is the Sorrentine haunt of poets and artists. Live pop/rock/jazz/folk music and club nights are held in an evocative and intimate setting. Excellent food and a fabulous cocktail bar/birreria.
Sat 8pm–late €5–€10

CIRCOLO DEI FORESTIERI
Via Luigi de Maio 35, 80067 Sorrento
Tel 081 877 3263
An impressive villa with elegant salons and panoramic views of Vesuvio and the Gulf of Naples. Things hot up later with live music and karaoke.
Daily 9pm–3am; closed Dec–end Feb

MATILDA CLUB
Piazza Tasso 1, 80067 Sorrento
Tel 081 877 3236
www.matildaclub.net
A superb, six-level nightclub. Live acts and regular club nights with house, Latin and dance music. Style and decor varies from elegant exposed walls to British pub to contemporary chic. Internet access is also available.
Daily 7.30pm–4am €12

TENNIS SORRENTO
Viale Montariello 4, 80067 Sorrento
Tel 081 807 4181
Tennis Sport Sorrento
Via Califano, 80067 Sorrento
Tel 081 8071616
There are two tennis clubs in Sorrento, both very busy in the summer. Each has half a dozen clay and concrete courts. Equipment rental is available.
Daily 10–10 €10 per hour

FESTIVALS AND EVENTS

MAY

FESTA DI SAN DOMENICO
Cocullo
This pre-Roman festival was adopted by the early Christian Church. It's dedicated to San Domenico Abbate, who delivered the town from poisonous snakes. On his feast day, his statue is carried through the town, and draped en route with hundreds of live snakes.
1st week in May

SAGRA DI SAN NICOLA
Bari
Three festivities honour St. Nicholas, patron saint of Bari. A parade processes to the basilica to deliver symbolically the saint's bones, which sailors brought back to the city in 1807. The next day, the saint's statue is carried to a fishing boat, where it is the focus of another three days of celebration. It's a festival untouched by tourism.
1st weekend in May

MAY/SEPTEMBER/ DECEMBER

FESTA DI SAN GENNARO
Naples
The fourth-century martyr San Gennaro is Naples' patron saint, and his blood has been kept in a vessel in an opulent sidechapel of the duomo since 1497. Three times a year, the blood is exhibited to a seething crowd and it liquefies. The time it takes to do so is said to portend the city's fortunes for the next year.
Saturday before the 1st Sunday in May, 19 September, 16 December

SICILY AND SARDINIA

Sicily's buzzing markets are one of Italy's great sights, where you'll be spoiled for choice if you want to track down local food to take home. Palermo's are the best, but towns like Siracusa, Agrigento and Noto also warrant a visit. These are also the places to head for other shopping—high-street fashion, wonderful food, interesting wine and above all, the bright ceramics made at Caltagirone.

For some unusual entertainment, catch a performance in the ancient Greek theatres at Taormina, Siracusa or Segesta, or hit Palermo for the island's funkiest nightlife.

Sardinia's capital, Cagliari, has the best of the island's shopping, though trendsetters might want to trawl the chic little shops tucked away in the Costa Smeralda developments. Sardinian cakes and pastries found all over the island are delicious and great presents to take home. Entertainment is strongest in Cagliari, but the clubs hot up in summer at resorts like Cala Gonone, and you shouldn't miss the traditional festivals in the island's interior.

KEY TO SYMBOLS	
⊕	**Shopping**
⊕	**Entertainment**
⊕	**Nightlife**
⊗	**Sports**
⊕	**Activities**
♡	**Health and Beauty**
⊗	**For Children**

Sicily

PALERMO

⊕ SICILY'S FOLK
Corso Vittorio Emanuele 450,
90133 Palermo
Tel 091 651 2787
Sicilian ceramics are among the most collectable in Italy. Caltagirone ceramics use blue, green and yellow glazes, depicting flowers, foliage and birds, and are Arab in style. There are some interesting, detailed figurines here, too.
🕐 Mon–Sat 8.30–1, 3.30–7.30 🚍 101, 122, 212

⊕ VUCCIRIA
Via Meli, 90213 Palermo
The Vucciria, near San Domenico, has a host of fresh produce, including the shiny swordfish, plump San Marzano tomatoes and tasty figs. The sights and smells of the Vucciria are unforgettable.
🕐 Mon–Sat 8–1 🚍 101, 212, 250

⊕ TEATRO MASSIMO
Piazza Verdi, 90138 Palermo
Tel 091 605 3111
www.teatromassimo.it
Completed in 1897, this opera house heralded the beginning of Palermo's *belle époque*. The house is certainly one of Europe's finest. The year-round entertainment includes opera, ballet and classical music.
💶 €60

⊕ AGRICANTUS
Via XX Septembre 82a, 90141 Palermo
Tel 091 309636
www.agricantus.org
More than just a bar, this place hosts world music bands, jazz groups, art exhibitions and dance productions. The multicultural crowd are always up for a good night out.
🕐 Daily 8pm–1.30am 💶 €6, free when there is no event

😊 MUSEO INTERNAZIONALE DELLE MARIONETTE
Via Butera 1, 90133 Palermo
Tel 091 328060
www.museomarionettepalermo.it
Children will love this museum of puppetry. It has a wonderful collection of puppets from all over the world, such as Britain's Punch and Judy and some sinister local characters.
🕐 Mon–Fri 9–1, 4–7 🎫 Adult €3, child €1.50

SIRACUSA
🌐 LA BOTTEGA DEL PUPARO
Via della Giudecca 19, 96100 Siracusa
Tel 0931 465540
Puppet shows are very much enjoyed in this part of Sicily. These traditional marionettes make great gifts or mementoes.
🕐 Mon–Sat 10–1, 5–8 🚋 1

🌐 ISTITUTO DEL PAPIRO
Via XX Settembre 19, 96100 Siracusa
Tel 0931 483342
www.papiro.it
The institute creates beautiful writing paper, bound books and lampshades out of papyrus. Many of the designs are heavily influenced by Greek and Egyptian art.
🕐 Mon–Sat 9.30–1, 4.30–8 🚋 1, 2

🌐 PESCHERIA
Molo Arezzo della Targia, 96100 Siracusa
The partially walled island of Ortigia is a fabulous setting for Siracusa's fish market. Ask for a tub of seafood salad, which you can eat on the *lungomare* (seafront).
🕐 Mon–Sat 8–1 🚋 1

🎭 TEATRO DELL'OPERA DEI PUPI
Via della Giudecca 17, 96100 Siracusa
Tel 0931 465540
www.pupisiciliani.com/eng/Default.htm
The Sicilian nobility, despite being toppled in the 19th century, are still very well represented in these puppet shows. Although staged for children, the shows have enough political commentary

and black humour to keep parents entertained.
🕐 Open all year for visits; performances Apr–end Dec 🎫 €8

TAORMINA
🎭 TEATRO GRECO
Via Teatro Greco, 98039 Taormina
Tel 0942 232220
Built by the Greeks around 250BC, this is arguably one of the greatest auditoriums in the world. Perched on the cliffs, it has stunning views of Mount Etna and the Bay of Axons. A variety of theatre, opera, cinema and music is shown here in the summer, but it's the views that steal the show.
🕐 Jul, Aug 🎫 €60

Searching for hidden treasure at Il Mercato del Bastione, Cagliari

Sardinia
CAGLIARI
🌐 IL FERRO BATTUTO
Via Oristano 18, 09127 Cagliari
Tel 070 502480
Ferro Battuto makes wrought-iron candlesticks, mirrors, lamps and furniture, all from original designs. Good reproductions of more classical designs are also produced.
🕐 Mon–Sat 9–1, 5–7 🚋 7, 8

🌐 IL MERCATO DEL BASTIONE
Bastione di San Remy, 90127 Cagliari
Among the bric-à-brac at this antiques flea market are retro

clothing, stylish crockery, photographs, newspapers and personalized recipe books.
🕐 Sun 🚋 7, 8

🌐 PASTICCERIA PIEMONTESE
Via Cocco Ortu 39, 09128 Cagliari
Tel 070 41365
Stop off at this shop for traditional Sardinian pastries such as *pistoccheddu prenu* (almond cream-filled pastry). They also make beautifully wrapped sweets and pralines.
🕐 Mon–Sat 9–1, 5–7 🚋 30, 31

🎭 CINEMA SOTTO LE STELLE
Marina Piccola, Viale Poetto, 09128 Cagliari
This 'cinema under the stars' shows general releases and cult films on a huge open-air screen at Marina Piccola—a magical way to watch a film on a warm summer's evening.
🕐 Jul, Aug 🎫 €7

🎭 NOTTE DEI POETI
Nora, 09010 Cagliari
Tel 070 270577
Evenings of prose and poetry are held in the Roman amphitheatre in the town of Nora, just south of Cagliari. Events are organized by a local theatre company.
🕐 Jul, Aug 🎫 €35 🚋 Cagliari–Nora A/R

😊 SHIPWRECKS OFF SARDINIA AIRSUB
Via Balilla 24–26, 09134 Cagliari–Pirri
Tel 070 506863
www.airsub.com
This company organizes year-round dives to the Roman and Spanish wrecks off the south coast of Sardinia. All equipment can be rented, and their shop sells a good range of snorkelling and diving gear.
🕐 Mon–Sat 8.30–1, 4.15–8.15
🎫 Dives €30–€250, equipment €8–€21

SICILY

JANUARY

FESTIVAL SUL NOVECENTO
Palermo
www.comune.palermo.it/Eventi
www.italiafestival.it/novecento
A performing arts festival with classical music, dance and opera to cheer the winter months. Initiated in 1995, it's been growing annually and takes place in venues all over the city.

FEBRUARY

ALMOND BLOSSOM FESTIVAL
Agrigento
www.festedisicilia.it/febbraio
Almond trees bloom early in Sicily and this festival, founded in 1937, celebrates both the coming of spring and folklore and popular culture from all over the world. Events take place in the Greek temples, and the week culminates with parades and fireworks.

CARNEVALE
All over Sicily and especially at Taormina and Acireale
www.festedisicilia.it/carnevale
Carnevale is enthusiastically celebrated with floats, parades, bands, dancing and fireworks all over Sicily, and particularly at Acireale and Taormina. Acireale festivities take place over 10 days and involve the entire town, with spectacular pyrotechnics on the final Tuesday.

MARCH–APRIL

HOLY WEEK CELEBRATIONS
Towns all over Sicily mark Holy Week with religious processions of great intensity. Statues are paraded through the streets and re-enactments of the Passion of Christ take place. Enna's parades are particulalry entertaining.
🕐 Week before Easter

MAY–JUNE

TEATRO GRECO
Siracusa, Sicily
www.siracusanet.it
The excellently preserved Greek theatre in the archaeological zone at Siracusa is the main venue for a festival of classical drama, when Greek plays are performed in their original setting.

AUGUST

FERRAGOSTO
www.festedisicilia.it/agosto
The great feast of the Assumption is celebrated in towns and villages all over Sicily with processions, parades, music and fun. Expect to see sumptuously decorated statues carried shoulder-high and the whole community letting its hair down late into the night.
🕐 15 August

SARDINIA

JANUARY

SAN ANTONIO ABATE FIRES
This pagan festival takes place in Mamoiada, Orisei, Torpè and other villages in the province of Nuovo. Villagers perform religious rites and blessings, and the festivities culminate in the lighting of huge bonfires.
🕐 16/17 January

FEBRUARY

LA SARTIGLIA
Oristano
Riders test their skills to the limits at this horseback tournament in Oristano—mounted competitors try to pierce a star that hangs above the streets with a sword and a carved wooden stick.
🕐 Last Sunday in Carnival and the following Thursday

APRIL

SA DIE DE SA SARDIGNA (SARDINIA'S DAY)
Cagliari
This festival commemorates the Sardinian Vespers, who brought about a popular rebellion on 28 April 1794 that led to the expulsion of the Piedmontese and the Viceroy Balbiano from Cagliari and Sardinia.
🕐 28 April

MAY

SAGRA DI SANT EFISIO
Cagliari, Sardinia
Sardinia's most important religious festival commemorates Sant'Efisio, a fourth-century Roman martyr. The feast dates from 1657, when prayers to the saint were believed to have delivered Cagliari from the plague. Decorated oxcarts and horsemen accompany the statue of the saint through the streets, and there is feasting, dancing and general jollity into the night.
🕐 1 May

AUGUST

SS. REDENTORE
Nuoro
This festival is a wonderful visual display of traditional costumes, horses, *traccas* (decorated carts), handicrafts and folk traditions. A singing competiton gives budding tenors the opportunity to showcase their talents.
🕐 29 August

WHAT TO DO

This chapter describes 9 walks and 17 drives that explore national parks, historic towns and areas of natural beauty from the Cinque Terre in the north to Sicily in the south. The walks and drives are marked on the map on page 278. The drives are plotted on individual maps and the start points of the walks that are on the drives are marked with a green numbered circle. Walks follow well-trodden paths, but it is advisable to buy a detailed map when walking in remote areas.

Out and About

THE CINQUE TERRE

This scenic route winds around a dramatic part of the Ligurian coastline, past secluded villages that cling to the steep cliffs (▷ 68). This area, the Cinque Terre or Five Lands, is a national park and a UNESCO World Heritage Site. There are plenty of hairpin bends so this drive is not for the faint-hearted, but there are some superb views.

THE DRIVE

Distance: 103km (64 miles)
Allow: 3 hours
Start/end at: Levanto

From Levanto, pick up the SP43 and drive through the industrial outskirts of the town. After 1km (0.6 mile) you reach a fork in the road where you turn left and begin to climb. Go through Busco, and then past Legnaro, where there is a very sharp bend. There are good views from here of the pretty village of Chiesanovo on the right. When you come to an intersection, turn left, following signs to La Spezia. Continue, passing the little church of Santuario di Soviore, and after another 1km (0.6 mile) take a right turn signposted for Vernazza.

❶ The views over the sea from now on are spectacular, with pink and toffee houses dotted over the hillsides below. The hills are terraced for the cultivation of vines, grown in small-layered patches held up by dry-stone walls *(muri a secco)*.

After 3km (2 miles) you come to another intersection—keep going straight for La Spezia. The road dips, then after 5km (3 miles) you come to another intersection where you turn left. (If you want to visit the village of Corniglia, turn right).

Vernazza on the Riviera Levante

❷ Corniglia is perched on the ridge of a rocky promontory at the foot of terraced vineyards. This fishing and farming community is similar architecturally to inland agricultural villages. The parish church of San Pietro, built in 1334 on the ruins of an 11th-century chapel, has a baroque exterior and is one of the most beautiful Gothic-Ligurian buildings in the Cinque Terre.

After thick patches of conifer woodland, the landscape opens out again with good views of Manarola, which juts out precipitously into the sea.

❸ While you drive you may occasionally see the quaint monorail trucks used by the farmers to help harvest their grapes from the terraced fields. The rare wine Sciachetra is produced in this area. The proximity of the vines to the sea and their exposure to the sun creates the ideal conditions for maturing grapes with high sugar content. The sweet flavour and golden colour of Cinque Terre wines make them an excellent complement to cheese, seafood and desserts.

Now head downhill to another intersection where you can turn right into the village of Manarola, or left to continue driving. This road, the SS370, climbs again for about 4km (2.5 miles), after which you enter a tunnel.

Continue straight ahead when you leave the tunnel and on your left-hand side you will see La Spezia, framed by mountains.

You soon come to an intersection, where you need to take a sharp right-hand turn at the traffic lights to join the SS530, which takes you to Portovenere. Follow this road as it climbs away from the harbour and after 8km (5 miles) you come to an intersection. Keep to the right, following signs for Portovenere.

After 3km (2 miles) you enter Portovenere (▷ 77), a pretty wedge of coloured houses. After exploring follow the road back to La Spezia. There is a NATO base in the port, so be prepared for heavy traffic and large vehicles.

La Spezia **❹** is the biggest naval base in the country. The public gardens in the west of the town are just a short distance away from Piazza Chirodo and La Spezia's naval Arsenale, rebuilt after World War II. Just off the complex is the Museo Tecnico Navale, celebrating La Spezia's naval history with impressive displays of battle relics and models.

Follow the road going through the centre of La Spezia, then turn left at the next intersection and pick up the SS1 for Ricco del Golfo. You no longer overlook the coast now and the landscape has a quiet, rural feel to it. Drive through the village and on to Borghetto di Vara, where you follow signs for the SS1 and continue to Cornice.

After 1.5km (0.9 mile) you will reach another intersection; turn left, following signs to 'Levanto 14'. Drive on for another 3km (2 miles), then turn left at the intersection onto the SS566. In about 45m (50 yards) you turn right again, go under a road bridge, through a tunnel and emerge at Ponte d'Osso. Continue downhill, enjoying views of Levanto as you descend into the village.

OUT AND ABOUT

The coastline near Vernazza (left) and the brightly painted houses that line the waterfront of Portovenere (right)

WHEN TO GO
Late spring and early autumn are quieter than summer.

WHERE TO EAT
Taverna Garibaldi in Levanto is an excellent pizzeria (Via Garibaldi 57, tel 018 7808098, 12–2, 7.30–11).

PLACE TO VISIT
Museo Tecnico Navale
Viale Amendola, 19122 La Spezia
☎ 0187 783016
🕐 Mon–Sat 8–6.45, Sun 8–1

Small boats in the harbour beneath the bright umbrellas of a café in Vernazza (above)

The dramatic coastline of the Cinque Terre attracts many artists (left)

A WINE TOUR FROM ALBA TO CUNEO

A vast array of wines is produced in northwest Italy, and the best of them come from the Langhe hills in southern Piedmont. From the medieval town of Alba this tour takes you through a picturesque landscape of hilltop villages and castles, passing many *enoteche*, *cantine* and private cellars en route, where you can sample the local produce.

THE DRIVE	
Distance: 92km (57 miles)	
Allow: 1 day	
Start at: Alba	
End at: Cuneo	

Capital of the Langhe district, Alba ❶ is famous for wine and white truffles. It was formerly known as the City of 100 Towers and although few of these survive, much of the town has kept its medieval appearance.

From Alba (▷ 67) follow the signs for Diano d'Alba, a village about 8km (5 miles) to the south, set among rolling vineyards.

❷ The vineyards here produce the fruity and fresh Dolcetto DOC table wine. This easy-drinking, sociable wine is renowned for its purplish ruby-red colour, plum and cherry flavours and distinctive bitter-almond aftertaste.

Backtrack to the left turn for Grinzane Cavour in the Gallo d'Alba direction.

Castello di Cavour ❸, which used to belong to Count Camillo Benso di Cavour (▷ 38), offers tours. It is home to the Museo dell'Enoteca Regionale Piemontese (Museum of Piedmont Vintage Wines), with a collection of tools used in wine production and the finest *enoteca*

Annunziata Barcio wine in the private cellar of the former abbey at Grinzane Cavour

(specialist wine shop) in the region. Established in 1967, it stocks an impressive range of Piedmont wines.

From the castle turn left for Gallo d'Alba, then left again, following signs for Serralunga d'Alba. Drive up the hillside to this medieval hilltop village, where the houses huddle around the foot of a 14th-century fortress. After exploring Serralunga, return in the direction of Gallo d'Alba. When you come to the main road turn left for Barolo.

The medieval village of Barolo ❹, home of 'the king of wines, the wine of kings', perches on the hill, its castle visible for miles around. Its elaborately decorated rooms are open to visitors and include the famous Silvio Pellico Library. The antique wine cellar houses the prestigious Enoteca Regionale del Barolo (Regional Wine-store of Barolo), which represents 11 boroughs in the Barolo area. Here you can stop and sample the wines and discover why they are so popular. On the upper floors is the Farming Museum, which illustrates the meticulous care and attention involved in producing Barolo's wines.

Leave Barolo following signs for La Morra, about 6km (4 miles) to the north.

La Morra ❺ is the capital of Barolo and produces a third of the wines; it also has superb views from the belvedere at the top of the town. Taste the local wines at the Enoteca Civica, which also has a wine exhibition, and at the Cantina Comunale (Via Carl Alberto 2, tel 0173 509204, Wed–Mon 10–12.30, 2.30–6.30).

Leave La Morra and take the road to Cherasco, crossing the River Tanaro.

Barolo, nestling in the rolling Piedmontese countryside

❻ Cherasco has much to explore: a well-preserved 14th-century castle, historic palaces and churches. It is also the centre of the National Association of Snail Breeders and hosts gourmet gastropod events in September.

From Cherasco, take the Bra road and turn left onto the SS231, which leads to Cuneo ❼.

Cuneo is the main town of southern Piedmont and is renowned for its Tuesday market, which fills the huge, arcaded Piazza Galimberti. The deconsecrated 13th-century Church of San Francesco houses the local museum and is also worth exploring.

OUT AND ABOUT

New casks containing wine in a cellar of one of the many vineyards in the Piedmontese hillsides around La Morra

Right: Lines of young vines neatly staked out on the slopes of the Piedmontese hills, near the town of Barolo

WHEN TO GO

October is the best time to go, for the grape harvest and the famous white truffles, though fog and rain may dampen your trip. Alternatively visit in late spring.

WHERE TO EAT

The Piedmont region takes its food very seriously. Truffles, cheese, hazelnuts and Barolo wine are just a few of the regional items often found on the menu. Try the Trattoria del Castello on the road up to Serralunga d'Alba (closed Wed) or the more expensive and elegant Locanda nel Borgo Antico in the centre of Barolo (closed Thu lunch). If you prefer a picnic there are some wonderful food shops in Alba.

PLACES TO VISIT

Enoteca Regionale and Museo dell'Enoteca Regionale Piemontese
Via Castello, 5, 12060 Grinzane Cavour
☎ 0173 262159
🕐 Wed–Mon 9–12, 2.30–6.30; closed Jan

Castello Falletti di Barolo
Piazza Falletti, 12060 Barolo
☎ 0173 334030. Enoteca 0173 56277
🕐 Fri–Wed 10–12.30, 3–6.30; closed Jan
www.barolodibarolo.com

LAGO DI COMO–LOWER LARIO

This drive follows the shores of the southern arms of Lake Como, past sumptuous villas and gardens, historic towns, resorts and fishing villages. High points are the village of Varenna, the Villa Carlotta at Tremezzo and the ferry trip across the lake. The hills above the lake, easily accessed from many resorts, provide fine views and excellent opportunities for hiking.

OUT AND ABOUT

THE DRIVE

Distance: 95km (59 miles)	
Allow: 1 day	
Start/end at: Lecco	

From Lecco take the SS36 Sondrio road north, through a series of tunnels. Come off at the Mandello/Varenna exit (7km/4 miles). Drive along the shore to the village of Varenna ❶, lying at the foot of the Grigna Mountains.

Narrow alleys and stepped streets lead down to the lake, with its promenade.

Take the car ferry (every 30–45 minutes in peak season) across to Menaggio, a lively resort with a pleasant lakeside promenade. Drive south along the SS340 to the Villa Carlotta, between the resorts of Cadenabbia and Tremezzo.

The famous Villa Carlotta ❷ was built by Marquis Clerici in the 18th century and was partially modified by Count Sommariva in the neoclassical style. Although it's now somewhat faded, you can still admire the original furniture and fine works of art inside. The villa has landscaped gardens, particularly lovely in spring, laid out by the subsequent owners, the Dukes of Sachsen Meiningen.

Continue south to Ossuccio, with its distinctive Romanesque tower topped by an unusual late-Gothic belfry. Just beyond Ossuccio take a boat from Sala Comacina to Isola Comacina ❸.

Tiny Isola Comacina is Lake Como's only island, an influential political and military base in the Middle Ages. After siding with Milan in the 10-year war between Como and Milan, it was ravaged in 1169 by the people of Como. Ruins and a baroque oratory are all that remain of the strategic settlement.

Drive another 4km (2.5 miles) around to Argegno, at the south of the delightful Val d'Intelvi. A cableway here climbs to the

The bell tower of Ossuccio

village of Pigra, commanding a splendid view of the lake. A stretch of fairly wild coastline leads to the pretty village of Moltrasio, via Brienno. Perched on the rugged lakeshore, it was once famous for the grey stone in its quarries, which is used in the buildings all around the shores of the lake. The next resort is Cernobbio, renowned for the exclusive villas built here from the 16th to 18th century.

The most famous is the 16th-century Villa d'Este ❹, once the home of Princess Caroline, wife of King George IV of England. Since 1873 it has been a luxury hotel, and every one of the 161 sumptuously decorated rooms in this historic building are unique. Overlooking the lake and surrounded by 10ha (25 acres) of parkland, the hotel has an 18-hole golf course and a wide range of outdoor and indoor sports and leisure facilities, including tennis courts, water-skiing, windsurfing, canoeing, squash courts, a gym and a spa.

The lakeside road leads south to Como.

❺ The fine walled city of Como is one of the most elegant places on the lake (▷ 69 and town walk ▷ 287).

From Como follow the signs for Lecco, which bring you to the SS639. Fork left after 6km (4 miles), keeping to the SS639. The road bypasses Erba—a former resort, it is now a major industrial hub. Another 10km (6 miles) brings you to Civate, departure point for San Pietro al Monte, a major Lombard Romanesque complex with fine views and rare 11th- and 12th-century frescoes. Return to the main road, which passes through several tunnels before reaching Lecco (7km/4 miles).

Lake Como viewed over the terracotta rooftops of the town of Menaggio, on the west side of the lake (left).
Small boats moored on the lakeside jetties in Varenna on the shores of Lake Como (right)

Lecco town on the shores of Lago di Lecco (above)

A ferry docked in front of the fine buildings of the town of Bellagio, strategically positioned where the three basins of Lake Como intersect (above)

WHERE TO EAT

There are plenty of lakeside cafés and restaurants to choose from en route. In Sala Comacina the delightful La Tirlindana (Piazza Matteotti 5, tel 0344 56637, daily 12.15–2.30, 7.30–11; closed Mon lunchtime) has wonderful homemade pasta.

PLACES TO VISIT

Villa Carlotta
Via Regina 2, 22019 Tremezzo
☎ 0344 40405
⏰ Apr–end Sep daily 9–6; Mar and Oct 9–11.30, 2–4.30
💶 Adult €7, students €3.50, under 6s free
www.villacarlotta.it

Villa d'Este
Via Regina 40, Como 22012 Cernobbio
☎ 031 3481
www.villadeste.it

DIFFERENZA F'A ... MERIDIANI

PARIGI
TORINO I.ᵃ del Ferro
COSTANTINOPOLI
BAGDAD LONDRA
PIETROBURGO LISBONA
NAPOLI
ROMA
VIENNA
VENEZIA

TEMPO MEDIO A MEZZODI VERO

GEN.
FEBBR.
MARZO
APRILE
APRILE
MAGGIO
GIUGNO
LUGLIO
AGOSTO
SETTEMBRE
OTTOBRE
NOV. DIC.

XII

DECLINAZIONE ORIENTALE DEL PIANO 34°.17'

LATITUDINE GEOGRAFICA DEL LUOGO 45°48'.15".

COMO TOWN

Off the lakeside drive (▷ 284–285), this walk meanders through the old centre of Como town (▷ 69) past fine monuments, silk and leather shops and inviting *pasticcerie* and cafés, ending with a funicular ride up to the village of Brunate with fine views above and across the lake.

THE WALK

Length: 2.7km (1.7 miles)
Allow: 2 hours
Start at: Piazza Cavour
End at: Brunate

From the 19th-century Piazza Cavour, with its open-air cafés and views of the lake, take Via Caio Plinio Secondo to the left of the Hotel Barchetta Excelsior. This leads into Piazza Duomo, the heart of the old centre and the finest square in the city.

Here you see the towering Torre del Comune, dating from 1215, the Broletto, a former law court from the same period, with stripes of pink, white and grey marble, and the magnificent Gothic/Renaissance duomo, with its lavish marble exterior and 15th- to 16th-century sculpture.

From the duomo head down Via Vittorio Emanuele II.

Halfway down on the right is the five-sided apse of the Church of San Fedele and the carved 'door of the dragon'. The building opposite (16th–17th century) has been the town hall since 1853.

The street ends in Piazza Medaglie d'Oro, dominated by the archaeological and historical museums, occupying the palazzi Giovio and Olginati respectively. Pass under the arch on the

*A sundial on the duomo (left).
A statue of Alessandro Volta, the inventor of the battery (right)*

left, along Via Serafino Balestra, formerly called Vicolo delle Orfanelli (Little Orphans Alley). Follow the medieval wall to the Torre di San Vitale, an imposing tower in the city walls. Turn right when you reach the busy Viale Battisti, keeping to the old city walls.

Continue south here and you come to the Basilica di Sant'Abbondio, a Romanesque construction that stands out in a rather dreary part of town.

Como's duomo

From Viale Battisti turn right by the medieval tower, best viewed from the far side. Turn right at the end of the road, down Via Giuseppe Rovelli, take the first left and turn right for Piazza San Fedele.

This square was built on the site of the Roman

forum, and until the 1800s the town market was held here. Today it is a small, intimate space, with cafés, arcades and a couple of finely preserved medieval buildings, which contrast with the uninspiring façade of San Fedele, rebuilt in the early 20th century.

Exit the piazza on the side facing San Fedele, crossing Via Indipendenza, one of the main shopping streets. Continue straight ahead to return to Piazza

Cavour. At the lakeside—a busy scene of boats and ferries—turn right, following the waterfront until you reach Piazza di Gasperi. The funicular here departs every 15 minutes and takes just over 6 minutes to reach Brunate, a village 720m (2,362ft) above the city, with magnificent views over Lake Como and the Alps.

WHEN TO GO
Avoid doing this walk between 12 and 3, when the churches and museums are closed.

WHERE TO EAT
There are plenty of good cafés and restaurants to choose from en route.

LIMONE–SIRMIONE

This drive skirts the northern and eastern shores of Lake Garda (▷ 71), stopping at historic towns along the way, dominated by Scaligeri castles, built by the della Scala family from Verona. In the north, dramatic peaks rise sheer from the deep waters; in the south, the lake broadens into a vast expanse of blue water.

THE DRIVE

Distance:	93km (58 miles)
Allow:	1 day
Start at:	Limone
End at:	Sirmione

❶ Limone sul Garda, which lies below white cliffs, is named after the lemon trees that once made it prosperous. A small resort, it has a centre of narrow alleys and a popular waterfront with lake-view cafés and restaurants.

From Limone sul Garda take the SS45 north through a series of tunnels for Riva del Garda.

At the northern tip of the lake, sitting spectacularly below the mountains, is Riva del Garda ❷. Formerly a trading port, today it is a thriving resort with a prominent castle, home to the Museo Civico, and an attractive medieval core.

Follow the signs for Torbole (4km/2.5 miles to the east), a small resort that is a magnet for windsurfers as the north winds guarantee action. Follow the main road (SS249) down the eastern shore of the lake, passing through tunnels, and continue as far as Malcesine.

❸ Dominated by the striking Castello Scaligero and set below the scenic Monte Baldo, Malcesine is the highlight of the lake's eastern shore. From the castle tower you can appreciate views of the surrounding walls and steep cliffs. Inside the castle there is a museum featuring a collection of weapons, archaeological finds and objects from the Italian Risorgimento (resurgence), the 50-year struggle for liberation from foreign rule that culminated in the Unification of Italy in 1870. Malcesine's panoramic cable car will take you up to Monte Baldo, for excellent views and rare mountain flora, an ideal spot for a walk.

Continue south through a series of villages, the prettiest of which is Castelletto, where old houses group around Piazza dell'Olivio. Travel along this road to reach Torri del Benaco.

❹ Despite being a ferry terminus, Torri del Benaco still retains its old character—a charming port with a castle on the lakeside. The della Scala family rebuilt the castle between 1383 and 1393 on Roman foundations and it now houses a museum. From Torri del Benaco to Peschiera del Garda most of the lakeside has been developed for tourism.

Stop at Punta di San Vigilio, occupied by the lovely Villa Guarienti, a church, park and beach. Beyond the resort of Garda is Bardolino ❺.

This area is synonymous with light, fruity red wine.

Bardolino's wine museum, the Museo del Vino at the Cantina Zeni, has some interesting exhibits on the history of wine-making in the region, the highlight being the opportunity to taste (for free) the full range of wines made in the Gardesana area. Bardolino also has an olive-oil museum, with an exhibition illustrating the history of olive-oil production in rural society that stretches back over 1,000 years. Many different kinds of extra-virgin olive oil can be tasted and bought in the museum shop, which is also stocked with a wide variety of Italian delicacies including spiced oils, aromatic vinegar, pesto and a selection of wines from the Garda region.

Continue south towards Peschiera del Garda.

For many visitors the main attraction of Peschiera del Garda ❻ is the popular Gardaland (on the right before you reach the resort), northern Italy's answer to Disneyland. The town itself is a busy intersection, with a formidable fortress.

From Peschiera del Garda take the SS11, following the signs to Sirmione.

The loveliest of Garda's resorts and a mecca for day-trippers, Sirmione ❼ stands on the tip of a thin, craggy peninsula extending 4km (2.5 miles) into the lake; the remains of a huge Roman villa (Grotte di Catullo) occupy a spectacular position there. A beautiful 13th-century castle, surrounded by a moat, dominates the old quarter. Visitors' cars must be left outside the town.

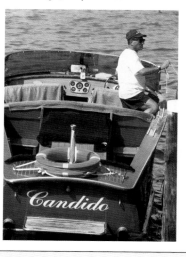

A boat mooring at Sirmione on Lake Garda

The hotel at Punta di San Vigilio, near Garda town (left)

A streetside stand selling lemons close to the central castle in Sirmione on Lake Garda (below)

WHEN TO GO

Avoid July and August, when the roads are choked with traffic. Spring is the ideal time to go.

WHERE TO EAT

The lakeside resorts have no shortage of cafés, pizzerias and restaurants. There are plenty of places by the lake where you can picnic. One of the prettiest spots to stop for a drink or meal is the old port in Torri del Benaco.

PLACES TO VISIT

Gardaland
Castelnuovo del Garda, 37014 Verona
☎ 045 6449777
🕐 Late Mar to mid-Jun daily 10–6; mid-Jun to early Sep 9am–midnight; early Sep–end Sep 10–6; Oct–early Nov weekends only 10–6; closed early Nov–late Mar
💶 Adults €24, under 10s €20
www.gardaland.it

Museo del Vino
Cantina Zeni, Via Costabella 9, Bardolino
☎ 045 7210022
🕐 Mon–Fri 8–12, 2–6; Apr–end Sep also Sat 9–12
www.kilkelly.com/Garda.html

Oleificio Cisano del Garda
Via Peschiera 54, 37011 Cisano di Bardolino VR–Lago di Garda
☎ 045 6229047
🕐 Mon–Sat 9–12.30, 2.30–7; Sun and public holidays 9–12.30; closed Jan, Feb, Sun, 15 Aug, 25–26 Dec, 1 and 6 Jan
💶 Free
www.museum.it

Museo Civico
Piazza Battisti 3, Riva del Garda
☎ 046 4 573869
🕐 Jul, Aug Tue–Sun 4–10; rest of year Tue–Sun 9.30–12.30, 2–6
www.garda.com/museocivico

Torri del Benaco
Via Costello, 370018 Malcesine
☎ 045 7400837
🕐 Daily 9.30–7.30; closed Oct–end Mar
💶 €4

Museo del Castello Scaligero di Torri del Benaco
Informazione Turistica, Viale F.lli Lavanda 2, 37010 Torri del Benaco
☎ 045 7225120
🕐 Mon–Sun 9.30–1, 4.30–7.30
💶 €3

OUT AND ABOUT

GRANDE STRADA DELLE DOLOMITI

This drive follows the Grande Strada delle Dolomiti (Great Dolomites Road), which was constructed in 1909 to link Bolzano and Cortina d'Ampezzo. It cuts through some of Europe's most breathtaking mountain scenery, navigating high passes and fertile alpine valleys. Pretty villages line the route, and cable cars and chairlifts give access to the higher slopes.

THE DRIVE	
Distance: 90km (56 miles)	
Allow: 3 hours' driving time	
Start at: Bolzano	
End at: Cortina d'Ampezzo	

Leave Bolzano/Bozen and head northeast in the direction of Bressanone/Brixen (▷ 104). Take the SS241, which is signposted in brown for the Eggental, and head along the Valle d'Ega (Eggental) towards Lago di Carezza.

❶ As you hit the SS241 the road immediately twists and climbs as it cuts through a narrow gorge into the mountains. As it gradually opens up the high peaks of the Latemar and Catinaccio/Rosengarten massifs begin to appear, giving you the first taste of the area's scenic glories. Make your first stop at Carezza al Lago, beside a beautiful lake whose

Lago di Carezza

turquoise waters reflect the surrounding dark fir trees and mountain ridges. You can stretch your legs by following the well-made track around the lake, approximately a 30-minute stroll. From the lake the road continues to climb up to the Passo di Costalunga (1,745m/5,725ft), the first of the high passes along this route, which forms the boundary between the Alto Adige and Trentino regions.

Continue on the SS241 over the Passo di Costalungo, which drops down into the beautiful Val di Fassa.

Once over the pass, the road descends into the Val di Fassa **❷**, a lovely alpine valley that attracts mountain sports enthusiasts in summer and winter. The River Avisio runs through the valley past a string of pretty villages, among them Vigo di Fassa, all catering to

holidaymakers. From Vigo di Fassa you can head up into the hills for a high-altitude walk through the Catinaccio mountains (▷ 292–293).

About 1.5km (0.9 mile) past Vigo di Fassa turn left onto the SS48 towards Canazei. Drive up the valley past Canazei and stay on the SS48 towards the Passo Pordoi **❸** (2,239m/7,346ft).

For the next 12km (7.5 miles) you will wind around 27 hairpin bends and the road becomes increasingly challenging, with dramatic views of soaring mountains all around and the green meadows of the Val di Fassa below. Passo Pordoi is the highest pass along the drive and you're likely to find yourself above the snowline at most times of year.

More hairpins snake down to Arabba **❹**, a mountain village that is a popular resort with winter skiers. Stay on the SS48 through Arabba.

From Arabba the road threads its away along the sides of a heavily wooded valley, where houses are few and far between and there's a real sense of isolation amid the upland countryside. Another steep section of road snakes up to the Passo di Falzarego (2,105m/6,906ft). Look for the stark outline of the ancient Castello di Andraz on your left and the relatively rare stone pines that dot the slopes of the high meadows around here. At Falzarego the views open up across new mountain ranges and peaks before the road begins its descent.

Stay on the SS48 towards Cortina d'Ampezzo. The contrasts of landscape are stark on this last section of the drive, where rocky mountain slopes tower above deciduous forests and alpine

OUT AND ABOUT

doesn't appeal, you can glide around the Olympic skating rink or ride on a horse-drawn sleigh or dog sled. Thrill-seekers can rent skidoos or experience an Olympic bobsleigh run via the Taxi-bob-sleigh, which takes you to speeds of over 120kph/75mph (tel 0436 860808).

A lonely mountain hut: Canazei in the Dolomites

OUT AND ABOUT

pastures. The road passes through the village of Pocòl and emerges into the mountain bowl that encircles Cortina d'Ampezzo.

Affectionately known as the pearl of the Dolomites, Cortina d'Ampezzo **5** is Italy's glitziest winter resort. It hosted the first televised Winter Olympics in 1956, and the awesome peaks formed the backdrop for some jaw-dropping scenes in the James Bond film *For Your Eyes Only* (1981), and *Cliffhanger* (1993), starring Sylvester Stallone. There are pistes for all skiing abilities, but if that

Campitello, with the Sassolungo rock pillars behind

THE HEART OF THE CATINACCIO

This straightforward walk is one of the easiest and most spectacular of the high-altitude Dolomite trails, giving you a true taste of the power and beauty of the mountains (▷ 107). The route plunges deeper and deeper into the peaks of the Catinaccio (Rosengarten), lined with alpine flowers, trees and shrubs and all without struggling on foot from the valley bottom.

THE WALK

Length: 6km (3.7 miles)

Allow: 1.5–2 hours

Ascent: 100m/328ft

Start/end at: Vigo di Fassa

Paths: Excellent, wide stony mountain trails. Can be slippery in icy/snowy conditions. Late spring and early autumn snow can hang around in patches, so shoes or walking boots with good grip are essential outside the peak summer season

Parking: Funivia Ciampedie (Ciampedie cable car) parking in Vigo di Fassa

Toilets: At rifugi alpini (mountain refuges)

After parking the car, buy a return ticket for the *funivia* (daily, every 15 minutes, 8.30–1, 3.30–6; €9). The cable car takes the strain, whisking you over 600m (1,970ft) up the mountain. As it ascends there are ever-widening views over the Val di Fassa and the Monzoni massif to the southeast. Leave the cable car at the top and walk out onto the Ciampedie plateau (1,998m/6,555ft).

Look for the waymark signpost (a little to the left) showing 540 and follow the trail down the hill with the *rifugio alpino* (mountain refuge) on your right. About 200m (218 yards) after the path flattens, take trail 540 (way-marked) contouring to the right. This splendid path leads right into the heart of the Catinaccio (Rosengarten) range, some of the Dolomites' most impressive mountain scenery.

The German name for these peaks means 'Rose Garden', an apt reference to the blush pink of the stone, which looks its deepest at dawn and by twilight. Legend has it that, betrayed by the colour and splendour of his roses, the king of the dwarves was dragged away from his mountain kingdom. He cursed the roses, binding them with a spell to

A snowy path in the Dolomites

make them invisible by day and night. While he ranted, he forgot to mention dawn and dusk, which is when the mountains glow a vibrant pink.

Follow the trail through the woods, across two ski slopes, grassy in summer, and under the cables of two ski lifts.

The woods are pine, carpeted with alpine shrubs. The most common are juniper, alpenrose *(Rhododendron ferrugineum)*, whose lovely pink azalea-like flower blooms from late June to August, and bilberry. Bilberries have small dark berries with a lustrous bloom and intense flavour; look for ripe fruit if you're walking in late August and September. The juniper berries that grow here have been used for centuries to flavour spirits and liqueurs and are still used today in many of the locally distilled *digestivi* and *aperitivi*.

Head deeper into the circle of peaks where the path undulates and the summits grow ever closer and more dramatic.

The highest peaks of the Catinaccio/Rosengarten group are the Cima Scalieret (2,887m/9,472ft), to your right, and Punta Emma (2,919m/9,577ft), ahead and to your left. All these peaks are popular with rock climbers and many of them have *vie ferrate* (fixed iron ladders) to help mountaineers on the precipitous rock walls (▷ 13).

The path descends out of the woods and ahead of you stands the pink-washed building of the Rifugio Catinaccio (1,960m/6,430ft), where you can rest and admire the mountain peaks.

There are hundreds of *rifugi alpini* throughout the Dolomites, some providing food and drinks, others offering

accommodation for hikers following the long-distance paths through the mountains.

Retrace your route back to the cable car. With the Catinaccio behind you, wide views open out to the mountains of the southeast.

The lumpy peak is the unmistakable silhouette of Marmolada, at 3,246m (10,650ft) the highest peak in the Dolomites, with its permanent glacier draped down one side.

If you are feeling fit you can tackle the other side of the range. Take the Paolina chairlift from Passo di Carrezza and follow trails 539 and 549 to Baita Pederiva. This is a 5km (3-mile) walk with more stupendous views.

A sign pointing the way through the pine woods in Catinaccio

WHERE TO EAT

Rifugi alpini at Ciampedie (top of the cable car) or Rifugio Catinaccio at the far end of the walk.

WHEN TO GO

The path is open all year round, but the less sure-footed should avoid the route during late autumn and winter, when the trail can get icy and slippery.

OUT AND ABOUT

THE GARFAGNANA

This drive takes you through the cool mountains of the Garfagnana (▷ 141), the region north of Lucca that stretches between the rugged national parks encompassing the Alpi Apuane in the west and the softer slopes of the Orecchiella in the east. Towns and villages are sprinkled about the hills, and there are plenty of paths if you wish to stop and explore on foot.

THE DRIVE

Distance:	170km (106 miles)
Allow:	8 hours
Start/end at:	Lucca

Leave Lucca (▷ 142) through Porta San Donato and pick up the SR12 signposted for Abetone. At the next turn follow the signs for Castelnuovo di Garfagnana. After 4km (2.5 miles) you will see the Lucchesi hills in front of you. Shortly afterwards, turn left at the brown signpost indicating Garfagnana and cross the bridge over the River Serchio onto the road that runs parrallel to the SR12 on the opposite bank. Go through two tunnels and after about 4km (2.5 miles) turn left again. Stay on this road, which passes through Diecimo, flanked by papermaking factories, an old local industry in this area. Drive on to the village of Borgo a Mozzano, where there is a bell tower on the left-hand side. Just after this is a sign saying 'Barga 18'; go over a bridge.

To the left of the road, spanning the river, is the distinctive 12th-century hump-back bridge known locally as Ponte del Diavolo ❶ (Devil's Bridge). According to legend the builder sought help from the Devil to build it and in return the Devil demanded the soul of the first being who

The Ponte del Diavolo just outside Bargo a Mozzano

crossed the river. The builder is said to have outwitted the Devil by making sure that a dog went over the bridge first.

After about 8km (5 miles) take a right-hand turn signed 'Barga', cross the river, turn left into Calavorno, then drive on through Piano di Coreglia to reach Fornaci di Barga. Just at the

entrance to this village take the right-hand fork to Barga, after which the road climbs uphill and the scenery becomes craggier and more alpine in appearance.

Barga ❷ is a hilltop town with a fine Romanesque cathedral (▷ 139). Don't miss the panoramic views of the mountains from the terrace by the cathedral entrance.

The red-roofed houses of Castelnuovo di Garfagnana

Drive on through Barga and follow the sign for Castelnuovo di Garfagnana. Cross another river and drive through Castelvecchio Pascoli, close to which is the house of Giovanni Pascoli, the celebrated 19th-century Italian poet. Continue through Ponte di Campia and follow the SR445 for about 9km (6 miles) through the thickly wooded hills to reach Castelnuovo di Garfagnana. This is the largest town in the area, where the Regional Park Office provides maps, books and information on the region. When you reach the crossroads take the SP72 signposted for San Pellegrino in Alpe.

Drive through Campori ❸. As you leave, the road begins to wind steeply upwards, cutting through hills cloaked with chestnut trees. For many years the economy of the Garfagnana depended on chestnuts, cheese and spelt (a type of wheat).

After 13km (8 miles) you will reach San Pellegrino in Alpe ❹.

Continued on page 296

OUT AND ABOUT

SR324

Sant'Anna Pelago

4 10

San Pellegrino in Alpe

SS324

Pievepelago

SR12

Fiumalbo

3

Abetone

La Regine

Campori

1991 ▲ Mte Giovo

Pian di Novello

Cutigliano

Castelnuovo di Garfagnana

SR445

Castelvecchio Pascoli

Piano degli Ontani

SR12

Barga

2

La Lima

Fornaci di Barga

Piano di Coreglia

Calavorno

SR12

Popiglio

5

Bagni di Lucca

Borgo a Mozzano

1 **Ponte del Diavolo**

Diecimo

G a r f a g n a n a

A l p i   A p u a n e

0 ___ 8 km
0 ___ 5 miles

Serchio

SR12

Pescia

SS435

A11

A11 / A12

A11

Lucca

OUT AND ABOUT

Spring and autumn are the best times to visit; August is the most crowded time and in winter snow and ice can make driving hazardous.

Barga's historic Caffè Capretz (Piazza Salvo Salvi 1, tel 0583 723001, closed Tue) is close to the Tourist Information Office. Here you can sit outside on a sunny day and enjoy a cappuccino and a pastry. Further along the route at San Pellegrino in Alpe is Albergo l'Appennino da Pacetta (Piazza San Pellegrino 5, tel 0583 649069, daily 12–2, 7–9.30), a relaxed family restaurant and inn with a sister café on the other side of the

road (tel 0583 649069). All the food is homemade, from the cakes and pasta to the bread

and jam. There are also several places in Bagni di Lucca where you can grab a quick coffee.

Museo Etnografico Provinciale

Via del Voltone, San Pellegrino in Alpe
☎ 0583 649072
🕐 Apr, May Tue–Sun 9–12, 2–5; Jun–end Sep 9.30–1, 2.30–7; Oct–end Mar Tue–Sat 9–1, Sun 9–12, 2–5; Jul, Aug, also open Mon
🎟 Ticket €1.50

Thermal waters running from the mouth of a fountain in Bagni di Lucca, a resort founded by Elisa Baciocch, sister of Napoleon and princess of Lucca

---

Continued from page 294

The spa resort of Bagni di Lucca

San Pellegrino is a little mountain village that has attracted pilgrims and artists for centuries, including Michelangelo and the poet Shelley. This is a good spot for a walk (▷ 297) and a bite to eat. It is also the home of the Museo Etnografico Provinciale, an excellent folk museum.

Drive on from San Pellegrino and join the SR324, which winds downhill. Follow the road as it passes through Sant'Anna Pelago and Pievepelago. At the

crossroads, turn right, taking the SR12 towards Abetone. Here you cross the river and start to climb again. Drive for 7km (4 miles) until you reach Abetone, a ski resort with a distinct alpine feel.

From Abetone the SR12 winds downhill to La Regine. You can continue following the SR12 here, or take an alternative route through the mountain woods and villages by turning off to the right at the brown sign just outside Abetone indicating Piano degli Ontani. Drive along this quiet little road for about 2km

(1.3 miles), then take the left-hand fork and continue through the woods to reach Pian di Novello, a small skiing village. From here the road winds steeply downhill, through Piano degli Ontani, eventually rejoining the SR12, where you turn right and follow the road to La Lima. Bear right in La Lima on the SR12, then drive through Popiglio, following the road for 17km (11 miles) until you reach Bagni di Lucca. Cross the small bridge on the right-hand side to reach the heart of the town.

⑤ Bagni di Lucca gained a reputation as a spa town in the 19th century, attracting many illustrious visitors who came to take the waters including Lord Byron, Shelley, and Robert and Elizabeth Barrett Browning.

Cross back over the bridge and continue along the SR12, which passes the Ponte del Diavolo and takes you back to Lucca.

The River Lima, with some of Castelnuovo di Garfagnana's buildings reflected in the clear, still waters

THE PILGRIM TRAIL FROM SAN PELLEGRINO

This is an easy, but rewarding, circular walk high in the mountains of the Garfagnana (▷ 141). It starts and ends in the hamlet of San Pellegrino in Alpe, a settlement that grew up around the relics of St. Pellegrino and that has attracted countless pilgrims since the eighth century. You can enjoy striking views over the mountains at several points along the trail.

THE WALK

Length: 4km (2.5 miles)
Allow: 1 hour
Start/end at: Middle of San Pellegrino in Alpe, with the L'Appennino da Pacetto inn on your left and the museum on your right
Paths: Wide, firm tracks and one section of quiet road
Parking: Free parking in the centre of San Pellegrino in Alpe

Begin in the heart of the village, in the square between the museum and the inn. With the museum on your right, walk forward until you find a red-and-white sign on the side of a building marked 'In giro monte Spicio'. Go up the steps. Pass the mobile phone mast on the right-hand side and follow the wide path flanked by trees. Follow this wooded path for just over 1km (0.6 mile).

The landscape now begins to open up, taking on the appearance of lonely moorland, with heather dotting the land on either side of the track. It can get foggy up here, but on clear days you should be able to enjoy some good views on the right-hand side.

Continue to follow the main track, ignoring any side routes, until the path intersects with a wide gravel track. You'll know you've reached it as there is a green post marking the point where the paths cross.

If you turn to the right here you will come to a tiny stone building, known as the Capella di San Pellegrino. Pellegrino, who was said to be the son of the king of Scotland, came to this area on a pilgrimage in the seventh century and stayed to provide refreshment and accommodation for other pilgrims.

To return to the main route, turn left and follow the wide track. Keep walking until you reach a bend in the path.

On the left-hand side of this bend is a rocky outcrop with an excellent viewpoint, a good photo opportunity. From here you can also appreciate just how high up you are.

Continue following the wide track, walking down until you reach a tarmac road. At this point you are on the border between Tuscany and Emilia-Romagna. Turn left and walk downhill, along the tarmac road. It's generally quiet, but still keep a sharp look-out for any passing cars. Follow this road until you return to San Pellegrino. There are some fantastic views of the mountains as you approach the village.

WHERE TO EAT

L'Appennino da Pacetto café in San Pellegrino, opposite the inn in Piazza San Pellegrino (tel 0583 649069).

WHEN TO GO

This area can be covered with snow as early as October so, despite the easy tracks, you should do this walk only in good weather.

An autumnal view of the hills around San Pellegrino in Alpe

OUT AND ABOUT

SIENA–VOLTERRA AND SAN GIMIGNANO

The delightful rolling countryside that characterizes Tuscany features on this drive. You travel along quiet roads through gently undulating hills, past olive groves, cypress trees and immaculately preserved hilltop towns and villages, many of which are generally overlooked by visitors.

THE DRIVE	
Distance: 154km (96 miles)	
Allow: 8 hours	
Start/end at: Siena	

From Siena, follow the road from Porta Romana and turn right at the sign for the A1. Turn left shortly afterwards, signposted Firenze, and follow the road *(tangenziale)* around the outskirts of Siena. After 6km (4 miles) go through a tunnel and follow the signs on the right for Monteriggioni (▷ 144).

You will soon see the walls of Monteriggioni sitting high on the hill. Park at the bottom of the village ❶ and climb to the top. The climb is worth it to see this extraordinarily well-preserved medieval fortified town, encircled by tower-studded walls.

From Monteriggioni follow the signs saying 'Firenze 46'. Turn left at the sign for Colle di Val d'Elsa.

❷ The landscape now becomes flatter and is covered with vineyards–this area is known as Chianti Colle Senesi (Sienese Hills Chianti). When you reach a roundabout (traffic circle) you will see a large sign on the left saying CALP—one of the biggest producers of rock crystal in the world.

Drive into Colle di Val d'Elsa ❸, going uphill to reach Colle Altao, the old part of town, and parking in the parking area on Via della Porta Vecchia.

Defined by three levels—Borgo, Castello and Piano (the Town, Castle and Plain)—Colle di Val d'Elsa is renowned for the production of fine handcrafted crystal. The town is entered through the monumental Porta Nuova that forms the gateway to a string of fine

16th- and 17th-century noble houses: the town hall, Palazzo Usimbardi, Palazzo Buoninsegni and the magnificent, but unfinished, Palazzo Campana, which marks the entrance to the castle, the oldest part of Colle di Val d'Elsa. The Piazza del Duomo is overlooked by the Praetorial Court, the seat of the Museo Archeologico (Archaeological Museum), the 17th-century cathedral, the Bishop's Palace, housing the Museo Civico e d'Arte Sacra (Museum of Religious Art), and the Via delle Volte, easily the most evocative corner of the town.

From Colle take the SS68, following signs for Volterra. After 6km (4 miles) the road starts to

A stand selling ceramic masks and local guidebooks in San Gimignano

climb into the heart of the country. Go through Castel San Gimignano, after which there are glorious views of vine-dotted hills, olive groves, dark cypresses and fields of sunflowers. There is a thermal electric plant at Lardarello, 33km (21 miles) from Volterra. Look for steam rising from the underground

thermal springs that spurt from these hills. After about 8km (5 miles) you should begin to see Volterra on the horizon as you reach the top of the hill and shortly you will see a sign saying 'Casciana Terme/Pontedera 44', where it is possible to turn right and make a diversion for a short walk up Monte Voltraio.

After 1km (0.6 mile) you come to Volterra ❹, a delightful Etruscan town containing fine medieval buildings and a Roman theatre (▷ 156).

Leave Volterra and follow signs for Pontedera. After 4km (2.5 miles) you will see a yellow sign on the left-hand side for San Cipriano, a little church that is an ideal spot for taking some photographs of the extensive views. Alternatively, keep going and follow the SP15 as it winds its way downhill, taking the right-hand fork and going over a modern bridge until you reach an intersection. Take the turn for Firenze and follow the SP4 for about 9km (6 miles). Turn right and follow the signs for San Gimignano. You will soon see the town perched on a hill in the distance; drive up and park outside the town walls. This may be difficult unless you arrive early in the day.

San Gimignano ❺ (▷ 151) is frequently referred to as the medieval Manhattan, due to its striking crown of ancient towers. It's worth stopping to walk around the streets.

Drive around the town walls to reach an intersection, where you turn right for Poggibonsi. Go straight over the next roundabout towards Poggibonsi. When you reach the uninspiring industrial town, go left at the next roundabout, and get on the SS2 (Cassia) back to Siena.

OUT AND ABOUT

Cafés and restaurants on the Campo in Siena (left)

Looking down on Piazza della Cisterna, from Torre Grossa in San Gimignano (right)

The view across the sun-kissed olive groves at Volterra in Tuscany, a steep tree-covered valley dropping down in the distance

WHERE TO EAT

There are several places to choose from in Volterra, including the Trattoria da Bado (Borgo San Lazzero 9, tel 0588 86477, 12–2, 7–9.30; closed Wed) at the entrance to the town, which serves typical Tuscan dishes. Alternatively, if you just want a snack, there is an Internet Café on Via Porte Lago, which has a glass floor revealing the remains of a Roman grain silo. Just outside the town, off the SR439, is Villa Palagione, an elegant villa that is happy to cater for non-residents—a lovely rural spot for a snack or a meal. You have several choices of restaurants, cafés and pizzerias in San Gimignano. The Gelateria di Piazza in Piazza della Cisterna has a reputation for serving the best ice cream in town.

WHEN TO GO

The scenery makes this drive good at any time of the year, but to miss the crowds you should try to visit in early spring or late autumn. Arrive early in San Gimignano to park your car.

PLACES TO VISIT

Museo Archeologico

Palazzo del Duomo, Piazza del Duomo, 53034 Colle di Val d'Elsa
🕐 May–end Sep Tue–Fri 10–12, 5–7, Sat–Sun 10–12, 4.30–7.30; Oct–end Apr Tue–Fri 3.30–5.30, Sat–Sun 10–12, 3.30–6.30
💶 €3

Museo Civico e d'Arte Sacra

Via del Castello 31, 53034 Colle di Val d'Elsa
☎ 0577 923888
🕐 Apr–end Oct Tue–Sun 10–12, 4–7; Nov–end Mar Sat–Sun 10–12, 3.30–6.30
💶 €3

THE HEART OF FLORENCE

This walk starts and ends with two of Florence's great churches and is a good way to get a general feel of the city (▷ 115–134). Weaving in and out of the main tourist route, it takes in some of the *centro storico's* quieter lanes, lesser-known churches, palaces and small museums along the way.

THE WALK

Length: 2km (1.3 miles)
Allow: 1.5 hours
Start at: Duomo
End at: Piazza Santa Maria Novella

Begin at Piazza del Duomo, Florence's religious heart and one of the city's three main squares.

Florence's Duomo (▷ 118) is one of Italy's most familiar landmarks, while the ancient Battistero (▷ 120) holds a significant place in Florence's spiritual history. The views from the top of Giotto's campanile (▷ 121) are stunning. At the top right-hand corner is the 14th-century Loggia del Bigallo, built for the Misericordia, a charitable institution whose members cared for plague victims in the 13th and 14th centuries. The beautifully carved porch served as a drop-off point for unwanted babies.

On the southwest side of the square is Via de' Calzaiuoli, (Shoemakers' Street), built on the site of a Roman road. Follow this pedestrianized, shop-lined street, the medieval city's main thoroughfare, to Piazza della Signoria, passing the unusual church of Orsanmichele (▷ 126) on your right along the way. Piazza della Signoria is one of two large piazzas in the city and has been home to Florence's civic forum since medieval times. Leave the square on Via Vaccherecchia, which emerges near the top of Via Por Santa Maria, once lined with medieval palaces that were destroyed by German bombing in 1944. A right turn brings you out to the Mercato Nuovo.

The Mercato Nuovo is also known as the Straw Market or 'Il Porcellino', after the famous bronze statue of a boar, a copy of the original by Pietro Tacca (1612)—its snout is worn shiny by the daily affections of thousands of tourists. There has been a market on this site since the early 11th century. The elegant loggia was built by Cosimo I in 1547 and has been restored; it now shelters stands selling souvenirs and leather goods.

Pass the market, turn left and walk down Via Porta Rossa.

On the left is the Palazzo Davanzati or the Museo della Casa Fiorentina Antica, complete with top-floor loggia. At the end of the street lie Piazza Santa Trinità and its church, full of artistic treasures. In the middle of the square is the tall Column of Justice, a monolith brought from the Baths of Caracalla in Rome and given to Cosimo I in 1560 by Pope Pius IV. On the left stands the fine Palazzo Bartolini-Salimbeni, built between 1520 and 1523 by Baccio d'Agnolo, and beyond this the splendid Palazzo Spini-Feroni, one of the best-preserved medieval palaces in Florence, now housing Ferragamo's flagship store and shoe museum. To its left, Borgo Santi Apostoli leads to the tiny sunken Piazza del Limbo, so-called because it stands on the site of a cemetery for unbaptized babies, and the Church of Santi Apostoli. Founded in the 11th century, it is one of the oldest churches in the city with a series of marble columns and capitals and a carved tomb by Benedetto da Rovezzano inside.

Once back in Piazza Santa Trinità, take the Via del Parione to the right of the church, then head down one of the two narrow alleys on the right. This emerges onto the intriguing Via del Purgatorio (Road of Purgatory). Turn left here into Via della Vigna Nuova.

The elegant façade of the Palazzo Rucellai, designed by Leon Battista Alberti and built by Bernardo Rossellino between 1446 and 1451, faces you across a little square *(piazzetta)*. The lovely Loggia dei Rucellai, now home to a fashion store, is on your right.

Cross over Via della Vigna Nuova, turn right up Via dei Palchetti (at the corner of the Palazzo Rucellai), then right again into Via dei Federighi. This leads into Piazza San Pancrazio.

Here you will find the ancient, deconsecrated Church of San Pancrazio, now home to the Museo Marini, which is dedicated to the work of the Florentine sculptor Marino Marini (1901–80). Just around the corner, on the right at Via della Spada 18, is the tiny Cappella di San Sepolcro. Built by Alberti in 1467 for the Rucellai family, it features a superbly carved marble inlay model of the Church of the Holy Sepulchre in Jerusalem.

From the Cappella di San Sepolcro, walk back a little way along Via della Spada and turn left down Via del Moro, which is full of antique shops. At Piazza Goldoni, turn right and continue along Borgo Ognissanti.

No. 60r is one of Florence's more unusual buildings, a well-preserved example of art deco architecture. A few doors down are the church and convent that give the street its name. It faces the river across the wide Piazza d'Ognissanti. To the right side is the 15th-century Palazzo Lenzi. Covered in elaborate sgraffito (incised patterning), it now houses the French Consulate. Across the river you can see the Church of San Frediano in Cestello, one of the many in Florence whose façade was left unfinished.

The Campanile by Giotto

Detail of the façade of the Palazzo Davanzanti, which contains the Museum of the Early Florentine Home

Backtrack a little and turn left up Via della Porcellana, lined with artisan workshops, then turn right at the top to emerge into the huge Piazza Santa Maria Novella. At the north end stands the magnificent Gothic church of the same name.

WHEN TO GO

Morning is the best time to explore Florence, when all the churches and museums are open. During the afternoon many of the smaller churches are closed and you will not be able to appreciate their remarkable interiors.

WHERE TO EAT

There are plenty of bars and cafés to choose from in this part of town. One of the nicest is Caffè Rivoire (Piazza della Signoria 5r, tel 055 293045, Mon–Sat 8am–midnight), which has a beautiful terrace. The Cantinetta dei Verrazzano (Via dei Tavolini 18–20r,

tel 055 268590, Mon–Sat 8am–9pm), just off Via Calzaiuoli, serves coffee and cakes along with excellent wines and snacks.

PLACES TO VISIT

Santi Apostoli
Piazza del Limbo, Firenze
🕐 Mon–Sat 10–12, 4–6, Sun 4–6

Museo Marini
Piazza San Pancrazio, Firenze
🕐 Wed–Mon 10–5; closed in Aug

Cappella di San Sepolcro
Via della Spada 18, Firenze
🕐 Mon–Fri 10–12

The Fontana di Porcellino (Fountain of the Little Wild Boar) in the Mercato Nuovo. It is a bronze copy of a marble statue by Pitro Tacca (1612)

SIENA AND SOUTHERN TUSCANY

From Siena, this drive takes you south past the ancient abbeys of Sant'Antimo and Monte Oliveto Maggiore and the hilltop towns of Montalcino, Pienza and Montepulciano. Some of Italy's finest wines are produced in this region, so look for *enoteche* (specialist wine bars and shops) where any non-drivers can try a glass or two.

THE DRIVE

Distance: 261km (162 miles)
Allow: 11 hours (best spread over 2 days)
Start/end at: Siena

From Siena take the SR2. In 3km (2 miles) you will see signs saying 'Buonconvento 25'. After another 8km (5 miles) turn left, staying on the SR2 for Buonconvento. When you come to a crossroads, keep driving along the SR2 to Buonconvento. Bear right after the bridge to park outside the town.

A Buonconvento blacksmith

Buonconvento **❶**, unusual in this area in that it is not perched on a hill, has a medieval old town and a small museum of religious art, the Museo d'Arte Sacra. It was once an important stop on the Via Francigena, the historic pilgrims' route that stretched from Canterbury to Rome (▷ 139).

Leave Buonconvento, following the SR2 past the outlying *zona industriale*. Turn right and take the SP45 for Montalcino. The scenery becomes prettier and you will soon see Montalcino on the hill ahead of you.

❷ As you climb uphill you will start to notice a large number of signs for *enoteche*, many of which offer free wine-tasting.

After about 9km (6 miles), bear right at the top of the hill and join the SP14, following signs for Montalcino. Follow the city wall in an anticlockwise direction until you arrive at the roundabout (traffic circle) at the top of the hill. There is free parking left of the roundabout. Alternatively there is pay parking on the right-hand side next to La Fortezza.

Montalcino **❸** (▷ 143) is particularly famous for its rich ruby red Brunello wine, characterized by an intense aroma and delicate, warm flavour with a hint of vanilla.

After exploring Montalcino, follow the brown signs from the roundabout at the top of the hill for the Abbazia di Sant'Antimo, joining the SP55. The road now starts to wind downhill to the valley bottom and in about 2km (1.3 miles) you should spot the abbey, nestling below the hills on the right-hand side. Shortly turn right to reach the abbey, a good starting point for a walk.
From here, return to the road and drive up the hill to Castelnuovo dell'Abate.

Turn right at the top of the hill, following the sign saying 'Stazione Monte Amiata' on the SP22. You will now traverse the Val d'Orcia, from where the road begins to wind downhill. Pass over a level crossing by Monte Amiata station and cross the River Orcia and you will come into the hamlet of Monte Amiata, after which the road begins to climb uphill again. When you reach the intersection, go to the left towards Castiglione d'Orcia. From here the road climbs even more steeply, with rewarding views. When you come to an intersection, take a left turn and join the SR323. Continue driving towards Castiglione d'Orcia.

At the centre of Castiglione d'Orcia **❹** is Piazza il Vecchietta (Square of the Old Women), dedicated to Lorenzo di Peter (1412–80). It is overlooked by the Palazzo Comunale, home to a fresco of the Madonna and Child with two saints (Sienese school) taken from the nearby Rocca d'Orcia. There are two churches worth seeing here: the Romanesque Church of Santa Maria Maddalena, and the Church of Santo Stefano with its 16th-century façade and two Madonnas by Simone Martini and Lorenzetti.

Drive through the village, then head downhill. After 5km (3 miles) turn left at the intersection to join the SR2. Continue until you reach the side road to Bagno Vignoni **❺**. Turn left to park just outside town, on top of the hill.

This ancient spa has been used since Etruscan times and is dominated by an enormous outdoor pool of warm, sulphurous water (▷ 138).

Go back downhill from the town, turn left at the end of the road and then take the next right to

Continued on page 304

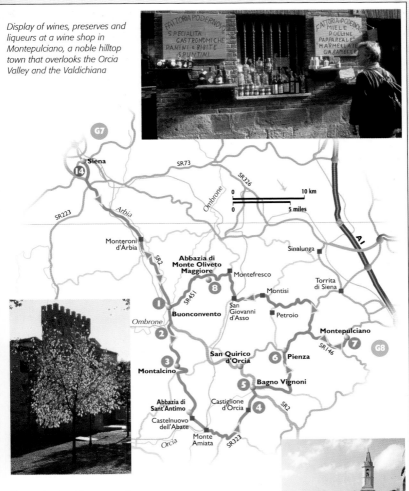

Display of wines, preserves and liqueurs at a wine shop in Montepulciano, a noble hilltop town that overlooks the Orcia Valley and the Valdichiana

The north gate at Buonconvento

WHERE TO EAT

In Montalcino, the Fiaschetteria Italiana (Piazza del Popolo 6, open 7.30am–midnight), a lovely old café with an imposing interior, serves coffees, cakes, light meals and wine. There are plenty of cafés and restaurants to choose from in Bagno Vignoni, but particularly good is La Parata (tel 0577 887508, Thu–Tue 10.30–2.45, 7.30–9.30). It serves a wide selection of *pannini* and cakes, along with local cheese, biscuits and olive oil, and you can sit outside on fine days. In Montepulciano you can enjoy cakes, snacks and a glass of wine at the art nouveau Caffè Poliziano (Via di Voltaia nel Corso, open daily), which also serves meals in its restaurant.

WHEN TO GO

You can do this drive any time of year, but July and August are the hottest and busiest months, while the countryside is at its best in spring and autumn.

PLACES TO VISIT

Museo d'Arte Sacra
Via Socini 18, Buonconvento
☎ 0577 807181
🕐 Mar–end Oct Tue–Sun 10.30–1.
3–7, Sat–Sun 10–1, 3–5; Nov–end Feb
Sat–Sun 10–1, 3–5
💶 €3.10
🚻

Abbazia di Sant'Antimo
Castelnuovo dell'Abate, Siena 53024
☎ 0577 835659
🕐 Mon–Sat 10.30–12.30, 3–6.30, Sun
9.15–10.45, 3–6
💶 Free

City wall and duomo, Pienza

Abbazia di Monte Oliveto Maggiore
Near Asciano
☎ 0577 707611
🕐 Daily 9.15–12, 3.15–5.45 (until 5
Oct–end Apr)
💶 Free
🅿 ♿ 🚻

The castle at Castiglione d'Orcia

Continued from page 302

join the SP53 for Pienza. Turn left onto the SP18 and drive uphill. The striking golden sandstone town of Pienza is in front of you. Park outside the walls.

The focal point of Pienza ❻ is the Piazza Pio II. The square, a UNESCO World Heritage Site, is lined by the Palazzo Piccolomini and Palazzo Borgia and the cathedral. With a pure Renaissance exterior, the cathedral has a Gothic interior similar to those of German churches.

Leave Pienza and continue uphill until you come to an

The landscape around Monte Oliveto Maggiore

intersection. Turn right here for the SR146 and Montepulciano ❼. Follow the road until you reach Montepulciano, again parking outside the city walls.

The Tuscan town of Montepulciano has sweeping views and a maze of steep, winding streets and alleyways. Besides the Renaissance church of San Biagio, the town has many wine shops where you can purchase bottles of Vino Nobile, the famous local wine (▷ 144). Aged in oak barrels for two years (three years for Reserva), this dry wine has a delicate bouquet with violet scents.

From Montepulciano, drive downhill. Turn right for Pienza on the SS146 and after 7km

(4 miles) turn right to join the SP15, a twisty road heading towards Torrita di Siena. Turn left just in front of a bar on the corner to join the SP57. Follow the road to an intersection where you take a sharp left past Petroio and then drive on for another 4km (2.5 miles), after which you turn right for Montisi.

The road now winds tightly downhill, passing through the woods until you reach an intersection. Turn left here and follow the SP14 through Montisi, on to the outskirts of San Giovanni d'Asso. When you come to the next intersection, turn right towards the remote Abbazia di Monte Oliveto Maggiore. Follow this road to Montefresco, then turn left at the intersection and drive for another 3km (2 miles). At the next intersection go left, then shortly turn off to visit the late 13th-century Abbazia di Monte Oliveto Maggiore.

❽ This Benedictine abbey (▷ 138) stands in a wooded park on a scenic rise and is still inhabited by monks. Pause a while to admire the famous frescoes in the main cloister.

Leave the abbey and continue along the SR451 until you reach Buonconvento. From here, pick up the SR2 that leads back to Siena.

OLD SIENA

Wander through the heart of old Siena, beginning in the north of the city and winding south past medieval churches and palaces to the Campo (▷ 152–153). The route then takes you through the city's less-visited southern quarters, finishing in Piazza del Duomo, overlooked by the cathedral and the Spedale di Santa Maria della Scala.

THE WALK

Length: 2km (1.3 miles)
Allow: 2–3 hours
Start at: Piazza San Domenico
End at: Piazza del Duomo

Begin your walk in Piazza San Domenico, home to the church of the same name, containing frescoes by Sodomo (1477–1549). With your back to the church, walk down Via della Sapienza opposite San Domenico, and after 100m (110 yards) you will come to the Biblioteca Comunale degli Intronati.

This library was founded in 1759 in what was probably a 13th-century hospital. It contains more than 500,000 books and other documents, including letters by St. Catherine of Siena and many medieval Sienese painters and architects. At the next minor crossroads is the Church of San Pellegrino alla Sapienza, built in 1767 over the site of a much older chapel.

Continue straight on at the church to emerge on Banchi di Sopra, a major street that follows the path of Via Francigena, a centuries-old pilgrimage route between Rome and northern Europe. Ahead is Piazza Salimbeni, home to a trio of fine palaces: Palazzo Tantucci (1548) on the left, the 14th-century Palazzo Salimbeni to the rear, and Palazzo Spannocchi (1470) to the right (only open to the public during the Palio, ▷ 259). The Salimbeni family were prominent bankers and silk and grain traders, while Ambrogio Spannochi was the treasurer to the Sienese Pope Pius II.

A short diversion left on Banchi di Sopra brings you to the church of Santa Maria delle Nevi (rarely open), renowned for its high altarpiece, the *Madonna della Neve* (1477) by Stefano di Giovanni. Known as Sassetta,

he was considered to be the first person to paint a cloudy sky.

Retrace your steps on Banchi di Sopra and look for the church of San Cristoforo on the left.

Romanesque in origin, San Cristoforo was rebuilt in the late 18th century after earthquake damage. Opposite is the Palazzo Tolomei, part of the original fortress home of the Tolomei, one of Siena's most powerful medieval dynasties of bankers and merchants. It is the oldest surviving private residence in the city, dating from 1205. Pause to admire the statue of the she-wolf suckling Romulus and Remus.

Continue south to the intersection with Banchi di Sotto and Via di Città, where you will find the Loggia della Mercanzia (1428–44), an attractive Gothic three-arched loggia. Little alleys either side take you into Piazza del Campo. Here you can admire the Campo from a café or visit the Museo Civico. Leave the piazza by Vicolo dei Pollaiuoli or Via dei Rinaldini. Both bring you to Banchi di Sotto, where you turn right.

Immediately on your right stands the Palazzo Piccolomini, a majestic palace begun in 1469. Inside, on an upper floor, is the little-known Archivio di Stato (State Archive), full of fascinating works of art. Beyond the palace is the Logge del Papa (Loggia of the Pope) built in 1462 on the orders of the Tuscan-born Pope Pius II (Enea Silvio Piccolomini).

Take the right-hand fork in front of the loggia and follow it around to the intersection with Via del Porrione, named after the *emporium*, the marketplace that stood nearby in Roman times.

Cross Via dei Porrione and walk through the arch down the Vicolo delle Scotte, passing Siena's Sinagoga (synagogue) on the right, the heart of the city's Jewish ghetto, created in 1571 by Cosimo I de Medici. Turn left on Via di Salicotto, then take the first right to emerge on Piazza del Mercato. Cross the square and bear right to pick up Via del Mercato, then turn left almost immediately to follow Via Giovanni Dupre, with attractive alleys branching off either side. At the Chiesa di San Giuseppe on the left take Via Sant'Agata straight onto a gravel area on your left towards the 13th-century Chiesa di Sant'Agostino, which contains paintings by Sodoma and Ambrogio Lorenzetti.

Head through the arch to Via San Pietro and the Church of San Pietro (set back on your right) and the red-brick Pinacoteca Nazionale beyond. Just before the church take a sharp left onto Via di Castelvecchio (an easily missed alley) and bear right for Via di Stalloreggi. Turn left towards the Arco delle Due Porte, an arch that formed part of the city's 11th-century walls, passing a house on the left (No. 91–93) where Duccio (c1260–1320) painted his famous *Maestà*. Turn right after the arch and follow the peaceful Via del Fosso di San Ansano to Piazza della Selva, where either Via Franciosa or Via Firolamo leads you to Piazza del Duomo or Piazza San Giovanni.

In Piazza San Giovanni you can visit the Battistero di San Giovanni and then walk up the steps to your right to see the Duomo, and the Ospedale di Santa Maria della Scalla.

WHERE TO EAT

The Nannini café at Banchi di Sopra 95–99 is a good place for a break, as is Bar Il Palio on Piazza del Campo (tel 47 0577282055).

OUT AND ABOUT

THE VALLE UMBRA

This drive through undulating, fertile countryside intersects with the Roman Via Flaminia, an ancient trade route that contributed to the prosperity of the towns that face each other across the valley. Saints, poets and painters have all lived and left their mark in this area.

THE DRIVE

Distance: 122km (76 miles)
Allow: 4.5 hours' driving time
Start/end at: Piazza Garibaldi, Santa Maria degli Angeli, near Assisi

From Piazza Garibaldi take the road south for Foligno, following signs for Perugia and Roma. Pass under the *superstrada* (main road), following signs for Costano and Bettona. The road now heads into open, flat countryside. Shortly after the *superstrada*, turn left at the intersection towards Bettona on the SP404 and head for Passaggio. Turn right at the roundabout (traffic circle) signposted for Bettona, Torgiano and Deruta and take a left, signposted for Bettona. Continue up the narrow SP403, with views to the north of the plain and Assisi, and drive through the terraced olive groves until you reach Bettona ❶. Go clockwise around the town and park by the town walls.

Overlooking the River Chiascio to the north, Bettona is an unspoiled town enclosed by medieval walls. It was the only Etruscan settlement on the east bank of the River Tiber.

Leaving Bettona, drive down the hill signposted for Torgiano. Turn right at the main road heading for Montefalco, Passaggio and Assisi, and continue to the roundabout at Passaggio. Go straight over the roundabout, towards Bevagna on the SP403. The road gently climbs as you near the town. Use the parking area on the right in front of the large tower, with its arched entrance that leads into the town.

❷ Bevagna's asymmetrical Piazza Silvestri is an extremely well-preserved example of medieval town planning. The 13th-century Palazzo dei Consoli, with its theatre and 12th-century Church of San Silvestro, are highlights of the town.

Drive out of Bevagna, following signs for Montefalco (7km/ 4.5 miles away), passing down an avenue of trees. About 100m (110 yards) beyond the town limit sign, fork left onto the SP443, past vineyards and farmland dotted with trees. Turn right at the intersection and continue through Montepennino up towards Montefalco. Turn left at the intersection outside the town and at the walls bear right. Park in the large parking area on your right.

With its panoramic views, Montefalco ❸ (▷ 144) is known as the Balcony of Umbria and is renowned for its Sagrantino DOCG wine. The former Church of San Francesco (now the Museo Civico di San Francesco) contains world-famous Renaissance frescoes by the artist Benozzo Gozzoli.

From Montefalco, take the road for Spoleto and Terni which heads down through thick olive groves onto the SP445, with views of Trevi across the valley. Drive through Turrita, passing the ornate Madonna della Stella sanctuary on the left (8km/ 5 miles from Montefalco). Go straight across at the lights and at the intersection turn right onto a long straight road. Bear left at the next intersection at Mercatello. In Bruna go over the bridge and take the sharp left signposted for Trevi. Drive 7km (4 miles) along the SP457, across the valley floor and past Castel San Giovanni. Go straight across the roundabout, following the signs for Trevi. About 600m (650yd) farther along, turn left at the intersection onto the busy SS3, in the direction of Fano, Perugia and Foligno.

Shortly on the left, you will come to the ancient springs at Fonti del Clitunno ❹ and the Tempio sul Clitunno, a church built on the site of a Roman temple, which incorporates some of its stones.

Continue north along the SS3 for a further 6.5km (4 miles), and at the traffic lights and petrol (gas) station turn right onto the road signposted for Parrano and Trevi. Drive up the SP425 past the Church of the Madonna delle Lacrime and Bovara turning. Head through the gates of Trevi and circumnavigate the town towards the large parking area above in Piazza Garibaldi.

❺ Trevi (▷ 156) is known as the City of the Olive, and the old town is surrounded by olive groves. In nearby Bovara there is an olive tree dedicated to St. Emiliano, which, at around 1,700 years old, is thought to be the oldest in Italy.

Leave Trevi, following signs for Foligno. Continue up the hill and turn left at the top. Drive down through Santa Maria in Valle towards the SR3. Follow the signs for Perugia at the roundabout, heading up onto the *superstrada* north. This fast road takes you past the industrial area around Foligno. About 8km (5 miles) from the roundabout, take the right towards Perugia onto the SS75. Come off the *superstrada* at the Spello exit. Turn right into the centre of Spello ❻. Park in Piazza Kennedy near Porta Consolare at the south end of town, or around the corner on the Collepino road.

The winding alleyways of Spello (▷ 155) are constructed from the local pink stone. There are more Roman remains here than in any other Umbrian town. The frescoes by Pinturicchio (1454–1513) in the Church of Santa Maria Maggiore are considered to be the artist's finest.

Take the road to the right of Porta Consolare and follow the signs for Collepino and Monte Subasio. Continue around the east side of town, branching up to the left after 1km (0.6 mile) to the town's Porta Montanara.

OUT AND ABOUT

The lush green vineyards surrounding the city of Assisi (left)

Via Garibaldi, Spello (right)

Follow the signs for Monte Subasio and head up the narrow SP249. Just past the fortified hamlet of Collepino, turn left at the Monte Subasio sign onto a so-called white (rough) road.

7 St. Francis retreated to the Eremo delle Carceri near the top of the massive limestone summit that forms the backdrop to Assisi. The top is 1,290m (4,232ft) above sea level, and 4.5km (3 miles) past the summit, the Eremo delle Carceri comes into view.

Continue down the hairpins of the SP251, past Assisi's 14th-century Porta Cappuccini. Turn left at the intersection at the bottom. Bear right past the petrol (gas) station towards Perugia along the SS147 and follow the road beneath the massive ramparts of the Basilica di San Francesco. Turn left to Santa

Maria degli Angeli (3km/2 miles from the intersection), cross the level crossing (grade crossing) and drive straight on towards the basilica until you arrive back in Piazza Garibaldi.

An olive tree in Spello

WHERE TO EAT

In the medieval hamlet of Bettona you can sit out on a terrace of the Relais La Corta di Bettona overlooking the plain towards Assisi. The Taverna del Guillare serves traditional Umbrian dishes such as homemade pasta with truffles (Via Caterina, 2 Bettona, tel 075 987114, Easter–end Nov daily 12–2.30, 7.30–10; closed Mon in winter).

Other options include Da Nina (Piazza Garibaldi 6, tel 0742 360161, closed Tue) in Bevagna and Ristorante il Molino (Piazza Matteotti 6–7, tel 0742 651305, closed Tue) in Spello.

PLACE TO VISIT

Museo Civico di San Francesco
Via della Ringhiera Umbra, 06037 Montefalco
☎ 0742 379598
🕐 Jul, Aug daily 10.30–1, 3–7.30; Mar–end May, Sep, Oct Tue–Sun 10.30–1, 2–6; Nov–end Feb Tue–Sun 10.30–1, 2.30–5
💶 €6

THE VALNERINA AND PIANO GRANDE

Beginning in Spoleto, this drive takes in the dramatic upper sections of the Nera Valley–the Valnerina (▷ 156), the lower Corno Valley and the Piano Grande on the southern edge of Monti Sibillini National Park (▷ 147).

THE DRIVE	
Distance: 183km (114 miles)	
Allow: 5.5 hours' driving time	
Start/end at: Spoleto	
Overnight stop: Norcia	

From Piazza della Vittoria on the north side of Spoleto follow the signs for Flaminia SS3, and Norcia and Foligno. Continue along the SS3, following signs for Fano, Perugia and Foligno for 2.5km (1.5 miles) and then bear right towards Cascia and Norcia. Passing Eggi on your left, drive into the long tunnel. You will emerge in the Valnerina. Follow the signs for Norcia, heading along the SS209 and up the valley for 14.5km (9 miles). The breadth of the valley fluctuates, sometimes narrowing dramatically to a gorge. Poplars and oaks border the Nera, and fortified towers and settlements punctuate the sides of the valley, pointing to its turbulent past.

Castel San Felice ❶, with its lovely 12th-century Romanesque church, is up to your right. High up on the left above Borgo Cerreto stands Cerreto di Spoleto and its tower.

About 500m (550 yards) past Borgo Cerreto, turn right at the intersection towards Norcia, over the elevated bridge into the tunnel. You will emerge on the SR320, which takes you along the narrow Corno Valley. The road cuts through tunnels and narrow gorges and passes under concrete galleries. At the sign for Cascia, where the main valley heads south, continue for a further 6km (4 miles) on the SR396 towards Norcia. The valley widens into a fertile bowl at the foot of the Sibillini Mountains, with the walled town of Norcia set on a mound before you (▷ 144–145).

Park outside Norcia's city walls at Porta Romana, and walk

into town ❷. Have a coffee in Piazza San Benedetto, or sample some of the best salami in Umbria.

Drive around the town walls clockwise and turn left towards Pescara, down a long straight avenue, following signs for Castelluccio. Turn left after 2.5km (1.5 miles) and head for Castelluccio, climbing up the SP477, enjoying views of the green valley below and the steep slopes of the Monti Sibillini foothills. Where the main road continues to the Adriatic, turn left for Forca Canapine and Castelluccio.

As you climb you can admire the dramatic views of Norcia below and the Monti Reatini to the south. Around 17km (11 miles) from Norcia the landscape becomes more rugged as you rise above the tree line. A little farther on, turn left towards Castelluccio, past a modern restaurant and over the brow of the hill. The massive slopes of Monte Vettore greet you, with the Piano Grande (▷ 145) overlooked in the distance by Castelluccio, below. Cross the plain following the sign for Visso. Drive up into the village and park by the low wall facing the Sibillini.

Castelluccio ❸, the last outpost in Umbria, is famous for the tiny lentils grown by local farmers on the valley floor.

From here, drive north towards Visso. After 5km (3 miles), from the pass above the village, there is a good viewpoint suitable for a picnic. As you continue into the Marche, down below the tree line the landscape becomes increasingly steep. Deep ravines cut through the white rock, and the conically shaped Monte Cardosa rises up on your left.

About 11km (7 miles) from Castelluccio ❹, just above the pretty village of Gualdo, turn left to Dell'Erborista Ristorante and

Pizzeria, a good lunch stop. Continue down to Visso, bearing left onto the SP134 at Castelsantangelo sul Nera.

The small town of Visso ❺ with its square towers nestles in a valley, surrounded by hills. The parish Church of Santa Maria contains some interesting remains of old frescoes.

Leaving Visso, follow the signs for Rome and Terni and drive out via Il Gole della Valnerina ('the throat of the Valnerina', a narrow gorge between high rocks) on the SR209, to emerge into a wild, narrow valley with overhanging rock formations. The valley floor opens up gradually as you drive on, and more settlements come into view. A further 11km (7 miles) down the Valnerina, take the turning left to Norcia if you are staying there for the night.

Otherwise continue on the SR209 past the tall, bleak towers of Triponzo that rise precariously from the cliff face. Ignore the turning to the right to Spoleto and continue in the direction of Terni through Scheggino, with its crumbling towers. Continue past Ceselli, where hamlets dot the hillside to the south. Slow down as you approach Sambucheto, and turn sharply right to San Pietro in Valle at the battered yellow sign just inside the village limits. Drive up the narrow lane past the cottages at Macenano and park in the parking area down past the abbey.

❻ The Abbazia di San Pietro in Valle was founded in 720. Steeped in history, it contains some of the most important examples of Romanesque frescoes in Italy (▷ 138).

Rejoin the main road, and continue south past Ferentillo as far as the intersection. Before turning right to Spoleto, make a detour and have a quick stop at Arrone to the left.

OUT AND ABOUT

A bridge across the River Nera in the Valerina (left)

Paragliding in the Monti Sibillini National Park (right)

7 Arrone's church, Santa Maria Assunta, contains frescoes by Vincenzo Tomagni and Giovanni da Spoleto. The immaculate upper village has a medieval close with a tree growing out of the clock tower.

Return to Spoleto, crossing the SR209 and Via Montefranco on the SP4, a winding road with good views of the distant hills. Turn right onto the fast Flaminia SR3 and after 15.5km (9.5 miles) you will see Spoleto's unmistakable Rocca.

WHEN TO GO

The best time to see the Piano Grande (Great Plain) is in May and early June, when the wild flowers are at their best. Check the weather with the tourist information office in Norcia before you head off (tel 0743 816090, Sep–end May closed Wed). Don't cross the Piano Grande in snow—Castelluccio can be cut off.

WHERE TO EAT

In Norcia: Cafe-bar Vignola (tel 0743 817086) and Ristorante Beccofino (tel 0743 817031) in Piazza San Benedetto.
In Castelluccio: Bar del Capitano (Via della Bufera Castelluccio 10, tel 0743 821159).
In Sant'Eutizio: Locanda Biancofiore (Via Santa Caterina 8, Preci, tel 0743 9399319, closed Mon).
In Gualdo: Dell'Erborista Ristorante and Pizzeria (Frazione Gualdo, Castelsantangelo sul Nera, tel 0737 98134, reserve at weekends).
In San Pietro in Valle: Ristorante Abbazia (Abazia di San Pietro in

Lentils, Monti Sibillini

Valle, SS 209 Valnerina, Loc. Macenano, 05034 Ferentillo, Terni, tel 0744 380011, closed in winter).

WHERE TO STAY

Hotel and Restaurant Grotta Azzura (Via Alfieri 12, Norcia, tel 0743 816513).

TIP

● It is better to break up the journey with an overnight stop in Norcia, concentrating on the upper circuit on the first day and Norcia and the lower circuit on the second.

OLD PERUGIA

From the medieval Via dei Priori this walk around old Perugia (▷ 148) winds out to the northerly Porta Sant'Angelo and one of the oldest churches in Italy. You return to the city along the 13th-century aqueduct, ending the walk on Piazza IV Novembre.

THE WALK	
Length: 3.7km (2.3 miles)	
Allow: 2–3 hours	
Start at: Via dei Priori (from Palazzo dei Priori)	
End at: Piazza IV Novembre	

Begin by walking down Via dei Priori, the steep street that descends from the Arco dei Priori beneath the Palazzo dei Priori tower. As you go down, passing the baroque Chiesa Nuova on your right, you will walk over a fragment of the *decumanus*, a thoroughfare through the Roman town. As you continue, you will pass the Sciri tower and the Oratory of San Francesco on Via degli Sciri on your left.

The street now bends past the Piazzetta della Madonna della Luce, with its two churches. Stop and go inside the Church of the Madonna della Luce to take in the miraculous *Vision of the Virgin* by Tiberio d'Assisi, and the cupola covered in frescoes by Giovan Battista Caporali.

Go down the steps to the left, through the Etruscan Porta Trasimeno, the old exit to Trasimeno and Tuscany, and turn right to enter Piazza San Francesco.

The Oratorio di San Bernardino, with its softly tinted façade, has a grassy area in front of it where students often relax in the sun—a good picnic spot on a sunny day.

Go back up Via San Francesco and take the next left up the steps along Via del Poggio. From here you can look down onto the front of the Church of San Francesco al Prato, built in 1230, and undergoing a lengthy restoration. Turn right up Via della Tartaruga, passing Piazza San Paolo on the right. At the top turn left and join Via Francolina towards Piazza Giuseppe Ermini and continue right onto Via del

Verzaro. This narrow street, with tall buildings on both sides, runs along the back of the Teatro Morlacchi, built in 1778.

Before you emerge onto Piazza Morlacchi, part of the university, pass by the little Church of San Martino del Verzaro on your left (1163), which has frescoes by Giannicola di Paolo inside.

Bear left and you will come to Piazza Cavalotti. Cross over and walk down Via Baldeschi. Pass the steps marked Via Appia on your left and continue until you join Piazza Ansidei. Cross the square and walk down to the left along Via Ulisse Rocchi, following the signs to the Arco Etrusco. As you continue down, go through the Etruscan Arch and cross the road with the big red 18th-century Università per Stranieri building on your left. Cross over to Corso Garibaldi.

This area is evidence of the city's expansion in medieval times, and is where the artisan quarters sprang up during the 13th and 14th centuries. On your right are Piazza Lupatelli and the Church of Sant' Agostino, with its pink-and-white checked front.

Continue walking along Corso Garibaldi and you will pass a little *madonnina* (shrine) on your left and the Complesso della Mercanzia.

This 14th-century building belonged to one of the powerful guilds—you can still make out a granary sign above the door lintel. It was also used as a hospital for the poor.
As you wander along the Corso you pass a series of monastic settlements, each with its own church. The Benedictine Santa Caterina on your right was restructured by Galeazzo Alessi in 1547, and the Dominican monastery of Beata Colomba at No. 191 was

where St. Francis and St. Dominic allegedly met in 1220.

Go straight on under a brick arch and you immediately find the graceful approach to the Tempio Sant'Angelo, the oldest church in Umbria, to your right.

Stop and admire the views from this peaceful spot, which marks the end of the medieval boundary. You can see over towards the restored Convent of San Francesco del Monte outside the city walls. Cassero di Porta Sant'Angelo has a little museum and panoramic terrace.

Return to Corso Garibaldi, passing the monastery of Santa Lucia. About two-thirds of the way down, just after the Complesso della Mercanzia building, turn right down Via Domenico Lupatelli, a narrow street lined with houses and picturesque side alleys. At the end of Via Lupatelli turn right. Go along Via Fabretti until you come to Via dell'Aquedotto on the left. Walk along the aqueduct, looking down onto the houses and gardens below.

The aqueduct was built between 1254 and 1276 by Fra Bevignate to bring water down from Monte Pacciano to the city's Fontana Maggiore, 5km (3 miles) away. It became a pedestrian way in the 1830s after a new water supply was built. This is a popular spot with artists and photographers. Turn around to admire the rooftops and buildings behind you.

The ancient Via Appia merges with Via dell'Aquedotto, and 200 steps take you up through the arch of the aqueduct to Via Baldeschi. Return to Piazza Cavalotti and bear left up Via Maestà delle Volte.

A fresco of the Virgin and Child was painted on this dark medieval thoroughfare in 1297.

OUT AND ABOUT

The church of San Pietro (left)

Piazza IV Novembre, with the 15th-century Palazzo dei Priori and the 13th-century Fontana Maggiore (bottom)

Corso Venucci (above)

Bronze statues on the front of the Palazzo dei Priori (below)

The Maestà delle Volte Oratory was built in 1335 to protect the fresco, but was rebuilt in 1576 after a fire. The medieval archway is a remnant of the portico, and Angelini built the fountain in the hollow beneath the church. On the right is a wall fresco by Beletti (1945).

Walk through the arches to Piazza IV Novembre, where you will find many cafés and bars selling ice cream.

WHERE TO EAT

Il Padrino serves fish dishes and is a good lunch stop (Via Baldeschi 5, closed Sun and Aug). There is also the Osteria del Gambero (Via Baldeschi 9, 075 5735461, daily 12.30–2.30, 7.30–11; closed Mon pm).

PLACE TO VISIT

Cassero di Porta Sant'Angelo
Porto Sant'Angelo
☎ 075 41670
🕐 Jul, Aug daily 11–1.30, 3–6.30; Apr–Jun, Sep, Oct Wed–Mon 11–1.30, 3–6.30; Nov–end Mar Wed–Mon 11–1.30, 3–5 💶 €3
www.sistemamuseo.it

OUT AND ABOUT

A CIRCUIT OF LAGO TRASIMENO

From Passignano this drive takes you anticlockwise (counterclockwise) around Lago Trasimeno (▷ 141), Italy's largest inland lake south of the River Po. You will pass by olive-studded slopes north of the lake, through the lowlands and marshy areas near the Tuscan border, and the gentle undulating countryside in the south.

THE DRIVE	
Distance: 80km (50 miles)	
Allow: 5.5 hours' driving time	
Start/end at: Passignano	

From the ferry pier drive west and north out of town, over the level crossing (grade crossing) on the old road (SR75) following signs for Tuoro and under the *superstrada*. After 6km (4 miles) turn right at the intersection and start climbing up, past the characteristic umbrella pines and cypress trees, to Tuoro **❶**, which is approached up an avenue.

Park at the top and admire the view of Isola Maggiore from Piazza Municipio. This unassuming village is historically famous as the sight of the bloody massacre of the Roman legions by Hannibal at the Battle of Lago Trasimeno in 217BC.

Turn back down the hill, and after 300m (330 yards) take a right, following the battle signs, then turn right again at the intersection to Castiglione del Lago. You will pass occasional signs for battle sites as the old road meanders past reed beds to the lake. Farther along from the intersection (at a bend in the road to the right), turn left, following the signs for Borghetto, Chiusi and Castiglione del Lago. Drive over the level crossing, and under the dual carriageway (divided highway). At Borghetto, turn right onto the SR75 then turn left at the intersection onto the SR71. Continue for 8km (5 miles) across the low-lying country near the lake's shore as far as Castiglione del Lago, which can be seen jutting out into the lake. Turn left and drive up to the large intersection just outside the town and park by the ramparts.

This fortified town ❷ was an island on the lake in Etruscan and Roman times. Later, it was defended by the Tuscia Lombards against Byzantine

Perugia and subsequently fought over by Arezzo, Cortona and Perugia. Its present form dates from the middle of the 13th century.

Drive out from town on the SR71, following signs for Chiusi, and continue along the long straight road towards Città della Pieve. Come off at the exit sign for Paciano and turn left onto the SP310, which goes under the main road. The landscape becomes more undulating and the fields widen to reveal vineyards, oaks and occasional red-brick houses. Approach Paciano up a road lined with cypresses and olives, turning left and driving up towards the centre. Park at the side of the road and walk up through the red-brick Porta Fiorentina.

Set among olive groves and oak woodland, Paciano ❸ is a quiet, well-preserved medieval village dating back to the 13th century. With its extensive views, this is a good base for walking and there are plenty of places to enjoy picnics in the surrounding countryside.

Leave Paciano and return down the hill. Turn right onto the SP310 and shortly afterwards

turn right again towards Panicale. After 2km (1.3 miles) turn right at the intersection and up, past olive trees, to the attractive *borgo*. Park immediately outside Panicale, near the lace museum, and walk up through the gate.

Panicale ❹ once belonged to the Etruscan town of Chiusi, which became strategically important to the Perugians in controlling the Nestor Valley to the south as well as Lago Trasimeno. From its vantage point it provides lovely views over to Isola Polvese. The town's street layout has developed in a circular pattern, with its three main squares on different levels.

Continue driving around the town; turn left at the intersection and drive northwest through Macchie. At the SR599 turn right for Magione. Go through Panicarola, past reed-fringed ditches, and the Sant'Arcangelo ferry stop on your left. After some 13km (8 miles), turn left for San Feliciano onto the SP316 and past San Savino. Follow the signs for the village, past the turning for the *traghetti* (ferries) to Isola Polvese, and park where you can or in the square.

San Feliciano ❺ is a traditional fishing village. Its fishing museum, the Museo della Pesca, is at the end of a narrow cul-de-sac near the lakeside and boatyards.

Take the SP316 north out of the village, through Monte del Lago, and follow the signs for the resort of Torricella. Go over the level crossing and follow the signs for Passignano, which take you up onto the fast *superstrada*. Come off at the next exit at Passignano Est, cross the level crossing and head back to the start point.

Fishing nets at San Feliciano, a hamlet on Lago Trasimeno

The Fortress of Castiglione sul Lago overlooking the lake (left)

The waterfront of Passignano sul Trasimeno, a little village on Lago Trasimeno (right)

WHERE TO EAT

In Castiglione del Lago there are several café bars and the restaurant La Cantina (Lione del Lago, Centro Storico, Via Vittorio Emanuele 93, tel 0759 652463, daily 12.30–3.30, 6.45–11; Oct–end Mar closed Mon). For refreshment in Panicale visit Bar del Gallo. About 2km (1.3 miles) south of San Feliciano is Da Massimo, specializing in lake fish (Via dei Romani 16, San Savino, tel 075 8476094/075 8476269, daily 11–11; closed Mon). Back in Passignano, Del Molo (Via A Pompili 7, San Savino, tel 075 827151, Tue–Sun 12.30–2.30, 7–10) is a reasonably priced restaurant and there is a good pizzeria opposite the ferry stop (Hotel Cavalieri, Via delle Ginestre, Passignano sul Trasimeno, tel 075 829292, daily 12.30–2.30, 7.30–10.30).

Street entertainment during a wine festival in Panicale

TIPS

● Time your drive to enjoy the evening views across the lake from the east and north.
● This drive is best arranged with a lunch stop at Castiglione del Lago or a picnic stop on the hill around Paciano.

PLACE TO VISIT

Museo della Pesca
Via Lungolago della Pace e del Lavoro 20, 06063 Magione
☎ 0758 479261
🕐 Jul, Aug daily 10.30–1,4–7; Apr–end Jun and Sep Tue–Sun 10–12.30, 3–6; Feb, Mar and Oct Thu–Sun 10.30–12.30, 2.30–5.30; Nov–end Jan Sat–Sun 10.30–1,2.30–5.30
💶 €3

THE CASTELLI ROMANI HILLS

From the frenetic centre of Rome to the quiet Albani hills, this route takes you past secluded villas, bustling towns and the serene lakes of Albano and Nemi. Wealthy Romans have escaped to the cool hills and lakes for centuries, and they remain a popular weekend retreat.

THE DRIVE

Distance: 76km (47 miles)	
Allow: 4 hours	
Start/end at: Rome	

Leave Rome on the Via Appia Antica (▷ 180), the ancient road from the city lined with catacombs, where you will find the tomb of Romulus, legendary founder and first king of Rome. About 12km (7.5 miles) from the city centre you will pass the remains of an ancient Roman aqueduct on the right-hand side. After the turning for the airport (Ciampino) the road becomes the SS7. Continue along this road, following signs for Albano/Ciampino and you will soon see the town of Castel Gandolfo in the distance.

About 8km (5 miles) from the aqueduct take a left turn and join the SS140 for Castel Gandolfo, after which the route becomes quieter and rural. The road soon starts to climb and shortly you reach the outskirts of Castel Gandolfo **1** (▷ 183).

You won't be able to park in the heart of Castel Gandolfo, but it is worth the walk uphill into the middle to see the Church of San Tommaso di Villanova and the exterior of the Pope's summer residence,

Castel Gandolfo, the Pope's summer residence, from where he gives his Sunday blessings

and to admire the views over Lago Albano (▷ 184).

Leave the town and continue along the Via Appia, following signs to Albano Laziale, home to a small museum and the tomb of the legendary warriors Horatius and Curiatii. From Albano Laziale it is about 2km (1.3 miles) to Ariccia, entered over a high bridge.

Ariccia **2** is a popular destination for Romans, who come here to enjoy al-fresco pizza on summer evenings. The town also contains the Palazzo Chigi, in which there is a museum.

Leave Ariccia and follow the SS7. There are large villas on either side of the road and bushy umbrella pines that provide welcome shade in the summer months. After about 2km (1.3 miles) you reach the outskirts of Genzano di Roma, where you will see a large church on the left-hand side. Continue past a large sports stadium on the left, where the landscape has a more industrial appearance. Just outside Genzano, take a left turn for Nemi (it is easy to miss it) onto Via Sardegna. At the next intersection, turn left in the direction of Nemi, and go right at the intersection, which brings you to Piazzale Cina. Follow the SP76D, and after 1km (0.6 mile)

you will approach the outskirts of Nemi, with the lake of the same name down on the left-hand side.

The ancient Romans were so inspired by the still azure waters of Lago di Nemi **3** that they named it Mirror of Diana and built a temple to the goddess on the lake's angled shores, surrounded by a sacred grove.

The road now winds uphill, and is lined with bars and restaurants. You will soon spot the town, which overlooks the lake, with its distinctive tower and narrow streets. If you want to explore further, park in the outskirts rather than in the crowded town.

4 Nemi became famous in 1930 when the remains of a Roman ship were discovered at the bottom of its lake. See them in the Museo delle Navi Romane. Staircases run up and down this village, which is famous for its miniature strawberries *(fragoline di Nemi)*, grown along the lake's shores. The tiny fruit, soaked in lemon juice and topped with fresh cream, is a local treat in the bars lining the belvedere overlooking the water.

Leave Nemi, and about 1km (0.6 mile) from the middle of the town turn right. The road winds uphill and passes under a bridge. Follow the signs for Velletri/Roma. Shortly there is an intersection, where you turn left to join the SS217, a fairly busy, winding road. Turn right for Rocca di Papa, joining the SS218, which climbs uphill through rows of mature chestnut trees. After 2km (1.3 miles) you will reach Rocca di Papa, with broad views over Rome on the left. Continue and go left as the road forks and follow the SS218 into the heart of Rocca di Papa **5**. Once again it is best to park in the outskirts if you want to explore the town.

OUT AND ABOUT

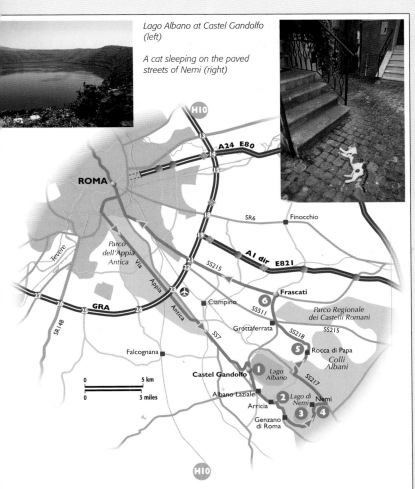

Lago Albano at Castel Gandolfo (left)

A cat sleeping on the paved streets of Nemi (right)

The narrow streets and houses of Rocca di Papa are built up around the hillside. From here it is possible to admire the 360-degree views of Rome, the battlefields where Hannibal met the Romans and the sea.

Now go downhill to leave the town, following the SS218 for about 4km (2.5 miles) to Grottaferrata, famous for its wine and 11th-century abbey. Leave Grottaferrata, following the SS218 until you reach Frascati **6** (▷ 184).

Frascati is the most famous of the Castelli towns, noted for its wine and sumptuous villas. The Villa Aldobrandini is occasionally open to the public and with a large cascade in its grounds is particularly impressive.

After exploring the town, follow the signs back to Rome.

WHERE TO EAT

Castel Gandolfo, Genzano and Frascati are full of restaurants and pizzerias. In Albano, La Taverna da Rosa in Piazza Luigi Sabatini (tel 06 9324381, closed Tue) and La Volpe e L'Uva on Via Collegio Nazareno (tel 06 9322251) are both worth a try.

WHEN TO GO

Spring or autumn to avoid the summer crowds. This drive is popular with locals at weekends.

PLACES TO VISIT

Museo Civico
Via Risorgimento 3, Albano
☎ 06 9323490
🕐 Daily 9–12.30, Wed–Thu 9–12.30, 4–7.30
💶 €2.50

Museo delle Navi Romane
Via Diana, Nemi
☎ 06 9398040
🕐 Tue–Sun 9–1.30, 2.30–4.30
💶 Adult €2, child (under 18) free

Villa Aldobrandini
Via Cardinal Massaia, Frascati, Tivoli
☎ 06 9420192
🕐 Gardens open daily except Sun and public holidays. Open Mon–Fri 9–1, 3–6. In winter closes at 5
💶 Free. Permits available for villa from visitor centre in Piazza G. Marconi

Palazzo Chigi
Piazza di Corte 14, Aricia
☎ 06 9330053
🕐 Tue–Fri 11, 4 and 5.30, Sat and Sun 10.30, 11.30, 12.30. 4, 5, 6, 7
💶 €10

THE PARCO NAZIONALE DEL GRAN SASSO

This drive takes you through the breathtakingly beautiful Gran Sasso National Park (▷ 202–203). Its unusual mountain landscape has earned it the name 'little Tibet'. With so much to explore en route you may want to take your time and spread it over two days.

THE DRIVE

Distance:	444km (276 miles)
Allow:	8 hours
Start/end at:	L'Aquila
Roads:	Although the route is full of tight mountain bends the road surface is generally good

Take the motorway from L'Aquila (A24) in the direction of Teramo. Pass through the tolls and after 10km (6 miles) you will reach the Assergi Valley, where the area becomes fertile and green. Go through the tunnel, Traforo del Gran Sasso d'Italia, that cuts straight through the mountain. Exit the motorway at San Gabriele Colledara and follow the sign for Prati di Tivo. Drive through the middle of the resort following signs for Cima Alta. After 1km (0.6 mile) there is a parking area. From here walk about 200m (220 yards) up the hill, where you can admire an extraordinary view over the mountain range that stretches right down to the sea.

Prati di Tivo ❶ is both a ski and summer resort at one of the highest points in the Gran Sasso mountain range. There are several bars and restaurants where you can find refreshments, and various places where you can ride horses or rent a bicycle.

From here take the ST43 in the direction of Ponte di Rio Arno Sotto. After 14km (9 miles) turn right onto the SS80 trunk road in the direction of Teramo. Ignore signs for the motorway marked Roma/L'Aquila, and continue along the main road following the signs for Castelli–San Gabriele.

Castelli ❷ sits 550m (1,805ft) above sea level under the picturesque Monte Camicia. This is a good starting point for trekking as you can cross over and climb the eastern face of the Gran Sasso Mountains from here. Castelli is renowned for its majolica ceramics, which

became famous in the 16th century. There are a number of ceramic shops and factories to visit in this pretty little village, where you can see the painters at work.

Drive through the village in the direction of Rigopiano.

On the left you will see signs for a steep path that leads 1km (0.6 mile) up to the tiny Church of San Donato in Martire ❸. It has a majolica ceiling dating back to 1615. If the church is closed, the caretaker who lives in the house opposite will let you in. A further 500m (1,640ft) up the slope is the Castelli majolica museum, in a former Franciscan convent.

Fresh produce in the marketplace of the ancient city of L'Aquila

Take the southbound road to Rigopiano, which after 47.5km (30 miles) of bends takes you to Castel del Monte.

This is a tortuous road, but it is worth navigating all the hairpin bends for the scenery. Castel del Monte ❹ (▷ 192) is another quaint stone village with a fortified quarter, Ricetto, and steep streets with flights of stone steps.

From Castel del Monte descend down the same road for 9km (6 miles) in the direction of Calascio/Rocca Calascio.

At 1,450m (4,757ft) above sea level, Calascio ❺ was one of the starting points of the migratory shepherds' trail, the Via della Transumanza. The shepherds would accompany their sheep from the Abruzzo to the more temperate region of Puglia, farther south, in the winter, and then bring them back in the spring. They slept in stone huts, some of which are still visible en route.

From Calascio you can visit the 16th-century Church of Santa Maria della Pietà or leave the car and climb up the scenic path that leads to the ruins of the 13th-century fortress of Rocca Calascio, a further 3km (2 miles) from the village. If you wish to drive, then bear in mind that the last 300m (330 yards) are rough and the road is not surfaced, which can be treacherous in wet conditions. From this vantage point 1,464m (4,800ft) above sea level the eye can roam freely over the mountain peaks and valleys of the Maiella and Mount Sirente. The *rifugio alpino* (mountain refuge) contains a small restaurant and has four charming rooms—an ideal place to stop for lunch or an overnight stay. Several panoramic trails start from here, suitable for all abilities during the warmer months, the longest going as far as Campo Imperatore (13km/8 miles).

Continue driving in the direction of Santo Stefano di Sessanio ❻, the last port of call on this drive.

This partially abandoned village lies 1,251m (4,104ft) above sea level. Its 120 inhabitants produce some of the country's best lentils, and you can buy them from one of the tiny

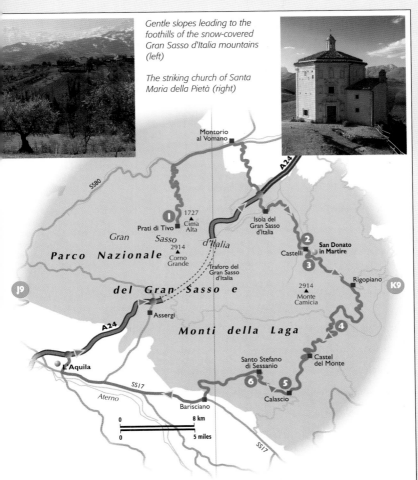

Gentle slopes leading to the foothills of the snow-covered Gran Sasso d'Italia mountains (left)

The striking church of Santa Maria della Pietà (right)

shops. Grey stone houses line the steep cobbled slopes, and at every turn there are views over the barren mountain range visible through the gaps in the narrow alleys.

From Santo Stefano di Sessanio descend to Barisciano and turn onto the SS17, which leads back into L'Aquila.

WHEN TO GO

Fine, dry weather is essential for this drive because of the hairpin bends. Avoid November to late March, when the roads are icy. Spring and autumn are the prettiest months, when the flowers are at their best, but high summer is refreshingly cool. Remember that August is the main holiday month for Italians and everywhere will be crowded.

WHERE TO EAT

There are many places to eat in Prati di Tivo and Castelli and plenty of good picnic spots. Rocca Calascio, Agriturismo al Borgo, is a mountain refuge that serves meals and snacks made from local produce (tel 338 8059430, open daily). Hotel Prati di Tivo is a hotel and restaurant that serves good local and Italian food (Località Prati di Tivo, Pietracamela, tel 0861 959636). Ristorante Ostello del Cavaliere in Santo Stefano di Sessanio is a nice place to stop to sample traditional food at a moderate price (Via della Giudea, tel 0862 89679, closed Thu).

TIPS

• Some of the mountainous roads and tortuous bends are unmarked and the signposts are often hidden.
• Consider an overnight stop or divide the drive into two half-day itineraries: L'Aquila–Prati di Tivo–Castelli on the first day and L'Aquila–Santo Stefano–Calascio–Castel del Monte on the second day.
• It is possible to cut the drive short and return directly to L'Aquila from Castelli.

PLACE TO VISIT

Centro Ceramico Castellano
Castelli
☎ 0861 979121
🕐 Jul–end Sep daily 10–7; rest of year Tue–Sun 10–1
💶 €2.60
www.castelliceramica.it

THE AMALFI COAST

This drive from the historic centre of Sorrento to the beautiful gardens and villas of Ravello follows a stretch of coastline in the middle of the protected marine area of Punta Campanella, stopping off at the enchanting Emerald Grotto along the way.

THE DRIVE

Distance:	32km (20 miles)
Allow:	7–8 hours
Start at:	Sorrento
End at:	Ravello

From Sorrento (▷ 209) take the road for Massa Lubrense, passing the hotels Bristol and Brittania on your left. After 50m (55 yards) you come to an intersection. Take the left-hand fork signposted Sant'Agata–Positano, a fairly wide but winding road. After 6km (4 miles) you reach Sant'Agata sui Due Golfi, with the Hotel Due Golfi on your left. Go straight on along the winding road with hairpin bends and after 4km (2.5 miles) you will come to an intersection at the end of the road with the Ristorante Teresinella facing you. Turn right onto the main Positano–Amalfi road.

After 1km (0.6 mile) there is a good stopping place to view the Galli Islands ❶. Continue along the road to a wide lay-by (pull-off), with a prominent white statue of the Virgin Mary on the right. From here you can look down onto Positano and appreciate the view across the sea.

Shortly take the right-hand turn down a narrow one-way road with hairpin bends that leads into Positano. Ignore the first parking area you see and continue along this road until you come to the petrol (gas) station and Mandara, which is the largest parking area. If it's full, a few metres farther along on the right is the Di Gennaro parking area. Park, walk past the second parking area and a few metres along to the right is a pathway that leads to the beach.

❷ The path is fairly steep, but it is lined with a variety of small shops. After 150m (165 yards), steps lead down to a square, to the left of which is the Church of Santa Maria Assunta with its imposing majolica dome. Take time to see the 13th-century Byzantine painting known as *The Black Madonna* and the ceiling covered with frescoes. Opposite the church more steps lead down to another path. Turn left and you will pass through a narrower pathway, lined with shops whose outer walls are adorned with a variety of wares. At the end of the pathway is a terrace with steps leading down to the beach. It is worth walking part of the way down the beach to get a view of the houses above that seem to have tumbled over the edge of the cliff.

Return to your car and follow the one-way road out of Positano. When you reach the intersection, turn right onto the road that passes through the village of Praiano (▷ 209). You will soon come to the entrance to the Grotta di Smeraldo (Emerald Grotto) on your right. There is parking here and two bars. Farther on, a tunnel leads down into the port of Amalfi (▷ 209). There is a small island in the road here where a statue of Flavio Gioia, the inventor of the compass, stands. Turn right here into the parking area.

Walk back to the statue and cross over into Amalfi's main square ❸. To the right is the cathedral, which dates back to the 11th century. Steps lead down under the right aisle to the crypt of Sant'Andrea, the patron saint of Amalfi (16th century), which contains some interesting Florentine mosaics. Continue up this street for 200m (220 yards) and you will pass the papyrus maker next to the bank (Monte dei Paschi di Sienna). The tourist information office is next to the post office, close to the statue on the road leading out of Amalfi towards Ravello.

Go back to your car and turn right in front of the statue onto the Ravello road. After 1km (0.6 mile) at the first intersection on your left go left and follow the road to Ravello. The parking area is in front of you, with steps leading up to the main square.

Ravello ❹ is famous for providing refuge to the people of Amalfi when the Saracens landed in AD877. The Church of San Pantaleone stands in the square. At the top of the left aisle is a small altar with a phial containing the solidified blood of the saint, which miraculously liquefies twice a year. To the right of the church you will find the entrance to the Villa Rufolo, dating back to the 11th century, with its beautiful gardens that overlook the coastline and the resort of Maiori. Richard Wagner wrote his opera *Parsifal* here (1879), and during the summer season the villa is the venue for Wagner concerts. Tickets are available from the villa or the tourist information office to the left of the church. Another villa with magnificent gardens is the 11th-century Villa Cimbrone.

Detail of the campanile, with its small towers and interwoven Arab-style arches dating from 1180–1276, crowning the duomo in Amalfi

OUT AND ABOUT

A line of open boats drawn up the shore and the terracotta rooftops of buildings clustered around the harbour area in the resort of Sorrento (left)

WHERE TO EAT

If you walk along the seafront in Amalfi you will pass the Lido Azzurro, which serves good food at a reasonable price. The Compà Cosimo in Ravello also serves lovely food.

PLACES TO VISIT

Villa Rufolo
Piazza del Duomo, Ravello
☎ 089 857657
🕐 Apr–end Sep daily 9–8; Oct–end Mar 9–6
💶 €4

Villa Cimbrone Gardens
Via Santa Chiara 26, Ravello
☎ 089 857459
🕐 Daily 9 until 1 hour before dusk
💶 €5

Positano perched on a cliff (above left and right)

The town of Ravello, built high in rocky hills (right)

OUT AND ABOUT

SORRENTO–MASSA LUBRENSE

On this walk, make the most of the rich scenery and memorable views over the Bay of Sorrento and the surrounding hills (▷ 209).

THE WALK

Length: 3.5km (2 miles)	
Time: 1 hour	
Start at: Piazza Tasso, Sorrento	
End at: Massa Lubrense	

From Piazza Tasso head down Via Cesareo, a narrow, cobbled shopping street selling wood and leather goods and liqueurs.

shoulder to admire the view over the bay. Negotiate the bends by taking the three paths that act as a short cut. Continue up on the road that climbs away from Sorrento. The road curves left but goes straight over onto Via Priora, which is little more than a path. This takes you over a main road—beware of scooters.

the many pieces of art inside are paintings by Cardisco and Negroni. Noteworthy is the sacristy, with oval portraits of the bishops of Massa Lubrense and 18th-century wooden furniture.

Frequent buses run back to Sorrento from Massa Lubrense.

Towards the end of the road you will see the Church of Sant'Annunziata on the left.

At the end of the road go right, then continue straight ahead and turn left at the parking sign, which leads to the restaurant Zintonio Mare. Here there is a slightly sloping road with a sheer rock face in front. Pass along the high walled path, which narrows and becomes a tight passage between two houses, one yellow and one pink. Walk up the steps, go around the railing, and you will find yourself on the busy main road.

At the International Camping sign, a little farther up on the right, turn left up the steep, cobbled road. Look over your

Looking down the hillside at people picnicking near Massa Lubrense (opposite)

Continue uphill to a shrine of the Madonna and Child and fork left.

You are now on a country trail in the middle of vineyards and lemon groves. It is around 600m (655 yards) to the top of the hill. Continue for another 400m (440 yards) to a crossroads and join Via Bagnulo. Pass under the arch below the white house and take the first right. Go down around two bends to an intersection and turn left, then take the first right heading straight towards Massa Lubrense.

The Church of Santa Maria delle Grazie, on Largo del Vescavado, stands on the foundations of the 16th-century cathedral of Massa Lubrense. The original structure was completely rebuilt in 1760 by Bishop Bellotti when the Episcopio was added. Among

The resort of Sorrento on the Amalfi coast

WHEN TO GO
Don't attempt this walk in August, when it is intensely hot.

WHERE TO EAT
You can stop for refreshment either in Sorrento or at Massa Lubrense, but there is nothing on the walk itself. The Red Lion in Sorrento, despite its name, has typical local and national dishes on the menu at reasonable prices served in a pub-like atmosphere. Meals begin with a free tomato bruschetta and end with a free limoncello liqueur.

TIPS
● This walk is quite steep and isolated in some parts.
● Take plenty of water and some snacks with you.

THE GARGANO PENINSULA

Spend a day touring the spur on Italy's boot, along the winding roads of the rugged coast and through the interior's limestone plateaux and forests that make up Gargano National Park. Starting out near the old imperial city of Manfredonia, this tour takes you past medieval castles, pilgrimage churches, fishing villages, sandy beaches and the beautiful Foresta Umbra.

THE DRIVE

Distance:	208km (129 miles)
Allow:	1 day
Start at:	Santa Maria di Siponto (south-west of Manfredonia)
End at:	San Severo/A14 *autostrada*

From the A14 *autostrada*, take the Foggia exit and follow signs for Manfredonia on the SS89. Just before Manfredonia, follow the road as it forks right onto the SS159, past the Church of Santa Maria di Siponto.

Santa Maria di Siponto ❶ is a handsome 11th-century Romanesque church built over a fifth-century crypt.

Continue for 3km (2 miles) to Manfredonia ❷.

Manfredonia is a good place to shop for picnic refreshments. Its castle, built by King Manfred (1232–66), now serves as a museum preserving the history of the Gargano Peninsula.

From Manfredonia, continue northeast on the SS89 and follow the road as it forks left towards Monte Sant'Angelo. The road winds north into the hills with several hairpin bends—beware of oncoming tour buses.

❸ Monte Sant'Angelo is a popular pilgrimage town,

A souvenir stand in Monte Sant'Angelo, a sanctuary that dates back to the sixth century

with many souvenir shops. It is celebrated for its Santuario di San Michele Arcangelo, a cave-shrine 90 steps down, where Archangel Michael appeared in the fifth century to the Bishop of Siponto.

Continue east towards the coast and Mattinata. Continue until you reach Baia di Zagare.

East of Baia delle Zagare is the Grotta Smeralda ❹, one of several caves along this stretch of coast.

A vast array of ceramics to choose from in a souvenir shop in Vieste

From Baia delle Zagare you can bypass some of the corniche's hairier bends by taking a detour inland to Testa del Gargano, heading back on the coast road towards Vieste.

❺ The peninsula's eastern-most point, Vieste (▷ 210), is a pleasant resort with good sandy beaches, ideal if you feel like a swim.

The coast road from Vieste continues in a northwest direction to Peschici.

Peschici ❻ is a pretty fishing village perched on a promontory with good swimming on the sandy beach (▷ 203).

Beyond Peschici, turn south off the coastal highway at the village of Valazzo and wind your way inland to Vico del Gargano ❼.

Vico del Gargano, with views over the Adriatic, is renowned for its olive oil.

From here, a narrow road winds up to the heart of the Foresta Umbra ❽.

The woodland road passes groves of beech trees, Foresta Umbra's pride (▷ 194), as well as maple, hornbeam and birch. You may glimpse rare orchids, deer or moufflon (wild sheep) on the plateaux.

The SS528 continues south through the forest and meets the SS272 (west of Monte Sant'Angelo). Drive through San Giovanni Rotondo via San Marco in Lamis. This tour ends at the San Severo entrance to the A14 *autostrada* (73km/45 miles).

Vieste rises sheer from the rocks to overlook the sea (left)

Small boats on the sandy shoreline beneath the town of Peschici (right)

M9

Parco Nazionale del Gargano

Golfo di Manfredonia

The serrated, heavily wooded Adriatic coastline with steep limestone outcrops that form the many promontories of the Gargano Peninsula (right)

M10
N10
M11

WHERE TO EAT

The Locanda Dragone in Vieste is a good place to stop for lunch. (Via Duomo 8, tel 0884 701212). Alternatively, you could wait and eat later at La Collinetta in Peschici (Madonna di Loreto, tel 0884 964151).

PLACES TO VISIT

Parco Nazionale del Gargano
Tourist Information Office
Via S. Antonio Abate 121, 71037 Monte Sant'Angelo, tel 0884 568911
www.parcogargano.it

Castello Manfredonia
Castello Svevo-Angioino, Manfredonia
☎ 0884 587838
🕐 Daily 8.30–7.30; closed first and last Mon of month except Jul and Aug
💶 €2.50

Santuario di San Michele Arcangelo
71037 Monte Sant'Angelo
☎ 0884 561150
🕐 Daily 8.30–6

OUT AND ABOUT

THE SALENTINE PENINSULA

From the baroque town of Lecce, this drive traces the varied coastline around the rocky Salentine Peninsula. The cliff-top road occasionally descends to sea level, running along sandy shores, across creeks and through small fishing villages. At the tip of the heel of Italy, Capo di Santa Maria di Léuca, the road turns north to Gallipoli, with its medieval *centro storico*.

THE DRIVE	
Distance: 150km (93 miles; plus 190km/118 miles back to Lecce)	
Allow: 1 day	
Start at: Lecce	
End at: Gallipoli	

❶ Enjoy Lecce's baroque jewels on Piazza del Duomo, the Chiesa di Santa Croce and the palazzi on Via Palmieri (▷ 196).

On the east side of Lecce's ring-road, the Via della Libertà meets up with the SS543 highway to San Cataldo (7km/4 miles). The highway to the coast passes through olive groves and past farmland and small fields reclaimed from the once malarial marshes on the coast. You will then pass the fine sands and pine woods of San Cataldo with its ancient Roman port, an area now known as the Lido di Lecce. From San Cataldo, turn back west for 1km (0.6 mile) on the SS543, then turn south onto the SS611 through the Riserva Naturale Le Cesine, past the Roca Vecchia towards Otranto.

The World Wide Fund for Nature Riserva Naturale Le Cesine ❷ covers 620ha (1,532 acres) of pine and holm-oak woodland and shrub (myrtle, mastic, broom and juniper). The wetlands are the migratory home for herons, coots, mallards and moorhens.

The 14th-century castle ruin of Roca Vecchia has a grand cliff-top view of the sea and there is good swimming at Torre dell'Orso's sandy beach. West of the coast road is the fishing lake of Alimini Grande.

The fishing and ferry port of Otranto ❸ has a Norman cathedral, famous for its 12th-century mosaic (▷ 202).

From the SS173 just outside Otranto, turn east onto the coast road that leads out towards Capo d'Otranto.

Capo d'Otranto ❹ is the Italian mainland's easternmost point, close to Albania. On a clear day you can see the island of Sazan and beyond to the Acrocerauni Mountains. Along the dramatic rocky coastline is Porto Badisco, a fishing hamlet where Aeneas, legendary hero of the Trojan Wars, is said to have landed in Italy.

Rejoin the SS173 at Porto Badisco. Continue south via Santa Cesarea Terme.

In the spa resort of Santa Cesarea Terme ❺ (recommended for respiratory ailments and tired bones), you can admire the art nouveau and Moorish-style Villa Sticchi over the thermal baths.

Continue to Castro ❻.

The ancient Roman cliff-top garrison-town of Castro overlooks a superb bay, where you can explore the subterranean Grotta Zinzulusa.

The SS173 continues south from Castro to Capo Santa Maria di Leuca ❼.

Capo Santa Maria di Leuca, is on the heel tip of Italy's boot. Its sanctuary, also known as Santuario de Finibus Terrae (Land's End), marks the point where St. Peter is said to have begun his mission to bring the Gospel to Italy.

Follow the coast road through Marina di Leuca, which winds its way past Punta Ristola northwest to Gallipoli. Punta Ristola is the boot's southernmost point. The coast road is punctuated by a series of Spanish-built watchtowers and modern beach resorts, notably Torre San Giovanni, Posto Racale and Baia Verde. Alternatively take a faster route inland along the SS274 (45km/28 miles).

The medieval *centro storico* (old town) of Gallipoli ❽ was originally an island. Now joined to the mainland by a causeway, it has a Byzantine *castello* (castle) and a baroque cathedral (▷ 194).

From Gallipoli, the SS101 returns north to Lecce.

The Roman amphitheatre in Lecce (second century AD)

OUT AND ABOUT

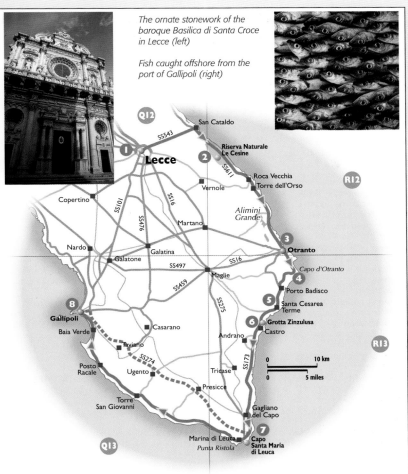

The ornate stonework of the baroque Basilica di Santa Croce in Lecce (left)

Fish caught offshore from the port of Gallipoli (right)

San Cataldo

SS543

Lecce

Riserva Naturale
Le Cesine

SS611

Roca Vecchia
Torre dell'Orso

Vernole

Copertino

SS101

SS16

SS476

Martano

Alimini
Grande

Nardo

Galatina

Otranto

Galatone

SS497

Maglie

SS16

Capo d'Otranto

SS459

SS275

Porto Badisco

Santa Cesarea
Terme

Gallipoli

Casarano

Grotta Zinzulusa
Castro

Baia Verde

Taviano

Andrano

SS173

10 km

0

0   5 miles

Posto
Racale

SS274

Ugento

Tricase

Torre
San Giovanni

Presicce

Gagliano
del Capo

Marina di Leuca
Punta Ristola

Capo
Santa Maria
di Leuca

OUT AND ABOUT

Try the Grotta del Conte (Via Duca del Mare, tel 0836 943 859) in Castro Marina.

PLACES TO VISIT

WWF Riserva Naturale Le Cesine

Approximately 5km (3 miles) away from Santo Catlado

☎ 0832 892264
🕐 Daily Oct–end Apr
📅 Sat–Sun 9.30–2.30
www.wwf.it/puglia

Grotta Zinzulusa

🚩 Organized from Castro Marina
☎ 0836 943812
🕐 Daily 9.30–7
✋ €3

A local fisherman mending his nets in Gallipoli (right)

SIRACUSA— THE VALLE DELL'ANAPO

Drive through the rural countryside west of Siracusa, past the towns of the Monti Iblei plateau to the valleys of the Anapo and Calcinara rivers, part of a large nature reserve.

THE DRIVE

Distance:	177km (110 miles)
Allow:	7 hours (7.5 hours including the short walk)
Start/end at:	Siracusa

From the middle of Siracusa (▷ 216) follow the SR124 in the direction of Solarino. At the entrance to the Parco Archeologico della Neapolis turn west along Viale Paolo Orsi and follow the SR124 signposted to Floridia. The road is lined with evergreen trees and there is a huge cemetery on the right. The road then passes through orange and olive groves interspersed with some less attractive commercial premises, until you reach the unprepossessing town of Floridia.

On entering the town look for a sharp right-hand turn off the one-way system. From here, head towards the northwest. The limestone escarpments of the Monti Climiti can be seen in the distance. At the next intersection turn left at the sign for Sortino and Pantalica and then look for signs to Solarino, a further 3km (2 miles) away.

After reaching Solarino continue along the main street that climbs upwards through the town. Follow signs to the SR124 and the elegant baroque town of Palazzolo Acreide.

A fishing boat moored near Siracusa harbour

This road now passes through a landscape of old fields divided by limestone walls, olive groves and scattered farmsteads, with natural vegetation including the caruba, or carob tree, on some of the higher ground ❶. After about 6.5km (4 miles) the beautiful valley of the Cava Monasterello can be seen to the left and, a little farther on, Mount Etna is visible towards the north on a clear day. The road now dips into a valley whose pleasant views are rather marred by pylons and a grain silo.

After about 6.5km (4 miles), Palazzolo Acreide comes into view, perched upon the hilltop ahead. As the road descends, watch out for the sharp bends. Cross the bridge just before entering Palazzolo Acreide ❷. Continue uphill, turning right at the intersection. Follow the signs to the middle of town and try to park near Piazza del Popolo.

It is only a short walk from here to the Museo Antonino Uccello, in Via Machiavelli, a fascinating museum of rural life and folklore. If time is not pressing, you can visit the Greek theatre and other ruins to the southwest of the town, at the archaeological site of Akrai, founded by the Greeks of Siracusa around 664BC.

From the centre of Palazzolo Acreide continue on the SR124,

following the road downhill from the piazza to the next town, Ferla (signposted to Caltagirone). After about 8km (5 miles) the road forks; turn right off the SR124 and follow signs to Ferla. This road winds through mountainous limestone-covered slopes, alongside a gorge containing a tributary of the Anapo. Farther on, the landscape softens into olive groves, and after 6.5km (4 miles) you drive through Cassaro. Continue up the main street past the Chiesa Madre on your right, following the SP10 to Ferla.

From Ferla, continue uphill along the main street and follow brown tourist signs on the right to Pantalica (ancient Hybla). As you enter this region, look for the ancient tombs cut into the limestone hillsides. The 12th-century BC ruins of the Castello del Principe can be found along a short, unmade track to the right, about 9km (6 miles) from Ferla.

Between the confluences of the Anapo and Calcinara rivers is the ancient Bronze Age settlement of Pantalica ❸, the remains of a necropolis (burial chamber) that was part of the pre-Greek settlement of the Siculi, which flourished from around 1250BC until Greek domination in the eighth century BC. The enigmatic ruins of Castello del Principe (Prince's Palace or Anaktoron) have been described as dating anywhere from the 12th century BC to between the sixth to ninth centuries AD.

From the parking area close to Castello del Principe, it is possible to take a circular walk (2–3 hours) down to the river in the valley, returning along a winding path up the mountainside (▷ 329). Continue for 1.5km (0.9 mile) to the end of the road, at the edge of the Valle del Calcinara.

Prehistoric cave tombs at the necropolis in Pantalica, in the Monti Iblei, all that remains of the Siculi civilization, which colonized the Calabrian mainland in the second century BC (left)

A spiral column adorning the Church of the Annunciation in Palazzolo Acreide (below)

PLACES TO VISIT

Museo Antonino Uccello
Via Machiavelli 19, Palazzolo Acreide
☎ 0931 881499
🕓 Daily 9–1
💶 Free
www.palazzoloacreide.com

Museo Civico dell'Opera dei Pupi
Piazza San Francesco 9, Sortino
☎ 0931 952079
🕓 Daily 9–1
💶 Free. Shows €2 (2 hours)
www.comune.sortino.sr.it/musei.htm
www.operadeipupi.it/home.htm

WHEN TO GO

July and August are extremely hot and it is probably better to make this long car journey during the cooler months, especially if you are also considering doing the walk in the Valle dell'Anapo (▷ 329).

WHERE TO EAT

Palazzolo Acreide has a reasonable choice of bars and restaurants, including the Trattoria La Casareccia (Ronco Cannarella 13, off Via Duca d'Aosta, closed Wed). Ferla has less choice, but it is a more suitable place for lunch as it's halfway along the drive. Dell'Arco (Via Arco Lantieri, open daily) is an unpretentious but pleasant family-run trattoria and pizzeria. Another family concern, La Bomba (Via Bordonali 2), is a friendly and well-run restaurant and pizzeria. If you are visiting off-season and you want to linger in Pantalica, you may want to take a picnic, as the nearest restaurant, the Ristorante Pizzeria Pantalica (open May–early Oct only), is about 5km (3 miles) back along the Ferla-Pantalica road. Sortino has a number of eateries and bars. Close to the Puppet Museum is a very good pizzeria, Pizzoleria (Via della

Libertà 152, closed Mon), while nearby in Corso Umberto, Bar Arcadia serves excellent coffee and light refreshments.

TIP

● Parts of this drive are quite exposed and it is very hot in the summer. Carry plenty of water with you.

Iron railings mark the entrance to a short walk on the left, down to the stream and pool of the riverbed (1.6km/1 mile).

Those unwilling to clamber down the valley can walk a few steps beyond the railings to view the tombs of the 13th-century BC Necropolis Nord-Ovest, and the aptly named Grotta Pipistrelli (Bat Cave).

Return to Ferla and look for the right-hand turn to the SP10 and Sortino. This road winds through olive and oak trees. After about 4km (2.5 miles) turn right at the road intersection and continue to Sortino.

4 Keep an eye out for the wonderful view of Mount Etna with the sprawl of Catania on its seaward base. To the right, and shortly before entering the town of Sortino, there is a lovely view of the Cava Cugni, a small river gorge leading to

The River Anapo that cuts through the Valle dell'Anapo near Ferla

the Cava Grande, the gorge of the Calcinara River.

Sortino is straight ahead of you on top of a cliff (not showing its best side). To enter the town, do not take the right-hand turn signposted Sortino, but take the left-hand turn signposted Siracusa and Carlentini.

5 The Sicilian puppet museum, the Museo Civico dell'Opera dei Pupi, in north-west Sortino, was founded by Don Ignazio Puglisi, whose father was also a master puppeteer, in 1996. Puppet theatre is a traditional form of entertainment for Sicilians that can be traced back to the first millennium AD, but some experts believe that the history of Sicilian puppet theatre goes back as far as the Greek period in Sicily. The themes of the Opera dei Pupi (puppet plays) are generally based upon the struggles of the Christian king Charlemagne and his knights (or paladins) against the

The ancient akrai*, the Greek theatre in Palazzolo Acreide*

Saracens, mixed with liberal amounts of folklore, comedy, romance and myth. The emphasis on the Christians' struggle against the Saracens very much reflects Sicily's own history, when the island was under Arab rule for around 200 years. The museum is famous for its collection of large puppets: Some are around 1.5m (5ft) tall and weigh up to 35kg (77lb). In May the theatre hosts the Festival delle Marionette, attracting groups of puppeteers from all over Italy.

Leave Sortino, following signs to Siracusa along Viale Mario Giardino. The road passes eastwards out of the town, with the large Municipio building set back from the road on the right.

Shortly after leaving the town look for the right turn onto the SP28 to Siracusa. This road roughly follows the course of the River Anapo, crossing and re-crossing it several times.

After about 18km (11 miles), it joins the SR114 to Siracusa. Ignore the turn-off to Siracusa Nord and continue along the SP114 to the Siracusa SR124 exit. Pass the large cemetery again on the outskirts of Siracusa, this time on your left.

At the next roundabout (traffic circle) keep left and follow the brown tourist signs that will direct you back to the Parco Archeologico della Neapolis.

ANCIENT PANTALICA— THE VALLE DELL'ANAPO

This walk winds past remnants of an ancient age, through tall stands of wild fennel, thistle and a myriad of other plants, down to the floor of the Valle dell'Anapo. Birds, including bluetits, goldfinches and stonechats, thrive in the tall vegetation, often heard rather than seen. Back on high ground, the views over the valley are spellbinding.

THE WALK

Length: 4km/2.5 miles (4.8km/3 miles with detour to Filiporto)
Allow: 2–3 hours
Ascent: 200m (655ft)
Start/end at: Castello del Principe parking area, 9.5km (6 miles) from Ferla along the Ferla-Pantalica road. Turn right off the main road and drive 200m (220 yards) to the end of the unmade track
Paths: Narrow, winding and sometimes steep. Slippery in parts
Parking: Castello del Principe
Toilets: Old railway station (Stazione Ferroviaria) in the valley

From the parking area, follow the path uphill to the tumbled blocks of stone marking the site of the Castello del Principe. Bear left down the hillside along the path towards the Necropolis Sud, passing the tomb chambers of the Grandi Tombe a Camere, a group of tombs that are part of the Necropolis Sud, dating from the ninth to eighth century BC, which you can see stretching out across the valley.

Part of the Monti Iblei mountain range, this limestone plateau bisected by the valleys of the Calcinara and Anapo rivers is famous for the ancient settlement of Pantalica.
Originally named Hybla, the town was founded in the mid-second century BC by the Siculi, who colonized from mainland Calabria. The foundations of the Castello del Principe (Prince's Palace, or Anaktoron), once a thriving township, and the cave-like tomb chambers of Europe's largest *necropoli*, are virtually all that is left of this early civilization.

At the next intersection (300m/330 yards) keep left and follow the path downwards. After 200m (220 yards) you can take a short and rather overgrown detour on the right to the Church of Santo Nicolicchio.

The Byzantines who settled around Pantalica converted earlier tombs and chambers in the area into churches and dwellings, and constructed the tiny rock-church of Santo Nicolicchio here in the ninth century AD.

Continue for another 200m (220 yards), keeping right where the path branches, and follow the steep, winding path down to the valley floor. Occasional splashes of red paint on the rocks help to define the route. On the valley floor, turn right and follow the broad dirt track, once part of the Siracusa–Vizzini railway line, for about 250m (275 yards) to where the road briefly crosses the river.

The Stazione Ferroviaria

Near here on the left is a small, shady picnic area by the side of a citrus orchard. Continue along the track, which shortly re-crosses the river, and you will come across the old railway station building on your right, with a small grove of walnut trees opposite. Its toilet blocks are clean if rudimentary, but do not rely on being able to find drinking water here. From the station, follow the right-hand curve of the track, flanked on the left by the river and abundant vegetation, including blackberry, willow and holm-oak growing at the foot of sheer limestone cliffs.

This part of the Anapo is home to trout, freshwater crayfish and several varieties of dragonfly, and along the river's

calmer stretches water mint, watercress and water iris are prevalent.

Approximately 800m (875 yards) from the station house turn right off the track through a gateway in the stone wall and follow the path back up the mountainside. Look for splashes of red paint on the rocks, again marking the route. To begin with this path is fairly hard work as it zigzags steeply up through a swath of wildflowers, including cistus, asphodel, wild salvia and broom. After about 450m (490 yards) the path is bisected by another— the right leads back to Castello del Principe, the left to Filiporto.

Continue to Filiporto to see the necropolis, or the tiny Byzantine rock-tomb church of Santo Micidiario. A detour there and back adds approximately 1km (0.6 mile).

Turn right and enjoy the wonderful view of the valley. After 800m (875 yards) the path rejoins the one from the Castello del Principe; keep left and continue back to the parking area (300m/330 yards).

TIP

● This is a strenuous walk and, apart from on the valley floor, quite exposed, so cover up to protect yourself from the sun.

WHERE TO EAT

There are no bars or restaurants in the valley so it is essential to carry food and water. There is a small shady picnic area in the valley near the river.

WHEN TO GO

The best time to visit the Valle dell'Anapo is in spring (Mar–end Apr), before the heat of summer, when most of the wildflowers are in bloom. To enjoy the valley at its best, avoid weekends and August crowds.

OUT AND ABOUT

Numerous companies specialize in organized tours across Italy. Whether you're an art-lover, gourmet, fitness freak or thrill-seeker, there is probably something to suit. You may want to seek some guidance to help you get the most out of your trip. Below are a few of the many tours led by expert tour guides who can help you get to grips with Italy's abundant attractions and long history.

For a virtual guided tour of Italy visit www.italytour.com. You'll find plenty of information on sports clubs, activities and cultural pursuits in Italy. There is also a searchable database of specialized tours and operators.

ART AND ARCHITECTURE
ACE Study Tours
Tel 01223 835055 (UK)
www.study-tours.org
A long-established charity that organizes guided art and architecture trips and makes donations to restoration projects throughout the world.

Eurogroups
Tel 800 337-2577 (US)
www.eurogroups.com
10-day escorted rail tours, taking in the art and architecture of Rome, Florence, Pisa and Venice.

Road to Italy
Tel 800 848-8163 (Canada)
www.roadtoitaly.com
Escorted city breaks to Rome, Florence and Venice.

BICYCLING AND WALKING
ATG Oxford
Tel 01865 315678 (UK)
www.atg-oxford.co.uk
Award-winning travel company that organizes walking tours around scenic parts of Italy for groups and individuals.

Charnes Tours
Tel 866 665-0324 (US)
www.charnestours.com

A US-based company running fully supported bicycle and walking tours in Italy.

Headwater's
Tel 01606 720099 (UK)
www.headwater-holidays.co.uk
Guided walking, bicycling and gastronomic holidays in areas such as the Dolomites, Umbria, the Amalfi coast, Capri, Sardinia, Sicily and the major art cities.

Odyssey Tours
Tel 320 838 9551 (Italy)
www.odyssey-tours.com
This Rome-based tour operator runs guided walking and coach tours in popular tourist areas.

FOOD AND CULTURE
JMB Opera Holidays
Tel 01905 422282 (UK)
www.jmb-travel.co.uk
JMB's tours include tickets to music festivals and concerts in some of the great opera houses in Italy.

Kudu Travel
Tel 01722 716167 (UK)
www.kudutravel.com
A company running guided walking tours specializing in culture, food, wine and music.

LUXURY
Benvenuto
Tel 334 307 8342 (Italy)
www.benvenutolimos.com
An Italian company providing exclusive chauffeur-driven half-day and full-day excursions along the Amalfi coast, and the

Sorrento Peninsula and around Naples, Salerno, Livorno, Florence, Civitavecchia and Rome.

MOTOR RACING
Everlast Tour and Travel
Tel 06 4741644 (Italy)
Tel 06 4827625 (Italy)
www.italytourtravel.com
Everlast, based in Rome, caters to a range of interests. It runs gastronomic, cultural, language, bicycling and walking tours as well as Formula 1 Grand Prix excursions.

Page and Moy
Tel 08700 106 226 (UK)
www.pagemoy.com
A leading specialist with a varied choice of tours, city breaks and trips to Grand Prix motor-racing events.

MOTORCYCLING
CIMT (Central Italy Motorcycle Tours)
Tel 06 9761 8377 (Italy)
www.cimt.it
Based in Rome, CIMT's specialist knowledge ensures that you will see the best of the country on two wheels.

Mototouring
Tel 02 2720 1556 (Italy)
www.mototouring.com
This Milan-based company runs guided motorcycle tours across Italy including gastronomic trips and an Italian motorcycle factories tour. It can also help you organize motorcycle rental.

CULTURAL COACH TOURS
Archers, tel 0870 460 3894, www.archersdirect.co.uk
Citalia, tel 0870 909 7555, www.citalia.co.uk
Consort Travel, tel 0845 345 0300, www.consort-travel.co.uk
Crystal Italy, tel 0870 888 0024, www.crystalitaly.co.uk
Leger, tel 0800 018 9898, www.leger.co.uk
Magic of Italy, tel 0870 888 0222, magicofitaly.co.uk
Shearings, tel 01942 824824, www.shearingsholidays.com
Woods, tel 01243 870870, www.woodstravel.co.uk

OUT AND ABOUT

This chapter lists places to eat and to stay alphabetically by town within the book's regional divisions.

Eating and Staying

EATING OUT IN ITALY

Eating is definitely one of life's pleasures in Italy. Italian food is fresh, seasonal and, above all, regional. There's really no such thing as Italian cooking, rather, there's Tuscan, Roman, Bolognese, Milanese, Neapolitan…and so on. Each region's cooking is dictated by its produce— so expect to find rice in the regions near the Po, truffles in Piemonte and Umbria, beans and pulses in Tuscany, and fresh fish at the coast.

Gnocchi alla romana (left), a well-stocked cellar in Lucca (middle) and rare expensive truffles (right)

FRESH REGIONAL PRODUCE

Italian cooking is straightforward, its quality dictated by the superlative standard of ingredients. Italian cooks are obsessed with freshness and food shopping is a daily social event in smaller places. This is beginning to change in cities though, as huge supermarkets begin to take over. Outside the big cities, you're also unlikely to find restaurants serving anything other than local food, so don't expect to eat Venetian dishes in Tuscany, let alone exotic cuisine. If you're desperate for international cooking, head for Milan, Rome or Turin; cities this size are also the places to find regional restaurants specializing in food from all over Italy.

MEALS AND MEALTIMES

Many working Italians eat breakfast *(prima colazione)* in a bar—a *cappuccino*, strong coffee with plenty of hot milk, and a sweet pastry, a *brioche* or *cornetto*, a jam- or custard-filled croissant. Hotels catering for foreigners usually serve a buffet-style breakfast with fruit juice, cereal, cold meat and cheeses. If you are heading for breakfast in a bar, most open for business around 7–7.30; hotel breakfast normally starts at 8, or earlier in business hotels.

Lunch *(pranzo)* and dinner *(cena)* both follow the same pattern—though its unlikely that you will want to tackle the full menu twice a day. The first course is the *antipasto* (starter, but literally 'before the meal'), a selection of *crostini* (bread with a savoury topping), cold meats and salami, seafood or vegetable dishes. The next course, *il primo* (first course) is designed to fill you up and consists of pasta, soup or risotto. This is followed by the *secondo* (second course), a portion of a meat or a fish dish, served on its own—if you

want vegetables *(contorni)* or a salad *(insalata)* order them separately. You finish with puddings *(dolci)* or cheese *(formaggio)*. The former is often a bowl of fruit, fruit salad *(macedonia)* or an ice cream *(gelato)*, though fancier places will have desserts such as *tiramisù*, *zuppa inglese* (trifle) or something rich made with ricotta cheese or chocolate. There's no pressure to wade through the whole menu, and it's quite acceptable to order a primo and salad, or an *antipasto* and *secondo*.

Italians drink mineral water *(acqua minerale)* with every meal, either sparkling *(frizzante* or *con gas)* or still *(senza gas)*, accompanied by a relatively modest amount of wine or a beer. Excessive drinking is frowned upon in Italy, where it is rare to see anyone inebriated. Bread is automatically included with every meal. Restaurants normally open for lunch around 12.30 or 1 and stop serving at 3; they close for the afternoon and reopen for dinner around 7.30–8. All restaurants have one official closing day a week, usually indicated on the door or front window, but many places open daily during the summer.

Smoking is not allowed in restaurants and bars, except at tables in the open air such as on a terrace or in a garden.

WHERE TO EAT AND WHAT TO EXPECT

● ***Trattorie*** are usually family-run, serving home-style cooking *(casalinga)*. They are generally simpler than restaurants. Sometimes there is no written menu and the waiter will reel off the list of the day's specials. They are open during lunchtime and in the evening.

● ***Ristoranti*** are more up-market and are not always open for lunch. The food and surroundings are usually more sophisticated than

EATING

that of a *trattoria*. Both *trattorie* and *ristoranti* add a cover charge (*coperto*), which includes bread, and a service charge to the bill.

• *Pizzerie* specialize in pizzas, but often serve simple pasta dishes as well. Look out for the sign *forno al legno*, wood-fired pizza oven.

• *Osterie* can either be old-fashioned places specializing in home-cooked food or extremely smart, long-established restaurants.

PAYING THE BILL (IL CONTO)

Pay by requesting the bill (*'il conto, per favore'*), and check to see whether service is included

(*'il servizio è incluso?'*). Scribbled bills on scraps of paper are illegal; if you don't get one, say that you need a receipt (*'Ho bisogno di una ricevuta, per favore'*), which all restaurants, bars and shops are legally obliged to issue. Both they and you can be fined if you do not take this with you.

• Smaller establishments will normally expect to be paid in cash; you'll be able to use a credit card in more expensive establishments. If service isn't included, it's customary to leave a small tip—some loose change will do.

SNACKS AND ICE CREAM

• Bars serve hot and cold drinks, alcohol and snacks throughout the day. It's customary to eat or drink standing up; you will pay a surcharge if you sit down either inside or at a table outside. In busier city bars make your request and pay at the cash desk, then take the receipt (*scontrino*) and go to the bar where you will be served. Snacks include *panini* (filled rolls), *tramezzini* (sandwiches made on soft white bread), *mini-pizze*, toasted sandwiches (*toast*) and sometimes vol-au-vent. Smarter bars will bring a saucer of olives, crisps or nuts with your drink if you're sitting down. All bars have toilets (*toiletti*); you may have to ask for the key (*chiave*).

• *Alimentari* (general grocer) sell breads and will often make you up a *pannino* (filled roll).

• **Pizza**, Italy's own contribution to fast food, is available all over the country and served by the slice from tiny *pizzerie* to takeaway—look for the sign *pizza al taglio*. There are also a few international chains.

• *Tavole calde* are stand-up snack bars that serve freshly prepared hot food; some have seating as well.

• *Forni* (bakers) sell *foccace*, flat oil and herb bread.

• *Rosticcerie* serve spit-roasted and ready-cooked food, particularly chicken, pasta and vegetable dishes to eat in or take away.

• *Gelateria* sell a range of varieties of ice cream, served in a cone (*cono*) or a tub (*coppa*) of varying sizes. The best ice cream is home-made on the premises; *produzione propria*. Many bars sell commercial ice cream.

• **Fast food** Larger towns and cities have branches of McDonalds and Burger King.

• **International cuisine** is very limited in Italy. Chinese restaurants are becoming increasingly popular in medium- to large-size towns, but you'll have to go to places such as Rome or Milan for a wider choice.

WHAT TO DRINK

• **Coffee** (*caffè*) is served in bars and cafés. Choose from either a small black coffee (*caffè* or *espresso*), a *cappuccino* (with frothy milk), *caffè con latte* (very milky coffee), *caffè macchiato* (an espresso with a drop of milk) or a *caffè corretto* with a slug of spirits. If you want weaker coffee, ask for a *caffè lungo* or an *Americano*. Decaffeinated coffee goes by the generic name Hag.

• **Tea** (*tè*) is generally served black; ask for *latte freddo* (cold milk) if you want milk. In summer *tè freddo* (ice tea), with lemon or peach, is popular.

• **Hot chocolate** (*cioccalata calda*), often served with whipped cream (*panna*), is available during the winter months.

• **Beer** (*birra*) is widely drunk, either bottled or draught (*alla spina*). Preferred Italian brands include Nostra Azzura, Peroni and Moretti, and imported beers are widely available.

• **Wine** is served in bars as well as in restaurants. Ask for white (*bianco*), red (*rosso*) or the less common rosé (*rosato*). House wine is either *vino de la casa* or *vino sfuso*, and can be very good. Bottled wines are locally produced, except in smarter restaurants; the best are DOCG wines (*Denominazione d'Origine Controllata e Garantita*); the label guarantees its origin. Many producers are marketing some superb wines as *vino da tavola*, which are well worth sampling.

• **Spirits** are known by their generic names, and you will find all the usual ones on sale. Italians are also fond of *aperitivi* such as Martini, Campari, Cinzano and the artichoke-based Cynar, and firmly believe in settling the stomach after eating with a *digestivo*. Fiery *grappa* is the most common, but herb-based liqueurs (*amari*), such as Averna and Montenegro, are drunk everywhere and there are dozens of local varieties—Amaretto, based on almonds, Strega, made from herbs and saffron, and Limoncello, a lemon liqueur. Stock and Vecchia Romagna are Italy's preferred brandies.

• **Cocktails** are popular in Venice. Why not try a *bellini*, peach juice and sparkling wine, a *rossini*, strawberry juice and sparkling wine, or a *puccini*, mandarin juice and sparkling wine.

• **Soft drinks** such as coke and lemonade compete with native refreshments—*spremuta di aranci* (freshly pressed orange juice), *granita* (fruity crushed ice), *sugo di alicocca* (bottled apricot juice) and *frullata*, a type of milk shake.

To fully appreciate Italian cuisine you will need to venture away from the beaten track and the sanctuary of tourist resorts and sample the local dishes. If you don't speak Italian this can be a daunting prospect, but knowledge of a few key words will help you to work out what's on the menu, order what you want and avoid any embarrassing blunders. Below is a menu reader, to help you translate common words and familiarize yourself with dishes and ingredients that you are likely to see on an Italian menu.

Whole cheeses in Sulmona (left), lemon liqueur (middle) and freshly picked green olives (right)

Piatti–Courses
antipasti starter
stuzzichini appetizers
primi piatti first courses
secondi piatti main courses
contorni vegetables/side dishes
dolci desserts
spuntini snacks

Carne–Meat
agnello lamb
cacciagione game
coniglio rabbit
fegato liver
maiale pork
manzo beef
pancetta bacon
pollame poultry
pollo chicken
prosciutto Parma ham
prosciutto cotto cooked ham
salsiccia sausage
tacchino turkey
vitello veal

Pesce–Fish
alici anchovy
baccalà dried salt cod
branzino sea bass
dorate bream
fritto misto mixed fried fish
merluzzo cod
pesce spada swordfish
sarde sardines
sogliola sole
tonno tuna
triglia mullet
trota trout

Frutti di Mare–Seafood
aragoste lobster
calamari squid
canestrelli scallops
cozze mussels
gamberetti prawns
granceola spiny spider crab
molluschi shellfish
ostriche oysters
seppia cuttlefish
vongole clams

Verdure–Vegetables
asparagi asparagus
broccolo broccoli
carciofo artichoke
carote carrots
cavolfiore cauliflower
cavolo cabbage
cetriolino gherkin
cetriolo cucumber
cicoria chicory
cipolla onion
fagioli beans
fagiolini green beans
finocchio fennel
latuga lettuce
melanzane aubergines
  (egg plant)
patate potatoes
peperone red/ green pepper
  (capiscum)
piselli peas
pomodori tomatoes
spinaci spinach
verdure cotte cooked greens
zucchini courgettes
  (zucchinis)

Metodi di Cucina—Cooking Methods
affumicato smoked
al forno baked
alla griglia grilled
arrosto roast
bollito boiled
casalingo homemade
crudo raw
fritto fried
frulatto whisked
ripieno stuffed
stufato stewed

La Pasta–Pasta
cannelloni meat- or cheese-
  filled tubes
conchiglie shell shapes
farfalle butterfly shapes
fettucine wide strips
fusilli spiral shapes
lasagne layers of pasta, meat
  sauce and béchamel or
  tomato sauce
linguine thin strips
pappardelle rippled strips
penne quill shapes
ravioli pasta cushions filled
  with meat, cheese or spinach
tagliatelle thin ribbons or strips
tortellini little 'hats' with meat
  or cheese filling
trenette long narrow strips

Salsi/Sugi–Sauces
amatriciana bacon, tomato and
  onion
arrabbiata tomato and hot chilli

EATING

brodo broth
cacciatore sauce for meat: tomato, onion, garlic, wine
carbonara smoked bacon, egg, cream and black pepper
passata sieved tomatoes
pesto basil, garlic, pine nuts, olive oil and pecorino cheese
puttanesca tomato, garlic, hot chilli, anchovies, capers
ragù minced meat, tomato and garlic
salsa sauce

frittata omelette
gnocchi small dumplings made from potato and flour or semolina
minestra soup
minestrone thick vegetable soup with pasta
risotto rice cooked in stock with meat, seafood or vegetables
risotto alla Milanese risotto with saffron
zuppa soup

Bevande–Drinks
acqua minerale mineral water
birra beer
caffè corretto coffee with liqueur/spirit
caffè freddo iced coffee
caffelatte milky coffee
caffè lungo weak coffee
caffè macchiato coffee with a drop of milk
caffè ristretto strong coffee
digestivo after-dinner liqueur
dolce sweet

Fresh fish in Gallipoli (left), fennel (middle) and oyster mushrooms, funghi di ostriche (right)

salsa di pomodoro tomato
salsa verde piquant/vinaigrette
sugo sauce
sugo di carne gravy

Specialità–Special Dishes
carpaccio thinly sliced raw beef served with a cold vinaigrette. Invented in 1961 at Harry's Bar in Venice and named after the painter Vittore Carpaccio
pastiera Neapolitan Easter grain pie, filled with ricotta and seasoned with orange
peperonata sweet pepper and tomato stew
polpetti meatballs
saltimbocca veal escalopes with ham and sage cooked in white wine
scaloppini thinly sliced veal cooked in white wine
stracotto beef stew
timballo baked meat and vegetable pie

Contorni–Side Dishes
insalata mista mixed salad
insalata tricolore mozzarella, tomato and fresh basil
insalata verde green salad
pane bread
patate fritte chips (french fries)
polenta maize meal dish

Altri Piatti–Other Dishes
antipasto misto mixed cold meats: salami, ham etc.

Dolci–Cakes/Desserts
cassata Sicilian fruit ice-cream
cioccolata chocolate
crema custard
gelato ice cream
macedonia fruit salad
panna cream
una pasta a cake/pastry
semifreddo chilled dessert made with ice cream
tiramisù chocolate/coffee sponge dessert
torta tart
zabaglione egg, sugar and Marsala dessert
zabaione di Verduzzo custard pudding with Friuli wine
zuccotto ice-cream sponge
zuppa inglese trifle

Frutti-Fruit
arancia orange
fragole strawberries
lamponi rasperries
mele apples
melone melon
pere pear
pesca peach
pesca noci nectarine
uve grapes

Formaggi–Cheeses
fontina smooth, rich cheese
formaggio di capra goat's cheese
formaggio nostrano local cheese
parmigiano parmesan

frizzante fizzy
ghiaccio ice
liquore liqueur
porto port wine
rinfreschi refreshments
secco dry
spumante sparkling wine
succo di arancia orange juice
tè tea
tè al latte tea with milk
tè freddo ice tea
vini da tavola table wines
vini pregiati quality wines
vino bianco white wine
vino rosato rosé wine
vino rosso red wine

Condimenti–Seasonings
aglio garlic
aromatiche herbs
basilico basil
capperi capers
pepe pepper
peperoncino chilli
prezzemolo parsley
sale salt
salvia sage
senape mustard
zucchero sugar

Il Conto–The Bill
IVA VAT (value added tax)
paghi alla cassa pay at the till
servizio compreso service charge included
servizio non compreso service charge not included
coperto cover charge

EATING

THE NORTHWEST

Typical Milanese dishes are *risotto alla milanese*, rice simmered in saffron-flavoured stock, and the classic *osso buco*, slow-cooked shin of veal. Farther north the cooking is simpler; polenta, maize meal, and *bollitto misto*, mixed boiled meats, spiced up with Cremona's *mostarda di frutta* (pickled fruit with mustard).

Outside Milan the fertile farms of Lombardy produce the cheeses that are the main ingredient in the region's cooking; masacarpone, Bel Paese and Gorgonzola. Basil is the essential ingredient in Ligurian cuisine. The best pesto in Italy is made here, the famous basil, cheese and pine-nut sauce served with pasta. This is usually followed by seafood and fresh mixed salads. Try the local anchovies, served as an *antipasto*, *ciuppin* (fish soup), and *bacalà* (dried cod), a traditional sailors' dish. Local dishes often rely heavily on chick-peas, while *torta pasqualina*, a spinach-and-cheese pie, makes an excellent snack. Try white Cinque Terre wine, produced on the region's cliff-top terraced vineyards.

Piemonte's forte is white truffles, whose intense taste enhances pasta and risottos, and sets off porcini mushrooms. This region borders France, so the food here has a touch of finesse and is beautifully presented. Good-quality meats are served with sauces made from the excellent regional wines. *Bagna caoda*, a hot sauce made with anchovies, garlic, butter and cream, and used as a vegetable dip, is also worth trying. Asti is the area's major sparkling wine. Be prepared to pay a lot for the illustrious red wines such as Barolo, Bardolino and Barbera.

AOSTA (GRAN PARADISO)

VECCHIO RISTORO

Via Tourneuve 4, 11100 Aosta
Tel 0165 33238
This quietly elegant restaurant offers top-notch cooking, with plenty of local recipes—try the *polenta con funghi* (polenta with wild mushrooms) in autumn. There's an excellent *bollitto misto* (mixed boiled meat with sauce *verde*); or sample the *degustazione* menu for a full range of dishes. Great puddings; the amaretto-stuffed peaches with raspberry coulis shines. They have the best of Val d'Aosta wines and some good French varieties.

🕐 Tue–Sat 12.30–2.30, 7.30–10.30, Mon 7.30–10.30; closed Jun
🍷 L €20, D €27, Wine €12

BERGAMO

ANTICA HOSTERIA

Piazza Mercato delle Scarpe, 24129 Bergamo
Tel 035 247993
Antica is brimming with local specialities such as polenta with porcini mushrooms. Choices include veal and rabbit, although the simple menu changes every week. Some famous Italian actors

EATING

The restaurants are listed alphabetically within each town. The prices are for a two-course lunch (L) and a three-course dinner (D) for one person, without drinks. The wine price is for a bottle of house wine.

For a key to the symbols, ▷ 2.

have been known to eat here. Within easy walking distance of Piazza Vecchio.
🕒 Daily 12–2.30, 7–10.30pm; Sep–end Jun closed Mon
🍷 L €17, D €27, Wine €10

GENOVA (GENOA)
LA MADELEINE
Via Maddalena 103, 16124 Genova
Tel 010 2465312
www.madeleinecafe.com
This tiny restaurant and bar (pictured on page 336) comes highly recommended by trendy Genoese. Chalk-boards advertize a daily menu with a small yet delicious range of modern Italian dishes, with an emphasis on fresh local seafood. As with most of the city's simpler eateries, reservations aren't necessary—just turn up and find a table.
🕒 Mon–Sat 11am–3am; closed Aug
🍷 L €17, D €30, Wine €15
🚌 1, 2, 3, 4, 7, 8, 12 or 15 to the Porto Antico complex

LAGO DI COMO
RESTAURANT TERMINUS
Lungo Lario Trieste 14, 22100 Como
Tel 031 329216
www.albergoterminus.it
A fine restaurant overlooking Lake Como. First courses such as *penne arrabbiata* (pasta quills with a spicy tomato, onion and garlic sauce) are priced at around €10. Main courses, including tiger prawns, are around €20. In summer diners can enjoy views of the lake while seated outside on the large terrace.
🕒 Daily 12–2.30, 7.30–10pm
🍷 L €33, D €40, Wine €13

LAGO DI GARDA
AL FATTORE
Via Roma 8, 25015 Desenzano
Tel 030 9141937
www.gardalake.it/alfattore
The crusty pizzas here are loaded with Italian goodies at bargain prices. Toppings include olives, roasted courgettes (zucchini), aubergine (eggplant), Parma ham, mozzarella and crispy Parmesan cheese. Fine dining in the restaurant's modern interior. There is also plenty of room outside in the summer.
🕒 Thu–Tue 12–2.30, 7–11
🍷 L €20, D €33, Wine €10

Restaurant Terminus is ideally located for Lago di Como

L'ARCIMBOLDO
Via Vittorio Emanuele 71, 25019 Sirmione del Garda
Tel 030 916409
This restaurant, with a terrace overlooking the lake offers simple dishes made with the finest ingredients. Highlights include beef, rocket (arugula) and Parmesan cheese, grilled swordfish or trout fillet in white wine. The restaurant's jazzy music makes this a lively place to eat.
🕒 Wed–Mon noon–3, 7–11pm
🍷 L €20, D €37, Wine €14
♿

GRAND HOTEL VILLA SERBELLONI
Via Roma 1, 22021 Bellagio
Tel 031 950216
www.villaserbelloni.it
Lakeside opulence without comparison. This is one of the most prestigious hotels on Lake Como. The attached restaurant, with a terrace overlooking the lake, is one of the area's best. Predominantly meat-based, menu choices range from *carpaccio* to succulent lamb and partridge. A jacket is required at dinner.
🕒 Apr–end Nov daily 12.30–2.30, 8–10pm
🍷 L €67, D €93, Wine €15

LAGO MAGGIORE
LA BAITA
Strada Cadorna 1, 28818 Piancavallo di Oggebbio
Tel 0323 587396
The rustic two-storey cottage has a panoramic view over the surrounding area. Sample tagliatelle in a venison sauce, roe with polenta, or cheese from the local valleys.
🕒 Daily 8–7
🍷 L €27, Wine €6

LA TERRAZZA
Via Mazzini 83, 28832 Belgirate
Tel 0322 7493
www.ristoranteterrazza.com
Surrounded by trees and shrubs, this lakeside restaurant is a special place to enjoy fantastic views and delicious fish dishes. The menu includes smoked herring, Norwegian salmon and grilled lake fish.
🕒 Thu–Tue 12.30–2.30, 7–11pm
🍷 L €20, D €24, Wine €12

EATING

MANTOVA (MANTUA)

IL CIGNO-TRATTORIA DEI MARTINI
Piazza d'Arco 1, 46100 Mantova
Tel 0376 327101
Mantovan cooking returns to its roots in this long-established restaurant. Homely dishes such as *tortelli di zucca* (pasta stuffed with pumpkin) and *maccheroni con pancetta e fagioli* (macaroni with pancetta and beans) are gorgeous. Main courses are seasonal—expect guinea fowl (*faraona*), pigeon (*piccione*) and *rognone trifolate* (kidneys with garlic and herbs). Fantastic puddings and an excellent wine list.
🕐 12.30–1.45, 7.30–9.45 Wed–Sun; closed Aug and 1–5 Jan
🍽 L €40, D €60, Wine €13

MILANO (MILAN)

BACI E ABBRACCI
Via de Amicis 44, 20123 Milano
Tel 02 89013605
www.bacieabbracci.it
Inter Milan striker Christian Vieri and AC Milan midfielder Christian Brocchi own this high-tech but informal restaurant. All profits are donated to charity. The kitchen serves up a very light, traditional Italian menu. Octopus with potatoes, prawns in vinegar, and rice with pears and cheese all make an appearance, alongside more than 70 varieties of pizza.
🕐 Mon–Fri 12.30–2, 6.30pm–2am, Sat–Sun 12–3, 6.30pm–2am; closed Aug
🍽 L €30, D €50, Wine €15
🚇 Sant'Ambrogio

LE BICICLETTE
Via Torti angolo Corso Genova, 20123 Milano
Tel 02 8394177
www.lebiciclette.com
Housed in a former bicycle shop, this restaurant is decorated with modern paintings by emerging artists. Ultra-busy at aperitif time, when there is a giant buffet of pasta, sandwiches and tasty delights to accompany the €5 cocktails. The short menu includes artichoke salad, fish ravioli with black butter, and Argentinian steak.
🕐 Sun–Thur 8pm–2am, Fri–Sat 8pm–1am
🍽 L €21, D €48, Wine €11.50
🚇 Sant' Agosina
🚃 84

LA COZZERIA
Via Muratori 7, 20135 Milano
Tel 02 54107164
Gigantic portions at competitive prices are served at this seafood restaurant. The menu is almost entirely mussel-based—you'll find mussel soup, mussels with

All profits at Baci e Abbracci, in Milan, go to charity

pepper, mussels with saffron, onions and cognac, and even curried mussels. This restaurant is quite small and the furniture is very simple, but it's certainly worth visiting.
🕐 Tue–Sun 7–11pm; closed Aug
🍽 D €30, Wine €10
🚇 Porta Romana

INNOCENTI EVASION 1
Via Privata della Bindellina 1, 20155 Milano
Tel 02 33001882
www.innocentievasioni.com
A small place with a tiny garden where guests can dine in summer. Beautifully presented nouvelle cuisine at very affordable prices. Four seasonal fixed-price menus are available, including one based on truffles. The restaurant is tricky to find, as it is on a street that looks like a private road. Reservations advised.
🕐 Tue–Sat 8pm–10pm; closed Aug
🍽 D €47, Wine €11
🚇 Certosa

JUST CAVALLI
Viale Camoens, 20121 Milano
Tel 02 311817
Fashion designer Roberto Cavalli owns this glitzy restaurant and his style is reflected in the interior and the menu. The fusion of international and Italian styles is evident in dishes such as tuna with basmati rice, coriander (cilantro) and onion marmalade.
🕐 Daily 6.30pm–2am, Sun lunch from 12.30; closed Aug
🍽 L €67, D €80, Wine €10
🚇 Cadorna

OSTERIA DEL BINARI
Via Tortona 1, 20144 Milano
Tel 02 89406753
This restaurant serves fixed-price meals, which diners select from the à la carte menu. The cooking style is traditional but extremely elegant. The atmosphere is great, thanks to both the restaurant's rustic style and the beautiful garden. There is no parking for cars and no metro station nearby, so the best way to get here is by taxi.
🕐 Mon–Sat 7–11pm
🍽 D €48, Wine €13
🚇 Porta Genova

PIXX
Via Maria Segreta 2, 20122 Milano
Tel 02 89015457
This classy take-away sandwich shop is a rare find in the middle of Milan. Tasty sandwiches, salads and other quick lunch options come at refreshingly low prices. Pastries and healthy desserts are also available. Most customers dash in and out, and eat their purchases in the nearby Piazza Duomo, sadly

EATING

missing the stylish modern interior. No credit cards.

🕐 Mon–Sat 8.30–7

🥪 Sandwich or salad €4, pastry €1.50

Ⓜ Cordusio

TANO PASSAMI L'OLIO

Via Vigevano 32a, 20144 Milano

Tel 02 8394139

www.tanopassamilolio.it

In this creative eatery dishes are made with one of 40 types of oil. Main courses are a mix of creative and traditional, including duck with truffles, king prawn tempura, and ravioli with ricotta. Reservations advised.

🕐 Mon–Sat 12–3, 8–10.30pm

🍴 L €80, D €90, Wine €12

Ⓜ Porta Genova

ZEN SUSHI

Via Maddalena 1, 20122 Milano

Tel 02 89013557

www.zenworld.it

Here at one of Milan's few sushi bars, you grab your rice, seaweed and raw fish as they revolve on a giant conveyor belt. The evening menu is à la carte only. This Italian-run Zen establishment is fun and friendly. Sake (rice wine) and Kirin beer are served, as well as some Italian wines.

🕐 Mon–Sat 12.30–3, 7–11.30pm; closed Aug

🍴 L €23, D €37, Wine €10

Ⓜ Missori

RIOMAGGIORE

BAR A PIE' DE MA'

Via dell'Amore, Riomaggiore 55, 19010 Riomaggiore

Tel 0347 7373985

www.buonenuove.net/?c=riomaggiore

After a stroll along the Via dell'Amore, there's nowhere nicer to pause than this terrace bar, perched high above the sea. You can drop in for a drink, a snack or a full meal for a group if you reserve ahead. The emphasis is on fish, with whatever came off the boats that morning on the menu. Expect light meals such as mixed fried fish and shellfish and seafood salad with

peppers, onions and piquant dressing. Wash it all down with Cinque Terre white wine, a flinty tipple.

🕐 Daily 10am–1am; Oct to mid-Nov, Mar, Apr closed Wed; closed mid-Nov to end Feb

🍴 L €13, D €23, Wine €6

SANTA MARGHERITA LIGURE

IL FRANTOIO

Via Giuncheto 23, Santa Margherita Ligure, 16038 Genova

Tel 0185 286667

When in Liguria eat basil and fish, and you'll find them both here; a delicate and intense lasagne al pesto, and a huge variety of risottos. Homemade

Delicious local produce is a speciality of Montagna Viva

pasta includes tagliolini served with a fish sauce. Wild strawberry tart and a bittersweet *semifreddo al caffé* stand out on dessert menu. Huge wine list.

🕐 Thu–Tue 2.30–2.30, 8–midnight; closed Nov

🍴 L €9, D €37, Wine €4.50

TORINO (TURIN)

L'ABERO DI VINO

Piazza della Consolata 9, 10122 Torino

Tel 011 5217578

www.club2006.com

This restaurant, renowned for its selection of wines, many from the Piedmont region, has a sumptuous menu that changes daily. Choices include duck, Alpine lamb and fillet of

FINESTRE SUL PO

Lungo Po Caderna 1, 10100 Torino

Tel 011 8123633

With a view of the river, this restaurant has an elegant simplicity. Meat and game are typical options in the main courses section of the menu, while *pappardelle* (pasta strips with rippled edges) and risotto make up some of the first courses.

🕐 Tue–Sun 7.30pm–2am; closed 10–25 Jul

🍴 D €38, Wine €10

♿

🚃 11 and 12 to Piazza Vittorio Veneto

beef. There's often a fixed-price lunch menu.

🕐 Tue–Sat 12–3, 7.30pm–midnight

🍴 L €8, D €27, Wine €9

🚃 4, 11, 12 and 63 to Piazza della Repubblica

MONTAGNA VIVA

3 Piazza Emanuele Filiberto, 10122 Torino

Tel 011 5217882

The main ingredients for MV's simple but delicious menu are provided by a union of local farmers. Set menus feature local hams, mountain lamb and scores of *antipasti*. Wide variety of local cheeses and excellent wines.

🕐 Mon–Fri 12–3, 7–10.30, Sat noon–3

🍴 L €23, D €33, Wine €9

🚃 Buses to Piazza della Repubblica

TOSCANA

Via della Misericordia 4, 10122 Torino

Tel 011 5628953

Frequented by locals, this restaurant is as typical as they come in Turin. The emphasis is on fine fresh food rather than interior design, and hearty Tuscan classics, thick soups, stews and light pastas dominate the menu. Few people (staff included) speak English here.

🕐 Mon–Fri noon–2.30, 7.30–10pm, Sat 7.30–10pm; closed Aug

🍴 L €12, D €30, Wine €8.20

🚃 4, 11, 12, 52, 56, 63, 67 and 72 to Piazza della Repubblica

EATING

VENICE

The waters of the lagoon and the Adriatic yield an extraordinary variety of seafood and fish. Try *seppie* (cuttlefish), used in risotto, *granceola* (spider crab) drizzled with oil and lemon, and *spaghetti alle vongole verace* (spaghetti with clams). Fish to sample include grilled *sarde* (sardines), *dorata* (bream) and *branzino* (sea bass). Rice and polenta are the Venetian 'fillers'—try *risi e bisi*, made with rice and the season's first peas, and *pasta e fagioli*, a hearty stew of pasta and dried beans. Artichokes *(carciofi)*, served raw, stewed or deep-fried, are another delicacy, while autumn visitors should try the intense, bittersweet *radicchio di Treviso*, a ruby-red leafy vegetable that's served braised or grilled.

Venetians often pop into a *bàcaro*; these are traditional bars selling wines by the glass and a range of *cicheti*, homemade snacks. Drinks on offer will include *un'ombra* (a glass of plonk), and the seemingly innocuous *spritz*, an aperitif made with wine, long drinks made with Campari, and sparkling water. Alternatively try a *bellini*, the classic mix of fresh white peach juice and *prosecco*, a champagne-like dry white wine from the Veneto.

EATING

AI GONDOLIERI

Dorsoduro 366, Fondamenta Venier, 30123 Venezia
Tel 041 5286396
The accent here is firmly on well-hung, beautifully cooked meat served in elegant surroundings.
🕐 Wed–Mon 12–3, 7–10pm; closed lunchtime Jul, Aug
🍽 L €28, D €50, Wine €14.50
💲
🚤 Accademia

ALLA MADONNA

San Polo 594, Calle della Madonna, 30125 Venezia
Tel 041 5223824
The food here is fairly simple but tasty, the service charming, and the wine list small but well considered. The queuing is the only bad thing about it (no reservations).
🕐 Thu–Tue 12–3, 7–10pm
🍽 L €28, D €44, Wine €10
🚤 Rialto

AL MASCARON

Castello 5225, Calle Lunga Santa Maria Formosa, 30122 Venezia
Tel 041 5225995
Al Mascaron offers great *ciccheti* (Venetian tapas) and an anything-goes attitude. It also has a menu for pasta, risotto and salads if you fancy grazing a little longer.
🕐 Mon–Sat 11–3, 6.30pm–midnight; closed over Christmas and New Year
🍽 Ciccheti €8, D €44 Wine/beer €1.50
🚤 San Zaccaria

AL TESTIERE

Calle del Mondo Novo, 5801 Castello, 30122 Venezia
Tel 041 522 7220
Local seafood and fish are imaginatively cooked at this tiny restaurant. There's a well-chosen cheeseboard and an excellent wine list.
🕐 Tue–Sat 12–2, 7–10.30; closed last week Dec, 2 weeks Jan, last week Jul, 3 weeks Aug
🍴 L €25, D €39, Wine €8
🚊 Rialto

ANTICA LOCANDA MONTIN

Dorsoduro 1147, Fondamenta di Borgo, 30123 Venezia
Tel 041 5227151
www.locandamontin.com
The tempting menu here includes an impressive steak tartare and a tantalizing *tiramisù*.
🕐 Thu–Mon 12.30–2.30, 7.30–10pm, (also open Wed Mar–end Jun and Sep, Oct, Christmas and Carnivale); closed 2 weeks Jan and 1 week Aug
🍴 L €22, D €45, Wine €12
🚭
🚊 Accademia

CIPRIANI RESTAURANT

10 Giudecca, Hotel Cipriani and Palazzo Vendramin, 30133 Venezia
Tel 041 5207744
www.hotelcipriani.it
This outstanding restaurant specializes in matchless regional Italian cuisine. The menu and wine list are very carefully thought out to ensure a memorable meal.
🕐 Daily 12–11pm; closed early Nov–early Apr
🍴 L €66, D €125, Wine €39
🚊 Giudecca

CORTE SCONTA

Calle di Pestrin, 3886 Castello, 30122 Venezia
Tel 041 522 7024
One of Venice's finest, and most famous, restaurants, focusing on fresh fish. Superbly imaginative *antipasti* are followed by light fish dishes, homemade pasta and traditional puddings. The wine

list is admirably matched with the cuisine. Reservations essential.
🕐 Daily 12–3, 6–10; closed early Jan–early Feb, mid-Jul to mid-Aug
🍴 L €33, D €50, Wine €9

DAL PAMPO (OSTERIA SANT'ELENA)

Calle Generale Chinotto, 24 Castello, 30122 Venezia
Tel 041 520 8419
Dal Pampo provides hearty cooking and robust wines.
🕐 Fri–Wed 12–2.30, 7.30–9; closed Christmas, May and Aug (check to see which week)
🍴 L €17, D €22, Wine €4
🚊 Sant'Elena

The Cipriani is the perfect choice for a memorable meal

HARRY'S BAR

San Marco 1323, Calle Vallaresso, 30124 Venezia
Tel 041 5285777
This stylish restaurant is very popular with Americans, and is famous for its *bellinis* and its *carpaccio* of beef.
🕐 Daily 10.30am–11pm
🍴 L €44, D €105, Wine €24
🚭
🚊 San Marco

OSTERIA OLIVA NERA

Castello 3417/18, Calle della Madonna, 30122 Venezia
Tel 041 5222170
The menu here shows that Venetian cooking can be given a contemporary edge. Delicious examples include

ANTICHE CARAMPANE

San Polo 1911, Rio Terra delle Carampane, 30125 Venezia
Tel 041 5240165
Carampane is dedicated to the history of Venetian cooking. Renaissance and medieval dishes are cleverly reinterpreted–try the shellfish with olive oil and Parmesan or the filleted St. Peter's fish with Treviso chicory.
🕐 Tue–Sat 12.30–3.30, 7.30–10.30pm
🍴 L €21, D €52, Wine €12
🚊 San Silvestro

scallops with wild mushrooms, and lamb cooked in thyme. The dessert menu includes a rich mascarpone cheesecake.
🕐 Fri–Tue 12–2.30, 7–10pm
🍴 L €28, D €47, Wine €9
🚊 San Zaccaria

OSTERIA LA ZUCCA

Santa Croce 1762, Ponte del Megio, 30135 Venezia
Tel 041 5241570
www.lazucca.it
The predominantly vegetarian dishes here are cooked with style and imagination. Reservations recommended.
🕐 Mon–Sat 12–2.30, 7–10.30pm; closed Aug
🍴 L €14, D €33, Wine €12.50
🚭
🚊 San Stae

VINI DA GIGIO

Fondamenta San Felice, 3628A Castello, 30122 Venezia
Tel 041 528 5140
www.vinidagigio.com
This increasingly famous place is one of the best-value restaurants in Venice, known for its superlative *antipasti*, fresh fish and meat and game; in season, try the wild duck from Burano. The wines come from all over the world. Reservations are essential.
🕐 Tue–Sun 12–2.30, 7.30–10.30; closed 3 weeks Jan into Feb, 3 weeks Aug into Sep
🍴 L €28, D €36, Wine €7
🚭
🚊 Ca' d'Oro

EATING

THE NORTHEAST AND EMILIA-ROMAGNA

It's generally accepted that you eat better in Emilia-Romagna than anywhere else in Italy. This is the home of *parmigiano-reggiano* (parmesan cheese), *prosciutto di Parma* (Parma ham), *ragù* (rich meat sauce) and egg pasta. Meat dishes include *bollito misto* (mixed boiled meats) and *zampone*, a stuffed pig's trotter usually served with lentils. Emilia's big-name wine is Lambrusco, golden and intensely scented.

Cooking in Trentino Alto-Adige is geared to long, cold winters. You'll find hearty soups rather than pasta, dumplings *(canerderli)*, spicy smoked meat *(speck)*, game and rabbit, while puddings are based on locally grown apples, plums and pears. Farther north, German influence is evident; goulash, sauerkraut and apple strudel all find their way onto the menu, and coffee gets weaker and creamier by the kilometre. More DOC wine is produced in the region than anywhere else in Italy—look out for Pinot Grigios and Chardonnays.

Friuli-Venezia Giulia's cuisine relies heavily on yoghurt and rye bread, piquant sweet-sour dishes and fish broths spiced with cumin and fennel. The region borders Yugoslavia, and some of the cooking has Slav influences and the pasta fillings are heavily spiced. The famous San Daniele ham is produced here, delicious with the local wines such as Tocai, Verduzzo and Pinot Nero.

BOLOGNA

BROCCAINDOSSO
Via Broccaindosso 7/a , 40125 Bologna
Tel 051 234153
At this rustic establishment, with rough tables and long wooden benches, they only serve one course and desserts, and there is no menu; although you can order pasta, it's better to wait and see what the staff bring you. Reservations essential. No credit cards.
🕐 Mon–Sat 8.30pm–2am; sometimes closed Aug

C'ENTRO
Via dell'Indipendenza 45, 40100 Bologna
Tel 051 234216
This modern, clean restaurant has an excellent range of local dishes and salads—all at very reasonable prices. C'entro is a safe haven for vegetarians, who can pile up as many of the raw ingredients as they like on their plates.
🕐 Mon–Sat 11.45–3, 6.30–9.30pm
🍴 L €11, D €17, Wine €7
🚌 20, 27

EATING

CESARI

Via de' Carbonesi 8, 40123 Bologna
Tel 051 237710

Stately establishment, five minutes' walk south of the main square, that has long been a star in Bologna's gastronomic sky. Specialties include homemade ravioli stuffed with rabbit and white truffle with celery and Parmesan. The wine list is extensive and good and includes wines produced by the owner. Reservations essential. Air-conditioned.

ⓒ Mon–Sat 12.30–3, 7.30–11pm; closed Sat in Jul and Aug
🍽 L €33, D €40, Wine €12
🚇 20, 29, 38, 39, 52

FANTONI

Via del Pratello 11, 40122 Bologna
Tel 051 236358

This small, lively trattoria serves simple local dishes with homemade pasta and wines and fresh fish from Thursday to Saturday. The small menu changes daily. You can sit out on the terrace in summer. Be prepared to queue at the door if you haven't made a reservaton. No credit cards.

ⓒ Tue–Sat 12–2.30, 8–10.30pm
🍽 L €13, D €21, Wine €8

VICTORIA STATION

Via Zanardi 76, Bologna
Tel 051 6346062
www.victoriastation.it

Easily recognized by the red London bus standing outside! A lively party place where British style meets old-fashioned Bolognese hospitality, with a large garden area and seating for 500 guests. A popular hangout for trendy young Bolognesi and celebrity visitors to the city. The daily menu is viewable on the website.

ⓒ Daily 7.30pm–2.30am
🍽 D €17 Wine €8

CANAZEI

RISTORANTE DE TOFI

Via Roma 88, Canazei, 38032 Trento
Tel 0462 601 302
www.hotel-astoria.net

Good restaurants are rare in this area, and locals consider the restaurant at the Hotel Astoria to be the best. Local dishes include *polenta al ragù* (maize meal with meat sauce), *funghi* (mushrooms) in autumn and some game.

ⓒ Daily 12.30–1.30, 7–8.30; closed May to mid-Jun and Oct, Nov
🍽 L €13, D €30, Wine €9
🚗 From the A22 (Brennero) exit Egnaora then follow signs for Cavalezei and Val di Fassa. From here follow signs to the hotel

Cesari is one of the finest restaurants in Bologna

CIVIDALE DEI FRIULI

ANTICA TRATTORIA DOMINISSINI

Stretta Jacopo Stellini 18, Cividale dei Friuli, 33043 Udine
Tel 0432 733763
www.anticatrattoriadominissini.it

Make your way through the bar area and down a couple of steps into this traditional restaurant, decorated with local pottery. The menu is faithful to straightforward Friulian cooking, so you'll be able to try traditional cheese and potato cakes, thick vegetable soups and grilled meat. The owner doubles as the waiter and he is passionate about wine;

ask his advice on local vintages or try the smooth white Tocai bursting with depth.

ⓒ May–end Oct Tue–Sun 10.30–3, 6–11; rest of year Tue–Sat 10.30–3, 6–11
🍽 L €20, D €29, Wine €7

MERANO (MERAN)

FLORA

Via Portici 75, Merano, 39012 Bolzano
Tel 0473 231484

An intimate restaurant in a 15th-century building. Cooking here is remarkably varied–the accent's Italo-Austrian. The black-and-white pasta with prawns and wild herbs is a signature dish; try the crayfish and the excellent lamb fillet.

ⓒ 12.30–2.30, 8–12; closed Sun, Mon lunch and mid-Dec–Feb
🍽 L €23, D €33, Wine €14

PADOVA (PADUA)

ANFORA

Via Soncin 13, 35122 Padova
Tel 049 656629

This is a lively place with a bohemian air. Anfora concentrates on local produce and fish dishes, and its prices are very reasonable. Arrive early or make a reservation.

ⓒ Mon–Sat 12.30–3, 8–10.30pm
🍽 L €13, D €27 Wine €9

BELLE PARTI

Via Belle Parti 11, 35122 Padova
Tel 049 8751822

A charming restaurant with wooden beams, white tablecloths and art nouveau stained glass. The menu includes regional and international dishes such as steamed mullet with potatoes and olives, cuttlefish with polenta, bigoli pasta with duck *ragù* and foie gras, and risotto with prawns and saffron. Excellent wine list. Reservations advisable.

ⓒ Mon–Sat 12.30–2.30, 8–11; closed Aug
🍽 L €40, D €53, Wine €14
Ⓢ

EATING

NANE DELLA GIULIA
Via Santa Sofia 1, 35121 Padova
Tel 049 660742
This *osteria*, reputed to be the oldest in town, is in the university quarter. The menu is strong on the cooking of the Veneto region and vegetarian dishes, making good use of local cheeses and vegetables; all items are very reasonably priced. Popular dishes include pasta with beans. Gay-friendly. No credit cards.
🕐 Tue–Sun 11.30–2.30, 7–midnight
🍴 L €11, D €27, Wine €8

OSTERIA DEI FABBRI
Via dei Fabbri 13, 35122 Padova
Tel 049 650336
This *osteria* in the old Jewish ghetto serves simple local pasta and polenta dishes, such as *pasta e fagioli* (pasta with beans) and grilled meats, including rabbit and beef. Reservations advisable.
🕐 Mon–Sat 12.30–2.30, 7.30–midnight
🍴 L €16, D €40, Wine €7.50

PEPEN
Piazza Cavour 15, 35100 Padova
Tel 049 8759483
There's a wide range of pizzas, as well as other dishes. Try the fish and puff pastry with cream cheese, barley and candied fruit. A reservation is essential, even at lunchtime, as it's hugely popular with local office workers.
🕐 Mon–Sat 12–3, 7–11pm; closed Aug
🍴 L €17, D €47, Wine €10
🔲

PARMA

SANTA CROCE
Via Pasini 20, 43100 Parma
Tel 0521 293529
www.ristoratori.it/santacroce
Restrained elegance in three rooms—glowing damask, polished wood floors and fresh flowers, all warm and welcoming. They serve up authentic Parma cuisine with a twist; try the mixed *salumi* to sample Parma ham in its birthplace, or delicate crab roulade, then move to seasonal

dishes prime fillet steak and mousses and *semifreddi* for dessert. Huge wine list.
🕐 Mon–Fri 12.30–2, 8–10, Sat 8–10
🍴 L €27, D €40, Wine €10
🔲

RAVENNA

BIZANTINO
Piazza A. Costa, 48100 Ravenna
Tel 054 432073
A self-service restaurant on the big market square in the centre of old Ravenna. It's ideal for a quick bite while you're out sightseeing. Expect good, simple food with plenty of fresh produce. No credit cards.
🕐 Mon–Fri 11.45–2.45
🍴 L €9, Wine €2

Al Rustichello has an enviable reputation in Ravenna

CA' DE VEN
Via Corrado Ricci 24, 48100 Ravenna
Tel 0544 30163
This 'House of Wine' has a large selection of wines, including local sweet varieties. The simple menu has salads, cold meats, fresh pasta and the local dish, *piadine*: a round flat bread filled and rolled up. The long tables are often crowded with locals.
🕐 Tue–Sun 11–2, 6–10pm
🍴 L €13, D €27, Wine €10

LA GARDELA
Via Ponte Marino 3, 48100 Ravenna
Tel 0544 217147
A bustling and friendly restaurant that's close to the main visitor attractions. They

specialize in homemade pasta, such as *tortelloni della casa* with ricotta, cream, spinach, tomatoes and herbs, tagliatelle with porcini mushrooms, and ravioli stuffed with truffles. If you fancy something more substantial they also serve grilled meats, fresh fish and vegetables.
🕐 Fri–Wed 12–2.30, 7–10pm
🍴 L €13, D €20, Wine €7.50

L'OSTE BACCO
Via Salara 20, 48100 Ravenna
Tel 0544 35363
A small, family-run *trattoria* serving tasty traditional Romagnolo cuisine, with good fish and *antipasti*. The wine list is also good. It is worth reserving a table.
🕐 Wed–Mon 12–2.30, 7.30–10.30pm
🍴 L €13, D €21, Wine €7
🔲

AL RUSTICHELLO
Via Maggiore 21/23, 48100 Ravenna
Tel 0544 36043
Just outside the old town walls west of the town, the Rustichello has gained a reputation for both the quality of its food and the size of its portions. The restaurant has a modern, light and elegant interior. English is spoken and the owner comes and tells you what's on the menu. Top dishes here include a marvellous *cappelletti* (a type of meat-filled ravioli) with asparagus. Reservations recommended. No credit cards.
🕐 Mon–Fri 12–2, 7–10pm, Sat 7–10pm
🍴 L €27, D €35, Wine €6

TRIESTE

ANTICA TRATTORIA SUBAN
Via Comici 2, 34128 Trieste
Tel 040 54368
This old coaching inn serves the best food in Trieste, and is well worth a trip out to the suburbs. Try the bean soup, ham and sauerkraut, or risotto with wild local herbs. Follow it up with veal simmered in wine

EATING

and a thoroughly modern chocolate soufflé.

⏰ Wed–Sun 12–3, 7–10.30, Mon 7–10.30; closed Tue

🍴 L €20, D €40, Wine €10

🚇 35

VERONA

AL CARRO ARMATO

Vicolo Gatto 2/a, 37121 Verona
Tel 045 8030175
www.carroarmato.it

Delightful bar/restaurant near the Gothic church of Santa Anastasia, with its mysterious name meaning 'armoured car'. Delicious *antipasti* are served from the narrow bar or on large trestle tables in the adjoining high-ceilinged hall. The good-humoured staff occasionally burst into song. Wines are served either from the barrel or by the bottle. Card games are often played here, and there's occasional live music. Young clientele. No credit cards.

⏰ Thu–Tue 11–3, 6pm–2am, Sun 1–5, 6pm–midnight

🍴 L €13, D €33, Wine €5

LA BOTTEGA DEL VINO

Via Scudo di Francia 3, 37121 Verona
Tel 045 8004535
www.bottegavini.it

A major player on the Veronese gastronomic scene, this elegant restaurant with its flamboyant interior is always crowded and bustling, but the service is slick and professional. As the name suggests, they have a very good wine list. Excellent Italian cheese served with honey.

⏰ Jul, Aug daily 10.30–3, 6pm–midnight; rest of year Wed–Mon 10.30–3, 6pm–midnight; open until 3am on opera nights

🍴 L €40, D €67, Wine €17

LEON D'ORO

Via Pallone 10a, Verona
Tel 045 595076

Relax with pizza and pasta in the garden of this unpretentious pizzeria, just a short walk from the Arena, and away from the crowds of Piazza Brà. Popular at lunchtime with locals; German beer is served more than wine. In the late evenings there is live music and a disco at weekends.

⏰ Daily 11.30am–2am

🍴 L €13, D €27, Wine €12

OSTERIA LA PIGNA

Via Pigna 4, 37121 Verona
Tel 045 8004080
www.osteriapigna.it

At this large and elegant restaurant diners are given a glass of sparkling *prosecco* while they peruse the menu. Try the duck *pappardelle*, risotto with Amarone or

Verona has a wide range of enticing eateries

stracotto (beef stew) and Amarone wine. A good range of wines is available.

⏰ Mon–Sat 12–3, 7–11pm

🍴 L €20, D €35, Wine €10

♿

TRATTORIA ALLA COLONNA

Largo Pescheria Vecchia 4, 37121 Verona
Tel 045 596718

This very popular establishment takes its name from the large column in the middle of the room. It's packed with locals, so if you haven't reserved make sure you arrive before 9pm for dinner. Expect excellent regional cooking that is good-value for money. Top dishes include horse meat, rabbit and *bigoli* pasta. The wines served are from the Veneto region. There is a fixed-price menu available for €13.

⏰ Mon–Sat 12–2.30, 7.30pm–2am

🍴 L €16, D €35, Wine €9

LA VECETE

Via Pellicciai 32A, 37121 Verona
Tel 045 594748
www.grupporialto.it

The best bar in town for tasting a very wide selection of wines. Five minutes' walk north from Piazza Brà, it's simply decorated with an enormous array of bottles to choose from. They also have excellent food, both snacks and full meals, served at the bar or at tables. It is advisable to make a reservation during July and August.

⏰ Mon–Sat 9am–midnight; til 3am during opera season (Jul, Aug)

🍴 L €19, D €40, Wine €13

VICENZA

ANTICA TRATTORIA TRE VISI

Corso Palladio 25, 36100 Vicenza
Tel 0444 324868
www.trevisi.vicenza.com

This lovely 15th-century building has a great team of staff making this a particularly enjoyable place to eat. The food is firmly mainland Venetian, made with top-quality seasonal ingredients, raised and grown locally. Try *porca l'Oca in pignatti con funghi*, a traditional dish of long-simmered goose with wild mushrooms, or *bigoli al radicchio di Treviso con acciughe*, the bittersweet long red radicchio from Treviso served with homemade pasta and anchovy—an intense and rich dish. The wine list consists of some good, mainly local, wines.

⏰ Tue–Sat 12.30–2.30, 7.30–10.30pm, Sun 12.30–2.30

🍴 L €20, D €40, Wine €12

EATING

FLORENCE

Florentine cooking is Tuscan, simple food prepared with good-quality ingredients. Although on offer in every restaurant and *trattoria*, pasta is not a traditional staple, though *pici*, a local variety of thick spaghetti, is a well-known Florentine *primo*. Bread is a favourite ingredient, toasted with a drizzle of olive oil in the form of *bruschetta*, spread with savoury toppings and served as *crostini*. The excellent vegetable soups (*ribollita*) are well worth trying. Beans are another local treat, appearing in soups or served as a *contorno*, livened up with olive oil and sage. Grilled meat (*alla fiorentina*) is popular—the first choices here are the *bistecca alla fiorentina*, a prime-quality steak slowly chargrilled over log embers, or *tagliata*, T-bone steak served with rocket and Parmesan cheese.

Wines to try include Chianti, Brunello and Vino Nobile di Montepulciano; Sfuso wine can be excellent, usually made from the locally favoured Sangiovese grape.

EATING

L'ANTICO RISTORO DI CAMBI
Via Sant'Onofrio 1r, 50124 Firenze
Tel 055 217134
This eatery is a rare find, serving lighter dishes at lunch. The menu concentrates on fresh ingredients. Try one of the excellent salads or platters, which are piled high with fresh produce including basil, rocket (arugula), pecorino cheese, buffalo mozzarella and cured meats.
🕐 Mon–Sat 12.30–2.30, 7.30–10.30pm
🍴 L €15, D €25, Wine €12
🚫
🚇 D, 6

BALDOVINO
Via San Giuseppe 22r, 50122 Firenze
Tel 055 241773
A bustling yet relaxed *trattoria* not far from Piazza Santa Croce that is especially good for those with children, as it serves great pizzas. The changing menu includes lots of soups, beef, various grilled meats and some inventive plates of *pastasciutta*. The wine list includes many Tuscan classics.
🕐 Mar–Oct daily 12–2.30, 7pm–midnight; rest of year Tue–Sun noon–2.30, 7pm–midnight
🍴 L €14, D €25, Wine €14
🚇 C, 14

CAFFÈ RIVOIRE
Piazza della Signoria 3r, 50122 Firenze
Tel 055 293045
The Rivoire opened in the 1870s and is a must for the chocolate connoisseur. It produces arguably the best chocolate in town. Eat an

exquisite ice cream or sample the famous hot chocolate.

🕐 Tue–Sun 8am–midnight; closed for 2 weeks in Jan

💶 Cappuccino €6, ice cream from €6 to eat in

🚌 A, B

CAPOCACCIA

Lungarno Corsini 12–14r, 50123 Firenze
Tel 055 210751
www.capocaccia.com

This upper-crust café bar serves finger foods, sandwiches and light fare, and is famed for its sumptuously filled *panini* and American-style brunch menu. There are more than 200 wines available.

🕐 Tue–Sun 12–1am, Tue–Fri dinner

💶 Filled *panini* €5–€14, smoked salmon and salad €16

🚌 B

CARABÈ

Via Ricasoli 60r, 50121 Firenze
Tel 055 289476
www.gelatocarabe.com

This Siciliana *gelateria* sells ice cream reminiscent of the first ice dessert recipes that arrived in southern Italy from the ancient Arabic world. The tastes of pistachio, fig, apricot and vanilla make for a stimulating change. No credit cards.

🕐 Daily 10am–1am

💶 Ice cream cone €2–€6

🚌 1, 6, 11, 14, 17, 22

DA BENVENUTO

Via della Mosca 16r, 50122 Firenze
Tel 055 214833

Lots of solid Tuscan food to choose from at this quirky establishment in Santa Croce. Among the good-value offerings is pasta with a meaty *ragù* sauce. Ask about the latest beef and pork dishes, seasoned with herbs and accompanied by crunchy vegetables and potatoes. The house red goes down very well.

🕐 Mon–Sat 11–3, 7–12

💶 L €17, D €30, Wine €8

🚫

🚌 B, 23

DOLCI E DOLCEZZE

Piazza Beccaria 8r, 50121 Firenze
Tel 055 234 5458

This old-style bakery deserves its international renown. If you are only in Florence for a day, make sure you come here for a cake break.

🕐 Tue–Sun 8–8

🚌 A, 6, 31, 32

ENOTECA PINCHIORRI

Via Ghibellina 87, 50122 Firenze
Tel 055 242777
www.enotecapinchiorri.com

This French-influenced establishment is one of Italy's best. The magical rose-scented *cortile* (courtyard) and elegant

Capocaccia is a place to be seen in

dining areas are a fitting complement to the exquisite nouvelle cuisine and unrivalled wine list.

🕐 Thu–Sat 12.30–2, 7.30–10pm, Tue–Wed 7.30–10pm; closed Aug, 24–25 and 31 Dec

💶 L €65, D €110, Wine €25

🚫

🚌 A, 14

OLIVIERO

Via delle Terme 51r, 50123 Firenze
Tel 055 287643
www.ristorante-oliviero.it

Excellent service and superb Tuscan food are the main characteristics here. Specialties include wild boar, guinea fowl and rabbit. Sublime soups, exquisite vegetables and

IL LATINI

Via de' Palchetti 6r, 50123 Firenze
Tel 055 210916
www.illatini.com

A traditional rustic *osteria* with large, hearty helpings of Tuscan classics. Highlights include a traditional *zuppa di farro* (a meat, grain and vegetable soup) and the wild boar dolceforte stew. The *tiramisù* is outstanding.

🕐 Tue–Sun 12.30–2.30, 7.30–10.30pm

💶 L €14, D €30, Wine €10

🚌 A, 6, 14, 17, 26

innovative pasta creations make up the rest.

🕐 Mon–Sat 7.30pm–1am; closed Aug

💶 D €50, Wine €17

🚌 A, B, 6, 11, 36, 37

OSTERIA DEL CAFFÈ ITALIANO

Via Isola delle Stinche 11/13r, 50122 Firenze
Tel 055 289020
www.caffeitaliano.it

Classic Tuscan fare including wild boar and chunky soups. There's an excellent choice of pasta dishes. The wine list includes lots of Chiantis and 'Super Tuscans'.

🕐 Tue–Sun noon–1am

💶 L €20, D €55, Wine €14

🚌 A

OSTERIA SANTO SPIRITO

Piazza Santo Spirito 16r, 50125 Firenze
Tel 055 2382383

A trendy *osteria* that excels in creating adventurous, mountainous salads—chunks of Parmesan and *prosciutto crudo* ham are mixed with pine nuts and various leaves such as rocket (arugula). There's a superb choice of cheeses and a decent wine list.

🕐 Daily 12.30–2.30, 8–12

💶 L €15, D €30, Wine €12

🚌 D, 11, 36, 37

EATING

PERCHÈ NO!
Via dei Tavolini 19r, 50122 Firenze
Tel 055 2398969
Customers can sit down in this
ice cream parlour, which is a
welcome bonus. There are
plenty of new tastes to
discover. Try the favourite
Malaga, which is dotted with
rich wine grapes. No credit
cards.
🕐 Mar–end Oct Wed–Mon 11am–
12.30am; Dec–end Feb Wed–Mon
12–7.30pm; closed Nov
🍦 Cone €2.50
🚌 6, 17, 23

PITTI GOLA E CANTINA
Piazza Pitti 16, 50125 Firenze
Tel: 055 212 704
Wine shop, culinary library and
wine bar, this stylish little oasis
provides a pleasant respite.
Snacks and light dishes are
served, including salads and
plates of cheese and salami, as
well as cakes to accompany
sweet wines.
🕐 Tue–Sun 11–10; closed mid-Aug
🍴 Light dishes €8–€15, Wine €3.50
glass

RISTORANTE PERSEUS
Piazza Mino da Fiesole 9, 50014 Firenze
Tel 055 59143
One of the best places for
sampling *bistecca alla
fiorentina*. All dishes are
accompanied by delicious
salads, Tuscan cannellini
beans and cooked vegetables.
Try the *pannacotta* (set cream
pudding) with forest fruits or
the sublime cheesecake. This
is a good place to bring
children.
🕐 Jun–end Sep daily 12.30–3,
7.30–11.30pm; winter Wed–Mon
12.30–3, 7–11pm
🍴 L €14, D €25, Wine €13
🚌 7

RISTORANTE RICCHI
Piazza Santo Spirito 8–9r, 50125 Firenze
Tel 055 215864
www.ristorantericchi.it
Choose to eat al fresco in
the gloriously leafy Piazza
Santo Spirito, or opt for the
clean, contemporary dining

rooms. The menu is a feast
of all-fresh fish and seafoods.
Imaginative salads and
vegetables are there to
accompany them.
🕐 Mon–Sat 7.30–11pm, café
7am–1am; closed last 2 weeks Aug
🍴 D €40, Wine €15
🚌 D, 11, 36, 37

SABATINI
Via dei Panzani 9a, 50123 Firenze
Tel 055 282802
www.ristorantesabatini.it
This elegant restaurant serves
solid Tuscan dishes with
international touches, and the
restaurant is known for
bistecca alla fiorentina.
Seafood enthusiasts can opt

*Oliviero offers a range of Tuscan
delights*

for the *risotto con scampi*.
An excellent wine list and
multilingual service.
🕐 Tue–Sun 12.30–3, 7–11
🍴 L €35, D €80, Wine €14
🚌 A, 1, 4, 7, 10, 11, 22, 23, 36, 37

LA SPADA
Via della Spada 62, 50123 Firenze
Tel 055 218 757
www.laspadaitalia.com
The deceptively simple menu
here offers well-prepared
dishes, from rabbit or pork
roasted on a spit to delectable
homemade pastas. Friendly
service and informal
atmosphere.
🕐 Tue–Sat 12–3, 6–10.30
🍴 L €12, D €25, Wine €15
🚌 A, 11, 36, 37

TARGA BISTROT FIORENTINO
Lungarno Cristoforo Colombo 7, 50136
Firenze
Tel 055 677377
www.targabistrot.net
Enjoy international cuisine
at its finest amid sleek
contemporary surroundings.
There are lots of innovative
delights and some inspiring
uses of typically southern
European ingredients. There
are many cheeses, a detailed
wine list and some delectable
desserts. Reserve well in
advance.
🕐 Mon–Sat 12.30–2.30, 8–11pm;
closed Aug and 1–8 Jan
🍴 L €22, D €50, Wine €19
🚌 14, 31, 32

TRATTORIA ANTICHI CANCELLI
Via Faenza 73r, 50123 Firenze
Tel 055 218927
Hearty Tuscan food is the
mainstay here. Feast on hearty
soups and *bruschetta* topped
with sweet tomatoes and olive
oil. The seasonal menu always
features a satisfying meat or
fish dish. Vegetarians have a
variety of side dishes to
choose from.
🕐 Daily 12–2.30, 7.30–10.30pm
🍴 L €10, D €20, Wine €6
🚌 4, 7, 10, 12, 13, 25, 31, 32, 33

ZIBIBBO
Via di Terzollina 3r, 50139 Firenze
Tel 055 433383
www.zibibbonline.com
Zibibbo's forte is fish. But
there are also tasty vegetable
side dishes and typically
Tuscan creations such as
tagliatelle with duck *ragù*.
There are plenty of Tuscan
wines and a wide choice of
desserts, including chestnut
mousse.
🕐 Mon–Fri 8–11, Sat 8–12, Sun 10–3;
closed Aug
🍴 L €25, D €40, Wine €14
♿
🚌 14c, 40

EATING

TUSCANY AND UMBRIA

Tuscan food is simple and straightforward, with an emphasis on local ingredients. Regional dishes include *cinghiale*, a robust wild boar casserole, *coniglio alla vernaccia*, rabbit cooked with white wine and herbs, and pheasant when in season. Southern Tuscany produces excellent *pecorino*, sheep's-milk cheese, while Siena's *panforte*, a spicy nut and fruit flat cake, and *cantuccini*, hard almond biscuits, will satisfy a sweet tooth. You will see Chianti wines everywhere; other excellent local wines include Montepulciano's Vino Nobile and Vernaccia, an interesting white from San Gimignano.

Umbrian cooking has much in common with Tuscan cuisine. Umbria is renowned for truffle-based dishes, while the area around Norcia is noted for its wonderful prosciutto and salami. Mountain food, such as tiny lentils from Castelluccio and local cheese, is excellent in the east of the region. Umbria's best-known wines are the whites from Orvieto, but Montefalco produces some superb red wines.

AREZZO

LE TASTEVIN
Via de Cenci 9, 52100 Arezzo
Tel 0575 28304
Le Tastevin is buzzing with local life. One room resembles a traditional *trattoria*, another, with pictures of film stars, is a jazz bar where the owner performs at weekends. There's also outside seating in summer. The restaurant claims Roberto Benigni, among other celebrities, as a regular. The food is traditional with some modern additions such as truffle and asparagus risotto. It is so popular that it is advisable to make a reservation.

Tue–Sun 12.30–2.30, 7.30–11.30
L €25, D €39, Wine €10

LA TORRE DI GNICCHE
Piaggia San Martino 8, 52100 Arezzo
Tel 0575 352035
This small bar seats just 30 people, but there is a terrace with more seating overlooking Piazza Vasari in summer. A menu is available, but regular customers here trust the staff to decide between the snacks, sandwiches and local main dishes, which change regularly with the seasons. They also have a good selection of cheeses made in the area and

PRICES AND SYMBOLS
The restaurants are listed alphabetically within each town. The prices are for a two-course lunch (L) and a three-course dinner (D) for one person, without drinks. The wine price is for a bottle of house wine.

For a key to the symbols, ▷ 2.

a great wine list, including the local Colli Aretini.
Thu–Tue 12–3, 6pm–1am
L €7, D €22, Wine €12

ASSISI

LA BUCA DI SAN FRANCESCO

Via Brizi 1, 06081 Assisi
Tel 075 812 204

Despite the huge numbers of tourists, La Buca still retains, and deserves, its reputation as Assisi's best restaurant. The ambiance plays its part, with a cosy, stone-walled interior and airy pergola for hot-weather dining, but the food can be outstanding, with a touch of elegance given to traditional Umbrian meat and vegetable dishes. A good wine list and highly professional service add to the experience.

🕐 Tue–Sun 12–2.30, 7.30–10
🍴 L €22, D €28, Wine €7

RISTORANTE MEDIO EVO

Via Arco dei Priori 4, 06081 Assisi
Tel 075 813068

This is a good option if you want to try out Umbrian delicacies. Truffles and wild boar turn up on the list of hearty local dishes. The fabulous grilled beef fillet with truffles as a main course costs €15, and the tasty homemade *strangozzi* spaghetti with tomatoes is €9.50 as a first course. Dust from the 13th-century roof covers the vast range of wines, some of which are priced up to €60 and beyond.

🕐 Thu–Tue 12–2.30, 7.30–10.30pm
🍴 L €17, D €35, Wine €10
🚌 The Linea A bus runs the 3km (2 miles) from Assisi's rail station into Piazza Unità d'Italia every half hour

CORTONA

LA GROTTA

Piazzetta Baldelli 3, 52044 Cortona
Tel 0575 630 271

Tucked away from the crowds, this restaurant, which has courtyard tables for summer eating, is a real find. A friendly family cooks the best of straightforward Tuscan food, with robust meat dishes and specialties such as *ribollito*, a twice-cooked vegetable broth, and *fagioli in fiasco*, white beans cooked in a covered flask. Size and popularity make advance reservations essential.

🕐 Wed–Mon 12–2.30, 7.30–9.30
🍴 L €11, D €17, Wine €4

IL PRELUDIO

Via Guelfa 11, 52044 Cortona
Tel 0575 630 104

Just down the hill from Cortona's main piazza, an intimate old palazzo is the setting for one of southern Tuscany's best restaurants. Start with a selection of their hot *antipasti*, before moving on to traditional pasta, stuffed *crespelle* (pancakes) or fine cuts of meat served with a modern twist. The staff are friendly and will advise on a

Buca di San Antonio is one of Lucca's finest restaurants

choice of wine from the comprehensive and interesting list.

🕐 Tue–Sun, 7.45–9.30
🍴 D €35, Wine €8

GREVE (IN CHIANTI)

TRATTORIA DEL MONTAGLIARI

Via Montagliari 29, Panzano in Chianti, 50020 Firenze
Tel 0558 52014
www.montagliari.it

An idyllic wine estate, founded in 1720, 5km (7 miles) from Greve. It has a big dining room, with a beamed ceiling, checked cloths and old prints; tables outside in summer. Go for the *pappardelle al cinghiale* (wide pasta ribbons with a rich wild boar sauce), the homemade ravioli or the *faraona al vinsanto* (guinea fowl with an intense wine sauce). Wines are serious; the estate produces Chianti Classico and Riserva, grappa, Vinsanto and Amaro— you can buy them in the estate shop.

🕐 12.30–2.30, 7.30–9.30; closed Mon and Jan 7–Feb 10
🍴 L €17, D €35, Wine €7
🚌 Take the SS222 from Firenze. The restaurant is on this road, at the 28.800km marker, 1km (0.6 mile) before Panzano

LUCCA

BUCA DI SAN ANTONIO

Via della Cervia, 56100 Lucca
Tel 0583 55881

This is one of the oldest and most popular restaurants in Lucca. The à la carte menu focuses on Lucchese cuisine and changes with the season. Offerings generally include grilled and roasted meats such as filleted and stuffed oven-cooked rabbit, pork with rosemary and garlic, and grilled beef with rocket (arugula) and parmesan. The waiters are happy to recommend something from the extensive wine list. Reservations recommended for dinner.

🕐 Tue–Sat 12.30–2.30, 7.30–11, Sun 12.30–2.30
🍴 L €28, D €45, Wine €13

RISTORANTE GAZEBO

Via Nuova per Pisa 1952, 55050 Massa Pisana
Tel 0583 379737
www.locandalelisa.com

In the stately conservatory of the 5-star Locanda l'Elisa hotel, Il Gazebo prides itself on using local produce in its menu of classic regional dishes. Main courses like *costolette d'agnello al rosmarine con purea di patate al tartufo* (lamb with rosemary served on mashed potato with truffles) reflect the chef's aim to serve traditional country food

EATING

with a modern twist.
Reservations essential.
- Daily 12.30–2.30, 7.30–10; closed Jan
- L €25, D €55, Wine €20
- From Pisa during the day
- A11 Firenze/Pisa Lucca exit, drive towards San Giuliano Terme/Pisa

MONTALCINO

GRAPPOLO BLU
Via Scale di Moglio, Montalcino, 53024 Siena
Tel 0577 847150
Down some steps from the main piazza you'll find this great little restaurant, serving up real Montalcino cooking. Terracotta floors, scrubbed tables and rush-seated chairs marry happily with the white walls and beamed ceiling—true Tuscan style. Try the *zuppa di fagioli* (Tuscan bean soup) *crostini* (toasted bread with different toppings) and *stinco all'aceto balsamico* (shin of beef in balsamic vinegar)—but leave room for the delicious *crostata di limone* (lemon tart). The local wines are excellent value.
- 12–3, 7–10; closed Fri and mid-Jan to mid-Feb
- L €17, D €22, Wine €8

ORVIETO

GROTTE DEL FUNARO
Via Ripa Serancia 41, 05018 Orvieto
Tel 0763 343276
Orvieto has no more stunning restaurant than the Grotte del Funaro. This giant cellar with views over the Umbrian valleys below has been open for business for more than 20 years. Several chambers with hefty stone walls are great for groups. More than 1,000 wines are stacked up in front of the huge casks. Sliced wild boar with truffles on toast is a first course at €12. Suckling pig, roasted on an open fire, is €8.50.
- Tue–Sun 12–2.30, 8–midnight
- L €25, D €33, Wine €9
- Five minutes' walk from the funicular rail station at Piazza Cahen. The funicular connects the *città alta* with Orvieto's main rail station

I SETTE CONSOLI
Piazza Sant'Angelo 1/A, 05018 Orvieto
Tel 0763 343 911
This Michelin-starred restaurant is blessed with a garden at the back, ideal for summer dining. The young brigade here is passionate about food, and it shows, with Umbrian specialties and the freshest possible produce served with a modern take. The wine list features over 700 vintages, and the staff will enjoy matching your wine to your menu choice; service can sometimes be slow, but eating here is an experience to enjoy at leisure.

Ristorante Gazebo, near Lucca, offers classic regional cuisine

- Apr–end Sep daily 12–2.30, 7.30–9.30; Oct–end Mar closed Wed and Sun pm
- L €28, D €45, Wine €9
- ♿

PERUGIA

CANTINONE
Via Ritorta 6, 06123 Perugia
Tel 075 5734430
A stunning restaurant in a 500-year-old dining hall with brick ceilings, stained with decades of wine residue, as this cellar was once used as a fermentation area. Several small rooms provide private dining away from the huge main medieval chamber. Chicken in white wine and the beef with Umbrian truffles are

GRANARO DEL MONTE
Via Alfieri 12, Norcia, 06046 Perugia
Tel 0743 816513
The Granaro del Monte was once a tithe barn for offerings to the church. Today its lovely vaulted rooms are a national monument and home to one of Umbria's best restaurants. Every local dish appears on the menu—mountain lentils from Castelluccio, pork products and hams from the town, black truffles and *funghi* from the wooded valleys. *Degustazione* menus let you sample the lot. The wine list is serious, the welcome friendly, and there's a roaring log fire where you can watch your grilled meat cooking.
- 12.30–2.30, 7.30–10
- L €13, D €24, Wine €10

great main courses. A wide range of cheeses and more than 50 wines are available. No credit cards.
- Wed–Mon 12.30–2.30, 7.30–10.30pm
- L €14, D €28, Wine €6
- 6, 7, 9, 11 to Piazza Italia

OSTERIA DEL TURRENO
Piazza Danti 16, 06100 Perugia
Tel 075 572 1976
If you've never tried eating at a *rosticceria/tavola calda*, Il Turreno is a great place to start. Tucked behind the Duomo, this traditional self-service fast-food eating house features a daily-changing and vast array of splendid hot and cold *antipasti* of every description, as well as pasta and meat dishes. There are tables outside if you want to take your time.
- Mon–Sat 11.30–8
- L/D €9, Wine €4

LA TAVERNA
Via delle Streghe 8, 06100 Perugia
Tel 075 572 4128
A narrow medieval street leads to this big popular restaurant. It offers a superb range of elegant dishes, created for the 21st century while paying homage to the region's culinary traditions. Expect subtle tastes and beautifully prepared meat dishes, and be sure to sample the *mousse di Baci Perugina*, a featherlight confection based on Perugia's own chocolate specialty.
🕐 Wed–Mon 12–2.30, 7.30–10
🍽 L €19, D €28, Wine €5
♿

PISA

DA BRUNO
Via Luigi Bianchi 12, 56100 Pisa
Tel 050 560818
www.pisaonline.it/trattoriadabruno
The self-proclaimed best restaurant in Pisa, Da Bruno serves traditional Pisan cuisine. The two dining rooms have wood-beamed ceilings, long, elegant tables and whitewashed walls covered with photos of famous people who have dined here. The menu is made up of rustic country dishes such as *baccalà con i porri* (salt cod cooked with leeks and tomatoes) and a variety of grilled fish dishes. Reservations are recommended.
🕐 Wed–Sun 12–3, 7–11, Mon 12–3
🍽 L €22, D €28, Wine €10

OSTERIA LA MESCITA
Via Cavalca 2, 56100 Pisa
Tel 050 544294
Family-run restaurant and *enoteca* in central Pisa which serves traditional but light Tuscan cuisine strongly influenced by local and seasonal produce. The menu changes weekly but generally includes *spaghetti alla mescita* (spaghetti flavoured with pork fat), light salads of wild fennel and ricotta cheese, and fresh fruit desserts. The *enoteca* has a cellar of more than 300

varieties of wine. The restaurant is small, but reservations aren't usually necessary.
🕐 Tue–Sun 12.30–3, 7.45–10.45pm; closed 3 weeks in Aug
🍽 L €17, D €39, Wine €12
🚍 3, 5, 7

LA PERGOLETTA
Via delle Belle Torri 36, 56127 Pisa
Tel 050 542458
La Pergoletta, inside an attractive medieval tower, has a menu that combines rustic Tuscan cuisine with modern flair. Specialties include *minestra di farro* (minestrone with farro grain), *arosto dagnello* (roast lamb with rosemary and garlic) and a

Osteria La Mescita, in Pisa, serves traditional Tuscan fare

fresh fish of the day. The chef's special is pasta stuffed with pears. Reservations recommended for evening meals.
🕐 Tue–Fri and Sun 8–11.30, Sat 12.30–2.30, 8–11.30; closed 1 week in Aug
🍽 L €28, D €36, Wine €10

SAN GIMIGNANO
RISTORANTE DORANDÒ
Vicolo dell'Oro 2, 53037 San Gimignano
Tel 0577 941862
www.ristorantedorando.it
This restaurant is tucked away in the heart of San Gimignano, between Piazza del Duomo and Piazza della Cisterna. Some of the dishes on the menu are based on recipes

from the Middle Ages and Etruscan times. Meals are given a modern twist, each accompanied by an intriguing story. The homemade desserts are also delicious. It is essential to reserve in advance.
🕐 Mar–end Oct daily 12.30–2.30, 7.30–9.30; Nov, Dec Tue–Sun 12.30–2.30, 7.30–9.30; closed 6 Jan–1 Mar, 10–26 Dec
🍽 L €33, D €50, Wine €10

LE TERRAZZE
Albergo la Cisterna, Piazza della Cisterna 24, 53037 San Gimignano
Tel 0577 940328
www.hotelcisterna.it
In the Braccieri's Palace Hotel, this restaurant has amazing views over the town's striking towers and defensive walls. Although the restaurant does not have outdoor seating, one wall in the 14th-century dining room is all glass, providing panoramic views. Traditional Tuscan and San Gimignano cuisine and a wide selection of wines.
🕐 Fri–Mon 12.30–2.30, 7.30–9.30pm, Wed–Thu 7.30–9.30pm; closed Jan, Feb
🍽 L €19, D €36, Wine €10
♿

SIENA
AL MARSILI
Via del Castoro 3, 33100 Siena
Tel 0577 47154
www.ristorantealmarsili.it
This restaurant in Siena's old town occupies a medieval building dating from the 14th century and is furnished with traditional heavy wood. There's a large main dining room and smaller brick niches with banqueting tables for larger parties. The wine bar is in a cellar carved out of rock below the Marsili Palace. Classical Tuscan cuisine is on the menu, including *gnocchetti* (little potato dumplings) with duck, homemade *crespelle* (crêpes) and vegetarian options. Reservations advised.
🕐 Tue–Sun 12.30–2.30, 7.30–9.30
🍽 L €28, D €45, Wine €10

EATING

ROME

Roman cuisine is based on gutsy down-to-earth foods, with more than a touch of Jewish flavour. Dishes are strong in taste—try *spaghetti aglio e olio* (garlic and oil), or *alla carbonara* (with pancetta cubes, cheese and beaten eggs). Romans are fond of offal, and you'll see *lingua* (tongue), *milza* (spleen), *rognone* (kidneys) and *trippa* (tripe) on the menu. Other local dishes include *abbacchio*, meltingly tender milk-fed lamb, and the delicious *saltimbocca alla romana*, thin veal slices wrapped in prosciutto and seasoned with sage. Artichokes *(carciofi)* are deep-fried *alla giudea* (Jewish-style), peas are tossed through pasta with delicate pasta sauces. Local wines include Frascati from the Castelli Romani and Est! Est! Est! from Montefiascone—it gets its name from the words Est! Est! Est! (Here it is! Here it is! Here it is!) that were scribbled on the door of an *enoteca* by a medieval papal envoy, sent to find the best wine shop in the town.

ALBERTO CIARLA

Piazza San Cosimato 40, 00153 Roma
Tel 06 5818668
www.albertociarla.com
This fish restaurant owes its renown to its innovative menu and the supreme skills of master chef Alberto Ciarla. Bean soup with seafood and lentils from Ponza with lobster are just a couple of the highlights. Vast wine cellar.

◉ Mon–Sat 8.30pm–midnight
🍽 D €55, Wine €20
🚇 H to Piazza Santa Maria in Trastevere
🚋 Tram 3, 8

PRICES AND SYMBOLS
The prices are for a two-course lunch (L) and a three-course dinner (D) for one person, without drinks. The wine price is for a bottle of house wine.

For a key to the symbols, ▷ 2.

AL BRIC

Via del Pellegrino 51, 00186 Roma
Tel 06 6879533
This is a very stylish *osteria* and wine bar. There are many small tables in the large room overlooking Via del Pellegrino, near Campo dei Fiori. The wine list is huge, with more than a thousand labels to choose from, while the menu has a wide selection of creative dishes matched perfectly with the wine suggestions. Try spaghetti with anchovies and pecorino or pears with Gorgonzola cheese. Among the homemade desserts, don't miss the strudel with cinnamon ice cream. The bread is homemade, too.

◉ Tue–Sun 7.30–11.30pm
🍽 D €55, Wine €8
🚌 64, 87, 492 to Largo Argentina
🚋 Tram 8

ANTICO CAFFÉ GRECO
Via dei Condotti 86, Roma
Tel 06 6791700
This famous old café was founded in 1767 by a Greek, hence the name. It has always been popular with the rich and famous, and English poets John Keats, George Byron and German poet and scientist Johann von Goethe all sought refreshment here. Look out for the pictures of some of the café's well-known past customers in the back room.
🕐 Daily 8–8
🍴 Table service: coffee €5, capuccino €5.50, cake €7
🚌 119 to Piazza di Spagna, or 52, 53, 58, 61, 71, 85, 160 to Piazza San Silvestro
Ⓜ Spagna

BAIRES
Corso Rinascimento 1, 00186 Roma
Tel 06 6861293
www.baires.it
Vibrant walls and floors and the sounds of the tango create a South American mood just behind Piazza Navona. Argentinian grilled meat served with various sauces is the obvious dish of choice. First courses include Argentinian-style marinated chicken (pollo all'escabeche) and there's a choice of salads and soups. The wine list similarly focuses on Argentinian varieties.
🕐 Daily 12–3.30, 7–midnight
🍴 L €27, D €40, Wine €12
🚌 87, 116, 492

IL BOOM
Via dei Fienaroli 30a, 00153 Roma
Tel 06 5897196
www.ilboom.it
This restaurant is dedicated to the Italian 1960s, with retro-style chairs, an original jukebox and photos of La Dolce Vita celebrities hanging on the walls. The granmisto has a selection of different first courses, from fried vegetables to creative bruschette (toasted bread). Sardines with rocket and ricotta is the chef's special. The wine list focuses on southern Italy.

🕐 Mon–Sat 7.30–midnight
🍴 D €33, Wine €8.50
🚌 H, 23, 44, 75, 280, 780
🚊 Tram 3, 8

I BUONI AMICI
Via Aleardo Aleardi 4–6–8, 00185 Roma
Tel 06 70491993
One of the best-value restaurants in Rome. Tables with traditional red-and-white chequered tablecloths are stacked with an array of delicious antipasti. Try the fresh pasta with lobster and chargrilled fish to follow, or the roast lamb. Remember to leave room for the homemade tiramisù and pannacotta.

Da Baffetto is one of Rome's best pizzerias

🕐 Mon–Sat 12.30–3, 7.30–11pm
🍴 L €16, D €30, Wine €4
Ⓜ Manzoni
🚌 16, 81, 87, 117, 714

CAFÉ CAFÉ
Via de' SS Quattro Coronati 44, 00184 Roma
Tel 06 7008743
The Swedish owner serves up coffee, cakes, fresh juice, and light Italian fare. It fills up quickly for Sunday brunch. Highly recommended for vegetarians and vegans.
🕐 Tue–Sun 10am–2am; closed Aug
🍴 L €11, D €10, Wine €12.50
🚌 3, 60, 75, 87, 117
Ⓜ Colosseo

SPECIAL

ANTONIO AL PANTHEON
Via dei Pastini 12, 00186 Roma
Tel 06 6790798
A family-run restaurant in a pedestrian street near the Pantheon. You can be sure of good food and a warm welcome. The large, brick-vaulted room has 1960s paintings on the walls. Food is quintessentially Roman and the clientele reassuringly local. Try the fresh fettuccine with creamy walnut sauce and for a main course the calves' liver cooked in chilli, olive oil and wine. The portions are very generous and the service is outstanding.
🕐 Mon–Sat 12–3, 7–11; closed 2 weeks in Aug
🍴 L €13, D €33, Wine €8
🚌 30, 40, 46, 63, 116

CUL DE SAC
Piazza Pasquino 73, 00186 Roma
Tel 06 68801094
Cul de Sac has a reputation for its pâtés. Try the sweet and sour wild boar pâté and the veal and Tabasco pâté. The interior is reminiscent of a 1950s train. Wide range of wines.
🕐 Daily 12–4, 7pm–12.30am
🍴 L €17, D €25, Wine €8
🚌 46, 62, 64, 87, 116, 492

DA BAFFETTO
Via del Governo Vecchio 114, 00186 Roma
Tel 06 6861617
Eat early or prepare to queue outside one of Rome's best pizzerias. Don't miss the savoury bruschetta al pomodoro (toasted bread topped with tomato, basil and olive oil). No credit cards.
🕐 Daily 6.30pm–1 am
🍴 D €20, Wine €5
🚌 46, 62, 64, 87, 116, 492

L'EAU VIVE
Via Monterone 85, 00186 Roma
Tel 06 68801095
This restaurant is run by nuns. The cuisine is mainly French in

EATING

origin. The wine list is excellent. Profits from the restaurant help the nuns raise funds for Third World missions.
- ⊕ Mon–Sat 12.30–4, 7.30–11pm; closed Aug
- 🍽 L €35, D €53, Wine €6
- 🚌 87, 492
- 🚋 Tram 8

F.I.S.H.
Via dei Serpenti 16, 00184 Roma
Tel 06 47824962
www.f-i-s-h.it
An Australian-inspired sushi restaurant that has echoes of Sydney harbour. Try an aperitif with oysters in the bar, then head into the restaurant. Select from three very contrasting menus: Mediterranean, Oriental and Antipodean. Finish with the crème brûlée or a sashimi of exotic fruits.
- ⊕ Tue–Sun 1–3, 8pm–2am
- 🍽 L €47, D €55, Wine €12
- 🚇 Cavour or Colosseo
- 🚌 40, 60, 70, 75, 117

GELATERIA DELLA PALMA
Via della Maddalena 20, 00186 Roma
Tel 06 68806752
This ice-cream shop has a great number of varieties to choose from. There are also mousses and ice cream with meringues on sale. If you prefer fruit, the raspberry ice-cream is unforgettable. No credit cards.
- ⊕ Daily 8am–2am
- 🍽 Ice creams from €2.50
- 🚌 64, 87, 492
- 🚋 Tram 8

IL GURU
Via Cimarra 456, 00184 Roma
Tel 06 4744110
Excellent Indian food, including vegetarian dishes, are served at Il Guru. You can order tandooris and curries of varying strengths or choose from one of three fixed-price menus or order à la carte. Traditional desserts are available along with Indian beer.

- ⊕ Daily 7.30pm–1am
- 🍽 D €25, Wine €6
- 🚇 Cavour
- 🚌 68

IL MARGUTTA
Via Margutta 118, 00187 Roma
Tel 06 32650577
www.ilmargutta.it
This is the only real vegetarian restaurant in the city. There are more than 40 vegetarian dishes and 120 wines to choose from, all at reasonable prices. A very good choice of dessert wines.
- ⊕ Daily 12.30–3.30, 7.30–11pm; closed 2 weeks in Aug
- 🍽 L €10–€16, D €40, Wine €15

F.I.S.H. offers an Australian take on Japanese cuisine

- 🚇 Flaminio or Spagna
- 🚌 116, 117

PIERLUIGI
Piazza de' Ricci 144, 00186 Roma
Tel 06 6861302
www.pierluigi.it
This excellent fish restaurant is reasonably priced considering its quality and setting—on the edge of a piazza, with plenty of tables outside. The scampi risotto is fantastically smooth and tasty, as is the *carpaccio* of tuna or swordfish. The fresh fish of the day are displayed behind a glass cabinet.
- ⊕ Tue–Sun 12–3, 7.30pm–midnight
- 🍽 L €28, D €55, Wine €14
- 🚌 46, 62, 64, 87, 116, 492

ROOF GARDEN 'LES ÉTOILES'
Via dei Bastioni 1, 00193 Roma
Tel 06 6873233
www.atlantehotels.com
For unparalleled views of St. Peter's and food to match, this roof terrace restaurant is a must. Sumptuous Mediterranean cuisine, including a raw tuna and tomato pasta and château filet with foie gras and sliced truffle. The imaginative wine list includes one of Umbria's best-kept secrets, the red Sagrantino di Montefalco.
- ⊕ Daily 12.30–2.30, 7.30–10.30pm
- 🍽 L €40, D €96, Wine €15
- 🚇 Ottaviano
- 🚌 70, 492

SORA LELLA
Via di Ponte Quattro Capi 16, 00153 Roma
Tel 06 6861601
www.soralella.com
Set on Isola Tiberina, near Trastevere, this is possibly one of the most unusual places to eat in Rome. Here you will find Roman cuisine at its best. All the typical dishes, from oxtail with cinnamon, cloves, raisins and pine nuts to memorable fried artichokes. Reservations recommended.
- ⊕ Mon–Sat 12.30–2.30, 8–11pm; closed Aug
- 🍽 L €27, D €65, Wine €13
- 🚌 23
- 🚋 Tram 8

T-BONE STATION
Via Crispi 29/31, 00186 Roma
Tel 06 6787650
Black-and-white movie stills and high-tech design liven up this trendy steakhouse. Steaks dominate the menu, but the salads are huge and appetizing too, especially the fresh crispy spinach and the classic chicken Caesar with Parmesan topping. Excellent cocktails.
- ⊕ Daily 12.30–3, 7.30pm–1.30am; Jul, Aug evening only
- 🍽 L €13, D €40, Wine €12
- 🚇 Barberini
- 🚌 52, 53, 61, 62, 63, 80, 95, 16, 119, 175, 492, 590

EATING

LAZIO AND THE MARCHE

The cuisine of Lazio is very like that of Rome, and you'll find many of the same dishes that are served in the capital. Along the coast, there's plenty of seafood and fish, appearing as crisp *fritto misto*, tiny mixed fried fish, *alla griglia*, grilled, or *al forno*, baked. A popular antipasto is *insalata di frutta di mare*, mixed shellfish and squid in a piquant salad. In summer look out for *gelaterie* selling homemade ice cream (*produzione propria*).

The rural region of the Marche is renowned for its tradition of real country cooking—rabbit (*coniglio*), lamb (*agnello*) and *porchetta*, roast suckling pig stuffed with a secret blend of wild herbs and spices. Don't miss the chance to try *olive ascolani*, huge meat-stuffed olives coated with egg and breadcrumbs, and deep-fried. The luscious *vincisgrassi*, layered pasta with *ragù* and béchamel, is another local special and along the coast you'll come accross *brodetto*, a delicate fish soup. The best wines in the Marche are Verdicchio and Rosso Conero, one of Italy's finest reds.

EATING

ALBANO

LA VOLPE E L'UVA

Via Collegio Nazzareno 14, 00042 Albano
Tel 06 9322251

Beside Albano's duomo, this restaurant-wine bar is a harmonious blend of good food, wine and art. The fixed menu changes weekly, with dishes paired with their complementary wines. This is the best place in the Castelli Romani for food and wine. Reservations essential. No credit cards.

🕐 Sep–end Jun Tue–Sat 7–11.30pm
🍽 D €27 including wine, Wine €6

PRICES AND SYMBOLS

The restaurants are listed alphabetically within each town. The prices are for a two-course lunch (L) and a three-course dinner (D) for one person, without drinks. The wine price is for a bottle of house wine.

For a key to the symbols, ▷ 2.

ASCOLI PICENO

GALLO D'ORO

Corso Vittorio Emanuele 13, 63100
Ascoli Piceno
Tel 0736 253520

First courses here include fried calamari, while main courses are topped with truffles or wild porcini mushrooms. The house special is *fritto misto* with fried olives, lamb cutlet, veal brain and courgettes (zucchini). A tourist menu is available for €20.

🕐 Mon–Fri 12–4, 7.30pm–12.30am, Sat 12–4
🍽 L €14, D €35, Wine €10
♻

GASTRONOMIA ENOTECA MIGLIORI

Piazza Arringo 2, 63100 Ascoli Piceno
Tel 0736 250042

Ascoli Piceno's most famous foodstuff is the *oliva ascolane*, and nobody makes them better than the Enoteca Migliori. This is a great place for cocktails or afternoon snacking, and it has a vast wine selection.

🕐 Tue–Sat 9–9, Sun 9–3
🍴 L €15, Wine €3
♿

FRASCATI

CANTINA TRINCA

Piazza San Rocco 4, 00044 Frascati
Tel 06 9409246, 338 8181955 (mobile)
www.cantinatrinca.it

Ask for a selection of prosciutti, salami, cheeses, olives and the delicious *porchetta di Ariccia* (roast pork served cold). No credit cards.

🕐 Jun–end Sep daily 4pm–midnight;
Oct–end May Tue–Sun 11–11
🍴 €10 per person including wine
🚇 Metro A: Anagnina, then bus to Frascati
🚂 From Termini station

RISTORANTE ZARAZÀ

Viale Regina Margherita 45, 00044 Frascati
Tel 06 9422053

This is the place to enjoy traditional Roman cuisine. Among the typical dishes are spicy tomato and bacon and oxtail cooked with a vegetable sauce. There's also a selection of mouth-watering creative dishes. Most wines are from Lazio and, of course, Frascati. Finish off the meal with a homemade pastry. Reserve in advance.

🕐 Tue–Sun 12.30–2, 8–10
🍴 L €35, D €35, Wine €5
🚇 From Roma take Metro A to Anagnina then bus
🚂 From Termini station to Frascati

SAN LEO

CASTELLO

Piazza Alighieri 11, San Leo, Pesaro e Urbino 61018
Tel 0541 916214

This is the town's best hotel (▷ 390) and restaurant. In the dining room genuine local dishes are served.

🕐 Closed 2 weeks in Nov and Jan
🍴 L €21, D €27, Wine €6
🚂 From Rimini
🚂 From Rimini take the SS258 west and turn left at Pietracuta for San Leo

TIVOLI

RISTORANTE ANTICHE TERME DI DIANA

Via dei Sosii 19, 00019 Tivoli
Tel 0774 335239
www.termedidiana.it

The choice is vast and appetizing at this underground restaurant, but don't miss the fresh egg pasta. There is a

The subterranean Ristorante Antiche Terme di Diana, Tivoli

lovely garden for summer dining.

🕐 Tue–Sun 12.30–2.30, 7.30–10pm
🍴 L €13, D €33, Wine €7
🚂 33km (21 miles) from Rome: Follow the Via Tiburtina or the Gran Raccordo Anulare (GRA). Turn off at Tivoli Città and follow signs for Villa d'Este; from the A24 (Rome/L'Aquila) take the exit for Tivoli (3km/2miles)

RISTORANTE SIBILLA

Via della Sibilla 50, 00019 Tivoli
Tel 0774 335281
www.ristorantesibilla.com

An elegant 18th-century restaurant serving typical Roman cuisine, homemade pasta and succulent grilled meat. Reservations recommended at weekends.

🕐 Tue–Sun 12.30–3, 7–10.30pm
🍴 L €20, D €40, Wine €8
🚂 33km (21 miles) from Rome: From the A24 (Rome/L'Aquila) take the exit for Tivoli (3km/2 miles)

URBINO

L'ANGOLO DIVINO

Via Sant'Andrea 14, 61029 Urbino
Tel 0722 327559
www.angolodivino.com

This is a paradise for truffle-lovers. Casciotta d'Urbino cheese and spicy salami will whet your appetite, and the lamb in a balsamic vinegar and truffle sauce will satisfy. All meals are served with plenty of Urbino's famous white and black truffles.

🕐 Tue–Sat 12–4, 7pm–midnight, Sun 11.30–4
🍴 L €16, D €33, Wine €7.80
♿
🚂 From Pesaro and Roma
🚌 Pesaro then frequent local bus service

TAVERNA LA VECCHIA FORNARINA

Via Mazzini 14, 61029 Urbino
Tel 0722 320007

This is a place to go to find rustic charm, a local clientele and hearty food smothered in decadent sauces. Two popuar dishes are the pasta with a meat sauce and stewed rabbit. No credit cards.

🕐 Wed–Mon 12–2.30, 7–10.30pm
🍴 L €16, D €33, Wine €8
♿

| SPECIAL IN URBINO |

LA VECCHIA URBINO

Via dei Vasari 3/5, 61029 Urbino
Tel 0722 4447
www.vecchiaurbino.it

This is a gastronomic wonderland, and one of the most famous restaurants in the Marche. Dishes to look out for include *delizia del Montefeltro* (ravioli with white truffles). There is a sommelier on call and an encyclopaedic wine list.

🕐 11–4, 7–11
🍴 L €16, D €23, Wine €7
🚂 To Porta Lavagine

THE SOUTH

Home of the pizza, Naples has some of Italy's best cuisine—tasty, fresh and imaginative. Try the ultra-thin classic *pizza marinara*, and other food-to-go such as *arancini*, fried rice balls, and *fiorilli*, stuffed and battered courgette flowers. Expect mounds of pasta, simply served with tomato and basil sauce, superb fish and seafood with fresh mozzarella, and vegetables such as peppers, aubergines and courgettes. Neapolitans are also famed for their pastries, often stuffed with sweetened ricotta and candied fruit.

The Puglian countryside yields huge quantities of wine, olive oil and vegetables, much used in local dishes. Short, thick pasta is mixed with bitter vegetable sauces, while lamb, roasted with thyme and rosemary, is the favourite meat dish. The cheeses, particularly the fresh milk varieties such as mozzarella and ricotta, are delicious. Puglian wines are on the up—pick of the bunch are Salice Salentino and Primitivo di Manduria.

Calabria and Basilicata are still relatively poor regions. Despite this the food is full of variety. Local cooking predominantly consists of homemade pasta and sauces made from local produce including tomatoes, pimentos, chillies, aubergines, pine kernels and olive oil, livened up with plenty of garlic, ginger and spices. In remote areas, menus will be limited, but the freshness and quality of the ingredients still shines through.

PRICES AND SYMBOLS

The restaurants are listed alphabetically within each town. The prices are for a two-course lunch (L) and a three-course dinner (D) for one person, without drinks. The wine price is for a bottle of house wine.

For a key to the symbols, ▷ 2.

AMALFI

TARI
Via Capuano 9–11, 84011 Amalfi
Tel 089 871832
This family-run restaurant is an intimate place to dine on quality traditional cookery. Expect some wonderful pasta and seafood creations using the freshest of produce, or simply opt for a delicious pizza for €6. The wine list has something to suit most tastes and includes lots of good local labels.

🕒 Wed–Mon 11.30–3, 8–11pm; closed Nov
🍴 L €9, D €45, Wine €6
🚭

BARI

AI DUE GHIOTTONI
Via Putignani 11, 70121 Bari
Tel 0805 232240
Old stone walls and modern design combine to give this buzzing restaurant a great sense of style. They serve genuine Puglian cooking, with lots of fresh fish, seafood

EATING

SPECIAL IN AMALFI

CARAVELLA

Via Matteo Camera 12, 84011 Amalfi
Tel 089 871029
www.ristorantelacaravella.it
This acclaimed restaurant has been producing excellent cuisine that marries traditional elements with innovative twists since 1959. There are plenty of seafood dishes to choose from and lightly boiled filleted fish with freshly squeezed lemon. Simplicity is the key, using fresh local ingredients. The service is first class and the choice of wines exemplary.
🕐 Wed–Mon 12–2.30, 7.30–10.30pm; closed 10 Nov–25 Dec
🍴 L €53, D €85, Wine €16
💲

and high-quality vegetables, is on offer here. Try the *risotto ai due ghiottoni*, a rich rice dish with spinach, cream, ham and fontina cheese, then move on to simply grilled fish, or *branzino al sale* (sea bass baked in salt). There is an excellent *macedonia* (fruit salad) along with some creamier treats on the dessert menu. Italian and foreign wines.
🕐 Mon–Sat 12.30–3.30, 7.30–12
🍴 L €25, D €45, Wine €12
💲

CAPRI

CAPANNINA

Via le Botteghe 12/14, 80073 Capri
Tel 081 8370732
www.capannina-capri.com
The menu at this prestigious establishment includes *ravioli alla caprese*, aubergines stuffed with ricotta cheese, luscious avocados and prawns and fresh local lobster. The wine list has more than 200 labels, and the desserts are devilishly rich. Reservations are required.
🕐 Thu–Tue 12–3, 7.30–11.30; closed Nov–Mar 15 except Christmas period
🍴 L €28, D €45, Wine €12

DA GEMMA

Via Madre Serafina 6, 80073 Capri
Tel 081 8370461
Gemma's has been the hangout of the *bella gente* since the 1930s. Savour the wonderful *pizza napoletana* and soak up the history documented on the walls. Highlights include fisherman's risotto, *ravioli alla caprese* and *maccheroncelli* with potatoes and mussels. There is an *antipasti* buffet and dessert-lovers have a mouth-watering choice. Excellent wine list.
🕐 Daily 12–3.30, 7–12; closed 3 weeks in Jan
🍴 L €23, D €40, Wine €10
💲

Capannina has attracted several celebrity diners

DA TONINO

Via Dentecalla 12, 80073 Capri
Tel 081 8376718
For quality wine and traditional southern Italian fare, look for Tonino's, near the Arco Naturale. Of particular note is the *millefoglie d'alici* (delicate pastry with anchovies) and the quail with chestnuts. Afterwards, enjoy iced *zabaione di Verduzzo* (a custard pudding made with Friuli wine).
🕐 Daily 12.30–2.30, 7–10.30pm; closed 6 Jan–15 Mar
🍴 L €13, D €45, Wine €9

GARGANO PENINSULA

GELATERIA ARTIGIANALE MAGGIORE

Via Deputato Petrone & Via Santa Maria di Merino 40, 71019 Vieste
The best ice cream in the area can be found at these *gelaterie*. Ask the friendly staff to guide you through the many choices: try a combination of fruits and the creamy chocolate. No credit cards.
🕐 Daily 10–10
🍴 Ice cream from €4

MEDIOEVO

Via Castello 21, 71013 Monte Sant'Angelo
Tel 0884 565356
www.ristorantemedioevo.it
Pilgrims often miss this wonderful restaurant in Monte Sant'Angelo. Start with some of the region's best *salumi* and cured meats and order from the small but excellent wine list. You can't leave Puglia without sampling the local *orecchiette* (ear-shaped pasta) with a meaty lamb sauce. The dried figs with almonds bathed in rum must be tasted.
🕐 Daily 12.30–3.30, 8–10pm; closed 15–30 Nov
🍴 L €16, D €35, Wine €7

LECCE

PICTON

Via Idomeneo 14, 73100 Lecce
Tel 0832 332383
www.acena.it/picton
Deep in the heart of the baroque city is Lecce's finest restaurant. You'll find a menu largely filled with traditional Puglian meals and the odd surprise. Seafood dominates the *antipasti* and pastas. The potato gnocchi with swordfish is outstanding, and steak and other meat choices sit alongside main-course fish dishes. Divine *dolci* and excellent regional wines complete this great-value culinary journey.
🕐 Tue–Sun 12.30–2.30, 8–11.30
🍴 L €20, D €45, Wine €10
💲

EATING

MARATEA

TAVERNA ROVITA
Via Rovita 63, Maratea, 85046 Potenza
Tel 0973 876588
On one of old Maratea's most picturesque streets is the Rovita, an elegantly laid-back establishment with touches of rustic charm. The cooking is regional, the bread and pasta homemade. Expect dishes like the delicate citron-spiked seafood risotto, plainly grilled fish and fruit-studded *cassata*. Some French wines augment the local and Italian list.
Ⓒ Daily 12.30–2, 7–11pm
Ⓦ L €20, D €45, Wine €4

MATERA

DA MARIO
Via XX Settembre 14, 75100 Matera
Tel 0835 336491
www.ristorantedamario.net
Mario's is a *rosticceria*, bar, *pizzeria* and little restaurant serving local food at low prices. Various set menus include local dishes such as turnip tops with homemade pasta, and pasta with wild mushrooms. Meat is simply grilled or *en brochette* and the vegetables are fresh.
Ⓒ Mon–Sat 2–3, 8–10
Ⓦ L €13, D €35, Wine €8

NAPOLI (NAPLES)

DORA
Via Ferdinando Palasciano 30, 80100 Napoli
Tel 081 680519
Traditional fish dishes make up the bulk of the impressive menu here. Well worth trying is the famous *pasta alla Dora* (pasta with a tomato sauce and shellfish), but the menu also offers a choice of grilled and baked fish dishes. Some very good wines are available and dessert is worth saving room for.
Ⓒ Mon–Sat 12–3, 8pm–midnight
Ⓦ L €47, D €80, Wine €13
Ⓟ Piazza Amedio
🚌 C18, 1, 150

EXCELSIOR
Via Partenope 48, 80121 Napoli
Tel 081 7640111
www.excelsior.it
The Hotel Excelsior's restaurant, La Terrazza, is hard to beat, with its stunning views, exquisite food and luxurious touches. The wine list has been compiled by a professional sommelier, so you can expect top quality. There are some inventive pasta creations and a superb mixed grill garnished with mussels.
Ⓒ Mon–Sat 12.30–3, 8–11pm
Ⓦ L €55, D €85, Wine €14
Ⓢ
🚌 C52, E5, 140, 152

Matera's Da Mario specializes in good-value local fare

TRATTORIA SAN FERDINANDO
Via Nardones 117, 80132 Napoli
Tel 081 421964
This welcoming place is full of artwork evocative of the nearby San Carlo theatre. Choose from a dozen excellent first and second courses: The delicious peppers and buffalo cheese and penne pasta with courgettes stand out. There is a great selection of desserts and the wine list is faithful to local producers.
Ⓒ Mon and Sat 12–3, Wed–Fri 12–3, 8–11.30
Ⓦ L €20, D €35, Wine €8
🚌 C4, C22

POMPEI

DE VIVO
Via Roma 36/38, 80045 Pompei
Tel 081 8631163
This superb bar/ice cream parlour/pastry shop has a good range of beverages and snacks, including small pizzas and filled flat-bread sandwiches and *panini*. There are lots of pastries and cakes, including Neapolitan *pastiera* (Easter orange and ricotta-filled grain pie), *sfogliatelle* (crunchy pastry wth a custard filling) and *babà al limoncello* (a soft cake with limoncello liqueur). The *gelati*, *sorbetti* and *semifreddi* will delight kids. No credit cards.
Ⓒ Aug daily 9am–10pm; rest of year Wed–Mon 9am–10pm; closed 2 weeks Jul
Ⓦ Pastries from €1.20, ice cream from €1.60

RISTORANTE-PIZZERIA CARLO ALBERTO
Via Carlo Alberto 15, 80045 Pompei
Tel 081 8633231
A small, well-designed eatery not far from the archaeological site. Choose from a wide selection of pastas and pizza. Delicious creations include seafood served in a tangy, slightly spicy lemon sauce. The wine list is adequate and the desserts top notch. Polish off the meal with a drop of *grappa del Vesuvio*, made from the Lacrima Christi grape that grows on the slopes of the dormant volcano.
Ⓒ Daily 12–3, 7–11.30pm
Ⓦ L €13, D €26, Wine €5
Ⓢ

PRESIDENT
Piazza Schettino 12, 80045 Pompei
Tel 081 8507245
www.uniplan.it/president
This is an excellent choice for seafood-lovers. The fish is freshly caught and of the highest quality—the choice catches of the day are cooked in the oven using traditional methods. There is a superior selection of wines. There is

EATING

also a water and an oil list
(24 oils!).
Tue–Sun 12.30–3.30, 8–11; closed
10–25 Aug
L €50, D €50, Wine €11

POSITANO

CAPITANO
Via Pasitea 119, 84017 Positano
Tel 089 811351
A feeling of elegant refinement
pervades the Capitano. Dine
under the pergolas on the
terrace, which has magical sea
views. First courses include a
delicious calamari and scampi
salad. Seafood dishes
dominate. You shouldn't leave
this part of the world without
trying fried prawns with orange
mayonnaise.
Daily 12.30–3.30, 7.30–11pm
L €33, D €50, Wine €14

AL PALAZZO
Via dei Mulini 23, 84017 Positano
Tel 089 875177
www.palazzomurat.it
This refined restaurant in the
Palazzo Murat hotel is covered
in luxuriant foliage. Of
particular note is the spaghetti
ai frutti del mare—a perfect
marriage of various types of
seafood and pasta. Their
Neapolitan aubergine
(eggplant) *parmigiana* is alive
with the fresh essential tastes
of this fertile region.
Daily 7.30–11; closed Nov–Easter
D €100, Wine €18

LA SPONDA
Via Cristoforo Colombo 30, 84017
Positano
Tel 089 875066
www.sirenuse.it
Lemon trees and
bougainvillaea fill the air with
scents in the summer months.
The Sersale family are famed for
their classic Neapolitan pasta
dishes and produce a very
special *spaghetti al pomodoro e
basilico* (tomato and basil).
Mar–end Nov daily 1–3.30,
8–10.30pm
L €53, D €115, Wine €30
Train from Napoli to Sorrento then
local bus

RAVELLO

CUMPÀ COSIMO
Via Roma 44/46, 84010 Ravello
Tel 089 857156
A magnet for visitors thanks
to its great-value dishes and
famous matriarch, Netta
Bottone. The spicy *penne
all'arrabiata* is particularly
tastebud-tingling. Main
courses include catches of the
day from land and sea. There
is a limited selection of wines.
The homemade ice cream
is excellent.
Apr–end Oct daily 12.30–3.30,
8–11pm; rest of year Tue–Sun
12.30–3.30, 8–11pm
L €23, D €40, Wine €9

*President in Pompei specializes
in seafood*

ROSSELLINIS
Via San Giovanni del Toro 28, 84010
Ravello
Tel 089 818181
www.palazzosasso.com
This acclaimed restaurant
is perched 300m (984ft)
above the sea. Look out
for the asparagus *raviolini*
with artichoke and carrot
sauce, and the classic
aubergine (eggplant)
cannelloni. There are
wonderful fish dishes and an
irresistible dessert selection.
Daily 7.30–10.30pm; closed
Nov–end Mar
D €120, Wine €38

SORRENTO

BUCO
Rampa Seconda Marina Piccola 5,
80067 Sorrento
Tel 081 8782354
www.ilbucoristorante.it
Dishes of particular note
here include the *fusilli al ragù
Genovese* (pasta in a lamb
sauce). Fish dishes include
red mullet served on a bed
of orange slices and pecorino
cheese. There are pleny of
decent wines and some
scrumptious desserts.
Thu–Tue 12.30–2.45, 7–11pm;
closed Jan
L €27, D €58, Wine €13

CARUSO
Via Sant'Antonino 12, 80067 Sorrento
Tel 081 8073156
www.restorantemuseocaruso.com
This restaurant is named
after Enrico Caruso, the
celebrated tenor and
gastronomic genius. The
gramophone plays crackling
classics by the maestro in
the background. The menu
has lots of vegetable and
seafood dishes.
Daily 12–3.30, 7.30–11.30pm; closed
Mon in Jan
L €55, D €70, Wine €15

LA FAVORITA–
O' PARRUCCHIANO
Corso Italia 71, 80067 Sorrento
Tel 081 8781321
www.parruchiano.it
Dining is quite an event in
this cavernous greenhouse
filled with luxuriant foliage.
Highlights include the
traditional stuffed peppers
and ravioli filled with
mozzarella, tomatoes
and basil.
Apr–end Oct daily 12.30–3.30,
8–11pm; rest of year Thu–Tue
12.30–3.30, 8–11pm
L €16, D €40, Wine €6

SICILY AND SARDINIA

Sicilian cooking reflects the influence of the island's foreign invaders; Greek, Arab, Norman and Spanish. Like southern Italy, street food is popular in the shape of pizza, *arancini*, croquettes and fritters, and there's a plethora of sweets. Fish is everywhere and the quality and variety of fruit and vegetables is superlative. Marsala, a sweet fortified wine, is made here; for mealtime drinking, pick one of the excellent Corvo wines.

Unlike that of the rest of Italy, Sardinian cuisine features very little pasta. Instead, roasted vegetables, meats and fish dominate the menu. There are some excellent local cheeses. Carnivores will find plenty of suckling pig and young lamb on the menu, best enjoyed with Cannonau di Sardegna, a punchy, full-bodied red wine. Another delicious meal is *Bottarga*, mullet-egg caviar; it's often served with the papery, crisp *carta di musica*, just one of Sardinia's excellent breads. Look out for the delicate gnocchetti, made from durum wheat tinted with saffrona, unique to the island.

EATING

Sicily

AGRIGENTO

BLACK HORSE
Via Celauro 8, 92100 Agrigento
Tel 0922 23223
Dishes to savour at this tiny eating house include spaghetti with sardines, pasta with aubergines, tomato and mozzarella, and mixed vegetables with a hint of sweet and sour.
🕐 Mon–Sat 2.30–2.30, 7.30–10pm; closed 1 Jan
🍴 L €10, D €20, Wine €4.50
💲

PRICES AND SYMBOLS

The restaurants are listed alphabetically within each town. The prices are for a two-course lunch (L) and a three-course dinner (D) for one person, without drinks. The wine price is for a bottle of house wine.

For a key to the symbols, ▷ 2.

CEFALÙ

OSTARIA DEL DUOMO
Via Seminario 5, Cefalù, Palermo 90015
Tel 0921 421838
The grilled fish, seafood, pasta and *antipasti* are particularly

good here. It can be busy at lunchtime, but it is worth waiting to get a table.
🕐 May–end Sep daily 12.30–3, 7–midnight; rest of year Tue–Sun 12.30–3, 7–midnight
🍴 L €20, D €37, Wine €10
💲

LIPARI

FILIPPINO
Piazza Municipio, Lipari, Isole Eilie, Messina
Tel 0909 811002
www.filippino.it/new/eng/index.asp
A big, bustling restaurant whose signature dishes include pasta with a caper, almond, basil, pecorino and

anchovy sauce, and sea bass-stuffed ravioli.

🎯 Tue–Sat 12.30–2.30, 7.30–10.30; closed 10 Nov–26 Dec

🍴 L €23, D €25, Wine €10

♿

PALERMO

FRUTTI DI MARE

Via Messina Marine 204, 90100 Palermo
Tel 091 471699

This well-known seafood restaurant beautifully prepares the catch of the day. Great value. No credit cards.

🎯 Daily 12–3, 7–midnight

🍴 L €20, D €27, Wine €8

🚌 101, 212, 250

OSTERIA DEI VESPRI

Piazza Croce Dei Vespri 6, 90133 Palermo
Tel 091 6171631

One of Sicily's finest restaurants. The penne pasta with tuna sauce is recommended.

🎯 Sep–end Jul Mon–Sat 12–3, 8–midnight; rest of year Mon–Sat 8–midnight; closed 1 week in Aug

🍴 L €25, D €45, Wine €10

🚌 101, 122, 220

SIRACUSA

747

112 Via Roma, Siracusa
Tel 0931 68 747

On the menu at this distinctively chic modern restaurant are fresh fish and Arab-influenced couscous.

🎯 Daily 8–2.30, 7–11

🍴 L €16, D €30, Wine €8

DON CAMILLO

Via Maestranza 96, 96100 Siracusa
Tel 0931 67133
www.ristorantedoncamillosiracusa.it

The raw shrimp, octopus and squid are top choices at this creative restaurant.

🎯 Mon–Sat 12–3, 7–10pm; closed 2 weeks in Nov, and 23–27 Dec

🍴 L €16, D €50, Wine €12

♿

🚌 1

JONICO A RUTTA 'E CIAULI

Riviera Dionisio il Grande 194, 96100 Siracusa
Tel 0931 65540

RISTORANTE DA LORENZO

Via Roma 12, 98039 Taormina
Tel 0942 23480

Squid and fish are imaginatively prepared here. Make room for the *tiramisù* or the local strawberries.

🎯 Thu–Tue 12–3, 7–11pm; closed 10 Jan–10 Feb

🍴 L €20, D €40, Wine €7.50

The menu here offers plenty of opportunity to be adventurous; try fresh pasta and marinated octopus.

🎯 Wed–Mon 12–3, 8–10.30pm

🍴 L €12, D €23, Wine €11

🚌 1

Escape Taormina's crowds at one of its fine restaurants

TAORMINA

CASA GRUGNO

Via Santa Maria de' Greci, 98039 Taormina
Tel 0942 21208
www.casagrugno.it

The sumptuous fare at this restaurant includes shellfish doused in Cognac.

🎯 Mon–Sat 7–10.30pm; closed Feb and Nov

🍴 L €40, D €65, Wine €16

Sardinia

ALGHERO

AL TUGURI

Via Maiorca 113, Alghero, 07041 Sassari
Tel 0799 76772
www.altuguri.it

Elegant fish restaurant.

🎯 Mon–Sat 2.30–2, 8–10.30pm; closed 20 Dec–20 Jan

🍴 2 courses minimum: L €33, D €37, Wine €13

CAGLIARI

ANTICA HOSTARIA

Via Camillo Benso Cavour 60, 09124 Cagliari
Tel 070 665870

Highlights of the menu include mussels and lobster cooked in local white wine.

🎯 Mon–Sat 1.30–3, 7–11; closed Aug and 23 Dec–6 Jan

🍴 L €27, D €40, Wine €10

♿

🚌 1, 6, 7

CORSARO

Viale Regina Margherita 28, 09125 Cagliari
Tel 070 664318

Notable dishes include *saccaia* (lamb with broth) and pasta stuffed with ricotta and vegetables.

🎯 Mon–Fri 12.30–3, 7.30–11pm, Sat 7.30–11pm; closed 2 weeks in Aug and 23–27 Dec

🍴 L €33, D €50, Wine €17

♿

🚌 5, 6

CALA GONONE

AL PORTO

Piazza del Porto 2, Cala Gonone, 08020 Nuòro
Tel 0784 93185

Try the fish soup with lobster or the day's catch *alla griglia* (charcoal-grilled).

🎯 12.30–3.30, 7.30–11.30; closed first 2 weeks in Dec and last 2 weeks in Jan

🍴 L €20, D €24, Wine €11

PORTO ROTONDO

DA GIOVANNINO

Piazza Quadrata, Porto Rotondo, 07020 Sàssari
Tel 0789 35280

This elegant restaurant is renowned for its wines.

🎯 Apr to mid-Nov daily 12.30–2.30, 8–10.30pm; mid-Nov to end Mar Tue–Sat 12.30–2.30, 8–10.30pm, Sun 12.30–2.30pm

🍴 L €65, D €80, Wine €15

♿

EATING

STAYING IN ITALY

There is a wide range of accommodation all over the country, but central and northern Italy have a greater choice than the south. On the whole, accommodation is more expensive in the major cities, Tuscany and Umbria, and the smarter coastal resorts during high season. In areas with fewer foreign visitors, you may be pleasantly surprised at the value for money, especially if you stay somewhere fairly simple; top-end business hotels often have good deals at weekends and in low season.

Choose from deluxe hotels in historic buildings, ultra-chic boutique hotels and family-run pensiones

HOTELS

Italian hotels (*alberghi*) are graded by regional authorities on a star rating of 1–5. These refer to the facilities provided—air-conditioning, telephone and television, lift (elevator), swimming pool—rather than character or comfort. You can expect 5-star hotels to be grand, with superb facilities and a high level of service; they will sometimes be in converted historic buildings, combining antique furnishings with 21st-century luxury. Four-star establishments will be almost as good and the accommodation first class. Three-star hotels are more idiosyncratic. Prices can vary enormously between them, as can the public areas, and staffing levels will be considerably lower. All 3-star rooms will have television, telephone, and sometimes air-conditioning. One- and 2-star hotels are relatively inexpensive, but are clean and comfortable, and rooms in 2-star places almost always have private bathrooms. Breakfast is usually included. During the high season at seaside resorts it's common to be forced to take half- or full-board, and single people may have to pay full price for a double if all singles are taken.

Smoking is not allowed in Italian hotels, except in the open air such as on a terrace or in a garden.

PRICING

● Italian hotels are legally required to post rates for high and low season on the back of every bedroom door. Note that some hotels have only one price.
● Rates vary according to the season, sometimes by as much as 25 per cent. Some hotels have high season (*alta stagione*) and low season (*bassa stagione*) rates; others charge the same rate year round (*tutto l'anno*).
● Hotels often quote their most expensive rates; ask if they have cheaper rooms.
● City-centre hotels sometimes have reduced weekend rates.
● Smaller hotels can be open to gentle bargaining, particularly during quieter times.
● Hotels are often willing to put another bed in a room for an extra 35 per cent, ideal for families with young children.

AGRITURISMI

The *agriturismo* scheme encourages farmers and landowners to convert redundant farm buildings into holiday accommodation. This can take the form of a small and luxurious hotel, a self-catering apartment, or a handful of rooms in a converted barn. Accommodation can be on a weekly basis, but many owners will let rooms by the night, and meals are often provided. *Agriturismi* are often in beautiful surroundings and frequently provide activities such as riding, escorted walking and mountain bicycling. Many have swimming pools and serve home-grown produce at meal times. The movement is particularly strong in Tuscany and Umbria. You'll need a car as *agriturismi* can be well off the beaten track. Most require advance reservations, but a couple of days ahead will often be fine.

CAMPSITES

There are plenty of campsites, especially along the Adriatic coast, which are normally open between April and September. The better sites will have swimming pools, bars, children's play areas, restaurants and shops; these look more favourably on caravans (trailer houses) and camper vans (RVs), so if you're in a tent, stick to the smaller sites.

SELF-CATERING

There are a great number of old farmhouses and villas to choose from, particularly in the affluent north and in Tuscany and Umbria. You can also rent apartments or houses in many of the coastal resorts, but Italian families tend to snap these up for the whole summer season. Tour operators sell villa packages, which include flights and car rental, but if you want to be independent, contact the local visitor offices well in advance. There are also websites devoted to private house rentals: www.holidayrentals.com

RIFUGI

If you're hiking or climbing in the mountains, you can stay in a network of *rifugi alpini*, mountain huts, owned by the Club Alpino Italiano. Most are fairly basic, and you'll probably find yourself in a dormitory bunk bed and washing in cold water. However, they are all very reasonably priced and surrounded by wonderful countryside with spectacular views.

ROOMS TO RENT

In popular areas you may see signs saying 'rooms', '*camere*' or '*zimmer*'. These are rooms to rent in private houses and are a good option if money is tight or you can't find a hotel. Local visitor offices keep a list.

RESERVATIONS

Reserve in advance in the main cities and popular resorts during the high season. In Rome, Florence and Venice you will need to reserve in advance all year round. Italians are on holiday during August, when you'll be competing with them for beds. If you're reserving in advance from home, make certain you get written confirmation by fax or email and take it with you. Without this, you may turn up and find all knowledge of your reservation denied.

FINDING A ROOM

- If you haven't reserved in advance, start looking around the main piazza or in the *centro storico*. In hilltop villages and towns it is also worth looking outside the *centro storico* or town walls. The local visitor information office will have lists and may be willing to make a reservation for you.
- Yellow signs direct you to hotels on the outskirts of towns and villages.
- In big cities, there is often a cluster of hotels near the railway station. Check them before you reserve as some are more respectable than others.
- It's perfectly acceptable to ask to see the room before you decide to stay somewhere.
- You will be asked to leave your passport at reception. Don't forget to ask for it back when you leave.
- Check-out time is normally noon, but hotels will usually store your luggage till the end of the day.

FURTHER SOURCES OF INFORMATION

HOTELS

- *Perfect Places to Stay in Italy*, published by the AA in conjunction with Touring Club Italiano, lists 500 recommended bed-and-breakfasts, farmhouses and town houses across Italy (£14.99, www.theaa.com).
- The Touring Club Italiano, the Italian equivalent of the AA in Britain, publishes *Alberghi e Ristoranti d'Italia*, which lists hotels in all price ranges. It comes out in early spring every year and is €20 (www.touringclub.it).
- An agency can reserve a room for you in the major cities, the Lakes, the Amalfi coast and Tuscany. Contact: Accomodation Line Ltd, 3rd Floor, 22–23 Princes Street, London W1B 2LT, tel 020 74091343, www.accomodationline.co.uk

AGRITURISMI

Contact:
Agriturist
Corso V Emanuele 101,
00168 Roma
Tel 06 8521342
www.agriturist.com

Agriturist also publishes *Vacanze in Fattoria*, a guide to farm holidays in English.
The TCI publishes *Agriturismo e vacanze in campagna* annually at €40.

CAMPING

The TCI publishes an annual guide to campsites, *Campeggio e Villaggi Turistici* (€20).

VILLAS
CV Travel

High-standard villas, palazzi and farmhouses.
Tel 020 7591 2800
www.cvtravel.riet

Magic of Italy

Villa rental packages.
Tel 0870 888 0228
www.magictravelgroup.co.uk/italy

Vacanze in Italia

Farmhouses, villas and apartments, mainly in Tuscany and Umbria and the Lakes.
Tel 0870 078 0193
www.britishtravel.com/vacanze.htm

STAYING

MAJOR HOTEL CHAINS

Name of hotel chain	Description	Hotels in Italy	Website and phone number
Accor Hotels	The fast-growing French group operates hotels in Italy under the Ibis, Mercure, Novotel and Sofitel brands.	43	www.accorhotels.com/italia tel 0226 90449
Baglioni	A chain of luxury hotels in fine buildings and top locations.	8	www.baglionihotels.com tel 02 773331
Best Western	The world's largest group, with 4,000 independently owned hotels in 80 countries.	112	www.bestwestern.it tel 0800 393130
Boscolo Hotels	Seventeen luxury hotels in some of the most sophisticated cities in Italy.	11	www.boscohotels.com tel (0039) 049 8287777
Charming Hotels	The Charming Hotels group was founded in 1995, but its popularity has grown rapidly and they now have 60 luxury hotels worldwide.	53	www.charminghotels.it tel 840 707575 (in Italy) tel (00) 800 24276464
Golden Tulip (inc Tulip Inns)	This Netherlands-based company has around 440 hotels in 51 countries, branded as either Golden Tulip (4-star) or Tulip Inns (3-star).	10	www.goldentulip.com tel (31) 332544800
Hilton	This American-based chain of top-class hotels has almost 500 branches throughout the world.	4	www.hilton.com tel 08705 909090 tel 800 878346 (in Italy)
ITI Hotels	A group of 30 hotels, mostly in Sardinia, but also in Rome, South Central and North America.	10	www.itihotels.it tel (0039) 06 6781341
Jolly Hotels	Jolly has been running hotels in Italy since 1949, and now has establishments in 26 Italian cities.	41	www.jollyhotels.it tel (0039) 0445414018
Le Méridien	Le Méridien is a well-established global hotel group with over 135 luxury hotels in 56 countries.	5	www.lemeridien.com tel 08000 282840
Orient Express Hotels	There are three luxurious hotels under the Orient Express brand in Italy, including their flagship hotels, the Hotel Cipriani in Venice and the Hotel Splendido in Portofino.	3	www.orient-express.com tel 20 78055060
Quality Inn Comfort Inn	Quality Inns offer mid-price accommodation, while Comfort Inns is a limited service chain.	10 7	www.choicehotels.com tel 0800 444444
Rocco Forte Hotels	Rocco Forte have luxury hotels in key locations around the world, with one hotel in Florence and one in Rome.	2	www.roccofortehotels.com tel (0039) 05527351
Roscioli Hotels	A family-owned chain of prestigious 4-star hotels, all in the heart of Rome.	4	www.rosciolihotels.it tel 800 840000 (in Italy)
Sina Hotels	Founded by the Bocca family in 1959, the Sina Hotels Group now has 6-, 4- and 5-star hotels in key cities throughout Italy.	9	www.sinahotels tel 800 273226 (in Italy)
Starhotels	A group of fine hotels owned by a Florence family, including one in New York	19	www.starhotels.com tel 0800 313132 (UK) tel 1800 816 6001 (US) tel 055 36925 (IT)
Starwood Hotels	Starwood is the name behind the prestigious hotel chains Sheraton, Westin and St. Regis, owning, leasing or managing around 750 hotels in 79 countries.	28	www.starwood.com tel 1 800 6255144 (US) tel 1 800 3253589 (US)
Utell International	The world's largest representative company, handling hotel reservations for nearly 5,000 luxury, business, and value hotels, resorts and apartments worldwide.	225	www.utell.com tel 08705 300200

STAYING

THE NORTHWEST

Big-city pleasures and convenience are found in Milan and Turin, where you will find the full range of hotels that you'd expect to see in any prosperous town, but both are major business destinations, so prices can be steep and you should certainly reserve in advance. The same applies in Genoa—a cheaper option here would be to stay in one of the resort villages along the coast. To the east lie the Riviera di Levante and the Cinque Terre, and to the west is the Rivieria di Ponente. The latter is a pleasant lower-key choice, patronized mainly by Italian families, while east lie the chic and glitzy ex-fishing villages of Portofino and Rapallo. North into Piemonte and the Valle d'Aosta you'll find hotels in the beautiful mountains of the Gran Paradiso. Mountains also form the backdrop to many of the popular places to stay in the east around Lake Como and Lake Garda. This is a prime holiday area so reserve ahead if you're planning a high-season trip. South from the Lakes lie the prosperous towns of Lombardy—Bergamo, Mantova and Cremona—good bases from which to explore the area.

STAYING

AOSTA (GRAN PARADISO)

HOTEL MILLELUCI
Porossan Roppoz 15, 11100 Aosta
Tel 0165 235 278
Fax 0165 235 284
www.hotelmilleluci.com
Located above Aosta, with splendid views of the Alps and the Aosta Valley, the Milleluci is ideal for exploring the Parco Nazionale del Gran Paradiso. Most rooms have a balcony and are furnished with period pieces.
€110–€200
24 rooms, 7 suites Outdoor

GENOVA (GENOA)

ACQUAVERDE
Via Balbi 29, 16126 Genova
Tel 010 265427
www.hotelacquaverde.it
This moderately priced hotel is within easy walking distance of the Via XX Settembre shopping area and the Porto Antico complex. The rooms are spacious, and there is private parking nearby.
€65–€100 excluding breakfast (€5)
30

PRICES AND SYMBOLS
Prices are the lowest and highest for a double room for one night including breakfast, unless otherwise stated. Note that rates can vary depending on the time of year.

For a key to symbols, ▷ 2.

SAVOIA CONTINENTAL
Via Arsenale di Terra 5, 16126 Genova
Tel 010 261641
Fax 010 261883
www.hotelssavoiagenova.it
The closest hotel to Genoa's Principe station. Spacious yet simple rooms have classic furniture and balconies. The large public facilities are shared with its 4-star sister hotel next door, the Savoia Majestic. The restaurant is somewhat uninspiring.
€162–€233
40

LAGO DI COMO
ALBERGO FIRENZE
Piazza Volta 16, 22100 Como
Tel 031 300333
www.albergofirenze.it
A high-quality, affordable hotel (pictured on page 367) in the heart of Como. The newly renovated rooms are sleek and most have great views. The hotel also has rooms specially fitted for use by people with disabilities.
€105
44

LAGO DI GARDA
BELLEVUE
Via Zanardelli 81, 25083 Gardone Riviera
Tel 0365 20235
www.hotelbellevuegardone.com
A small, quiet lakeside hotel brimming with amenities. The outdoor pool never gets too busy, as the hotel has just 30 rooms, most of which have balconies. Private parking.
Apr–end Sep
€96–€105
30 Outdoor

FLAMINIA
Piazza Flaminia 8, 25019 Sirmione
Tel 030 916078
www.hotelflaminia.com
A hotel with large rooms and a stunning location. The wooden terrace built over the lake is perfect for swimming and sunbathing.
€125–€140
41 rooms, 4 suites

MIRAMAR
Via XXV Aprile 22, 25018 Sirmione
Tel 030 916239
www.hotelmiramar.it
Real value for money, especially in the low season. Most rooms have balconies, and all are very modern. A huge lounge and bar area caters for all the summer visitors and the gardens lead down to the water.
€38–€50 including breakfast
30

LA PAUL
Via XXV Aprile 26, 25019 Sirmione
Tel 030 916077
This 3-star hotel is a five-minute walk from Sirmione.

Milan's Carlyle Brera is a stylish option

Adventurous guests can rent rowing boats and bicycles. Many of the rooms have balconies overlooking the hotel grounds.
€72–€150
45 Outdoor

LAGO MAGGIORE
GRAND HOTEL DES ÎLES BORROMÉES
Corso Umberto I 67, 28838 Stresa
Tel 0323 938938
www.borromees.it
Distinguished guests have been staying at this 5-star luxury hotel since 1861. Commanding fine views of the lake, the hotel offers watersports, mountain bicycling, horseback riding and

golf. Rooms have fireplaces, giant balconies and huge baths.
€230–€390
161 rooms, 11 suites

SPERANZA AU LAC
Piazza Marconi 6/9, 28838 Stresa
Tel 0323 31178
www.milansperanza.it
Overlooking both the lake and the main square, this 4-star hotel has the best location in town. The modern rooms have wide balconies. The hotel restaurant is recommended, although there are several places to eat within a minute's walk.
€90–€180
86 rooms, 3 suites

MANAROLA
MARINA PICCOLA
Via Birolli 20, 19010 Manarola
Tel 0187 920103
Fax 0187 920966
www.hotelmarinapiccola.com
Literally a stone's throw from the sea, this is a simple seaside hotel, with quirky elegance and touch of style. The rooms are plain and some have sea views, and it combines good taste with a totally relaxed atmosphere. Great restaurant overlooking the sea, serving nothing but fish.
Closed Nov
€105
13
Take the SS566 from La Spezia, then head on the SS370 to Manarola. You will need a permit from your hotel to take the car into the village

MANTOVA (MANTUA)
RECHIGI
Via Calvi, 30, 46100 Mantova
Tel 0376 320781
Fax 3762 220291
www.rechigi.com
Contemporary art, polished marble and interesting lighting enliven the interior of this modern hotel, near the Palazzo Ducale. The rooms are functional, comfortable and well equipped, though the bathrooms are small.

€176 not including breakfast
60
From Parma take the SS343 to Mantova. Immediately before the station, turn right along Corso Vittorio Emanuele II and continue across the intersection at Piazza Cavalloti into Corso Umberto I. At the end (Piazza Marconi) turn right into Via Calvi

MILANO (MILAN)

BAVIERA
Via Castaldi 7, 20124 Milano
Tel 02 6590551
www.hotelbaviera.com
This comfortable and gracious hotel is within walking distance of Centrale rail station. The rooms have old-fashioned bedding; some are larger than others, so ask for the biggest possible.
€80–€300
50
Repubblica

BRISTOL
Via Scarlatti 32, 20124 Milano
Tel 02 6694141
www.hotelbristolmil.it
Exit Centrale rail station via the stairs and you'll find yourself at the front door of this classic, stylish hotel. The style is refined, with modern amenities such as soundproofed rooms, direct-dial phones, in-room Jacuzzis and internet facilities. There is no restaurant, but the bar serves snacks and drinks until late at night.
€170; closed August
68
Centrale FS

CARLYLE BRERA HOTEL
Corso Garibaldi 84, 20121 Milano
Tel 02 29003888
www.carlylebrerahotel.com
The stylish Carlyle Brera is a cut above most business hotels. The Moscova Metro station is a stone's throw from the front door. Bicycles are also available to guests, free of charge.
€290
94 rooms (2 suites)
Moscova

MICHAELANGELO
Via Scarlatti 33, 20124 Milano
Tel 02 67551
www.milanhotel.it
This elegant 4-star hotel offers hydrotherapy suites, opulent lounges and fine dining. The guest rooms are vast and most bathrooms have Jacuzzis.
€250–€350
300 rooms, 4 suites
Centrale FS

MINI HOTEL AOSTA
Piazza Duca d'Aosta 16, 20124 Milano
Tel 02 669 1951, numero verde (free in Italy) 800 719888
www.minihotel.it
Functional modern hotel right outside Milan's central train

The Lido Palace is redolent of the Edwardian era

station. The rooms are soundproofed and simply furnished.
€80–€170
63
Centrale FS

SANTA MARGHERITA LIGURE

LIDO PALACE
Via A Doria 3, Santa Margherita Ligure, 16038 Genova
Tel 0185 285821
Fax 0185 284708
www.lidopalacehotel.com
Redolent of gracious Edwardian days, all the rooms at this seafront hotel have sea views and many have balconies. The four-people suites are excellent value.

Closed Nov to mid-Dec
€126–€232
54
From north exit the A12 at Rapallo and follow signs to Santa Margherita Ligure. The hotel is on the seafront opposite the marina

TORINO (TURIN)

BOLOGNA
Corso Vittorio Emanuele II 60, 10121 Torino
Tel 011 5620191
www.hotelbolognasrl.it
A convenient hotel opposite Porta Nuova rail station. Most of the rooms have televisions, private bathrooms and telephones. The hotel has no restaurant, but there are plenty of eating options nearby.
€85
45
Porta Nuova

TURIN PALACE
Via Sacchi 8, 10128 Torino
Tel 011 5625511
www.thi.it
An elegant 4-star hotel where the rooms have giant beds. The buffet breakfast is a rich spread of Piedmontese hams, cheeses and local Lavazza coffee. Turn left out of Turin's Porta Nuova rail station and you are right outside the hotel's doors.
€170–€244
122 rooms, 2 suites
Porta Nuova

VARESE

LOCANDA DEI MAI INTEES
Via Nobile Claudio Riva 2, 21022 Azzate, Varese
Tel 0332 457223
www.mai-intees.com
Small romantic hotel a few minutes from the centre of Varese, set in a renovated 14th-century villa. The rooms are furnished individually, some with antique furniture.
€185–€215
11 rooms, one suite
Located in the town of Azzate, off the A8 motorway
Varese
Milano Malpensa 25km (16 miles)

STAYING

VENICE

If you're spending a few days discovering Venice, stay in the heart of the city, though the Lido, with its sea and sand, can be a good bet for families. Within the city, decide where you want to be and reserve well ahead, particularly during Carnival or the summer. Most first-time visitors tend to stay in and around the *sestiere* (district) of San Marco, but other areas worth considering are Dorsoduro, the city's most elegant residential area, Castello, where you'll pay a lot less for a room with a view and Cannaregio, a wonderfully diverse *sestiere*. Across the Grand Canal, San Polo and Santa Croce have plenty of mid-range hotels and *pensione*. Room prices are among the highest in Italy and wherever you stay, you'll find there's a hefty supplement for a view over the water. Bear in mind, too, that there are no door-to-door taxis and you may have to walk some distance carrying your luggage. If you're planning to stay for a week or so, self-catering is well worth considering.

RESERVATIONS
The Associazione Veneziana Albergatori (Venetian Hoteliers' Association) has booths at the train station, the arrivals hall at Marco Polo airport and the Piazzale Roma parking area. The official tourist board, the APT, publishes a list of all Venetian accommodation available at their offices at the train station, Marco Polo airport, Piazza San Marco 71 and Viale Santa Maria Elisabetta 6/A, Lido (www.provincia.venezia.it/aptve).

PRICES AND SYMBOLS
Prices are the lowest and highest for a double room for one night including breakfast, unless otherwise stated. Note that rates can vary depending on the time of year.

For a key to symbols, ▷ 2.

AL PONTE ANTICO
Cannaregio 5768, Calle dell'Aseo, 30131 Venezia
Tel 041 2411944
www.alponteantico.com
This magnificent 15th-century palazzo has been well appointed with antiques, chandeliers, frescoes and preserved beamed ceilings. Public rooms have large windows with stunning views of the Canal Grande. Take breakfast and later sip *aperitivi bellini* on the terrace or in the light and elegant *salone*. Guest rooms and junior suites have Venetian flourishes and modern bathrooms. Other facilities include safe, television, minibar, hair-dryer, internet connection, room service and hydromassage bath.

📱 €220–€550
🛏 8 🔼
🚉 Rialto

ANTICA LOCANDA AL GAMBERO

San Marco 4687, Calle dei Fabbri, 30124 Venezia

Tel 041 5224384

www.locandaalgambero.com

This is a comfortable, well-run hotel between the Rialto and San Marco. Immaculate private bathrooms add to the good value here. Other amenities include television, telephone, safe, internet connection, hair-dryer and minibar. As with its sister hotel the Locanda Sturion (▷ 372), there are tea/coffee-making facilities in each room. Discount meals are available in the excellent Le Bistrot downstairs.

€110–€170

6

San Marco

BISANZIO

Castello 3651, Calle della Pietà, 30122 Venezia

Tel 041 5203100

www.bisanzio.com

This restored 16th-century palazzo hotel is near the so-called Chiesa di Vivaldi. Guest rooms have parquet flooring, beamed ceilings and unfussy Venetian touches. The most expensive rooms have charming balconies with rooftop views. All have telephone, satellite television, hair-dryer and minibar. The Brown Lounge, bar and breakfast room share a functional, understated appearance. Continental breakfast is included.

€120–€350

50

San Zaccaria

LA CALCINA

Dorsoduro 780–783, Fondamenta Zattere ai Gesuati, 30123 Venezia

Tel 041 5206466

www.lacalcina.com

A perennial favourite along the Zattere, this hotel has wonderful views of the Giudecca. The simple rooms have parquet flooring and attractive period touches. Each

has a private bathroom, telephone, hair-dryer and safe. There are no televisions or minibars in the bedrooms. Take breakfast on the canalside platform, then relax on the roof terrace. La Piscina bar/restaurant serves unfussy Venetian fare.

€120–€240

29

Zattere

CA' MARIA ADELE

Rio Terà dei Catecumeni, 111 Dorsoduro, 30123 Venezia

Tel 041 520 3078

www.camariadele.it

Right next to Santa Maria della Salute and a minute's walk

The Bisanzio is in a 16th-century palazzo

from the *vaporetto*, this luxurious little hotel provides the ultimate in sybaritic and romantic living. You can choose between one of the themed suites, where the décor ranges from cosy fireside to Oriental, or relax in the comfort of a more conventional room.

€390–€500

7 rooms, 7 suites

Salute

CA' PISANI

Dorsoduro 979/a, Rio Terra dei Foscarini, 30123 Venezia

Tel 041 2401411

www.capisanihotel.it

Smooth lines, exposed beams and art deco furnishings mix

with modern minimalist touches here. Each room is individually designed and has a relaxing, sophisticated charm. The facilities, including sauna, are excellent and the bathrooms ultra-modern. La Rivista restaurant continues the modern theme with simple Italian cuisine.

€220–€300

29   Access

Accademia

DANIELI

Castello 4196, Riva degli Schiavoni, 30122 Venezia

Tel 041 5226480

www.danieli.hotelinvenice.com

A spellbinding lobby and a rooftop terrace overlooking the lagoon give the Danieli luxury status and celebrity appeal. This former home of Doge Dandolo is dramatically lit and filled with marble and antiques. Dine Venetian-style at the pricey Terrazza Restaurant, then sip a spritz at the Dandolo Piano Bar. Guest rooms vary immensely, but most have flowery furnishings and excellent amenities.

€482–€2,400

233 rooms

San Zaccaria

LA FENICE ET DES ARTISTES

San Marco 1936, Campiello della Fenice 193, 30124 Venezia

Tel 041 5232333

www.fenicehotels.com

This is popular with musicians and opera aficionados as it's close to the famous La Fenice. Exposed beams, classic seating, antique furnishings and marble give it a refined yet comfortable character. The best rooms have balconies and unusual artwork. Facilities include telephone, television, private bathroom, hair-dryer and safe. La Taverna restaurant serves traditional Venetian dishes.

€155–€250

67 rooms, 1 suite

San Angelo or San Marco

STAYING

GIORGIONE

SS Apostoli, 4587 Cannaregio,
30131 Venezia
Tel 041 522 5810
www.hotelgiorgione.com
This 15th-century palazzo is
located down a tranquil *calle*
off the bustling campo Santi
Apostoli, and spreads its
rooms between the old
palazzo and a newer building;
all have air-con, minibars,
satellite TV and internet
connection. The public areas
are welcoming and warm, and
you can eat breakfast in the
courtyard with its flowers and
lily pond. Buffet breakfast is
included. The attached
Giorgione pub/wine bar serves
traditional Venetian cuisine.
€130–€330 including breakfast
76
Cà Doro or Fondamente Nuove

LOCANDA ARMIZO

Campo San Silvestro, 1104 San Polo,
30125 Venezia
Tel 041 520 6473
www.armizo.com
This small hotel in a converted
merchant's premises
offers excellent value and
comfortable rooms. Four big,
airy and spacious rooms
overlook the *campo* and will
sleep up to five; rates are per
room, not per person. Good
bathrooms, friendly welcome
and well-presented breakfasts
served in the bedrooms. All
rooms have satellite TV.
€69–€249
7
San Silvestro

LOCANDA LA CORTE

Castello 6317, Calle Bressana, 30122
Venezia
Tel 041 2411300
www.locandalacorte.it
Within easy reach of many
shops, restaurants and
entertainment venues, this
pleasant hotel is in an
attractive part of the Castello
Sestiere, near Chiesa Santi
Giovanni e Paolo. The rooms
have been completely restored
and refurbished using rich

fabrics and luxury Venetian
furniture. Facilities include
private bathroom, television,
hair-dryer and telephone. The
secluded courtyard full of trees
and flowers at the heart of the
hotel is a great place to relax
and enjoy the buffet breakfast.
€130–€200
16
San Zaccaria or Fondamente Nuove

LOCANDA SAN BARNABA

Dorsoduro 2785–2786, Calle del
Traghetto, 30124 Venezia
Tel 041 2411233
www.locanda-sanbarnaba.com
Just a few steps from the Ca'
Rezzonico *vaporetto* stop, the
San Barnaba is acknowledged

*The Pausania is in a refurbished
14th-century palazzo*

as one of the best hotels in
this price range in this area. All
rooms are tastefully furnished.
Public areas are elegant, and
there's a small courtyard and a
rooftop terrace. The hotel has
ground-floor rooms and there
are no bridges between it and
the *vaporetto*, making it useful
for those with limited mobility.
€120–€170
13
Ca' Rezzonico

LOCANDA STURION

San Polo 679, Calle del Sturion, 30125
Venezia
Tel 041 5236243
www.locandasturion.com
A convivial well-run hotel with
marble floors and dark wood.

Most rooms face a quiet *calle*
and each has a television, safe,
hair-dryer, minibar and even a
kettle! The breakfast room and
the best bedrooms have views
of the Rialto. There is no lift.
€100–€260
11
San Silvestro Rialto

LONDRA PALACE

Riva degli Schiavoni, 4171 Castello,
30122 Venezia
Tel 041 5200533
www.slh.com/londra
This handsome 19th-century
palazzo along the busy Riva
was renovated in 1999. In
1877, Tchaikovsky composed
his fourth symphony in room
106, while gazing out towards
San Giorgio Maggiore. Dark
wood furniture and marble
floors blend with the light
walls and modern lighting,
creating an air of calm and
restrained elegance. Enjoy
the stunning views from
the terrace while you dine
at Do Leoni, which serves
regional dishes. Rooms are
comfortable, if a little
characterless. The ample pink
marble bathrooms come with
bathrobe, shower and Jacuzzi.
€270–€850
53
San Zaccaria

METROPOLE

Castello 4149, Riva degli Schiavoni,
30122 Venezia
Tel 041 5205044
www.hotelmetropole.com
This hotel is handy for San
Marco. Rooms with views face
the bustling Riva and may be
noisy. Rooms have chandeliers
and elegant fittings, and some
of the suites have canopied
beds. The bathroom floors are
heated. Live dinner-time music
in the courtyard restaurant.
€230–€500
56 rooms, 14 suites
San Zaccaria

NOVECENTO

Calle delle Dose, Campo San Maurizio,
2683 San Marco, 30124 Venezia
Tel 041 241 3765
www.locandanovecento.it
This San Marco gem is another
stunning boutique hotel that's
right up with the best of
Venice's new-wave designer
lodgings. There's a tiny
courtyard, a breakfast room
and honesty bar, but you'll
probably want to spend time
in your room, equipped with
every comfort.
🛏 €130–€240
🚪 9 🔅
🚎 Giglio

PAUSANIA

Dorsoduro 2824, Fondamenta
Gheradini, 30123 Venezia
Tel 041 5222083
www.hotelpausania.it
This 14th-century palazzo,
complete with quadruple
lancet windows, stunning
staircase and an original well,
was refurbished in 2002.
Public areas have marble
floors, understated furnishings,
Murano glass chandeliers and
frescoed ceilings. The similarly
decorated bedrooms are
spacious and well equipped,
all with a private bathroom,
telephone, television, radio
and minibar. The buffet
breakfast is served in a room
overlooking the wonderful
garden—a rarity in Venice.
Make sure you reserve a room
early as this is a very popular
hotel.
🛏 €150–€280
🚪 26 🔅
🚎 Ca' Rezzonico

LA RESIDENZA

Castello 3608, Campo Bandiera e Moro,
30122 Venezia
Tel 041 5285315
www.venicelaresidenza.com
This handsome palazzo hotel
is reasonably priced by
Venetian standards. The Gothic
façade, with its 10th-century
sculptural details, overlooks
the peaceful Campo Bandiera
e Moro to the south. The

wonderful lobby has elegant
furnishings amid ornate
ceilings and walls. Request
one of the refurbished rooms,
which have a fresh, bright feel
and period pieces. Facilities
include private bathroom with
shower, television, safe and
minibar.
🛏 €100–€180
🚪 15 🔅
🚎 Arsenale

SAN SAMUELE

San Marco 3358, Salizada San Samuele,
30124 Venezia
Tel 041 5228045
www.albergosansamuele.it
This above-average 1-star
hotel is in a wonderful

*La Residenza enjoys a peaceful
setting*

location near the San Samuele
vaporetto stop. Staff are
friendly and the hotel is tidy
and well run. The lounge area
has the usual Venetian
trappings: patterned wallpaper,
marble floors, antiques and
chandeliers. For the price, the
rooms are nothing special, but
in contrast to the competition
they are clean and
comfortable. Most have shared
bathrooms and basic facilities.
No credit cards.
🛏 €50–€105
🚪 10
🚎 San Samuele

PENSIONE ACCADEMIA

Dorsoduro 1058, Fondamenta Bollani,
30123 Venezia
Tel 041 5210188
www.pensioneaccademi.it
Verdant courtyard gardens,
Grand Canal views and
helpful staff complement this
hotel that is in a great
location for art-lovers. Once
called Villa Maravege, it is a
former Russian embassy. The
stately rooms have wooden
floors, 19th-century furniture
and chandeliers. Private
bathroom, television and
phone in all the rooms.
Continental breakfast spread
provides a bountiful choice
and can be enjoyed on the
tranquil canalside terrace.
Early reservations are
recommended.
🛏 €150–€300
🚪 27 🔅
🚎 Accademia

WESTIN EXCELSIOR VENICE LIDO

Lido 41, Lungomare Marconi, 30126
Venezia
Tel 041 5260201
www.starwood.com
A Moorish building, with
fountains and lemon trees in
the courtyard, once frequented
by the belle-époque set. The
terraces lead down to a
swimming pool. Facilities
include television, safe,
dry-cleaning and 24-hour
concierge service. Dine in the
elegant Tropicana salon or
Terrazza restaurant, then sip
cocktails in the Blue Bar. Clay
tennis courts, watersports and
a beauty parlour are available.
🕐 Mid-Mar to end Nov
🛏 €850–€2400
🚪 197 rooms and suites 🔅
🚎 Outdoor
🚎 Lido Casino

STAYING

THE NORTHEAST AND EMILIA-ROMAGNA

You'll find plenty of accommodation choice in the northeast and Emilia-Romagna, an area of immense diversity. If you're on the artistic and cultural trail, it's likely you'll be heading for Emilia-Romagna and Bologna. Many hotels in the regional capital are aimed at business visitors and can be busy, but you should have no trouble in the region's smaller cities of Padua, Ravenna, Verona, Parma and Vicenza. Heading east into Friuli-Venezia Giulia, whose main towns are Trieste and Udine, there is plenty of accommodation. Northwest lies the scenic splendour of the mountains of the high Veneto and Trentino-Alto-Adige, where you're more likely to find yourself staying in an Austrian-style chalet than a splendid palazzo. Except for the peak months of July and August, you should have no trouble finding somewhere to stay, but remember that German is the first language in the Alto-Adige. Good areas for a few nights include the valleys of the Dolomites and the beautiful, historic town of Trento.

STAYING

PRICES AND SYMBOLS
Prices are the lowest and highest for a double room for one night including breakfast, unless otherwise stated. Note that rates can vary depending on the time of year.

For a key to symbols, ▷ 2.

BOLOGNA

CENTRALE
Via della Zecca 2, 40121 Bologna
Tel 051 225114
Small central third-floor hotel with lift. Best-value and most pleasant of the city's cheaper hotels. The hotel is simply

furnished, but there is a television in all the rooms.
🛏 €78–€96 excluding breakfast
🛈 20 🔖

GRAND HOTEL BAGLIONI
Via Indipendenza 8, 40121 Bologna
Tel 051 225445
www.baglionihotels.com
Housed in the Palazzo Ghisilardi Fava, rooms here are luxuriously furnished and superbly equipped, with 24-hour room service, adjustable heating and air-conditioning, satellite television, minibar and safe. Restaurant. Parking and computer access.
🛏 €319–€390
🛈 124 🔖

OROLOGIO
Via IV Novembre 10, 40123 Bologna
Tel 051 231253
www.orologio.hotel-bologna.net
The elegant rooms are well equipped, and service is excellent. Pets allowed. Bicycles available. Garage parking. Reservations essential.
🛏 €320–€351
🛈 34 🔖

CIVIDALE DEI FRIULI

LOCANDA POMO D'ORO
Piazza San Giovanni 20, Cividale dei Friuli, 33043 Udine
Tel 0432 731489
www.alpomodoro.com
There are plenty of traditional touches here but the

bathrooms are very modern and the rooms spacious.

🛏 €75

ℹ 17

🚗 From the north exit the A23 at Udine and follow signs to Cividale dei Friuli (S54). Turn right opposite the station and follow signs into town and the hotel. From the south exit A23 Udine Sud and follow signs to Cividale (S54).

MERANO (MERAN)
EINSIEDLER EREMITA
Via Val di Nova 25, Merano, 39012 Alto Adige
Tel 0473 232191
Fax 0473 211575
www.einsiedler.com
This great-value hotel makes a good base for families, with tennis courts, a sauna and a playground for young children. There's a good bus service into town 5km (3 miles) away and a cable car nearby.

🕐 Apr–end Nov

🛏 €51–€75

ℹ 37 🏊 Outdoor and indoor

🚗 Exit the A22 at Merano Sud. The city is divided into six hotel zones. The Einsiedler is in the yellow zone, so follow the yellow arrows to the correct zone, where you will pick up signs directing you to the hotel

PADOVA (PADUA)
CITTÀ DI PADOVA YOUTH HOSTEL
Via Aleardo Aleardi 30, 35122 Padova
Tel 049 8752219
www.ctgveneto.it/ostello2
This hostel is in a modern building 10 minutes' walk southwest of the middle of town. Reserve ahead (May–end Oct). Membership is required.

🕐 Closed 20 Dec–6 Jan

🛏 €15.50

ℹ 112 beds

🚌 3, 8, 12, 18 from Bay 3 at the rail station

MAJESTIC TOSCANELLI
Via dell'Arco 2, 35122 Padova
Tel 049 663244
www.toscanelli.com
This is the nicest of the city's 4-star hotels. The rooms are equipped with satellite

television and a safe. Other services include laundry and child-minding.

🛏 €172–€199

ℹ 34 🚭 🅿

SANT'ANTONIO
Via San Fermo 118, 35137 Padova
Tel 049 8751393
www.hotelsantantonio.it
This inexpensive hotel is on the northern edge of the town. It overlooks the old stone bridge that spans the river. Rooms are large and pleasant, and there is a bar and a lift. Pets are welcome.

🛏 €78–€82 excluding breakfast (€7)

ℹ 33 🚭

The Alpine-style Einsiedler Eremita stands amid vineyards

PARMA
VERDI
Via Pasini 18, 43100 Parma
Tel 0521 293 539
Fax 0521 293 559
www.hotelverdi.it
A stylish, traditional Italian hotel of the old school. Private parking and good restaurant.

🕐 Closed 2 weeks in Aug and over Christmas

🛏 €110–€190 excluding breakfast (€12)

ℹ 20 🚭

🚗 From Mantova, Bologna, Piacenza or Milan take the *viale* that circles the *centro storico*. Via Pasini is the section opposite the Parco Ducale

RAVENNA
ALBERGO CAPPELLO
Via IV Novembre 41, 48100 Ravenna
Tel 0544 219813
www.albergocappello.it
An elegant, mid-price hotel with very stylish rooms. Some accessible for guests with disabilities. Babysitting service available.

🛏 €110–€160

ℹ 7 🚭

TRENTO
ANDES
Piazza Massar 3, Vigo di Fassa, 38039 Trento
Tel 0462 764575
Fax 0462 764598
www.hotelandes.com
Facilities at this chalet-style hotel include a health and beauty centre and a kids' playground.

🕐 Closed end Oct–30 Dec

🛏 €42–€81 minimum 3 days. Special rates Christmas and Easter

ℹ 31 🏊

🚗 From SS 48 take the N242 to Vigo di Fassa. Turn left in village to Funivia Catinaccio; hotel is on left

TREVISO
VILLA ABBAZIA
HOTEL DEI CHIOSTRI
Piazza IV Novembre 3, 31051 Follina, Treviso
Tel 0438 971277
Fax 0438 970001
www.hotelabbazia.it
www.hoteldeichiostri.com
Two hotels well located for exploring the Veneto Alpine mountains and Venice, Vicenza and Treviso. The Abbazia is a cosy romantic hotel, in the style of a private house. The Hotel dei Chiostri is a light, airy boutique hotel furnished in contemporary style. They share a classy restaurant.

🛏 Abbazia: €180–€210; dei Chiostri: €100–€120

ℹ Abbazia: 12 rooms, 4 suites; dei Chiostri: 15 rooms

🚗 Located in Follina, north of Treviso, off the A27 motorway taking the exit for Conegliano.

🚉 Conegliano

🚆 Treviso

STAYING

TRIESTE

DUCHI D'AOSTA
Piazza Unità d'Italia 2, 34121 Trieste
Tel 040 7600011
A great combination of old-world style and modern comforts makes this elegant hotel Trieste's top choice.
€253–€285
55
Follow the signs to *centro città*; the hotel is on the main piazza facing the sea

UDINE

LA' DI MORET
Viale Tricesimo 276, 33100 Udine
Tel 0432 545096
Fax 0432 545096
www.ladimoret.it
Immensely comfortable, with classically simple, large bedrooms.
€120–€140
82 Outdoor and indoor
Exit the A23 at Udine Nord and follow signs to Tarvisio, then Udine – Cividale; the hotel is on the right at the second set of traffic lights

VERONA

COLOMBA D'ORO
Via Carlo Cattaneo 10, 37121 Verona
Tel 045 595300
www.colombahotel.com
There is beautiful antique furniture in many of the rooms at this luxury hotel. Parking is free or you can pay €18 to park in the hotel garage.
€135–€245
41 rooms, 10 suites

HOTEL DUE TORRI
Piazza Sant'Anastasia 4, 37121 Verona
Tel 045 595044
www.baglionihotels.com
This luxurious hotel occupies a 13th-century palazzo in central Verona, right next to Sant'Anastasia church. It's spread over five floors, and the public areas and the guest rooms are magnificently furnished. There is a restaurant and a bar.
€390–€635
90

IL TORCOLO
Vicolo Listone 3, 37121 Verona
Tel 045 8007512
www.hoteltorcolo.it
The rooms at this small, friendly hotel are simply equipped but elegantly furnished and include a television and a refrigerator. There is a lift, and parking is available at €8 per day.
€70–€112 excluding breakfast
19

VICTORIA
Via Adua 8, 37121 Verona
Tel 045 590566
www.hotelvictoria.it
This friendly hotel is just southwest of the heart of the

Il Torcolo is very handy for Verona's Arena

city. The rooms are equipped with satellite television, phone, safe and minibar (whirlpool baths on request). The superior class rooms are magnificent. The hotel has a bar and lounge area, and a sauna and solarium. Garage parking costs €20 per night, but advanced reservations are recommended.
€190–€270
66

VILLA DEL QUAR
Via Quar 12, Pedemonte, Verona
Tel 045 6800 681
www.hotelvilladelquar.it
This 5-star hotel is just outside Verona, and has attracted awards for its fine dining room, Ristorante Arquade.

SPECIAL IN TRENTO

VILLA MADRUZZO
Via Ponte Alto 26, Cognola, 38050 Trento
Tel 0461 986220
Fax 0461 986 361
www.villamadruzzo.it
If you don't have a car, there are regular buses up the hill to this beautiful 18th-century villa. Bedrooms are classy and the rooms airy and well equipped. The restaurant is excellent and good value.
€95–€102
51
Exit the A22 at Trento or Trento Nord and follow signs to Padua. Climb the hill and go through the tunnel, then turn almost immediately left towards Cognola. At the round-about turn right to Via Ponte Alto, continue for about 100m (109 yards) then take the sharp right between the walls into the hotel

€260–€335
28 Outdoor
Take the A22 motorway and exit Verona North, then follow the super-strada SS12 to San Pietro in Cariano.
Verona

VICENZA

CRISTINA
Corso SS Felice e Fortunato 32, 36100 Vicenza
Tel 0444 323751
Fax 0444 324297
www.paginegialle.it/hotelcristinavicenza
This modern, family-run hotel is ideal for an overnight stay. A stroll away from the *centro storico*, it has its own parking, a real bonus, and a good level of comfort. There's plenty of parquet flooring, marble-clad walls and deep sofas in the public areas and the bedrooms are well equipped although some are a little small.
Closed 24 Dec–2 Jan
€90–€160
33
From the A4 follow signs to the city; you will arrive on the Corso SS Felice e Fortunato

STAYING

FLORENCE

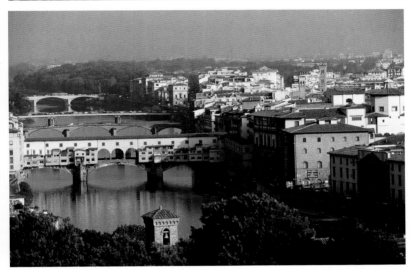

Florence has some of Italy's greatest hotels, with superb standards of luxury and service, but prices are high. More modest hotels and *pensioni* often occupy one or two floors of a much larger building and rarely have much in the way of public areas. It's worth paying more for quiet surroundings and air-conditioning during the summer. If you are making Florence part of a touring holiday, consider staying outside the city, possibly in Fiesole, Certosa, Prato or Pistoia, and using public transport to travel into Florence. Visitors on a budget can stay in one of the clean and relatively cheap hostels.

RESERVATIONS

Branches of APT can be found at Vía Manzoni 16, Vía Cavour 1r and Piazza Mino 7, Fiesole. They publish complete lists of accommodation, but do not make reservations. The Consorzio Informazioni Turistiche Alberghiere (Hoteliers' Tourist Information Consortium) has offices at the train station, at the AGIP service station in Peretola on the A11 Firenze-Mare Autostrada, at the Chianti Est service station on the A1 Autostrada del Sole and at Vespucci airport. The station office will reserve rooms for personal callers only; others only have lists of accommodation (www.firenze.turismo.toscana.it).

PRICES AND SYMBOLS

Prices are the lowest and highest for a double room for one night including breakfast, unless otherwise stated. Note that rates can vary depending on the time of year.

For a key to symbols, ▷ 2.

ANNALENA

Vía Romana 34, 50123 Firenze
Tel 055 222402
www.hotelannalena.it
This building, close to the best restaurants of Oltrarno, has housed all manner of guests over the years from tragic young widows during the Medici era to Mussolini's fascist police. The accommodation is simple and clean—one room has a terrace, others look out onto the garden. Each room has a private bathroom, television and telephone.

€95–€166

20

D, 11, 36, 37

BELLETTINI
Via de' Conti 7, 50123 Firenze
Tel 055 213561
www.hotelbellettini.com
Close to the duomo, this hotel dates from the 15th century and is one of the oldest and best-run in the city. There are some lovely Tuscan touches in the decor, and rooms vary in size, making it perfect for families. Facilities include private bathroom (optional), television, telephone, internet access and safe.
€105–€170
28, 5 suites
1, 4, 6, 7, 10, 11, 14, 17, 23

CASCI
Via Cavour 13, 50129 Firenze
Tel 055 211686
www.hotelcasci.com
This family-run hotel, near the duomo, was once the home of the opera composer Rossini. There are some original 14th-century touches, but overall it has been thoroughly modernized, with immaculate, functional rooms. The triple-glazed windows deaden street sounds. The hotel is especially good for families. Many of the simple but comfortable rooms have balconies. Facilities include private bathroom, safe telephone, cable television and minibar.
€90–€150
25
1, 6, 7, 10, 11, 17, 31, 32

CRISTINA
Via della Condotta 4, 50122 Firenze
Tel 055 214484
This friendly, small hotel with largish rooms is a great place for families, as the owners go out of their way to make children and their parents feel at home. The rooms are clean and spacious, and four have private bathrooms. Great value for money, so you'll need to reserve well in advance.
€57–€90
9
A, 14, 23

GOLDONI
Borgo Ognissanti 8, 50123 Firenze
Tel 055 284080
www.hotelgoldoni.com
Hotel Goldoni is great value for money. The well-tended rooms have a smart, Parisian feel. Each guest room has a private bathroom, telephone, internet access, television and safe.
€100–€200
20
A, B, 6, 11, 36, 37

GRAND HOTEL MINERVA
Piazza S Maria Novella 16, 50123 Firenze
Tel 055 27230
www.grandhotelminerva.com

Guests at the Goldoni have included Mozart in 1700

Locations don't get much better than this one, where guests step out to face the church of Santa Maria Novella, behind which is the main train station. Rooms have modern décor, with good views. Amenities include internet access, free WiFi, and garage parking.
€155–€307
102
A, 11, 36, 37

HELVETIA & BRISTOL
Via dei Pescioni 2, 50123 Firenze
Tel 055 287814
www.thecharminghotels.com
Once popular with English ladies on the Grand Tour, this hotel preserves the refined air of the 19th century. Each room has been individually designed. Modern amenities include private bathroom, hair-dryer, television, telephone, minibar and safe. The Bristol restaurant serves contemporary Tuscan food.
€310–€530 excluding breakfast
67
A, B, 6, 11, 22, 36, 37

HOTEL VILLA LA VEDETTA
Viale Michelangelo 78, 50125 Firenze
Tel 055 681 631
www.villalavedettahotel.com
Overlooking Florence from the hillside, Villa la Vedetta is an oasis of genteel calm. The art nouveau villa has bright modern rooms featuring enormous windows, marble and mosaic bathrooms, whirlpool tubs, internet and smart décor. A free courtesy bus transports guests to Piazza Santa Maria Novella. The classy ambiance extends to the contemporary menu of the villa's restaurant, Onice.
€159–€420, excluding breakfast
18 Outdoor
12

JOHANNA I
Via Bonifacio Lupi 14, 50129 Firenze
Tel 055 481896
www.johanna.it
The rooms here are small but beautifully furnished, with private bathrooms, coffee- and tea-making facilities, television and telephone. There is a comfortable communal room with a fridge. No credit cards.
€80–€95
11
8, 11, 12, 20

LOGGIATO DEI SERVITI
Piazza Santissima Annunziata 3, 50122 Firenze
Tel 055 289592
www.loggiatodeiservitihotel.it
This former Servite monastery, with vaulted ceilings, dark wood antiques and rich fabric, is in a charming square. Many of the refurbished rooms look onto the arcades of Piazza

STAYING

Santissima Annunziata. Rooms have a private bathroom, telephone, minibar, safe, hair-dryer and television.

€140–€205, includes breakfast

29

C, 6, 31, 32

MALASPINA
Piazza Indipendenza 24, 50129 Firenze
Tel 055 489869
www.malaspinahotel.it

Right on the beautiful Piazza Indipendenza, the elegant Malaspina Hotel was built in the 14th century. The sound-proofed rooms are quite modern but they have kept some of their traditional touches and are spotless. Each has a television, minibar, safe and telephone.

€80–€209

31

7, 10, 20, 25, 31, 32, 33

MONNA LISA
Borgo Pinti 27, 50121 Firenze
Tel 055 2479751
www.monnalisa.it

This 15th-century palazzo is a wonderful mix of old and contemporary design. The reception has stuccoed walls and a striking staircase. Many rooms have elaborate ceilings, wall hangings and antiques. Facilities include private bathroom, hair-dryer, television, telephone, minibar and safe. The flower-filled garden is perfect for relaxing with a drink.

€182–€350

55

14, 23

RELAIS CERTOSA HOTEL
Via di Colle Ramole 2 (off Via Chiantigiana, Certosa), 50124 Firenze
Tel 055 204 7171
www.florencehotelcertosa.it

Near the Certosa exit of the A1, this guesthouse is set in wooded grounds. It has spacious rooms and suites, some in rustic Tuscan style, others modern. Tuscan dishes predominate at lunch and dinner, served in the garden in

good weather. The hotel's occasional complimentary shuttle or a bus takes guests to the city in 10 minutes.

€95–€247 includes breakfast

69

RIVOLI
Via della Scala 33, 50123 Firenze
Tel 055 27861
www.hotelrivoli.it

Close to Santa Maria Novella, the Rivoli is a beautifully renovated Franciscan monastery. The public spaces have cross vaulting, arches and pillars, which recall its serene and austere past. The rooms are simple with large marble bathrooms, and some have a

The Malaspina offers Renaissance elegance

balcony or terrace. Expect 24-hour room service, laundry, coffee- and tea-making facilities, television, radio, telephone and trouser press. On fine days, breakfast is served on the flower-filled patio.

€227–€320, including breakfast

69

Outdoor heated whirlpool

A, 11, 36, 37

SCOTI
Via dei Tornabuoni 7, 50123 Firenze
Tel 055 292128
www.hotelscoti.com

This impressive 15th-century building stands opposite the Palazzo Strozzi in the shopping mecca of Via Tornabuoni. It is

SOGGIORNO ANTICA TORRE
Piazza della Signoria 3, 50122 Firenze
Tel 055 216402
www.anticatorre.com

The Soggiorno Antica Torre is part of a tower that was built in the 11th century beside the Piazza della Signoria, the venue for many of the city's most notable historical events. Even after extensive refurbishments and renovations, the original ceilings remain intact, complemented by handsome parquet floors. The distinctly Florentine rooms are beautifully furnished. Each one has a private bathroom (with shower or bath), hair-dryer, minibar, television and telephone.

€100–€200 excluding breakfast (€3)

6

A, B

small with simple but light-filled bedrooms. None with private bathrooms. The lounge has beautiful 18th-century frescoes depicting an Arcadian landscape. Electric fans are available in the summer.

€70–€95

11

A, 6, 11, 36, 37

TORRE GUELFA
Borgo Santi Apostoli 8, 50123 Firenze
Tel 055 2396338
www.hoteltorreguelfa.com

Sleep in a 13th-century tower and enjoy some excellent views from the former home to the extremely wealthy Acciaiuoli family. High ornate ceilings give the building an airy feel and some rooms have canopied beds and balconies. The facilities include telephone, private bathroom, minibar, safe and television.

€150–€185

20

B, D, 11, 37

STAYING

TUSCANY AND UMBRIA

There are dozens of lovely places to stay throughout Tuscany and Umbria, Italy's top destination for foreign visitors, from 5-star opulence to *agriturismo*. Tuscany's main towns are Siena, Pisa, Lucca and Arezzo, all with a wide range of accommodation. Reserve in advance in summer, and remember that rooms will be reserved months in advance in Siena during the July and August Palio. If you're driving, you'll find an excellent choice in the Chianti villages, San Gimignano and the southern Tuscan hill towns. Umbria's main town is Perugia, where you should aim to stay in the *centro storico*. Like Tuscany, Umbria has a clutch of appealing small towns and villages with excellent accommodation—reserve in advance if you want to stay in Orvieto and Assisi during high season, but two to three days in advance should be sufficient for the towns of Todi, Gubbio, Spello and Norcia. Lago di Trasimeno is busy on summer weekends and during July and August, and Spoleto is packed during its summer festival.

ASSISI

FONTEBELLA
Via Fontebella 25, 06081 Assisi
Tel 075 812883
www.fontebella.com
This slightly crumbling, 16th-century palazzo can be found between Piazza del Pool and the Basilica di San Francesco. Golden swags, old paintings and tapestries cover the walls, and the rooms are traditionally furnished. The garden restaurant is the perfect place for dining if you don't fancy venturing farther afield.
€105–€230
46

SAN FRANCESCO
Via San Francesco 48, 06082 Assisi
Tel 075 812281
www.hotelsanfrancescoassisi.it
This hotel, opposite the basilica, is perfectly positioned for exploring Assisi. There are both spacious and cramped rooms in this old building so chose your room wisely, but they are all comfortable and cheerful. The owners take great delight in making you feel welcome, and make a particular effort to ensure you start the day well fed. Don't miss the views over the rooftops from the terrace upstairs.
€110–€160
44

PRICES AND SYMBOLS
Prices are the lowest and highest for a double room for one night including breakfast, unless otherwise stated. Note that rates can vary depending on the time of year.

For a key to symbols, ▷ 2.

BEVAGNA

HOTEL PALAZZO BRUNAMONTI
Corso Matteotti 79, 06031 Bevagna
Tel 0742 361 932
www.brunamonti.com
Right in the heart of Bevagna, this charming hotel combines

18th-century elegance in the public rooms with low-key Umbrian traditional style in the well-equipped bedrooms. There are splendid parquet floors and frescoed ceilings, while the dining room oozes a great combination of formality and style. Staff are friendly, and all rooms are equipped with all you'd expect from a top-class hotel.

🏨 €47–€155
🛏 16 ♿

L'ORTO DEGLI ANGELI

Via Dante Alighieri 1, 06031 Bevagna
Tel 0742 360 130
www.ortoangeli.it

This stunning Residenza d'Epoca (Historic Hotel) comprises two old palazzi, surrounded by beautiful courtyards and gardens, in the heart of the walled town of Bevagna. Every bedroom is different, those in the Palazzo Andreozzi having frescoed ceilings, those in the Palazzo Alberti a more rustic style. A loggia overlooks the garden, and there are comfortable public rooms, an excellent restaurant, a fitness and beauty centre, and helpful multilingual staff.

🏨 €220–€350
🛏 14 ♿

CORTONA

RELAIS VILLA BALDELLI

San Pietro a Cegliolo 420, 52044 Cortona
Tel 0575 612406
www.villabaldelli.com

Dating from the 1600s, this 4-star country villa built of *pietra serena* (the local grey stone) sits in peaceful parkland. Rooms are simple but elegant with beamed ceilings, wrought-iron beds and wooden furnishings. The shared lounge has a large, original fireplace. Facilities include a bar and wine-tasting room. Traditional breakfasts are served on the terrace in summer. Walks, horseback riding and excursions can be arranged.

There is also an on-site golf academy and driving range.

🏨 €200–€300
🛏 15 ♿ 🏊 Outdoor
�GF Camucia, then taxi 2km (1.3 mile)
🚗 Take the Valdichiana exit on the A1 and follow signs for Cortona. At Camucia take the SS71 in the direction of Arezzo. The Villa Baldelli is on the right just after Sodo, 2km (1.3 mile) from Arezzo

GREVE (IN CHIANTI)

DEL CHIANTI

Piazza Matteotti 86, Greve, 50022 Firenze
Tel 0558 53763
Fax 0558 53763

Greve is a classic Chianti village and this historic hotel

The Relais Villa Baldelli, in Cortona, offers simple elegance

(parts of the building are nearly 1,000 years old) is right on the central piazza. Bedrooms are light and airy, with wrought-iron bedheads and cool white drapes, while downstairs there are terracotta floors, white walls and a mix of modern and antique furniture. The vine-shaded eating area under a pergola in the garden is a bonus.

🗓 Mar–end Nov and 15 Dec–7 Jan
🏨 €100–€120
🛏 16 ♿ 🏊 Outdoor
🚗 Greve is on the SS222, the old Via Chiantigiana that links Florence and Siena

LUCCA

ALBERGO SAN MARTINO

Via della Dogana 7/9, 55100 Lucca
Tel 0583 469181
www.albergosanmartino.it

This 3-star hotel in Lucca's old town is only a brief stroll from the cathedral from which it takes its name. Bedrooms are comfortably furnished and have a television and refrigerator. An English speaker pops into the hotel at 6pm every evening to give guests a talk on what to see and do in Lucca. The talk comes with a complimentary afternoon tea or summer drink. Parking is €10 per day and bicycle rental is also available.

🏨 €100–€130
🛏 9 ♿
🚆 300m (330 yards) from the central rail station
🚗 Drive into the old city through Porta Eliza. Turn left at Via dei Fosso until you get to Corso Garibaldi where you take the first left

VILLA ROMANTICA

Via Barbantini 246, 55100 Lucca
Tel 0583 496872
www.villaromantica.it

Villa Romantica is an imposing town house surrounded by trees only a few minutes' walk from Lucca's famous walls. The rooms are brightly decorated with busy fabrics in the fashion of the period. For a romantic trip, reserve into the suite with its four-poster bed, living room and terrace. There is a shuttle service to the town that runs four times an hour. You can also park here for free and rent a bicycle.

🏨 €100–€150 excluding breakfast
🛏 4 (1 junior suite, 1 suite) ♿
🏊 Outdoor
🚶 5 minutes' walk from Lucca. At the city walls, just before the football stadium, turn right into Via dello Stadio. The hotel is at the end of the road

VILLA LA PRINCIPESSA
Via Nuova per Pisa 1616, 55050 Massa Pisana
Tel 0583 370037
www.hotelprincipessa.com
This 4-star hotel is one of the most elegant lodgings in Tuscany. The luxurious guest rooms are decorated with antiques and period furnishings. Facilities include a lounge, bar and restaurants. Bedrooms come equipped with telephone, satellite television and minibar.
€240–€290
42 Outdoor
Regular buses run from both Lucca and Pisa. From Pisa, there is a stop near the hotel

MONTALCINO
AL BRUNELLO DI MONTALCINO
Strada Provinciale Traversa dei Monti, 53024 Montalcino
Tel 0577 849 304
www.hotelalbrunello.it
Don't let the modern brick exterior deter you from stopping at this ultra-comfortable hotel, in a peaceful location just outside Montalcino. Rooms in the new wing are huge and beautifully appointed, with traditional Tuscan furniture and sumptuous bathrooms; many have private balconies with superb views. Cheaper rooms in the original building are smaller, though equally well equipped. The restaurant serves local specialties and has an excellent wine list, and there's a pool for relaxing at the end of a hot day.
€95–€110 (new wing); €50–€85 (original building)
32 Outdoor
2 km (1.3 mile) southeast of Montalcino on Grosseto road

DEI CAPITANI
Via Lapini 6, Montalcino, 53042 Siena
Tel/Fax 0577 847227
www.deicapitani.it
Almost all the rooms in this beautifully converted late medieval building have

sweeping views over the archetypal Tuscan landscape of the Val d'Orcia. The bedrooms are lofty and come in cool shades with lovely beamed ceilings and plenty of space. Family-run, the hotel prides itself on personal service. The buffet breakfast could keep you going all day, and if the private parking's full, they'll help you find a space in town.
Closed 5 Jan–15 Feb
€110
29 Outdoor
Exit the Autosole at Firenze Certosa from the north, Chiusi Chianciano from the south, and follow signs to Montalcino. On arrival follow the yellow signs to the hotel in the *centro storico*

The Villa La Principessa is in the hills surrounding Lucca

MONTEPULCIANO
CAMERE BELLAVISTA
Via Ricci 25, 53045 Montepulciano
Tel 03478 823 314
If you're looking for good-value accommodation right in the historic heart of Montepulciano, these privately run rooms are an excellent choice. Light, simply furnished and airy, many have superb views, and all have wonderful beamed ceilings and are equipped with private bathrooms.
€49–€65
6

NORCIA
GROTTA AZZURRA
Via Alfieri 12, 06046 Norcia
Tel 0743 816513
The building's beautiful stuccoed walls, cavernous rooms and fabulous furnishings create comfortable surroundings. Suits of armour preside over those eating in the impressive dining rooms, where local roast lamb is served. Most of the bedrooms are fairly simple, but the slightly pricier rooms look like film sets and are worth paying extra for.
€35–€120
46
Follow signs for the hotel from Spoleto

ORVIETO
VIRGILIO
Piazza del Duomo 5, 05018 Orvieto
Tel 0763 341882
www.hotelvirgilio.com
You won't find better value in one of Orvieto's most popular areas. The sound of church bells can always be heard in this hotel, set right on the main piazza, never letting you forget you're in a small Italian town. The rooms are small but cared for, and every room has private facilities. Try to get a room with a view of the magnificent duomo. The breakfasts are simple but tasty.
Closed Feb
€52–€90
13
Funicular from railway station and then take a taxi or hop on the city-circuit bus

PASSIGNANO SUL TRASIMENO
HOTEL LA VELA
Via Rinascita 2, 06065 Passignano sul Trasimeno
www.hotellavela.it
The lakeside village of Passignano makes a good stop-off point heading into Umbria from Tuscany, and you'll find a warm welcome at this family-run, well-priced hotel. On a quiet street a few

STAYING

minutes' walk from the heart of town and water's edge, the hotel has comfortable, simple bedrooms, all with bathrooms, telephone and TV, a pleasant bar and breakfast room and a good restaurant serving everything from pizza to Umbrian specialties.

€50–€75
29

PERUGIA

SANGALLO PALACE

Via Masi 9, 06100 Perugia
Tel 075 5730202
www.sangallo.it

This modern hotel is in Perugia's old heart. Almost all rooms have balconies, allowing guests to enjoy splendid views of the city and the hills that surround the property. The guest rooms are slightly impersonal since they are geared towards business visitors, but they have every standard amenity. There is a state-of-the-art gym and an impressive indoor pool.

€100–€170
94 Indoor

PIENZA

RELAIS IL CHIOSTRO DI PIENZA

Corso Rossellino 26, Pienza, 53026 Siena
Tel/Fax 0578 748400
www.relaisilchiostrodipienza.com

Walk through the luminous cloister of this 15th-century ex-monastery to one of southern Tuscany's most atmospheric hotels. The restoration has been beautifully done, leaving the vaulted ceilings, beams and architectural details untouched, while sensitively adding 21st-century comfort. The bedrooms are big and antique pieces enhance the public areas. A good restaurant, dreamy terraces and geraniums add to the magic, all a minute's walk from Pienza's main piazza.

Closed 7 Jan–15 Mar
€180–€220
37 Outdoor

Exit the Autosole at Valdiciana from the north, Chiusi Chianciano Terme from the south, and follow signs to Pienza. The hotel is inside the town walls on the right

PISA

FRANCESCO

Via Santa Maria 129, 56126 Pisa
Tel 050 554109
www.hotelfrancesco.com

Close to the Leaning Tower and the botanical gardens, this small hotel and restaurant is in the heart of Pisa. Rooms are whitewashed, with wooden furnishings, and most have panoramic views. Bedrooms have a television and minibar. Facilities include a family-run

The Relais Fattoria Vignale offers traditional Tuscan luxury

pizzeria, bicycle rental and a courtesy airport shuttle.

€95–€120
13
4

RADDA IN CHIANTI

RELAIS FATTORIA VIGNALE

Via Pianigiani 8, Radda in Chianti, 53017 Siena
Tel 0577 738300
Fax 0577 738592
www.vignale.it

Fattoria Vignale started life as the manor house of a big wine estate; today, it's one of Italy's top hotels, aimed at well-heeled foreigners. The conversion is very successful—expect traditional Tuscan architecture, well-polished

antiques, fireplaces big enough to roast an ox and huge sofas. The bedrooms, some with private terraces, are opulent and luxurious, with service to match. The vaulted wine cellars house a taverna, and there's a smarter restaurant near the main building.

Mid-Mar–end Nov and Christmas–6 Jan
€180–€250
42 Outdoor
From the Autosole (A1): from the north exit Firenze Certosa, take the superstrada Firenze–Siena towards Siena. Exit at S Donato (22km/14 miles) and follow signs to Radda in Chianti. From the south exit at Valdarno, take the N408 to Gaiole in Chianti. After 17km (11 miles) take the road to Radda in Chianti. The hotel is signposted (yellow signs) and is in the middle of Radda

SAN GIMIGNANO

L'ANTICO POZZO

Via San Matteo 87, 53037 San Gimignano
Tel 0577 942014
www.anticopozzo.com

This 3-star hotel, in a superbly restored 15th-century, town house, is located in the middle of San Gimignano. The building sits on a cobbled street near the Piazza della Cisterna. The interior is medieval in character and contains a well-preserved lobby with a high, vaulted ceiling. There's an atmospheric bar in the brick cellar and a first-floor garden terrace. Rooms have satellite television, minibar and safe. Guests get a discount when parking in lot 3.

Closed Dec to mid-Jan
€140–€160
18
From Florence, Siena, Volterra
Poggibonsi then bus to San Gimignano
Take the Poggibonsi Nord exit of the Firenze/Siena highway and follow signs to San Gimignano

HOTEL RELAIS SANTA CHIARA
Via Matteotti 15, 53037 San Gimignano
Tel 0577 940701
www.rsc.it
A short walk from the medieval hill town of San Gimignano, the 4-star Relais Santa Chiara combines contemporary architecture with superb views. To ensure the best outlook, request a room with a balcony when you make your reservation. The hotel has no restaurant, but a generous breakfast is served. There are also a cocktail bar and meeting room on site. The rooms have satellite television and a minibar.

€140–€220
41 Outdoor
On arrival at San Gimignano turn left at the roundabout in the direction of Volterra, then take the next right. The hotel is 450m (550 yards) south of Porta San Giovanni, outside the city walls

SIENA
MINERVA
Via Garibaldi 72, 53100 Siena
Tel 0577 284474
www.albergominerva.it
A 10-minute walk from Piazza del Campo and the rail station, this 3-star hotel has good views over the city and hills beyond. Good value, with modern, fully equipped bedrooms.

€80–€122
59
3, 4, 7, 8, 10, 17, 77

SPELLO
PALAZZO BOCCI
Via Cavour 17, Spello, 06038 Perugia
Tel 0742 301021
Fax 0742 301464
www.emmeti.it/pbocci.it
Built in the 18th century and renovated in the 1990s, this romantic hotel is set in the heart of one of Umbria's prettiest towns. You'll find high frescoed ceilings, public rooms with deep sofas and terracotta floors scattered with Persian rugs, a pretty breakfast room

and terraces with views over the plain below. The bedrooms are all different and spacious, with luxury fabrics, huge beds and state-of-the-art bathrooms. The staff are charming, efficient and multilingual.

€130–€150
23
Spello old town is a short walk from the rail station
Exit the Autosole (A1) from the north at Valdichiana, from the south at Orte, and follow signs to Spello. Follow the signs to *centro storico* and then the yellow hotel signs. The hotel is on the left up the main street

Siena's Grand Hotel Continental provides aristocratic luxury

SPOLETO
PALAZZO DRAGONI
Via del Duomo 16, 06049 Spoleto
Tel 0743 222220
www.palazzodragoni.it
Next to the cathedral, this 14th-century building was the home of the Dragoni family, who more than contributed to the prosperity of Spoleto. Now owned by the local bakers, the Diotallevi family, it has kept much of its original charm with the added bonus of modern facilities and the best breakfast pastries in town. The rooms are all different, but each is comfortable and well kept. The dining area has wonderful views of the city.

GRAND HOTEL CONTINENTAL
Via Banchi di Sopra 85, 53100 Siena
Tel 0577 56011
www.ghcs.it
This luxurious hotel in a former aristocratic home is part of Siena's cultural heritage. It has been faithfully restored to its former glory right down to the magnificent frescoes, a wall painting of St. Christopher dating from the 15th century, and the ornamental motifs from the 19th century. A covered courtyard has been coverted into a winter garden. Full leisure facilities are available at the nearby Park Hotel via a courtesy bus service.

€394–€730
51
3, 9, 10, 5 from Florence to La Lizza

€119–€145
15
CA from station

TODI
FONTE CESIA
Via L Leony 3, Todi, 06059 Perugia
Tel 0758 943737
Fax 0758 944677
www.fontecesia.it
The Fonte Cesia was originally an 18th-century palazzo, complete with private chapel—today, it's a top-class luxury hotel. Bar, breakfast room and lounge all retain their brick vaulting. The bedrooms are decorated with heavy brocades and have ultra-comfortable beds and marble bathrooms. The staff are friendly, the breakfast excellent, and there's a smart, expensive restaurant on the premises. Free parking.

€130–€170
32 bedrooms, 5 suites
Ponte Rio (Terni/Perugia line)
Route C
Exit the Autosole at Orvieto and take the SS448 to Todi. Follow the yellow signs to the hotel in the *centro storico*

STAYING

ROME

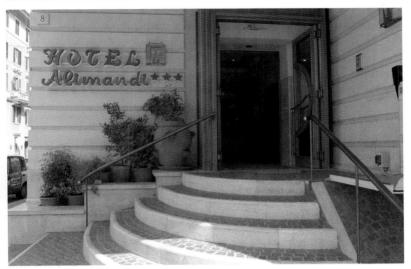

Rome's busiest months are from Easter to the end of October but, for peace of mind and better choice, it's worth making reservations in advance whenever you visit the capital. There's a good range of accommodation in the *centro storico*, Rome's tightly packed heart, west of Via del Corso. From here, there's plenty to see within walking distance, with the bonus of a wide choice of bars and restaurants. Heading farther east, classy hotels are clustered around Piazza di Spagna and towards Via Vittorio Veneto, with plenty of mid-range options to the southwest between the Quirinale and the Forum. You could also consider staying across the River Tiber in the pleasant district of Prati, near the Vatican and St. Peter's, or check in somewhere in the vibrant Trastevere area. Budget hotels are mainly found near Stazione Termini; pick carefully here—some are distinctly unappealing. If money's tight, consider a stay at one of the well-appointed convents run by religious orders.

RESERVATIONS
Rome's APT (tourist) offices will not reserve accommodation for you, but they do have lists of hotels. The main office is five minutes' walk from Stazione Termini at Via Parigi 5 (Mon–Fri 8.15–7.15, Sat 8.15–1.45, tel 06 48899253, www.romaturismo.com or www.provincia.roma.it).

For a key to symbols, ▷ 2.

PRICES AND SYMBOLS
Prices are the lowest and highest for a double room for one night including breakfast, unless otherwise stated. Note that rates can vary depending on the time of year.

ALIMANDI
Via Tunesi 8, 00192 Roma
Tel 06 39726300
www.alimandi.org
This is a superior 3-star, family-run hotel that is very good value for money. Close to the Vatican Museums and totally refurbished, the 19th-century building has kept some original features, including elegant Venetian stuccowork. Rooms are spacious, with modern furnishings and pastel hues. All have satellite and pay television, roomy bathrooms with hair-dryer, and internet connection. They cater very well for visitors with disabilities. The Continental buffet breakfast is served on the roof terrace or in the dining room. The hotel provides a free airport shuttle, and garage parking is available.
🕒 Closed 10 Jan–10 Feb
💶 €130–€155
🛏 35 🛗 📺
🚇 Cipro-Musei Vaticani or Ottaviano
🚌 81, 95, 492

STAYING

ANNE AND MARY
Via Cavour 325, 00184 Roma
Tel 06 69941187
www.anne-mary.com
This welcoming bed-and-breakfast occupies part of an elegant 19th-century building near the Colosseum. Rooms are simple but they are dramatically appointed, with clean lines and swooping curtains. Each has a private bathroom with an enclosed shower. Via Cavour is a large, somewhat frantic road, but the proximity of this hotel to the major sights means it is worth putting up with the noise.
🛏 €110–€135
🛎 6 ♿
🚇 Cavour, Colosseo
🚌 75, 81, 85, 87, 116, 117

ATLANTE STAR
Via G Vitelleschi 34, 00193 Roma
Tel 06 6873233
www.atlantehotels.com
Nestled between Vatican City and Castel Sant'Angelo, this establishment exudes class and nobility, with richly upholstered sofas, heavy drapes, stuccoed ceilings and plush carpets. The guest rooms are equally lush and spacious. Half of them have whirlpool baths. There is a bar and gourmet restaurant and you can enjoy views of the Basilica di San Pietro. The hotel provides a free airport shuttle service.
🛏 €248–€388; under 12s free
🛎 61 ♿
🚌 32, 81, 492
🚇 Ottaviano–San Pietro

CAPO D'AFRICA
Via Capo d'Africa 54, 00184 Roma
Tel 06 772801
www.hotelcapodafrica.com
This is a handsome 19th-century building close to the Colosseum in a trendy district. The hotel is a fusion of contemporary and classic design with Japanese touches. The rooms are a joy to behold, with warm ochre and saffron shades and perfectly fitted bathrooms in marble and wood. The breakfast room on the roof looks out over the Collosseo. There's a large, well-equipped gym and a solarium. The hotel is accessible for guests with disabilities. American buffet breakfast.
🛏 €340–€380
🛎 65 ♿ 🚭
🚇 Colosseo, San Giovanni
🚌 81, 85, 87, 117
🚊 Tram 3

THE DUKE
Via Archimede 69, 00197 Roma
Tel 06 367221
www.thedukehotel.com
The Duke is in the heart of the well-heeled Parioli district,

The Hotel de Russie is one of Rome's finest

between the parks of the Villa Borghese and the Villa Gloria. Inside, it looks like an English country home with classical flourishes and there is a delightful art nouveau glass cupola in the Polo lounge. The rooms are luxurious and intimate, spacious and light, with minibar, safe, satellite television and a games console. The large marble bathrooms are very luxurious. Children get welcome packs and free tickets to the zoo.
🛏 €320–€480
🛎 78 ♿ 🚭
🚇 Flaminio
🚌 910
🚆 From Piazza del Popolo, train to Viterbo, 1st stop–Termini

GENIO
Via G Zanardelli 28, 00186 Roma
Tel 06 6832191/6833781
www.LeonardiHotels.com
This is a hotel with a nice touch of the Old World about it. Antique furniture and rich red carpets throughout give it a regal air. The high-ceilinged rooms are a good-size, with embroidered armchairs and marble-fitted bathrooms. The bar and roof terrace have fine views of the Basilica di San Marco and Castel Sant'Angelo. It is very convenient for the Renaissance quarter of Rome and just seconds away from Piazza Navona. A free airport shuttle is available.
🛏 €104–€340
🛎 60 ♿
🚌 70, 81, 87,116, 492

HOTEL DE RUSSIE
Via del Babuino 9, 00187 Roma
Tel 06 328881
www.roccofortehotels.com
In the heart of the city amid all the top designer shops, this is one of the top hotels in Rome. The Bonaparte brothers lived and died here. It's a unique blend of contemporary and classic styles. The guest rooms have high ceilings and are well furnished. The bathrooms are a work of art with all the amenities. If that's not enough there is a spa with a hydropool, sauna, Turkish baths and beauty treatments. The first-class restaurant is elegant and, when open onto the gardens, one of the most romantic spots in Rome.
🛏 €720–€1100 excluding breakfast (€30)
🛎 125 ♿ 🚭
🚇 Flaminio
🚌 117

HOTEL FENIX
Viale Gorizia 5/7, Roma
Tel 06 8540741
Fax 06 8543632
www.fenixhotel.it
An elegant, but not expensive, hotel in the Trieste residential area, away from the crowds

but within easy reach of Rome's centre and numerous historical and cultural attractions. The rooms are decorated and furnished in neoclassical style and the hotel has its own secluded garden off the restaurant/ breakfast room. The Fenix was built in the 1960s, so the architecture is bland and unimpressive, but inside the hotel is bright, with a mix of antique furniture and modern art, just like a private residence. The atmosphere is relaxed and comfortable, and the staff aim to make you feel at home.

🍽 €132–€220
🛏 65 rooms, 8 suites 🆒
🏠 On the corner of Viale Gorizia and Via Nomentana
🚌 36, 60, 62, 84

INTERNAZIONALE
Via Sistina 79, 00187 Roma
Tel 06 69941823
www.hotelinternazionale.com
Wisteria winds up the front of this palazzo, which was as a convent in the 16th and 17th centuries. The breakfast lounge is swathed in soothing pastel shades of blue and mauve. The scheme continues throughout the hotel, from the cupids in the cupola to the moiré wall coverings in the bedrooms.

🍽 €190–€260
🛏 42 🆒
🚇 Piazza di Spagna
🚌 62

ITALIA
Via Venezia 18, 00184 Roma
Tel 06 4870919
www.hotelitaliaroma.com
This inexpensive, family-run hotel is very central and just off the second-largest shopping street in town. The reception is on the first floor. The 19th-century building was refurbished simply in 2002. The rooms are functional with television, minibar, air-conditioning (€8 extra per day), bathroom and hair-dryer. The hotel has a bar and a safe

at the reception. Continental buffet breakfast.

🍽 €52–€87
🛏 23 🆒 15 rooms (€8 extra)
🚇 Repubblicà
🚌 64

LOCARNO
Via della Penna 22, 00186 Roma
Tel 06 3610841
www.hotellocarno.com
Artists and intellectuals such as Umberto Eco, author of *The Name of the Rose*, favour this art deco refuge on a sleepy street near the Piazza del Popolo. The 1925 building still has some original features, including a cast-iron elevator. The decorating is delicate and

The Lord Byron is splendidly furnished

deft, using period lamps, furniture and fabrics. Each room is different. Free use of the business facilities, and vintage bicycles.

🍽 €130–€600
🛏 68 🆒
🚇 Flaminio
🚌 117

LORD BYRON
Via Giuseppe de Notaris 5, 00197 Roma
Tel 06 3220404
www.lordbyronhotel.com
The Lord Byron is a romantic hideaway in pastoral Parioli, overlooking the Villa Borghese. The art deco villa has been elegantly restored, with scarlet sofas, lacquered furniture, gilded mirrors and marble bathrooms.

LANCELOT
Via Capo D'Africa 47, 00184 Roma
Tel 06 70450618
www.lancelothotel.com
Don't let the high-rise appearance put you off this welcoming, family-run hotel just above the Colosseum. The lounge and dining room have period furniture and Murano glass chandeliers. There is a bar, library and a delightful courtyard. The rooms are spacious and most have wooden floors and pastel walls. All the rooms have bathrooms with a shower, a safe and satellite television. Some of the guest rooms have terraces. Continental breakfast.

🍽 €158
🛏 60 🆒
🚇 Colosseo, San Giovanni
🚌 81, 85, 87, 117; tram 3

Rooms 503, 602 and 603 have spectacular views. Its restaurant, Relais Le Jardin, is considered to be one of Italy's finest.

🍽 €325–€495
🛏 32 🆒
🚇 Flaminio
🚌 117
🏠 West side of Via Giuseppe de Notaris 5, just north of Via Mangili

NAZIONALE A MONTECITORIO
Piazza Montecitorio 131, 00186 Roma
Tel 06 695001
www.nazionaleroma.it
This hotel is close to the Fontana di Trevi and the Scalinata di Trinità dei Monti. It has dark wood panelling and marble floors and columns in the lobby. The moderately sized rooms, with high ceilings and period furnishings, are decorated in gold and brown shades. All have private bathrooms, satellite/pay television, minibar and a safe. The restaurant serves Italian and Continental cuisine.

🍽 €325–€455
🛏 95 🆒
🚌 46, 62, 116

STAYING

NORD NUOVA ROMA

Via Giovanni Amendola 3, 00185 Roma
Tel 06 488 5441
Fax 06 481 7163
www.romehotelnord.it
This recently renovated hotel is near Diocletian's Baths and the Roman Archaeological Museum. It has preserved its 1930s art deco style with marble and hardwood flooring, and décor. It is one of the better hotels in the area close to Termini station. The rooms are rather small, but the convenient location makes up for that, and there are all modern facilities including TV, WiFi internet connections and telephone. On the seventh floor there is a fitness room and a terrace with a bar and great views over the city. The staff speak English and are very helpful with making reservations for city tours and restaurants and giving directions to sights and attractions.
€105–€206
155
Located close to Termini station and Piazza della Repubblicà
Termini

PORTOGHESI

Via dei Portoghesi 1, 00186 Roma
Tel 06 6864231
www.hotelportoghesiroma.com
This hotel is tucked away in the Tor di Nona area, north of Piazza Navona. From here you can feel the heartbeat of Rome as mopeds sputter and locals chatter nearby. It's easy to miss the unassuming entrance, but keep an eye out for the row of dainty flags. Highlights include the sunny breakfast room and the roof terrace.
€185–€210
27
Spagna
116, 280

RAPHAEL

Largo Febo 2, 00186 Roma
Tel 06 682831
www.raphaelhotel.com
Day or night, the ivy-covered façade of this hotel, a short distance from Piazza Navona, always looks romantic. The antique-filled lobby, golden velvet sofas and gilt tables give it a period feel. The rooms are littered with *objets d'art* and furnished in the Imperial style. There are plenty of modern facilities though; satellite television, a safe and a minibar. The restaurant has an international reputation and a roof terrace where you can have breakfast, with unparalleled views of the city.
€450–€700 excluding breakfast (€35)
59
40, 62, 64, 87, 116, 492, 628 to Piazza Navona

The Scalinata di Spagna is hugely popular

SCALINATA DI SPAGNA

Piazza Trinità dei Monti 17, 00187 Roma
Tel 06 6793006
www.hotelscalinata.com
Reserve months—if not years—in advance at this boutique hotel atop the Scalinata di Trinita dei Monti. La Scalinata's 16 rooms are highly coveted (especially numbers 10 and 12). The breakfast terrace, overlooking the red-tiled roofs and cupolas, is a riot of blossom. Active visitors can jog in the nearby Villa Borghese park, which also has a modern underground gym. You can also plug in your laptop, or try the free internet television with e-mail.
€100–€400
16
Spagna
116

STARGATE HOSTEL & HOTEL

Map 428 H3
Via Palestro 88, 00185 Roma
Tel 06 445 7164
www.stargatehotels.com
A rough-and-ready hostel/hotel near Termini station. There is an age limit of 35 on hostel rooms. The hotel rooms are more private. An Italian breakfast of coffee and brioche is included.
Hostel: €10–20; hotel: €40–90
Hostel: 20; hotel: 20
Castro Pretorio or Termini
492

VISCONTI PALACE

Via Federico Cesi 37, 00193 Roma
Tel 06 3684
www.viscontipalace.com
This hotel has recently had a complete refurbishment. The rooms are spacious and furnished in contemporary style, and there is a range of room types to suit your budget. The outside of the building is not impressive, but the interior is bright and airy with displays of modern art by Rome artists; the public areas also have fresh flowers every day. The lavish buffet breakfast in the spacious basement dining area makes a great start to the day. The Visconti Palace is popular with business visitors and there are good deals for leisure stays, especially in the summer months. Given that some of Rome's major attractions are within 10 minutes' walk, this is a near-ideal location. The hotel is adapted for disabled access throughout, with ramps wherever steps occur. WiFi and internet access in rooms and the lobby bar.
€185–€290
247 (13 junior suites)
Valet parking service

STAYING

LAZIO AND THE MARCHE

Apart from the hill towns around Rome—Albano, Frascati and Tivoli—much of Lazio, and certainly the Marche, is relatively untouched by tourism. If you are heading east across the Apennines, Tivoli is a good overnight stop. North along the Lazio coast from Rome, Tarquinia is a good base from which to explore the Etruscan sites. Inland from here is Viterbo and placid Lago Trasimeno, a cool oasis in the summer with plenty of hotels around the lake. Heading south from Rome, the coast around Monte Circeo and Terracina is a picturesque place to stay, but busy in summer, so reserve in advance if you want to stay in high season. East into the Marche, the main focal points are Urbino and the compact Ascoli Piceno in the Tronto Valley; both have good hotels and restaurants. If you're looking for a typical Italian resort, head for Pèsaro or Fano, both of which have plenty of family-run hotels.

PRICES AND SYMBOLS

Prices are the lowest and highest for a double room for one night including breakfast, unless otherwise stated. Note that rates can vary depending on the time of year.

For a key to symbols, ▷ 2.

ASCOLI PICENO

GIOLI

Viale A de Gasperi 14, 63100 Ascoli Piceno
Tel 0736 255550

This is Ascoli Piceno's most highly recommended hotel, although it loses points for sketchy service. It is just steps away from the busy Piazza Arringo and the tower-lined Piazza del Popolo. It even has a small garden, which adds a refreshing touch of green. The interior is light and modern but comforting and classy, with fresh cut flowers and newly plumped pillows. There is 24-hour room service and parking is available.

€125
🛏 56
🅿 2, 3
🚉 Ascoli Piceno; train to San Benedetto del Tronto and change for Ascoli Piceno
🚗 From the A14 take the San Benedetto del Tronto exit and follow signs to Ascoli Piceno and then to the *centro storico*; from Rome take Via Salaria

FRASCATI

BELLAVISTA

Piazza Roma 2, 00044 Frascati
Tel 06 9421068
www.hbellavista.it

In Palazzo Senni, this hotel looks out over Frascati's main square. The rooms are comfortable and simply furnished, designed to make the best of the original architecture. They have televisions and telephones and a tiny bathroom with a shower. Private parking in the courtyard.

€78–€93
🛏 18 🔹 5 rooms
🚇 From Rome take Metro A: Anagnina, then bus
🚌 Blue bus from Rome to Frascati
🚉 Train from Termini station to Frascati

FLORA
Viale Vittorio Veneto 8, 00044 Frascati
Tel 06 9416110
The rooms in this art nouveau hotel are refined and spacious. Some have a terrace with excellent views. There is a veranda, terrace and roof garden. Airport transfers are available on request.
💷 €150–€180
🛏 37 🔲
🚇 From Rome take Metro A: Anagnina, then bus
🚌 Blue bus from Rome to Frascati
Ĥ Train from Termini station to Frascati

MACERATA
VILLA SIBILLINI
Contrada Collalto 10, 62026
San Ginesio, Macerata
Tel 0733 653081, 3206 935510
www.villasibillini.com
A country house hotel offering bed-and-breakfast and overlooking the Sibillini mountains. Guest rooms are spacious, with good views. There is a full restaurant service.
💷 €85 bed-and-breakfast, or villa rental with staff €2,500 per week
🛏 5 🏊 Outdoor
🚇 From Ancona take the A14 motorway and exit for Macerata
❌ Ancona, Pescara

SAN LEO
CASTELLO
Piazza Dante Alighieri 11, San Leo, Pesaro e Urbino 61018
Tel 0541 916214
This 16th-century palazzo is the town's only hotel and its best restaurant (▷ 357). The simple and spotless bedrooms are peaceful.
🔵 Closed 2 weeks in Nov and Jan
💷 €50–€63
🛏 14
🚇 From Rimini
🚇 From Rimini take the SS258 west and turn left at Pietrocuta for San Leo

SPERLONGA
LA SIRENELLA
Via Cristoforo Colombo 25, Sperlonga, Latina 04029
Tel 0771 549186
Fax 0771 549189
www.lasirenella.com

A typical, family-run, good-value holiday hotel, right on the beach. The clean, simply furnished rooms have good bathrooms. The rooms at the front have sea views and the hotel has access to the private beach. Half- or full-board is compulsory and a three-day package is excellent value for money.
🔵 Closed Dec
💷 €130–€206
🛏 40 🔲
🚇 Fondi Sperlonga (Roma/Napoli line) then bus
🚇 Exit the Autosole at Ceprano and take the N82 to Sperlonga. The hotel is on the seafront

The Raffaello in Urbino is close to Raphael's birthplace

TIVOLI
LA PANORAMICA
Viale Arnaldi 45, 00019 Tivoli
Tel 0774 335700
www.villadestetivoli.it
Rooms in this 19th-century building are all comfortable, with private bathroom and television. Double rooms with extra bunk-beds are available for families. The terrace has a splendid view of Rome. The hotel is close to Villa d'Este.
💷 €55
🛏 10
🚇 Ponte Mammolo or Rebibbia, then bus to Tivoli
🚇 33km (21 miles) from Rome: from the A24 (Rome/L'Aquila) take the exit for Tivoli (3km/2 miles)

SPECIAL IN TIVOLI
SIRENE
Piazza Massimo 4, 00019 Tivoli
Tel 0774 330605
In this 19th-century villa the rooms are spacious and gracefully decorated. All have private bath and some have a private terrace. There is a restaurant and café with a panoramic terrace.
💷 €145
🛏 40 🔲
🚇 Ponte Mammolo or Rebibbia, then bus
🚇 33km (21 miles) from Rome: Follow the Via Tiburtina or the Gran Raccordo Anulare (GRA). Turn off at Tivoli Citta and follow signs for Villa d'Este; from the A24 (Rome/L'Aquila) take the exit for Tivoli (3km/2 miles)

URBINO
BONCONTE
Via della Mura 28, 61029 Urbino
Tel 0722 2463
www.viphotels.it
Urbino's most luxurious hotel. Embedded in the thick southern walls of the city, with cityscapes to the north, and cypress-lined hills to the south. The restaurant serves good local cuisine.
💷 €133
🛏 23 🔲
🚇 Exit A14 at Pesaro/Urbino and then follow signs to centro storico. From here follow signs for hotel

RAFFAELLO
Via Santa Margherita 40, 61029 Urbino
Tel 0722 4784
www.albergoraffaello.com
This hotel is in a 14th-century palace on a hill in the old town. The top-floor rooms look out over San Francesco's bell tower and the Palazzo Ducale.
💷 €115
🛏 14 🔲
🚇 Exit A14 at Pesaro/Urbino and then follow signs to the centro storico. From here follow signs for hotel

STAYING

THE SOUTH

Naples, the Amalfi coast and the Sorrento peninsula have something to suit everyone, all within easy reach of Naples, the great classical ruins of Pompei, and the off-shore islands of Capri and Ischia. Across the Apennines lies the Gargano peninsula, a well-kept secret with pretty villages and comfortable hotels. This is a great place from which to explore south into Puglia. Vibrant Bari is Puglia's capital, but the best place for accommodation is in the *trulli* country round Alberobello and baroque Lecce. Further south again in the regions of Calabria and Basilicata, there are some good hotels in Matera and Maratea, and there are many simple, family-run establishments along the coast and in the other main towns.

For a key to symbols, ▷ 2.

PRICES AND SYMBOLS

Prices are the lowest and highest for a double room for one night including breakfast, unless otherwise stated. Note that rates can vary depending on the time of year.

ALBEROBELLO

DEI TRULLI

Via Cadore 32, Alberobello, 70011 Bari
Tel 080 4323555
Fax 080 4323560
www.hoteldeitrulli.it
Sample the full *trulli* experience in this deluxe hotel converted from a group of Alberobello's distinctive conical stone houses. Totally traditional from the outside, the interior has been skillfully converted to provide the comfort that its numerous foreign guests expect. This hotel is popular with group tours, but the gardens and pines provide a calm setting and the bedrooms' white-washed walls, simple decoration and well-equipped bathrooms are oases of tranquility.

🛏 €140–€180
🛌 28 🔶 🏊 Outdoor
🚌 From Bari
🚉 Alberobello from Bari
🚗 Exit the A14 at Bari Nord and follow signs to Alberobello, then follow signs to the hotel

AMALFI

LA BUSSOLA

Lungomare dei Cavalieri 16, 84011 Amalfi
Tel 089 871533
www.labussolahotel.it
This former mill and pasta factory is on the outskirts of Amalfi (pictured above). Its attractions include a small private jetty and a terrace with views of the azure waters below. The restaurant serves very good regional dishes. The lobby has a 1970s feel, while the lounge area has some elegant 18th/19th-century furnishings. Guest rooms are simply furnished with amusingly kitsch artworks, and have basic facilities. Private parking is €10 per day.

🛏 €94–€154
🛌 62 🔶 12 rooms only (€10 extra)

STAYING

LIDOMARE

Largo Piccolomini 9, 84010 Amalfi
Tel 089 871332
www.lidomare.it

The Lidomare is in a 14th-century building just off the main piazza. It is good value for this part of Italy. Many of the rooms have high ceilings, bright tiled floors, and a mixture of modern and dark wood furniture. Facilities include private bathroom, television, safe, heating and telephone. There's a pleasant terrace with superb views where breakfast is served.

€90–€120

15

From Naples or Salerno

Salerno then bus to Amalfi

Take the A3 from Naples then turn right to Amalfi and follow signs for *centro*

BARI

VICTOR

Via Nicolai 71, 70122 Bari
Tel 0805 216600
Fax 0805 212601
www.victorservice.com

Bari can be noisy, so the soundproofed rooms here are welcome. This is a modern and efficient hotel, and it wins for its position and parking—a nightmare in Bari. The rooms are comfortable and well equipped.

€106–€126

77

From Rome, Naples, Milan, Lecce

Bari from Rome, Naples, Milan, Lecce

From the north, exit Bari Nord and fork left towards Bari Fiera on *tangenziale* SS16, take exit 4 Fiera Porto–Via Napoli. From the south take exit 4

CAPRI

BELSITO

Via Matermania 11, 80073 Capri
Tel 081 8370969
www.hotelbelsito.com

This hotel, in an attractive 18th-century villa, is in an excellent spot, only a short stroll from the Piazzetta di Capri and Arco Naturale. Some of the light and cheery guest rooms have balconies that overlook the Marina Piccola. The white walls blend well with bright modern furnishings. The terrace restaurant serves traditional Neapolitan dishes, and there are some enchanting views of the island from here.

€62–€180

13

From Naples and Sorrento then funicular to town (also from Salerno and Positano in Aug). Hotel is 10 minutes from the centre

DA GELSOMINA MIGLIERA

Via Migliara 72, 80071 Anacapri
Tel 081 8371499
www.dagelsomina.com

Capri's La Tosca offers splendid views

This hotel provides good-value accommodation, near the sublime Migliera cliff-top vantage point. It has excellent facilities and a wonderful restaurant. The rooms are decorated in cool hues and have tiled floors. All have television, telephone, minibar, hair-dryer and private bathroom. There are jaw-dropping views from each balcony and a large swimming pool and sundeck.

€115–€125

5 Outdoor

From Capri town

From Naples and Sorrento then funicular to town (also from Salerno and Positano in Aug)

GRAND HOTEL QUISISANA

Via Camerelle 2, 80073 Capri
Tel 081 8370788
www.quisi.com

Marble floors, elegant statues, chesterfield sofas and chandeliers greet you in the lobby of this well-established luxury hotel—quality and service are the watchwords here. The rooms are filled with a blend of cool and warm pastel shades, and a mixture of comfy modern and elegant Venetian-style furnishings. There are superb views throughout and top-class facilities, including a spa and a first-rate restaurant.

Closed Nov to mid-Mar

€300–€730

150 Indoor and outdoor

LA TOSCA

Via Birago 5, 80073 Capri
Tel 081 8370989
www.latoscahotel.com

This is a lovely little hotel with wonderful views of the monastery of San Giacomo and the distinctive Faraglioni rocks. The comfortable rooms are light and airy. Facilities include private bath in most rooms and telephone. Breakfast costs an additional €8 per person.

€63–€125

From the port take the funicular to Piazzetta di Capri (Piazza Umberto VII and La Tosca is a five-minute walk away)

GARGANO PENINSULA

ALBA DEL GARGANO

Corso Matino 102, 71030 Mattinata
Tel 0884 550771
www.albadelgargano.it

For great value on the Gargano coast, this is a sure-fire hit. The guest rooms are simply furnished with modern fittings, and facilities include a television, telephone and compact bathroom with shower. The restaurant serves decent regional cooking. The hotel's wonderfully sandy private beach (2km/1.3 miles away) is well equipped.

STAYING

€56–€86 bed-and-breakfast, except Aug half-board rate only €132
40 10 rooms
Bari to Foggia
Foggia then local bus
A14 to Foggia exit then SP89 to Mattinata

HOTEL DEI MANDORLI
Località Montagna, Ruggiano, 71043 Manfredonia
Tel 0884 530400/1
www.hoteldeimandorli.it
Set in the Gargano National Park, this hotel is a good base for exploring the area. The rooms are functional but comfortable. There is a decent pizza restaurant. Horseback riding can be arranged, and there are plenty of outdoor activities.
€52
19
Bari to Foggia
Manfredonia then local bus to Ruggiano
Take the SP89 from Foggia and turn left at Manfredonia

LECCE
CENTRO STORICO B&B
Via Andrea Vignes 2b, 73100 Lecce
Tel 0832 242727
www.bedandbreakfast.lecce.it
On the second floor of a 16th-century palazzo, this hotel offers excellent value just a short walk from the rail station. The guest rooms are simply furnished and clean. The suite sleeps two to three people, with a kitchen area. Enjoy the cityscape from the terrace. No credit cards.
€52–€80
6
From Bari, Napoli, Taranto
Lecce

PATRIA PALACE
Piazzetta Riccardi 13, 73100 Lecce
Tel 0832 245111
www.starwoodhotels.com
This 5-star hotel is in the 17th-century Palazzo D'Anna. The guest rooms, decorated in warm hues, are immaculate and refined. Feast on quality cucina pugliese served in

the evocative restaurant, or enjoy a drink in Danny's Bar.
€188–€320
67

MARATEA
VILLA DEL MARE
Acquafredda, Maratea, 85046 Basilicata
Tel 0973 878007
Fax 0973 878102
www.hotelvilladelmare.com
A week or more can be happily spent at this resort hotel. Inside, the style is Mediterranean; cool and white, with shady, flower-filled terraces. Many of the bedrooms are big enough for families. There's also a crèche for kids. A lift will whisk you down to the private beach. If

The Villa del Mare, Maratea, offers guests yacht excursions

you want total peace, check when the in-house disco operates. Parking.
Closed Nov–end Mar
€110–€215
75 Outdoor
Sapri (Napoli/Reggio di Clabria line) then bus to Acquafredda
Exit the Autosole at Lagonegro-Nord and follow the Valle del Noce superstrada to the Sapri exit. At Sapri, turn left onto the N18 towards Maratea. The hotel is 6km (9.5 miles) along this road

MATERA
ITALIA
Via Ridola 5, 75100 Matera
Tel 0835 333561
Fax 0835 330087
www.albergoitalia.com

Hotels as comfortable as this are thin on the ground in Basilicata. The building is an old palazzo, so there are high ceilings, marble and flagged floors and gracious architecture. Bedrooms are big, and the staff will happily add a couple of beds to your room for the kids.
€98–€130
45
From Naples, Bari, Taranto and Potenza
Exit the A14 at Taranto Nord and take the N7 west to Matera. From the town outskirts follow yellow signs to the hotel

NAPOLI (NAPLES)
GRAND HOTEL EUROPA
Corso Meridionale 14, 80143 Napoli
Tel 081 267511
www.sea-hotels.com
A convenient location and decent service make this a good bet for accommodation near the centro storico. Most of the soundproofed rooms have cheerful paintings hung on whitewashed walls. Facilities include television, phone, safe, hair-dryer and minibar. Traditional music is often played in the adjoining La Grande Abbuffata restaurant.
€78–€180
80
Piazza Garibaldi, Napoli Centrale
ALIBUS to Piazza Garibaldi

GRAND HOTEL VESUVIO
Via Partenope 45, 80121 Napoli
Tel 081 7640044
www.vesuvio.it
Many notable figures such as Grace Kelly and tenor Enrico Caruso have passed through the doors of the Grand Hôtel Vesuvio since it opened in 1882. Public rooms and guest rooms are filled with antiques and exquisite fabrics. Dine in style at Caruso, the rooftop restaurant, or take advantage of the fitness, health and beauty facilities.
€380–€850
163 rooms, 16 suites
C52, E5, 140, 152

STAYING

SPECIAL IN NAPLES

COSTANTINOPOLI 104
Via Santa Maria di Costantinopoli 104, 80138 Napoli
Tel 081 5571035,
Fax 081 5571051
www.costantinopoli104.it
A hidden gem, this elegant, homely hotel is in the historical city centre. An enormous art nouveau stained-glass window dominates the main façade of the building. The interior is bright and airy with all modern comforts. Try to get a room on the roof level, which has a terrace with sunbeds. The hotel has a charming secluded garden with a swimming pool and terrace. Garage parking.
€205–€220
13 rooms, 6 suites
Outdoor
Naples
Piazza Dante, Piazza Cavour

HOTEL IL CONVENTO
Via Speranzella 137/A, 80132 Napoli
Tel 081 403977
www.hotelilconvento.com
This handsome 17th-century palace, next to the convent of Santa Maria Francesca, is newly renovated and has subtle lighting and attractive antique furniture. Two junior suites have balcony views, but all the rooms have excellent amenities.
€83–€180
10 rooms, 4 suites
R2 from the Naples train station

MIRAMARE
Via Nazario Sauro 24, 80132 Napoli
Tel 081 7647589
www.hotelmiramare.com
The American consulate in the 1950s, this beautiful building has been transformed into an attractive hotel. The bedrooms come with all modern comforts. You can relax and enjoy the sublime vistas on the terrace.

€202–€314
31
152

STARHOTEL TERMINUS
Piazza Garibaldi 91, 80142 Napoli
Tel 081 7793111
Fax 081 206689
www.starhotels.com
Standing right outside Napoli Centrale station, the Terminus resembles a dull concrete block. Inside is a chic, sophisticated hotel with soundproofing to create an oasis of peace in the bustling city. This is largely a business hotel. The result is that July, August and Christmas are considered low season,

The Albergo Casa Albertina, in Positano, has fabulous sea views

and the Terminus could be a good choice for a bargain leisure break in the heart of Naples. There is garage parking and a restaurant and roof terrace.
170
€105–€209
Naples
Napoli Centrale
Piazza Garibaldi

POMPEI

AMLETO
Via Bartolo Longo 10, 80045 Pompei
Tel 081 8631004
www.hotelamleto.it
The Amleto is a great base from which to explore the ruins of Pompei, Ercolano and the Vesuvio. The marble floors,

subtle lighting and fresh, vibrant walls give the hotel an air of spacious tranquillity. The roof garden and solarium have bird's-eye views of Pompei. Free parking.
€99–€155
26
Circumvesuviana train from Naples to Pompei

HOTEL FORUM
Via Roma 99, 80045 Pompei
Tel 081 850 1170
Fax 081 850 6132
www.hotelforum.it
A charming hotel in the heart of Pompei town, with some rooms overlooking the ruins and Vesuvio. The rooms are tastefully decorated, and some have been converted into suites. The hotel has secure parking.
€90–€130
36
From the Naples-Salerno motorway, Via Roma is one of the main roads into the town centre
Circumvesuviana from Naples Piazza Garibaldi, Trenitalia main line trains from Napoli Centrale

HOTEL DEL SOLE
Via Roma 133, 80045 Pompei
Tel 081 863 1700
www.hoteldelsole.it
This hotel is well located for exploring Capri, Sorrento, the Amalfi coast and Naples, and is ideal for Pompei. Some rooms overlook the ruins.
€75–€80
52
From the Naples-Salerno motorway, Via Roma is one of the main roads into the town centre
Circumvesuviana from Naples Piazza Garibaldi, Trenitalia main line trains from Napoli Centrale

POSITANO

ALBERGO CASA ALBERTINA
Via Tavolozza 3, 84017 Positano
Tel 089 875143
www.casalbertina.it
A flight of 60 steps descending from the road leads to this family-run hotel on the cliffs above Positano. Whitewashed

vaulted ceilings and cool, blue-tiled, majolica flooring create a relaxing air. There are first-rate facilities in the guest rooms—some have hydromassage baths and all have a private terrace with a sublime panorama. A twisting path leads down to the beach. The restaurant serves excellent seafood and traditional Neapolitan dishes. Parking available.

€220–€250. Half-board only
20
Hydrofoil from Naples Jun–end Sep

LA FENICE
Via Marconi 4, 84017 Positano
Tel 089 875513
A small hotel with spectacular views on the beach side. Guest rooms are beguiling, although the facilities are basic. There is a seawater pool and Jacuzzi, and a private beach. Private boat tours can be reserved from here, too. The traffic can be noisy.

€100–€125
13 (2 suites)
Outdoor

HOTEL DI SAN PIETRO
Via Laurito 2, 84017 Positano
Tel 089 875455
www.ilsanpietro.it
This luxury hotel has stunning views, excellent facilities and sumptuous suites. Each room has a huge marble bathroom and a private terrace. Relax in the tranquil gardens and dine in the first-rate terrace restaurant. There is a private beach, a swimming pool and a tennis court.

€380–€500
62 Outdoor
Take the A3 from Naples and follow signs for Sorrento, then pass Positano and follow signs for the hotel (1.5km/0.9 mile) on the SS163 towards Amalfi

VILLA FRANCA
Viale Pasitea 318, 84017 Positano
Tel 089 875655
www.villafrancahotel.it
The cool blue-and-white façade hints at the relaxing

qualities of this hotel's interior. Guest rooms vary in size, but all have subtle shades and bright decorative touches. The pool and terrace overlook the beach and the terrace restaurant serves excellent Neapolitan food. Facilities include a health club and gym.

€220–€320
37
Outdoor

RAVELLO
VILLA AMORE
Via Santa Chiara, 84010 Ravello
Tel 089 857135
A peaceful hotel just a short stroll from Piazza Duomo that is good value in the chic,

The Hotel di San Pietro, Positano, is famed for its celebrity guests

pricey town of Ravello. There are spellbinding views from the terrace and a very good bar/restaurant serving traditional local dishes. Guest rooms are compact with modern furnishings. Most have views of the gardens and the Thyrrhenian Sea. Reserve well in advance.

€68–€82
12

VILLA MARIA
Via Santa Chiara 2, 84010 Ravello
Tel 089 857255
www.villamaria.it
Villa Maria has whitewashed interiors that blend well with antiques and vibrant tiling. Guest rooms have dark wood

furniture, tiled floors and are equipped with private bathroom, telephone and television.

€180–€280
23
Turn off the A3 Naples/Salerno road at intersection Vietri S. Mare. Follow signs for Ravello and then signs for the hotel. Guests can be escorted from Naples by prior arrangement

SORRENTO
GRAND HOTEL EXCELSIOR VITTORIA
Piazza Tasso 34, 80067 Sorrento
Tel 081 8071044
www.exvitt.it
This magnificent hotel brims with Victorian style. The guest rooms and suites have many belle époque decorative touches and top-class facilities. Many have terraces with views of the gardens or sea. Self-catering apartments are also available. At the restaurant you can dine in style under a celestial ceiling or by candlelight on one of the terraces.

€325–€525
96 Outdoor
From Naples and Sorrento

IMPERIAL TRAMONTANO
Via Vittorio Veneto 1, 80067 Sorrento
Tel 081 878 2588
www.tramontano.com
This 16th-century palazzo, a hotel since 1812, has been the choice of royalty as well as literary icons such as Byron, Shelley and Goethe. Most guest rooms have parquet flooring and elegant furnishings. Many have magnificent views, and there is access to a private beach and swimming pool.

Closed Jan–end Feb
€280
116 Outdoor

SICILY AND SARDINIA

Unless you're visiting Sicily for a seaside holiday, the chances are you'll be touring, staying just a couple of nights at different bases. Most visitors take in Palermo, the capital, where there's plenty of choice, before heading on. Good options include historic Siracusa, Agrigento for the classical sites, and picturesque Erice on the west coast. Taormina is Sicily's prime resort town, but Cefalù, on the north coast, has a lot going for it, while Enna, high in the interior mountains, makes a great stopover. The off-coast island groups, the Egadi and Aeolian, are popular holiday destinations in summer, and it is advisable to reserve in advance.

Sardinian possibilities include Olbia, handy for the Costa Smeralda, the lovely west-coast Cala Gonone, and Alghero, the island's main holiday destination, on the east coast. In Cagliari, the capital, staying in the old Castello quarter is to experience the city at its best.

Sicily

AGRIGENTO

KAOS
Villagio Pirandello, 92100 Agrigento
Tel 0922 598622
Fax 0922 598770
www.athenahotels.com
This 18th-century villa has been sensitively converted into one of the area's nicest hotels. The rooms are big and cool, and facilities include tennis courts, spacious grounds and a private beach. It's a great place to stay to escape the crowds.
🛏 €130–€155
🛎 105 🅿 🏖 Outdoor
🚌 From Catania and Palermo
🚉 Agrigento from Catania and Palermo

🚗 Take the A20 from Messina to Palermo and the Caltanisetta exit. Follow the signs to Agrigento on the SS640, then take the SS189 to Agrigento and follow signs to the hotel

CEFALÙ

KALURA
Via V Cavallaro 13, Cefalù, 90015 Palermo
Tel 0921 421354
Fax 0921 423122
www.kalura.it
Nearly all the big, airy rooms here have balconies overlooking the sea. One of the most beautifully positioned hotels in Sicily, with lovely gardens, tennis courts and a children's playground; steep steps lead down to the beach.

🛏 €120–€196
🛎 68 🅿
🏖 Outdoor and private beach
🚌 From Palermo
🚉 Cefalù then bus
🚗 From Palermo or Messina take the A20 and exit at Cefalù Ovest. Follow the yellow hotel signs to the hotel; approx 1.5 km (0.9 mile) east of the old town on the coast

ENNA

GRANDE ALBERGO SICILIA
Piazza Colojanni 7, 94100 Enna
Tel 0935 500850
Fax 0935 500488
www.hotelsiciliaenna.it
A charming hotel in the heart of this little town. The facilities are modern, and it has large

MODERNO

Via Vittorio Emmanuele 67, Erice, 91016 Tràpani
Tel 0923 869300
Fax 0923 869139
www.pippocatalano.it

You're in for a treat at this hotel. There is a lovely courtyard for breakfast and an excellent restaurant serving Sicilian cuisine.
€95–€116
40
From Trapani (10km/16 miles)
Take the A29 from Palermo and exit at Trapani, then follow signs to Erice and yellow signs to the hotel

rooms, some with a spectacular view of Etna. Garage parking.
€102–€130
60
Take the A19 between Catania (84km/52 miles) and Palermo (119km/75 miles)
Palermo, Catania
Palermo, Catania

ISOLE EGADI

FAVIGNANA

Corso da Badia, Via Circonvallazione 8, 91023 Favignana, Isola Egadi
Tel 0923 925 449
Fax 0923 921 727
www.favignanahotel.com

The rooms in this tastefully furnished hotel have satellite TV, phone and minibar, and there is an internet point.
€90–€180
17
Hydrofoil service from Tripani

ISOLE EOLIE

GATTOPARDO PARK

Via Diana, Lipari, Isole Eolie
Tel 0909 811035
Fax 0909 880207
www.netnet.it/hotel/gattopardo

The rooms to go for here are in the private dwellings that nestle in the flowery garden. Close to some of the island's best beaches.
Closed Nov–end Feb
€112–€248
50

From Messina, Naples and Palermo May–end Oct
Take a taxi from the port

PALERMO

PRINCIPE DI VILLA FRANCA

Via Giuseppina Turrisi Colonna 4, 90140 Palermo
Tel 091 6118523
www.principedivillafranca.it

Villa Franca is near the Teatro Politeama. The large guest house showcases Sicilian craftsmanship, from the bed spreads to the furniture. The restaurant is worth a visit for its traditional cooking.
€185
34
101, 107, 614

Many of Siracusa's hotels have views out to sea

SIRACUSA

DOMUS MARIAE

Via Vittorio Veneto 76, 96100 Siracusa
Tel 0931 24858
www.sistemia.it/domusmariae

This seafront hotel's terrace has mesmerizing views of Mount Etna. The rooms are spacious and have balconies and bathrooms.
€135–€150
12
Circolare 1, 8, 20
Siracusa from Milan, Rome, Naples and Palermo

GRAND HOTEL VILLA POLITI

Via Politi 2, 96100 Siracusa
Tel 0931 412121
www.villapoliti.com

This hotel's 18th-century elegance and level of service set it apart from other hotels.
€186
100 Outdoor
Circolari 1, 3

GUTKOWSKI

Lungomare Vittorini 26, 96100 Siracusa
Tel 0931 465861
www.guthotel.it

Take your breakfast on the terrace at this simple, airy hotel and soak up the dazzling Mediterranean views.
€75–€90
15
Circolare 20
Take the Catania–Siracusa motorway and exit at Siracusa Sud. Follow this to the centro storico. The hotel is on the east coast of the Isla di Ortiga

TENUTA DI ROCCADIA

Contrada Roccadia, Carlentini, 96013 Siracusa
Tel 0959 90362
www.roccadia.com

This agriturismo hostel (pictured on page 396) provides guests with the opportunity to experience rustic Sicily. It arranges outdoor activities such as horseback riding. The rooms sleep two to four and have private bathrooms. A car is essential.
€35–€45 per person
20 2 Outdoor
Train to Lentini
Take the Catania–Siracusa motorway and exit at Brucoli–Carlentini, 30km (19 miles) from Siracusa

TAORMINA

GRANDE ALBERGO CAPOTAORMINA

Via Nazionale 105, 98039 Taormina
Tel 0942 572111
www.atahotels.it/capotaormina

With bright rooms, inspiring views and a lift to the hotel's private caves, beach and saltwater pool, this hotel has a lot to offer. Every room has a balcony or sea-view terrace.
Closed Oct–end Mar
€125–€270
206 Outdoor

STAYING

VILLA BELVEDERE

Via Bagnoli Croce 79, 98039 Taormina
Tel 0942 23791
www.villabelvedere.it
This is one of the area's best places to stay. The rooms have small balconies, many with beautiful views.
🌐 Closed Nov to mid-Dec, mid-Jan to end Mar
💶 €120–€205
🛏 47 ♿ 🏊 Outdoor

VILLA DUCALE

Via Leonardo da Vinci 60, Taormina
Tel 0942 28153
Fax 0942 28710
www.taormina-hotels.villaducale.com
This hotel's terrace offers spectacular views of Naxos Bay and Mount Etna. It is outside the centre of Taormina and away from the bustle. The hotel has a free bus shuttle or you can walk into the town in 10–15 minutes.
🛏 16 ♿
💶 €160–€250
🚗 Off the A18 motorway; from Taromina centre take the road in the direction of Castelmola
🚆 Taormina-Giardini Naxos station 5km (3 miles)

VILLA FIORITA

Via Pirandello 39, 98039 Taormina
Tel 0942 24122
www.villafioritahotel.it
Each room in this old inn has a terrace, and there is a shady garden and a pool.
💶 €120–€235
🛏 31 rooms, 3 suites ♿ 🏊 Outdoor
✈ From Catania airport 40km (25 miles)
🚆 Taormina, then local bus or taxi
🚗 Exit Taormina from the A18 and head for *centro storico* and follow signs for hotel

Sardinia

ALGHERO

CONTINENTAL

Via F.lli Kennedy 66, Alghero, 07041 Sassari
Tel 0799 75250
Fax 0799 81046
www.hotelcontinentalalghero.it
Outside the city but with a regular bus service into town,

this is a good choice if you want to escape the crowds. Some rooms have balconies. You can use the facilities of its more expensive sister hotel, the Calabona, nearby.
🌐 May–end Sep
💶 €74–€124
🛏 32
🏊 Use of pool and private beach at Hotel Calabona

CAGLIARI

FORTE VILLAGE

Santa Margherita di Pula, 09010 Cagliari
Tel 070 92171
www.fortevillageresort.com
This sprawling, 5-star resort is the ideal place to be pampered. An extensive range

The Villa Belvedere looks over the Ionian Sea

of accommodation, bars and restaurants is available. The resort has plenty of sport and recreation facilities such as golf, go-carting and outdoor ice-skating.
🌐 Mar–end Oct
💶 €400–€896. Half-board only
🛏 771 rooms, suites and bungalows
♿ 🏊 Outdoor 🍴
🚆 From Piazza Matteotti rail station and Elmas bus from the airport on request
🚗 Follow road SS195

CALA GONONE

CALA LUNA

Lungomare Palmasera 32, Cala Gonone, 08020 Nùoro
Tel 0784 93133
Fax 0784 93162
www.toplevelhotel.com/calaluna

This good-value hotel stands less than 50m (55 yards) from the beach. The rooms have good beds, though they're plain and simply furnished.
💶 €57–€78
🛏 27
🚗 Take the SS125 north from Cagliari. Turn right down to Cala Gonone just before Dorgali

OLBIA

OLLASTU

Località Costa Corallina, 07026 Olbia
Tel 0789 36744
Fax 0789 36760
www.ollastu.it
In a village 8km (5 miles) south of Olbia, the Ollastu Hotel is great for getting away from it all. The complex is sited on a promontory with magnificent sea views, and each room is a separate mini-villa with its own entrance. A beach is near and there is also a swimming pool and tennis court.
🌐 Mar–end Oct
💶 €55–€120
🛏 54 ♿ 🏊 Outdoor
🚗 Take the main coast road south from Olbia towards Nuoro/San Teodoro
✈ Olbia
⛴ Ferry from Genoa to Porto Torres/Olbia, Livorno, Piombino or Cittavecchia to Olbia

PORTO ROTONDO

GREEN PARK

Località Aldia Manna, Porto Rotondo, 07020 Sàssari
Tel 0789 380100
Fax 0789 380043
Stay in the main building, or opt for one of the cheaper, single-storey dwellings in the grounds—they all have a balcony or terrace with a sea view and the beach is less than 1km (0.6 mile) away.
🌐 Closed mid-Oct to mid-Apr
💶 €52–€139
🛏 50 ♿ 🏊 2 outdoor
🚗 Take the 125 north from Olbia then after 9km (5.5 miles) turn right to Porto Rotondo and follow signs to the hotel
✈ Olbia then taxi; hotel will arrange transfer

STAYING

Planning

BEFORE YOU GO

CLIMATE AND WHEN TO GO

Contrary to the picture-postcard image of perpetual sunshine and blue skies, Italy has variable weather. Apart from the summer months, when temperatures soar and the sun shines all day, this mountainous country has the full range of conditions. The climate is predominantly Mediterranean, with the far north experiencing Alpine trends and the far south arid and hot. Spring is pleasant everywhere, but there's frequent rain right through into May, and temperatures north of Rome only start to climb in June. Farther south, April and May see the start of summer. Italy's hot months are from July to late September, when average temperatures are around 30°C (86°F) and the sirocco, a hot wind from Africa,

WEATHER STATIONS

Venezia
6m
20ft

Milano
210m
689ft

ROMA
3m
10ft

Palermo
34m
112ft

pushes humidity up. In summer, the area around the Alps experiences numerous thunderstorms, which regularly help clear the air, but inland parts of southern Italy suffer extremely hot nights, often making sleeping difficult. As in the spring, the sirocco may well bring very high temperatures to parts of Italy during the autumn, accompanied by high humidity. Temperatures start to drop everywhere towards the end of September, with increasingly frequent bouts of rain and the first frosts in the Alps. Winter in the north is cold, with snow in the mountains, heavy frosts and thick fog on the plains. These conditions are also found to an extent in central Italy, with Tuscany and Umbria both experiencing bitter spells during the winter months. Winter is the wettest season in the south, and average daytime temperatures range from 7°C to 13°C (45°F to 55°F). November is dank and wet everywhere. Around Christmas you can hope for some crystal-clear, cold, sunny days. Mountain regions are colder, with heavy winter snowfalls (see below).

WEATHER REPORTS

BBC World news and CNN news have websites and broadcast regular global weather updates in English, and The Weather Channel and the Met Office in the UK have

TIME ZONES		
City	Time difference	Time at 12 noon in Italy
Amsterdam	0	noon
Auckland	+11	11pm
Berlin	0	noon
Brussels	0	noon
Cairo	+1	1pm
Chicago	-7	5am
Dublin	-1	11am
Johannesburg	+1	1pm
London	-1	11am
Madrid	0	noon
Montreal	-6	6am
New York	-6	6am
Paris	0	noon
Perth, Australia	+7	7pm
San Francisco	-9	3am
Sydney	+9	9pm
Tokyo	+8	8pm

Italy is one hour ahead of GMT/UTC. The clocks are moved forward an hour for daylight saving time on the last Sunday in March. The clocks go back an hour on the last Sunday in October. The chart shows time differences from Italy.

global weather websites too (www.bbc.co.uk, www.CNN.com, Weather Channel—www.weather.com, www.metoffice.com).

MOUNTAINOUS AREAS

The weather can change very quickly in the mountains throughout the year, so prepare for all eventualities. Always carry

VENICE
TEMPERATURE
Average temperature per day
per night

°C
30
20
10
0

°F
86
68
50
32

J F M A M J J A S O N D

RAINFALL
Average rainfall

mm
120
80
40
0

in
4.5
3
1.5
0

J F M A M J J A S O N D

MILAN
TEMPERATURE
Average temperature per day
per night

°C
30
20
10
0

°F
86
68
50
32

J F M A M J J A S O N D

RAINFALL
Average rainfall

mm
120
80
40
0

in
4.5
3
1.5
0

J F M A M J J A S O N D

ROME
TEMPERATURE
Average temperature per day
per night

°C
30
20
10
0

°F
86
68
50
32

J F M A M J J A S O N D

RAINFALL
Average rainfall

mm
120
80
40
0

in
4.5
3
1.5
0

J F M A M J J A S O N D

PLANNING

waterproofs and extra clothing, as sudden drops in temperature and changes in conditions are common even in summer. Remember to carry enough water when you are in remote areas. At high altitudes the sun can be fierce and it is magnified in winter when it reflects off the snow, so cover up and wear plenty of sun block. Most ski resorts monitor avalanche reports and close runs that are at risk, but if you intend to go off-piste or climb in remote areas without a guide, you should check the weather and avalanche reports beforehand (www.eurometeo.com www.csac.org).

NATURAL HAZARDS

These include landslides, avalanches, mudflows and flooding, mainly in the winter months. Earthquakes are occasionally felt in many parts of the country. Northern and central Italy may experience bad flooding in winter and shorter periods of localized flooding during dramatic summer thunderstorms, particularly around the northern lakes. Flooding and land subsidence

PALERMO
TEMPERATURE

RAINFALL

DUTY-FREE AND DUTY-PAID GUIDELINES

There are few restrictions on the personal items you may bring into Italy—illegal drugs and firearms are not permitted, of course—but you should carry receipts for valuable items to prove you owned them before visiting Italy.

Duty-paid allowances for US citizens

US citizens can bring home up to $800 of duty-paid goods, provided they have been out of the country for at least 48 hours and haven't made another international trip in the past 30 days. This limit applies to each member of the family, regardless of age, and allowances may be pooled.

- 1 litre of alcohol
- 200 cigarettes
- 100 cigars (non-Cuban)
- 1 bottle of perfume (if trademarked in the US)

For the most up-to-date information, see the US Department of Homeland Security's website: www.customs.treas.gov

Duty-paid guidelines for UK citizens

You cannot buy goods duty-free if you are travelling within the EU. If you bring back goods on which you have paid tax in Italy, you will not normally have to pay any tax or duty on them in the UK. However, any alcohol or tobacco you bring from Italy must be for your own use and not for sale back home. HM Revenue and Customs considers anything over the following limits to be commercial quantities and may demand payment of some UK tax and duty unless you can prove the quantities are for your personal use, such as a wedding reception or a big party.

- 3,200 cigarettes
- 400 cigarillos
- 110 litres of beer
- 90 litres of wine
- 3kg of tobacco
- 200 cigars
- 10 litres of spirits
- 20 litres of fortified wine (such as port or sherry)

You cannot bring back goods for payment (including payment in kind) or for resale. These are considered to be commercial items and you could be made to pay UK taxes and duties, or have the goods seized by Customs officers.

For up-to-date information see the website of HM Revenue and Customs: http://customs.hmrc.gov.uk where there is a section on advice for travellers. There is also a telephone advice line: 0845 010 9000.

are an ongoing problem in Venice. In autumn, especially in October and November, tides flood houses, churches and shops, causing damage to businesses and affecting visitors and residents alike. Parts of southern Italy lie on a major seismic fault line, and minor tremors and earthquakes are almost a daily occurrence. There

has been renewed volcanic activity on Mount Etna in Sicily. The eruptions themselves appear to have subsided for the time being, but if you plan to climb Etna you should always follow the advice of guides near the summit and keep to the designated routes at all times. There is ongoing volcanic activity on the island of Stromboli.

PLANNING

WHAT TO TAKE

You will need lightweight cottons and linens to wear during the summer, except in the mountains, where sudden drops in temperature and changes in weather conditions are common. Natural fabrics are more comfortable than synthetics in humid conditions. Light- to medium-weight clothing is worn in the south during winter, while warmer clothes are worn elsewhere. Alpine wear is needed during winter in the mountain resorts.

In fashion-conscious cities such as Rome, Milan and Venice, people tend to dress smartly at all times. Bring clothes that cover your shoulders and knees if you are intending to visit churches or other religious buildings.

REMEMBER TO PACK...

- Waterproofs
- A folding umbrella
- A small bag for daily use, such as a shoulder bag that can be worn across the body, or a money belt
- Your driver's licence and passport
- Comfortable shoes
- A compass
- Your address book, for emergency contacts or postcards
- Photocopies of all important documents: passport, insurance details, credit card, debit card and passport numbers and registration numbers for mobile phones, cameras and other expensive items
- A torch (flashlight) and binoculars
- A first aid kit, including plasters (Band Aids), antiseptic cream, painkillers and any prescribed medication
- An Italian phrasebook—any attempt at Italian is appreciated (▷ 417–420)
- Toiletries and sunscreen in screw-top containers inside plastic bags to guard against leakage caused by variable pressure in aircraft luggage holds

LUGGAGE ALLOWANCES

On international flights within Europe, IATA allowances are 20kg (44lb) for economy class and 30kg (66lb) for first class, but ask your airline before you fly as there may be restrictions (particularly budget airlines) and you may have to pay excess baggage charges. You can usually take more luggage on transatlantic flights as you are only restricted to two pieces of luggage no larger than 170cm (67in) across.

PASSPORTS

- You will need a passport to enter Italy, which should be valid for at least another six months from the date of entry.
- If you lose your passport, you should contact your embassy (▷ 411).
- Keep a note of your passport number or carry a photocopy of the information page separately from your passport. Alternatively, scan the information pages of your passport and any other important documentation and email them as attachments to a secure email account that can be accessed from anywhere in the world.
- If you intend to work or study in Italy, make sure your passport is stamped with your date of entry. You will need it to apply for a *permesso di soggiorno* (permit to stay) (▷ below).

VISAS

- If you are an EU national, or from Australia, Canada, New Zealand or the United States, you do not need a visa for stays of up to 90 days. To extend your visit you can, one time only, apply to any police station for an extension of a further 90 days. This extension cannot be used for studying or employment, and you will have to prove that you can support yourself financially.
- Regulations can change at short notice so check before making your travel arrangements.
- If you are a citizen of a country other than those mentioned above, you should contact the Italian Embassy in your home country to check visa requirements.

WORKING IN ITALY

EU citizens do not need permits or visas to work in Italy but you must register at the police station and apply for a *permesso di soggiorno* (permit to stay), essential if you intend to live, work or study in Italy. This will necessarily involve an experience of Italian bureaucracy—it can be a lengthy process. The documentation you need changes every year, but will usually include your passport (with your date of entry into the country stamped inside), four passport-sized photographs, and proof that you will be able to support yourself financially while in the country. You can apply for a *permesso di soggiorno* at the foreigners' bureau (*ufficio stranieri*) at any police station.

Non-EU citizens must apply for a *permesso di lavoro* (work permit). If you are working for an Italian company, it will organize the permit and forward the documents to your home country's Italian consulate, which will then issue you with a visa. If you are going to work for a non-Italian company (or if you are self-employed or paid in a foreign currency), you will have to organize the permit yourself through the Italian consulate in your own country. Allow plenty of time—the process can take several months.

STUDYING IN ITALY

EU citizens will need a *permesso di soggiorno* (▷ above).

Non-EU citizens will need a visa. You should apply to the Italian consulate in your home country, who will need proof of your enrolment, proof of payment of fees and evidence of your financial support. The visa will only cover you for the length of your course.

TRAVEL INSURANCE

Check your insurance cover and buy a supplementary policy if necessary. Most policies cover cancellation, medical expenses, accidents, personal liability, and loss of personal belongings (including money). It should cover the cost of getting you home in case of medical emergency. If you have private medical cover, check your policy, as you may be covered while you are away.

HEALTH DOCUMENTS

European citizens should carry a European Health Insurance Card (EHIC), which provides access to state-provided medical treatment (▷ 406). However travel insurance is still recommended for all visitors to Italy, and is essential for non-EU visitors.

PRACTICALITIES

ELECTRICITY
Electricity in Italy is 240 volts, and electrical appliances are fitted with sockets that have two round pins. If your appliances are manufactured for 240 volts, you just need a plug adaptor. If your voltage is different (eg in the US), you need an adaptor and transformer.

LAUNDRY
Most visitors trust their cleaning to their hotel, where your clothes are returned to your room and the (often high) charge added to your bill. Self-service launderettes (la lavandaria automatica) are few and far between, but they are emerging in the larger cities. A wash will cost around €4. Dry cleaning (lavasecco) starts from around €3 for a shirt up to €7.50 for larger items such as jackets and coats, but the quality of the service varies immensely.

MEASUREMENTS
Italy uses the metric system, with all foodstuffs sold by the kilogram or litre. They also use the ettogrammo (100g), usually abbreviated to etto.

PUBLIC TOILETS
There are public toilets at railway stations and in larger museums, but otherwise they are rare. You will probably end up using the facilities in a bar or café. Facilities can be basic, to say the least. Toilet paper may or may not be provided, and sometimes there is only one toilet for both men and women. In some places there is a dish for gratuities—you should leave around 25c.

SMOKING
● Smoking is not permitted on public transport, inside airport buildings and in public offices and buildings.
● Cigarettes and other tobacco products can only legally be sold in tabacchi (tobacconists) to those over 16. The stand-alone tabacchi are only open during normal shop hours (▷ 413). Those attached to bars stay open longer.

VISITING ITALY WITH CHILDREN
Children are welcomed at most hotels and in almost all

(▷ 413)

CLOTHING SIZES

Clothing sizes in Italy are in metric. Use the chart below to convert the size you are at home into metric.

UK	Metric	US	
36	46	36	SUITS
38	48	38	
40	50	40	
42	52	42	
44	54	44	
46	56	46	
48	58	48	
7	41	8	SHOES
7.5	42	8.5	
8.5	43	9.5	
9.5	44	10.5	
10.5	45	11.5	
11	46	12	
14.5	37	14.5	SHIRTS
15	38	15	
15.5	39/40	15.5	
16	41	16	
16.5	42	16.5	
17	43	17	
8	36	6	DRESSES
10	38	8	
12	40	10	
14	42	12	
16	44	14	
18	46	16	
20	48	18	
4.5	37.5	6	SHOES
5	38	6.5	
5.5	38.5	7	
6	39	7.5	
6.5	40	8	
7	41	8.5	

restaurants. Disposable nappies (diapers) and baby foods are available in many food shops (il negozio di alimentari or il supermercato). On the down side, the lack of public toilets and changing facilities, most of which may not be as clean as you are used to, can make things difficult for people with very young children.
● Italian children stay up late—if parents are eating out, the kids go too. This means that most hotels do not offer a baby-sitting/listening service.
● Put on a high-factor sunblock and keep children covered up. If they're swimming, persuade them to cover up and swim in a T-shirt.
● Children are susceptible to heat stroke, so seek shade in the middle of the day and keep

---

CONVERSION CHART

From	To	Multiply by
Inches	Centimetres	2.54
Centimetres	Inches	0.3937
Feet	Metres	0.3048
Metres	Feet	3.2810
Yards	Metres	0.9144
Metres	Yards	1.0940
Miles	Kilometres	1.6090
Kilometres	Miles	0.6214
Acres	Hectares	0.4047
Hectares	Acres	2.4710
Gallons	Litres	4.5460
Litres	Gallons	0.2200
Ounces	Grams	28.35
Grams	Ounces	0.0353
Pounds	Grams	453.6
Grams	Pounds	0.0022
Pounds	Kilograms	0.4536
Kilograms	Pounds	2.205
Tons	Tonnes	1.0160
Tonnes	Tons	0.9842

their heads and necks protected.
● Most hotels will put up to three or four beds in a room so families can stay together; the add-on cost is around 30 per cent of the room price.
● Italian hotels are unheated until the end of October, and, in the south, some remain so.
● If you are bottle-feeding your baby, you might want to bring the formula with you.
● Children between 4 and 12 qualify for a 50 per cent discount on trains; those under 4 go free.
● Books with ideas on how to keep children occupied are available in Rome, Florence and Venice bookshops, and local tourist information offices are also able to help.
● Strollers and pushchairs can be hard work on cobbled streets in hill towns.

VISITORS WITH DISABILITIES
Wheelchair access is improving in the larger cities, but it is virtually non-existent in the rest of the country. It is always worth asking individual establishments what access is like. The narrow, cobbled streets and lack of pavements (sidewalks) in many of the old towns can prove difficult and places like Venice present their own unique set of problems for people with mobility issues (▷ 64).
● Holiday Care in the UK publishes information on

(▷ 64)

PLANNING

accessibility on holiday in Italy (Holiday Care, Sunley House, 4 Bedford Park, Croydon CR0 2AP, tel 0845 124 9971, fax 0845 124 9972, www.holidaycare.org.uk).
● In the US, SATH (Society for Accessible Travel and Hospitality) has lots of tips for holidaymakers with visual impairment or reduced mobility (www.sath.org).

PLACES OF WORSHIP
If you are Catholic you will have no problem finding somewhere to practise your faith in Italy. You will find Catholic churches in even the smallest towns and villages and there are plenty of famous pilgrimage sites to track down. Religious festivals are celebrated enthusiastically throughout the year (▷ 413). Every Wednesday at 11am the Pope celebrates Mass in St. Peter's or Aula Paolo VI in Vatican City (see www.vatican.va for details).

In Rome, members of other Christian denominations are well catered for. The church of All Saints (Ogni Santi) in Via del Babuino is an Anglican church, and St. Paul's within the Wall (San Paolo entro le Mura) in Via Napoli is an American Episcopalian church. The Presbyterian Church of Scotland is at 7 Via XX Settembre. There are several Methodist and Baptist churches in the city and a Lutheran church in Via Sicilia. Seventh Day Adventists meet at Lungotevere Michelangelo 7.

There is a large Jewish community in Italy too. Rome has a Jewish quarter and the religion is widely practised in Venice, Florence, Ferrara and the north. To find synagogues and Jewish community centres in Italy, try visiting www.kosherdelight.com or www.maven.co.il

There are few mosques in Italy, but the main centre for Islam is in Milan. For information contact the Unione delle Comunite ed Organizzazione Islamiche in Italia (UCOII) (Via Padova 38, 20127 Milano, tel 01 83660253) or the Islamic Cultural Society Milano (Via Staro 5, Milano, fax 02 26413204). For details of mosques, halal restaurants and Muslim shops in Italy visit www.muslimtraveller.com

MONEY

A bancomat, the Italian name for a cash machine (ATM)

Italians traditionally use cash, but this is changing. Credit and debit cards are widely accepted, but not for small sums. Food bills are paid for in cash and market traders don't take cards.

CREDIT AND DEBIT CARDS
MasterCard, Diners Club and Visa are widely accepted, as well as Eurocheque cards. Credit cards *(carta di credito)* are becoming more widely accepted, but some smaller establishments still do not take them. Look for the credit card symbols in the shop window or check with the staff.

ATMs
Cash machines, called bancomats in Italy, are plentiful and many are accessible 24 hours a day. Most have instructions in English and other languages. You avoid commission and the exchange rates are better when you withdraw cash with a debit card (Cirrus/Maestro/Delta) from ATMs rather than using a bureau de change, although you may incur bank charges.

TRAVELLERS' CHEQUES
With the growth in the use of plastic cards for payments and cash withdrawals, there has been a decline in the acceptance of travellers' cheques and few places now accept them for payment. The exchange rate for

LOST/STOLEN CREDIT CARDS
American Express
06 7228 0371
Diners Club
800 864064
Maestro
+44 870 6000 459
MasterCard/Eurocard
800 870866
Visa/Connect
800 877232

travellers' cheques is most favourable for those issued in euros, but is generally poorer than for banknotes. Personal cheques drawn on a bank outside Italy cannot easily be changed for cash.

CURRENCY EXCHANGE
Travellers' cheques, cheques and foreign currency can be changed at banks, railway stations and airports, and very often at major hotels (generally at a poorer rate). Many banks in you home country have differing exchange rates depending on the currency being bought or sold. Check with banks for details and shop around before you buy.

10 EVERYDAY ITEMS AND HOW MUCH THEY COST	
Sandwich	€2.50
Bottle of water	50c
Cup of tea or coffee	€1.50–€4
0.5 litres of beer	€3.20–€6.50
Glass of wine	85c–€4.50
Daily newspaper	90c–€3
Roll of camera film	€5
20 cigarettes	€2.50
An ice cream cone	€2
A litre of petrol (gas)	€1.05

PLANNING

BANKS AND POST OFFICES

The largest banks in Italy are Unicredito and Intesa-BCI. Most major banks have cash machines and exchange facilities, although they are often very busy. Banks are usually open from 8.30 until 1 or 1.30, and again for a short time in the afternoon. Some open on Saturday morning. Central post offices usually have a currency exchange that is open throughout the day until 6.30.

BUREAUX DE CHANGE

There are bureaux de change (cambio) in all the main cities, usually open throughout the day until around 7.30. They often change money commission-free, but the exchange rates are not as good as those from banks.

CURRENCY RESTRICTIONS

Import and export of local and foreign currency is limited to €10,330, but check with your embassy before departure if you need to bring large sums into the country. Amounts greater than this should be declared and validated in Italy.

WIRING MONEY

Wiring money is quite a lengthy process and the bureaucracy involved means that it is probably not worthwhile unless you are planning to spend quite a long time in Italy. Ask your bank at home for a list of affiliated banks. You can get money wired out to any bank from home, but if your bank is already in contact with certain banks in Italy it will make the process a lot easier. Always ask

for a separate letter, telex or fax confirming that the money has been sent and ask that it be sent to Swift. It can take up to a week for the money to transfer. If you have a bank account in Italy and at home, you can transfer money directly if both the banks are part of the Swift system of international transfers. Again it takes about 5–7 days, if not longer. American Express Moneygram and Western Union Money Tranfers are faster from the US, but more expensive. Citibank can transfer money for a flat fee of $10 to anywhere in the world (www.c2it.com). Do not wire more money than you need; you can only export €10,330.

TAX REFUNDS

All non-EU shoppers are entitled to an IVA (sales tax) refund on major purchases. Ask for a *fattura* (invoice) when shopping, then present this at customs for stamping when leaving the EU. Return the stamped invoice to the store within four months of the date of purchase and the shop will refund the IVA direct.

BANKNOTES AND COINS

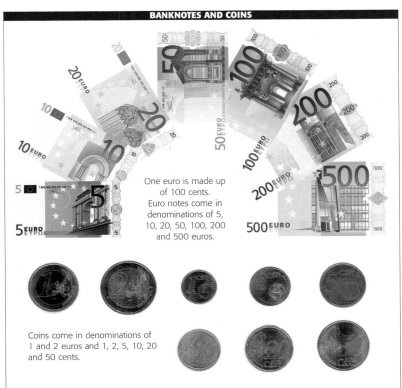

One euro is made up of 100 cents. Euro notes come in denominations of 5, 10, 20, 50, 100, 200 and 500 euros.

Coins come in denominations of 1 and 2 euros and 1, 2, 5, 10, 20 and 50 cents.

PLANNING

BEFORE YOU GO

No vaccinations are necessary for a trip to Italy, unless you are coming into the country from an infected area. If you have any doubts, contact your doctor before you leave.

You should always take out health insurance, and most people do so as part of their travel insurance (▷ 402). You should ensure that it covers the cost of getting you home in an emergency. If you already have health insurance to cover treatment at home, check with your insurer before you leave that you will be covered while abroad.

In addition to health insurance, which is normally included in travel insurance, European nationals should carry a European Health Insurance Card (EHIC). This gives you access to state-provided medical treatment, and you'll be treated on the same basis as an 'insured' person living in the country you're visiting. In Italy this could include free medicines on a doctor's prescription, but it might not cover all the things you'd expect to get free of charge from the NHS in the UK. You may have to make a contribution to the cost of your care.

The EHIC also covers any treatment you need for a chronic disease or pre-existing illness. You need to make arrangements in advance for kidney dialysis and oxygen therapy. To arrange for kidney dialysis while you're away, contact your NHS renal unit in the UK before you travel. For information on oxygen supply services in the countries covered by the EHIC arrangements, including Italy, call the Department of Health's Customer Service Centre on 020 7210 4850. The EHIC won't cover you if the main purpose of your trip is to get medical treatment.

You can apply for an EHIC online through the Department of Health website (www.dh.gov.uk) or by calling 0845 606 2030, or by collecting an application form from a post office.

MEDICAL ASSISTANCE
Ambulance (emergencies)
118

HEALTHY FLYING

• People visiting Italy from as far as the US, Australia or New Zealand may be concerned about the effect of long-haul flights on their health. The most widely publicized concern is deep vein thrombosis, or DVT. Misleadingly known as economy class syndrome, DVT is the formation of a blood clot in the body's deep veins, particularly in the legs. The clot can move around the bloodstream and could be fatal.

• Those most at risk include the elderly, pregnant women and those using the contraceptive pill, smokers and the overweight. If you are at increased risk of DVT, see your doctor before departing. Flying increases the likelihood of DVT because passengers are often seated in a cramped position for long periods of time and may become dehydrated.

To minimize risk:
drink water (not alcohol);
don't stay immobile for hours at a time;
stretch and exercise your legs periodically;
do wear elastic flight socks, which support veins and reduce the chances of a clot forming.

EXERCISES

1 ANKLE ROTATIONS	2 CALF STRETCHES	3 KNEE LIFTS

Lift feet off the floor. Draw a circle with the toes, moving one foot clockwise and the other anticlockwise	Start with heel on the floor and point foot upward as high as you can. Then lift heels high keeping balls of feet on the floor	Lift leg with knee bent while contracting your thigh muscle. Then straighten leg, pressing foot flat to the floor

Other health hazards for flyers are airborne diseases and microbes spread by the plane's air-conditioning system. These are largely unavoidable but seek advice from a doctor before you leave if you have a serious medical condition.

For up-to-date information on travel health issues, see the Department of Health's website on www.doh.gov.uk (in the UK), or the website of the National Center for Infectious Diseases on www.cdc.gov/travel (in the US).

WHAT TO TAKE WITH YOU

It is a good idea to take photocopies of all important documentation, such as travel insurance and your EHIC, which should be kept separate from the originals. You could scan the photocopies and send them to an email address that can be accessed anywhere in the world.

If you are on regular medication, you should ensure that you have adequate supplies for your trip. Make a note of the chemical name (rather than the brand name) in case you need replacement supplies.

HOW TO GET A DOCTOR (UN MEDICO)

• To get in touch with a doctor, ask at your hotel or consult the Yellow Pages

(*Pagine Gialle*) under *Unità Sanitaria Locale*.
- For an ambulance, call 118.
- If you need emergency treatment, go directly to the Pronto Soccorso (casualty department/emergency room) of the nearest hospital.

HOW TO GET TREATMENT WITH YOUR EHIC
- If you need medical treatment while you are away, take your EHIC to the USL (*Unità Sanitaria Locale*) office, which will provide you with a certificate of entitlement.
- Take this to any doctor or dentist on the USL list to receive free treatment. If they need to refer you to a hospital, they will give you a certificate that entitles you to free treatment.
- If you go to a hospital without being referred by a doctor, make sure you show your EHIC to the member of staff who attends to you.
- If you do not have a USL certificate, you will have to pay for treatment and it may be difficult to get the money back afterwards, and then you will probably only receive a partial refund.
- It is advisable to carry a photocopy of your EHIC.

HOW TO GET TREATMENT WITH INSURANCE
- You are strongly advised to take out comprehensive health insurance before you travel. This can be for a single trip or for a period up to one year for several trips. You should also check that it covers all activities you intend to pursue; an extra premium must be paid for winter sports or hazardous activities such as scuba diving.
- Take a copy of your insurance documents to the doctor or hospital—they may be able to bill your insurance company direct.
- If you have to pay for treatment, keep all of your receipts for your insurance claim.

PHARMACIES (FARMACIA)
Most pharmacies (indicated by green crosses outside) are open during normal shop hours, but a rota system operates in major cities such as Rome so that there is at least one open at all times—a copy of the rota is displayed in pharmacy windows.

Enjoying the sun near the fortress of Rocca Scaligera in Sirmione on Lake Garda

DENTAL TREATMENT (UN DENTISTA)
If you have an EHIC, contact the USL, as above. If you do not have an EHIC, contact a private dentist (in the Yellow Pages under *Dentista*). Again, take a copy of your insurance details and keep your receipts.

OPTICIANS
Opticians can usually carry out minor repairs to your glasses, such as replacing screws, on the spot, for little or no charge. Lenses can often be replaced overnight. If you really cannot survive without your glasses or contact lenses, bring a copy of your prescription with you so that you can have replacements made up if necessary.

FOOD AND DRINK
Italy's tap water is generally safe to drink, but you should look out for signs that say *acqua non potabile*, which means the water is not drinkable. Local meat, dairy products, poultry, seafood, fruit and vegetables are all safe to eat.

SUMMER HAZARDS
From April to the end of September the sun is extremely strong and you will need to wear a high-factor sunblock.
Insect bites are not usually dangerous. There is no malaria in Italy, but there is an ongoing mosquito problem, even inland—Milan is particularly bad. Use insect repellent or a mosquito net at night in the summer months and be vigilant near water and woodland areas.

SELECTED HOSPITALS WITH EMERGENCY DEPARTMENTS

CITY	Address	Telephone
ROME		
Policlinico Gemelli	Largo Gemelli 8	06 68371
FLORENCE		
Santa Maria Novella	1 Piazza Santa Maria Novella	055 27581
VENICE		
San Giovanni e Paolo	Campo San Giovanni e Paolo	041 529 4111

ALTERNATIVE MEDICAL TREATMENTS

You can buy homeopathic remedies in most pharmacies. For more detailed advice, contact one of the following associations for practitioners in your area:

Italian Medical Association of Acupuncture (AMIA), Piazza Navona 49, 00186 Roma, tel 06 6868 556

Associazione Terapie Naturale (A.Te.Na), Piazza Wagner 8, 20145 Milano, tel 02 468798

Research Institute in Clinical Homeopathy, Acupuncture and Psychotherapy (CSOCAP), Via Sabotino 2, 00195 Roma, tel 06 3751 6391

COMMUNICATION

Public phones can be found on the streets and in train stations, larger stores and call centres

COUNTRY CODES FROM ITALY	
Australia	00 61
Belgium	00 32
Canada	00 1
France	00 33
Germany	00 49
Greece	00 30
Ireland	00 353
Netherlands	00 31
New Zealand	00 64
Spain	00 34
Sweden	00 46
UK	00 44
USA	00 1

USEFUL TELEPHONE NUMBERS

International operator-assisted service and Italian operator: **170**

Italian directory enquiries: **12**

Information in foreign languages: **176**

Information on addresses from phone numbers: **1412**

AREA CODES FOR MAJOR CITIES	
Bologna	051
Brindisi	0831
Florence	055
Genoa	010
Milan	02
Naples	081
Palermo	091
Perugia	075
Pisa	050
Rome	06
Siena	0577
Turin	011
Venice	041
Verona	045

Calling Abroad
● A call from outside Italy would be dialled as 0039 (011 39 from the US) + 06 (code for Rome) + phone number.
● A call from Rome to the UK would be dialled as 0044 + the area code missing off the first 0 (eg: 01780–1780) + the number.
● A call from Rome to the US would be dialled as 001 + the area code + the number.
● For all calls within Italy, local and long distance, you must dial the regional area code *(prefisso)*, which begins with a 0, as 06 for Rome, 041 for Venice.

CALL CHARGES

Free phone numbers *(numeri verdi)* usually begin with 800 and national call rate numbers begin with 848 or 199. Hotels tend to overcharge for long-distance and international calls, so it is best to make calls from public phones, using telephone cards. Rates are lowest all day Sunday and between 10pm and 8am on weekdays and Saturday.

REVERSE-CHARGE (COLLECT) CALLS

From major Italian cities, you can place a direct call abroad by reversing the charges or by using a phone credit card number. To reverse the charges, call the International Operator on 170 or, for a cheaper alternative, dial the country's operator direct on one of the following free numbers:
Australia (Optus): 800 172 611
Australia (Telstra): 800 172 601
Canada: 800 172 213
France: 800 172 226
New Zealand: 800 172 641

UK: 800 172 440
US (AT&T): 800 172 444
US (MCI): 800 905 825
US (Sprint): 800 172 405

PUBLIC TELEPHONES

If you are calling from a public phone you must deposit a coin or use a phone card to get a dial tone. Note that some pay phones will only accept coins and others only a *carta telefonica* (phone card). Phones that only take coins tend to be less reliable than phone card phones. Call-centre telephones are a better bet than the often poorly maintained public telephones. Here you are assigned a booth to make your call and you pay for the call when you have finished.

PHONE CARDS

Prepaid *carte telefoniche* (phone cards) are used widely. You can buy them from post offices, tobacconists, newsstands and bars. Tear off the corner of the card and insert it in the slot of the public phone. When you dial, the number of units that it holds appears in the window. After you hang up, the card is returned so you can use it until it runs out. The Time phone card is good

value, allowing you to call Europe and the United States at 28c per minute during peak time, but if you are calling between 10pm and 8am, or on Sunday, conventional phonecards are cheaper.

You can also make cheap international calls from the call centres in all major cities.

MOBILE PHONES

It can be very expensive to use your mobile phone abroad and you will often be charged to receive calls as well as make them. If you travel abroad frequently and intend to use your phone, consider swapping your SIM card for a card from an alternative provider—either a foreign network or a dedicated provider of international mobile phone services. You can buy these at mobile phone shops before you leave.

Text messages are often a cheaper alternative to voice calls, but check the charges for making calls and text messages with your service provider. Italian mobile numbers begin with 330, 335, 347, 368 etc.

PLANNING

INTERNET CAFÉS

Internet points, as the Italians prefer to call them, are relatively widespread and cheap—expect to pay around €5 per hour, except in hotels when it can be up to €10 per hour. There is an online directory of internet points in Italy listed by region at http://cafe.ecs.net

After using a public-access computer, make sure you log off fully. Make sure that no-one using the computer after you can gain access to your credit card number, password etc. At the start, select the options instructing the computer not to retain your details. It is also a wise precaution to delete the history of any web browsing before logging off.

Many hotels are now equipped with WiFi or HotSpot facilities that enable you to use your own laptop computer to access the internet. You will need a wireless notebook network card compatible with 802.11g slotted into your computer.

LAPTOPS

If you intend to use your own laptop in Italy, remember to bring a power converter to recharge it and a plug socket adaptor. A surge protector is also a good idea. To connect to the internet you need an adaptor for the phone socket.

If you use an international internet service provider, it's cheaper to dial up a local node rather than the number in your home country. Dial-tone frequencies vary between countries, so set your modem to ignore dial tones.

A post box in Naples

POSTAL SERVICES

Poste Italiane, the Italian postal service, has 14,000 post offices (*posta, ufficio postale* or *PT*) across Italy. You can buy stamps and send letters and packages from here and send faxes and telegrams from larger post

INTERNET CAFÉS	
Region/Town	**Popular Internet Cafés**
The Northwest	
Milan	Gr@zianet, Piazza Duca d'Aosta 14, Stazione Centrale, tel 02 670 0543
	Phone@Point, Viale Sabotino 5, tel 02 5830 7274
Turin	BU.NET, Internet Wine Café, Via San Quintino 13f, tel 0114407517
Venice	TheNetgate, Crosera San Pantalon, Dorsoduro 3812a, tel 041 244 0213
The Northeast and Emilia-Romagna	
Bologna	Net Arena, Via de' Giudei 3/b, tel 051 220850
Padua	Bowling Padua, Via Venezia 124, tel 049 776465
Ravenna	Bowling, Via Romea Nord 231 Savio-Cervia, tel 0544 927982
Verona	Internet Idea, Via Sforza 1, tel 045 8550545
Florence	Internet Point, Via del Moro 58, tel 055 265 8221
Tuscany and Umbria	
Gubbio	Gubbio On Line, Via Madonna di Mezzo Piano 25, tel 075 922 3000
Perugia	The NetGate, Via Cesare Battista 19, tel 075 572 0771
Pisa	Internet Planet, Piazza Cavallotti, tel 050 830702
Rome	TreviNet Pl@ce Internet Point, Via Arcione 103 (Fontana di Trevi), tel 06 6992 2320
	Excape, Via Somalia 227, tel 06 8632 9492
	Stargate I-Café, Via Marrucini 12, tel 445 4953
The South	
Capri	Capri Internet Point, Marina Grande, tel 081 837 8518
Naples	I-cafe Piazza Garibaldi 73 - Staz. Centrale, tel 081 563 4836
	InternetNapoli, Piazza Cavour 146, tel 081 298877
Sicily	
Palermo	Everalways, cso Tukory 198, tel 091 217652
Siracusa	Fermento SRL, Via del Crocifisso 44/46, tel 0931 60762
Sardinia	
Cagliari	Intermedia Point, Via Eleonora d'Arborea 4, tel 070 652201

POSTAGE RATES		
Airmail *(via aerea)*	**Letter (20g)**	**Delivery time**
Europe	€0.41	up to 2 weeks
US	€0.77	up to 2 weeks
New Zealand and Australia	€0.77	2–3 weeks

Posta Prioritaria	**Letter (20g)**	**Letter (21–100g)**	**Delivery time**
Europe	€0.62	€1.25	3 days
US, Africa, Asia	€0.77	€1.55	4–8 days
New Zealand and Australia	€0.77	€1.55	4–8 days

COURIERS	
DHL	800 345345
Federal Express	800 833040
UPS	199 199 345
EMS–International Express Courier (Italian postal service)	800 009966

offices. Although notoriously unreliable, the introduction of a priority mail service (posta prioritaria) has provided a more efficient alternative, relieving the pressure on the old State post service, which has improved.

Vatican City has its own postal service, which is more efficient than the Italian State system. There is a Vatican City post office in the square in front of the Basilica di San Pietro.

Stamps (francobolli) are also available from tobacconists. The value of the stamps they sell you for a letter will be an approximation of the delivery cost. If you need to send a heavy letter or a package, you are better off taking it to a post office where it can be weighed.

For information on all Italy's postal services, contact Poste Italiane (tel 800 222666, www.poste.it). In general, post offices are open Monday to Saturday from 8 to 1.45.

POSTCARDS

These are classed as low priority, so if you want them to arrive at their destination within a couple of weeks, send them *priorità* and put them in an envelope.

SENDING ITEMS OF VALUE

You can use the registered post (raccomandato) to send valuable items; add €2.60 to the price of normal postage. The cost of insured mail (assicurato) depends on the value of the items (€5.15 for packages up to €55.65 in value). Insured mail services are not available to the US.

RECEIVING POST IN ITALY

Poste restante, or general delivery, is known as *fermo posta.* These letters are held at the *fermo posta* counter in the main post office of the town to which the letter is addressed. To pick them up you must present your passport as identification and there is a small charge. *Fermo posta* letters should be addressed in the following way:

> Rebecca Brown,
> Fermo Posta,
> 00185 Roma,
> Italy

If you are receiving items in Italy via courier, you may have to pay IVA of up to 20 per cent to pick up the package.

FINDING HELP

EMERGENCY NUMBERS

From anywhere in Italy	
Ambulance (Ambulanza)	118
Automobile Club d'Italia (ACI)	803 116
Fire Brigade (Vigili del Fuoco)	115
Police (Carabinieri)	112
Police (Polizia)	113
Roadside Rescue (Soccorso Stradale)	803 116
Roadside Rescue (Europ Assistance Vai)	803 803
Samaritans (English-speaking volunteers available 1–10pm)	06 7045 4444

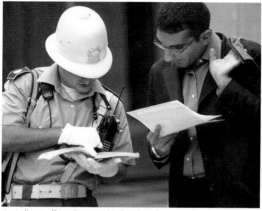

An Italian traffic policeman (vigile urbano) *giving directions*

PERSONAL SECURITY

● Though levels of crime are low, you should take care around railway stations, on public transport and in crowded areas in the larger cities where pickpockets and bag snatchers may be operating. Be particularly wary of groups of children, who may try to distract your attention while stealing from you.

● Passports, credit cards, travel tickets and cash should not be carried together in bags or pockets. Only carry with you what you need for the day and consider making use of safe deposit facilities in hotels.

● An increasing number of robberies are taking place from cars at rest stops/petrol (gas) stations on motorways. You should treat with caution offers of help if you find yourself with a flat tyre, particularly on the motorway from Naples to Salerno, as sometimes the tyre will have been punctured deliberately.

● Lock your vehicle and never leave valuables in the vehicle even if you will only be away for a short time or are nearby.

Recently cars containing luggage have been the targets of car thieves, so avoid leaving luggage in cars overnight or for any length of time.

● Be vigilant when on sleepers/night trains as thieves sometimes operate on the trains and may take the opportunity during the night to rob sleeping passengers. Theft can also take place on trains during the day, so do not leave bags containing valuables unattended.

● Never carry money or valuables in your back pocket. Always keep them secure in a money belt or similar.

● Do not flaunt your valuables. Leave valuable jewellery in hotel safes and, if you are a woman walking around on you own, consider turning any rings with stone settings or similar around so that only the band is visible and not the jewels.

● Never put your camera or bag down on a café table or on the back of a chair, from where it could be snatched.

● Carry bags or cameras on the side of you that is farthest away from the road, to

PLANNING

CREDIT CARD EMERGENCY NUMBERS

Credit Card/Travellers' Cheques	
American Express	tel 06 7228 0371
American Express travellers' cheques	tel 800 914912
Diners Club	tel 800 864064
Eurocard/CartaSi	tel 800 870866
MasterCard	tel 800 870866
Visa	tel 800 819014

minimize the risk from bag snatchers.

● Keep a close eye on your bags and possessions in crowded areas.

● Wear bags across your body, rather than just over your shoulder, from where they can be easily snatched.

● If you have a programmable safe in your hotel room, do not use your date of birth as the code. It is on your passport and your hotel registration.

LOST PROPERTY

ATAC has lost property offices for articles left on buses or trams, as do FS trains for anything left on their trains.

● If you will be making an insurance claim, you need to report the loss to the police to get a statement (denuncia).

● If your passport is lost or stolen, report it to the police and your consulate. The whole process of getting a replacement is easier if you have kept a copy of your passport number or a photocopy of the information page safe (▷ 402).

● If your credit card or bank card is stolen, report it to the police and phone the appropriate bank card/credit card emergency number to cancel your card. All are open 24 hours a day and have English-speaking staff.

● If your travellers' cheques are stolen, notify the police, then follow the instructions given with the cheques.

REPORTING THEFT

Report thefts to a police station, where you will need to make a statement. It is unlikely that you will get your belongings back, but you need the statement (denuncia) to make a claim on your insurance. You can find the address and contact details of your nearest police station in the Yellow Pages (Pagine Gialle) under Commissariato, commando di polizia or stazione dei carabinieri.

POLICE

There are three branches of the police in Italy, any of whom should be able to help you if you are in difficulty.

The carabinieri are military police, easily recognizable by the white sash they wear across their bodies. They deal with general crime, including drug control.

The polizia is the State police force, whose officers wear blue uniforms. They too deal with general crime, and if you are unfortunate enough to be robbed (or worse) they are the ones you will need to see.

The vigili urbani, the traffic police, wear dark blue uniforms and white hats.

WHAT TO DO IF YOU ARE ARRESTED

If you are taken into custody by the police, you could be held for up to 48 hours without appearing before a magistrate. You can also be interviewed without a lawyer present. You do, however, have the right to contact your consul, who is based at your country's consulate, but you are still bound by Italian law. Your consul will not be able to get you out of prison, but will visit you and put you in touch with English-speaking lawyers and interpreters, offer advice and support and contact your family on your behalf. Try to keep hold of your passport and contact your travel insurance company, as your insurance may cover you for legal costs.

EMBASSIES AND CONSULATES

Lists of embassies and consulates are available from tourist offices. You can also look under Ambasciate or Consolati in the phone book or visit www.embassyworld.com

EMBASSIES AND CONSULATES

Australia			
Embassy	Via Antonio Bosio 5, 00161 Roma		tel 06 852721
Consulate	Via Borgogna 2, 20122 Milano		tel 02 7770 4217
	www.italy.embassy.gov.au/		
Canada			
Embassy	Via G B de Rossi 27, 00161 Roma		tel 06 445981
Consulate	Via Vittorio Pisani 19, 20124 Milano		tel 0267581
Ireland			
Embassy	Piazza di Campitelli 3, 00186 Roma		tel 06 697 9121
Consulate	Piazza F Pietro in Gessate 2, 20122 Milano		tel 02 5518 8848
	www.ambasciata-irlanda.it		
New Zealand			
Embassy	Via Zara 28, 00198 Roma		tel 064 417171
Consulate	Via Guido d'Arezzo 6, 20145 Milano		tel 02 4801 2544,
	www.nzembassy.com/home.cfm?c=7		fax 024801 2577
US			
Embassy	Via Vittorio Veneto 119a–121, 00187 Roma		tel 06 46741,
	www.usembassy.it		
Consulate	Lungarno Amerigo Vespucci 38, 50123 Firenze	tel 055 239 8276	
Consulate	Largo Donegani 1, Milano		tel 02 290351
Consulate	Piazza della Repubblica, 80122 Napoli		tel 081 583 8111
Consulate	Via Vaccarini 1, 90141 Palermo		tel 091 625 2426
Consulate	Via Dante 2/43, 16121 Genova		tel 010 584492
UK			
Embassy	Via XX Settembre 80a, 00187 Roma		tel 06 4220 0001
Consulate	Lungarno Corsini 2, 50123 Firenze		tel 055 284133,
			fax 055 219112
Consulate	Via S Paolo 7, 20121 Milano		tel 02 723001,
			fax 02 864 65081
Consulate	Via dei Mille 40, 80121 Napoli		tel 081 423 8911,
			fax 081 422434
Consulate	Piazzale Donatori di Sangue 2/5, 30171		tel 041 5055990,
	Venezia Mestre		fax 041 950254
	www.britain.it		

MEDIA

MAGAZINES

Many Italian magazines are adorned with pictures of scantily clad women, but this isn't necessarily a reflection of their content. If you read a little Italian, magazines such as *Panorama* and *l'Espresso* are good for news, while *Oggi* is a more light-hearted alternative with the focus on celebrity gossip and lifestyle. *L'Espresso* is renowned for its restaurant reviews and is highly respected in Italy.

English-language magazines can be hard to track down in Italy. *Roma C'è* and *Time Out Roma* (monthly) both have English-language sections. *Wanted in Rome* is aimed at resident English-speakers, but also has what's-on listings for the city. *Italy* is a monthly magazine with an associated website at www.italymag.co.uk, which has informative and stimulating articles on all things Italian.

ENGLISH-LANGUAGE NEWSPAPERS

Newsstands in airports and central train stations of major Italian cities carry English-language newspapers such as *The Times*, *Financial Times*, *The Guardian*, *Daily Telegraph*, *The New York Times* and *International Herald Tribune*. Some British papers are available only in their shorter international editions, and you will not get all the supplements in the Sunday papers. Expect to pay about €4 for a foreign newspaper. Some hotels can order a British or US newspaper for you, but it may be a day late. In Milan and Rome it's usually possible to get newspapers on the day of publication after about 2pm.

ITALIAN-LANGUAGE NEWSPAPERS

La Repubblica has a good what's-on section on Thursdays and a glossy magazine supplement on Saturdays called *La Repubblica delle Donne* with excellent articles reflecting all aspects of Italian life and society. There are two daily sports papers published in Italy—*La Gazzetta dello Sport* (pink paper) and the *Corriere dello Sport*; these are mainly

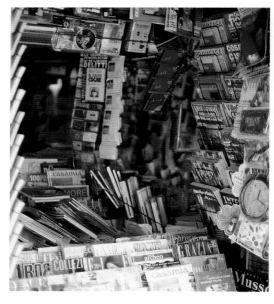

There is a vast array of listings magazines and newspapers to choose from at most newsstands

dominated by football and motor sports news. *La Gazzetta dello Sport* also publishes a supplement on Saturday called *Sport Week*, which tends to cover a wider range of sports and contains excellent full-colour photos and features on the week's events.

Il Messaggero is a local paper, popular with Romans. *La Repubblica, Corriere della Sera, La Stampa* and *Il Sole/24 Ore* are the main national newspapers. *La Repubblica* and *Corriere della Sera* both publish special editions in Rome.

TELEVISION

Italy has three State-run television stations (RAI-1, -2 and -3), which broadcast some worthy entertainment, three stations run by Silvio Berlusconi's Mediaset group (Italia Uno, Rete Quattro and Canale Cinque), and a number of local channels. RAI-3 has international news broadcasts, which include an English-language section. It starts at 1.15am. Italian television is generally pretty frivolous, usually comprising a mixture of soaps, chat shows and American imports dubbed into Italian. Quiz shows also remain popular.

Most hotels, from mid-range upwards, have satellite television, so you can keep up to date with the news and sport on BBC World, CNN and Eurosport.

RADIO

RAI Radio 1, 2 and 3 (89.7FM, 91.7FM and 93.7FM), the State-run stations, have a mixture of light music, chat shows and news—all in Italian. If you are in Rome, Radio Vaticano (93.3FM) broadcasts news in a number of languages, including broadcasts in English at 5.10pm and 9.50pm daily. Radio Italia Network (90–108FM) is the best national radio station for dance music and Radio Deejay (99.7–107FM) plays a variety of popular music and also broadcasts chat shows.

If you have your computer with you while travelling, you can get BBC radio stations including Radio 1, Radio 2, Radio 3, Radio 4, 5 Live and 6 Music on the internet via www.bbc.co.uk/radio. The BBC World Service frequencies in Italy are MHz 12.095, 9.410, 6.195 and 0.648. Visit www.radio-locator.com to track down information on US radio stations online.

OPENING TIMES AND TICKETS

OPENING TIMES

Banks
Usual opening times are 8.30 to 1.30, and 3 to 4.30, Monday to Friday. Some larger branches also open on Saturdays to 1.30.

Post Offices
These are generally open 8 to 1.45, Monday to Saturday.

Pharmacies
Pharmacies are usually open the same hours as shops, but use a rota system to stay open during the afternoon and late into the evening. Look for the list displayed in the shop window providing details of other pharmacies in the area and their opening times.

Museums and Galleries
The opening times for museums and galleries vary greatly, according to the season and the location. Some are open all day, while others close at lunchtimes. Many close one day each week, usually Mondays. Check the Sights section of this book (▷ 65–220), or contact the museum or gallery concerned for the most up-to-date information.

Churches
Most churches open early in the morning for Mass, often around 7. They close at lunchtime, opening again around 4 and closing at 7. Some of the larger churches are open all day, and some may be closed to visitors during services. Check the Sights section of this book (▷ 65–220) for specific opening times or contact the church.

Cafés and Bars
The hours kept by Italy's cafés and bars vary considerably from place to place and according to the season. Some are open for breakfast, others open in time for lunch, and some are only open in the evenings. Wine bars usually close at midnight or later. See the listings in the What to Do section of this book for specific opening times (▷ 221–276).

Restaurants
Restaurants that serve lunch open from 11am and usually close during the afternoon. They reopen, along with those that only serve dinner, sometime after 7pm and stay open late. Pizzerias are usually only open in the evening.

Some restaurants close in August—look for the sign *Chiuso per ferie*. See the Eating and Staying section of this book for specific opening times (▷ 331–398).

Shops
Traditionally, shops open in the morning between 8 and 9 and close for lunch at around 1. They reopen in the afternoon at 3.30 or 4 and close at 8. Most are closed Sundays and Monday mornings, but shops in the larger cities are beginning to stay open all day—look out for the sign *Orario continuato*. See the What to Do section of this book for specific opening times (▷ 221–276).

NATIONAL HOLIDAYS
Shops and banks generally close on public holidays. The road and rail networks are usually very busy at this time. There is a limited public transport service on Labour Day and the afternoon of Christmas Day. However, with the exception of Labour Day, Assumption and Christmas Day, most bars and restaurants remain open.

ENTRANCE FEES
Admission to churches tends to be free, but you may be asked to make a small donation or pay to see inside a church, or part of a church, that is of particular artistic or historic interest; the dome of St. Peter's in Rome, for example. You should expect to pay around €2, but charges can be as high as €8 for main attractions and pilgrimage sites. Museums charge for admission. Expect to pay €5–€10, but discounts apply for students and people over 65. Larger archaeological sites have an entrance fee of around €5, but expect to pay up to €10 for the larger sites such as Pompei, and extra for a guided tour.

Combined Tickets
If you are intending to do a lot of sightseeing in a particular area, it is worth enquiring about combined tickets. For example, in Venice, you can buy a combined ticket for the 15 churches in the CHORUS group of artistically important churches for €8: If you went to see all of them and paid separately it would cost you €30. You can purchase a *Carta Musei* (Museums Card) in Umbria, and Siena has a combined ticket giving access to all of its museums, again providing significant savings. Most major tourist towns or regions have combined tickets covering museums and areas of cultural interest. Further details of these are available from tourist offices (▷ 414).

PLANNING

TOURIST OFFICES

Most major towns and cities have a tourist office within their main railway stations and airports. Known as Azienda Promozione del Turismo (APT), they tend to keep normal shop opening hours (▷ 413). They provide maps and information and can also offer help and advice in finding accommodation.

The Ente Provinciale per il Turismo (EPT) is usually devoted more to the bureaucracy of the tourism industry rather than providing information for tourists. Villages may have a small office known as a Pro Loco, but they often have limited opening hours.

The table below shows the addresses and contact details for the main regional tourist ofices across Italy.

Tourist offices provide free maps, guides and leaflets for visitors

OVERSEAS TOURIST OFFICES

Italian State Tourist Offices Overseas (ENIT)
www.enit.it or www.italiantourism.com

Australia	Level 4, 46 Market Street, Sydney 2000, NSW, tel 02 9262 1666
Canada	175 Bloor Street E, Suite 907, South Tower, M4W3R8 Toronto, Ontario, tel 416 9254 882
UK	1 Princes Street, London W1 8AY, tel 020 7408 1254
US	630 Fifth Avenue, Suite 1565, New York, NY 10111, tel 212-245-5618
	12400 Wilshire Blvd, Suite 550, Los Angeles CA 90025, tel 310-820-1898
	500 North Michigan Ave, Suite 2240, Chicago, Illinois 60611, tel 312-644-0996

TOURIST OFFICES

THE NORTHWEST

Genoa
Via Acqua Verde–Stazione Piazza Principe, tel 010 576791, fax 010 581408, www.apt.genova.it

Turin
Atrium Torino, Piazza Solferino, tel 011 535181, fax 011 530070, www.turismotorino.org

Como
Via Cavour 17, tel 031 3300 111, fax 031 261152, www.lakecomo.org

Mantova
Piazza Mantegna 6, tel 0376 328253, fax 0376 204389, www.aptmantova.it

Milan
Via Marconi 1, tel 02 7252 4301, fax 02 7252 4350, www.milanoinfotourist.com

VENICE
Castello 4421, tel 041 5298711, fax 041 5230399, www.turismovenezia.it

THE NORTHEAST AND EMILIA-ROMAGNA
Padua
Riviera dei Mugnai 8, tel 049 876 7911, 049 650794, www.padovanet.it

Verona
Piazza Brà, Via degli Alpini 9, tel 045 8068680, fax 045 800 3638, www.tourism.verona.it

Vicenza
Piazza Duomo 5, tel 0444 544122, fax 0444 325001, www.ascom.vi.it/aptvicenza

Bologna
Palazzo della Podestà, Piazza Maggiore 1, tel 051 246541, fax 051 639 3171, www.comune.bologna.it/bolognaturismo

Ravenna
Via Salara 8–12, tel 0544 35755, fax 0544 35094, www.turismo.ravenna.it

FLORENCE
Via Manzoni 16, tel 055 23320, fax 055 234 6286, www.firenzeturismo.it

TUSCANY AND UMBRIA
Lucca
Piazza S. Maria, tel 0583 919931, fax 0583 91663, www.lucca.turismo.toscana.it

Pisa
Via Pietro Nenni 24, tel 050 929777, fax 050 929764, www.pisa.turismo.toscana.it

Siena
Piazza del Campo 56, tel 0577 280 551, fax 0577 281041, www.terresiena.it

Assisi
Piazza del Comune, tel 075 812 450, fax 075 813727, www.bellaumbria.net/assisi

Perugia
Piazza IV Novembre 3, tel 075 573 6458, fax 075 572 0988, www.umbriaturismo.it www.perugiaonline.com

ROME
Via Parigi 5, tel 06 488991 or 06 3600 4399, fax 06 481 9316, www.romaturismo.com

LAZIO AND THE MARCHE
Ascoli Piceno
Piazza Arringo 7, tel 0736 298204, fax 0736 298232, www.comune.ascoli-piceno.it

Tivoli
Largo Garibaldi, tel 0774 334 522, fax 0774 331294, www.comuneditivoli.it

THE SOUTH
Capri
Piazza Umberto I 19, tel 081 837 0686, fax 081 837 0918, www.capritourism.com

Naples
Palazzo Reale, Piazza del Plebiscito, tel 081 252 5720, fax 081 418619, www.inaples.it

Pompei
Via Sacra 1, tel 081 850 7255, fax 081 863 2401, www.uniplan.it/pompei

Sorrento
Via T. Maio 35, tel 081 807 4033, fax 081 877 3397, www.sorrentotourism.it

SICILY AND SARDINIA
Palermo
Piazza Castelnuovo 34, tel 091 583847, fax 091 605 8366, www.aapit.pa.it

Siracusa
Via Maestranza 33, tel 0931 464 255, fax 0931 60204, www.flashcom.it/aatsr

Taormina
Palazzo Corvaja, Piazza Santa Catarina, tel 0942 23243, fax 0942 24941, www.gate2taormina.com

Cagliari
Piazza Matteotti 9, tel 070 669255, fax 070 664923, www.cagliaridascoprire.it

PLANNING

FILMS AND BOOKS

FILMS

Italy has been making films from the earliest days of cinema art. Mussolini recognized the cultural value of cinema and in 1937 established Cinecittà outside Rome, a huge campus of studios and technical facilities that is still in operation today.

Italy has produced some world-class filmmakers, including Federico Fellini, Pier Paolo Pasolini, Dino De Laurentii, Michelangelo Antonioni and Roberto Rossellini, to name but a few.

● The so-called spaghetti westerns were the creation of Sergio Leone, who counted Clint Eastwood among his favourite leading men, in films such as *Per Un Pugno di Dollari* (A Fistful of Dollars, 1964) and *Il Buono, Il Brutto e Il Cattivo* (The Good, The Bad and the Ugly, 1967).

● The golden age of Roman filmmaking was in the 1950s and 1960s. The much-acclaimed *Roman Holiday* (1953) thrust Audrey Hepburn into the limelight. You'll recognize many of the landmarks the stars visit, including the Bocca della Verità (▷ 177).

● *Three Coins in a Fountain* (1954) is still a great travelogue for Rome.

● Probably the most famous movie image of Rome is Anita Ekberg's dip in the Trevi Fountain in *La Dolce Vita* (1960), which was also filmed in Tivoli (▷ 188–189) and Viterbo (▷ 187).

● *The Italian Job* (1969), an action-packed comedy with Michael Caine, is famous for its car chases around the streets of Turin. In *Death in Venice* (1971) the city is as big a star as the leading man, Dirk Bogarde; and views of Florence feature strongly in *A Room with a View* (1985).

● Travelling around Italy you may recognize some locations made famous in movies. Scenes in Kenneth Branagh's adaptation of Shakespeare's *Much Ado About Nothing* (1993) were shot in the rolling countryside of Tuscany, and the hilltop Villa Vignamaggio, with its knot gardens and vineyards.

● Terni in Umbria and Arezzo in Tuscany feature in *La Vita è Bella* (Life is Beautiful, 1997), a movie set in 1940s Italy telling the dark

Anthony Hopkins (seated) in Piazza della Signoria in Florence, filming Hannibal

but heartwarming story of a Jewish bookkeeper who struggles to hold his family together during WWII.

● The streets of Ancona are the setting for Nanni Moretti's drama *La Stanza del Figlio* (The Son's Room), which won the Palme D'Or at the 2001 Cannes Film Festival.

● The village of Follina, near Treviso, and the mountainous landscape of the Veneto Alpine foothills provided the backdrop for Richard Attenborough's film *In Love and War* (1997).

● *The Talented Mr Ripley* (1999) was filmed all over Italy, including Rome, Isola d'Ischia and Isola di Procida near Naples, Palermo, Positano and Venice. The sequel, *Ripley's Game* (2002), was shot mainly in the north of Italy and captures the classical architecture of Asolo and Vicenza in the Veneto region.

BOOKS

There are many good books covering Italy's long, vibrant and eventful history and social life in the present day.

● For history in novel form, try *I, Claudius* (1934), by Robert Graves, or Irvine Stone's *The Agony and the Ecstasy* (1965).

● Research is going on all the time at Italy's archaeological sites, and new books emerge offering fresh insights into how people lived in past ages. *Pompeii: History, Life and Afterlife* is a major new work by Roger Ling, of Manchester University, while in *Pompeii the Living City* a historian and a dramatist have collaborated to describe what life was like in the

25 years before the city was engulfed in AD79.

● For younger readers, Caroline Lawrence's *Roman Mysteries* series is set in the Roman Empire, and *The Rotten Romans*—part of the *Horrible Histories* series—takes a light-hearted look at ancient times.

● Anyone interested in Italian politics and society should read *The Dark Heart of Italy* (2003) by Tobias Jones, which describes Italian life under Silvio Berlusconi's administration. The theme is also taken up by Geoff Andrews in *Not a Normal Country*, which explores the rise of Berlusconi at a time of widespread cynicism about politics.

● The Teach Yourself series now includes an introduction to Italian life. *Teach Yourself World Cultures—Italy* by Derek Aust and Mike Zollo (2004) gives you a basic overview that will enrich your time in Italy.

● *Venice—Tales of the City* (2003) is a collection of essays on Venice, edited by Michele Lovric.

● Marlena de Blasi is an Italian who made a name for herself as a food writer and for her book *A Thousand Days in Venice*, which describes her life and recipes in the city. Now she's back with *A Thousand Days in Tuscany*, in which she explores the culinary traditions of the region.

● In *We Etruscans* Anna Rist observes life in a Tuscan hill town over 30 years, and charts changes in lifestyle and landscape, aspirations and habits among the locals.

● *The Humorists' Guide to Italy* is an anthology to keep you amused on a long train journey or on a quiet afternoon by the pool. It includes pieces by D.H. Lawrence, Charles Dickens, Edward Lear, E.M. Forster, Henry James and Mark Twain.

● The Touring Club of Italy has teamed up with the tourism promotion boards of various regions and cities to produce a series of English-language guidebooks with detailed road and city maps. *Vicenza and its Province*, for example, describes how to reach scores of Palladian villas in the countryside.

PLANNING

WEBSITES

HOTELS
www.florencehotelsnetwork
.com
www.1stvenicehotels.com
www.italyhotels.it
www.allitalianhotels.com

WEATHER
www.initaly.com/travel/weather
www.weather.com
www.weatheronline.co.uk/
Italy.htm
www.wunderground.com/global/
IY.html

TELEPHONE NUMBERS
Italian Yellow Pages
www.paginegialle.it

TRANSPORTATION
www.atac.roma.it
www.trenitalia.it

AIRPORTS
www.adr.it
www.ancona-airport.com
www.pisa-airport.com
www.sea-aeroportimilano.it
www.travel-library.com/airports/
europe/italy/
www.veniceairport.it

NEWS
www.repubblica.it
www.ilmessaggero.it
www.corriere.it

TOURISM
Abruzzo and Molise
www.laquila.com
www.moliseweb.com
Basilicata
www.aptbasilicata.it
Calabria
www.turismo.regione.calabria.it
Campania
www.ept.napoli.net
Emilia-Romagna
www.apt.emilia-romagna.it
Florence
www.firenze.net
www.firenzeturismo.it
Friuli-Venezia Giulia
www.regione.fvg.it
Lazio
www.apt.rieti.it
www.apt.viterbo.it
Liguria
www.regione.liguria.it
Lombardy
www.primitaly.it/lombardia
www.turista.it/cerca/italia/
Lombardia/regione-lombardia
Marche
www.turismo.marche.it
Piemonte
www.regione.piemonte.it
Puglia
www.comune.bari.it
Rome
www.enit.it
www.enjoyrome.com
www.romaturismo.it
Sicily
www.aapit.pa.it/default_eng.asp
Sardinia
www.regione.sardegna.it
www.sardegnamediatime.com/
index_en.php
Trentino-Alto-Adige
www.trentino.to
Tuscany
www.turismo.toscana.it
Umbria
www.umbri-turismo.com
Val d'Aosta
www.regione.vda.it/turismo

The Vatican
www.vatican.va
Veneto
www.regione.veneto.it
Venice
www.turismovenezia.it
www.comune.venezia.it

GENERAL
www.estateolie.it
www.firenzemusei.it
www.fodor.com
www.italiansrus.com
www.italiantourism.com
www.itwg.com
www.museionline.it
www.parks.it
www.theaa.com
www.travel-guide.com
www.virtualtourist.com

ITALIAN WORDS AND PHRASES

Once you have mastered a few basic rules, Italian is an easy language to speak: It is phonetic, and unlike English, particular combinations of letters are always pronounced the same way. The stress is usually on the penultimate syllable, but if the word has an accent, this is where the stress falls.

Vowels are pronouned as follows:

a	casa		as in	mat short 'a'
e	vero closed		as in	base
e	sette open		as in	vet short 'e'
i	vino		as in	mean
o	dove closed		as in	bowl
o	otto open		as in	not
u	uva		as in	book

Consonants as in English except:
c before i or e becomes ch as in church
ch before i or e becomes c as in cat
g before i or e becomes j as in Julia
gh before i or e becomes g as in good
gn as in onion
gli as in million
h is rare in Italian words, and is always silent
r usually rolled
z is pronounced tz when it falls in the middle of a word

All Italian nouns are either masculine (usually ending in o when singular or i when plural) or feminine (usually ending in a when singular or e when plural). Some nouns, which may be masculine or feminine, end in e (which changes to i when plural). An adjective's ending changes to match the ending of the noun.

MONEY

Is there a bank/currency exchange office nearby?
C'è una banca/un ufficio di cambio qui vicino?

Can I cash this here?
Posso incassare questo?

I'd like to change sterling/dollars into euros
Vorrei cambiare sterline/dollari in euro

Can I use my credit card to withdraw cash?
Posso usare la mia carta di credito per prelevare contanti?

CONVERSATION

What is the time?
Che ore sono?

I don't speak Italian
Non parlo italiano

I only speak a little Italian
Parlo solo un poco italiano

Do you speak English?
Parla inglese?

I don't understand
Non capisco

Please repeat that
Può ripetere?

Please speak more slowly
Può parlare più lentamente?

Write that down for me, please
Lo scriva, per piacere

Please spell that
Come si scrive?

My name is
Mi chiamo

What's your name?
Come si chiama?

Hello, pleased to meet you
Piacere

This is my friend
Le presento il mio amico/la mia amica

This is my wife/husband/daughter/son
Le presento mia moglie/mio marito/mia figlia/mio figlio

Where do you live?
Dove abiti?

I live in …
Vivo in …

I'm here on holiday
Sono qui in vacanza

Good morning
Buon giorno

Good afternoon/evening
Buona sera

Goodbye
Arrivederci

How are you?
Come sta?

Fine, thank you
Bene, grazie

I'm sorry
Mi dispiace

USEFUL WORDS

yes	thank you	where	when	why
sì	grazie	dove	quando	perchè
no	you're welcome	here	now	who
no	prego	qui	adesso	chi
please	excuse me!	there	later	may I/can I
per favore	scusi!	la	più tardi	posso

Could you help me, please?
Può aiutarmi, per favore?

How much is this?
Quanto costa questo?

I'm looking for …
Cerco …

Where can I buy …?
Dove posso comprare …?

How much is this/that?
Quanto costa questo/quello?

When does the shop open/close?
Quando apre/chiude il negozio?

I'm just looking, thank you
Sto solo dando un'occhiata

This isn't what I want
Non è quel che cerco

I'll take this
Prendo questo

Do you have anything less expensive/smaller/larger?
Ha qualcosa di meno caro/più piccolo/più grande?

Are the instructions included?
Ci sono anche le istruzioni?

Do you have a bag for this?
Può darmi una busta?

I'm looking for a present
Cerco un regalo

Can you gift wrap this please?
Può farmi un pacco regalo?

Do you accept credit cards?
Accettate carte di credito?

I'd like a kilo of …
Vorrei un chilo di …

Do you have shoes to match this?
Ha delle scarpe che vadano con questo?

This is the right size
Questa è la taglia (misura— for shoes) giusta

Can you measure me please?
Può prendermi la misura, per favore?

This doesn't suit me
Questo non mi sta bene

Do you have this in …?
Avete questo in …?

Should this be dry cleaned?
Questo è da lavare a secco?

Is there a market?
C'è un mercato?

NUMBERS

0 zero	6 sei	12 dodici	18 diciotto	40 quaranta	100 cento
1 uno	7 sette	13 tredici	19 diciannove	50 cinquanta	1000 mille
2 due	8 otto	14 quattordici	20 venti	60 sessanta	million milione
3 tre	9 nove	15 quindici	21 ventuno	70 settanta	quarter quarto
4 quattro	10 dieci	16 sedici	22 ventidue	80 ottanta	half mezza
5 cinque	11 undici	17 diciassette	30 trenta	90 novanta	three quarters tre quarti

IN TROUBLE

Help!
Aiuto!

Stop, thief!
Al ladro!

Can you help me, please?
Può aiutarmi, per favore?

Call the fire brigade/police/an ambulance
Chiami i pompieri/la polizia/un'ambulanza

I have lost my passport/ wallet/purse
Ho perso il passaporto/il portafogllio/il borsellino

Where is the police station?
Dov'è il commissariato?

I have been robbed
Sono stato/a derubato/a

I need to see a doctor/ dentist
Ho bisogno di un medico/ dentista

Where is the hospital?
Dov'è l'ospedale?

I am allergic to …
Sono allergico/a a…

I have a heart condition
Ho disturbi cardiaci

COLOURS

black nero	green verde
brown marrone	light blue celeste
pink rosa	sky blue azzuro
red rosso	purple viola
orange arancia	white bianco
yellow giallo	grey grigio

AROUND THE TOWN

English	Italian	English	Italian	English	Italian	English	Italian	English	Italian
on/to the right	a destra	near	vicino a	west	ovest	castle	castello	town hall	municipio
on/to the left	a sinistra	cross over	attraversi	free	gratis	museum	museo	boulevard	corso
around the corner	all'angolo	in front of	davanti	donation	donazione	monument	monumento	square	piazza
opposite ...	di fronte a ...	behind	dietro	open	aperto	palace	palazzo	street	via
at the bottom (of)	in fondo (a)	north	nord	closed	chiuso	gallery	galleria	avenue	viale
straight on	sempre dritto	south	sud	cathedral	cattedrale	town	città	island	isola
		east	est	church	chiesa	old town	centro storico	river	fiume

lake **lago**

bridge **ponte**

no entry **vietato l'accesso**

push **spingere**

pull **tirare**

entrance **ingresso**

exit **uscita**

GETTING AROUND

Where is the train/bus station?
Dov'è la stazione ferroviaria/degli autobus (dei pullman–long distance)?

Does this train/bus go to …?
È questo il treno/l'autobus (il pullman–long distance) per …?

Where are we?
Dove siamo?

Do I have to get off here?
Devo scendere qui?

When is the first/last bus to …?
Quando c'è il primo/l'ultimo autobus per …?

Please can I have a single/return ticket to …
Un biglietto di andata/andata e ritorno per … per favore

I would like a standard/first-class ticket to …
Un biglietto di seconda/prima classe per …

Where is the timetable?
Dov'è l'orario?

Do you have a subway/bus map?
Ha una piantina della metropolitana/degli autobus?

Where can I find a taxi?
Dove posso trovare un tassi?

Please take me to …
Per favore, mi porti a …

How much is the journey?
Quanto costerà il viaggio?

Please turn on the meter
Accenda il tassametro, per favore

I'd like to get out here, please
Vorrei scendere qui, per favore

Is this the way to …?
È questa la strada per …?

Excuse me, I think I am lost
Mi scusi, penso di essermi perduto/a

TOURIST INFORMATION

Where is the tourist information office/tourist information desk, please?
Dov'è l'ufficio turistico/il banco informazioni turistiche, per favore?

Do you have a city map?
Avete una cartina della città?

Can you give me some information about …?
Puo darmi delle informazioni su …?

What sights/hotels/restaurants can you recommend?
Quali monumenti/alberghi/ristoranti mi consiglia?

Please could you point them out on the map?
Me li può indicare sulla cartina?

What is the admission price?
Quant'è il biglietto d'ingresso?

Is there a discount for senior citizens/students?
Ci sono riduzioni per anziani/studenti?

Is there an English-speaking guide?
C'è una guida di lingue inglese?

Are there organized excursions?
Ci sono escursioni organizzate?

Do you have a brochure in English?
Avete un opuscolo in inglese?

Could you reserve tickets for me?
Mi può prenotare dei biglietti?

Can we make reservations here?
Possiamo prenotare qui?

TIMES/DAYS/MONTHS

Monday **lunedì**	Friday **venerdì**	week **settimana**	January **gennaio**	May **maggio**	September **settembre**
Tuesday **martedì**	Saturday **sabato**	today **oggi**	February **febbraio**	June **giugno**	October **ottobre**
Wednesday **mercoledì**	Sunday **domenica**	yesterday **ieri**	March **marzo**	July **luglio**	November **novembre**
Thursday **giovedì**	day **giorno**	tomorrow **domani**	April **aprile**	August **agosto**	December **dicembre**

RESTAURANTS

Waiter/waitress
Cameriere/cameriera

I'd like to reserve a table for ... people at ...
Vorrei prenotare un tavolo per ... persone a ...

A table for ..., please
Una tavola per ..., per favore

Could we sit there?
Possiamo sederci qui?

Is this table taken?
Questa tavola è occupata?

Are there tables outside?
Ci sono tavole all'aperto?

We would like to wait for a table
Aspettiamo che si liberi una tavola

Could we see the menu/wine list?
Possiamo vedere il menù/la lista dei vini?

Do you have a menu/wine list in English?
Avete un menù/una lista dei vini in inglese?

What do you recommend?
Cosa consiglia?

What is the house special?
Qual è la specialità della casa?

I can't eat wheat/sugar/salt/pork/beef/dairy
Non posso mangiare grano/zucchero/sale/maiale/manzo/latticini

I am a vegetarian
Sono vegetariano/a

I'd like ...
Vorrei ...

May I have an ashtray?
Può portare un portacenere?

I ordered ...
Ho ordinato ...

Could we have some salt and pepper?
Può portare del sale e del pepe?

The food is cold
Il cibo è freddo

The meat is overcooked/too rare
La carne è troppo cotta/non è abbastanza cotta

This is not what I ordered
Non ho ordinato questo

Can I have the bill, please?
Il conto, per favore?

Is service included?
Il servizio è compreso?

The bill is not right
Il conto è sbagliato

We didn't have this
Non abbiamo avuto questo

HOTELS

I have made a reservation for ... nights
Ho prenotato per ... notti

Do you have a room?
Avete camere libere?

How much per night?
Quanto costa una notte?

Double/single room
Camera doppia/singola

Twin room
Camera a due letti

With bath/shower
Con bagno/doccia

May I see the room?
Posso vedere la camera?

I'll take this room
Prendo questa camera

Could I have another room?
Vorrei cambiare camera

Is there a lift in the hotel?
C'è un ascensore nell'albergo?

Is the room air-conditioned/heated?
C'è aria condizionata/riscaldamento nella camera?

Is breakfast included in the price?
La colazione è compreso?

When is breakfast served?
A che ora è servita la colazione?

The room is too hot/too cold/dirty
La camera è troppo calda/troppo fredda/sporca

I am leaving this morning
Parto stamattina

Please can I pay my bill?
Posso pagare il conto?

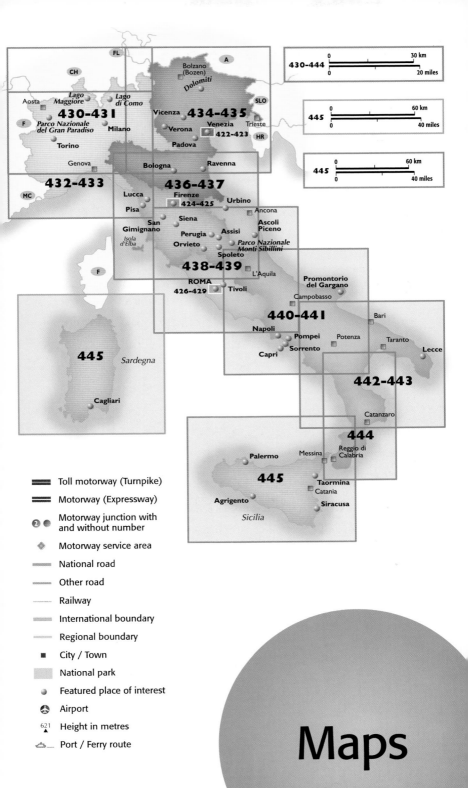

| 430–444 | 0 _____ 30 km |
| | 0 _____ 20 miles |

| 445 | 0 _____ 60 km |
| | 0 _____ 40 miles |

| 445 | 0 _____ 60 km |
| | 0 _____ 40 miles |

FL
CH
A

Bolzano
(Bozen)
Dolomiti
SLO

Aosta
Lago Maggiore
Lago di Como
430–431
Vicenza **434–435**
Venezia
Trieste

F
Parco Nazionale del Gran Paradiso
Milano
Verona
422–423
HR

Torino
Padova

Genova
Bologna
Ravenna

MC
432–433
436–437

Lucca
Firenze
424–425
Urbino
Ancona

Pisa
Siena
Ascoli Piceno

San Gimignano
Perugia
Assisi

Isola d'Elba
Orvieto
Parco Nazionale Monti Sibillini
Spoleto

438–439
L'Aquila

F
ROMA
426–429
Tivoli
Promontorio del Gargano

Campobasso
440–441
Bari

Napoli
Pompei
Potenza
Taranto
Lecce

445
Sardegna
Capri
Sorrento

Cagliari
442–443

Catanzaro
444

Reggio di Calabria
Messina

Palermo
445
Taormina
Catania

Agrigento
Sicilia
Siracusa

— Toll motorway (Turnpike)

— Motorway (Expressway)

❷ ● Motorway junction with and without number

◆ Motorway service area

— National road

— Other road

---- Railway

— International boundary

— Regional boundary

■ City / Town

▨ National park

● Featured place of interest

✈ Airport

621 Height in metres
▲

⚓ Port / Ferry route

Maps

VENEZIA

0 — 200 m
0 — 200 yds

CANNAREGIO

SANTA LUCIA

SANTA CROCE

SAN POLO

SAN MARCO

DORSODURO

MARITTIMA

LA GIUDECCA

Fond Contarini
Rio di S Alvise
Tre Archi
Rio di San Girolamo
Rio del Battello
Rio Mad dell'Orto
Madonna dell'Orto
Rio della Sensa
Rio della Misericordia
Calle d Cerena
Rio de S Giobbe
Canale
Rio della Crea
Cannaregio Piccolo
Canale d Misericordia
Fondamenta Nouv
Gesuiti
Rio di S Caterina
Rio dei Gesuiti
Rio Terra Farsetti
Calle Rielto
Rio Terra Leonardo
Guglie
Campo S Geremia
San Marcuola
Rio di Noale
Rio di Felice
Ca' d'Oro
Ca' d'Oro
Riva de Biasio
San Stae
Rio Terra lista di Spagna
Ferrovia
Fond S Lucia
Fond San Simeon Piccolo
Rio di S Zan Degola
Rio Ca Tron
Rio di S Stae
Rio d Pergola
Rio delle due torri
Rio di S Cassiano
Rio di S S Apostoli
Santa Maria degli Miracoli
Ponte d Libertà
Rio Marin
Rio di S Zuane
Piazzale Roma
Rio d S M Maggiore
Rio d Burchielle
Rio Terra del Pensieri
Rio Nuovo
Rio di Ca' Foscari
Santa Maria Gloriosa dei Frari
Campo S Polo
Beccarie
Rialto
Rialto
San Silvestro
Calle d Fabbri
Calle d Salvador
Scuola Grande di San Rocco
Frescada
Rio del Madonetta
Rio di S Polo
Sant' Angelo
Rio di S Luca
Fuseri
Piazza San Marco
Basilica San Ma
Rio d Tintor
Scuola Grande dei Carmini
Campo S Margherita
Ca' Rezzonico
Ca' Rezzonico
San Samuele
San Toma
Campo Santo Stefano
Rio di S Maurizio
Rio di S Moise
Museo Correr
Pa D
Rio di S Barnaba
Rio di A Raffaele
Rio di S Nicolo
Rio Malpaga
Accademia
Rio di S Trovaso
Rio di S Vio
Rio di S Vidal
Rio di S Santissimo
Rio di S Mauritio
Vallaresso (san Marco)
DORSODURO
Rio Ognissanti
Galleria dell'Accademia
Giglio
Salute
Fond Zattere al Ponte Lungo
San Basilio
Collezione Peggy Guggenheim
Rio della Fornace
Santa Maria della Salute
Zattere
Fond Zattere allo Spirito Santo

Canale dei Lavraneri
Fond San Biagio
Fond d Convertite
Rio del San Biaggio
Fond S Eufemia
S Eufemia
Giudecca
Fond S Eufemia
Canale della Giudecca
Zitelle
Fond de Zitel
Fond San Giacomo
Redentore
Fond della Croce
Calle del Squero
LA GIUDECCA
C delle Scuole
Rio del P Lungo
Calle S Giacomo
Rio d Croce

① ② ③ ④ ⑤

Ⓐ Ⓑ Ⓒ

422

Fonta dei Vetrai

Murano

Murano

Burano
Torcello

San Michele
in Isola

Cimitero

Isola
di San Michele

...a Mendicanti Nuove

Ospedale

Santi Giovanni
e Paolo

d. S G Laterano

Rio d Giustina

Rio di S Francisco

ta Maria
mosa

Scuola di
San Giorgio
degli Schiavoni

Rio d.S Lorenzo

S Ternita

Canale d Galeazze

San Giorgio
dei Greci

S Martino

Rio d Greci

Rio d la Pietà

Rio d Côrne

Canale di Porta Nuova

Darsena
Grande

Rio d Vergini

Isola di
S Pietro

San
Zaccaria

Rio d Ca Dio

Rio San Daniele

Canale di S Pietro

C A S T E L L O

Riva   degli   Schiavoni

Rio del Arsenale

Rio della Tana

Rio di Quintavale

San Zaccaria

Arsenale

Museo
Storico
Navale

Via Giuseppe Garibaldi

Fond a Sant'Ana

Canale   di   San   Marco

Riva dei Sette Martiri

Viale Garibaldi

Secco Marina

Rio di S Giuseppe

Vle 24 Maggio

San
iorgio

San Giorgio
Maggiore

Viale Trento

Viale dei Giardini Pubblici

Rio dei Giardini

Isola
di
S Elena

Isola di
San Giorgio
Maggiore

Canale della Grazia Della Grazia

Viale 4 Novembre

Viale Plave

Canale di S Elena

Via S Elena

(D)   (E)   (F)

423

FIRENZE

0 — 200 m
0 — 200 yds

ROSSELLI

VLE FRATELLI

Viale F Strozzi

V della Pratello
Via F. Dionisi
Via della Fortezza
Via Barbano
Piazza dell'Indipendenza

Via Jacopo da Diacceto
Via Luigi Alamanni
Via Valfonda
Via B Cennini
Via Guelfa
Via Nazionale

Via Magenta
Il Prato
della Scala
Via degli Orti Oricellari
Via Faenza
Via Fiume
Via Nazionale

Via Montebello
Garibaldi
V Giuseppe Corso Italia
Via Solferino
Palestro
Curtatone Via
Via Borgo
Montebello
Vespucci
Amerigo

STAZIONE SANTA MARIA NOVELLA

Piazza della Stazione

Via del Melarancio
Piazza dell'Unità Italiana
Via Sant'Antonino
Via Faenza

Cappelle Medicee
San Lorenzo
Piazza S Lore

Santa Maria Novella

Via Maso Finiguerra
Via Palazzuolo
V di Canaca
Via Benedetta scala
Via del Moro
Via del Porcellana
Palazzuolo

Piazza di Santa Maria Novella

Via Panzani
V del Giglio
V dell'Alloro
Via de' Conti

Via de'Cerretani
Battistero
S Giova
Campa

Via de'Pecori
Via degli Strozzi
Via de' Vecchietti
Via de'Pescioni
Via de' Tornabuoni

Piazza della Repubblica

Orsanmichele

Via de'Lam

PONTE AMERIGO VESPUCCI

Lungarno di Santa Rosa

Ognissanti

Vespucci

Via del Fossi
Via del
Via de'Federighi
Via delle Belle Donne
Via dei Banchi
Via del Trebbio
Via de' Sole

Arno

Via L Bartolini
Via San Giovanni
Via S Onofrio
Borgo
Lungarno Vespucci
Lungarno del Piaggione
Soderini
Frediano
San
Lungarno Corsini
Lungarno Guicciardini

Museo della Casa Fiorentina Antica
Via Porta Rossa
delle Terme

Santa Trinità
Via Porta
Via del Parione
Via delle Terme
Via Borgo Santi Apostoli
Lung degli Acciaiuoli

Piazza de' Signo

PONTE ALLA CARRAIA

Via di Camaldoli
Via dell'Orto
Piazza de' Nerli
V del Drago d'Oro
San Leone
V del Drago d'Oro
Via

Piazza del Carmine
Borgo della Stella
Borgo de'Serragli
Via Santo Spirito
Via Sant'Agostini

Cappella Brancacci

Santa Maria del Carmine

Maffia
Via del Leone
Via Ardiglione

Santo Spirito

Piazza Torquato Tasso
Via Villani

Piazza Santo Spirito

Via del Vellutti
Via Sguazza
Via Toscanella
Borgo San Iacopo

Ponte Santa Trinità
Ponte Vecchio

Galleria degli Uffizi

Museo di St della Scie
Via de'Bardi
Piazza d S Maria sopr'Arn

VIALE
FRANCESCO
V Giano della Bella
V del Casone
PETRARCA

Giardino Torrigiani

Via delle Caldaie
Via del Campuccio
Via Santa Maria
Via della Chiesa
Via Mazzetta
Borgo Tegolaio
Via dello Sdruccolo
V de'Pitti
Via de' Marsili

Piazza de'Pitti

Palazzo Pitti

Via Romana
Via della
Meridiana

Via Guicciardini
San Costa di Glorgi
Via di San Leonardo

Giardino di Boboli

Via Ugo Foscolo
Via P Metastasio
VIA SENESE
Viale N Machiavelli

Via Madonna della Pace
Via del Bobolino

A   B   C

Zanobi
Reparata
Callo
VII Aprile
Santa
Via degli Arazzieri
San Via degli
Guelfa
Camillo
Cavour
Via Giorgio La Pira
Museo di
San Marco
Piazza
San
Marco
Galleria
dell'Accademia
Via Ricasoli
Via Ricasoli de'Pucci
Piazza
della
SS Annunziata
Santissima
Annunziata
Via
Servi
del
V dei Castellaccio
degli
Museo
Archeologico
Nazionale
Ospedale
degli Innocenti
Piazza
Palazzo Medici-
Riccardi
Duomo
del Duomo
Via
ell'oche
Via del Proconsolo
Museo Nazionale
del Bargello
Badia
Fiorentina
della Condotta
Palazzo
Vecchio
d Ninna
V del Corno
Via del Castellani Via de'
Via de Neri
V del Saponai V dei Vagellai
Lung Generale Diaz
Museo dell'Opera
del Duomo
Via Folco Portinari
Via Sant'Egidio
Via dell'Oriuolo
del Corso
Borgo
degli
Albizi
Via
de'Pandolfini
Via Ghibellina
V della Vigna Vecchia
V delle Burella
V Matteo Palmieri
V dei Lavatoi
Via dell'Anguillara
Borgo de' Greci
V Vinegia
V delle Brache
V de' Benci
Borgo Santa
Croce
Corso dei Tintori
Lung delle Grazie
Giardino
dei Semplici
Via Pier Antonio Micheli
Gino
V L S Cherubini
Venezia
Capponi
VIE GIACOMO MATTEOTTI
VIA
DEI
VIA DEGLI ARTISTI
Via Pier
Capponi
Via Giambologna
Giardino della
Gherardesca
Piazzale
Donatello
DELLA
VIA G LA
FARINA
ROBBIA
Via Iacopo Nardi
Via Benedetto Varchi
VIA S C
Pellico
VIA
B SEGNI
VIALE
Via
Giuseppe
Borgo Pinti
Giusti
Via V Alfieri
Laura
della
Pergola
Alfani
Via Nuova
de'Caccini
Borgo
Pinti
Via della Mattonaia
Via I C Farini
Mattonaia
Fiesolana
Colonna
ANTONIO
Piazza
Massimo
d'Azeglio
Via
de'
Pepi
di
Mezzo
Via Pietrapiana
Piazza
dei Ciompi
dell'Ulivo
Allegri
Borgo
La
Croce
Via G B Niccolini
Via
della
CRAMSCI
Via A Manzoni
Via G
Leopardi
Via
Fernando
Paolieri
Piazza
Cesare
Beccaria
Via Giosue Carducci
Pilastri
Pinti
del
V della Vigna Nuova
V Giuseppe Verdi
V dela Rosa
Pepi
Via
de' Macci
Pepi
Via delle Casine
Casa
Buonarroti
Borgo
V San Cristofano
Via dei Pinzochere
Via del Fico
Piazza di
Santa Croce
Via di San Giuseppe
Via delle
Concie
Ghibellina
Via Pietro Thouar
Piazza
Lorenzo
Ghiberti
dell'Agnolo
GIOVINE
ITALIA
VIALE
GIOVANNI
AMENDOLA
Santa
Croce
Tripoli
Via
Via dei Malcontenti
PONTE
ALLE GRAZIE
Torrigiani
Bardi
Piazza
de' Mozzi
Via
dei Renai
Via di San Niccolo
Lungarno
Serristori
Arno
Lungarno della Zecca Vecchia
Piazza
Piave
Lungarno
G PECORI GIALDI
LUNGARNO
PONTE SAN
NICCOLO
Via
del
Bastioni
Vle Giuseppe Poggi
Belvedere
Via
di
Via del Monte alle Croci
Via dell'Erta Canina
Piazzale
Michelangelo
Via San Miniato a Monte
VIALE MICHELANGELO
VIALE GALILEO GALILEI
Via delle Porte Sante
San Miniato
al Monte
Vico delle
V Cramonte
Corti
Via di
Miniato
Via del Bastioni
Via della Fornace
Benvenuto
Cellini
PONTE SAN
NICCOLO

D   E   F

ROMA

500 m
500 yds

I1

BARI

SS16

Capurso   Mola di Bari

delfia   Rutigliano

asamassima   Conversano   Polignano a Mare

Turi   Monopoli

  Savelletri

Castellana   Torre Canne

Putignano   Grotte

  Fasano

Gioia   Noci   **Alberobello**   SS379

del Colle   Locorotondo

  Ostuni

astellaneta   Martina Franca   San Vito

  dei Normanni

Mottola   Ceglie Messapica   SS379   E55

  SS16   **Brindisi**

Massafra   **PUGLIA**   SS613

Palagiano   Grottaglie   SS172

  SS7

Marina di Ginosa   SS7   E90   Latiano   Mesagne   San Pietro

TARANTO   Francavilla Fontana   Vernotico

  Oria   SS613

  San Donaci

SS7ter   Manduria   San Cataldo

  San Pancrazio   Squinzano

  Salentino

  Campi

  Salentina   **Lecce**

Campomarino   Copertino   SS16

  Porto   Martano   **Otranto**

  Cesareo   SS101

  Nardo   Galatina   SS16

Golfo di   Galatone   Maglie

Taranto   Parabita   Santa Cesarea

Gallipoli   Casarano   SS275   Terme

  Ugento   SS274

  Gagliano del Capo

  Marina

  di Leuca

I2

I3

Cariati

  SS106

Campana

  Ciro Marina

  E90

velli   Strongoli

  SS107

  E846

Petilia

Policastro   Crotone

  Cutro

SS106   E90   Isola di

  Capo Rizzuto

I4

Mario Mameli 445 D14
Marotta 437 J7
Marradi 436 G6
Marsala 445 H17
Marsciano 438 H8
Marsico Nuovo 442 M12
Marta 437 G9
Martigny 430 B2
Martina Franca 443 P12
Martis 445 D11
Massa 436 E6
Massa Marittima
 436 F8
Massafra 443 P12
Matelica 437 J8
Matera 442 N12
Mazara del Vello
 445 H17
Medicina 437 G5
Mel 435 H3
Melegnano 431 E4
Melfi 441 M11
Melito di Porto Salvo
 444 M16
Menaggio 431 D3
Merano 434 G2
Mesola 435 H5
Messina 445 M16
Mestre 435 H4
Metaponto 442 P12
Migliarino 434 H5
Migliarino 436 F7
Miglionico 442 N12
Milano 431 D4
Milano Marittima
 437 H6
Milazzo 445 M16
Mileto 444 N15
Minervino Murge
 441 N11
Minozzo 436 F6
Minturno 440 K11
Mira 435 H4
Mirandola 433 E4
Mirandola 434 G5
Missanello 442 N12
Modena 436 F5
Modica 445 L18
Modigliana 437 G6
Moena 434 G2
Moglia 434 F5
Mola di Bari 443 P11
Molare 433 D5
Molfetta 441 N11
Molinella 437 G5
Moliterno 442 M12
Molveno 434 F3
Moncalieri 432 C4
Mondolfo 437 J7
Mondovi 432 C5
Mondragone 440 K11
Moneglia 433 E6
Monfalcone 435 J3
Monguelfo 435 H2
Monopoli 443 P11
Monreale 445 J16
Monselice 434 G4
Monsummano Terme
 436 F6

Montagnana 434 G4
Montalcino 436 G8
Montalto delle Marche
 439 K8
Monte Argentario
 438 F9
Monte San Savino
 437 G7
Monte Sant'Angelo
 441 M10
Montebelluna 435 H3
Montecchio Maggiore
 434 G4
Montecchio 438 H8
Montecchio 431 D3
Montecorvino Rovella
 442 L12
Montefalco 438 H8
Montefiascone 438 H9
Montefiorino 436 F6
Montegrotto Terme
 434 G4
Montella 441 L12
Montenero di Bisaccia
 439 L10
Montepulciano 437 G8
Montereale 439 J9
Monteriggioni 436 G7
Monterotondo 438 H10
Montesano sulla Marcellana
 442 M12
Montesarchio 440 L11
Montevarchi 436 G7
Monti 445 D11
Montichiari 434 F4
Monticiano 436 G8
Montorio al Vomano
 439 K9
Monza 431 D4
Morano Calabro
 442 N13
Morbegno 431 E3
Morciano di Romagna
 437 H6
Morcone 440 L11
Mores 445 D12
Moretta 432 B5
Morgex 430 B3
Mormanno 442 N13
Mortara 433 D4
Motta di Livenza 435 H3
Mottola 443 P12
Muccia 437 J8
Muggia 435 K4
Muravera 445 D14
Muro Lucano 442 M12

Napoli (Naples) 440 K12
Narni 438 H9
Naturno 434 G2
Navelli 439 K9
Nepi 438 H9
Nereto 439 K8
Nervi 433 D5
Nettuno 438 H10
Nicastro 444 N15
Nice 432 B7
Nicosia 445 L17

Nizza Monferrato
 432 C5
Nocera Umbra 438 J8
Noceto 433 E5
Noci 443 P12
Noepoli 442 N13
Nogara 434 G4
Nola 440 L11
Noli 432 C6
Nora 445 D14
Norcia 439 J8
Noto 445 L18
Nova 441 M11
Nova Levante 434 G2
Novafeltria 437 H6
Novara 431 D4
Novellara 434 F5
Noventa Vicentina
 434 G4
Novi Ligure 433 D5
Numana 439 K7
Nuoro 445 D12

Occhiobello 434 G5
Oderzo 435 H3
Offida 439 K8
Ogliastro Cilento 442 L12
Olbia 445 D11
Oleggio 431 D3
Omegna 431 C3
Oppido Lucano 442 N12
Oppido Mamertina
 444 N16
Ora 434 G2
Orbassano 432 B4
Oria 431 D3
Oriolo 442 N13
Oristano 445 C13
Ormea 432 C6
Orosei 445 E12
Orsogna 439 K9
Orta 441 M11
Ortisei 434 G2
Ortona 439 K9
Orvieto 438 H8
Orvinio 439 J9
Oschiri 445 D12
Osimo 439 J7
Ospedaletti 432 B6
Ostiglia 434 G4
Ostra 437 J7
Otranto 443 R12
Ottana 445 D12
Ottaviano 440 L11
Ottone 433 D5
Oulx 432 B4
Ovada 433 D5
Ozieri 445 D12

Pachino 445 M18
Padova 434 G4
Paesana 432 B5
Paestum 442 L12
Palagiano 443 P12
Palau 445 D11
Palazzo San Gervasio
 441 N11

Palazzolo Acreide 445 L18
Palena 439 K10
Palermo 445 J16
Palestrina 440 J10
Palinuro 442 M13
Palmanova 435 J3
Palmi 444 M16
Palombara Sabina
 438 H9
Paluzza 435 J2
Pandino 431 E4
Paola 444 N14
Papasidero 442 M13
Parabita 443 Q13
Parma 434 F5
Passignano sul Trasimeno
 437 H8
Paterno 442 M12
Paterno 445 L17
Paternopoli 441 L11
Pavia 433 D4
Pavullo nel Frignano
 436 F6
Pedraces 434 H2
Pegli 433 D5
Pejo 434 F2
Pellaro 444 M16
Pellegrino Parmense
 433 E5
Pennabilli 437 H7
Penne 439 K9
Pergola 437 J7
Perugia 437 H8
Pesaro 437 J6
Pescara 439 K9
Pescasseroli 440 K10
Peschici 441 M10
Peschiera del Garda
 434 F4
Pescia 436 F6
Pescina 439 K10
Pescocostanzo 439 K10
Pescolanciano 440 K10
Pescopagano 441 M12
Petilia Policastro 444 P14
Petrella Tifernina 440 L10
Piacenza 433 E4
Piadena 434 F4
Piana Crixia 432 C5
Pianoro 436 G6
Piazza al Serchio 436 F6
Piazza Armerina 445 L17
Picerno 442 M12
Pico 440 J11
Piedimonte Matese
 440 K11
Pienza 437 G8
Pietra Ligure 432 C6
Pietrasanta 436 E6
Pieve di Teco 432 C6
Pieve di Cadore
 435 H2
Pieve Santo 437 H7
Pievepelago 436 F6
Pila 435 H5
Pinerolo 432 B5
Pineto 439 K9
Pinzolo 434 F3
Piobbico 437 H7

ACKNOWLEDGMENTS

Abbreviations for the credits are as follows:
AA = AA World Travel Library, t (top), b (bottom), c (centre), l (left), r (right), bg (background)

UNDERSTANDING ITALY

4cl AA/Clive Sawyer; 4cc AA/Max Jourdan; 4cr AA/Terry Harris; 5cr AA/Ken Paterson; 6cl AA/Max Jourdan; 6cc/cr AA/Clive Sawyer; 8tl AA/Max Jourdan; 8tr AA/Clive Sawyer; 8cc AA/Simon McBride; 8br AA/Clive Sawyer; 8br AA/Eric Meacher; 9tl AA/Ken Paterson; 9cl AA/Jerry Edmanson; 9cl AA/Tony Souter; 9bl AA/Simon McBride; 10tr AA/Clive Sawyer; 10tc AA/Max Jourdan; 10cl/cr/br AA/Clive Sawyer.

LIVING ITALY

11 AA/Max Jourdan; 12bg AA/Clive Sawyer; 12cl AA/Ken Paterson; 12tr AA/Ken Paterson; 12cr AA/Tony Souter; 12cc AA/Clive Sawyer; 12br Ingo Arndt/Nature Picture Library; 13tl AA/Ken Paterson; 13tr AA/Ken Paterson; 13cl Asgeir Helgestad/Nature Picture Library; 13cc AA/Max Jourdan; 13cr AA/Clive Sawyer; 14bg/cl AA/Clive Sawyer; 14tr AA/Clive Sawyer; 14cl Lamalfafoto/Team/Grazia Neri; 14cr AA/Clive Sawyer; 14br Alex Kouprianoff; 14 vertical strip AA/Clive Sawyer; 15tc Franco Origlia/Getty Images; 15cl AA/Clive Sawyer; 15cc AA/Max Jourdan; 15cr AA/Dario Miterdiri; 15bc AA/Alex Kouprianoff; 16bg AA/Max Jourdan; 16tc AA/Simon McBride; 16cl AA/Simon McBride; 16cr AA/Max Jourdan; 16cc/r AA/Simon McBride; 16br AA/Simon McBride; 17tl Marco Galbiati/Grazia Neri; 17tr AA/Tony Souter; 17cr AA/Max Jourdan; 17 horizontal strip AA/Simon McBride; 18bg AA/Simon McBride; 18tl AA/Clive Sawyer; 18tr Giulio Andreini/Marka; 18cr AA/Max Jourdan; 18cl AA/Clive Sawyer; 19tl AA/Clive Sawyer; 19tr AA/Simon McBride; 19cc AA/Tony Souter; 19cl AA/Dario Miterdiri; 19cr Giulio Andreini/Marka; 20bg AA/Clive Sawyer; 20tl AA/Clive Sawyer; 20tc AA/Jim Holmes; 20cc AA/Alex Kouprianoff; 20b AA/Simon McBride; 21tl AA/Simon McBride; 21tr SIPA/Rex; 21cl Sipa Press/Rex Features; 21cc AA/Jim Holmes; 21cr AA/Alex Kouprianoff; 21cl AA/Ken Paterson; 22bg AA/Alex Kouprianoff; 22tr AA/Pete Bennett; 22c AA/Clive Sawyer; 22br Clive Rose/Getty Images; 22 vertical strip AA/Max Jourdan; 23tl AA/Terry Harris; 23tr AA/Max Jourdan; 23cl Michael Steele/Getty Images; 23cc Luca Lozzi/Getty Images; 24bg AA/Max Jourdan; 24tl AA/Ken Paterson; 24tc AA/Dario Miterdiri; 24tr AA/Simon McBride; 24cl AA/Max Jourdan; 24cc AA/Dario Miterdiri; 24cr AA/Allstar/Cinetext Collection; 24cl AA/Ken Paterson.

THE STORY OF ITALY

25 AA/Dario Miterdiri; 26bg AA/Clive Sawyer; 26cc AA/Ken Paterson; 26cr AA/The Story of the Nations - Carthage; 26bl AA/Ken Paterson; 26br AA/Clive Sawyer; 27cl AA/Pat Aithie; 27cc AA/The Story of the Nations - Carthage; 27cr AA; 27cc AA/Tony Souter; 27cr AA/Clive Sawyer; 27bc AA/Jim Holmes; 28bg AA/Max Jourdan; 28cc AA/Story of the Nations - Rome; 28cr AA; 28bl AA/Max Jourdan; 28br AA/Clive Sawyer; 29cl AA/Max Jourdan; 29cc AA; 29cr AA; 29bc AA/Alex Kouprianoff; 29br Giraudon/Bridgeman Art Library; 30bg AA/The Story of the Nations - The Goths; 30cr AA; 30bl Mary Evans Picture Library; 30bc Giraudon/Bridgeman Art Library; 31cl AA/The Story of the Nations - The Goths; 31cc AA/James Tims; 31cr AA; 31cl/cc AA/Clive Sawyer; 31bl Bridgeman Art Library; 31bc Bridgeman Art Library; 31br AA/Tony Souter; 32bg/br AA/Ken Paterson; 32cl Roger-Viollet, Paris; 32bl AA/Max Jourdan; 32bc AA/Clive Sawyer; 33cl AA; 33cc AA; 33cr AA; 33bc AA/Clive Sawyer; 33br AA/Simon McBride; 34bg/br AA/Jim Holmes; 34cc AA/Simon McBride; 34cr AA; 34bl Giraudon/Bridgeman Art Library; 35cl Biblioteca Marucelliana, Florence/Bridgeman Art Library/Alinari; 35cc both AA; 35cr AA/Simon McBride; 35cr AA; 35bc AA/Dario Miterdiri; 35br AA/Clive Sawyer; 36bg AA; 36cl AA; 36cc AA; 36bl AA/Clive Sawyer; 36bc AA; 36br AA; 37cl Mary Evans Picture Library; 37cc AA; 37cc Mary Evans Picture Library; 37cr AA; 37bc

AA/Peter Wilson; 37br AA/The Story of the Nations - Venice; 38bg/br Illustrated London News; 38cc Mary Evans Picture Library; 38cr Illustrated London News; 38bl Mary Evans Picture Library; 39cl Mary Evans Picture Library; 39cr AA/Clive Sawyer; 39bc Mary Evans Picture Library; 39br Mary Evans Picture Library; 40bg AA/Simon McBride; 40cl SIPA/Rex; 40 all others AA/Clive Sawyer.

ON THE MOVE

41 AA/Clive Sawyer; 42-47t Pierfabrizio di Marco/Trieste Airport; 42cl Pierfabrizio di Marco/Trieste Airport; 44c Aeroporto di Venezia Marco Polo; 46c AA/Simon McBride; 48-55t AA/Simon McBride; 48c AA/Simon McBride; 50cr AA/Simon McBride; 50cc AA/John Miller; 50bl Alessio Pedretti; 51c AA/Simon McBride; 51bl EsseBi Italia; 52c AA/Terry Harris; 52 Tunnel Sign - Automobile Club d'Italia; 52 Other Signs - EsseBi Italia; 54c AA/Jim Holmes; 56-59t AA/Simon McBride; 56c AA/Simon McBride; 57/58 AA/Simon McBride; 60-61t Pierfabrizio di Marco/Trieste Airport; 60c Air One; 61cr Turrin Fotografia/Trieste Airport; 61b Aeroporto di Venezia Marco Polo; 62-63t AA/Dario Miterdiri; 62c AA/Max Jourdan; 63c AA/Max Jourdan; 64t AA/Nicholas Sumner; 64b Regency San Marino.

THE SIGHTS

65 AA/Clive Sawyer; p66-219bg AA/Richard Ireland; 67tl AA/Tony Souter; 67tr AA/Max Jourdan; 68tl AA/Tony Souter; 68tr World Pictures; 69 AA/Max Jourdan; 70 AA/Max Jourdan; 71 AA/Max Jourdan; 72tc AA/Pete Bennet; 72cl AA/Clive Sawyer; 72cr/bc AA/Max Jourdan; 73 AA/Clive Sawyer; 75cl AA/Max Jourdan; 75cr AA/Clive Sawyer; 76 Robert Harding Picture Library/Alamy; 77tl AA/Clive Sawyer; 77tr AA/Tony Souter; 78tc Carlo Cerchioli/Grazia Neri; 78cl Fiat Auto; 78cc Claudio Penna/Marka; 78cr John Heseltine; 79 Ermes Lasagni/Marka; 80tl Pictures Colour Library; 80tr AA/Clive Sawyer; 82cl AA/Simon McBride; 83tl AA/Clive Sawyer; 83tr AA/Simon McBride; 84tc/cl/cc AA/Clive Sawyer; 84cr AA/Dario Miterdiri; 84b AA/C Sawyer; 85tl AA/Peter Wilson; 85cr AA/Clive Sawyer; 86tc/cl/cc/cr AA/Simon McBride; 87tl/cr AA/Simon McBride; 87b AA/Clive Sawyer; 88tl/tr AA/Simon McBride; 89tl/tr/b AA/Clive Sawyer; 90tc AA/Simon McBride; 90cl AA/Simon McBride; 90cr Bridgeman Art Library; 90b Giraudon/Bridgeman Art Library/Alinari; 91tl Bridgeman Art Library; 92t/cl AA/Simon McBride; 93tc AA/Rich Newton; 93cl AA/Simon McBride; 93cr AA/Clive Sawyer; 94 AA/Clive Sawyer; 95 AA/Simon McBride; 96t AA/Simon McBride; 96cl AA/Clive Sawyer; 97 AA/Simon McBride; 98 AA/Simon McBride; 99t AA/Simon McBride; 99cr AA/Rich Newton; 100tl AA/Clive Sawyer; 100tc AA/Simon McBride; 100tr AA/Clive Sawyer; 101 AA/Dario Miterdiri; 102tl AA/Simon McBride; 102tr AA/Clive Sawyer; 104tl Italian Tourist Board; 104tr James Davis Worldwide; 105 AA/Clive Sawyer; 106tl AA/Clive Sawyer; 106tr World Pictures; 107 World Pictures; 108 Italian Tourist Board; 109tl AA/Tony Souter; 109tr World Pictures; 110 AA/Tony Souter; 111tl AA/Clive Sawyer; 111tr Pierfabrizio di Marco/Trieste Airport; 112 AA/Clive Sawyer; 113 AA/Pete Bennett; 114 AA/Clive Sawyer; 116cl AA/Ken Paterson; 117tl AA/C Sawyer; 117tc/tr AA/Simon McBride; 118tc/cl AA/Simon McBride; 118cc AA/Clive Sawyer; 118cr AA/Ken Paterson; 119 AA/Simon McBride; 120 AA/Simon McBride; 121 AA/Simon McBride; 122tc AA/Barrie Smith; 122cl AA/Jerry Edmanson; 122cr/bl AA/Simon McBride; 123 AA/Simon McBride; 124tl AA/Simon McBride; 124tc AA/Clive Sawyer; 124tr AA/Simon McBride; 125 AA/Simon McBride; 126tl AA/Simon McBride; 126tr AA/Simon McBride; 127 AA/Simon McBride; 128tc AA/Clive Sawyer; 128cl AA/Jerry Edmanson; 129t AA/Clive Sawyer; 129bc AA/Simon McBride; 130t AA/Simon McBride; 130cl AA/Barrie

Smith; 131 AA/Simon McBride; 132 AA/Simon McBride; 133 AA/Clive Sawyer; 134tl AA/Barrie Smith; 134tc/tr AA/Clive Sawyer; 136 AA/Ken Paterson; 137t AA/Peter Davies; 137tr AA/Terry Harris; 138tl AA/Simon McBride; 138tr AA/Ken Paterson; 139tl AA/Terry Harris; 139tr AA/Ken Paterson; 140tl AA/Clive Sawyer; 140tr AA/Terry Harris; 141tl AA/Ken Paterson; 141tr AA/Terry Harris; 142t AA/Clive Sawyer; 142cl AA/Jim Holmes; 143tl AA/Simon McBride; 143tr AA/Ken Paterson; 144tl AA/Terry Harris; 144tc AA/Simon McBride; 144tr AA/Ken Paterson; 145tl AA/Ken Paterson; 145tr AA/Simon McBride; 146 AA/Terry Harris; 147 World Pictures; 148t AA/Ken Paterson; 148cl AA/Terry Harris; 149 AA/Clive Sawyer; 150tl AA/Clive Sawyer; 150tc AA/Ken Paterson; 150tr AA/Clive Sawyer; 151t AA/Ken Paterson; 151cr AA/Simon McBride; 152tc AA/Jerry Edmanson; 152cl AA/Clive Sawyer; 152cc AA/Simon McBride; 152cr AA/Clive Sawyer; 152cb AA/Clive Sawyer; 153 AA/Clive Sawyer; 154 AA/Terry Harris; 155tl AA/Terry Harris; 155tr AA/Ken Paterson; 156tl AA/Ken Paterson; 156tc AA/Terry Harris; 156tr AA/Ken Paterson; 158tc AA/Dario Miterdiri; 158cl AA/Dario Miterdiri; 158cr AA/Peter Wilson; 158bl AA/Alex Kouprianoff; 158bc AA/Dario Miterdiri; 159tl/tr AA/Simon McBride; 160tc/cl AA/Dario Miterdiri; 160cr AA/Peter Wilson; 160bl AA/Alex Kouprianoff; 160bc AA/Dario Miterdiri; 161tl AA/Simon McBride; 161cr AA/Clive Sawyer; 161b AA/Peter Wilson; 162tc AA/Simon McBride; 162cl/cc AA/Jim Holmes; 162cr AA/Simon McBride; 162b AA/Alex Kouprianoff; 163 AA/Jim Holmes; 164tc/cl AA/Simon McBride; 164cr AA/Peter Wilson; 164bl AA/Simon McBride; 165c AA/Clive Sawyer; 165b AA/Peter Wilson; 166 AA/Peter Wilson; 167tl AA/Alex Kouprianoff; 167tc AA/Jim Holmes; 167tr AA/Peter Wilson; 168tc/cl/cr/b AA/Simon McBride; 169t/b AA/Jim Holmes; 170c Dario Miterdiri; 170b AA/Simon McBride; 171tl AA/Alex Kouprianoff; 171tc AA/Simon McBride; 171tr AA; 172t AA; 173t/cr AA/Jim Holmes; 174 AA/Jim Holmes; 175 AA/Jim Holmes; 176 AA/Simon McBride; 177tl AA/Jim Holmes; 177tr AA/Simon McBride; 178t AA/Dario Miterdiri; 179tl AA/Jim Holmes; 179tc AA/Simon McBride; 179tr AA/Dario Miterdiri; 180tl AA/Simon McBride; 180tc AA/Dario Miterdiri; 180tr AA/Peter Wilson; 182 AA/Clive Sawyer; 183tl AA/Clive Sawyer; 183tc/tr AA/Tony Souter; 184tl AA/Simon McBride; 184tr AA/Clive Sawyer; 185tl AA/Clive Sawyer; 185tr AA/Tony Souter; 186t AA/Tony Souter; 187tl AA/Clive Sawyer; 187tr AA/Tony Souter; 188 AA/Simon McBride; 189 AA/Simon McBride; 190 AA/Tony Souter; 192tl AA/Clive Sawyer; 192tc AA/Max Jourdan; 192tr AA/Clive Sawyer; 193 World Pictures; 194 World Pictures; 195t AA/Clive Sawyer; 195 AA/Clive Sawyer; 197 AA/Clive Sawyer; 198 AA/Max Jourdan; 199 AA/Max Jourdan; 201 AA/Max Jourdan; 202tl AA/Tony Souter; 202tr AA/Clive Sawyer; 203 AA/Clive Sawyer; 204 AA/Max Jourdan; 205 AA/Max Jourdan; 206 AA/Clive Saywer; 207tl AA/Max Jourdan; 207cr AA/Clive Sawyer; 208tl AA/Tony Souter; 208tr AA/Clive Sawyer; 209t AA/Clive Sawyer; 209cr AA/Max Jourdan; 210tl AA/Clive Sawyer; 210tr AA/Tony Souter; 212-219 AA/Clive Sawyer; 220tl AA/Clive Sawyer; 220tr John Miller.

WHAT TO DO

221 AA/Max Jourdan; 222-224t AA/Jim Holmes; 224l/r AA/Max Jourdan; 225-226t Archivio Teatro del Maggio Musicale Fiorentino/Gianluca Moggi/New Press Photo Firenze; 225cr AA/Clive Sawyer; 226cl Archivio Teatro del Maggio Musicale Fiorentino; 226cr AA/Clive Sawyer; 227t Brand X Pictures; 227cl Matilda Club, Sorrento; 227cr AA/Clive Sawyer; 228-232t AA; 229cl AA/Simon McBride; 229cr Corbis; 230l Nazionale Turismo Equistre; 230r AA/Clive Sawyer; 231l AA/Anna Mockford and Nick Bonetti; 232cl/cr AA/K Paterson; 233t/cl Time Elevator, Rome; 233cr AA/Max Jourdan; 234t AA/Dario Miterdiri; 234b AA/Simon McBride; 235-239t AA/Max Jourdan; 235c AA/Max Jourdan; 237c AA/Clive Sawyer; 239c AA/Molly Lynch; 240-244t AA/Dario Miterdiri; 240c AA/Clive Sawyer; 241c AA/Anna Mockford and Nick

Bonetti; 242c AA/Clive Sawyer; 245-246 AA/Clive Sawyer; 246c AA/Clive Sawyer; 247-251t AA/Simon McBride; 247c AA/Clive Sawyer; 248c AA/Simon McBride; 249c Archivio Teatro del Maggio Musicale Fiorentino; 252-260t AA/Simon McBride; 254c AA/Ken Paterson; 261-267t Flavio Raimondo/Fabriano; 261c AA/Alex Kouprianoff; 262c AA/Clive Sawyer; 264c AA/Jim Holmes; 265c AA/Jim Holmes; 268-269t AA/Clive Sawyer 268c AA/Clive Sawyer; 270-273t Brand X Pictures; 270c AA/Max Jourdan; 272 AA/Max Jourdan; 274-276t AA/Clive Sawyer; 274c AA/Clive Sawyer; 275c AA/Clive Sawyer.

OUT AND ABOUT

277 AA/Tony Souter; 279 AA/Tony Souter; 280 Pictures Colour Library; 281 AA/Tony Souter; 282 AA/Tony Souter; 283 AA/Tony Souter; 284 AA/Max Jourdan; 285tl/tr AA/Pete Bennet; 285bl AA/Max Jourdan; 285br AA/Clive Sawyer; 286 AA/Max Jourdan; 287 AA/Max Jourdan; 288 AA/Max Jourdan; 289t AA/Max Jourdan; 289br AA/Clive Sawyer; 290 Sally Roy; 291t World Pictures; 291b Travel Ink/Andrew Watson; 292 Sally Roy; 293 Sally Roy; 294c AA/Ken Paterson; 294b Rebecca Ford; 295 AA/Ken Paterson; 296 AA/Ken Paterson; 297 1990, Photo Scala, Florence; 298 AA/Ken Paterson; 299tl/tr AA/Simon McBride; 299b AA/Ken Paterson; 301tr AA/Simon McBride; 301cr AA/Ken Paterson; 301b AA/Jerry Edmanson; 302 AA/Simon McBride; 303t AA/Clive Sawyer; 303c/b AA/Simon McBride; 304t AA/Ken Paterson; 304b AA/Simon McBride; 307tl AA/Ken Paterson; 307tr/br AA/Terry Harris; 309 AA/Terry Harris; 311tl/tr/cr AA/Terry Harris; 311b AA/Tony Souter; 312 AA/Terry Harris; 313 AA/Terry Harris; 314 AA/Clive Sawyer; 315 AA/Clive Sawyer; 316 AA/Clive Sawyer; 317tl AA/Clive Sawyer; 317tr www.vittorebuzzi.it/Alamy; 318 AA/Clive Sawyer; 319t AA/Clive Sawyer; 319cc AA/Max Jourdan; 319cr/b AA/Max Jourdan; 320 AA/Max Jourdan; 321 AA/Clive Sawyer; 322 AA/Tony Souter; 323tl AA/Tony Souter; 323tr/b AA/Clive Sawyer; 324 AA/Tony Souter; 325tl AA/Clive Sawyer; 325tr/b AA/Tony Souter; 326 AA/Clive Sawyer; 327t John Heseltine; 327br Fausto Giaccone/Marka; 328t Maurilio Mazzola/Marka; 328b Danilo Donadoni/Marka; 329 Jenny Squillaci; 330tl AA; 330tr AA/Max Jourdan.

EATING AND STAYING

331 AA/Jim Holmes; 332cl AA/Jim Holmes; 332cc Isla Love; 332cr AA/Ken Paterson; 333 AA/Max Jourdan; 334cl AA/Tony Souter; 334cc AA/Max Jourdan; 334cr AA/Jerry Edmanson; 335cl AA/Tony Souter; 335cc AA/Ken Paterson; 335cr AA/Tony Souter; 336-363t AA/Clive Sawyer; 340c AA/Anna Mockford and Nick Bonetti; 342c AA/Anna Mockford and Nick Bonetti; 345c AA/Anna Mockford and Nick Bonetti; 346c AA/Simon McBride; 349c Photodisc; 353c AA/Clive Sawyer; 354c AA/Clive Sawyer; 355c AA/Clive Sawyer; 356c AA/Ken Paterson; 358c Photodisc; 362c Photodisc; 363c AA/Clive Sawyer; 364l AA/Jim Holmes; 364c AA/Barrie Smith; 364r AA/Clive Sawyer; 365 AA/Simon McBride; 367-398t AA/Clive Sawyer; 370c AA/Anna Mockford and Nick Bonetti; 374c AA/Anna Mockford and Nick Bonetti; 377c AA/Simon McBride; 380c AA/Tony Souter; 385c AA/Clive Sawyer; 386c AA/Clive Sawyer; 387c AA/Clive Sawyer; 389c AA/Terry Harris; 397c AA/Clive Sawyer.

PLANNING

399 AA/Max Jourdan; 404 AA/Clive Sawyer; 405 ECB; 406 AA/Clive Sawyer; 407 AA/Max Jourdan; 408 AA/Clive Sawyer; 409 AA/Max Jourdan; 410 AA/Max Jourdan; 412 AA/Clive Sawyer; 414 AA/Clive Sawyer; 415 AA/Simon McBride; 416 Stockbyte.

Every effort has been made to trace the copyright holders, and we apologise in advance for any accidental errors. We would be happy to apply the corrections in the following edition of this publication.

Project editor
Nicola Lancaster

Interior design
David Austin, Glyn Barlow, Alan Gooch, Kate Harling, Bob Johnson,
Nick Otway, Carole Philp, Keith Russell

Picture research
Liz Allen, Alice Earle, Debbie Ireland, Charlotte Lippmann, Vivien Little, Serena Mellish

Cover design
Tigist Getachew

Internal repro work
Susan Crowhurst, Ian Little, Michael Moody

Production
Lyn Kirby, Helen Sweeney

Mapping
Maps produced by the Cartography Department of AA Publishing

Main contributors
Sally Roy (consultant), Jack Altman, Anna Maria d'Angelo, The Content Works, Charlotte Eager,
Rebecca Ford, Alex Johnson, Simona Marchetta, Lee Marshall,
Jenny Squillaci, Vittorio Squillaci, Nicky Swallow

Copy editors
Sue Gordon, Janet Tabinski

Updaters
David Browne, Barbara Rogers, Sally Roy

Revision Management
Cambridge Publishing Management Ltd

See It Italy
ISBN 13: 978-1-4000-1703-4
ISBN 10: 1-4000-1703-3
Second Edition

Published in the United States by Fodor's Travel and simultaneously in Canada by
Random House of Canada Limited, Toronto.
Published in the United Kingdom by AA Publishing.

Color separation by Keenes
Printed and bound by Leo, China
10 9 8 7 6 5 4 3 2 1

Special Sales: This book is available for special discounts for bulk purchases for sales
promotions or premiums. Special editions, including personalized covers, excerpts of
existing books, and corporate imprints, can be created in large quantities for special needs.
For more information, write to Special Markets/Premium Sales, 1745 Broadway, MD 6-2,
New York, NY 10019 or e-mail specialmarkets@randomhouse.com

A02359
Mapping in this title produced from: Map data © 1998–2005 Navigation Technologies BV. All rights
reserved. Mapping © ISTITUTO GEOGRAFICO DE AGOSTINI, Novara–2006

Relief map images supplied by Mountain High Maps ® Copyright ©1993 Digital Wisdom, Inc

Weather chart statistics supplied by Weatherbase © Copyright 2003 Canty and Associates, LLC
Communicarta assistance with distance/time charts gratefully acknowledged

Important Note: Time inevitably brings changes, so always confirm prices, travel facts, and
other perishable information when it matters. Although Fodor's cannot accept responsibility
for errors, you can use this guide in the confidence that we have taken every care to ensure
its accuracy.

Fodor's Key to the Guides

AMERICA'S **GUIDEBOOK LEADER** PUBLISHES GUIDES FOR **EVERY KIND OF TRAVELER**. CHECK OUT OUR MANY SERIES AND FIND YOUR **PERFECT MATCH**.

FODOR'S GOLD GUIDES
America's favorite travel-guide series offers the most detailed insider reviews of hotels, restaurants, and attractions in all price ranges, plus great background information, smart tips, and useful maps.

COMPASS AMERICAN GUIDES
Stunning guides from top local writers and photographers, with gorgeous photos, literary excerpts, and colorful anecdotes. A must-have for culture mavens, history buffs, and new residents.

FODOR'S 25 BEST / CITYPACKS
Concise city coverage in a guide plus a foldout map. The right choice for urban travelers who want everything under one cover.

FODOR'S AROUND THE CITY WITH KIDS
Up to 68 great ideas for family days, recommended by resident parents. Perfect for exploring in your own backyard or on the road.

SEE IT GUIDES
Illustrated guidebooks that include the practical information travelers need, in gorgeous full color. Perfect for travelers who want the best value packed in a fresh, easy-to-use, colorful layout.

FODOR'S FLASHMAPS
Every resident's map guide, with 60 easy-to-follow maps of public transit, parks, museums, zip codes, and more.

FODOR'S LANGUAGES FOR TRAVELERS
Practice the local language before you hit the road. Available in phrase books, cassette sets, and CD sets.

THE COLLECTED TRAVELER
These collections of the best published essays and articles on various European destinations will give you a feel for the culture, cuisine, and way of life.

Dear Traveler

From buying a plane ticket to booking a room and seeing the sights, a trip goes much more smoothly when you have a good travel guide. Dozens of writers, editors, designers, and cartographers have worked hard to make the book you hold in your hands a good one. Was it everything you expected? Were our descriptions accurate? Were our recommendations on target? And did you find our tips and practical advice helpful? Your ideas and experiences matter to us. If we have missed or misstated something, we'd love to hear about it. Fill out our survey at www.fodors.com/books/feedback/, or e-mail us at seeit@fodors.com. Or you can snail mail to the See It Editor at Fodor's, 1745 Broadway, New York, New York 10019. We'll look forward to hearing from you.

Tim Jarrell
Publisher